CW00950952

DICTIONARY OF THE THEATRE: TERMS, CONCEPTS, AND ANALYSIS

Patrice Pavis
Translated by Christine Shantz
Foreword by Marvin Carlson

Patrice Pavis is one of France's most brilliant academics and a leading expert internationally in the theory of theatre. *Dictionary of the Theatre* is an English translation of Pavis's acclaimed *Dictionnaire du théâtre,* now in its second edition in France.

This encyclopedic dictionary includes theoretical, technical, and semiotic terms and concepts. Alphabetical entries range from 'absurd' to 'word scenery' and treat the reader to a vast panoply of theatre and theory. The extended discussions are supported by useful examples drawn from the international repertoire of plays and playwrights, both classic and contemporary.

This dictionary is remarkably well integrated, partly because of its excellent system of cross-referencing, but also because it represents the vision and scholarship of a single, recognized authority. There is no other source like it available and it will be warmly welcomed by the English-language theatre world.

PATRICE PAVIS is Professor of Theatre Studies at the University of Paris VIII.
CHRISTINE SHANTZ is Chief of Translation at the Inter-American Development Bank, Washington, D.C. She has held positions at the United Nations and Canada's Export Development Corporation, and has translated a number of literary and scholarly works.
MARVIN CARLSON is Sydney E. Cohn Professor of Theatre, City University of New York.

PATRICE PAVIS

Dictionary of the Theatre: Terms, Concepts, and Analysis

Translated by Christine Shantz

Preface by Marvin Carlson

UNIVERSITY OF TORONTO PRESS
Toronto and Buffalo

Toronto Buffalo London
Printed in Canada

ISBN 0-8020-4342-9 (cloth)
ISBN 0-8020-8163-0 (paper)

Dictionary of the Theatre: Terms, Concepts, and Analysis is a translation of *Dictionnaire du Théâtre* (édition revue et corrigée; Paris: Dunod 1996)

Printed on acid-free paper

Canadian Cataloguing in Publication Data

Pavis, Patrice, 1947–
Dictionary of the theatre : terms, concepts, and analysis

Translation of Dictionnaire du théâtre.
Includes bibliographical references and index.
ISBN 0-8020-4342-9 (bound) ISBN 0-8020-8163-0 (pbk.)
1. Theater – Dictionaries. 2. Drama – Dictionaries.
I. Shantz, Christine. II. Title.

PN2035.P313 1998 792′.03 C98-930987-8

This translation has been published with the assistance of grants from the Writing and Publishing Section of the Canada Council for the Arts and from the French Ministry for Culture.

University of Toronto Press acknowledges the financial assistance to its publishing program of the Canada Council for the Arts and the Ontario Arts Council.

Contents

Foreword

At the beginning of the 1980s I offered a seminar at Indiana University on the subject of "Theatre Semiotics," a theoretical approach to theatre studies that was at that point just being introduced among English speaking scholars. My class was made up of graduate students from theatre, comparative literature, and semiotic studies, a field which Tom Sebeok had pioneered at Indiana University. Much of the first day or two of the seminar was spent in introducing a number of basic terms from Saussure, Austin, Pierce, and other early theorists in this field – necessary preliminaries that no one in the class found particularly satisfying. The students from semiotic studies, long familiar with such terms as signifiers and signifieds, illocutions, and perlocutions, icons and indexes, found this introduction a little boring and elementary, while the theatre students felt barraged by a flood of odd and unfamiliar terms the immediate relevance of which to their own interests was anything but clear.

For the first couple of sessions I felt rather like a teacher of French attempting to introduce the language to a class composed partly of beginning students and partly of students in their second or third year of French studies, and I am sure the students shared this feeling. About the third session, however, there was a memorable moment when one of the theatre students, quite casually, referred in passing to the subtext of a scene. One of the semiotic students stopped him, confessing that he had never heard this apparently useful technical term and asking him to explain it. For both theatre and semiotic students this was a revelation. Suddenly both realized that the theatre students also had a technical vocabulary, useful and virtually transparent to them, that needed explanation for someone outside that particular intellectual world.

Now, twenty years later, the theoretical worlds and theoretical vocabularies of literary theory (and more recently cultural theory) and theatre studies have to a large degree interpenetrated each other, so my theatre students today find signifiers and signifieds (not to mention more complex and more current specialized terms that have appeared as the semiotic analysis of the early 1970s has been overtaken by a wide variety of competing analytic strategies) as common in their reading and their theoretical speculations as students of an earlier generation found such terms as subtext, denouement, or protagonist. Patrice Pavis has created the first dictionary of theatrical terms that reflects this blending of the specialized vocabulary that has been borrowed by theatre studies from many other intellectual disciplines.

It is particularly fitting that Professor Pavis should undertake this task, as one of the leading scholars to introduce the theoretical vocabulary of semiotics to theatre studies. As a French scholar he is also continuing a long tradition of such activity: the

French encyclopedists LaPorte and Chamfort produced the first theatre dictionary, the *Dictionnaire Dramatique* (1776), and a French scholar Alfred Bouchard produced *La langue théâtrale* (1878), the first dictionary to include both literary and technical theatre terms. The twentieth century has seen a variety of theatrical dictionaries: some specialize in certain dramatic traditions or in technical and backstage terminology, others seek to provide a general listing of specialized theatre vocabulary. The best known among these are W.G. Fay's *A Short Glossary of Theatrical Terms* (1930), Ken Carrington's *Theatricana* (1939), Wilfred Granville's *A Dictionary of Theatrical Terms* (1952), Bowman and Ball's *Theatre Language* (1961), and Joel Trapido's *International Dictionary of Theatre Language*.

Most of these earlier dictionaries attempt, with varying degrees of success, to provide a listing that mixes historical and literary terms that one is likely to encounter in writings about the theatre (for example, comedy, protagonist, minstrel, deus ex machina), with trade terms used by persons in the theatre, technical backstage terms (cyclorama, wings, batten), and theatrical slang (ham, rant, raspberry). Pavis has moved in a different direction; he has maintained the listing of historical and literary terms but replaced the technical and slang listings with entries that introduce some of the specialized theoretical vocabulary that is now regularly employed in theoretical writing about the theatre. This shift of emphasis makes his new dictionary a uniquely helpful guide for readers interested in understanding the special vocabulary of contemporary theatre scholarship.

MARVIN CARLSON

Preface

Alphabetical order can become destiny – the destiny of the articles in the first and second editions of this dictionary (1980 and 1987) placed the undertaking somewhere between "absurd" and "vraisemblable" (believable). This new edition is not beyond the reach of such alphabetical constraints, although it has been completely revamped and expanded considerably. An encyclopedia still seems an immoderate project in terms of both breadth and ambition, but one that is all the more legitimate and necessary if we are to grasp the diversity and comprehensiveness of the theatre phenomenon. This new edition, conceived in the same spirit as the earlier ones and subject to the same limitations, has been enriched with many new articles and additions. Is it merely a coincidence that "absurd" has given way to "abstraction"? And is not abstraction a better response than absurdity to the proliferation of new forms? This is much more than a cursory update or revision of old materials. The infinite play of cross-references imperceptibly weaves a text that needs to be continually revised and corrected in the light of current realities. This edition speaks of the innovations of the 1990s, of the cross-cultural, multimedia and interdisciplinary aspects of theatre today. Those influences mean that we must rethink theories and their categories, and see Western dramaturgy (as text "representation") from the standpoint of an anthropology of performance practices and an ethnoscenology.

Theatre is a fragile, ephemeral art that is particularly sensitive to what is in the air. It cannot be accounted for without from time to time questioning its foundations and reviewing the critical apparatus we use to describe it.

Theatrical activity has never been so intense or so marked by diversity in terms of languages, venues and audiences. Spectators today are more tolerant and more interested in avant-garde experiences. They are harder to surprise or shock. No longer content to be delighted, admiring or fascinated, they need technical or philosophical explanations. Theatre is not afraid of theorizing about its own practices, or even making them the subject of its plays, although the complacent self-contemplation of the glory years of theory (1965–1975) is now a thing of the past. Is it possible that theatre is finally being taken seriously as a major art in its own right rather than an offshoot of literature, a substitute for film, or a kind of tawdry entertainment?

During the 1960s and 1970s, theatre studies developed under the impetus of the human sciences, splintering off into many different objects of study and methodologies. The piecemeal, discontinuous approach of a dictionary is needed to put together the fragments without giving the illusion of unity or totality. Theory requires a precise metalanguage that will define complex notions without oversimplifying them. This is a methodological and epistemological undertaking, rather than a terminological or technical one. Rather than describing concepts within established boundaries, theory sets its own boundaries to account for an evolving subject-matter. In its infinite play of cutting, naming and making cross-references, the dictionary allows for reflection on theatre and the world being "talked about" (we no longer dare to say "represented").

The complexity of theory pales by comparison to the abundant wealth of theatrical experiments in our times. Many of these are having some success, whether research into space, body expression, rereadings of classics, or the fundamental relationship between actor and spectator. But beware those who proclaim the death of staging or history, the disappearance of theatre, a return to the evidence of the text or the uncontestable supremacy of the actor, for underlying such statements is often a rejection of reflection and meaning, a return to a critical obscurantism with sinister echoes. In these times of ideological uncertainty, as the humanist heritage is liquidated between two fire sales of concepts too soon shopsoiled, of hermeneutical gadgets and flashy postmodern devices, a process of historical and structural reflection seems ever more necessary to stave off the vertigo of theoretical relativism and aestheticism.

This dictionary of theatre concepts seeks first of all to clarify critical notions that have become muddled. Though it may contain borrowings from paths now blocked off, it reflects the practical work of staging analysis, i.e. the analysis of theatre creation as such. Rather than examining etymology or compiling definitions, it focuses on presenting different theses, on placing reflection about theatre within a broader intellectual and cultural context, evaluating the influence of the media, testing existing or imaginable methodological tools.

Any lexicon fixes language use at a particular point in its evolution, takes an inventory of naming signs and defines things named using existing terms. We started out, then, by drawing up a list of terms. And this gave us cause for concern, for although there are notions that are able to cross time and borders, there are also concepts that are historically dated or have fallen into disuse because they are identified with a particular genre or set of problems. We have had to look into both types of terms. Although we have confined ourselves to current usage, we have also kept the more classical concepts, especially since some of them are being used in a new sense (for example, *catharsis, fiction, actor*). A single entry therefore frequently refers to different, even contradictory, historical applications. These overlaps can only be perceived, however, if one takes a historical perspective and looks at concepts and theories in a relative light.

This reasoned dictionary essentially looks at our Western traditions of theatre, from Aristotle to Bob Wilson. Those traditions rule out a description of non-European forms, particularly traditional Oriental theatres with quite a different frame of reference, but they have been open through the 1980s and 1990s to cross-cultural practices and the mix of forms, genres and theories that characterizes contemporary art. We have been obliged to exclude – perhaps somewhat arbitrarily – lateral forms of spectacle such as ceremony, ritual, circus, mime, opera, puppetry, etc. These forms have been examined only as they relate to theatre (cf. marionette and actor, stage music). The influence of the media, on the other hand – particularly television, radio and the movies – is so pervasive that several articles have been included to account for the mark it has left on contemporary theatre practice.

This book contains not a list of creators, movements and theatres (although its articles naturally make constant references to them), but rather a presentation of major issues in dramaturgy, aesthetics, hermeneutics, semiology and anthropology. The constantly evolving vocabulary of theatre criticism is an equally important field, with problems defined in an often very specialized terminology that the dictionary must clarify.

Alongside these very technical entries, we have devoted considerable space to longer articles on key aesthetic issues, methods of analysis, and forms of representation. Here it is even less possible than elsewhere for lexicology to claim any objectivity. It must take sides in debates under way, stand on its own assumptions, and not hide behind the neutral columns of the dictionary.

The aim is to help students, theatregoers and practitioners, as well as critics and spectators, to articulate the major theoretical issues involved.

The general definition that opens most of the articles gives a preliminary orientation, making sure not to narrow down the terms or problems involved. It is therefore meant to be as general as possible and should not be understood as an absolute. Then a methodological discussion endeavors to remedy the simplification inherent in any definition by opening up the debate and placing it in a theoretical and aesthetic context. Here too, the tension between vocabulary and methodical treatise holds sway. Each article is seen as a presentation of the difficulties of usage within an overall theory, as a point of departure opening onto a dramatic and stage universe, and shows the veins of the construction that underlies and presupposes it. Hence the frequent cross-references (indicated with an asterisk), which are used to lighten the text and to trace pathways through a dense critical landscape. The reader may progress at will, guided by the thematic index.

As a snapshot of theatre at a particular point in its evolution, we hope this book will evince neither the calm assurance of a telephone book nor the easy conscience of the penal code. In putting forward a structural interpretation of how text and stage function, it is not to be considered definitive or normative.

The acuity of its vision rests upon its fragility. Removing any one term will bring down the whole building, as we have had occasion to see quite often in the course of the past twenty years...

The terms examined here, which were chosen as much for their tendency to recur in the history of criticism as for their usefulness in describing phenomena, can be grouped into the eight categories of the thematic index:

- *dramaturgy*, which examines action, character, space and time; all the issues that have contributed at once to founding theatrical, textual and stage practice;
- *text and discourse*, being the two faces of any representation of human actions;
- *genres and forms*, the major ones being listed here with no attempt to present an exhaustive account, which would be impossible in any case;
- *the staging* and how it is conceived and organized, excluding the technical terms of stage machinery that a specific study would require;
- *structural principles and aesthetic questions*, which do not relate solely to theatre but are essential to grasp its aesthetics and organization;
- *reception of the performance* from the spectator's point of view, with all the hermeneutical, sociosemiotic and anthropological operations that this entails;
- *semiology*, which, far from being a new science that can substitute for other disciplines, is rather a fundamental aesthetic reflection on the production, arrangement and reception of signs. This integrated approach to semiology, after weathering a crisis during the 1970s, has finally come into stride and lost its hegemonic pretensions, without losing any ground in terms of substance or intellectual rigour.

These eight categories provide us with stable frameworks – comforting reference points – as they sustain the gaze this book continues to level on theatre reality, holding fast against the incessant flow of creation, the irreducible gap between theory and practice, and the vagaries of theatre life.

TRANSLATOR'S ACKNOWLEDGMENTS

I would like to acknowledge the support provided by the Canada Council and the Government of France. Thanks also to Elena and Patrice Pavis for their generosity, to Isis Sadek for her careful work on the bibliography, and to my family – David, Marina, Cristóbal, and Leandro – for lighting the way.

CHRISTINE SHANTZ

Thematic Index

DRAMATURGY

TEXT AND DISCOURSE

ACTOR AND CHARACTER

GENRES AND FORMS

STAGING

STRUCTURAL PRINCIPLES AND AESTHETIC QUESTIONS

RECEPTION

SEMIOLOGY

EXPLANATORY NOTE

Words followed by an asterisk refer to other articles. Dates in parentheses after an author's name or title identify the article or book as listed in the bibliography at the end of this dictionary. Works cited in the body of an article are not included in the bibliography at the end of the article, but are naturally considered major references. Well-known works with many editions are often referred to by the first publication date, with the edition used indicated in the general bibliography.

The thematic index on pages xiii–xviii places terms in their conceptual context based on type of approach or critical field.

ABSTRACTION

Fr.: *abstraction*; Ger.: *Abstraktion*; Sp.: *abstracción*.

Although there is no such thing as abstract theatre (in the sense of abstract painting), it is possible to see a process of abstraction and stylization of theatrical material in both writing and staging. Any artistic work, and any staging in particular, is abstracted from surrounding reality, and (following the distinction made in ARISTOTLE's *Poetics*) is more like poetry, which deals with the general, than theatre, which deals with the specific. By its very nature, a staging organizes, filters, abstracts and extracts from reality. Under certain aesthetics, this process of abstraction becomes quite systematic: for instance, SCHLEMMER's Bauhaus pursues "simplification, reduction to the essential, the elemental, the primary, in order to oppose a unity to the multiplicity of things" (1978, 71). As a result, forms become geometric, individuals and movements are simplified, one becomes aware of codes, conventions, and overall structure.

ABSURD

Fr.: *absurde*; Ger.: *das Absurde*; Sp.: *absurdo*.

1. Absurd elements are felt to be unreasonable, nonsensical or lacking any logical connection with the rest of the text or performance. According to Existentialist philosophy, the absurd is that which cannot be explained by reason and denies man any philosophical or political rationale for his actions. A distinction must be made between absurd elements in theatre and the contemporary *theatre of the absurd*.

Elements of theatre are called absurd when we cannot place them in their dramaturgical, theatrical and ideological contexts. Such elements are found in theatrical forms well before the absurd theatre of the 1950s (ARISTOPHANES, PLAUTUS, Medieval farce, *commedia dell'arte**, JARRY, APOLLINAIRE). The theatre of the absurd, as a genre or central theme, came into being with IONESCO's *The Bald Soprano* (1950) and BECKETT's *Waiting for Godot* (1953). Some contemporary representatives are ADAMOV, PINTER, ALBEE, ARRABAL and PINGET. Reference is sometimes made to a *theatre of derision*, which "seeks to elude any precise definition, and gropes its way towards the unspeakable or, to borrow a title from Beckett, the unnameable" (JACQUART 1974, 22).

Beyond illogical dialogue or stage business, the absurd often implies an ahistorical, non-dialectical dramaturgical structure. Man is a timeless abstraction incapable of finding a foothold in his frantic search for a meaning that constantly eludes him. His actions have neither meaning nor direction; the *fabula** of absurd plays is often circular, guided not by dramatic action but by wordplay and a search for words.

2. The origins of this movement date back to CAMUS (*The Outsider, The Myth of Sisy-*

phis 1942) and SARTRE (*Being and Nothingness* 1943). In the context of the war and the post-war period, these philosophers painted a disillusioned picture of a world devastated by conflict and ideology.

Among the theatrical precursors to the contemporary theatre of the absurd are farce, *parades**, grotesque interludes in SHAKESPEARE and Romantic *drame*, playwrights who defy categorization such as APOLLINAIRE, JARRY, FEYDEAU and GOMBROWICZ. The plays of CAMUS and SARTRE (*Caligula, le Malentendu, Huis clos*) do not meet any of the formal criteria of the absurd, even though their characters are its philosophical spokesmen.

The absurd play was first seen as an anti-play in relation to classical dramaturgy, the Brechtian epic approach and the realism of popular theatre (*anti-theatre**). The preferred form of absurd dramaturgy is that of a play without a plot or clearly defined characters in which chance and invention reign supreme. The stage eschews psychological or gestural mimicry and illusion, so that the spectator is obliged to accept the physical conventions of a new fictional world. By centring the "*fabula*" around the problem of communication, the absurd play often becomes a discourse on theatre, i.e. *metatheatre**. From surrealist research into automatic writing the absurd inherited the ability to sublimate in a paradoxical form the "writing" of the dream, the subconscious and the mind, and to discover stage metaphors to represent this inner landscape.

3. There are several "strategies" of the absurd:
- the *nihilistic* absurd, in which it is practically impossible to draw any conclusions about the world view or philosophical implications of the text or acting (IONESCO, HILDESHEIMER);
- the absurd as a *structural* principle used to reflect universal chaos, the disintegration of language and the lack of a harmonious image of mankind (BECKETT, ADAMOV);
- the *satirical* absurd (satirical in its formulation and plot) gives a fairly realistic account of the represented world (DÜRRENMATT, FRISCH, GRASS, HAVEL).

4. Absurd theatre is already a chapter of literary history, with its own classical figures. A possible dialogue with realistic playwriting was cut short when BRECHT, who planned to write an adaptation of *Waiting for Godot*, was unable to carry out his project. The absurd has been revived in Eastern Europe by dramatists such as HAVEL or MROZEK, and in language games in the style of WITTGENSTEIN, also used in Western European drama by playwrights such as HANDKE, HILDESHEIMER and DUBILLARD. It continues to influence contemporary writing and deliberately provocative stagings of seemingly harmless and classical texts.

See also: tragic, tragicomic, comic.

Further reading: Hildesheimer 1960; Esslin 1962; Ionesco 1955, 1962, 1966.

ACT

(From the Latin *actus*, action.)
Fr.: *acte*; Ger.: *Akt*; Sp.: *acto*.

External division of the play into more or less equal parts on the basis of time and development of the action.

1. Structural Principles

Ways of distinguishing between acts and marking the transition from one act to another have varied considerably over the years in Western theatre. The same is true of devices used to indicate the end of one act and the beginning of another, which have included the use of a *chorus** (GRYPHIUS), the lowering of a curtain (beginning in the seventeenth century), a change of lighting or black-out, musical refrains, posters, etc. The division of plays into acts can be a response to very different needs (the need to change candles and scenery, for instance).

A. TEMPORAL DIVISIONS

The act may mark off a unit of time, a time of day (classical dramaturgy), one entire day (Spanish Golden Age drama), or, less frequently, a longer lapse of time (CHEKHOV, IBSEN).

The act is defined as a unit of time and as a narrative unit on the basis of its boundaries rather than its contents. It ends when all the characters exit or when a significant change occurs in the continuity of space and time, thus dividing the *fabula** into major moments.

B. NARRATOLOGICAL DIVISIONS
This is the basic criterion for dividing a work into acts. Ever since ARISTOTLE, it has been thought that drama ought to present a single action that can be broken down into organically interrelated parts, whether or not the *fabula** includes a reversal of the action. Such a structure is narratological, and the division is made on the basis of universally accepted major units of the narrative. There are three essential phases: (1) *protasis* (introduction and setting into motion of dramatic elements); (2) *epitasis* (complication and tightening of the knot); (3) *catastrophe* (resolution of conflict and return to normality). These three phases (which correspond fairly closely to the ternary narratological models used in *narrative** theory) form the nuclei of all plays cast in the Aristotelian mould, and three is the magic number for this kind of dramaturgy. Thus, HEGEL (1832), reflecting on theatre tradition, also distinguishes between three key moments: (1) birth of the conflict; (2) collision; (3) paroxysm and reconciliation. This model, which could be considered logical and canonical (for this type of dramaturgy), may give rise to many variations, since the external divisions do not necessarily coincide with the three phases of the narrative (*narrative analysis**, *dramatic structure**).

2. Evolution of Number of Acts
Greek tragedies were not divided into acts but rather structured by entrances of the chorus, which separated them into *episodes** (of which there were between two and six). Later, Latin playwrights (such as HORACE, or DONATUS in his commentary on TERRENCE) and, above all, Renaissance theoreticians introduced formal divisions, adding two intermediate elements to the ternary scheme and increasing the number of acts from three to five. Act two now contained the development of the plot and ensured the transition from protasis to climax. Act four prepared the dénouement or introduced a last suspense, a quickly dashed hope of resolution. Five acts are found in plays as early as those of SENECA (following the rules of HORACE). The five-act play was to become the norm in seventeenth-century France, imposed by a standardized dramatic structure. The basic principle was henceforth a conscious one: to achieve a smooth, constant progression that guided the action toward a necessary dénouement. The breaks between acts do not affect the quality or unity of action; they build up a rhythm for this progression and harmonize the form and content of the acts. According to the classical norm, the acts must be balanced, form an autonomous whole and each one must shine with "some special beauty, either an incident or a passion, or something of the kind" (D'AUBIGNAC 1927, VI: 4, 299).

Within this aesthetics, the act functions as a catalyst and a guide for the action: "It is a degree, a step in the action. It is in this division of the action as a whole into degrees that the work of the poet must begin [...] Dialogue marks off the seconds, scenes mark off the minutes, acts the hours." (MARMONTEL 1763, article on act).

3. Other Structural Models
The division of the play into three or five acts was claimed to be universal or natural in the classical (or neoclassical; cf. FREYTAG 1857) era. In fact, it works only for this particular kind of dramaturgy, which is based on the unity of time and space. As soon as the action is drawn out or no longer appears as a harmonious continuum, the five-act model is no longer valid. A series of *scenes** or *tableaux** gives a much better account of the texts of SHAKESPEARE, LENZ, SCHILLER, BÜCHNER or CHEKHOV (cf. SZONDI 1556). Although some of these playwrights retained the act (and the scene) in name, their texts are actually a series of loosely constructed *tableaux**.

This is true of SHAKESPEARE, whose work was later edited into acts and scenes, and the Spanish playwrights who arranged their plays into three *jornadas*, or "days," as well as most post-classical and post-Romantic authors.

Once the criteria for dividing a play into acts included not only action but time, the act tended to embrace a single dramatic moment, define a period in time, and take on the "status" of a tableau. Historically, this phenomenon occurred in the eighteenth century (bourgeois *drama**), continuing into the nineteenth (HUGO) and becoming a fundamental feature of epic dramaturgy in our own time (WEDEKIND, STRINDBERG, BRECHT, WILDER). DIDEROT noted, without realizing it, the transition from the act to the tableau, from the *dramatic** to the *epic**: "If a poet has reflected well on his subject and properly analyzed the action, he will be able to give a title to each of his acts; and just as in the epic poem one speaks of a descent into Hell, funereal games, the enumeration of the army, the opposition of the shadows, in the dramatic poem one would speak of the act of suspicion, the act of fury, the act of recognition or sacrifice" (DIDEROT 1975, 80–81).

ACTANT

Fr.: *actant;* Ger.: *Aktant;* Sp.: *actante.*
See ACTANTIAL MODEL

ACTANTIAL MODEL

Fr.: *modèle actantiel;* Ger.: *Aktantenmodell;* Sp.: *modelo actancial.*

1. Usefulness of the Actantial Model

The notion of actantial *model* (or *scheme* or *code*) has become indispensable in semiological and dramaturgical research as a means of visualizing the major forces at work in the drama and their role in the action. The advantage of such a notion is that it does not artificially separate *character** from *action** but reveals the dialectics between them and gradual transition from one to the other. Its success is attributable to the fact that it illuminates problems of dramatic *situation**, the dynamics of situations and characters, and the emergence and resolution of *conflicts**. In addition, the actantial approach is an indispensable *dramaturgical** analysis for any staging, which is also intended to clarify the physical relationships and configuration of the characters. Finally, the actantial model provides a new perspective on the character, no longer likened to a psychological or metaphysical being but rather to an entity that belongs to the overall system of actions, varying from the "amorphous" form of the *actant** (deep narrative structure) to the specific form of the *actor** (surface discursive structure that exists as such in the play). According to GREIMAS and COURTÈS (1979), the actant is "that which accomplishes or undergoes an act, independently of all other determinations" (1979, 3; Eng. 1982, 5). This notion was borrowed by GREIMAS (1966) from the grammarian L. TESNIÈRE (1965).

Nevertheless, scholars disagree as to the form this model should take and how its categories should be defined, and the differences between variations go beyond mere details in presentation. The basic idea, from PROPP (1929) to GREIMAS (1966), is to:

1. Divide the characters into a minimum number of categories to embrace all the combinations actually present in the play;
2. Identify the true protagonists of the action, beyond the individual expressions of character, by means of regrouping or splitting up the characters.

2. Refinements of the Model

A. POLTI (1895)

The first attempt to define the set of all theoretically possible dramatic situations was made by G. POLTI, who reduced the number of basic situations to 36, an oversimplification of theatrical action.

B. PROPP (1929)

On the basis of a corpus of folk tales, V. PROPP defined the typical narrative as one having seven actants corresponding to seven spheres of action:

1. Villain (commits the misdeed);
2. Donor (provides the magic object and values);
3. Helper (comes to the hero's rescue);
4. Princess (demands a feat and promises marriage;
5. Dispatcher (sends the hero on a mission);
6. Hero (acts and is subject to various peripeteia);
7. False hero (usurps the true hero's role for a time).

PROPP defines the functions of the characters as follows: "The names of the dramatis personae change (as well as the attributes of each), but neither their actions nor functions change. From this we can draw the inference that a tale often attributes identical actions to various personages. *This makes possible the study of the tale according to the functions of its dramatis personae.*" (1968)

C. SOURIAU (1950)
Six dramaturgical functions make up the framework of any dramatic universe:

- Lion (directed force): the desiring subject of the action;
- Sun (value): the good desired by the subject;
- Earth (receiver of the good): the one who benefits from the desired good;
- Mars (opponent): obstacle encountered by the subject;
- Scales (arbiter): decides to whom to allocate the good desired by rivals;
- Moon (helper).

These six functions exist only in their interactions. SOURIAU's system represents an important first step in the formalization of actants, and includes all imaginable protagonists. Only the arbitrating function (scales) appears to be less integrated into the system, having a superior position to the other functions, and being sometimes difficult to identify in the play under study. Otherwise, this model adapts easily to that of GREIMAS, who divides the six functions into three pairs.

D. GREIMAS (1966, 1970)

```
Sender  →  Object   →  Receiver
              ↑
Helper  →  Subject  →  Opponent
```

The *sender–receiver* axis controls values, hence ideology. It decides on what values and desires are to be created and how they will be allocated to the characters. It is the axis of "power" or "knowledge," or both at the same time.

The *subject-object* axis traces the trajectory of the action and the quest of the hero or protagonist. It is strewn with obstacles that the subject must overcome in order to advance. It is the axis of "desire."

The *helper-opponent* axis facilitates or hinders communication. It generates the circumstances and modalities of the action and is not necessarily represented by characters. Helpers and opponents are often only "projections of the will to act and imaginary resistance within the subject himself" (GREIMAS 1966, 190). (This is sometimes the axis of "knowledge," sometimes of "power.")

E. A. UBERSFELD (1977)
In her application of the GREIMAS model, A. UBERSFELD (1977a, 58–118) switches the places of the subject–object pair, making the subject the function manipulated by the sender–receiver pair, while the object becomes the function caught between helper and opponent. This brings about a major change in the operation of the model. The GREIMAS model did not allow one to base an analysis on a subject consciously created by a sender for the purpose of a receiver; the subject was defined only at the end of the journey in accordance with the quest for the object. This approach had the advantage of establishing the subject–object pair gradually, defining the subject not in itself but according to its actions. In UBERSFELD's model, however, there is a risk of overestimating the nature of the subject, of making it a datum easily marked out by the

	System of character	Level of existence
Surface structure Level IV (performance)	C Actors (players) c^1 c^2	Character perceptible through actor
Level III (textual surface)	a^1 a^2 Actors a a a^1 a^2 a^3	Discursive structure (motifs, themes of plot)
Deep structure Level II (syntax of the narrative)	A^1 A^2 A^3 Actants A	Narrative structure (logic of actions)
Level I (logical structure)	Logical operators Greimas's logical square	Elementary structures of meaning

ideological functions of the sender–receiver – which would not appear to be A. UBERSFELD's intention since she rightly remarks that "there is no autonomous subject in a text, only a subject–object axis" (1977a, 79). This modification of the GREIMAS model also affects the helper-opponent axis but does not have the same effect on the overall operation of the model, as it matters little whether help or hindrance affects the subject or the object pursued; the difference has to do with how effectively and quickly the help/hindrance operates.

F. PROBLEMS AND POSSIBLE IMPROVEMENTS OF ACTANTIAL MODELS

The most common disappointment concerning the application of the model is that it is too general and universal, particularly with respect to the sender and receiver functions (God, Humanity, Society, Eros, Power, etc.). It is recommended that several possibilities be tried out, particularly for the subject, which should be finalized last and in the most versatile manner possible. It should be remembered that the reason for using an actantial model is its flexibility, and that there is no final, ready-made solution; each new solution requires its own corresponding model. Moreover, each of the six categories can be subdivided into a new actantial model.

Care should be taken not to limit the use of the actantial code to the characters (and thus to textual analysis). Everything that is shown on the stage is to be taken as a combination of actants. For instance, in BRECHT's *Mother Courage*, the materials used and how they are destroyed or become worn constitute an actantial model in themselves. One could therefore generate a model in which the six actants would be represented by different states of the props and stage; this would avoid reducing the model to a combination of characters. Similarly, the system of the various *gestus** could be studied. (Concerning the problem of an ahistorical actantial model, see the entry under *character**.) This model was conceived on the basis of the concept of conflict in classical Western drama and does not apply well to modern drama (SZONDI 1956) or non-European forms of drama that involve neither conflict nor plot nor dramatic progression in the Western sense.

3. Actants and Actors

A. THEORY OF LEVELS OF EXISTENCE OF THE CHARACTER

Level I: *Elementary structures of meaning.* Relationships of opposition, contradiction and implication in different spheres of meaning make up the logical square (GREIMAS' semiotic square, 1966, 1970:137).

Level II: *Actants**, which are general, non-anthropomorphic and non-figurative entities (e.g. peace, Eros, political power). Actants exist only on a theoretical and logical plane within a logical system of action or narrativity.

Level III: *Actors** (in the technical sense, not in the sense of players or performers), which are individualized, figurative entities actualized in the play (similar to characters in the traditional sense).

Intermediate level between II and III: *Roles**, figurative, animate entities which are nevertheless general and exemplary (e.g. the braggart, the noble father, the traitor). Role is part of both the deep narrative structure (e.g. traitors always do X) and the surface of the text (a "Tartuffe" is a specific kind of traitor).

Level IV: Staging, actors (in the sense of players or performers) as they are played by one or more performers. This level is different and separate from that of characters.

Splitting up or regrouping of the character: Splitting up:

- One actant is represented by several actors, e.g. in *Mother Courage*, the actant "to survive" is represented by Mother Courage, the cook, the soldiers and the chaplain.
- One performer plays two characters, as in cases of double roles. In *The Good Person of Setzuan* (BRECHT), the same character represents two different actants (to be human, to make a profit at all costs).

Regrouping. Two performers play one character or different aspects of one character (a doubling-up procedure often used today). It is also possible for a single actor to bring together several spheres of action. For example, Mother Courage embodies the actants "to make a profit" and "to live in peace."

Further reading: Bremond 1973; Suvin 1981.

ACTING

Fr.: *jeu de théâtre*; Ger.: *Spiel*; Sp.: *actuación*

Acting is the visible and properly "scenic" part of the performance, through which the spectator receives the whole of the event with the force of its enunciation. Even a reading of the dramatic text requires one to visualize how it could be performed, as MOLIÈRE reminds his readers: "Comedies are made solely to be played, and I recommend that they be read only by those who have the eyes to discover, in reading, all of the play [acting] of theatre." (*l'Amour médécin*, "Au lecteur")

In order to grasp the actor's work, both reader and spectator must compare the enunciation as a whole (gesture, facial expression, intonation, vocal quality, rhythm) with the given text or situation. The acting can then be broken down into a sequence of signs and units that ensure the coherence of the performance and the interpretation of the text.

Acting was long seen in terms of the actor's sincerity or hypocrisy – should he believe in what he is saying and be moved by it, or should he distance himself and convey his role in a detached manner? The answer varies according to how one sees the effect to be produced in the audience and the social function of theatre. DIDEROT's solution (to be an insensitive actor) applies only to a kind of self-conscious acting in which the actor makes no attempt to have the onlookers believe that he is possessed by and somehow transmuted into the character: "It is extreme sensitivity that makes actors mediocre; it is sensitivity that makes most bad actors bad, and it is a complete lack of sensitivity that can make actors sublime." (*Paradoxe sur le comédien*)

At the present time, directors no longer see acting in terms of sensitivity or mastery. They ask themselves, above all, what dramaturgical and semiotic function gesture and facial expression fulfill in the sequence examined. There is no such thing as a natural kind of acting that can do without conventions and be received as self-evident and universal. Any acting is based on a codified system (even if the audience does not see it as such) of behaviour and actions that are considered to be believable and realistic or artificial and theatrical. To advocate the natural, the spontaneous and the instinctive is only to attempt to produce *natural** effects, governed by an ideological code that determines, at a particular historical time and for a given audience, what is natural and believable and what is declamatory and theatrical. The best actors are those who are most familiar with the rules but seem to be working freely and effortlessly.

How the text is interpreted depends on the acting and the rhythm the actor gives to his speeches, gestures and the performance as a whole. If the pace of the acting is slow, a discourse on the unconscious and the historicity of the text may appear, in the margins, so to speak, like a commentary or "subtext" (STANISLAVSKY) that parallels and contradicts the text acted. If it is rapid (as in the past), such commentary is less "audible" and is not expressly imposed on the spectator. "The tradition of rapid acting represents only what is written. The unconscious disappears." (VITEZ and MESCHONNIC 1982: 32.)

2. Acting and Theatre

A. RULES AND CONVENTIONS

Theatre is hand in glove with acting in its principles and rules, if not its forms. HUIZINGA (1950) gives the following overall definition of acting: "... This description of the principle of play also applies to acting. Fiction, mask, a defined stage, conventions, they are all there. To be sure, one thinks immediately of the stage/house division that so radically separates actors from spectators in an apparent contradiction of the principle of play. And it is true that only the *happening** or *dramatic play** can bring everyone together in an acting community. Still, there can be no theatrical representation without the complicity of an audience, and a play cannot succeed unless the spectator plays the game, accepts the rules, and plays a role as one who suffers or ... "

B. PLAY IN THEATRE

Rather than seeking a total correspondence between the play principle and theatre, we will look at what theatre shares with certain types of play. R. CAILLOIS' typology (1958) appears to cover what we understand intuitively, at least from our Western point of view, by *play*.

- *Mimicry* (simulacrum). Since ARISTOTLE, theatre has been seen to imitate the actions of men. This remains fundamentally true if we see *mimesis** mpt as a nonphotographic reproduction of reality but as a transposition – an abstraction and reconstruction – of human events. An actor always resorts to a *persona*, or mask, even when he is pointing.
- *Agon** (competition). Competition – rivalry, comic or tragic conflict] – is one of the essential devices of drama. The stage-house relationship also has an element of rivalry, without stretching the metaphor too far. In classical dramaturgy, the stage aims to win over the house *en bloc*, to have the audience's gaze turn the stage into an autonomous universe. Brechtian epic theatre, for its part, aims to bring the contradiction from stage to house, so that the audience is divided as to narrative and political solutions. Although this desire for radical division may seem somewhat like a naive fantasy of political activism, there is no doubt that this style of dramaturgy favors contradictions by bringing together opposing ideologies and solutions.
- *Alea* (chance). Many playwrights have experimented with chance. It was long thought that the outcome of the play had to be decided in advance and there were few ways to have chance intervene in the events of the performance. The boldest made use of it in the construction of their plays, as in theatre of the *absurd** and experimentation with alogical narrative (DÜRRENMATT) that surprised the audience with an unpredictable plot as the action took "the worst possible turn" which "happened by chance" (DÜRRENMATT, 1991). Sometimes it is the actors who decide at random what ending to give the play. But only *psychodrama**, *dramatic play** and the *happening** fully incorporate the randomness of play into their performances.

- *Illinx* (vertigo). Theatre does not physically play with the bodies of the spectators to the point of dizziness, but can simulate the most vertiginous psychological situations perfectly. *Identification** and *catharsis** in this sense can be seen as slipping into the indeterminate areas of fantasy or, as ROBBE-GRILLET would say, into "progressive drifts of desire."

If the main rule in theatre is, as playwrights are wont to reiterate, to please, the rules of the theatre game call for adapting the spectator's vision to some of the essential principles of play. From *ludus*, conventional play, to *païda*, spontaneous and anarchic play, there is a vast range of emotions and possible combinations thereof.

3. A Semiotic Theory of Acting?
To take away the metaphysical ground where these considerations on the universality of acting are rooted, to avoid repeating humanist speeches about the playful nature of man or copying the psychologist who – rightfully – points up the importance of play as a child matures psychologically and socially, we will put forward a semiological theory of acting viewed as a *modelling** and rendering into *signs** of reality. The actor, guided by the director and their reading of the text to be performed or the script to be produced, has available an acting program that he elaborates based on its expected reception by the audience. Which movements are visible and relevant? Should the utterances of the text be counteracted by mimicry? How to situate interaction with other actors? Should the character's existence be simulated or proposed by convention? The acting is built up in the course of the rehearsals, then in the choice of a *mise en scène* that will solve the technical problems. Each answer implies a production of gestural sequences that will endeavor to reconcile all these requirements, to establish the fictional status of the performance, and to give the audience what they expect and what will at the same time surprise them.

See also: Reception, spectator, theatrum mundi.

Further reading: Evreinoff 1930; Caillois 1958; Winnicott 1971; Schechner 1977; Dort 1979; Sarrazac 1981; Ryngaert 1985.

ACTION
Fr.: *action*; Ger.: *Handlung*; Sp.: *acción*.

1. Levels of Formalization of the Action

A. VISIBLE AND INVISIBLE ACTION
A series of stage events produced mainly through the behaviour of the characters, the action is both the entire *process* (*theatrical process**) of visible transformations on stage on a concrete level and, at the level of the *characters**, that which characterizes their psychological or moral progression.

B. THE TRADITIONAL DEFINITION
"A series of deeds and actions which constitute the subject of a dramatic work" (*Robert* dictionary).

The above definition is tautological and merely descriptive, since it simply replaces *action* with deeds and actions, and does not indicate the nature of this transforming process of doing, nor how the events are arranged in the dramatic text or on the stage. To say, as ARISTOTLE does, that the plot is "the organization of the events" (*Poetics*, section 1450a) still does not explain the nature and structure of dramatic action; one then has to show how this "organization of the events" is structured, how the plot is articulated and on the basis of what indications it can be reconstructed.

C. THE SEMIOLOGICAL DEFINITION
First, the *actantial** model is reconstituted at a given point of the play, by establishing the links between the actions of the characters, by determining the subject and the object of the action, and the opponents and helpers, until the model is modified and the *actants** take on new values and positions within the dramatic universe. The driving force of the action may, for example, shift from one character to another, the object pursued may be eliminated or appear in another form, the strategy of the opponents/helpers may change. Action takes

Level 3 Surface structure (manifest)	System of characters ↓	Actors ↓	Plot ↓
Level 2 Discursive structure (figurative level)	Actantial Model ↓	Actants ↓	Action ↓
Level 1 Deep structure Narrative structure	Elementary structures of meaning (Greimas's semiotic square, 1970)	Logical operators	Logical models of action

place as soon as one of the actants takes the initiative to change its position within the *actantial** configuration, thus upsetting the balance of forces within the drama. Action is therefore the dynamic, transforming element that makes the logical and temporal transition from one *situation** to another. It is the logical and temporal series of dramatic situations.

Any analysis of the *narrative** breaks down a story in terms of the axis of imbalance/balance or transgression/mediation, potential/fulfillment (lack of fulfillment). Any action may be accurately described as the transition from one phase to another, from a beginning situation to an ending situation. ARISTOTLE already implied as much when he divided *plot** into a beginning, middle and end (*Poetics*, section 1450b).

2. Actantial Model, Action and Plot

A. In order to differentiate *action* from *plot**, we must look at these notions within the context of the actantial model (table)and locate them at the different levels on which they appear (deep structure and surface structure). The table reads from bottom to top, moving from deep structure (which exists only theoretically, in a reconstituted model), to surface structure (the discursive structure of the text and the series of episodes in the plot); that is, the action insofar as it is perceptible in the narrative and on stage.

B. The action is situated at a relatively deep level, since it consists of very general figures of actantial transformation even before the complex arrangement of the narrative episodes that make up the plot becomes apparent.

The action may be summarized in a general, abstract *code*. It is sometimes crystallized in a very concise formula (BARTHES 1963, in his account of the "formula" of RACINE's tragedies). The plot is perceptible at the surface level of the individual message. For example, we could trace the action of *Don Juan* through its various literary sources, thus reducing it to a small number of basic narrative sequences. On the other hand, if we analyze each version, we must consider the episodes and the hero's specific adventures, carefully enumerating the sequences of *motifs**: this would be a study of *plot**. H. GOUHIER proposes a similar distinction between *action* and *plot* when he opposes *schematic action*, a kind of essence or concentrated formula of action, to *action that implies duration*, i.e. an action that is played out at the level of existence: "The action sketches out events and situations; as soon as it begins to unfold, it sets off a play of images that tells a story in itself and is thus located at the level of existence" (1958, 76).

C. The difference between action and plot corresponds to the difference between *fabula** (sense 1.B) as material and narrated story, i.e. the temporal and causal logic of the actantial system and *fabula** (sense 1.C) as structure of the narrative and *narrating discourse*, i.e. a series of actual speeches and episodes: *sjuzet* (see *fabula**) in the sense of the actual arrangement of events as presented by the narrative (TOMACHEVSKY 1965).

3. Action of Characters

Since ARISTOTLE, there has been controversy over which term of the action/character pair ought to prevail. Clearly, one determines the other and vice versa, but opinions differ as to which should take precedence.

A. "EXISTENTIALIST" CONCEPTION

Action prevails. "... it is not for the purpose of presenting their characters that the agents engage in action, but rather it is for the sake of their actions that they take on the characters they have. [...] What is more, without action there could not be a tragedy, but there could be without characterization." (*Poetics*, section 1450a) Action is considered the driving force of the plot (*fabula*), the characters being defined only secondarily. The analysis of the narrative or drama attempts to distinguish between spheres of action (PROPP 1968), minimal sequences of acts, actants as defined by their places within the actantial mode (SOURIAU 1950; GREIMAS 1966) and situations (SOURIAU 1950; JANSEN 1968; SARTRE 1973). All these theories share a certain distrust of psychological character analysis and a tendency to judge characters on the basis of their actions alone. SARTRE summarizes this attitude fairly well: "A play throws people into an enterprise; there is no need for psychology. There is, however, a need to define very precisely what position, what situation each character may take, on the basis of the pre-existing causes and contradictions that have produced it in relation to the main action" (1973, 143).

B. ESSENTIALIST CONCEPTION

Inversely, a philosophy that tends to judge man on his essence rather than his actions and situation begins by analyzing character, often very subtly, defining it according to consistency and psychological or moral essence, beyond the concrete actions of the plot; it is interested only in the personification of "greed," "passion," "absolute desire." The characters exist only as a list of moral or psychological attributes; they are identical to their speeches, contradictions and *conflicts**. Their actions would appear to be merely the consequence and externalization of their psychological and moral qualities.

4. Dynamics of Action

The action is linked, at least in *dramatic** theatre (*closed form**), to the emergence and resolution of contradictions and conflicts between the characters and between one character and his situation. It is the imbalance created by a conflict that obliges the character to act in order to resolve the contradiction, but his actions (and reactions) will lead to other conflicts and contradictions. This ongoing dynamic process creates the movement of the play. The action, however, is not necessarily expressed or apparent at the level of plot; it can sometimes be felt in the transformation of the protagonists' consciousness, a process that can be reflected only in discourse (classical drama). To speak, in theatre even more so than in daily life, always means to act (see *spoken action**).

5. Action and Discourse

Discourse is a way of doing. By virtue of an implicit convention, theatrical discourse is always a way of acting, even by the most conventional dramaturgical standards. According to D'AUBIGNAC, in the theatre speeches "must be like actions performed by those who appear there; for here *speaking* is doing" (*Pratique du théâtre*, vol. IV, ch. 2). When HAMLET says: "I must to England," one is to imagine him already on his way. Discourse on stage has often been considered the focus of verbal action and *presence**. "In the beginning was the Word ... in the beginning was Action. But what is a Word? In the beginning was the active Word" (GOUHIER 1958, 63).

Other forms of verbal action, such as performative utterances, the use of presuppositions and deictics, are at work in the dramatic text (PAVIS 1978a). They make the separation between the action visible on stage and the "work" of the text even more problematic: "To speak is to do, the *logos* takes over the functions of *praxis* and substitutes for it." (BARTHES 1963, 66; Eng. 1964b, 58). Theatre becomes a place of simulation where the spectator, by tacit agreement with the author and the performer, is asked to imagine performative acts on a stage other than that of reality (cf. *pragmatics**).

6. Constituent Elements of Action

Drawing on research done on the philosophy of action (VAN DIJK 1976), Elam identifies six constitutive elements of action: "an *agent*, his *intention* in acting, the *act* or *act-type* produced, the *modality* of the action (manner and means), the *setting* (temporal, spatial and circumstantial) and the purpose" (1980: 121). These elements define any kind of action, as long as it is conscious and non-accidental. By identifying these elements it is possible to determine the nature and function of action in theatre.

7. Forms of Action

A. RISING ACTION/FALLING ACTION

Until the *crisis** and its resolution in the *catastrophe**, the action rises. The sequence of events speeds up and becomes more and more inevitable as the conclusion approaches. Falling action occupies only a few scenes or even a few lines toward the end of the play (*paroxysm**).

B. PERFORMED ACTION/NARRATED ACTION

Action is shown directly or transmitted in a narrative. In the second case, it is itself *modalized** by the narrator's action and situation.

C. INTERNAL ACTION/EXTERNAL ACTION:

The action is mediated and internalized by the character or, alternatively, imposed on the character "from the outside."

D. MAIN ACTION/SECONDARY ACTION:

The first has to do with the progression of the protagonist(s); the second is grafted onto the first as a sub-plot of no fundamental importance to the *fabula** as a whole. Classical dramaturgy, in requiring unity of action, tends to limit action to the main action.

E. COLLECTIVE ACTION/PRIVATE ACTION:

Particularly in historical drama, the text often draws a parallel between the individual fate of the hero and the general or symbolic fate of a group or a people.

F. ACTION IN CLOSED FORM*/IN OPEN FORM*

(See entries under above headings)

8. Theatrical Action Within a Theory of Language and Human Action

A. THE AUTHORS OF THE ACTION

Among the innumerable meanings of theatrical action, the foregoing enables us to divide action into three fundamental branches:

1. *Action of the fabula** or action shown: includes everything within the fiction, everything the characters do.
2. *Action of the dramaturg and director*: gives utterance to a text through the staging, by making the characters *do* specific things.
3. *Verbal action of the characters* who speak the text, which contributes to their assumption of the fiction.

B. LINK BETWEEN ACTION OF THE FABULA AND SPOKEN ACTION OF THE CHARACTERS

Two kinds of action can be distinguished in theatre: the overall action of the *fabula*, which is an action as it is represented in the *fabula*, on the one hand, and the action spoken by characters on the other, which is realized in each of the characters' utterances (or *discourse**).

Action as *fabula* forms the narrative framework of the text or performance. It may be read and reconstructed in various ways in the staging, but always retains its overall narrative structure, within which the characters' utterances (spoken actions) are embedded.

This distinction tends to fade when the characters have no plan of action and replace visible action with a story about their utterances or their difficulties in communicating, as in BECKETT (*Endgame, Waiting for Godot*), HANDKE (*Kaspar*) and PINGET. This was already the case even in some of MARIVAUX's comedies (*les Serments indiscrets*), in which the speakers engage in directionless or plotless conversation and constantly refer to their way of speaking and the obstacles to their communication.

Further reading: Tomachevsky 1965; Greimas 1966; Jansen 1968; Urmson 1972; Bremond 1973; Rapp 1973; Hübler 1972; Stierle 1975; *Poetica* 1976; Van Dijk 1976; Suvin 1981.

ACTIONS

Fr.: *actions*; Ger.: *Handlungen*; Sp.: *acciones*.

Unlike theatrical actions, which are symbolic and representative of human behaviour, *actions* by *performance** or *body art** artists such as Otto MÜHL or Hermann NITSCH of the Fura dels Baus group or the Cirque Archaos are literal, real actions, often violent, ritual and cathartic in nature. They involve the actor's person and reject the simulation of theatrical mimesis.

In rejecting theatricality and the sign, actions seek out a ritual model of effective action, of intensity (LYOTARD 1973) that will elicit from the performer's body – and then from the spectator – a kind of force field, a physical vibration or shudder like ARTAUD's concept of a "culture in action that becomes like a new organ within us, a kind of second breath" (1964, 10–11).

ACTOR

Fr.: *acteur, comédien*; Ger.: *Schauspieler*; Sp.: *actor*.

1. Status of the Actor

Long the object of social opprobrium, the actor has acquired a certain social status, even prestige, once he "arrives." The actor's aesthetic role is very variable and uncertain. From the end of the nineteenth century, following a tradition of great actors and an actor-oriented theatre, there began an era of director's theatre, described here by MEYERHOLD: "The director will not be afraid to come into conflict with the actor at rehearsal, to the point of and including hand-to-hand fighting. His position is solid, because unlike the actor he knows (or should know) what the show will look like tomorrow. He is obsessed by the *whole*, and thus stronger than the actor" (1963, 283).

2. The Emancipation of the Actor

There may be a trend today toward a return to the actor and a collective conception of performances comprising extra-theatrical materials (reportage, *collage** of texts, gestural *improvisation**, etc.). Tired of their role as loudspeakers at the service of a paternalistic and tyrannical *director** and a *playwright** burdened with ideological issues, actors are claiming their share of creativity. The performance thus loses its fetishistic nature as a *monument* and becomes a series of entertaining *moments*.

3. Actor as Ham

An actor who falls prey to the temptation of showing off or ham-acting puts himself in the spotlight at the expense of his colleagues, the character, theatrical illusion, and the poor spectator who is expected to admire the monster. Apart from the social perversion of ham acting, it entails a demagogic complicity with the audience, who is aware that the actor is a virtuoso who masters his role and is even capable of interrupting himself to prove it.

Further reading: Diderot 1994; Jouvet 1954; Stanislavsky 1963; Duvignaud 1965; Villiers 1951, 1968; Strasberg 1969; Chaikin 1972; Eco 1973; Aslan 1974, 1993; Schechner 1977; Dort 1977b, 1979; *Voies de la création théâtrale*, 1981, vol. 9; Roubine 1985; Pavis 1996a.

ACTOR'S EXERCISE

Fr.: *travaux d'acteur*; Ger.: *Schauspielerübung*; Sp.: *ejercicio del actor*.

The programs at most acting schools include exercises (as in STANISLAVSKY, MEYERHOLD, COPIEAU, DULLIN, BRECHT, VITEZ, LASSALLE) that often involve painstaking preparation of part of a play. Hence the idea of providing for systematic acting exercises to work towards presentations within the school or for a group of friends or professionals (for example, at the TNS in Strasbourg or CDNA in Grenoble). The actors or apprentices often get organized themselves without a director, and try out experimental kinds of presentation. The results vary greatly. Sometimes the actors feel liberated without the presence of a director; sometimes, left to their own devices, they feel more disoriented than revitalized (see examples in *Théâtre/Public*, no. 64–65, 1985).

ADAPTATION

Fr.: *adaptation;* Ger.: *Bühnenbearbeitung, Adaptation, Adaption;* Sp.: *adaptación.*

1. The re-casting of a work in one genre to another (adaptation of a novel for the stage, for instance). The narrative content (*narrative** or *fabula**), which is retained more or less faithfully, although sometimes with significant differences, is adapted or dramatized (*dramatization**), while the discursive structure undergoes a radical change from one enunciative mechanism (*enunciation**) to another. A novel may be adapted for the stage, for the big screen or for television. Through this process of semiotic transferral, the novel is transposed into dialogues (which often differ from those of the original) and above all into staged actions that use all of the materials available to dramatic performance (gesture, image, music, etc.). Examples are the adaptations of DOSTOYEVSKY's works by GIDE and CAMUS.

2. The concept of adaptation also refers to *dramaturgical** work based on the text to be staged. All imaginable textual manoeuvres are permissible: cuts, rearrangement of the narration, stylistic polishing, the use of fewer characters or locations, a dramatic focus on certain strong points of the novel, the addition of external texts, *montage** and *collage** of foreign elements, different endings and changes in the *fabula* as required by the staging. Adaptation, unlike *translation** or *contemporization**, can be very free; it does not hesitate to change or even invert the meaning of the original play (cf. BRECHT's adaptations or *Bearbeitungen* of SHAKESPEARE, MOLIÈRE and SOPHOCLES and Heiner MÜLLER's "translations," e.g. *Prometheus*). To adapt is to entirely rewrite the text, using it as raw material. This practice has created a better awareness of the importance of the *dramaturg** in a production.

There can never be a perfect or definitive adaptation of plays from the past. At the most, like BRECHT in his "Modellbuch," one can set out certain dramatic premises and establish certain interpretations of the play from which future directors may benefit (*model**).

3. The term "adaptation" is often used in the sense of translation or a more or less faithful transposition, and it is not always easy to draw a line between the two. Adaptation here means a translation that adapts the source text to the new context of reception, making any additions or deletions that may be considered necessary to its reappraisal. Rereadings of classics – including abridged editions, new translations, the addition of other texts, new interpretations – are in themselves adaptations, as is the process of translating a foreign text and adapting it to the cultural and linguistic context of the target language. Most translations today are called adaptations, which corroborates the fact that any one of the range of operations from translation to rewriting of a play is a re-creation, and that the transfer of forms from one genre to another is never an "innocent" process but involves the production of meaning.

ADDRESS TO THE AUDIENCE

Fr.: *adresse au public;* Ger.: *Anrede ans Publikum;* Sp.: *apelación al público.*

Parts of the text (which may or may not be improvised) that the actor, leaving his role as a character, delivers directly to the audience, thus breaking the illusion and fiction of a *fourth wall** completely separating the auditorium from the stage. The Latin term *ad spectatores* is also used in this sense.

1. In the *dramatic** form of theatre, addressing the audience is strictly forbidden, in order to maintain the theatrical *illusion**. It exists only in the form of the *authorial intervention** or the moralizing discourse of the *raisonneur**. The latter form of *discourse** is a way of expanding the internal communication of characters into direct communication with the audience. It is disguised by the fiction of a character who is meant to instruct the audience in how the action should be viewed.

2. In epic theatre (BRECHT, WILDER, sometimes GIRAUDOUX), the address to the audience is quite common, and just as legitimate as *alienation-effects** or a parodic acting style. It takes place at a key point of the action when the character is reaching a decision, when he asks the audience for advice or ends the play with an *epilogue** (*The Caucasian Chalk Circle* by Brecht, for instance). These addresses are often an invocation to be virtuous (Jesuit theatre, medieval miracle plays) or to become aware of one's alienation. It attempts to establish a bridge between the fictional world and the real-life situation of the spectators.

3. The status of the character who addresses the crowd is, however, ambiguous. He introduces himself as a private person, as Actor X or Y who speaks on his own behalf and may even invite the audience to join him in a dialogue, but, on the other hand, he never succeeds in making the spectators forget his real situation and status as a character. Everything he says, as soon as it is uttered on the stage, takes on the value of *lines to be said* which are part of the fiction of the play and provided for in the staging, addressed to a fictitious spectator who is already anticipated by the performance. The address to the audience (except in a *happening**, in which there is theoretically no longer a sender or receiver of the text) is never direct *communication** outside the fiction, but indulges the audience's taste for play and demystification.
See also: aside, monologue, soliloquy, parabasis, semiotization

AD SPECTATORES

Fr.: *ad spectatores;* Ger.: *ad spectatores;* Sp.: *ad spectatores.*
See ADDRESS TO THE AUDIENCE

AESTHETICS OF DRAMA

Fr.: *esthétique théâtrale;* Ger.: *Theaterästhetik;* Sp.: *estética teatral.*

Aesthetics – the science of the beautiful and the philosophy of fine arts – is a general theory that looks beyond particular works to define the criteria by which a work of art should be judged and, as an indirect consequence, the work's links with reality. This leads to the notion of *aesthetic experience** and the question of the origins of the pleasures of contemplation, catharsis, tragic and comic elements: how can the performance be apprehended aesthetically, rather than according to a criterion of truth, authenticity or realism?

Theatre aesthetics (or *poetics**) sets out the laws of dramatic composition, indicating how text and stage function. It sees the theatrical system as part of a larger whole: *genre**, theory of literature, system of fine arts, dramatic or *theatrical categories**, theory of beauty, philosophy of knowledge.

1. *Normative aesthetics* examines the text or performance according to the criteria of the tastes of a particular period (even if they have been universalized in a general theory of art by aestheticians). This brand of aesthetics is founded on a pre-established definition of the *essence** of theatre and judges its object according to how well it conforms to the model or, in reception theories, according to the work's stylistic divergencies from that model and whether or not it calls into question the norm and the horizon of *expectation**. Normative aesthetics necessarily eliminates certain types of works; by characterizing theatre as being based on conflict, for instance, it has long excluded epic theatre. Each historical period is dominated by a series of such norms, has a different notion of *verisimilitude**, of *decorum**, of theatre's moral and ideological potential (the *rules** of the three *unities**, mixed *genres**, *total the-*

*atre**). Aesthetics formulates a value judgment about the text, and endeavours to base it on clearly-established criteria (cf. *questionnaire**).

2. *Descriptive (or structural) aesthetics* merely describes and enumerates the forms of theatre, classifying them according to various criteria. These criteria are supposed to be objective: whether the action is open-ended or closed, stage configuration, mode of *reception**, and so on. It is very difficult, however, to find a solid basis on which to formalize textual and stage language. The aesthetics of theatre has not (yet?) been integrated into a general theory of discourse or general semiotics. The field of aesthetics is subdivided into the study of the mechanisms of *production* of text and performance (*poiesis*), the study of the spectator's *reception** activity (*aisthesis*), and the study of emotional exchanges: identification or distance (catharsis) (JAUSS 1982b), although they can be considered to be dialectical (PAVIS 1983a).

3. *The aesthetics of production and reception* enables us to reformulate the above dichotomy between a normative and a descriptive approach. The aesthetics of production lists the factors that explain how the text is formed (historical, ideological and generic determinants) and how the stage functions (material working conditions, conditions of performance, acting techniques). Production is seen as a set of circumstances that have influenced the shaping of the text performed or show produced. The aesthetics of *reception** is situated at the other end of the chain, examining the spectator's point of view and the factors that have determined his or her correct or incorrect reception, the cultural and ideological horizon of expectation, the series of works preceding this text and performance, the mode of perception (distanced or emotional), the relationship between the fictitious world and the real worlds of the period represented and the spectator.

4. The areas covered by *aesthetics* and *dramaturgy** intersect, as both concern themselves with the way in which an ideology or worldview is related to literary technique and stage practice. *Semiology** addresses the internal functioning of the performance without making prior judgments on its place within a precise normative aesthetics. It borrows some of its methods from aesthetics, including the search for *units**, links and exchanges between *stage systems**, and the production of *effects*.

See also: theatricality, specificity, staging, essence of theatre, aesthetic experience.

Further reading: Hegel 1832; Zich 1931; Veinstein 1955; Gouhier 1958; *Revue d'esthétique* 1960; Souriau 1960; Aslan 1963; Adorno 1984; Borie, de Rougemont, Scherer 1982; Carlson 1984.

AESTHETICISM

Fr.: *esthétisme*; Ger.: *Ästhetizismus*; Sp.: *estetismo*.

This term, which is generally used rather negatively, applies to an element of the mise-en-scène:

- that stresses the purely aesthetic (rather than semantic or ideological) dimension of the mise-en-scène, seeking formal beauty alone (*formalism**);
- that pursues art for art's sake and advocates the autonomy of the work of art (ADORNO 1984), an attitude that is sometimes criticized from a political point of view as embodying a lack of commitment;
- that does not fit neatly into the overall discourse of mise-en-scène; for instance, overly-rich *costumes**, as pointed out by BARTHES, can be victims of an "aesthetic disease," "the hypertrophy of a formal beauty without relation to the play" (1964a, 55; Eng. 1972a, 44).

AGIT-PROP THEATRE

Fr.: *théâtre d'agit-prop*; Ger.: *Agit-Prop Theater*; Sp.: *teatro de agitación*.

1. Agit-prop theatre (from the Russian *agitatsiya-propaganda*, for agitation and propaganda) is a form of theatre *animation** designed to raise the audience's consciousness of a political or social situation. It

emerged after the Russian revolution in 1917 and developed mainly in the Soviet Union and in Germany between 1919 and 1932–1933 (when socialist realism was introduced by Zdanov and Hitler took power). It had little success in France; its sole publication, called *Scène ouvrière*, had only a fleeting existence.

2. Agit-prop has its distant ancestors in baroque Jesuit theatre and in the Spanish and Portuguese *auto sacramental**, which contained exhortations to action. But agit-prop is much more radical in its desire to serve as a political instrument for an ideology, whether one in opposition (as in Germany or the United States) or one propagated by the governing power (Russia in the 1920s). This is clearly a leftist ideology, with its criticism of bourgeois domination, initiation to Marxism, and attempts to promote a socialist or communist society.

The main contradiction of this critical movement is that it is sometimes at the service of a certain political line striving to prevail (as in Germany), other times at the mercy of directives from above that are to be disseminated and made to triumph (as in the Soviet Union). Depending on its political status, agit-prop is therefore led to invent forms and discourses or to apply a program that it did not necessarily refine itself, and from which it may wish to distance itself; hence its fragility and diversity as a hybrid genre that is both theatrical and political.

3. In its connections to current political events, agit-prop appears above all as an ideological activity rather than a new artistic form. It proclaims its desire for immediate action by defining itself as "agitatory play rather than theatre" or as "information plus stage effects." Its ephemeral and periodical nature makes it difficult for the researcher to follow: the text is only one means among many of stirring political awareness, and it is relayed by gestural and stage effects that are intended to be as clear and direct as possible – hence its attraction to the circus, pantomime, buffoonery and cabaret.

By giving priority to the easily comprehensible and visualizable political message, agit-prop allows itself neither the time nor the means to create a new genre and an ideal type; it is often nothing but a "steamroller" (F. WOLF) with no subtlety. Its forms and borrowings are as constantly changing as its contents, varying greatly from one country to another according to cultural tradition. Most often, "agitator-propagandists" base their work, albeit in a critical way, on such traditions as *commedia dell'arte**, circus or melodrama. The "inferior" genres, such as circus or pantomime, are quite effective, as they are very popular and supply a familiar form for new or revolutionary contents. Even when the play is so elaborate as to tell a story embodied by characters, it holds to a direct, simplified plot that leads to clear conclusions. The *Lehrstück* (a didactic play that is a "sophisticated" form of agit-prop – the works of BRECHT being the clearest examples) meets the same simple or simplistic criteria. The "living newspaper" presents the news in a critical light, showing the action's protagonists on stage. A political revue made up of barely dramatized numbers and "news flashes" most often provides the through-line for the agit-prop play. A *chorus** of storytellers or singers sums up and "inculcates" the political lessons or slogans. Art may even come into play, when agit-prop is inspired by and inspires avant-garde movements (Futurism, Constructivism) and mobilizes artists such as MAYAKOVSKY, MEYERHOLD, WOLF, BRECHT or PISCATOR (who staged the *Revue Roter Rummel* for the German Communist party).

4. Agit-prop appears suddenly at a time of acute political upheaval, when the humanist and "bourgeois" heritage seems irrelevant and dated. It disappears just as rapidly once the situation has stabilized (in Fascism and Stalinism, but also in a liberalism capable of withstanding any shock), or once the authorities no longer tolerate any questioning or statement. When its message begins to lose its relevance, agit-prop tends to become too repetitive – its schematic Manicheism makes the audience

laugh or squirm, rather than helping them "progress" ideologically. To avoid this pitfall, new forms of agit-prop theatre (*guerilla theatre**, the *collective creations** of groups like the Teatro Campesino, the San Francisco Mime Troupe, Bread and Puppet, L'Aquarium) try not to seem too schematic, and take pains with the artistic presentation of their radical political message. They realize, perhaps, that even the most inspired political speech can only convince if the actors keep in mind the aesthetic and formal dimension of the text and its stage performance.

See also: participation, history.

Further reading: Gaudibert 1977; *Théâtre d'Agit-Prop, Le 1978*; German agit-prop texts in Hoffmann and Hoffmann-Ostwald 1973; Ivernel and Ebstein 1983; Boal 1979.

AGON

(From the Greek *agon*, competition/contest.)
Fr.: *agon*; Ger.: *Agon*; Sp.: *agon*.

1. Every year in ancient Greece, contests were held in arts and sports. There was an *agon* for choruses, for playwrights (510 B.C.), and for actors (450–420 B.C.).

2. In attic comedy (ARISTOPHANES), *agon* is the dialogue and conflict between enemies that forms the heart of the play.

3. By extension, the *agon*, or "agonistic" principle, characterizes the conflict between the *protagonists**, who oppose each other in a dialectic of speech/reply. Each is totally involved in a debate that leaves its mark on the dramatic structure and constitutes its dramatic *conflict**. Certain theoreticians go so far as to make dialogue (and *stichomythia**) the hallmark of dramatic conflict, and, more generally, of theatre itself. It should be remembered, however, that some dramaturgies (e.g. epic or absurd) are not based on the agonistic principle of characters or action.

4. In the theory of R. CAILLOIS (1958), *agon* is one of the four principles governing play activity (along with *illynx*, the search for vertigo; *alea*, the role of randomness; and *mimesis*, the pleasure derived from imitation).

See also: dialogue, dialectic.

Further reading: Duchemin 1968; Romilly 1970.

ALEXANDRINE

Fr.: *alexandrin*; Ger.: *Alexandriner*; Sp.: *alejandrino*.
See VERSIFICATION

ALIENATION EFFECT

Fr.: *distanciation*; Ger.: *Verfremdungseffekt*; Sp.: *distanciación*.

A device that places the reality represented at a distance so that it appears in a new light, revealing its hidden or too-familiar aspects in a fresh way.

1. Alienation-Effect as Aesthetic Principle
The term *alienation-effect* comes from the translation of SCHKLOVSKY's *priem ostranenija*, or "making strange device." This is an aesthetic *device** that consists of altering our perception of a literary image by making it unfamiliar. "After we see an object several times, we begin to recognize it. The object is in front of us and we know about it, but we do not see it." (SHKLOVSKY, Eng. 1965, 21). "The technique of art is to make objects 'unfamiliar,' to make forms difficult, to increase the difficulty and length of perception" (1965, 20). The purpose of the image "is not to make us perceive meaning, but to create a special perception of the object – it creates a 'vision' of the object instead of serving as a means for knowing it" (1965).

This aesthetic principle applies to all artistic languages. In theatre, it has to do with "disillusioning" techniques that negate the impression of a stage reality and reveal the artifice of the dramatic construction or of a character. The spectator's attention is drawn to the way in which the illusion is created, the way in which the actors build their characters. All theatrical genres employ this device.

2. Brechtian Alienation-Effect

A. A POLITICAL PERCEPTION OF REALITY

BRECHT arrived at a notion similar to the Russian Formalist concept in seeking to modify the spectator's attitude and enhance his perception. For BRECHT, "A representation that alienates is one which allows us to recognize its subject, but at the same time makes it seem unfamiliar" (*A Short Organum for the Theatre*, sect. 42). The alienation effect is "a device that enables one to describe the processes represented as bizarre" (1972, 353). He saw this device as capable of transforming the spectator's approving attitude, based on identification, into a critical one.

For BRECHT, this is a political instrument as well as an aesthetic act. The purpose of the "estrangement" is not a new perception or comic effect, but a process of ideological "disalienation" (*Verfremdung* refers us to *Entfremdung*, or social alienation, cf. BLOCH 1973). The alienation-effect makes a transition from aesthetic device to ideological responsibility in the work of art.

B. LEVELS OF ALIENATION-EFFECT

The alienation-effect takes place simultaneously at several levels of the performance:

1. The *fabula** tells two stories: one is concrete and the other is an abstract and metaphorical parable of it.
2. The *scenery* presents the object to be recognized (e.g. a factory) and the criticism to be made (exploitation of workers) (BRECHT 1967, 15: 455–458).
3. *Gestures* provide information about the individual and his social status and relationship with the working world, his *gestus**.
4. The *diction* does not "psychologize" the text by trivializing it, but restores rhythm and artificial construction (e.g. musical delivery of the alexandrine).
5. Through his *acting*, the actor shows the character he plays, rather than incarnating him.
6. *Addresses to the audience**, songs and visible scenery changes are also devices which break the illusion.

See also: historicization, epic, metatheatre, play within a play, mise-en-abyme.

Further reading: Barthes 1964a; Ruelicke-Weiler 1968; Benjamin 1969; Chiarini 1971; Bloch 1973; Knopf 1980.

ALLEGORY

Fr.: *allégorie*; Ger.: *Allegorie*; Sp.: *alegoría*.

An allegory is the personification of a principle or abstract idea. In theatre this is done through a character with well-defined traits and characteristics (a scythe for Death, for instance). Allegory is used mainly in *morality plays** and medieval mysteries and in Baroque dramaturgy (GRYPHIUS). Its use waned as the character became more bourgeois and anthropomorphic, but returned in the parodical or militant forms of *agit-prop**, expressionism (WEDEKIND) and Brechtian parable (*Arturo Ui*; *The Seven Deadly Sins*).

Further reading: Benjamin 1928; Frye 1957; *Le Théâtre européen face à l'invention: allégories, merveilleux, fantastique*, 1989.

ALTERNATIVE THEATRE

Fr.: *théâtre alternatif*; Ger.: *Alternativtheater*; Sp.: *teatro alternativo*.

An alternative to commercial theatre and officially subsidized theatre is an *alternative theatre** or third theatre that puts forward its own original programming, style and modus operandi. Paradoxically, scarce resources lead to experimentation in new forms with more initiative, independently, economically and aesthetically.

AMBIGUITY

Fr.: *ambiguïté*; Ger.: *Doppeldeutigkeit, Mehrdeutigkeit*; Sp.: *ambigüedad*.

Quality which leaves open several alternative meanings or *interpretations** of a character, an action, a passage of the dramatic text or the entire performance.

One of the structural constants of the work of dramatic fiction is the way in which it produces and maintains ambiguity. A work of art is not encoded or deciphered in a single proper way, except in the case of *oeuvres à clef* (works in which actual persons appear as fictional characters) or *didactic plays**. The staging has full discretion to resolve or add to the ambiguity. Any stage interpretation necessarily favours a certain reading of the text, while opening the way to new possibilities of *meaning**.

See also: sign, isotope, hermeneutics, coherence.
Further reading: Rastier 1971; Pavis 1983a.

ANAGNORISIS

Fr.: *anagnorisis*; Ger.: *Anagnorisis*; Sp.: *anagnórisis.*
See RECOGNITION

ANALOGON

Fr.: *analogon*; Ger.: *Analogon*; Sp.: *analogón.*
See ICON

ANALYTICAL PLAYWRITING

Fr.: *technique analytique, drame analytique*; Ger.: *analytische Technik*; Sp.: *técnica analítica.*

1. A dramaturgical technique that consists of introducing into present action a narrative of events that took place before the play began and which are revealed, *a posteriori*, in the play. The most famous example is *Oedipus Rex* by SOPHOCLES: "Oedipus is, in a way, only a tragic analysis. Everything is already there in a developed form" (GOETHE to SCHILLER, letter of 2 October 1797, in 1970). Clearly, such a technique has much to offer to a style of writing intended to reveal character: in SOPHOCLES' *Oedipus Rex*, remarked Freud, "The action of the play consists in nothing other than the process of revealing [...] a process that can be likened to the work of a psycho-analysis" (*The Interpretation of Dreams*, Eng. in 1976, 4: 363).

2. The analysis of the reasons that led to the catastrophe becomes the sole object of the play, eliminating all dramatic *tension** and *suspense** and thereby favouring the appearance of *epic** elements. Some types of dramaturgy, rejecting the dramatic form, use an epic technique of construction to display past events and *flashbacks** (IBSEN, BRECHT), with the result that the drama is only a vast *exposition** of the *situation* (e.g. *The Bride of Messina* [*Die Braut von Messina*] by SCHILLER, *Ghosts* and *John Gabriel Borkman* by IBSEN, *The Broken Jug* [*Der zerbrochene Krug*] by KLEIST, *l'Inconnu d'Arras* by SALACROU).

3. Inversely, in synthetic playwriting and drama (i.e. in the dramaturgy of "pure" dramatic form), the action develops toward a destination that is unknown at the beginning, though necessary according to the logic of the *fabula* and therefore, to some extent, predictable.
Further reading: Campbell 1922; Szondi 1956; Green 1969; Strässner 1980.

ANIMATION

Fr.: *animation*; Ger.: *Animation*; Sp.: *animación.*

1. Theatrical or cultural "animation," at least in present-day France, very often accompanies cultural productions, providing an in-depth preparation for more effective reception. This notion, which emerged in France as part of the trend toward the decentralization of theatre and cultural activities in general, reflects the theatrical undertaking and its place in society today. Should animation be promoted in a general way on the cultural fringe, or should specific animation sessions take place before or after a show to "exploit" it, in all senses of the word? Generally speaking, this movement has understood that theatre cannot be reduced to the analysis of a text and its staging, but that any innovation or creation can be correctly received only when the audience has been properly prepared. Accordingly, the animation approach should begin with activities in schools and the workplace. By initiating young specta-

tors to dramatic play, by teaching them how to read a performance, animation invests in a future audience without being able to test the results of its efforts immediately.

2. Animation may take the form of anything from discussion after a show to the organization of a people's theatre (as in Jean VILAR's TNP, or National Popular Theatre, during the 1950s and 1960s) or an audiovisual presentation in the classroom or on television; from neighbourhood surveys designed to prepare for a show (Théâtre de l'Aquarium during the 1970s) to actually working with the people to prepare a production. Animation familiarizes a still ill-informed public about the mechanics of theatre, demystifying it and integrating it into society. This can only succeed if it takes place in the context of a cultural institution, a theatre with an adequate operating budget and a team of animators who consider theatre a political as well as an aesthetic act. Animation has become so important for the success of a show that the director must often function as manager, educator, activist and public relations officer. Carrying out so many thankless and time-consuming tasks frequently conflicts with the creative activity of theatre people and contributes to further widening the gap between accessible popular art and elitist art. Antoine VITEZ' call for an "elitist theatre for all" would appear to be a utopian search for a middle ground between animation and pure creation.

ANNOUNCER

Fr.: *orateur*; Ger.: *Ansager*; Sp.: *orador*.

The announcer of a troupe, in the seventeenth century, was in charge of passing on the usual compliments to open the season, greeting distinguished patrons, introducing the play, maintaining order during the performance, and conveying thanks and announcements at the end of it. As an intermediary, or even the playwright's stand-in, he played an important role in placing the play in its social context. MOLIÈRE and then LA GRANGE were announcers for the Illustre-Théâtre, MONTFLEURY and HAUTEROCHE for the Hôtel de Bourgogne, FLORIDOR for the Marais.

ANTAGONIST

Fr.: *antagoniste*; Ger.: *Gegenspieler, Antagonist*; Sp.: *antagonista*.

The *antagonists* of a play are characters in opposition or in *conflict**. The antagonistic nature of the theatrical universe is one of the essential principles of *dramatic** form.
See also: protagonist, obstacle, agon.

ANTHROPOLOGICAL THEATRE

Fr.: *théâtre anthropologique*; Ger.: *anthropologisches Theater*; Sp.: *teatro antropológico*.

This term, used principally in Latin America, refers not to non-European performance forms (i.e. "indigenous theatre") but rather to a trend in staging where human beings are examined in their relationships to nature and culture, expanding the European notion of theatre to include cultural performance practices and adopting an *ethnoscenological** approach to explain such practices. GROTOWSKY's Theatre of Sources, BARBA's theatre anthropology, SCHECHNER's productions (*Dionysus in 69*), and rites and *actions** by groups such as Fura dels Baus or Brith GOF are part of this anthropological trend.

ANTHROPOLOGY, THEATRE

Fr.: *anthropologie théâtrale*; Ger.: *Theateranthropologie*; Sp.: *antropología teatral*.

Theatre offers an exceptional testing ground for anthropology in that it shows human beings who play at representing other human beings, a simulation intended to analyze and show how they behave in society. By placing people in an experimental situation, theatre and theatre anthropology are able to reconstruct micro-societies and evaluate the individual's relationship with the group. What better way is there to present one's idea of a person than to represent him or her on stage? According to SCHECHNER, the paradigms of anthropology and theatre are converging: "Just as theater is anthropologizing itself, so anthropology is being theatricalized" (1985, 33). Such is the impeccable reasoning of theatre anthropology.

Unfortunately, however, things become much more complicated in the field, for although theatre anthopology can claim in theory to be able to organize knowledge about *theatre studies**, it is at present more of a rallying cry or a desire for knowledge than an actual discipline; a huge fallow field (or impenetrable virgin forest) rather than a well-defined area of culture. The process of definition, however, has already begun with Eugenio Barba's ISTA (International School of Theatre Anthropology), which has been organizing workshops since 1980. "ISTA is a place where a new way of teaching theatre is being transmitted, transformed and translated. It is an interdisciplinary research laboratory. It is the framework that enables a group of theatre people to participate in the surrounding social environment, through their intellectual work as well as their productions" (BARBA 1982b, 81). E. BARBA and N. SAVARESE's book, *Anatomie de l'acteur. Un dictionnaire d'anthropologie théâtrale* (1985, 1995 2nd ed.), describes the research being done at the School and defines the program of theatre anthropology: "The study of man's biological and cultural behaviour in a performance situation; that is, man using his physical and mental presence according to different principles than those governing everyday life" (1985, I). In view of the importance of BARBA's and ISTA's synthesis, we will review its principles in depth, after taking a brief look at the reasons for the emergence of anthropological thought in theatre, the conditions for epistemological success of such an enterprise, and a discussion of some of its theses.

1. Reasons for its Emergence

A. RELATIVITY OF CULTURES

The idea of considering theatre from the point of view of an anthropology or theory of culture is not a new one. Most writings on theatre include some sort of hypothesis about the origins of theatre. In the twentieth century, this genealogical line of thought has led, in the case of ARTAUD, for instance, to a desire for a return to the origins, a nostalgia for theatre's roots, a comparison with far-off, non-Western cultures. Anthropology as applied to theatre, even if it is not yet recognized as such, appears to have emerged through the awareness of a "malaise in civilization" (FREUD) and the inadequacy of culture and life as diagnosed by Antonin ARTAUD: "Never before, when it is life itself that is in question, has there been so much talk of civilization and culture. And there is a curious parallel between this generalized collapse of life at the root of our present demoralization and our concern for a culture which has never been coincident with life, which in fact has been devised to tyrannize over life" (1964b, 9; Eng. 1958, 7). This feeling that our culture is collapsing and that we have lost a dominant system of references leads theatre people (whether BROOK, GROTOWSKI or BARBA) to put their former practices into perspective, gain an awareness of exotic forms of theatre and take an ethnological look at the actor. These theatrical experiments have something in common with Lévi-Strauss' anthropology in so far as it attempts to understand man "from the moment when the kind of explanation one is seeking attempts to reconcile art and logic, thought and life, the perceptible and the intelligible" (BELLOUR and CLÉMENT 1979, 186).

B. INADEQUACY OF RATIONAL LOGIC

According to a non-Freudian school of thought, the symbol is placed above the concept, and thinkers such as JUNG, KERENYI or ELIADE (1965) relate it to "the effort to translate that which, in the intimate experience of the *psyche* or in the collective unconscious, goes beyond the boundaries of the concept, and escapes the categories of understanding, and therefore cannot be known in the strict sense, but can be 'thought,' recognized through forms of expression of the human aspiration to the unconditional, the absolute, the infinite, the totality; that is, to use the language of religious phenomenology, an openness to the sacred" (VERNANT 1974, 229). This "openness to the sacred" is often accompanied by a return to the religious, even if it is not always acknowledged; sometimes, as M. BORIE has shown, it shows up in Western anthropology's guilty conscience about idealized primitive societies, resulting in a quest for lost authenticity: "Theatre has been increasingly viewed, even before ARTAUD, not as a space intended as an illustration of text and subject to the supremacy of the written word, but as the best possible place for actual physical contact between actors and spectators. Does it not then offer a unique place for experiencing a return to the authenticity of human relationships?" (BORIE 1980, 345). *Theatre of participation**, the collective *happening** and autobiographical *performance art**: all draw on this source of authenticity that theatrical communication allows.

C. SEARCH FOR A NEW LANGUAGE

The quest for the sacred and the authentic requires a language that is not indebted to natural language or a too-rational approach to writing: "To break through language in order to touch life is to create or recreate the theatre; the essential thing is not to believe that this act must remain sacred, i.e., set apart – the essential thing is to believe that not just anyone can create it, and that there must be a preparation" (ARTAUD 1964b, 17; Eng. 1958, 13). This preparation for a language that rejects the facile and the sterile necessitates finding a kind of coded language that will belong at once to creators, participants in the theatrical ceremony and actors who are "like victims burnt at the stake, signaling through the flames" (1964b, 18; Eng. 1958, 13). One might as well say that the key is not easy to find or that it burns whoever would seize it. This *hermeneutics** that distrusts rationalism, and semiological positivism even more, seeks to decode a mythical theatrical language, whether it be called hieroglyph (MEYERHOLD), ideogram (GROTOWSKI), or "pre-expressive base of the actor" (BARBA 1982b, 83).

2. Epistemological Conditions of Theatre Anthropology

The founding of an anthropology of the theatre depends on the existence of a number of prerequisites.

A. NATURE OF ANTHROPOLOGY

A distinction is generally made between *physical* anthropology (studies on the physiological characteristics of man and race), *philosophical* anthropology (study of man in general, e.g. in the sense of KANT as *theoretical, pragmatic and moral* anthropology) and, finally, *cultural* or *social* anthropology (organization of societies, myths, everyday life, etc.): "Whether anthropology calls itself 'social' or 'cultural', it always aspires to know the *whole man*, viewed in one case according to what he produces and in the second according to how he represents" (LEVI-STRAUSS 1958, 391). Theatre anthropology, specifically that of BARBA, concerns itself with both the physiological and the cultural aspects of the actor in a performance situation. An ambitious program, indeed! In the study of the actor's *bios*, what exactly should we study and measure? Should we be content with a morphological and anatomical description of the actor's body? Should we measure the work done by the muscles, the heartrate, and the like? Should theatre research take a medical approach? The results of such studies in the past have not been easy to relate to other factors, particularly the sociocultural.

B. CHOICE OF POINT OF VIEW

According to LEVI-STRAUSS (1958, 397–403), the anthropologist's point of view is characterized by *objectivity*, *totality* and an interest in the *meaning* and *authenticity* of personal relationships and of actual exchanges between individuals. However, theatre anthropology as conceived by BARBA (who never refers to LEVI-STRAUSS' work) has taken a different route. He does not give priority to an external, objective point of view, that of the distant observer (the spectator) or a super-observer who, like the ethnologist, attempts to gather all observable data. On the contrary, as expressed by TAVIANI (in BARBA and SAVARESE 1985, 197–206), he opposes two points of view, that of the actor and that of the spectator, as he is concerned with the usefulness of observation for the actor, with an "authentically empirical approach to the phenomenon of the actor" (1985:1) and therefore with its feedback on dramatic practice: "When semiologists analyze a performance as a very dense stratification of signs, they are observing the theatre phenomenon through its outcome. There is no proof, however, that this procedure is of any use to the show's creators, who must begin at the beginning, and whose destination is what the spectators will see" (TAVIANI op. cit., 199).

The heart of BARBA's theatre anthropology, however, lies in the notion of "body technique" (MAUSS), which, unlike MAUSS, he identifies as the "particular, extraordinary use of the body in theatre" (BARBA op. cit., 1).

C. STATUS OF "BODY TECHNIQUE"

We could, as does VOLLI, albeit partially (in BARBA and SAVARESE 1985, 113–123), refer to Marcel MAUSS' article on "Body Techniques" (1936), i.e. the "ways in which men in each society, through tradition, know how to use their bodies" (1936). MAUSS gives many examples borrowed from all kinds of human activities, but does not mention theatre or art and in any case does not contrast them to everyday situations, as he considers any technique – whether everyday or artistic – to be determined by society. BARBA borrows this notion of a body conditioned by culture from MAUSS (1936), but introduces an opposition between the everyday situation and the performance situation: "We use our bodies differently in daily life than in 'performance' situations. In the everyday context we have a body technique conditioned by our culture, social status, and occupation. But in a 'performance' situation there is a totally different body technique" (1982b, 83).

BARBA appears to suggest that in performance, body technique changes radically and the actor is no longer subject to cultural conditioning. It is difficult to see what would cause this metamorphosis, however; what would make the actor change bodies when he changes contexts. Even in performance, the actor – particularly the Western actor – remains at the mercy of his original culture, particularly his everyday gestures. The very idea of separating life from performance is an odd one, since it is the same body that is used, and the performance cannot erase everything. This distinction between the everyday and the performance aspects runs the risk of establishing precisely the kind of radical opposition between nature (the everyday body) and culture (the body in performance) that anthropology endeavours to refute. One is reminded of the time when stylistics wished at all costs to distinguish ordinary language from poetical language, without explaining how to establish the *distinguo*. Here as well, the body in performance is defined tautologically: the body in performance is the body that is being performed, which possesses specific properties different from those of the everyday body. Although a distinction can be made pragmatically, it is a superficial one and does not give an acceptable account of gesture and presence (why reserve this presence to performance alone: in real life also is one not more or less "present"?).

D. SEARCH FOR UNIVERSAL PRINCIPLES OF CULTURE

Although anthropology sets itself the task of studying the human being in all its diversity, it often concludes that, despite the differences, there is a substratum common to all men, that the same myth appears in many different places, for instance. LEVI-STRAUSS seeks "to overcome the apparent antimony between the unicity of the human condition and the apparently inexhaustible plurality of the forms in which we apprehend it."

A similar concern guides GROTOWSKI, who arrives at the conclusion that "culture, each particular culture, determines the objective socio-biological basis, as each culture is linked to everyday body techniques.

It is important to observe, then, what remains constant in all cultures, what is cross-cultural" (in BARBA and SAVARESE 1985, 126).

BARBA shares this universalism with his master, GROTOWSKI, as he considers that "theatres do not resemble each other in their different manifestations, but rather in their principles." The book (BARBA and SAVARESE 1985) contains a wealth of iconographical material intended to show analogies between the poses and gestures of actors belonging to the most diverse theatre traditions.

BARBA identifies the cross-cultural element at "the pre-expressive level of the actor's art" (1985, 13), in the presence (particularly in Oriental actors) "that strikes the spectator and obliges him to look," a "nucleus of energy, a suggestive and knowing but unpremeditated radiance that overcomes our senses." "It is not yet a 'performance' or a theatrical 'image,' but a force that springs from a body that has been given a form" (1982b, 83).

Like GROTOWSKI (1971, 91), BARBA distrusts the intentionality of the actor and his desire for expression to signify something in particular. He therefore chooses to look at the actor before this expression, at a pre-expressive level that can be seen as universal, as "the force that springs from a body that has been given a form" (1982, 83) or the sources (or origins of man) that are found underlying different theatrical cultures which supposedly explain, like pre-expressive techniques, that "upspring of creative power" (BARBA and SAVARESE 1985, 124). Whatever the metaphor used – upspring of power, source, core of energy, pre-expressivity – one might well wonder whether this "body that has been given form" is not already expressive, even if its expressivity is unintentional and non-communicative. Can one not communicate? Is not the performance situation a communication of communication?

3. Other Perspectives

A. A RETURN TO THE QUESTION OF ORIGINS

One of the obsessions of philosophical anthropology, particularly in the nineteenth century, has traditionally been the question of the origin of languages. The debate has been closed since the advent of structural linguistics, but a similar concern has motivated and continues to motivate reflections on the origins of theatre (cf. NIETZSCHE, 1872) with respect to the origins of theatre, of the *pre-theatre* that precedes it (SCHAEFFNER, in *Encyclopédie des spectacles*, 1965). Regardless of when theatre appeared, there is a consensus that it reflects a gradual secularization of ceremonies or rites. It remains to be determined whether it conserves traces of its ritual origins in its modern forms. Even thinkers as close as BENJAMIN and BRECHT disagree on this matter. For BENJAMIN, every work of art, even "in the age of its mechanical reproduction" (according to the essay of the same title of 1936), "has its basis in ritual, the location of its original use value. This ritualistic basis, however remote, is still recognizable as secularized ritual even in the most profane forms of the cult of beauty" (1968, 224).

For BRECHT, on the other hand, the emancipation from cult is complete: "Theatre may be said to be derived from ritual, but that is only to say that it becomes theatre once the two have separated; what it brought over from the mysteries was not its former ritual function, but purely and simply the pleasure which accompanied this" (*A Short Organum for the Theatre*, sect. 4).

What BRECHT does not appear to admit here is the unending dialectics of the sacred and the profane, the possibility of "resacralizing" the theatre that has been in evidence since ARTAUD, BROOK and GROTOWSKI and given prominence by the religious anthropology of Mircea ELIADE. One could go so far as to say, like Paul STEFANEK (1976), that theatre never truly left ritual, since ritual was *theatricalized* from the very beginning. Thus we come back to SCHECHNER's circular and timeless formula about the theatricalization of anthropology and the anthropologization of theatre.

B. LIMITS AND PROSPECTS

All of these anthropological considerations, which have been revived by BARBA's reflections, have had the merit of questioning whole areas of Western aesthetics, such as the identification and psychology of the actor, illusion and characterization, notions that have dominated theoretical thinking from ARISTOTLE to BRECHT. Nevertheless, such considerations are based almost exclusively on Oriental traditions and do not really elucidate the behaviour of the Western actor, although they imply its inclusion. The epistemological basis of such studies, not to mention their exact object, is constantly shifting. As well, it is unfortunate that more reference is not made to "real" anthropologists such as LEVI-STRAUSS, TURNER (1982), LEROI-GOURHAN (1974) or JOUSSE (1974). Still, theatre anthropology, particularly that practised by BARBA and his colleagues at ISTA, is the most systematic and ambitious response to the political theorizing of BRECHT or the functionalism of *semiology**.

See also: Ethnoscenography, ethnodrama, anthropological theatre.

Further reading: Eliade 1963, 1965; *Esprit*, Nov. 1963; *Drama Review*, 59 (Sept. 1973) 94 (1982); Brook 1968; G. Durand 1969; Barba and Savanese 1985, 1995; Borie 1980, 1981, 1982, 1989; Innes 1981; Pradier 1985; Slawinska 1985, Pavis 1996a.

ANTI-HERO

Fr.: *antihéros;* Ger.: *Antiheld;* Sp.: *antihéroe.*

See HERO

ANTI-MASQUE

Fr.: *antimasque;* Ger.: *Antimasque;* Sp.: *antimáscara.*

See MASQUE

ANTIQUE COMEDY

Fr.: *comédie ancienne;* Ger.: *antike Komödie;* Sp.: *comedia antigua.*

In Greek theatre (500 B.C.), antique comedy, deriving from fertility rites in honour of Dionysius, was a violent, political, often grotesque and obscene brand of satire (CRATES, CRATINOS, and particularly ARISTOPHANES).

ANTI-THEATRE

Fr.: *antithéâtre;* Ger.: *Antitheater;* Sp.: *antiteatro.*

1. A very general term used to designate a *dramaturgy** and an acting style that negate all of the principles of theatrical *illusion**. The term was coined in the 1950s with the beginnings of the *theatre of the absurd**. The subtitle of IONESCO's *Bald Soprano* (1953) is "anti-play," which probably helped the critics to discover *anti-theatre* (e.g. G. NEVEUX in *Théâtre de France II*, 1952 and L. ESTANG in *La Croix* of 8 January 1953, who uses the term to label BECKETT's play, *Waiting for Godot*).

2. This type of theatre is not really an invention of our times, as each era invents its own counter-plays; for instance, the *théâtre de foire* parodied classical tragedy in France in the eighteenth century. It is futurism (MARINETTI) and surrealism, however, that best illustrate literature's rejection of tradition and the well-made psychological play. Theatre had grown tired of psychology, subtle dialogues and well-constructed plots; people no longer believed in theatre as a "moral institution" (SCHILLER). Anti-theatre is characterized by a critical and ironical attitude toward artistic and social tradition. Its precepts are that the stage is no longer capable of giving an account of the modern world and that illusion and identification are naïve. Action no longer obeys social causality (as in BRECHT) but the principle of randomness (DÜRRENMATT, IONESCO). Man is only a laughable puppet, even though he takes himself for a hero or simply a human being.

3. *Anti-theatre* is a catchword that belongs to journalistic rather than scientific language. It includes epic forms as well as *absurd** and actionless forms of theatre (HANDKE's *Sprechtheater*, for instance) or *happenings**. It does not specify whether the negation has to do with art in general, or a type of dramaturgy that is considered to be out of date. In the first case, exemplified by the Futurists and Dadaists, the rebellion has to do with the very notion of artistic activity, and theatre is made to self-destruct, as PIRAN-

DELLO, MROZEK, BECKETT or HANDKE often succeeded in doing. In the second case, it is merely the "palace revolution," a formal protest against the established order, as in BRECHT (cf. his desire for an anti-Aristotelian dramaturgy) or IONESCO, who states that he makes anti-theatre only because established theatre is considered to be *the* theatre.

4. Rather than an aesthetic doctrine, anti-theatre is characterized by a attitude that is critical of tradition. It rejects imitation and illusion and thus spectator *identification**, and embraces illogical action, randomness rather than causality, scepticism about the stage's didactic and political potential; the ahistorical reduction of drama to an absolute form or an existential literary typology; rejection of all values, particularly those of positive *heroes** (absurdism also develops as a counter-current to philosophical drama or psychological or social realism). This apolitical aesthetic attitude of absolute negation paradoxically helped to consolidate the metaphysical, transhistorical and therefore idealistic character of anti-theatre, which, in the last analysis, regenerated precisely the traditional form of theatre that the absurd and historical avant-garde movements had set out to eradicate.
Further reading: Ionesco 1955, 1962; Pronko 1963; Grimm 1982.

ANTONOMASIA

Fr.: *antonomase*; Ger.: *Antonomasia*; Sp.: *antonomasia*.

A figure of speech in which an epithet or common name is substituted for a character's name, for instance, the "bilious lover," the "miser" or the "tartuffe" for Alceste, Harpagon or Tartuffe. (In the latter case, the sound of the name subliminally gives the hearer the disagreeable impression of an unctuous man whispering his prayers.)

When names of characters are potentially expressive of their entire psychology, they are figures of antonomasia. In addition to the comic effect and the immediate information provided to the spectator about the characters' natures, this technique also gives an indication of the dramatist's point of view, prepares our critical judgment and facilitates abstraction and reflection on the basis of a particular aspect of the story narrated. This motivation of the poetic sign reinforces the link between the signifier (the characteristics of the name and the character) and the signified (the meaning of the character). Tartuffe is inseparable from his name and his speech, thus giving the impression of being an autonomous poetic sign. "A proper name," writes R. BARTHES, "should always be analyzed with care, as the proper name is, so to speak, the king of signifiers; it bears a wealth of social and symbolic connotations" (In CHABROL 1973, 34).
Further reading: Carlson 1983.

APHORISM

Fr.: *aphorisme*; Ger.: *Aphorismus*; Sp.: *aforismo*.
See MAXIM

APOLLONIAN AND DIONYSIAC

Fr.: *apollinien et dionysiaque*; Ger.: *das Apollinische und das Dionysische*; Sp.: *apolíneo y dionisíaco*.

In *The Birth of Tragedy* (1872), NIETZSCHE identifies two opposing tendencies in Greek art that he extrapolates into antithetical principles governing all art. His analysis attempts to discover the forces that drive and shape artistic creation, and according to which all art evolves.

The Apollonian represents moderation and harmony, knowledge of self and one's limits. The image of the sculptor giving form to matter, representing the real and absorbed in the contemplation of image and dream is the archetype of Apollonian art, a form that is subject to the limits of dream and the principle of individualization. Doric architecture, rhythmical music, the naive poetry of HOMER and the painting of RAPHAEL are some examples.

The Dionysiac does not represent the barbaric anarchy of pagan feasts and orgies. It is dedicated to inebriation, to the uncontrolled forces unleashed in men in spring, to nature and the individual reconciled. It is the art of a kind of music lacking articulate form that strikes terror in the hearer and the performer. Instead of a structured form, it presents only primitive suffering and resonance. Man experiences himself as a god, rejecting all barriers and upsetting traditional values, "man is no longer an artist but a work of art" (NIETZSCHE 1967, 25).

The Apollonian and the Dionysiac, despite – or perhaps because of – their opposite natures, could not exist without each other. They complement each other in creative work, giving rise to Greek art and, more generally, to the history of art. This polarity does not coincide exactly with the traditional oppositions such as classicism/ Romanticism, technique/inspiration, pure form/overflowing content, *closed form*/ open form**. However, it does take up and restructure certain contradictory characteristics of Western art of which theatre is but one example. A typology of staging styles would no doubt reveal these tensions: for instance, the opposition between a *theatre of cruelty** of Dionysiac inspiration (as proposed by ARTAUD) and a very controlled "Apollonian" theatre such as the Brechtian.

APPARITION

Fr.: *apparition*; Ger.: *Erscheinung*; Sp.: *aparición*.
See GHOST

APPLAUSE

Fr.: *applaudissement*; Ger.: *Beifall*; Sp.: *aplauso*.

Applause in the strict sense – the act of clapping the hands together – is a fairly universal phenomenon. First of all, it is a physical release for the *spectator** after a period of forced immobility. Applause always has a phatic function that says "I receive you and appreciate you." It also says, in a gesture of negation (*denial**), "I'm breaking the illusion to tell you that I enjoy the illusion you created for me." Applause is a barehanded encounter between the spectator and the artist, above and beyond the fiction.

The custom of applauding actors is a very old one. The Greeks even designated a charming little god, Krotos, just for this activity. The custom of clapping hands was standard all over Europe in the seventeenth century. In some cultures the audience shows its appreciation by shouting and whistling. There are differing opinions as to whether one should applaud during the performance, thus shattering the illusion. Applause is in fact an element of distantiation or alienation in which reality intrudes on art. Today, middle-class French audiences gladly applaud their favourite actors and their witticisms, or even the scenery, at the beginning of an act; they may applaud several times during a light "boulevard" comedy or at the Comédie-Française; while a more intellectual and "avant-garde" audience will show its enthusiasm only after the curtain has fallen, in order not to single out specific actors or production effects but to thank the performers collectively once the show is over. Then they may call for the actors, the director, the stage designer, even the author, if he dares to make an appearance.

Applause is sometimes literally staged. From the beginning, theatre entrepreneurs have paid professional clappers to encourage the audience to appreciate the show. The actors may do several curtain calls, or the whole ritual may be staged, with actors continuing to play their characters or doing a comic number (a questionable way of winning over the audience).

Further reading: Poerschke 1952; Goffman 1974.

ARCHETYPE

(From the Greek *archetypos*, original model.)
Fr.: *archétype*; Ger.: *Archetyp*; Sp.: *arquetipo*.

1. In Jungian psychology, archetypes represent a set of acquired and universal inclinations of human imagination. They are held in the collective unconscious and surface in consciousness through dreams, imagination and symbols.

Literary criticism (FRYE, 1957) has taken over this notion to identify, beyond specific works of art, a network of myths rooted in a collective vision. It looks for recurrent images which are typical of human experience and creation (misdeed, sin, death, the thirst for power, etc.).

2. A typological study of dramatic *characters** reveals certain figures that proceed from an intuitive and mythical view of man and reflect universal complexes or behaviours. In this sense, Faust, Phaedra and Oedipus are archetypal characters; they tend to escape the narrow framework of their particular situations, as determined by the individual playwright, to become universal archaic models. The archetype is therefore a type of character which is particularly general and recursive in a particular work or an era or in all literatures and mythologies.
See also: type, stereotype, actantial model, theatre anthropology, type character.
Further reading: Bodkin 1934; Jung 1937; Slawinska 1985.

ARISTOTELIAN THEATRE

Fr.: *théâtre aristotélicien*; Ger.: *aristotelisches Theater*; Sp.: *teatro aristotélico.*

1. Term used by BRECHT and taken over by critics to designate a *dramaturgy** that claims kinship with ARISTOTLE, a dramaturgy based on *illusion** and *identification**. The term has become synonymous with *dramatic** theatre, *illusionist** theatre or theatre of identification.

2. BRECHT (wrongly) identifies the Aristotelian conception with a single characteristic; he attacks the Aristotelian dramaturgy which seeks spectator identification in order to produce a *cathartic** effect, precluding a critical attitude. Identification, however, is only one of the criteria of the Aristotelian doctrine. Others are compliance with the three *unities** (particularly the principle of *coherence** and unity of action), and the role of fate and necessity in the presentation of the *fabula* – the play is constructed around a conflict, an "entangled" or dead-end situation which has to be "untied" or resolved (*knot**, *dénouement**).

3. It would be equally wrong to identify anti-Aristotelian theatre with the *epic** form. The use of epic techniques does not automatically guarantee a critical attitude that will transform the spectator. Inversely, forms of theatre that arise in the context of cathartic dramaturgy do not necessarily paralyze the spectator's faculties (Living Theater). A playwright does not have to slavishly follow the Aristotelian mould in order to produce strong cathartic effects.
See also: Brechtian, closed form and open form.
Further reading: Lukács 1914, 1975; Kommerel 1940; Kesting 1959; Benjamin 1969; Brecht 1963, 1972; Flashar 1974.

ASIDE

Fr.: *aparté*; Ger.: *Beiseitesprechen*; Sp.: *aparte.*

A speech by a character that is not meant for another character but for himself (and therefore the audience). It is distinguished from the monologue by its brevity and the fact that it is part of the dialogue. The aside appears to be a slip of the tongue that is heard "by chance" by the audience, while the monologue is a more structured speech that is meant to be heard and is clearly separate from the situation of dialogue. Words seemingly spoken by the characters to themselves should not be confused with words directly addressed to the audience.

1. The aside is a form of *monologue** that in theatre becomes a direct *dialogue** with the audience. Its essential property is to introduce a modality other than dialogue. Dialogue is based on a continuous exchange of points of view and colliding contexts; it develops the play of intersubjectivity and increases the possibility of the characters lying to each other. The aside, on the other hand, reduces the semantic context to that of a single character; it indicates the character's "true" intention or opinion, so that the spectator knows what is going on and can judge the situation on a well-informed basis. The monologuist never tells a lie in an aside because, as a rule, one does not voluntarily mislead oneself. These moments of

internal truth also function as pauses in the dramatic development that allow the spectator to form an opinion.

2. The typology of the aside coincides with that of the monologue: self-reflexivity, complicity with the audience, coming to a realization or decision, *address to the audience**, interior monologue, etc.

3. The aside is accompanied by stage business that is intended to make it believable (physical separation of the actor, a change in intonation, a look directed toward the audience). There are techniques that can be used to make it acceptable to the audience or believable while still drawing attention to it as a recognizable device, such as a projector directed at the monologuist, voices off or different lighting.

The use of the aside has been criticized in an ingenuously naturalistic conception of performance, but contemporary staging has rediscovered its virtues in terms of its dramatic force and dramaturgical effectiveness.

See also: Soliloquy, speech, authorial intervention, epic.

Further reading: Larthomas 1972; Gullí-Pugliati 1976; Pfister 1977.

ATELLAN FARCE

(From *fabula atellana*, Atellan fables.)
Fr.: *atellanes;* Ger.: *Atellane;* Sp.: *atelanas.*

Little buffoon-type farces that take their name from their village of origin, Atella in Campania (Italy). Invented in the second century B.C., the atellan farces present grotesque, *stereotyped** characters such as Maccus the fool, Bucco the greedy braggart, Pappus the silly old miser, and Dossenus the wily hunchbacked philosopher. They were revived by the Roman actors and performed along with tragedies. They are considered to be one of the predecessors of the *commedia dell'arte**.

ATTITUDE

Fr.: *attitude;* Ger.: *Haltung;* Sp.: *actitud.*

The way one holds one's body, in the physical sense. By extension, a psychological or moral approach to a given question.

1. The *actor's attitude*, i.e. his position in relation to the stage and other actors (isolation, adherence to the group, emotional relationships with others). *Attitude* is equivalent to pose, as a voluntary and involuntary way of holding oneself; and *to posture*, as the position of one part of the body in relation to the others. Attitude is often similar to a gesture that is *held*: "Gesture gives way, attitude remains ... [...] Mime is an art in movement in which attitude is only punctuation." (DECROUX 1963, 124)

2. For BRECHT, the attention of the director and the spectator should be directed toward human relations, particularly in their socioeconomic dimension. The attitudes (*Haltungen*) of the characters among themselves (or *gestus**) visualize the balance of power and contradictions. Attitude is employed as a link between man and the outside world, thus resembling attitude as defined by psychologists.

3. The attitude of the director towards the text is the way in which the text is interpreted or criticized and how this critical and aesthetic judgment is reflected in the staging.

Further reading: Engel 1979; Noverre 1978; Pavis and Villeneuve 1993.

AUDIENCE'S LEFT, AUDIENCE'S RIGHT

Fr.: *côté cour, côté jardin;* Ger.: *rechts vom Zuschauer, Links vom Zuschauer;* Sp.: *derecha e izquierda del escenario.*

See STAGE LEFT, STAGE RIGHT

AUTHORIAL INTERVENTION

Fr.: *mot d'auteur;* Ger.: *Einschreiten des Autors in die Handlung;* Sp.: *dicho de autor.*

A part of the dramatic text that appears to be words put into the character's mouth by the playwright rather than said by the character in accordance with his psychology and the situation – usually a witticism, a joke, an aphorism or a *maxim**.

The authorial intervention is a form of *quotation** announced as such, which is intended to "go over the characters' heads" to highlight the playwright's stylistic talents. Thesis drama and boulevard theatre, both of which like to bestow knowing winks on the audience, are particularly fond of this kind of allusion. This allows the director to short-circuit the *communication** between the characters and demystify the convention of a spontaneous speech invented by a character.

AUTO SACRAMENTAL

(From the Latin *actus*, act, and *sacramentum*, sacrament, mystery.)

An allegorical religious play performed in Spain and Portugal on Corpus Christi, dealing with moral and theological issues (the sacrament of Eucharist). The show was performed on carts and combined farce and dance with Biblical history, attracting a popular audience. These plays were performed throughout the Middle Ages, reaching their apogee in the Golden Age, and were banned in 1765. They had a profound influence on Spanish dramatists such as LOPE DE VEGA, TIRSO DE MOLINA and CALDERON, and on Portuguese dramatists such as VICENTE.

Further reading: Flecniakoska 1961; Sentaurens 1984.

AUTOBIOGRAPHICAL THEATRE

Fr.: *théâtre autobiographique*; Ger.: *Autobiographisches Theater*; Sp.: *teatro autobiográfico*.

1. Autobiography is generally understood to mean "a retrospective prose account of one's own existence, with the main accept on one's individual life and especially the history of one's personality" (LEJEUNE 1971, 14). This definition would appear to render the genre of autobiographical theatre impossible, since theatre is a present fiction taken on by imaginary characters other than the author, who have other concerns than simply telling their lifes. An impossible and infrequently seen genre, despite attempts as old as theatre itself: *parabasis** in ARISTOPHANES; *Le Jeu de la Feuillée* (1276), in which the author, ADAM DE LA HALLE, appears in person among his friends of Arras; *Le Drame de la vie* (1793) by RESTIF DE LA BRETONNE, who undertakes to "publish the life of a man and put it into drama with a truthfulness that makes him act rather than speak."

2. Autobiographical theatre (or performance) ought not be confused with *monodrama**, cerebral drama, self-dramaturgy (centred around a character that imposes his vision on the external world), or the monological trend seen in European theatre during the 1970s and 1980s (DANAN 1995). A distinction must also be made between autobiographical dramatic texts (regardless of their writing) and stage performance by an actor-author who speaks of himself.

The aim in the first instance is to examine how the writing constantly returns, through the different characters' voices, to the author's obsessive self. In the (today much more frequent) case of self-performances by actor-authors who are biographers of themselves, there is a real person before us whom we see, live, reflecting upon his past and present condition, while the autobiographical text read or carried by an actor is the written and narrated result of such a reflection. Thus the actor on stage is, by nature, autobiographical, since he is appearing in a show, speaking in the present tense, which he experiences before us. The actor always pays with his own person since, strictly speaking, he writes with his body upon himself. As soon as he opens his mouth, of course, he risks speaking of something other than himself and his current status as an actor in front of us, risks taking on a role. Thus – and this is the actor's paradox – as soon as he appears to be there, present and real, he is also taking on a role as a character which at the same time prevents him from bearing autobiographical witness. Or at least such an autobiographical communication will always be suspect because it will be subject to a particular set of movements, choice of props, in short a staging of the self for artistic and fictional purposes. There is always, in GOETHE's words, *Dichtung und Wahrheit* (poetry and truth) in what he says. The autobiographical actor is not only a "heart laid bare" but also a narrator, arranger, embellisher, demonstrator and exhibitionist who works with his material as a sculptor works with clay or a writer with words. As soon as he recounts (himself) he takes distance from his present self and stages himself in daily life (per GOFFMAN 1959). Paradoxically, the fact of having the actor's actual person on stage renders the process of autobiography, of stripping naked, suspect and artificial, or at least unbelievable. The spectator wonders, along with the actor: Who am I? How did I become myself? Where do I want to go?

Stripping naked and engaging in self-criticism in public is always suspect and stagey, so the actor must give a new confession every night, without altering it much. Hence the irony of those who confess: "I have asked you all to come here tonight to watch me make myself interesting" (DESPROGES, 1986, 8).

Forms of stage autobiography

A. LIFE STORY

The actor-author uses the stage to recount his past life, making reference to real persons and events. An example is *Le Roman d'un acteur* by Philippe CAUBÈRE. CAUBÈRE retraces, in a kind of *Bildungsroman*, his itinerary as an actor in the Théâtre du Soleil. He plays all the characters and himself, reproducing moments of real life and producing a living and moving fresco of theatre during the 1970s.

B. SHAMELESS CONFESSION

This may have to do with illness or sexuality; knowing that the actor is HIV positive and is playing out the final moments of his life gives the confession a real poignancy, but at the price of the spectator's extreme discomfort (*L'Avant-mort* by J.-D. PARIS, 1992, Théâtre de la Bastille; *Dumb Type-SN* by T. FURUHASHI 1995).

C. IDENTITY PLAY

This is the richest form, particularly in the United States with Spaulding GRAY, Laurie ANDERSON, GÓMEZ-PEÑA and Eleanor ANTIN (cf. CARLSON, 1996). Autobiographical theatre among these performers is an act of research into sexual, social, ethnic and cultural identity, an identity that fluctuates according to the occasion (the thief) and politics (the psychotic). Trying out different fictional selves (executed brilliantly by PIRANDELLO) leads to calling into question the absolute alternative between the real self and the stage self, to situating the subject in a continuous play of roles and mirrors, "making [us] recognize that character, role and identity are much more fluid categories than the traditional binary categories would lead us to believe" (CARLSON 1996, 8).

Further reading: Rougemont in Scherer 1986; Caubère 1994.

AVANT-GARDE

Fr.: *avant-garde*; Ger.: *Avantgarde*; Sp.: *vanguardia*.
See EXPERIMENTAL THEATRE

B

BALLET COMEDY

Fr.: *comédie-ballet;* Ger.: *Ballettkomödie;* Sp.: *comedia ballet.*

Comedy that includes ballet in the course of the action of the play or in the form of autonomous interludes between the scenes or acts (cf. MOLIÈRE and LULLY).

Ballet is often thought of as a complementary, if not a secondary element, as a decorative interlude, while the text of the comedy is seen as primordial. Some ballets, however, contain dramatic elements that are acted out with dialogue. The playwright sometimes chooses to relate the ballet to the plot, as MOLIÈRE did with *les Fâcheux*: "In order not to break the thread of the play with the interludes, we decided to tailor them to the subject as best we could, and to make a single whole of ballet and comedy" (Preface).

Ballet comedy is usually built around a succession of ballet entrances, danced passages that form an uninterrupted series of successive scenes, according to the principle of the episodic play.

Further reading: McGowan 1978.

BELIEVABLE

See VERISIMILITUDE

BIOMECHANICS

Fr.: *biomécanique;* Ger.: *Biomechanik;* Sp.: *biomecánica.*

Study of mechanics as applied to the human body. MEYERHOLD uses this expression to describe a method of training for actors that is based on the instant execution of tasks "which are dictated externally (by the author, the director) [...]. In so far as the task of an actor is the realization of a specific objective, his means of expression must be economical in order to ensure that *precision* of movement which will facilitate *the quickest possible realization of the objective*" (1969, 198).

The biomechanical technique is the opposite of the introspective, "inspirational" method of "authentic emotions" (199). The actor approaches his role from the outside rather than grasping it intuitively. Biomechanical exercises prepare him for fixing his gestures in "pose-positions" that will enhance the illusion of movement, the expressiveness of the *gestus** and the three stages of the acting cycle (intention, realization, reaction).

Further reading: *Drama Review*, 1973; Meyerhold 1963, 1969, 1973, 1975, 1980; Braun 1995.

BIT PART

Fr.: *utilité;* Ger.: *Nebenrolle;* Sp.: *rol secundario.*

An actor who is assigned a bit part is used as a foil for his partners. To play a bit part is to have a minor, walk-on part in the play.

See also: casting, typecasting, character.

BLACK COMEDY

Fr.: *comédie noire;* Ger.: *schwarze Komödie;* Sp.: *comedia negra.*

The genre of black comedy is close to the tragicomic. It is *comedy* in name only and presents a pessimistic and disillusioned perspective without even a tragic resolution. Values are negated and the play only ends "well" in an ironic tour de force (for example, *The Merchant of Venice, Measure for Measure,* ANOUILH's *pièces noires,* DÜRRENMATT's *The Visit*).

BLOCKING

Fr.: *mise en place;* Ger.: *szenisches Arrangement, Markieren;* Sp.: *planta de movimiento.*
See READING, STAGING

BODY

Fr.: *corps;* Ger.: *Körper;* Sp.: *cuerpo.*

1. Organism or Puppet?
Within the range of acting styles, the actor's body is situated somewhere between spontaneity and total control, between a natural, spontaneous body and a puppet-like body whose strings are held and manipulated by its subject or spiritual procreator, the director.

2. Transmitter or Material?
Views regarding the use of the body in theatre oscillate between the following two conceptions:

A. The body is only a *transmitter* or bearer of the theatrical creation, which is situated elsewhere – in the text or the fiction performed. The body is totally subordinated to a psychological, intellectual or moral meaning; it is self-effacing when confronted with dramatic truth, playing only a mediating role in the theatrical ceremony. The body's gestures are typically illustrative and only reinforce words.
B. The body is self-referential *material.* It does not refer to anything other than itself, nor is it the expression of an idea or a psychology. The dualism of idea and expression are replaced by the monism of body production: "The actor must not illustrate but accomplish an 'act of the soul' by means of his own organism" (GROTOWSKI 1968, 257). *Gestures** are (or at least appear to be) creative and original. Actors' exercises consist of producing emotions through the mastery and handling of the body.

3. Body Language and Body Expression
Today, it is the notion of body as material that predominates in staging practice, at least in experimental theatre. This is why avant-garde directors, freed from textual and psychological influences, have often tried to define the actor's body language: the "genuine physical language with signs, not words, at its root" of which ARTAUD speaks (1964b, 81; Eng. 1958, 124) being only one metaphor among many others. The common denominator is a search for signs that are not copied from language but have a figurative dimension. The iconic sign, halfway between the object and its symbolization, becomes the archetype of this body language – the hieroglyph in ARTAUD and MEYERHOLD, the ideogram in GROTOWSKI, etc.

The actor's body becomes the "conducting body" that the spectator desires, fantasizes about and identifies (by identifying with it). Any symbolization or *semiotization** runs up against the difficult-to-codify *presence** of the actor's body and voice.

4. Ranking of Body Parts
The body does not create meaning in a block; it is always broken down into parts which are hierarchically structured according to an acting style or aesthetic. Tragedy, for instance, tends to obliterate movements of the limbs and the trunk, while psychological drama uses the face and hands above all. Popular forms favour gestures that involve the whole body. Mime, countering psychologism, neutralizes the face and, to a lesser extent, the hands, concentrating on attitudes and the trunk (DECROUX 1963). Overriding these genre-based hierarchies is the body's general dependence on social *gestus** and cultural determinants. One of the ambitions of *body*

*expression** is precisely to promote an awareness of postural conditioning and gestural alienation.

5. Body Image

According to psychologists, body image takes shape at the "mirror stage" (LACAN). It is the mental representation of the body's biological, libidinous and social aspects. Any use of the body on or off stage requires a mental representation of body image. Even more than the non-actor, the actor has an immediate intuition of his body, its image and how it relates to its environment, particularly his fellow actors, the audience and surrounding space. By mastering the representation of his gestures, the actor enables the spectator to perceive the character and the situation, to identify with him in fantasy. In this way, he controls the look of the performance and its impact on the audience and ensures *identification**, transference or catharsis.

6. Anthropology of the Actor

An anthropology of the actor is beginning to emerge, based on the following hypotheses:

- An actor inherits and has at his disposal a certain body imbued with the surrounding culture. His body "expands" (BARBA) under the effect of the presence and gaze of the other.
- The body shows and hides at the same time. Each cultural context has rules about what is permissible to show.
- The body may be manipulated from the outside or control itself. Ergo, it is either acted upon by others or acts on its own.
- Sometimes it is centred upon itself and gathers everything into that centre; sometimes it is decentred and stands at the periphery of itself.
- Each culture determines what it considers to be a body under control or out of control; a fast, slow or normal pace.
- The actor's speaking and acting body invites the spectator to join the dance and adapt to synchronous interaction.
- The actor's body is not only perceived visually by the spectator, but also kinesthetically; it calls up the spectator's corporal memory, and motor and body awareness.
- Presence, facial expression, proxemics, actor, voice.

Further reading: Mauss 1936; Decroux 1963; Lagrave 1973; Bernard 1976; Chabert 1976; Dort 1977b; Hanna 1979; De Marinis 1980; Pavis 1981a: Laborit 1981; Krysinski 1981; Marin 1985.

BODY ART

Fr.: *art corporel;* Ger.: *Body Art;* Sp.: *arte corporal.*

Body art is "less a movement than an attitude, a worldview, a vision of the role an artist should play" (NORMAN 1993, 169). It consists of subjecting one's body to ill treatment in order to cross the threshold between reality and simulation, elicit a reaction from an audience or the police, stage a protest against war or massacre. Body art appeared in the 1920s with MARINETTI, DUCHAMP and Dada, and resurfaced with a vengeance in the 1960s in the form of *performance art** and *happenings**. It flirts with a pretence of death and suffering, as in Japanese Butoh and groups like Fura dels Baus, or the Punk aesthetic as embodied in Royal de Luxe, a postmodern revival of the old Grand-Guignol. (On the transformation of the body, see Michel JOURNIAC (1943–1995) and his *Vingt-quatre heures de la vie d'une femme ordinaire*).

BODY EXPRESSION

Fr.: *expression corporelle;* Ger.: *Körperausdruck;* Sp.: *expresión corporal.*

An acting technique used in workshop that activates the actor's expressivity, mainly by developing his vocal and gestural resources and his faculty for improvisation. It makes the actor aware of his physical and emotive potential, of his body image and his ability to project it in his acting.

This approach borrows techniques from *mime**, *dramatic play** and *improvisation**, but it is more an awareness-rousing, training activity than a full-blown artistic discipline.

Body expression was used in rehearsal by theatre groups during the 1960s (BROOK, Living Theatre) and their followers, and had a major influence on therapy art and the teaching of theatre.
See also: gesture, body, facial expression.
Further reading: Feldenkrais 1964; Levieux [n.d.]; Dars and Benoît 1964; Barret 1973; Pujade-Renaud 1976; Bernard 1976, 1977; Barker 1977; Boal 1979; Ryngaert 1977, 1985; Salzer 1981; Marin 1985.

BOULEVARD THEATRE

Fr.: *théâtre de boulevard;* Ger.: *Boulevardtheater;* Sp.: *teatro de bulevar.*

The term "boulevard theatre" comes from the famous Boulevard of Crime (destroyed in 1862), Saint-Martin Boulevard and Temple Boulevard, which housed in the nineteenth-century theatres such as la Gaité, l'Ambigu and les Funambules, on whose stages many sentimental deeds and misdeeds were performed – their melodramas, pantomimes, fairytale plays, shows of acrobatics, and bourgeois comedies (SCRIBE) were already being criticized by contemporary artists and intellectuals. Boulevard theatre had its high point before the second world war, with a vaudeville comedy branch and a serious, psychological branch (BERNSTEIN). After 1930 it still evinced quality, in the talents of GUITRY, BOURDET, BATAILLE, and later ANOUILH, AYMÉ, ACHARD and MARCEAU.

Today boulevard theatre is a quite different genre, an art of pure entertainment, though it retains from its melodramatic origins the art of entertaining at little intellectual cost. It represents a sector that is quantitatively and financially significant, separate from the highbrow genres of the Comédie-Française, experimental theatre and the popular forms of street theatre. It specializes in light comedies written by successful playwrights for a middle-class audience with traditional aesthetic and political tastes – plays that are neither disturbing nor original. The word "boulevard" refers to the kind of theatre and its characteristic repertory and style. Some successful boulevard playwrights in France are A. ROUSSIN, BARILLET and GRÉDY, F. DORIN, J. POIRET and, before them, FEYDEAU, LABICHE, BOURDET, COURTELINE, even ROSTAND. All have been fortunate enough to have had talented and successful actors at their service: COQUELIN, RAIMU, P. FRESNAY, P. BRASSEUR.

1. Boulevard Dramaturgy

Dramaturgically speaking, the boulevard play is the logical consequence of the *well-made play**, the *melodrama** and the *bourgeois drama**, all of which share a very tightly woven dramatic structure in which conflicts are always resolved at the end, with no surprises. The *fabula** is absolutely conformist, even when it appears to threaten order and prod (rather than shock) the bourgeois about the possible loss of his financial and moral security. For the pleasure of the entire family, this domestic tragedy/comedy revolves around the eternal triangle: Madame, Monsieur and the lover (or mistress). One topographical peculiarity is the all too frequent discovery of Monsieur (or Madame's lover) in shorts in the depths of a closet. The triangle is often adapted to the tastes of the day (introducing elements such as homosexuality, the timid appearance of infantile or mentally deficient characters, the eternal generation gap between the affluent character and the hippie). The play continues to be a well-made play whose form and outcome hold no surprises, unlike the radical avant-garde.

2. Themes

Boulevard theatre seeks to seduce with tantalizing themes that never question the fundamental complicity between playwright, staging and audience. It mocks the endearing failings of the bourgeois (often called "truly French" character traits), but does so only in order to recognize their intrinsic and reassuring permanence. At no point is an analysis of economic and ideological mechanisms introduced to spoil the party or the *joie de vivre* of these likeable average French people who drive around in Mercedes Benzes. Even the few working-class characters who venture into this frivolous world (the simple-minded Spanish maid, the stammering mailman, the brainless plumber: inoffensive creatures all) are charmed by the good life. By presenting only the glamourous surface of social life (conversations in the living room, the bedroom or at the country house), the playwrights never risk being disturbing; moreover, they have the indestructible alibi of humour and disenchanted *authorial interventions** about youth or the lunacy of the modern world, all served up with facile but effective jokes. Boulevard theatre – experienced in the same way as a cocktail party, a visit to the *Folies-Bergères* or climbing the Eiffel Tower, and covered regularly by television in *Au théâtre ce soir* – is decidedly a well-established genre in the best neighbourhoods and aesthetic consciences. While retaining the same conservative ideological function, it has a knack for appearing up-to-date by adopting themes that seem daring (superficial eroticism, homosexuality in *La Cage aux folles*, the "revolt" of the "heirs," adultery as lifestyle), for seeming to be eternally new and for justifying its own stupidity with "right-wing laughter."

3. The Bourgeois Style

The acting style (we dare not speak here of a staging system) is invariably pleasant. The actors, delightful hams that they are, strive for realism by showing tics familiar to the audience: a rolling of eyes, a whirling of arms, feverish movements, pregnant pauses and silences heavy with insinuation. The phatic function is put to a tough test, as the audience is never given the chance to "tune out." Within this living-room naturalism, everything must seem lifelike, larger than life in fact: elegant furniture, the subtle and relaxed "preppy" luxury of the interiors, the bourgeois comfort of a world that is close enough for the spectator to aspire to or feel at home in. This sociological slice of life must be cut with impeccable precision to fulfill both the need for ideological recognition and the dream of social mobility. Boulevard theatre is discreet agit-prop for the well-heeled.

Further reading: Corvin 1989.

BOURGEOIS COMEDY

Fr.: *comédie bourgeoise;* Ger.: *bürgerliche Komödie;* Sp.: *comedia burguesa.*

See BOURGEOIS THEATRE

BOURGEOIS DRAMA

Fr.: *drame bourgeois;* Ger.: *bürgerliches Drama, Trauerspiel;* Sp.: *drama burgués.*

See DRAMA

BOURGEOIS THEATRE

Fr.: *théâtre bourgeois;* Ger.: *bürgerliches Theater;* Sp.: *teatro burgués.*

1. A Negative Theatre

This expression is often used today in a pejorative sense in reference to *boulevard** theatre and repertory, produced for maximum profits, its themes and values addressed to a "(petit-)bourgeois" audience who spend large amounts of money to consume an ideology and aesthetic already familiar to them. The term is rather negative, and is used mainly by advocates of a radically different, *experimental** and militant theatre. As is often true of slogans and insults, it is difficult to describe its exact semantic field; however, it reflects an ideological opposition that eschews purely aesthetic categories and identifies the political enemy with an overall negative notion, as much in connection with the mode of production and style as with the play's themes. As P. BOURDIEU writes in *La Distinction, Critique sociale du jugement*: "Theatre divides and is divided: the opposition between right-bank and left-bank theatre, between bourgeois and avant-garde theatre, is inseparably aesthetic and political" (1979, 16). In the eighteenth century, however, bourgeois drama saw itself as an oppositional, even revolutionary form, carried by the ascendant class and fiercely opposed to the aristocratic values of classical tragedy, in which the personal sphere is poles apart from the bourgeois nuclear family. In the nineteenth century, the *bourgeois drama*, in both its elegant form (Romantic drama) and its popular form (*melodrama** and *vaudeville**), became the model of a dramaturgy in which the spirit of enterprise and the new myths of the bourgeoisie reigned supreme. With the arrival of a new class in direct opposition to bourgeois interests, however, bourgeois theatre took on an entirely different meaning and became, for the young BRECHT for instance, synonymous with "mass-consumption" dramaturgy, founded on the fascination with and reproduction of the dominant ideology. BRECHT's theorizing contributed to establishing an essentially negative image of bourgeois theatre, which does not however prevent it from continuing to prosper and from being identified in the minds of the public at large with quintessential theatre, and representing two thirds of all stage production in major cities all over the world.

2. The Ceremony of Bourgeois Theatre
This image is associated first of all with that of a rich theatre that does not skimp on materials: gold and velvet, evening dress in exchange for sumptuous costumes and scenery, famous actors, easily understood plays with a rich supply of reassuring stereotypes and *authorial interventions**. The little dramas of the bourgeoisie inevitably appear: broken families, adultery, the generation gap, the "natural" elegance of honest people. This does not rule out an apparent questioning of bourgois life, a way of "provoking the bourgeois" by making them believe, for one brief moment and in a kind of social catharsis adapted to their cultural horizon, that they risk losing all their worldly possessions and certainties. Fortunately, the genre calls for the good bourgeois to master "the art of the narrow escape" (cf. the title of an article on *boulevard theatre** by POIROT-DELPECH: "L'art de l'échappé belle") and for the "tragic" aspects of his existence to right themselves in the end. Just as domestic and bourgeois tragedy sealed the demise of tragedy and aristocratic individuality two centuries ago, bourgeois theatre today marks the advent of a culinary art based on wealth and expressivity in which all is quantifiable (the price of the ticket gives the spectator the right to experience a plethora of scenery, costumes, high sentiment, sweat, tears and laughter).

3. A Contradictory Notion
Apart from this caricaturesque form of theatre, one might well ask whether any theatre today can really escape being qualified as bourgeois, if we think of the term in the historical sense rather than as a slogan. How could dramaturgy (and not only the bourgeois production apparatus of theatrical manifestations) escape bourgeois individualism, when the whole history of theatre since Greek tragedy, through the European versions of classicism, has led to defusing the tragedy of man in the grip of fate and resituating the conflict among men, *caractères* (MOLIÈRE), types (melodrama), or conditions (DIDEROT). Unless another kind of society should redistribute values with no debt at all to bourgeois taste and ideology, will theatre not necessarily remain tied to so-called bourgeois culture? More than one branch of the avant-garde, claiming to break with the bourgeois vision and mode of production, remains tied to it in spite of its denials and ex-communications. We are far from having overcome bourgeois thought or practices, despite the socialist "intermission" between the Russian revolution and the collapse of the Berlin wall. The avant-garde has lost its radical nature. On the other hand, "bourgeois theatre" is sometimes subtle enough to flirt with the avant-garde (S. GUITRY, A. ROUSSIN, E. IONESCO, H. PINTER and some playwrights of *café theatre**) or to make "intelligent boulevard theatre" (BOURDET, ANOUILH, DORIN). Unfortunately, bourgeois theatre is not always or necessarily stupid, and it sometimes even satirizes itself (DORIN, OBALDIA) in self-apology to win over the audience with laughter, aiming its sarcasm at its "committed and intellectual" double and attacking its "bête noire," *experimental** avant-garde theatre, which it labours to show as empty and pretentious (as F. DORIN in *le Tournant*, 1973). All these ideological skirmishes speak of what is at stake in the battle of theatrical genres, barely concealing ideologies

in conflict or, to use the fashionable term, "societal choices."

BRAGGART

Fr.: *fanfaron;* Ger.: *Prahler;* Sp.: *fanfarrón.*

Traditional character who boasts of imaginary exploits. The tradition dates back to the Greek *alazon*, the Latin *miles gloriosus*, the Spanish *capitán* and English *braggadocio* (as in SPENSER's *The Faerie Queene*). Matamore in CORNEILLE's *l'Illusion Comique* and Falstaff in SHAKESPEARE's *King Henry the Fourth* are famous examples.

BRAVURA PIECE

Fr.: *morceau de bravoure;* Ger.: *Bravourstück, Glanzstelle, Paradestück;* Sp.: *trozo de bravura.*

BREAK

Fr.: *rupture;* Ger.: *Bruch;* Sp.: *ruptura.*

1. Break in Theatrical Illusion

A break (or rupture) occurs when one of the elements of the play comes into conflict with the principle of the *coherence** of performance and the fiction of the reality represented. Illusion in theatre is as quick and effective as it is fragile; at any moment all the enunciators risk breaking out of the framework of illusionist performance. Such breaks are effected by the actors. Breaks in tone are possible in literature as well, but they appear to be integrated into the fiction. In theatre they come from outside, brought about by actors who, by virtue of such breaks, appear to be external to the fictional universe.

2. Break in Acting

This may occur when the actor suddenly stops saying his lines (or fluffs them), adopts a scornful attitude toward his acting, voluntarily acts falsely, or changes register, mixes tones and destroys the unity of his character.

3. Function of Breaks

As primarily a method of producing an *alienation-effect**, breaks are the hallmark of an aesthetics of the discontinuous and fragmentary. They invite the spectator to "put the pieces back together," to participate by giving an ideological sense to the aesthetic device.

But contemporary *staging** should not forget that the break is a dialectical notion and can be effective only when a unity or *coherence** has first been established. Too many breaks, or the use of breaks for no reason, produce a new style of performance, a new coherence of the incoherent, and the production becomes unreadable.

See also: dramatic and epic, quote, collage, montage, rhythm.

Further reading: Benjamin 1969; Voltz 1974; Adorno 1984.

BRECHTIAN

Fr.: *brechtien;* Ger.: *Brechtisch;* Sp.: *brechtiano.*

An adjective derived from the name of Bertolt BRECHT, the German playwright (1898–1956), and used to describe a theatre called, variously, *epic**, critical, dialectical or socialist, and an acting style that favours audience participation, mainly through the demonstrative ("showing") nature of the acting.

The term is often used to describe a staging style that stresses the historical aspect of the reality represented (*historicization**) and encourages spectators to remain at a distance and not be taken in by its tragic, dramatic, or simply illusionist nature.

"Brechtian" often refers to "politics of signs" – stage and text provide a space for theatre practice and signify reality through a system of signs that are at once aesthetic (rooted in stage materials or in a given stage craft) and political (criticizing reality rather than imitating it passively). The Brechtian "system," whether one stresses those of its aspects which make it antidramatic (epic), realistic or dialectical (alliance of opposing principles such as identification and distance), is by no means a cut-and-dried philosophy that provides a recipe for staging.

On the contrary, it should enable plays to be staged according to the requirements of each era and in the appropriate ideological context. During the 1950s and 1960s, however, many troupes and young playwrights were content to slavishly imitate the Brechtian "style" – using certain props and colours, minimalist scenery and an "alienated" brand of acting – without attempting to adapt these aesthetic means to an historical analysis of reality and thus to a new way of making theatre. So "Brechtian" is a term that can be either admiring and "filial" or insulting and mocking, reflecting contemporary theatre's difficult (and at present quite distant) relationship with this playwright who has already become a classic – "poor B.B.".

See also: experimental theatre, narrative.

Further reading: Brecht 1961, 1963, 1967, 1976; Dort 1960; Barthes 1964b, 84–89; 1972a, 71–76; Ruelicke-Weiler 1968; Pavis 1978b; Lehmann and Lethen 1978; Knopf 1980; Banu 1981a; F. Toro 1984.

BUFFOON

Fr.: *bouffon*; Ger.: *Quacksalber, Possenreisser*; Sp.: *saltimbanqui*.

Wandering troupes of mountebanks and buffoons travelled Europe in days gone by, performing popular shows on stages mounted on trestles. These itinerant actors – clowns, acrobats, jugglers and sometimes singers and poets – always led an existence on the fringes of official theatre.

BURLESQUE

(From the Italian *burlesco, burla*; joke, farce.)
Fr.: *burlesque*; Ger.: *das Burleske*; Sp.: *burlesco*.

Burlesque is an exaggerated form of the *comic**, using trivial expressions to speak of the noble or elevated, making a travesty of a serious genre by using *grotesque** or vulgar pastiche. It is an explanation of the most serious things using laughable and ridiculous expressions.

1. The Burlesque Genre

Burlesque became a literary genre around the middle of the seventeenth century in France, with SCARRON (*Recueil de vers burlesques*, 1643; *Virgile travesti*, 1648), D'ASSOUCI (*le Jugement de Pâris*, 1648), PERRAULT (*les Murs de Troie*, 1653), in a reaction against the strictures of classical rules. This kind of writing, or rather rewriting, is particularly fond of mocking classical authors (SCARRON, MARIVAUX in *Télémaque travesti* and *Homère travesti*, 1736). Burlesque often uses pamphleteering and social or political satire. It had difficulties establishing itself as an independent genre, however, probably because of its links with the models it parodies (MOLIÈRE, SHAKESPEARE in the play of Pyramus and Thisby put on by Bottom in *A Midsummer Night's Dream*), in takeoffs on well-known texts, such as GAY's *Beggar's Opera* (1728), *The Rehearsal* by BUCKINGHAM satirizing DRYDEN, and FIELDING's *Tragedy of Tragedy or the Life and Death of Tom Thumb the Great* (1730). In France, burlesque ballet opened the way to the *ballet comedies** of MOLIÈRE and LULLY in the first half of the seventeenth century.

2. Aesthetics of the Burlesque

More than a literary genre, burlesque is a style, an aesthetic principle of composition that consists of inverting the signs of the world represented, treating the trivial nobly and the noble trivially. In this it follows the baroque principle of the world in reverse: "Burlesque, which is part of the ridiculous, consists in the incongruity between the idea one gives of a thing and its true idea. [...] This incongruity arises in two ways: first, by speaking in a low manner of the most elevated things, and second, by speaking in magnificent terms of the lowest things" (C. PERRAULT, *Parallèle des anciens et des modernes*, III, 1688). Contrary to a widely-held opinion, burlesque is not vulgar or coarse; it is a refined art that assumes that its readers are highly cultivated and have a sense of *intertextuality**. Burlesque writing – or rewriting – is a stylistic deformation of the norm, a mannered and precious way of expressing oneself and not a popular, spontaneous genre. It is the mark of a great style, of an ironic intellect who admires the object of parody and seeks comic effects of contrast and superlatives in form and theme. The debate (as expressed in MARIVAUX's preface to *Homère travesti*) as to whether the burlesque is embodied in the language used or the ideas developed (in the signifier or the signified) is ill-founded, since it is only by contrasting the two terms that the comic arises (principle of mixed genres and the mock-heroic).

It is difficult to distinguish the burlesque from other *comic** forms. Nevertheless, we could say that the burlesque rejects the moralizing or political discourse of *satire**; i.e., that it does not necessarily possess the catastrophic and nihilistic vision of the grotesque, and that it appears to be an "exercise in style" and a free and gratuitous exercise in writing. Its tendency to make a travesty of ideology has enabled it to develop on the fringes of literary and political institutions. It is the combination and intertextuality of all styles and types of writing that, even today, make it a modern genre *par excellence*, a kind of counterpoint (BAKHTIN's dialogism, BRECHT's *alienation-effect**).

Today the burlesque is best expressed in film: in the comic films of B. KEATON, the Marx brothers and M. SENNET, the visual *gags** reflect the stylistic distortions of classical burlesque. In this sense, the textual principle of the burlesque becomes a playful and visual one, as it contrasts serious behavior with its comic deconstruction through an unexpected upset.

Further reading: Bar 1960; Genette 1982.

BURLESQUE COMEDY

Fr.: *comédie burlesque*; Ger.: *burleske Komödie*; Sp.: *comedia burlesca.*

Comedy that represents a series of comic peripeteia and *burlesque** jokes (*burlas*) that happen to an extravagant or buffoon-like character (for example, *Dom Japhet d'Arménie* by SCARRON).

BY-PLAY

Fr.: *contre-intrigue*; Ger.: *Nebenhandlung, Gegenhandlung*; Sp.: *contra-intriga.*

See SUBPLOT

C

CAFÉ THEATRE

Fr.: *café-théâtre;* Ger.: *café-théâtre;* Sp.: *café-teatro.*

Café theatres, as we know them, are a recent invention. In 1961, M. ALEZRA opened *La Vieille Grille,* a café presenting poetry and songs. In 1966, B. DA COSTA opened *Le Royal,* the first café theatre to bear the name. They were followed by Café de la Gare, with Romain Bouteille, and the Vrai Chic Parisien with Coluche. Since then, some thirty more have opened in Paris, eighty in France overall, and the success of this kind of show has not diminished in the least.

Despite its very recent popularity, café theatre has older and more prestigious forerunners – the medieval tavern where we can visualize F. VILLON, the philosophers' cafés in the eighteenth century where philosophical thought took shape or confronted real life; the nineteenth-century tavern frequented by the lower classes (like Zola's *assommoir*), which was more a place of perdition than a venue for organized cultural exchange.

The novel aspect of today's café theatres is that they have become one of the last refuges for unknown playwrights and actors intent on challenging a theatre establishment that operates only with successful *boulevard** plays, recognized classical playwrights or low-risk subsidized shows. In this sense, café theatre is a response to the supposed shortage of playwrights and the very real difficulty of finding a place to work, but also to a young audience's insistent demand for new talent, liberating laughter and a changing and up-to-date repertoire.

Café theatre is not a new dramatic genre, nor does it utilize an original kind of stagecraft or space (drinks are not necessarily consumed during the show). But it is the result of a series of economic constraints that impose a rather uniform style – the stage is too small, limiting the number of actors to three or four and establishing a very close relationship with a house holding fifty to one hundred spectators. The two or three shows a night are necessarily short (fifty to sixty minutes) and depend largely on the (often comic) performance of the actors, who are "tragically" invited to take the financial risk of sharing the takings with the owner of the theatre. The scripts are often satirical (one-(wo)man shows) or poetic (montage of text, poems or songs). They are almost always productions which, if successful, go on to bigger theatres, the boulevard or the movies. Staging effects are deliberately sacrificed in favour of a virtuoso acting style that has led to the discovery of several new movie stars. The most striking dramatic innovation is the creation of comic or absurd monologues. Sometimes these plays provide a platform for little-known groups or for a powerful new feminist discourse.

The crisis of boulevard theatre and unemployment among actors have paradoxically favoured the rise of café theatre,

which already has a considerable repertoire of plays of varying quality in the boulevard theatre vein, including one (wo)man shows that may be somewhat flashy but are often original (ZOUC, JOLY, BALASKO). Café theatre has not yet managed to free itself sufficiently of commercial constraints to create a new and lasting genre.
Further reading: Merle 1985

CAPE AND SWORD PLAY

Fr.: *pièce de cape et d'épée*; Ger.: *Mantel-und-Degenstück*; Sp.: *obra de capa y espada.*

The Spanish *comedia en capa y espada* is a typical comedy presenting noble characters in a sophisticated plot that revolves around honour, chance and disguise (LOPE DE VEGA, CALDERÓN, TIRSO DE MOLINA). There is often a grotesque sub-plot centred around the *gracioso*, a *fool** or comic valet, a character who by contrast throws a parodic light on the refined world of the aristocracy.

CARACTÈRE

(From the Greek *Kharactêr*, engraved sign)
Fr.: *caractère*; Ger.: *Charakter*; Sp.: *carácter.*

1. The French term *caractère* designates the psychological and moral identity of the agents, or characters. The *caractères* of LA BRUYÈRE or MOLIÈRE, for instance, offered a fairly complete portrait of the inner selves of their characters. Character in this sense appeared during the Renaissance and the French classical period and was in full bloom in the nineteenth century, evolving in parallel to capitalism and bourgeois individualism and culminating in modernism and psychological analysis. Avant-garde theatre, with its distrust of the individual (that bourgeois invention), tends to go beyond it and the psychological approach in search of a syntax of types and characters which are "deconstructed and post-individual."

2. A *caractère* is presented as a set of characteristic (specific) traits of a temperament, a vice or a quality. *Types** and *stereotypes** tend to be an easily recognizable sketch and not as well-rounded as a *caractère*, which is much more profound and subtle. Certain individual traits may be permissible; thus, MOLIÈRE's great *caractères* (*l'Avare, le Misanthrope*), in spite of their general characterization, conserve certain individual traits that go beyond the "synthetic" representation of a simple *caractère*. A *caractère* is a reconstruction and an in-depth examination of the properties of a milieu or an era. The *caractère* is often a character with whom we cannot help identifying – who does not recognize himself or herself in the character who falls in love, suffers the pangs of jealousy, experiences anguish?

3. A *character comedy** focuses on an accurate description of the characters' motivations: in the Aristotelian dialectics between *action* and *character*, the action is only important to the extent that it characterizes, i.e. defines and visualizes the protagonists. This type of comedy contrasts with the *comedy of intrigue**, which is based on a succession of peripetia.

4. Dialectics of *caractère*: In classical dramaturgy, the *caractère* must guard against two opposite extremes – it must be neither an abstract historical force nor an individual pathological case (HEGEL 1832). The "ideal" *caractère* finds a balance between individual (psychological and moral) traits and sociohistorical determination (MARX 1868, in MARX and ENGELS 1967, 166–217). Generally speaking, a *caractère* that is effective on stage brings together universality and individuality, the general and the particular, poetry and history (cf. ARISTOTLE's *Poetics*). It is very precise but leaves room for adaptation to each spectator. Herein lies the secret of any character in theatre – he is both us (we identify with him through *catharsis**) and the other (we keep him at a respectable *distance**).
See also: history, character, characterization, motivation, denial, comedy of character.

CASTING

Fr: *distribution*; Ger.: *Besetzung, Rollenverteilung*; Sp.: *distribución.*

The way in which the roles of a play are assigned to actors. By extension, the word "cast" means the group of performers in a play.

It was long thought that casting should depend naturally and entirely on the text and the author's staging instructions. Most directors continue to cast on the basis of their reading of the text, though they are bound by institutional constraints and actor availability. Conversely, some directors now think that a more or less random casting will give a distinctive meaning to the staging: "Even if, hypothetically, it were done blindly (by drawing straws, for instance), it would find its own balance; everything always takes on (or produces) meaning." (VITEZ, *Annuel du théâtre*, 1982–83, p. 31). Theatre people are certainly no longer obsessed, as they were in the nineteenth century, with type-casting. No matter how it is done, casting is a crucial moment, the "most irremediable, and therefore the most serious" choice (LASSALLE, ibid., p. 20), "which involves the whole meaning of the play" (VITEZ, ibid. p. 31).

Opinion is divided as to the usefulness of casting all roles from a single "family" of actors, thus gaining time and benefiting from previous experience, or, alternatively, regenerating the group by adding new elements to it, while ensuring a variety of backgrounds and styles.

The tendency to recruit stars (film stars if possible) continues to prevail, but the theatre business sometimes needs to make such investments. Invested with the star's past and aura, the role may modify the meaning of the staging to enrich the character and the play with a mythical dimension that leads to a fresh interpretation.

CATASTROPHE

Fr.: *catastrophe*; Ger.: *Katastrophe*; Sp.: *catástrofe*.

The catastrophe (from the Greek *katastrophe*, unraveling) is the last of the four parts of the Greek tragedy. This concept designates the moment at which the action comes to an end, when the hero perishes and pays for the tragic flaw or error (*hamartia**) by sacrificing his life and recognizing his guilt. Catastrophe is not necessarily related to the notion of a disastrous event, but may sometimes entail a logical conclusion of the action: "A truly tragic unfolding consists in the irresistible progression toward the final catastrophe" (HEGEL 1832). The catastrophe is only one particular instance of the *dénouement**, one which is frequently seen in Greek drama, but is less "automatic" in the classical age in Europe.

The catastrophe represents the outcome of the hero's error in judgment and moral flaw. Whether the character is guilty without really being so, as in Greek tragedy, or responsible for "minor failings" (BOILEAU, *Art poétique*, III:107) as in modern classical tragedy, he must always yield. The difference is that resolution by catastrophe sometimes has a meaning (in Greek tragedy or in classical tragedy, which recentres the flaw on the individual responsible, his passion, his glory, etc.), such meaning being the expiation of an original defect, the error in judgment, refusal to compromise; at other times, however, it leads only to an existential tragicomic vacuum (BECKETT), an absurd situation (IONESCO) or total derision (DÜRRENMATT, KUNDERA).

Aristotle's *Poetics* recommends that playwrights locate the catastrophe in the fifth act with the hero's fall, but it may extend throughout the play when *flashbacks** have been used to situate it at the beginning of the play (the *analytical** technique which "unravels" the reasons and conflicts which led to the tragic outcome).

CATHARSIS

(From the Greek *katharsis*, purging.)

In his *Poetics* (1449b), ARISTOTLE describes how passions (essentially *fear and pity**) are purged through being produced in a spectator who *identifies** with the tragic hero. Catharsis also occurs when music is used in theatre (*Politics*, vol. 8).

Catharsis is one of the goals and one of the consequences of tragedy, which, "provoking pity and fear, effects a purging of such emotions" (*Poetics*, 1449b). This is a medical term that compares identification with an act of evacuation and discharge of emotion. The result is a "cleansing" and purification through the regeneration of the perceiving self. (For a history of the term, see F. WODTKE 1955.)

1. This purging, which has been likened to identification and aesthetic pleasure, is related to the work of the imagination and the production of stage illusion. In psychoanalysis, it is interpreted as pleasure experienced at one's own emotions at the sight of the other's emotions, and pleasure in feeling part of one's former inhibited self taking on the comforting appearance of the self of the other (*illusion**, *denial**).

2. Various interpretations of the term have renewed the ambiguous nature of the cathartic function. There is a Christian conception that tends to take a rather negative view of catharsis, from the Renaissance to the Age of Enlightenment, seeing it as a hardening induced by seeing evil and a stoic acceptance of suffering. This resulted in CORNEILLE's translation of ARISTOTLE's passage as "Which through pity and fear it purges of similar passions" (*Second Discours sur la tragédie*, 1660); and even ROUSSEAU's condemnation of theatre in reproaching catharsis for being nothing but a "fleeting and vain emotion which lasts no longer than the illusion which produced it; a vestige of natural feeling soon stifled by the passions; a sterile pity which feeds on a few tears and which has never produced the slightest act of humanity" (*Du contrat social*). The second half of the eighteenth century and bourgeois drama (particularly that of DIDEROT and LESSING) attempted to prove that catharsis is intended not to eliminate the spectator's passions but to turn them into virtues and emotional involvement in the pathetic and the sublime. For LESSING, tragedy is in the last analysis "a poem that evokes pity"; it invites the spectator to find a happy medium (a bourgeois notion *par excellence*) between the extremes of pity and terror.

Going beyond the purely psychological and moral conceptions of catharsis, late eighteenth century and nineteenth century thinkers sometimes attempted to define it in terms of harmonious form. In his essay *On the Sublime*, SCHILLER sees catharsis not only as an invitation to "become aware of our moral freedom," but also as a vision of formal perfection that must subjugate.

For GOETHE, catharsis helps reconcile contradictory passions. In his *Rereading of Aristotle's "Poetics,"* he makes it a formal criterion for an ending and dénouement closed upon itself (which reconciles passions and is "required by any drama and even any poetic work"). NIETZSCHE achieves this evolution toward a purely aesthetic definition: "Never since Aristotle has an explanation of the tragic effect been offered from which aesthetic states or an aesthetic activity of the listener could be inferred. Now the serious events are supposed to prompt pity and fear to discharge themselves in a way that relieves us; now we are supposed to feel elevated and inspired by the triumph of good and noble principles, at the sacrifice of the hero in the interest of a moral vision of the universe. I am sure that for countless men precisely this, and only this, is the effect of tragedy, but it plainly follows that all these men, together with their interpreting aestheticians, have had no experience of tragedy as a supreme art" (1872, sect. 22; Eng. 1967, 132).

The last revival of the debate on catharsis comes with BRECHT, who attributes it, with an ardour tempered in *A Short Organum for the Theatre* and its appendices, to the spectator's ideological alienation and the fact that a text gives prominence only to the characters' ahistorical values. Today, it would appear that theoreticians and psychologists have a much more subtle and dialectical view of catharsis, viewing it not as opposed to critical and aesthetic distance but as presupposing it: "The new awareness (distance) does not follow the emotion (identification), as what is *understood* is in a dialectical relationship with what is *felt*. There is less a transition from one (reflexive) attitude to another (existential) one than oscillations from one to the other, sometimes so close to each other that one can almost speak of two simultaneous processes whose very unity is cathartic." (D. BARRUCAND 1970).

CEREMONY

Fr.: *cérémonie;* Ger.: *Zeremoniell;* Sp.: *ceremonial.*
See RITUAL IN THEATRE

CHAMBER THEATRE

Fr.: *théâtre de chambre;* Ger.: *Kammerspiel;* Sp.: *teatro de cámara.*

Like chamber music (its linguistic parent), chamber theatre is a form of performance and dramaturgy that restricts the stage means of expression, the number of actors and spectators and the scope of the themes.

This type of theatre (performance) – of which STRINDBERG's *intimate theatre,* founded in 1907 (and his *Kammerspiel,* or chamber plays), are the best example – developed in reaction against a "heavy" dramaturgy based on multitudinous artistic and technical personnel, a wealth of scenery, the excessive importance of the audience conferred by the picture-frame or central stage or "theatre for the masses," the frequent interruptions of intermissions and the grandiose apparatus of bourgeois theatre. The dramatic writing is likewise refined, being stripped down to the essential conflicts and unified by the use of simple rules, described by STRINDBERG as follows: "If I were asked what the Intimate Theatre wants, what its aim is, I would answer this: to develop in drama a subject laden with meaning, but limited. We avoid expedients, easy effects, bravura pieces, numbers for stars. The author should not be tied in advance by any rule; it is the subject that determines the form. Complete freedom, then, in how the subject is dealt with, provided that the unity of conception and style are respected" (*Open letter on Intimate Theatre,* 1908).

A similarly intimate theatre existed between the wars with playwrights like GANTILLON, PELLERIN, BERNARD. It was meant to work "toward elucidating the mystery of inner life, toward deciphering the enigma that man constitutes for himself" (J.-J. BERNARD).

The popularity enjoyed by chamber theatre from the turn of the century to the present day is attributable to an acute sensitivity to psychological issues and the desire to turn the stage into a meetingplace and reciprocal confessional for actors and spectators. Here, behind closed doors, the actor seems to be directly accessible to the audience, who are compelled to become emotionally involved in the dramatic action and feel personally challenged by the actors. The themes – the couple, loneliness, alienation – are chosen to speak "directly" to the spectator, who is comfortably installed, almost as if on a psychiatrist's couch, and confronted, by the actor and the fiction, with his own inner self. The stage is almost an extension of his consciousness, or even of his unconscious self, as if he could alternatively open and close his eyes and continue to see a play or a fantasy on his "other stage" (cf. J. TARDIEU's *Théâtre de chambre,* 1955). Some directors (GROTOWSKI, BARBA) insist that the number of spectators be limited and that the stage and the auditorium be imbued with a "holy" atmosphere. Unlike the experience of a celebration, a ritual, a great dramatic or epic spectacle or a happening, the spectator of chamber theatre finds himself isolated and brought back to himself, as in the intimate space of the cinema. This is why *café theatre**, a genre that is today very popular and similar in the "poverty" of its resources, is quite the opposite of chamber theatre, which cannot endure its noise, disturbances and satirical themes that immediately awaken the "collectivity of funlovers." Dramaturgies that are resolutely addressed to the individual, such as psychological theatre, or to the social class, like the *theatre of everyday life** and the *chamber theatre* of M. VINAVER (1978, 1982, for theory) find in intimist theatre a listening situation that lends itself to their writing and their ideal relationship with the audience.

The same goes for chamber theatre as for chamber music – it must reconstruct the polyphony of dialogues and themes, the dissonances, the specific tonality of each instrument: a painstaking work of dramaturgical marquetry and intricate vocal composition.
Further reading: Strindberg 1964; Sarrazac 1989, 1995; Danan 1995.

CHANCE

Fr.: *hasard*; Ger.: *Zufall*; Sp.: *azar*.
See MOTIVATION

CHARACTER

Fr.: *personnage*; Ger.: *Person, Figur*; Sp.: *personaje*.

In theatre, the character easily takes on the features and voice of the actor, so that at first glance it does not appear to be problematical. In spite of this apparent identity between a living person and a character, however, the character began by being only a mask – or *persona* – corresponding to the dramatic role in Greek theatre. Through the use of *person* in grammar, the *persona* gradually acquired the meaning of an animate being and a person, and the character took on the illusion of being a human person.

1. Historical Metamorphosis of the Character

A. CHARACTER AND PERSON

In Greek theatre, the *persona* is the mask or role held by the actor; it does not refer to the character sketched out by the dramatist. The actor is clearly detached from the character as its executor rather than its embodiment, to the point of separating gesture and word in acting. The evolution of Western theatre is marked by a reversal of this perspective: the character is identified more and more with the actor and becomes a psychological and moral entity similar to other human beings, entrusted with producing an effect of *identification** on the spectator. It is this symbiosis between character and actor (culminating in the aesthetics of the great Romantic actor) that causes most of the problems in character analysis.

B. HISTORY OF AN ITINERARY

The above-mentioned development began to emerge with the beginnings of bourgeois individualism, in the Renaissance and the classical period (BOCCACIO, CERVANTES, SHAKESPEARE), and peaked from 1750 until the end of the nineteenth century, when bourgeois dramaturgy saw in this rich individuality the typical representative of its aspirations for recognition of its central role in the production of goods and ideas.

Thus the character, at least in its most precise and definite form, is bound to a bourgeois dramaturgy that tends to view it as a mimetic substitute for its consciousness. As a passionate force in SHAKESPEARE, the character had difficulty becoming a free, autonomous individual. In the French classical age, though with more difficulty, it was still able to meet the abstract requirements of universal or exemplary action, without exhibiting the attributes of a particular social type (except in bourgeois drama). At the beginning of the eighteenth century, the character still hesitated to throw itself into the battle against feudalism and clung to the codified forms of *commedia dell'arte** (at the Théâtre Italien, particularly in MARIVAUX's plays) and to the ossified structures of neoclassicism (VOLTAIRE). Not until DIDEROT came onto the scene with his *bourgeois drama* did the character represent a *condition** rather than an abstract and purely psychological *caractère**. Work and family (and, in the nineteenth century, the fatherland) became the milieu in which the characters, copied exactly from reality, developed toward naturalism and the beginnings of mise-en-scène. At that point the trend reversed itself and the character tended to be dissolved in symbolist drama, in which the world is populated solely with shadows, colours and sounds that correspond to each other (MAETERLINCK, STRINDBERG, CLAUDEL). Then the process of deterioration was reinforced, in the epic dramaturgy of the expressionists and

BRECHT; the character was fragmented and taken apart, given over entirely to the needs of the *fabula**, of the historicization and deconstruction of reality, and this marks the outcome of its "mise-en-scène." The beginnings of a new direction could be felt with the surrealist character, in which dream and reality are intermingled, and the self-reflexive character (in PIRANDELLO or GENET) in which various dimensions of reality are combined in the *play within a play** and the "character within a character."

2. The Character/Action Dialectic
All characters in theatre perform an action (even if, as in BECKETT, they do nothing visible); conversely, any action requires protagonists in order to be staged, whether they be human characters or simply *actants**. Hence the notion, fundamental to theatre and to any *narrative**, of an *action**/ *character** dialectic. This exchange can occur in three different ways.

A. Action is the main element of the contradiction and determines the rest. This is ARISTOTLE's thesis: "[...] it is not for the purpose of presenting their characters that the agents engage in action, but rather it is for the sake of their actions that they take on the characters they have. Thus, what happens – that is, the plot – is the end for which a tragedy exists, and the end or purpose is the most important thing of all" (1450a). Here the characters are agents, and the essential thing is to show the different phases of their actions in a well-structured plot. The conception of action as the engine of drama is regaining credence today; playwrights and directors refuse to start with a preconceived idea of the character but present actions "objectively," reconstructing series of physical actions without trying to justify them through a psychological study of motivations (cf. PLANCHON in his productions of the classics, as quoted by COPFERMAN 1969, 245–249).

B. Action is the secondary, and almost superfluous, consequence of an analysis of character, so that the playwright does not worry about making explicit the relationship between the two. Such is the conception of classical dramaturgy, or more specifically of seventeenth century French tragedy. Thus, in RACINE, the character was set up as moral essence; it was valid through its being and tragic opposition, and had no need to resort directly to action because it was that action: "To speak is to do, the *logos* takes over the functions of *praxis* and substitutes for it. All the disappointment of the world is gathered up and redeemed in speech, *praxis* is drained, language filled" (BARTHES 1963, 66; Eng. 1964b, 58). Here the character reached a point of no return in its essentialism. It was now defined only by an *essence* (the tragic) or a *quality* (greed, misanthropy), or by a list of physical and moral stock roles. Under these circumstances, the character tended to become an organic, autonomous individual. This did in fact happen later, with naturalistic aesthetics: although the character was no longer being defined ideally and in the abstract, it continued to be a self-sufficient substance (this time determined by an economic and social environment) which was bound to the action only indirectly, without being able to participate freely in its development.

C. Action and *actant** cease to be in contradiction in a functionalist theory of the narrative and of characters. They complement each other; the character identifies itself as the actant of a sphere of actions that are peculiar to it, and the action differs according to whether it is performed by the actant, the *actor**, the *role** or the *type**.

V. PROPP (1929) was the first to present this dialectical view of the character in action. Successive narrative theories (GREIMAS 1966; BRÉMOND 1973; BARTHES 1966a) have applied this principle by refining the analysis according to the various mandatory phases of any narrative and its properly dramaturgical functions (SOURIAU 1950). In this way, we can trace several necessary itineraries of the action and determine its main juncture points. In addition to this "horizontal" analysis, we seek to sound out the depths of the character, X-raying several levels or layers of real-

Degrees of Reality of the Character	
Particular	
individual	Hamlet
caractère	the misanthropist
*humour**	Sir Toby (*Twelfth Night*)
actor	the lover
role	the jelous lover
type	the soldier
*condition**	the merchant
stereotype	the knavish valet
allegory	death
archetype	the pleasure principle
actant	the search for profit
General	

ity from the general to the specific (see table).

3. The Character as a Sign within a Larger System

The character (rebaptized *agent*, *actant** or *actor**) is seen as a structural element that organizes the phases of the narrative, building the *fabula*, guiding the narrative material around a dynamic model, containing a concentrated bundle of signs in opposition to those of the other characters.

In order for the *action** and the *hero** to exist, a field of action must be defined that is normally off limits to the hero, one whose laws he transgresses. As soon as the hero "comes out of the shadows," as soon as he leaves his environment without conflict to enter a foreign domain, the mechanism of the action is set in motion. The action will not stop until the character has regained its original status or achieved one where the conflict no longer exists.

The character in a play is defined by a series of distinctive traits: hero/villain, woman/man, child/adult, lover/non-lover, etc. These binary traits make the character a paradigm, a crossroads of contradictory properties, completely destroying the conception of a character as an indivisible essence; there is always, just beneath the surface, a splitting of the character and a reference to its opposite. (In his alienation-effects, BRECHT merely applies this structural principle by making apparent the *duplicity* of the character and therefore the impossibility of the spectator identifying with such a split being.)

The result of these successive deconstructions is not a destruction of the notion of the character but a classification by traits and an establishment of the relationships among all the protagonists of the drama, who are seen in terms of a set of complementary traits, leading to the notion of *intercharacter*, which would be much more useful for analysis than the old, mythical view of the character's individuality. There is no reason to fear that the dramatic character will be fragmented in a multitude of different signs, as a character is generally performed by a single actor.

4. Semantics of Character

A. SEMANTIC ASPECT

Bearing the actor's features, the character is "placed" directly before the spectator (*ostension**). At first this means nothing beyond the character itself giving an image (*icon**) of its appearance in the fiction, producing a *reality-effect** and *identification**. This dimension of the here and now, of the immediate meaning and of self-referentiality, constitutes what BENVENISTE (1974) calls the *semantic* dimension, the overall (or intended) meaning of a sign system.

B. SEMIOTIC ASPECT

But the character is also part of the system of the other characters; it acquires validity and significance through difference, within a semiological system of correlated units. It is a cog in the machinery of characters and actions. Certain features of its personality are comparable to those of the other characters, and the spectator manipulates those characteristics like a file in which each element refers back to the others. This functionality and faculty for assembly and disassembly make the character a very malleable material that lends itself to all sorts of combinations.

C. CHARACTER AS "SHIFTER"

The fact that the character belongs to both the semantic and the semiotic spheres makes it a hinge between the event and its differential value within the fictional structure. As a shifter between *event** and *structure**, the character sets up relationships between elements that are otherwise irreconcilable: first, the reality-effect, identification and all the projections the spectator may experience; second, semiotic integration into a system of actions and characters within the dramatic and stage universe.

This interaction between the semantic and the semiotic extends to an actual exchange that constitutes the production of meaning in theatre. Everything that pertains to the semantic (the *presence** of the actors, *ostension**, the iconic nature of the stage, the performance *event**) can be experienced by the spectator, and also used and integrated into the system of the fiction and, finally, the dramatic universe: any event is subject to *semiotization**. Conversely, and dialectically, all the systems we may have built acquire dramatic reality only at the moment (in the event) of identification and emotion that we experience during the performance. Thus performance event and structure of action and characters complement each other and contribute to theatrical pleasure.

D. CHARACTER READ AND CHARACTER SEEN

The nature of the character in theatre is to be embodied by the actor, to be more than the paper being we know by its name, the length of its speeches and certain information that is given either directly (by this and other characters) or indirectly (by the playwright). Through the actor, the stage character acquires a precision and consistency that take it from the virtual to a real and iconic status. This physical aspect of the character as part of the event is specifically theatrical, and determines how the production will be received. Everything that we read between the lines about the character when reading the text (physical appearance, social milieu) has been dictatorially decided in the staging. While this diminishes our imaginary perception of the role, it also *adds* a hitherto unimagined perspective, by changing the *situation** of enunciation and therefore the interpretation of the spoken text.

We can, of course, compare characters read with characters seen, but under normal conditions of performance reception it is only the latter we will have to deal with. In this sense, when we are not familiar with the play we are about to see, our situation differs greatly from that of the director, and our analyses must be based on the character as staged who, as enunciator and element of the dramatic *situation**, imposes an interpretation of the text and the entire performance. The points of view of the reader and the "ideal" spectator are, here, irreconcilable; whereas the first requires the acting to correspond to a certain view of the characters and their actions, the second is confined to discovering the meaning of the text through the information provided by the staging and to observe whether the staging makes the text "speak" clearly and intelligently or whether it is redundant or contradictory (*textual and visual**). Both our view of the character *read* (by the reader) and of the character *seen* (by the spectator) require certain adjustments. A character in a book can only be visualized if we add information to those physical and moral traits that are explicitly stated, constructing a portrait on the basis of scattered information through a process of inference and generalization. In the case of a stage character, however, there are too many visual details to keep track of all of them and use them in arriving at a judgment: we must therefore abstract the relevant features and consider them in relation to the text, in order to choose the interpretation that seems right and simplify the complex stage image we receive in a process of abstraction and *stylization**.

E. CHARACTER AND DISCOURSE

Characters in theatre seem to invent their own speeches – herein lies both the hoax and their persuasive power. Actually, quite the opposite is true; it is the speeches, read and interpreted by the director and actor, that invent the character. It is easy to forget this when we see the confident acting of this inexhaustible speaker. On the other hand, the characters can only say and mean what their (read) texts appear to mean; their discourse depends on the *situation of enunciation**, on the other actors and their discursive presuppositions; in short, on the verisimilitude and believability of whatever they may say in a given situation.

Understanding characters means being able to make the connection between their lines and a situation shown on stage, and at the same time between a situation and the way it throws light on the text. It implies a mutual clarification of performance and text, enunciation and utterance.

It is important to grasp character construction according to the very different ways the information can be delivered: one "must consider who says or does [the act of utterance], to whom it is said or done, on what occasion, how, and from what motive" (ARISTOTLE, section 1461a). So we note and compare what each character says and does and what is said and done in relation to that character, rather than relying on an intuitive view of interiority and personality. An analysis of character necessarily leads to an analysis of speech, and an understanding that the character is both the *source* of his speeches (uttering them on the basis of his situation and character) and the *product* of them (being none other than their human representation). What is disquieting for the spectator, however, is that the character is never the owner of its discourse, and that this discourse often intertwines several "threads" of different origins: a character is almost always the more or less harmonious synthesis of various discursive formations, and conflicts between characters are never debates between distinct and homogeneous ideological and discursive points of view (PAVIS 1986a). All the more reason to distrust the *reality-effect** and to ask questions about its discursive and ideological construction.

5. Death or Survival of the Character?

It might be feared that, by the end of this process of experimentation, the character might not survive the deconstruction, and lose its age-old role as a support for signs. The director O. KREJCA recently wondered uneasily whether the semiological approach might not make the actor a monkey shut up in a *closed sign system** (1971, 9). It appears that there is every reason to reassure him: in spite of the "observed" death of the character in the novel, the blurred outlines of the character in the interior monologue, it is by no means clear that the theatre can likewise do without the character or that it is dissolving into a list of properties or signs. That the character is divisible, that it is not merely an awareness of self in which ideology, discourse, moral conflict and psychology coincide – that has been clear since BRECHT and PIRANDELLO. That does not mean, however, that contemporary texts and current productions no longer make use of the actor, or at least an embryo of character. The permutations, reduplications and grotesque magnification of characters only creates an awareness of the problem of the divided psychological or social consciousness. They contribute to bringing down the structure of the subject and person of a worn-out humanism. But they can do nothing to prevent new *heroes** or anti-heroes from being created: positive heroes of all imaginable causes, heroes created by the unconscious alone, parodic figures of the buffoon or the outcast, heroes of advertising or counter-

cultures. The character is not dead; it has merely become polymorphous and difficult to pin down: its only hope for survival.
See also: characterization, motivation.
Further reading: *Dictionnaire des personnages littéraires*, 1960; Stanislavsky 1966; Pavis 1976b; Ubersfeld 1977a; Hamon 1977; Abirached 1978; Suvin 1981.

CHARACTERIZATION

Fr.: *caractérisation*; Ger.: *Charakterisierung*; Sp.: *caracterización.*

Literary or theatrical technique used to provide information about a *character** or situation.

Characterization is one of the playwright's basic tasks. It consists of providing the spectator with the means of seeing and/ or imagining the dramatic world and thus creating a *reality-effect** by contriving to produce the credibility and verisimilitude of the character and his adventures. By the same token, it clarifies the motivations and *actions** of the characters. It occurs throughout the play, as the characters develop gradually, but is accentuated and essential in the exposition and establishment of the contradictions and conflicts. However, it is not possible to have total knowledge of the *motivation** and characterization of all of the characters; and this is fortunate, as the meaning of the play is the always uncertain result of its characterizations, and it is up to the spectator to extrapolate and define his own view of the characters (*perspective**).

1. Techniques of Characterization

A novelist can easily characterize externally by describing his characters' hidden motivations. But the playwright, because of the "objectivity" of theatre (SZONDI 1956), presents characters in actions and speech without the benefit of commentary: the result is a certain amount of imprecision as to the manner in which the character should be "read." There are several factors that facilitate this reading:

A. *Stage directions* indicate the psychological or physical state of the characters, the frame of the action, etc.

B. *Names of places and of dramatis personae* suggest a character's nature or fault (*antonomasia**) even before the action.

C. *Discourse of a character* and, indirectly, comments by other characters, provide self-characterization and offer several different points of view on the same figure.

D. *Stage business and paralinguistic factors* (intonations, *facial expression**, *gestures**) are clearly provided by the playwright, the director and the actor, but they appear to come from the characters themselves, through the way they express themselves and their "reality-effect." The author intervenes directly through *asides**, the *chorus** and *addresses** to the audience. These are anti-dramatic procedures used for instant characterization that circumvents the fiction of a character inventing his own discourse.

E. The action of the play is presented in such a way that the spectator necessarily draws conclusions about its protagonists and understands their motivations. Characterization always takes place through plot development, other actants' discourse, silence and sound, the ambiguity and unspoken discourse of the stage.

2. Degree of Characterization

Each dramaturgy has its own specific blend of characterization: classical theatre posits an essentialist and universal knowledge of man and has no use for materialist or sociological characterization. *Naturalism**, on the other hand, includes scrupulous descriptions of the characters' lives and gives an account of the *milieu** in which they move. As soon as the dramatic form presupposes the knowledge of a certain psychology or character types (for example, *commedia dell'arte**), it becomes useless to undertake further characterization, as they are already known by tradition and *convention**.

CHIRONOMY

(From the Greek *Kheir*, hand.)

The rules governing a symbolic use of the hands, as in classical Indian dance or the attitudes struck by tragedians in the seventeenth century.

CHOREOGRAPHY

Fr.: *chorégraphie*; Ger.: *Choreographie*; Sp.: *coreografía*.

Contemporary performance techniques tend to erase the boundaries between spoken theatre, song, mime, *dance theatre**, dance, etc. It is important, for instance, to pay attention to the melody of the *diction** or the choreography of a *staging**. There is a choreographical dimension in all acting, all movement on stage, in any organization of signs. Choreography has as much to do with the actors' movements and gestures, the pace or *rhythm** of the performance and the synchronization of word and gesture, as with the arrangement of the actors on the stage.

The *staging* does not reproduce movements and behaviour from everyday life as is. They are stylized, rendered harmonious or "readable," co-ordinated for the spectator's gaze, worked and repeated until the staging is, so to speak, "choreographed." BRECHT, who can hardly be accused of aestheticism, placed great emphasis on this altering of proportions or stylization for the stage: "...a theatre where everything depends on the gest cannot do without choreography. Elegant movement and graceful grouping, for a start, can alienate, and inventive miming greatly helps the story" (*A Short Organum for the Theatre*, sect. 73).

See also: gesture, mime, body, expression, dance theatre.

Further reading: Hanna 1979; Noverre 1978; Pavis 1996a.

CHORUS

(From the Greek *khoros* and Latin *chorus*, troupe of dancers and singers, religious holiday.)

Fr.: *choeur*; Ger.: *Chor*; Sp.: *coro*.

A term common to music and theatre. A device used in Greek theatre, the chorus is a homogeneous group of dancers, singers and narrators who speak collectively to comment on the action in which they are involved in various ways.

In its most general form, the chorus consists of non-individualized and often abstract forces (*actants**) that represent higher moral or political interests: "the *song of the chorus* expresses universal moods and feelings in language approaching now the solidity of the epic style, and now the impetuosity of lyric" (HEGEL 1832; Eng. 1975, 1172). The function and form of the chorus have varied so widely across the ages that a brief historical overview is in order.

Greek tragedy appears to have evolved from the chorus of masked dancers and singers. Such is the importance of this group of men who gradually gave form to individualized characters, after the leader of the chorus (*exarchôn*) had established the main actor, who gradually began to imitate an action (THESPIS' tragedies). AESCHYLUS, followed by SOPHOCLES, introduced a second and then a third actor.

The *choréia* achieved a synthesis between poetry, music and dance which is at the origin of Western performance. However, as R. BARTHES noted, "our theatre, even when it is lyrical, cannot give an idea of what the *choréia* was like, as music prevails to the detriment of the text and dance is relegated to interludes (ballets); whereas the *choréia* is defined by the absolute equality of the languages comprising it: all are 'natural,' that is they spring from the same mental framework, formed by an education that included letters and singing under 'music' (choruses were naturally composed of amateurs, who were by no means difficult to recruit)" (R. BARTHES, "Le théâtre grec," *Histoire des spectacles*, 1965, p. 528).

The tragic chorus was composed of a dozen chorists arranged in a rectangle, while the chorus in comedy had up to twenty-four members. As the responses and comments of the chorus began to be sung by the chorists and spoken by the coryphaeus (leader of the chorus), dialogue and the dramatic form gradually supplanted it, and the use of the chorus was restricted to marginal commentary (warnings, advice, supplications).

1. Evolution of the Chorus

The origins of Greek theatre, and by extension those of Western theatrical tradition, are to be found in the ritual celebrations of a group in which dancers and singers were both audience and ceremony. The oldest form of theatre was the recitation of the main chorist interrupted by the chorus. Later the responses to the chorus were made by one, then by several protagonists. The dramatic form (dialogue) became the norm, and the chorus became a medium for commentary in the form of warnings, advice and supplications.

In the comedy of Aristophanes, the chorus was largely integrated into the action and took part in the *parabasis**. Later, when it appeared at all, it was used as a lyrical interlude (as in Roman comedy).

In the Middle Ages the chorus took on more personal, more didactic forms, functioning as an epic co-ordinator of the episodes presented, and was subdivided within the action into sub-choruses that took part in the *fabula**.

In the sixteenth century, particularly in humanistic theatre, the chorus separated the acts (as in MARLOWE's *Faust*) or was used as a musical interlude. SHAKESPEARE personalized it, embodying it in an actor who delivered the *prologue** and the *epilogue**. The clown and the fool, precursors of the confidant of French classical theatre, represent a parodic form of the chorus.

French classicism largely renounced the chorus, preferring the more intimate illumination provided by *confidant** and *soliloquy**. (Notable exceptions are RACINE's *Esther* and *Athalie*.) The last classical use of the chorus is found in GOETHE and SCHILLER. For the latter, the chorus must favour catharsis and "depsychologize" the dramatic conflict by elevating it from its banal surroundings to a highly tragic sphere of "the blind force of the affections" and "illusion... he disdains to excite" (SCHILLER's preface to *The Bride of Messina*).

The use of the chorus was clearly in decline in the realism and naturalism of the nineteenth century, as an offense against verisimilitude. Sometimes it appeared in the form of collective characters such as "the people" (BÜCHNER, HUGO, MUSSET). Now that illusionist dramaturgy has been superseded, the chorus is reappearing as an alienation-effect (BRECHT, ANOUILH's *Antigone*), as a desperate attempt to find a force common to all (T.S. ELIOT, GIRAUDOUX, TOLLER), or in musical comedy (as a mystifying and consensual function of the group welded together by artistic expression – dance, song, text).

2. Powers of the Chorus

A. AESTHETIC FUNCTION AS DENIAL OF REALITY

In spite of its fundamental importance in Greek tragedy, the chorus was soon seen as an artificial element external to the dramatic debate among the characters. It became an epic technique that was often used to create distance, as it set up for the spectator another spectator/judge of the action authorized to comment on it, an "ideal spectator" (SCHLEGEL). Essentially, this epic commentary was used to incarnate on stage the audience and its gaze. SCHILLER says exactly what BRECHT was to say later about the epic narrator and the alienation-effect: "It is by holding asunder the different parts, and stepping between the passions with its composing views, that the chorus restores to us our freedom, which would else be lost in the tempest." ("On the Use of the Chorus in Tragedy," SCHILLER's preface to *The Bride of Messina*).

B. IDEALIZATION AND GENERALIZATION

By elevating itself above the "pedestrian" action of the characters, the chorus relays the dramatist's "deep" discourse, making the transition from particular to general. Its elevated lyrical style raises the realistic discourse of the characters to the highest possible level, and art's power of generalization and discovery is increased tenfold: "It forsakes the contracted sphere of the incidents to dilate itself over the past and the future, over distant times and nations, and general humanity, to deduce the grand results of life, and pronounces the lessons of wisdom (SCHILLER, ibid.)

C. EXPRESSION OF A COMMUNITY

In order for the real spectator to recognize himself in the "ideal spectator" of the chorus, the values transmitted by the latter must be his own, and total identification must be possible. Accordingly, the chorus has no chance of being accepted by the audience unless that audience is welded together by cult, belief or ideology. It must be spontaneously accepted as a game, i.e. as an autonomous world with rules known to all that we do not question once we have agreed to submit to them. The chorus is, or should be, according to SCHILLER, "a living wall for us which tragedy draws around itself in order to shut itself off completely from the real world and to reserve for itself its ideal basis, its poetic freedom" (Preface to *The Bride of Messina*). Once the community crosses the boundaries of this fortress or reveals its internal contradictions, the chorus is criticized as being unrealistic and is doomed to disappear. Since not all periods have the talent to "bring out the public character of life" (LUKÁCS 1965, 149), the chorus has often fallen into disuse, particularly as the individual emerged from the masses (seventeenth and eighteenth centuries) and became aware of his social force and class status.

D. CHORUS AS A VOICE OF PROTEST

The essentially ambiguous nature of the chorus – its cathartic and ritual power on the one hand and its distancing force on the other – explains how it has survived in times that have lost the belief in great individuals and have not (yet?) experienced the free individual of a society without contradictions. Thus, in BRECHT or DÜRRENMATT (*Der Besuch der alten Dame* [*The Visit*]), the chorus is used to denounce what it is theoretically supposed to represent: a unified power unchallenged from within that presides over human destiny.

In "neo-archaic" forms of theatrical communities, the chorus does not play this critical role, but is disguised as a unified group celebrating a rite. This is true of *happenings**, *performance art** that calls for physical involvement by the audience or theatrical communities (the Living Theater is the typical example of a continuous, though invisible, use of a chorus in both stage and social space).

See also: crowd scene, confidant, epic narrator.

CHRONICLE PLAY

Fr.: *chronique*; Ger.: *Chronik*; Sp. : *crónica*.

The chronicle play or history is a play based on historical events, sometimes taken from the chronicles of a historian (for example, HOLINSHED's chronicles of 1577 as used by SHAKESPEARE). John BALE's *King Johan* (1534) is considered to be the first chronicle play, but the most well-known examples continue to be those of Shakespeare which, from *King John* to *King Henry the Eighth*, paint a fresco of the *history** of England, as it was at the end of Elizabeth I's reign following the English victory over the invincible Armada (1588).

This genre, created by BALE and SHAKESPEARE but also attributable to SACKVILLE and NORTON (*Gorboduc*, 1561), PRESTON (*Cambises*, 1569) and MARLOWE (*Edward II*, 1593), was revived in the historical plays of SCHILLER (*Wallenstein*, *Mary Stuart*) and GOETHE (*Egmont*) and, today, in the epic theatre of BRECHT (*Galileo*) and *documentary theatre**. This genre has the advantage of being in direct contact with history, which it dramatizes with an eye to accuracy, taking into consideration, however, moral concerns and contemporary exemplarity. Despite their often chronological and event-centred form, the *fabulae* of chronicle plays are structured by the point of view and discourse of the historian-playwright and conveyed in a dramatic form in which literature and the stage come into their own.

CLAQUE

Fr.: *claque;* Ger.: *Claque, bezahlte Beifallsklastcher;* Sp.: *claque.*
See APPLAUSE

CLASSICAL DRAMATURGY

1. In France, classical dramaturgy developed between 1600 and 1670. J. SCHERER (1950) distinguishes between the archaic period (1600–1630), the pre-classical period (1630–1650) and the classical period in the strict sense (1650–1670). We do not use here the term "neo-classical," which is sometimes employed in reference to European classicism in the seventeenth and eighteenth centuries.

2. Classical dramaturgy in French has come to mean a formal type of dramatic construction and representation of the world, as well as an autonomous, logical system of dramaturgical rules and laws. The rules imposed by scholars and public taste in the seventeenth century were turned into a coherent set of distinctive criteria of *action**, structures of space and time, *verisimilitude** and mode of stage presentation.

3. The unified action is confined to one main event, and everything must converge in setting up and resolving the *complication** of the conflict. The world represented must be sketched out within fairly strict limits: a duration of twenty-four hours, a homogeneous place, a mode of presentation that offends neither good taste nor *decorum** nor verisimilitude.

This type of dramaturgy, thanks to its internal consistency and concordance with the literary and humanistic ideology of its time, remained in force until the neoclassical forms (MARIVAUX, VOLTAIRE), surviving through the ninenteenth century in the form of the *well-made play** and *melodrama** and in the twentieth century in *boulevard theatre** and television soap operas. Once this dramaturgical model had become doctrine (at the same time as human psycho-social analysis was being renewed by the humanities), it rejected any formal innovation or different approach to reality. Consequently, it was brutally rejected by new aesthetic trends in the nineteenth century by Romantic drama (although the latter continued to draw on it), and at the beginning of the twentieth by the naturalist, Symbolist and epic movements.

See also: poetics, theory of theatre.

Further reading: d'Aubignac 1927; Marmontel 1787; Benichou 1948; Bray 1927; Szondi 1956; Anderson 1965; Jacquot 1968; Pagnini 1970; Fumaroli 1972; Truchet 1975; R. Simon 1979; Scherer 1986; Forestier 1988; Regnault 1996.

CLICHÉ

Fr.: *cliché;* Ger.: *Klischee;* Sp.: *tópico.*
See STEREOTYPE

CLIMAX

Fr.: *clou;* Ger.: *Höhepunkt;* Sp.: *punto culminante.*

Point in the play which focuses the audience's attention and marks the moment of greatest tension (*obligatory scene**) or largest number of actors, or most ingenious point in the staging.

CLOSED FORM

Fr. *forme fermée;* Ger.: *geschlossene Form;* Sp.: *forma cerrada.*

The *closed form/open form* opposition is not an absolute one, as the two types of dramaturgy do not exist in a pure state. It is, however, a convenient way of comparing formal tendencies in the construction and mode of representation of a play. The distinction is significant only if one can establish a correspondence between each of the forms and certain characteristics of its dramaturgical approach, and perhaps even the conception of man and society underlying it. It corresponds only partially to the pairs *epic*/dramatic**, *Aristotelian*/non-Aristotelian**, *classical** dramaturgy/epic theatre.

1. Fabula

The *fabula* forms a whole that is structured around a series of a limited number of episodes, all centred around the main *conflict**. Each theme or motif is subordinated to the general scheme, which obeys a strict temporal and causal logic. The plot progresses dialectically (by action and counteraction), contradictions once resolved leading always to new contradictions until the final point that resolves the main conflict. All the actions are integrated with the guiding idea, which coincides with the quest of the main subject. Episodes that are too difficult to stage are transmitted through the character's consciousness and language by narrations or long monologues. The action tends to be dematerialized and to exist only through the mediation of the protagonists' discourse; it often appears typical, even parabolic (*narrative**). Much attention is given to effects of symmetry in the sequence of actions and speeches; each act adds to the general development of the dramatic curve.

The closed form is appropriate for tragedy, since all actions appear to converge inevitably on a *catastrophe**. The episodes succeed one another with an implacable logic, excluding any chance occurrence or deviation by the hero from his tragic trajectory (*analytical technique**).

2. Spatiotemporal Structures

What is imperative is not so much the *unity** of time and place as their homogeneity. Time has value as duration, as compact and indivisible substance, as a brief crisis concentrating all the dramatic phases of a unified action. It retains the same quality throughout the performance; as soon as it threatens to alter or distort the time of the main hero's inner action, it is mediated by a narrative and reconstructed by discourse.

Space also tolerates few changes. It remains homogeneous rather than differing according to the places represented. As a neutralized, "aseptic" place, it is perceived as a source of meaning and not an actual location.

3. Characters

Limited in number, they coincide with their speeches, and they display many common features in spite of their diversity. Their meaning proceeds from their relative positions within the *actantial* configuration**. Their properties are mainly intellectual and moral (their place within the dramatic or tragic universe) rather than material (social rank and naturalistic physical descriptions).

4. Discourse

Discourse also obeys the rule of homogeneity and artistic conventionality, being subject to a set form: for example, alexandrines, series of tirades, words echoed from speech to speech. Language is not intended to produce a *reality-effect** but to bring together protagonists with the same cultural and verbal background.

Typically, the use of the closed form results in the *well-made play**; i.e. a play constructed according to a classically-inspired dramaturgy that presents an autonomous, "absolute" fictional universe (SZONDI 1956, 18) and creates the illusion of a harmonious, self-enclosed and structurally seamless world.

Further reading: Wölfflin 1956; Klotz 1969; Bickert 1969.

CLOSET DRAMA

Fr.: *théâtre dans un fauteuil*; Ger.: *Lesedrama, Buchdrama*; Sp.: *teatro para leer.*

A dramatic text that is meant to be read rather than performed, at least in its original conception. The most common reason given for this kind of play is the excessive difficulty of staging it (length of text, number of characters, frequent scenery changes, poetic and philosophical difficulty of monologues, etc.). The plays are read only in a group or individually, which is meant to ensure a more sustained attention to the literary beauties of this "dramatic poem." Today, however, we tend to think, according to VITEZ's formula, that any text can be made into theatre.

The first author of such a "theatre for reading" was SENECA, but the genre flourished mainly in the nineteenth century, with *Spectacle dans un fauteuil* by MUSSET (1832); SHELLEY's *The Cenci* (1819) and *Prometheus delivered* (1820); BYRON's *Manfred* (1817). Many imposing Romantic dramas defy staging (TIECK, HUGO, MUSSET, GRABBE). Today, the drama is often called "poetic" and adapted for the stage (for example, CLAUDEL's *le Soulier de satin*). The contemporary trend is to stage all kinds of texts, including those considered unstageable. The notion of closet drama is therefore relative, as there is no criterion for deciding once and for all whether the play is literary or suited to the stage.

See also: dramatic and epic, reading, text and performance, dramatic text, documentary theatre, theatricality.
Further reading: Hogendoorn 1973, 1976.

CLOSE-UP

Fr.: *gros plan;* Ger.: *Grossaufnahme;* Sp.: *primer plano.*
See FOCALIZATION

CODES IN THEATRE

Fr.: *codes au théâtre;* Ger.: *Theaterkodes;* Sp.: *códigos teatrales.*

1. Code and Codes

The term is rarely seen in the singular, unless it is misused, as there is no *one* theatrical code that holds the key to everything that is said and shown on the stage (any more than there is one theatrical language). It would be naive to expect *semiology** to reveal one or even several theatrical codes that could reduce (or formalize) dramatic performance to a schematic outline. A code is thus a rule that associates one system with another arbitrarily in a manner established in advance. So, for example, the code of flowers associates certain flowers with certain emotions or symbolisms. Instead of this conception, typical of a semiology of communication, we prefer, for the theatre, the conception of a constantly changing code that is not pre-established and can be subjected to a *hermeneutic** interpretation.

2. Problems with the Notion of Theatrical Code

A. BASIC OBJECTION

Theatre critics often express the objection that to codify a performance (when a play is staged) or to look for definitive codes is to immobilize the performance and, in the short term, condemn it to death by pinning it to a single signifying outline. The objection seeks to refute an overly positivistic approach that is too squarely based on a theatrical message conceived as a set of signals sent and received as unequivocally as traffic lights. However, a more flexible approach to codes and a more *hermeneutic** view of performance interpretation in no way criticizes a semiological procedure on the grounds that it would immobilize the performance *event**.

B. DIFFICULTY OF ESTABLISHING A TYPOLOGY OF CODES

There is no one typology that prevails over the others. One can, however, make a useful distinction between codes specific to theatre (*specificity**) and codes common to other systems (painting, literature, music, narrative). The ideological code poses special problems in that it is very difficult to identify and is reflected in artistic, cultural and epistemological elements of the text and the stage. The codes specific to the work (idiolect) govern only the internal (syntactical) functioning of the performance.

The distinction between (a) *specific codes,* (b) *non-specific codes* and (c) *combined codes* is only one possible classification among others according to the criterion of theatrical *specificity**:

Specific codes

1. The codes of Western performance; for example, fiction, stage as a transformable place of action, *fourth wall** concealing action and revealing it to a voyeuristic audience.

2. Codes linked to a literary or dramatic genre, an era, a style of acting.

Non-specific codes: These are not specific to theatre, and even the spectator who knows nothing about the theatre takes them with him or her to the performance:
1. Linguistic codes.
2. Psychological codes: everything necessary to properly perceive the message.
3. Ideological and cultural codes: these are little known and therefore hard to formalize, but consitute the grid through which we perceive and assess the world. (ALTHUSSER 1965, 149–151) (*Socio-criticism**)

Mixed codes: This is the kind of code that holds the key to the specific and non-specific codes used in the performance. For instance, it is impossible to draw a line between gesture as belonging to the actor (i.e. not specifically theatrical) and as artifical and constructed (i.e. specific to the theatre). In other words, gesture, like performance as a whole, constantly operates on both levels – imitation of reality, reality effect, mimesis *and* artistic construction, theatrical *device**.

D. CODIFICATION AND THEATRICAL CONVENTION

Many theatrical *conventions** can undoubtedly be reduced to a set of codes, particularly in the case of highly stylized or ritualized forms of theatre (Peking Opera, classical dance, Nô, etc.) It is then easy to define the convention and limit it to a set of unchangeable rules. Other conventions, however, which are just as necessary for producing the show, are often "unconscious," whether they are too automatic to be noticed (laws of perspective, euphony, ideological markers that govern the staging, conventions necessary for the aesthetic perception of the performance on the basis of which we reconstitute a dramatic story and world using a few signs).

Further reading: Balcerzan and Osinski 1966; Barthes 1970; Helbo 1975, 1983; Eco 1976; de Marinis 1982.

CODIFICATION

Fr.: *codification*; Ger.: *Kodifizierung*; Sp.: *codificación*.

See CODES IN THEATRE

COHERENCE

(From the Latin *cohaerentia*, cohesion.)

Fr.: *cohérence*; Ger.: *Kohärenz*; Sp. : *coherencia*.

Harmony and consistency among the various elements of a whole. A text (in the semiotic sense of the term) is coherent when the actants remain the same and the relations between the initial and final propositions are identical (ADAM 1984, 15), when we are in a position to integrate the sign into "an overall system of interpretation" (CORVIN 1985, 10).

1. Dramaturgical Coherence

Classical dramaturgy is characterized by a high degree of unity and homogeneity as to the materials used and the way these are arranged. The *fabula** forms a whole that is logically and organically structured in the constituent parts of the action. Unity of time and place reduce the narrative to a homogeneous and continuous material. The dialogue is a series of speeches or tirades that are related to each other by thematic unity. Abrupt changes in subject matter are not permitted; one theme gives way smoothly to another and the style remains uniform. Conversation with no specific purpose and aimless discussions unrelated to the situation are not allowed. The character assumes and represents the contradictions of the play in his unified consciousness. He coincides perfectly with the *conflict**, and the debate that opposes him to the others is only an abstract debate of antagonistic consciousnesses which annihilate one another in the coherent and non-problematic ideological and moral system of the central consciousness that belongs to the playwright.

Dramaturgical coherence is the result of a unifying view of the conflicts between heroes or within one hero. Coherence means a narrative that can be read easily and with no surprises, according to a logic of action and a narrative order in tune with the socio-cultural model of a given society.

2. Dramaturgical Incoherence

Conversely, post-classical dramaturgy denounces the search for unity at any cost. The action is no longer continuous or logical, but fragmented and lacking a master plan. Time and place are multiple. The character is replaced by disparate voices or discourse. This "shattering" has little to do with a formal requirement for freedom in the use of time, place and space, but is the logical consequence of the end of the hero's unified and free consciousness. As the action is no longer unified or identical with its author, the *fabula** is fragmented, disjointed and, as in BRECHT, sometimes delivered by a narrator possessing the key to social analysis, which is generally passed on to the spectator for partial reconstruction.

3. Stage Coherence

Stage space can also establish coherence in the places represented. It can play all possible roles, being able to transform itself instantaneously by a theatrical convention. Another convention, however, dictates that once the stage has been set it keeps its identity and coherence and that everything appearing thereon is marked by the same *modality**. In this sense, the stage homogenizes the event represented. The characters who are brought together upon it move within a world governed by the same laws; their exchanges take place at the same level. Failure to comply with this law produces a comic effect (as in IONESCO, and as early as MOLIÈRE in *Amphytrion*).

4. Coherence of Performance

The coherence of the *performance text** (the *staging**) depends above all on the dramaturgical coherence that inspires it. In any case, the staging has the power to accentuate or deny the coherence/incoherence as read in the text and to establish its own coherence (*questionnaire**). A coherent staging does not produce any sign that transgresses the framework of dramaturgical analysis. It makes the spectator's task easier by linking up identical elements – the same tonality in the various elements of a scene design, co-ordinated acting, an even acting pace, a harmonious way of structuring action and stage business, etc.

An incoherent staging (in a non-pejorative sense, though incoherence may also be unintentional, of course) disorients the audience by causing the meaning to "explode" in all directions, making an overall interpretation impossible.

Coherence has to do with the organization of the various signifying systems, the way in which the signifiers produce comparable or even redundant signifieds. When there is a discrepancy between these systems, the incoherence takes on relevant meaning. The perception of such discrepancies affects the pace or *rhythm** of the staging. Our perception of the coherence/incoherence approach clarifies the staging discourse and the structure of the performance text (PAVIS 1985e).

The notion of coherence/incoherence is as much a category of *reception** as of *production**. It is produced by the staging as intentional meaning, but it is ultimately the spectator who is empowered to build it up on the basis of the performance signs. It is up to the spectator to discover unity or disparity in the signifying systems of the performance. An understanding of the way in which the various stage systems are combined enables the spectator to admit or reject certain signs and to construct *isotopies** for a reading of the performance as a whole – in other words, to establish his own reading coherence, even when using sign systems which might at first appear incoherent.

The notion of coherence is eminently dialectical and exists only in opposition to that of incoherence. Every *text*, and thus every staging, is a never-ending interplay of coherence and incoherence, norm and transgression. Once established in a "dominant narrative order," the spectator "attempts to impose a kind of intelligibility on the world proposed as coherent, constant, decipherable" (J.M. ADAM, *Langue française*, no. 38, 1978). The triumph of coherence also applies to modern or absurd plays, according to ADORNO: "The rigorously meaning-negating works are faithful to the same ideal of density and unity as the old meaning-constitutive ones" (ADORNO 1970, 231, Eng. 1984, 221). It may occur that the spectator does not perceive the coherence until long after the performance, theatre being, as it were, an "octopus" of *catharsis* and *nemesis*.

See also: semiology, semiotization, units, redundance.

COLLAGE

Fr.: *collage*; Ger.: *Collage*; Sp.: *collage*.

A painting term introduced by the Cubists, then the Futurists and Surrealists to designate the practice of juxtaposing two heterogeneous elements or materials, or artistic objects with real objects.

1. Collage is a reaction against the aesthetics of a visual work of art made of a single material and containing elements which are harmoniously melded within a specific form or frame. It uses all kinds of materials, thematizes the poetic act of fashioning them, entertains itself with daring and provocative juxtapositions.

Collage plays on the work's *signifiers*, on its materiality. The presence of common or unexpected materials guarantees a meaningful *openness** of the work and makes it impossible to find an order or logic within it. (Montage, on the other hand, compares sequences made from the same material, and the contrasts produced by the way it is organized are meaningful.)

Gluing fragments and objects together is one way of "quoting" a previous effect or painting (cf. DUCHAMP's addition of a moustache to the Mona Lisa). This act of quotation has a metacritical function as it splits the object and its contemplation, the factual level and the *distance** from which it is observed.

2. All these properties of collage in the visual arts apply to literature and theatre (both writing and staging) as well. Instead of an "organic" work made of a single piece, the playwright cobbles together fragments of texts from different sources – newspaper articles, other plays, recordings, etc. A stylistics of different kinds of collage is possible, though it is not easy to establish a typology. Based on the metaphor/metonymy axis, we can determine the movement that thematically brings together or separates the pieces juxtaposed. Even if the elements contradict one another in their thematic content or physical aspects, they are always correlated by the spectator's search for artistic perception. The success of the collage depends on this perception, be it original or banal.

Dramaturgical collage: Use of texts or elements of stage business of different origins – insertion in a play of theoretical texts, prefaces, commentaries (cf. D. MESGUICH using an interview with GODARD and a monologue by CIXOUS in his version of *Hamlet*; P. CHÉREAU making up a prologue of various texts by MARIVAUX for his staging of *La Dispute*; R. PLANCHON entirely recomposing his *Folies bourgeoises*).

Verbal collage: Collections of scraps of conversations or sounds (for example, R. WILSON in his *Letter to Queen Victoria*), the theatre of the *absurd** as it skips from one theme to another, a collage of social stereotypes in Joël DRAGUTIN's *La Baie de Naples*.

Collage in stage design: Pictorial technique of surrealistic inspiration that stresses displaced objects (PLANCHON, GRÜBER). Juxtaposition of incongruous props: the bicycle, the tent on an aquatic set in R. DEMARCY and T. MOTTA's *Disparitions* (1979).

Collage of acting styles: Parody of several acting styles (naturalistic or grotesque, etc.). Discrepancies between the text and the accompanying gestures. There is a distinction to be drawn between collages of heterogeneous materials (play, stage design, music, text, etc.) and the kind of patchwork or hybrid construction of a new production (*cross-cultural theatre**).

See also: quotation, intertextuality, play and counterplay, playwriting, coherence.
Further reading: Deloche 1977; *Revue d'Esthétique* 1978: no.3–4; Bablet (ed.) 1978.

COLLECTIVE CREATION

Fr.: *création collective*; Ger.: *Kollektive Arbeit, Kollektivarbeit*; Sp.: *creación colectiva.*

1. Artistic Method

A production not created by a single person (playwright or director) but developed by an entire theatrical company. The text is often finalized after improvisation during rehearsal as each participant suggests changes. The *dramaturgical** work follows the evolution of the working sessions, and only affects the global conception by trial and error. The division of labour may even go so far as to make each actor responsible for inventing and developing the material required for his character (Théâtre de l'Aquarium), the various parts being integrated into the whole only toward the end.

A process of historical, sociological and gestural research is required to refine the *fabula* (Théâtre du Soleil for *1789* and *1793*). The actor may start with a purely physical and experimental approach to his character by building up his part of the *fabula* on the basis of the *gestus** he has identified.

At some point during the team work, the need for coordination of the improvised elements begins to be felt. This is where the *dramaturg** and the director come in. This process of accumulation and centralization does not necessarily mean appointing one person to assume directorial duties, but it does encourage the team to reorganize its sketches stylistically and narratively, to move toward a "collective" staging (if the terms are not mutually exclusive).

This method of work is frequently encountered today in experimental theatre, but to be successful it requires participants to be highly qualified and versatile, not to mention the problems of group dynamics that may cause the whole enterprise to fail.

2. Sociological Roots

This form of creation has been in favour since the sixties and seventies. It arises in a sociological climate that encourages individual creativity within the group to overcome the "tyranny" of the playwright and his/her text and the director, who have tended so far to monopolize the power and to make all aesthetic and ideological decisions. This movement has to do with a rediscovery of the ritual and collective aspect of theatre, and with theatre people's fascination for improvisation, gesture freed of language, and non-verbal modes of communication. It is a reaction against the division of labour, specialization and technological dependence in theatre, a clear trend since theatre entrepreneurs have had access to all modern means of stage expression and make use of "skilled workers" rather than versatile artists. Politically, this promotion of the group goes hand in hand with the call for an art created by and for the masses, a direct democracy and a self-managed mode of production by the troupe. This process may go as far as the research carried out by the Living Theater or the Performance Group into merging theatre with life, in which living is no longer *making* theatre but *incarnating* theatre every day. Promoting the group eliminates the sacred notion of the masterpiece (A. ARTAUD wanted to "do away with the masterwork"). There is no longer one consciously organized central meaning; art is everywhere, anyone can respond to it, and the group masters the different facets of the creative act.

3. Methods of Creation

In improvisation, the actor is asked not to establish his character too soon but to experiment with *gestus**. The result is that multiple points of view come out on the themes dealt with, without a director deciding arbitrarily to unify and simplify the approach. At the most, at the end of this process, the dramaturg (literary adviser) or group leader may offer advice as to the contributions made by the actors, reorganize and compare their narrative sketches, or even suggest how a final staging might be established with the consent of the majority. The dynamics of the group and the ability of each participant to see beyond his own partial view will determine the success of the collective enterprise.

4. Features and Problem Areas

Collective creation is a systematic rediscovery of a forgotten fact – that theatre, as it is realized on stage, is a collective art par excellence, in which different techniques and languages are brought together: "The 'story' is set out, brought forward and shown by the theatre as a whole, by actors, scene designers, mask-makers, costumiers, composers and choreographers. They unite their various arts for the joint operation, without of course sacrificing their independence in the process" (BRECHT, *A Short Organum for the Theatre*, sect. 70). BRECHT defines collective work here as a pooling of knowledge, but it can also be conceived as an actualization of signifying systems in the stage utterance – the staging is no longer the discourse of a particular author (whether the playwright, the director or the actor), but the more or less visible and conscious result of a collective process. Here we go from the sociological notion of *collective creation* to the aesthetic *and* ideological notion of a *creative collective*, a collectivity of meaning and a collective subject of theatrical enunciation. The cause of the current crisis in collective creation is not only a return to the playwright, the text and the establishment after the collective euphoria of 1968. It is also attributable to the fact that the individual artistic subject is never unified and autonomous in any case, but always disperse, in the collective as well as the individual work.

Further reading: *Revue d'esthéthique*, 1977; Chabert 1981.

COMEDIA

Fr.: *comedia*; Ger.: *Comedia*; Sp.: *comedia*.

Spanish dramatic genre appearing in the fifteenth century. A comedia is generally divided into three days (*jornadas*). Typical themes are love, honour, conjugal fidelity and politics. Among the traditional types of the *comedia* are:

- *comedia de capa y espada* (comedy of cape and sword), representing the conflicts of nobles and knights;
- *comedia de carácter* (comedy of character);
- *comedia de enredo* (comedy of intrigue);
- *comedia de figurón*, a satirical comedy of social caricature.

COMÉDIE LARMOYANTE

Fr.: *comédie larmoyante*; Ger.: *Rührstück*; *Trauerspiel*; Sp.: *comedia lacrimógena*.

"Tearful comedy," a kind of melodrama, was a genre similar to the *bourgeois drama** in the eighteenth century (DIDEROT, LESSING). Its themes, drawn from the everyday lives of bourgeois people, evoke deep emotions, even tears, from the audience.

COMEDY

(From the Greek *komedia*, a ritual song accompanying the procession in honour of Dionysius.)
Fr.: *comédie*; Ger.: *Komödie*; Sp.: *comedia*.

1. Origins

Comedy is traditionally defined by three criteria that oppose it to its elder sister, tragedy. It has characters of humble origins and happy endings, and is intended to make the spectators laugh. Being "an imitation of persons worse than the average" (ARISTOTLE), comedy does not draw on a historical or mythological background but is dedicated to the prosaic reality of everyday people; hence its adaptability to all societies, its infinite diversity and the difficulty of establishing a coherent theory. Not only does it forego endings strewn with bodies or disenchanted victims, it almost always ends on an optimistic note (marriage, reconciliation, recognition). The spectators' laughter is sometimes born of complicity, sometimes of superiority, and acts as a protection against tragic anguish by producing a kind of "affective anesthesia" (MAURON 1963, 27). The audience feels protected by the silliness or frailty of the comic character and reacts with a feeling of superiority to the use of exaggeration, contrast or surprise.

Having come into existence at the same time as tragedy, Greek comedy – and consequently the comic play in general – is a double and an antidote to the tragic mechanism, for "Common to tragedy and comedy is the Oedipal conflict." (MAURON 1963, 49). "Tragedy plays on our deepest anxieties, comedy on our defence mechanisms against them" (1964, 36). Both genres are a response to human questioning, and the transition from tragic to comic (from the "paralyzed" spectator's anguished dream to liberating laughter) is ensured by the degree of the audience's emotional involvement, which FRYE calls the ironic mode: "Irony, as it moves away from tragedy, begins to merge into comedy" (FRYE 1957, 285). This movement produces structures which are very different in each case. Whereas tragedy is linked to a constraining and necessary series of motifs that lead protagonists and spectators toward catastrophe without their being able to disentangle themselves, comedy lives on the sudden brainwave, changes in pace, chance and inventiveness in dramaturgy and staging. This does not mean, however, that comedy always flouts the order and values of the society in which it appears; in fact, although order is threatened by the hero's comic failing, the conclusion reminds him of it, sometimes bitterly, and brings him back to the dominant social norm (hypocrisy, dishonesty, compromise, etc.).

Contradictions are finally resolved in an amusing way (though the smile may be strained) and balance is restored to the world. The comedy may have created the illusion that social foundations might be threatened, but it was "only for laughs." Here again, the restoration of order and the happy ending come only after a time of irresolution in which it seems that all is lost for the good guys, a "point of ritual death" (FRYE 1957, 179) that then leads to the optimistic conclusion and final resolution.

2. Comic Play

The comic play is intended to make people smile. For French classicism, comedy, as opposed to tragedy and *drama* (in the eighteenth century) shows characters, in a non-aristocractic environment and in everyday situations, who always manage to get out of trouble. MARMONTEL gives a very general but quite complete definition: "It is the imitation of manners in action: the imitation of manners, in which it differs from tragedy and the heroic poem; and imitation in action, in which it differs from the moral didactic poem and simple dialogue" (1787, 'Comédie').

Comedy is subject to the reign of subjectivity: "In comedy there comes before our contemplation, in the laughter in which the characters dissolve everything [...] the victory of their own subjective personality which nevertheless remains self-assured" (HEGEL 1832, 380; Eng. 1975, 1199). "What is comical [...] is a personality or subject who makes his own actions contradictory and so brings them to nothing, while remaining tranquil and self-assured in the process (HEGEL 1832, 410; Eng. 1975, 1220).

3. Minimal Sequence of Comedy

The *fabula* in comedy goes through the phases of *balance*, *imbalance* and *new balance*. Comedy presupposes a contrasted, even contradictory view of the world in which a normal world, generally a reflection of the spectator's world, judges and mocks the abnormal world of characters considered different, original, ridiculous ergo comic. These characters are necessarily simplified and generalized, as they embody a failing or an unusual view of the world in a schematic and pedagogical way. Comic action, according to ARISTOTLE (*Poetics*, chapter 5) is of no consequence and may therefore be entirely invented. It typically breaks down into a series of obstacles and reversals. It is basically driven by *mistaken identity**.

Unlike tragedy, comedy lends itself well to alienation effects and is quick to parody itself, laying bare its devices and fictional mode. It is highly self-aware and often functions as a critical *metalanguage** and as *a play within a play**.

Further reading: Voltz 1964; Olson 1968b; Chambers 1971; Pfister 1973; Issacharoff 1988.

COMEDY, HIGH AND LOW

Fr.: *comédie haute et basse;* Ger.: *Konversationstück, Schwank;* Sp.: *comedia alta y baja.*

A distinction based on the status of comic devices, applicable to Greek comedy as well as subsequent comedy. *Low* comedy uses comic devices from farce (visual comedy, *gags**, *lazzi**, blows); while *high* comedy uses wordplay, allusions and "witty" situations. The *Comedy of Humours,* which is attributed to JONSON, author of *Every Man in His Humour* (1598), is the prototype of high comedy, intended to illustrate the different humours of human nature considered as the result of psychological factors. Farce or buffoonery belong to low comedy. "'Low' comedy causes hearty laughter; 'high' comedy, on the other hand, most often invites only a smile, and tends to become serious, then grave" (MAURON 1963, 9).

COMEDY OF CHARACTER

Fr.: *comédie de caractère;* Ger.: *Charakterkomödie;* Sp.: *comedia de carácter.*

Comedy of character describes characters who are sketched out in fine detail as to their psychological and moral attributes. It tends to be fairly static in presenting a series of portraits that have no need of plot, action or perpetual motion in order to take shape. It flourished in the seventeenth and early eighteenth centuries under the influence of La Bruyère's *Caractères.*

Comedy of character renders an exact description of the characters' motivations. In the Aristotelian dialectics between *action* and *character,* action is important only in so far as it characterizes (defines and paints a faithful picture of) the protagonists. An overly-close study of character risks destroying the dramatic form (*epic treatment**) and turning the playwright into a psychologist or moralist (CHEKHOV). This type of comedy is the opposite of *comedy of intrigue**, which is based on repeated peripeteia.

COMEDY OF HUMOURS

Fr.: *comédie d'humeurs;* Ger.: *comedy of humours;* Sp.: *comedia de humores.*

This type of comedy came into being in the era of SHAKESPEARE and BEN JONSON (*Every Man out of His Humour,* 1599). The theory of the humours, based on the medical conception of the four humours governing human behaviour, aims to create stock characters who are physiologically determined by a particular humour and act accordingly, maintaining identical behaviour in all situations. This brand of comedy is similar to the *comedy of character**, which diversifies behavioural criteria by extending them to social, economic and moral traits.

COMEDY OF IDEAS

Fr.: *comédie d'idées;* Ger.: *Ideenkomödie;* Sp.: *comedia de ideas.*

A play in which systems of ideas and philosophies of life are debated in a comic or serious vein (for example, SHAW, WILDE, GIRAUDOUX, SARTRE.)

COMEDY OF INTRIGUE

Fr.: *comédie d'intrigue;* Ger.: *Intrigenstück;* Sp.: *comedia de intriga.*

Opposite of *comedy of character**. Characterization is vague and the many turns and twists of the action give the illusion of constant movement (for example, *Les Fourberies de Scapin, The Merchant of Venice*).

COMEDY OF MANNERS

Fr.: *comédie de moeurs;* Ger.: *Gesellschaftskomödie, Sittenkomödie;* Sp.: *comedia de costumbres.*

A study of human behaviour in society that stresses differences of class, milieu and character (for example, England and France in the seventeenth and eighteenth centuries with CONGREVE, SHERIDAN, MOLIÈRE, DANCOURT, LESAGE, REGNARD; naturalistic drama in the nineteenth).

COMIC

Fr.: *comique;* Ger.: *das Komische;* Sp.: *cómico.*

The comic element is not restricted to the genre of comedy; it can be grasped from various angles and in various areas. An anthropological phenomenon, it responds to the instinct for *play**, to man's love of joking and laughter, to his ability to perceive unusual and ridiculous aspects of physical and social reality. As a social weapon, it gives the ironist a means of criticizing his milieu, of masking his opposition with witticisms or grotesque farce. As a dramatic genre, it centres the action around conflicts and peripeteia that bear witness to human inventiveness and optimism in the face of adversity.

1. Principles of the Comic Element

A. DIMENSION OF UNUSUAL ACTION

The mechanics of the comic:
Since BERGSON's studies on laughter, the source of the comic has been attributed to the perception of a mechanism reproduced in human action: "something mechanical grafted onto the living." "Attitudes, gestures and body movements are laughable in as much as this body reminds us of a mere mechanism." (BERGSON 1899). This principle applies at all levels: stiff gestures, verbal repetition, a string of gags, the tables being turned on someone, the thief who is victim of a theft, mistaken identity, rhetorical or ideological stereotypes, juxtaposition of two concepts with similar signifiers (play on words).

An action that misfires:
The comic is produced in a situation in which the subject is unable to accomplish the action undertaken. KANT defined the comic as "an affect caused by the sudden transformation of an expectation which comes to nothing" (1790, in 1959, 190). Subsequently, the comic was associated with the idea of an action that is *displaced* from its accustomed place, creating an effect of surprise (STIERLE 1975, 56–97).

B. PSYCHOLOGICAL DIMENSION

Superiority of the observer:
The perception of a comic action or situation is related to the observer's judgment. The observer feels superior to the object perceived and derives an intellectual satisfaction from this: "Thus a uniform explanation is provided of the fact that a person appears comic to us if, in comparison with ourselves, he makes too great an expenditure on his bodily functions and too little on his mental ones; and it cannot be denied that in both these cases our laughter expresses a pleasurable sense of the superiority which we feel in relation to him. If the relation in the two cases is reversed – if the other person's physical expenditure is found to be less than ours or his mental expenditure greater – then we no longer laugh, we are filled with astonishment and admiration" (FREUD, Eng. 1976, 6, 256). FREUD describes and summarizes various characteristics of the spectator's attitude toward a comic event: moral superiority, perception of a failing in the other, realization of the unexpected and the incongruous, discovery of the unexpected through a change in perspective, etc. The sympathetic perception of the other's inferiority – and thus our own superiority and satisfaction – puts us halfway between perfect identification and total distance. Our pleasure, as in the case of theatrical illusion and identification, lies in the constant transition between identification and distance, between perception "from within" and "from without." In this process, however, it is the distant perspective that always wins. MARMONTEL remarked that the comic implies a comparison "between the spectator and the visible character, an advantageous distance for the former" (1787, 'comédie').

Liberation and release:
The comic effect provides a psychic release and is impervious to any prohibition or barrier; hence the insensitivity, indifference and "anesthaesia of the heart" (BERGSON 1940, 53) generally attributed to laughers. They put the ridiculous person into perspective, unmasking the importance of the body behind the spiritual façade of the indi-

vidual. All comic phenomena – *parody**, *irony**, satire, humour – contribute to "degrading the dignity of individuals by directing attention to the frailties they share with all humanity, but in particular the dependence of their mental functions on bodily needs." This unmasking is equivalent here to an admonition: "such and such a person, who is admired as a demigod, is after all only human like you and me" (FREUD, Eng. 1976, 6, 263). By laughing at the other, one laughs a bit at oneself; it is a way of getting to know oneself better and a way of surviving against all odds, always landing on one's feet no matter what the problems or obstacles. This is probably why HEGEL considers comedy to be the mode of human subjectivity and the ultimate resolution of contradictions: "what is comical [...] is a personality or subject who makes his own actions contradictory and so brings them to nothing, while remaining tranquil and self-assured in the process" (1832, 410; Eng. 1975, 1220). "In the dénouement, comedy should show that the world does not collapse under folly" (1832, 384). This indicates the essentially social dimension of laughter.

C. SOCIAL DIMENSION

Laughter is contagious; laughter calls for at least one partner to share the joke with. By laughing at someone funny, we establish a relationship with him, whether one of acceptance or exclusion (cf. below). Laughter presupposes definite sociocultural groups and the subtle relationships between them. It is a social phenomenon (BERGSON 1899).

The comic message and the laughing audience are joined in a process of communication. The fictional comic world is revealed only as a result of the spectator's customary perspective, which is offended and contradicted by the stage. Because the audience's expectations are not met, it can become detached from the comic event, keep its distance and laugh, strong in the assurance of its superiority. In tragedy, on the other hand, the exemplary and superhuman nature of the conflicts prevents the audience from replacing the action with its own perspective – it identifies with the hero and renounces criticism.

Comedy has a "natural" tendency to show a realistic representation of a social milieu. It constantly alludes to current events or aspects of civilization and unmasks ridiculous social practices – alienation comes naturally to comedy. Tragedy, on the other hand, mythifies existence and addresses itself not to a social group, but to a deep universal dimension of man, and reifies human relationships. The tragic requires the protagonists and spectators to accept a transcendent and immutable order. The comic, on the contrary, clearly indicates that social rules and values are only conventions that help human beings get along with each other, but which could be done without or replaced by others.

D. DRAMATURGICAL DIMENSION

The comic situation in theatre arises from a dramaturgical *obstacle** encountered by the characters either consciously or unconsciously. The obstacle, which is produced by society, prevents a project from being realized immediately and gives the advantage to the bad guys or the authorities. The hero is constantly coming up against a blank wall, so to speak. However, the conflict – and this is the main difference between comedy and tragedy - can be put aside to give the protagonists their way. Very often, the conflict has been created by the victims themselves. Unlike tragedy, the episodes in comedy are not linked to one another in a necessary, inevitable fashion.

2. Forms of the Comic

A. COMIC AND LAUGHABLE

A first distinction between the comic in real life and in art contrasts (1) the laughable (the ridiculous) and (2) the humourous. Between (1) *ridiculum* and (2) *vis comica* (JAUSS 1977, 177) lies all the difference between fortuitous comic productions (a natural event, an animal, a fall) and conscious productions of intellect and art. Spontaneous laughter in real situations is "a raw laugh, just a laugh and nothing more, the laughter of simple denial, refusal, spontaneous self-defence" (SOURIAU 1948, 154). Only what is reinvested by human invention with aesthetic intention is truly comic.

B. MEANINGFUL COMIC AND ABSOLUTE COMIC

BAUDELAIRE makes a distinction between the meaningful and the absolute comic elements. In the former, one laughs *at* something or someone; in the latter, one laughs *with*, and the laughter involves the whole body, the vital functions and the *grotesque** nature of existence (for example, Rabelaisian laughter). This kind of comic spares nothing, neither political nor moral values.

C. LAUGHTER OF INCLUSION AND LAUGHTER OF EXCLUSION

The necessary mutual support among laughers has the result of either rejecting the comic person as ridiculous or inviting him to join the laughers in a unanimous movement of the brotherhood of man.

D. COMIC, IRONY, HUMOUR

Humour is one of the favourite techniques of playwrights (particularly those who write brilliant dialogues for boulevard plays or philosophical dramas). It draws on the comic and irony but has its own tone. While *irony** and *satire** often give an impression of being cold and cerebral, humour is warmer and doesn't hesitate to laugh at itself or to be ironical at the ironist's expense. It seeks out the hidden philosophical aspects of existence and implies a great inner wealth within the humourist. "Humour is not only somewhat liberating, like jokes and the comic, but also something grandiose and edifying: characteristics that are not found in the other two kinds of pleasure through intellectual activity. Its grandiose aspect apparently proceeds from the narcissism and victoriously affirmed invulnerability of the ego" (FREUD 1976, 4:278).

E. AMUSING, RIDICULOUS, LUDICROUS

The comical comes across through a situation, a speech or stage business in an amicable or hostile way. In the first instance, we laugh moderately at what we perceive as being funny or *amusing*; in the second, we reject the situation as being ridiculous (*laughable*).

The *amusing* (a frequently-used term in the French classical era) evokes an aesthetic emotion and is addressed to the intellect and the sense of humour. As MARMONTEL explains, it is the opposite of the comic and the ludicrous, "the effect of a diverting surprise that causes a singular, striking and new contrast between two objects or between an object and the incongruous idea that it produces. It is an unexpected encounter which, through inexplicable connections, excites in us the sweet convulsion of laughter" (*Éléments de littérature*, 1787, "plaisant").

The *ridiculous* or laughable is much more negative, and evokes in us a slightly contemptuous sense of superiority without shocking us. According to ARISTOTLE, comedy is "an imitation of persons worse than the average. Their badness, however, does not extend to the point of utter depravity; rather, ridiculousness is a particular form of the shameful and may be described as the kind of error and unseemliness that is not painful or destructive. Thus, to take a ready example, the comic mask is unseemly and distorted but expresses no pain" (*Poetics*, sect. 1449b). For comic authors, the ridiculous becomes the object of satire and the mainspring of the action (theoretically, judging from their prefaces, playwrights consider it their highest mission to correct manners through laughter; practically speaking, they are mainly interested in making the audience laugh at a failing that may be their own). A perception of the ridiculous implies that the author and the spectator are in a position to judge what is reasonable and permissible in human behaviour. This is MOLIÈRE's goal as set out in his "letter on the comedy of *The Imposter*" (1667): "The ridiculous is the external and perceptible form that Providence has attached to everything that is unreasonable, to make us perceive it and force us to flee it. To know the ridiculous, we must know the reason why it signifies a defect, and see what it consists of." The *ludicrous** and the *grotesque** are a bit further down the scale of comic techniques, as they imply a magnification and distortion of reality that extends to caricature and excess.

3. Comic Techniques

There is no satisfactory typology of comic forms. Classifying them according to the source of comic pleasure (superiority, incongruity or psychic release) can explain them only in part (*satire** in the first case, wordplay in the second, risqué jokes in the third). The traditional classification is that of dramaturgical studies on comedy (cf. definitions of the different types of comedy). We will not cover all techniques here, as they have already been outlined in the sections on forms and types of comedy.

Further reading: Freud 1905; Monro 1957; Victoroff 1953; Mauron 1963; Escarpit 1967; Pfister 1973; Warning and Preisendanz 1977; Sareil 1984; Balme 1985; Issacharoff 1988.

COMIC RELIEF

Fr.: *détente comique;* Ger.: *komische Entspannung;* Sp.: *esparcimiento cómico.*

The moment or scene of comic relief takes place after or just before a dramatic or tragic episode to provide a radical change in atmosphere and defer the catastrophe (particularly in SHAKESPEARE and playwrights practising a mixture of genres). Comic relief provides a pause, *suspense** and preparation of dramatic action.

COMMEDIA DELL'ARTE

Fr.: *commedia dell'arte;* Ger.: *Commedia dell'Arte;* Sp.: *commedia dell'arte.*

1. Origins

Commedia dell'arte was once called *commedia all'improviso, commedia a soggetto, commedia di zanni* and, in France, Italian comedy or comedy of masks. Not until the eighteenth century (according to C. MIC, 1927) did this form of theatre, in existence since the middle of the sixteenth, take the name *commedia dell'arte. Arte* designates at once art, know-how, and the technique and professionalism of the actors.

It has not been proven that *commedia dell'arte* descended directly from the *Atellan farces** of Rome or from ancient mime. Recent research questions the etymology of *Zanni* (the comic valet), formerly attributed to *Sannio,* the buffoon of Atellan farce. It is likely, however, that these popular forms of comedy, in addition to the jugglers, buffoons and fools of the Renaissance and the popular comedies in dialect by RUZZANTE (1502–1542), prepared the way for *commedia.*

2. Acting Style

Commedia dell'arte is characterized by a collective creation of actors who elaborate a show by improvising words and gestures, using a scenario that is not written in advance by a playwright and is always very sketchy, giving instructions on entrances and exits and the major movements of the *fabula**. The actors draw inspiration from a dramatic subject borrowed from a (modern or ancient) comedy or invented. Once the acting script or scenario has been established, each actor improvises by drawing on *lazzi** characteristic of his role (comic stage business) and responding to the audience's reactions.

Grouped in homogeneous troupes, the actors travelled Europe, playing in rented halls and public squares or under contract to a prince, and keeping up a strong family and craft-oriented tradition. They represent a dozen fixed types, falling into two "parties." The serious party consists of the two couples in love. The ridiculous party comprises the comical old men (Pantalone and the Dottore), Capitano (from PLAUTUS' *miles gloriosus*), the valets or Zanni (named variously Arlecchino, Scaramuccia, Pulcinella, Mezzottino, Scapini, Coviello, Truffaldino) divided into first Zanni (a cunning and witty valet who carries the plot) and second Zanni (an ingenuous, awkward character). The ridiculous party always wear grotesque masks (*maschere*) which serve to designate the actor by the name of his character.

In this theatre of the actor (or actress, a novelty at the time), the accent was on mastery of the body, the art of replacing long speeches with a few gestures and "choreographing" the movements of the actors as a group, using space on the basis of a staging before its time. The actor's art is less total invention and a novel means of expression than an art of variation and verbal and gestural felicity. The actor must be able to return everything he improvises to a starting point, in order to feed his partner and ensure that his improvisation does not stray too far from the *scenario**. When the lazzi – mimetic and sometimes verbal improvisations that are more or less planned and written into the scenario – are developed into fully autonomous acting sequences, they become *burle*. This kind of acting fascinates actors today because of its virtuosity and subtlety and the identification and critical distance it demands of the actor. It foreshadows the reign of the director by entrusting the adaptation of texts and overall interpretation to a *capocomico* (or *corago*).

3. Repertoire

The actors' repertoire was extensive, and not restricted to the scenario of a comedy of intrigue. The *scenarios* that have survived give us a very limited view, since the objective was precisely to embroider on a schematic narrative. Novellas, classical and literary comedies (*commedia erudita*), popular traditions, all went into the *commedia*'s bag of tricks. Some troupes even staged tragedies, tragicomedies or operas (*opera regia, mista* or *heroica*), or, like the Comédie-Italienne in Paris, specialized in parodying classical and contemporary master works. They also performed the works of a particular author (MARIVAUX for Luigi RICCOBONI's troupe, GOZZI and GOLDONI in Italy). At the end of the seventeenth century, the art of the *commedia* began to "run out of steam," as the rationalist bourgeois tastes of the eighteenth century (for example, GOLDONI, and MARIVAUX in his later years) dealt it blows from which it would never recover.

4. Dramaturgy

Despite the diversity of its forms, *commedia* can be reduced to a series of dramaturgical constants – a subject that is modified and developed collectively; recurrent instances of mistaken identity; the typical *fabula* of lovers temporarily thwarted by libidinous old men; a penchant for disguise, women dressed as men, scenes of recognition at the end of the play in which the poor become rich and the missing reappear; complicated manoeuvres by a mischievous but astute valet. The art of this genre is to develop plots endlessly, using a limited stock of figures and situations. The actors do not try for verisimilitude but rather work on pacing and the illusion of movement. *Commedia* revived (rather than destroyed) "noble" but aging genres such as tragedy full of emphasis, overly-psychological comedy, too-serious drama; in this way it rediscovered ancient forms and acted as a catalyst for a new way of making theatre by stressing acting style and theatricality.

This is the aspect that probably explains the *commedia*'s major influence had on "classical" playwrights such as SHAKESPEARE, MOLIÈRE, LOPE DE VEGA and MARIVAUX. The latter, for instance, achieved a difficult synthesis of refined psychology and linguistic expression combined with the use of types and situations from the "comedy of masks." In the nineteenth century, *commedia dell'arte* disappeared completely, to be replaced by the pantomime and melodrama, the latter being based on Manichean stereotypes. Today it survives in burlesque film and clown work. Its training techniques for actors have become the model for a complete actor-based and collective-oriented theatre that seeks to rediscover the power of gesture and improvisation (MEYERHOLD, COPEAU, DULLIN, BARRAULT).

Further reading: Attinger 1950; Pandolfi 1957–1961; Nicoll 1963; Taviani and Schino 1984; Pavis 1986a; Fo 1991; Rudlin 1994.

COMMEDIA ERUDITA

Fr.: *commedia erudita*; Ger.: *Commedia erudita*; Sp.: *comedia erudita*.

An Italian brand of comedy of intrigue from the Renaissance, often written by Humanists to counterbalance the rather coarse imitations of the comedies of PLAUTUS or TERENCE and the popular genre of *commedia dell'arte** – for example, *I Suppositi* by ARIOSTO (1509), *La Mandragola* by MACHIAVELLI (1520).

COMMUNICATION IN THEATRE

Fr.: *communication théâtrale;* Ger.: *Theaterkommunikation;* Sp.: *comunicación teatral.*

This often used though imprecise term denotes the process whereby information is exchanged between stage and house. Obviously, the performance is transmitted to the audience through the actors and scenery. The question of how feedback from the audience influences the acting and how the actors interact with the audience, however, is not quite so clear, and there is no consensus as how important this factor is. Some researchers consider theatre to be the art and prototype of human communication: "What is exclusively specific to theatre is that it represents its object, human communication, *through human communication*: in theatre, human communication (communication between the characters) is therefore represented by human communication itself, through the communication of the actors" (OSOLSOBE 1980, 427).

1. Communication or Not?

A. Theatre research (both theoretical and practical) often confuses communication and audience participation, making communication between the actors and the audience the essential goal of theatre activity. But is this really what semiologists and information theorists understand by "communication"? If we define communication as a symmetrical exchange of information in which the listener becomes the receiver and uses the same code, then theatre is not communication (MOUNIN 1970). Apart from the extreme case of the *happening**, which seeks to eliminate the distinction between spectator and actor, the spectator always remains in his place, and can answer back only by applauding, booing or throwing tomatoes.

B. But if, on the other hand, communication is conceived as a way of influencing other people and recognized as such by those one wishes to influence (PRIETO 1966a,b), the reciprocal nature of the exchange is no longer necessary. Clearly, such a definition is applicable to theatre – we know that we are in the theatre and cannot fail to be "affected" by the show. It is a question of knowing how this *reception** takes place, as the mere *communication* (delivery) of stage signs must be distinguished from the *foregrounding* of the artistic and ideological effect. Or this communication must be defined as (1) "physical co-presence of sender and receiver" and (2) "coincidence of production and communication" (DE MARINIS 1982, sect. 6.2, 158, 162).

2. Forms of Response

A. Semiology of communication has not yet succeeded in establishing a theory of *reception**, despite its intention to associate theatre art with a "spectator art" (BRECHT). It still too often sees performance as a *message** comprising signals sent intentionally by the stage to a receiver who, in the position of a decipherer, needs do no more than decode each of the signals, without choosing or structuring the information received. It matters little where the spectator is physically located with respect to the performance – whether in front of, beside, in the middle of, scattered around, etc. The determining factor is the spectator's ability to combine a choice of signs into a meaningful structure that is "profitable," i.e. enables him to better understand the show. The audience must be able to *model* (abstract, theorize) its own social situation in order to compare it with the fictional *models** proposed by the stage. In other words, as demonstrated by BRECHT, the audience must take into account two *historical** dimensions – its own (its aesthetic and ideological *expectations**) and the play's (the aesthetic and social context, whether or not the text lends itself to a particular interpretation). This calls for a study of the mechanisms of perception. First the Russian Formalists, then BRECHT, showed how it is the effect of an unusual perception, the recognition of the aesthetic *device** and ideological strangeness that bring about the meaningful "click." Determining "horizons of expectation" (JAUSS 1970) for the performance (and the text) is an essential step in predicting audience response (*reception**).

B. Rather than true communication between actors and audience, there is a *hermeneutic** interaction between naive perception and perception of the *theatrical effect*, whether it be a Brechtian *alienation-effect**, a formal device or the gradual awareness of an ideology. The performance is "the coming into being, the production of a new awareness in the spectator, unfinished like any awareness but propelled by that very unfinished quality, that distance conquered, that inexhaustible work of criticism in action" (ALTHUSSER 1965, 151). That is to say, and this is BRECHT's legacy, there can be no true communication between stage and audience unless the play is capable of revealing itself as an artistic *effect** intended to discover an ideological effect.

3. Formalization of Reception Processes
Current research on reception aesthetics has shifted the perspective of literary analysis from *production* and the author to *reception* and the reader or spectator. If we hypothesize that the performance communicates with the spectator, we must ask ourselves to whom the dramatic text is addressed, how it speaks to the audience and how the latter reworks it.

The basic hypothesis is, first, that text and performance are capable of structuring or manipulating proper reception of the play; and second, that we can detect an "implied receiver" that may take the form of a theoretical model imposed on the reader, an ideal receiver for the entire play that is a kind of omniscient "super-spectator" or, in some plays, a character who acts as a mediator between us and the playwright.

Figures of the "implied receiver":
A. The staging is the first and most important decision that orients spectator interpretation in a direction that is often very clear.

B. The dramatic text asks the reader certain unavoidable questions. How is the action presented? Who are the main characters? Who appears to have the upper hand in discussions? Who is presented in a favourable light? Some of these questions find an immediate response in the way our sympathies and antipathies are manipulated. Others are impossible to resolve. For instance, who has the proper conception of life in society, Alceste or Philinte? Many questions are meant to elicit contradictory answers (for example, moral dilemmas in classical tragedy) or absurd ones.

C. The interplay of the *perspectives** of the characters in conflict often has a similar result. It is up to the spectator to put things back into perspective after uneven, subjective or misleading speeches by the characters. Identifying the *mouthpiece**, *chorus** or *raisonneur** will generally establish the image of the "right" reception (though not always). The ideal receiver may even be one of the *dramatis personae**, and though the latter may not be an actual spokesman of the playwright, we feel that the play's message is addressed to this kind of person.

D. This "implied receiver," or image of the spectator within the play itself, is not the exception but the rule in dramatic and stage structure. The image may or may not be a clear one, depending on the dramaturgical style – it will be hidden and vague in naturalistic drama, emphasized in didactic theatre or a theatre that bares its devices. The machinery of reception is most clearly in evidence in BRECHT, where it becomes an end in itself and an integral part of theatrical activity. The spectator realizes that all of the fiction and its interlocking discourses bring him back to his own situation, that one communicates through a story with one's own (hi)story.

See also: semiology, stage-house relationship.
Further reading: Barthes 1964a, 258–276; Eng. 1972a, 261–79; Mounin 1970; Miller 1972; Moles 1973; Styan 1975; Corti 1976; Corvin 1978a, b; Fieguth 1979; de Marinis 1979, 1982; Quéré 1982, Hess-Lüttich 1981, 1984, 1985; Winkin 1981; J. Martin 1984; *Versus* 1985.

COMPETENCE

Fr.: *compétence;* Ger.: *Kompetenz;* Sp.: *competencia.*
See PERFORMANCE

COMPLICATION

Fr.: *complication;* Ger.: *Komplikation;* Sp.: *complicación.*

The moment in the play (mainly in *classical** dramaturgy) when the *conflict** becomes "knotted" and the dramatic tension is intensified. The *action** is not simplified (resolution or final fall) but is complicated in new peripeteias, and the hero sees the exit doors slammed before him one by one. Each episode makes his situation more and more inextricable to the point of open *conflict** or final *catastrophe**.

COMPOSITION, DRAMATIC

Fr.: *composition dramatique;* Ger.: *dramatische Komposition;* Sp.: *composición dramática.*

Way in which a play, particularly the dramatic text, is constructed (synonym: *structure**).

1. Rules of Composition
A *poetics** constitutes a normative treatise on dramatic composition. It sets out the *rules** and methods of construction of the *fabula**, the balance between acts and the nature of the characters. Composition is treated as the scrupulous application of *rhetoric**, and a typical arrangement is considered as being obligatory.

It is possible to come up with a theory of dramatic composition (or of theatrical *discourse**), on the condition that the system's principles are descriptive rather than normative, and sufficiently general and specific to give an account of all imaginable types of dramaturgy.

Contemporary writing, particularly post-dramatic and post-Brechtian writing, no longer obeys a set of rules of composition. Those rules have disappeared with the advent of non-composed texts which come into being on the stage.

2. Structural Principles of Composition
Determining the composition of the dramatic text implies a description of the *point of view* (or *perspective**) from which the playwright speaks in organizing events and allocating the text to the characters. The next step is to identify changes in point of view, techniques used to manipulate the character's views and speeches, and the structural principles according to which the action is presented – is it presented as a single organic entity or is it broken up into a series of epic sequences? Is it interrupted by lyrical interludes or commentaries? Are there slow moments and more intense moments within the act?

Solutions in theatrical composition are borrowed from pictorial or architectural composition – the way masses, surfaces and colours are arranged, positioned and placed in sequence corresponds in theatre to the distribution of the events represented and the sequential arrangement of the actions.

The phenomena of framing of the *fabula* (*frame**), *closed** or open performance, change of perspective and *focalization** come within the scope of such a study of composition.

Composition in classical dramaturgy was strictly regulated, applying the *rules** of verisimilitude and narrative structure (*exposition**, *knot**, *dénouement**, *obstacle**). The composition of modern works obeys rules so diverse and contradictory that they are entirely irrelevant, and difficult even to describe.

See also: dramaturgy, dramatic structures, closed form, open form.
Further reading: Freytag 1965; Uspensky 1973; Eisenstein 1976.

COMPOSITION, PARADOXICAL

Fr.: *composition paradoxale;* Ger.: *paradoxe Komposition;* Sp.: *composición paradójica.*

A dramaturgical technique that consists of reversing the *perspective** of the dramatic structure by inserting a comic episode in a tragic situation (*comic relief**) or showing the *irony** of a tragic character's fate. This contrasting *device** was used, notably by

MEYERHOLD (1973–1992), to point up the contradictions of the action, and as a stylistic technique to reveal the artistic construction – the automatism of perception is blocked, promoting a new view of everyday events. MEYERHOLD was one of the first to identify and use this device systematically. He used paradoxical composition in acting, stage design (blue sun, orange sky) and, generally, in the overall structure of the *staging** (HOOVER 1974, 309).
See also: counterpoint, play and counterplay, alienation, foregrounding.
Further reading: Rudnitski 1988; Braun 1995.

CONCLUSION

Fr.: *conclusion*; Ger.: *Konklusion, Schluss*; Sp.: *conclusión.*
See FINAL RESOLUTION

CONCRETIZATION

Fr.: *concrétisation*; Ger.: *Konkretisierung*; Sp.: *concretización.*
See DRAMATIC TEXT

CONDITION

Fr.: *condition*; Ger.: *gesellschaftlicher Stand*; Sp.: *condición social.*

In the third *Entretien avec Dorval sur le fils naturel* (1757), DIDEROT refers to *characters** who are defined not by their attributes but by their social standing, occupation and ideology, i.e. their *condition*: "Up to now in comedy, character has been the main object, and condition only accessory; today condition must become the main object and character only accessory" (1951, 1257). The reason for this requirement of bourgeois drama was to place characters properly in their socioeconomic context.

CONFIDANT

Fr.: *confident*; Ger.: *Vertrauter*; Sp.: *confidente.*
1. A secondary *character** who listens to the protagonist's confidences and counsels or guides him/her. The confidant is found mainly in plays of the sixteenth to eighteenth centuries as a substitute for the *chorus**, playing the role of indirect narrator and contributing to the *exposition** and subsequent comprehension of the action. He/she is sometimes required to carry out the hero's dirty work (for example, Oenone in RACINE's *Phèdre*, Euphorbe in *Cinna*). The confidant is rarely raised to the level of the main character's *alter ego* or full partner (like Horatio in *Hamlet*), but does complement him/her. We are not given a very clear picture of the confidant, who is no more than an echo with no tragic conflict to assume or decision to take. Being the same sex as his/her friend, the confidant oftens guides the latter in his/her love project. Through confidences, curious couples are formed (Théramène and Hippolyte, Philinte and Alceste, Dorante and Dubois in *Les fausses confidences*) whose identities are questionable. Their relationships are characterized by an affinity of character or, in the case of the comic confidant, an obvious contrast (Don Juan and Sganarelle).

2. The confidant perpetuated the moderate, exemplary attitude of the chorus. He/she represents general opinion, the man in the street; and shows the hero to good advantage through his/her often timid or conformist behaviour. In bourgeois drama or tragedy the confidant may be used as an intermediary between the hero's tragic myth and the spectator's everyday existence. In this sense, he/she guides the spectator's *reception** and represents him/her in the play.

The confidant's influence has varied considerably over the course of literary and social evolution. His/her power increased as the hero's declined (end of the *tragic**, irony about great men and rise of a new class). In BEAUMARCHAIS, for instance, the confidants Figaro and Suzanne seriously oppose their masters' supremacy and glory. The tragic form and the pre-eminence of the aristocratic world disappear with them.
3. The confidant's dramaturgical duties within the play are just as variable as his/

her true relationship to the main character. He/she may be, by turns or simultaneously, a *messenger** bringing news, a narrator of tragic or violent events, the Prince's tutor, an old friend (Oreste and Pylade in *Andromaque*), teacher or nurse. He/she always lends an attentive ear to the important figures of the fictitious universe; a "passive listener" according to SCHLEGEL's definition, but also an irreplaceable listener to a hero in distress, a "psychoanalyst" before his time who knows how to provoke a crisis and relieve the tension. The confidant's more prosaic forms, in women, are nurse, lady's maid (CORNEILLE's *la Suivante* in 1632–1633), *soubrette** (MARIVAUX) or chaperone for romantic rendezvous; in men, the one who does the dirty work, the dishonest *alter ego* (Dubois in *les Fausses Confidences*). Although the confidant's role may vary, it is not simply that of a stand-in or a sounding-board for *monologues** (these are maintained in classical dramaturgy and the confidant does not seek to replace them). A kind of "dual" character (located both within and outside the fiction), the confidant sometimes stands in for the audience (whom he guides as to the proper meaning) and the playwright's *double** – thus he/she is often promoted to the rank of intermediary between the main characters and the creators.

Further reading: Scherer 1950, 39–50.

CONFIGURATION

Fr.: *configuration;* Ger.: *Konfiguration;* Sp.: *configuración.*

The configuration of the *characters** in a play is the schematic image of their relationships on stage or within the *actantial** model. The various forces of the dramatic work are joined together by this whole network.

1. To use the term *configuration* implies a structural conception of the characters – each *figure** has no reality or value in itself but only through its place in the system of relationships among the figures, *ergo* through difference and correspondence rather than because of their essential individuality.

2. The configuration changes whenever a character enters or exits and whenever the *actantial** model is altered by a change in the *situation** and development of the action.

3. The configuration of the characters is the image of the statistically possible relationships and those actually realized in the play. Some relationships are relevant to the dramatic universe, while others are fortuitous and have no bearing on characterization.

4. "The pure configuration of masterworks" is how COPEAU refers to what is done and said upon the stage "without ever overstating the meaning" (1974, 199). This is this configuration that the staging is invited to display and fill.

See also: mathematical approach.

Bibliography: Souriau 1950; Ginestier 1961 Ubersfeld 1977a.

CONFLICT

Fr.: *conflit;* Ger.: *Konflikt;* Sp.: *conflicto.*

The dramatic conflict is a result of the antagonistic forces of the drama. It opposes two or more characters, world views or attitudes in respect of a single *situation**.

According to the classical theory of *dramatic** theatre, the purpose of theatre is to present human actions, to follow the evolution of a crisis, the emergence and resolution of conflicts: "a dramatic action is not confined to the simple and undisturbed accomplishment of a specific aim; on the contrary, it rests entirely on *collisions* of circumstances, passions, and characters, and leads therefore to actions and then the reactions which in turn necessitate a resolution of the conflict and discord" (HEGEL 1832, 322; Eng. 1975, 1159). Conflict has become the hallmark of theatre, but this is justifiable only for an action-oriented dramaturgy (*closed form**). Other forms (for example the *epic**) or other theatres (Asian, for instance) are not characterized by conflict and *action**.

Conflict exists when a subject (regardless of its exact nature) pursuing a certain object (love, power, ideal) is "thwarted" in its enterprise by another subject (a character or a psychological or moral *obstacle**). This opposition is then translated into an individual or "philosophical" fight. The outcome will be either *comic** and lead to reconciliation, or *tragic** when none of the parties can yield without falling into discredit.

1. Place of Conflict

The conflict is most often contained and shown in the course of the action and constitutes its climax (cf. the *Zieldrama*, a drama constructed around an objective and goal, the catastrophe). But the conflict may have occurred before the play begins, in which case the action is an *analytical** demonstration of the past (*Oedipus* is the best example). Although the character must wait until the very end of the play to discover the secret of his action, the spectator knows it from the beginning. The *textualization** of the conflict (its place in the *fabula*) gives us an intimation of the playwright's tragic vision. It is often located in the same place in different plays by the same playwright – in RACINE, for instance, the transgression often takes place before the play begins, while in CORNEILLE it is a central part of the play.

2. Forms in Conflict

The various types of conflict may be very different. Were it possible to establish a typology scientifically, it would provide a theoretical model for all imaginable dramatic situations, thus specifying the dramatic nature of action in theatre. Such a typology would include the following conflicts:

- Rivalry between two characters for economic, amorous, moral, political or other reasons.
- Two conflicting world views or irreconcilable moral values (for example, Antigone and Creon).
- Moral debate between subjectivity and objectivity, inclination and duty, passion and reason. This debate takes place within a single figure or between two "camps," both of which try to win over the hero (*dilemma**).
- Conflict of interest between individual and society, particular and general motivations.
- Man's moral or metaphysical struggle against a principle or ideal that is larger than he (God, the absurd, the ideal, striving to better himself).

3. Forms of Conflict

In classical drama, the conflict is linked to the *hero** and is his hallmark. Since the hero is defined as self-awareness and in terms of his opposition to another character or a different moral principle, "hero and collision are united" (LUKÁCS 1965, 135). Not all conflicts, however, are externalized in the most visible form of the oratorical duel (*stichomythia**) or debate with arguments and counter-arguments. Sometimes the *monologue** is best suited to present a line of reasoning based on opposing and contradictory ideas. Most often, the *fabula* (or structure of events with peripeteias and reversals) has to do with the dialectics of the conflict between characters and of actions. Each episode or motif of the *fabula* is meaningful only in relation to other motifs that contradict or modify it: "what we see in front of us are certain ends individualized in living characters and very conflicting situations, and we see them in their self-assertion and display, in their reciprocal influence and design; and all this in the very moment of their mutual expression; and we see too the self-grounded final result of this whole human machinery in will and accomplishment, we see it in its criss-cross movement and yet in its final peaceful resolution" (HEGEL 1832, 322; Eng. 1975, 1159). All stage resources are available to the director to make these opposing forces take shape: physical appearance of the actors, blocking, *arrangement** and *configuration** of groups and characters on stage, lighting effects. Contextualization and staging necessarily impose choices on the visualization of human relationships and the "physical" translation of psychological or ideological conflicts (*gestus**).

4. Underlying Reasons for Conflict
Beneath the individual motivations of characters in conflict it is often possible to discern social, political or philosophical causes. The conflict between Rodrigue and Chimène (in *Le Cid*), apart from the opposition between duty and love, is prolonged by a sociopolitical dispute between their fathers – the principles of an archaic individualistic moral system as opposed to a centralizing and monarchical political vision (PAVIS 1980a).

According to a Marxist or any sociological theory, any dramatic conflict rests on a contradiction between two groups, two classes or two ideologies that happen to be in conflict at a given historical moment. In the last analysis, the conflict does not depend on the playwright's will alone, but on the objective conditions of the social reality represented. This is why historical dramas illustrating great historical upsets and describing the opposing parties succeed best at visualizing dramatic conflicts. Inversely, a dramaturgy that presents the internal or universal debates of man has much more difficulty in showing combats and conflicts dramatically (for example, French classical tragedy gains in fineness of analysis what it loses in dramaturgical effectiveness). Choosing overly individual or universal human conflicts leads to a disintegration of the dramatic elements and "novelizes" or "epicizes" theatre (LUKÁCS 1963; SZONDI 1956; HEGEL 1832). The epic form is much better equipped for describing action in detail and focusing the *fabula* not on the crisis but on the progression and development (*epic treatment of drama**).

5. Resolution of the Conflict
The underlying reasons for the conflict determine whether the contradictions are to be resolved or not. According to classical dramaturgy, the conflict must be resolved within the play: "The action must be complete and finished; that is, in the event that completes it the spectator ought to be so well informed about the feelings of all those involved that he leaves the theatre in peace of mind and no longer in doubt of anything" (CORNEILLE, *Discours du poème dramatique*). This resolution of the conflict is accompanied, in tragedy, by a feeling of reconciliation and relief in the spectator, who is simultaneously made aware of the end of the play (with all problems resolved) and the radical separation between imaginary conflicts and his own private problems. The dramatic conflict is then finally resolved through the "sense of reconciliation which the tragedy affords by the glimpse of eternal justice. In its absolute sway this justice overrides the relative justification of one-sided aims and passions because it cannot suffer the conflict and contradiction of naturally harmonious ethical powers to be victorious and permanent in truth and actuality" (HEGEL 1832, 380; Eng. 1975, 1198). This reconciliation takes places on all levels: subjective and idealistic when individuals renounce their own enterprises for the sake of a higher moral reason; objective when a political force cuts off the debate; artificial when a *deus ex machina** unties the knots of an insoluble debate, and so on.

A dialectical materialist dramaturgy such as that of BRECHT does not separate the fictitious conflicts from the audience's social contradictions, but refers the first to the second: "Everything related to conflict, collision or struggle can definitely not be treated without dialectical materialism" (BRECHT 1967, 16:927).

See also: action, actantial model.

Further reading: Szondi 1961; Marx 1967.

CONSTRUCTED SCENERY

Fr.: *décor construit*; Ger.: *Bühnenaufbauten*; Sp.: *decorado construido*.

"Scenery in which the essential planes of architecture are realized in space, taking into account the distortions necessitated by theatre perspective" (SONREL 1943).

CONTEMPORIZATION

Fr.: *actualisation;* Ger.: *Aktualisierung;* Sp.: *actualización.*

Operation consisting of adapting an old text to the present time, taking into account contemporary circumstances, the tastes of the new audience and changes in the *fabula** made necessary by social evolution.

Contemporization does not change the central *fabula**, and preserves the nature of the relationships between the characters. Only the period and sometimes the setting are changed.

A play may be contemporized on several levels, from a simple updating of costume to an *adaptation** for a different audience and sociohistorical situation. At one time it was naively thought that one had only to perform the classics in modern dress to enable the spectator to identify with the issues presented. In today's productions, more care is taken to provide the audience with the necessary tools for a proper *reading** of the play; the aim is to accentuate rather than eliminate the differences between yesterday and today. Contemporization thus tends to be a *historicization** (Brechtian *Aktualisierung*, for instance).

See also: translation, dramaturgical analysis.

Further reading: Brecht 1963, 1972; Knopf 1980.

CONTEXT

Fr.: *contexte;* Ger.: *Kontext;* Sp.: *contexto.*

1. The *context* of a play or scene is the set of circumstances surrounding the production of the linguistic text and/or the performance and which facilitate comprehension. These circumstances include spatiotemporal coordinates, the subject of the *discourse**, the deictics, anything capable of clarifying the linguistic and stage "message," its enunciation.

2. In a more restricted and more strictly linguistic sense, context is the immediate surroundings of the word or sentence, what comes before and after the isolated term, the *co-text* in the sense of verbal context as opposed to the situational context. A scene or speech is meaningful only in context, when viewed as a transition between two situations or actions.

3. A knowledge of the *context* is essential for the spectator in order to understand the text and the performance. Any staging takes a certain amount of knowledge for granted – elements of human psychology, the value system of a given milieu or period, the historical specificity of the fictional universe. This shared knowledge or set of implicit assumptions, this ideological and cultural competence common to the spectators, is essential to the production and reception of the dramatic text or staging.

4. The notion of context poses as many problems in theatre as it does in linguistics. One would have to list and formalize contextual features if one wanted to decipher the meaning of the situation. Finally, it is difficult to make out in the performance exactly what pertains to the dramatic situation, the ideology of the period represented, the ideology of the audience, or the cultural values of a specific group.

See also: reception, intertextuality, off stage, nontextual, dramatic situation, situation of enunciation.

Further reading: Veltrusky 1977, 27–36; Pavis 1983a.

CONVENTION

Fr.: *convention;* Ger.: *Konvention;* Sp.: *convención.*

Conventions are explicit or implicit ideological and aesthetic presuppositions that enable the spectator to receive the acting and the performance. Convention is the pact between the playwright and the audience whereby the former composes and stages his play according to rules that are known to and accepted by the latter. Conventions include everything that audience and stage must agree upon in order to produce dramatic fiction and pleasure in playacting.

1. Involvement

Like poetry or the novel, theatre comes into being only through a certain complicity between sender and receiver. This complicity goes only so far, however, or the playwright would never be able to surprise the spectator and create a work capable of going off the beaten track and eliciting astonishment.

Like *verisimilitude** or *device**, convention is a notion that is difficult to define in detail, given the wide variations in genres, audiences and staging styles over the centuries.

2. Typology

Accordingly, it is difficult to establish a sound typology. There are simply too many parameters to enable a definitive list of conventions to be established.

A. CONVENTIONS OF REPRESENTED REALITY

A good knowledge of objects in the dramatic universe and the ability to recognize them are absolutely essential: understanding a character's psychology, identifying his social status, having an idea of the ideological rules of the milieu represented; these are all conventions based on a set of *codes**.

B. CONVENTIONS OF RECEPTION

Conventions include all material and intellectual elements necessary for a proper "reading," for instance, showing things within the spectator's optical range, using the laws of perspective (for the picture-frame stage), speaking audibly in the appropriate language, etc., believing in the fiction, letting oneself get carried away by the performance or, on the contrary, being aware of the illusion being created.

C. SPECIFICALLY THEATRICAL CONVENTIONS

- the *fourth wall**
- monologues and *asides** as ways of supplying information about a character's internal thought processes
- use of the chorus
- polymorphous space
- dramaturgical treatment of time
- prosodic structure

D. CONVENTIONS PERTAINING TO A SPECIFIC GENRE OR FORM

- characterization of actors (for example, *commedia dell'arte**)
- colour system (Chinese theatre)
- simultaneous scenery (French classicism)
- *word scenery** (SHAKESPEARE).

3. CHARACTERIZING CONVENTIONS AND OPERATIONAL CONVENTIONS

To avoid the taxonomic chaos of the foregoing typology, we could oppose (a) conventions that serve to *characterize* and render credible, conventions that do not proclaim themselves as such; and (b) *operational* conventions or artificial tools that are used for a few minutes and then removed. This would involve identifying a kind of structure of conventions for a specific type of performance, and ranking the various conventions hierarchically.

A. CHARACTERIZING CONVENTION

A device that gives the performance authenticity and helps create a harmonious world that is legitimate and believable (elements of costume or physical bearing that immediately identify a character).

B. OPERATIONAL CONVENTION

This type of convention is very much used in the epic acting style which eschews imitation. It is a short-term agreement, often ironic – a chair means comfort, a banana skin denotes danger, bricks are food (cf. *Ubu aux Bouffes* by P. BROOK at Bouffes du Nord in 1977). Here convention is happy to show itself off as a play-*device**. In many modern stagings this false convention becomes a stylish gadget that the audience has come to expect, so that the operational convention becomes a characterizing convention (characteristic of a certain avant-garde). Thus it appears that staging and theatre constantly produce (operational) conventions that become accepted to the point of appearing characteristic of theatre, in use from time immemorial, so that there is a constant dialectics between operational and characterizing conventions.

4. Conventions and Theatrical Codes
Semiological theory explains the theatrical message in terms of structural laws and a set of *codes** at work in text and performance. It is tempting, therefore, to treat conventions as a kind of reception code (DE MARINIS 1978; PAVIS 1976a, 124–134). This is legitimate, however, only if codes are not conceived of – as they are in semiology of communication – as explicit systems given in advance (such as Morse code or traffic signals). Not all conventions are codes, as they are by no means all explicit and controllable, particularly ideological and aesthetic conventions which do not form closed, already-elucidated systems.

Rather, conventions are "forgotten" rules internalized by theatre practicians and decodable after an interpretation involving the spectator. The notion of a fixed code is replaced by that of a hermeneutical hypothesis or an operating/deciphering tool.

5. Dialectics of Conventions
Conventions are essential to the functioning of theatre, and every kind of performance will use them. Accordingly, certain aesthetic approaches deliberately play on using them to an extreme degree (*types**). Complicity with the audience is strengthened and these stylized forms (such as opera, pantomime, farce) seem to be marvellous artificial constructions in which everything has a precise meaning. But the excessive use of conventions risks tiring the audience, who can no longer expect anything of the action, characterization or specific message of the play. The use of conventions therefore requires great dexterity. Literary history is full of these dialectical reversals: conventions → formulation of a norm → standardization → violation of rules by inventing counter-conventions → formulation of new rules, etc.
Further reading: Bradbrook 1969; Swiontek 1971; Burns 1972; De Marinis 1982.

CONVERSATION

Fr.: *conversation*; Ger.: *Gespräch*; Sp.: *conversación*.
See DIALOGUE, PRAGMATICS

CORYPHAEUS

Fr.: *coryphée*; Ger.: *Koryphaios*; Sp.: *corifeo*.
See CHORUS

COSTUME

Fr.: *costume*; Ger.: *Kostüm*; Sp.: *vestuario*.

Costumes play an increasingly important and varied role in contemporary staging, truly becoming the "actor's second skin" that TAIROV spoke of at the beginning of the century. Although costume has always been the very token of character and disguise, for a long time its use was confined to merely characterizing and dressing the actor according to the verisimilitude of a condition or situation. Today costume has a much more ambitious role in performance: it has numerous functions and has become an integral part of the work on stage signifiers. As soon as it appears on stage, clothing becomes costume and is subject to the effects of magnification, simplification, abstraction and readability.

1. Evolution of Costume
Costume is as old as the representation of men in ritual or ceremonial, where dress has always been a major element. The Greek priests of Eleusis and priests in medieval mystery plays wore garments also used in theatre. The history of costume in theatre is related to the history of fashion, but extends and aestheticizes it considerably. Costume has always existed, sometimes in a very visible and exaggerated manner: until halfway through the eighteenth century, actors dressed as luxuriously as possible in court clothes given to them by their protectors as an external sign of wealth, without paying much attention to the characters they were supposed to be playing. With the rise of a realistic aesthetics, costume gained in imitative accuracy what it lost in material wealth and imaginative excess.

During the second half of the eighteenth century in France, theatre reformers such as DIDEROT and VOLTAIRE, and actresses and actors such as CLAIRON, FAVARD, LEKAIN and GARRICK, made the transition to a more realistic aesthetics in which costume imitated the dress of the character. Nowadays, it often continues to be used simply to identify the character, using only the most typical and obvious signs, with little aesthetic value of its own. With the stage revolutions of the twentieth century, however, costume has found a place for itself in relation to the staging as a whole. In addition to this shifting nature of dress as a signifier, certain theatre traditions reproduce fixed costume systems whose colours and forms refer to an unchangeable code known to the initiated (Chinese theatre, *commedia dell'arte**, etc.).

2. Function of Costume

Like dress, costume's first function is to clothe, since nudity, although it is no longer an aesthetic or ethical problem on the stage, is not carried off easily. The body is always socialized by ornament or an effect of disguise or concealment, always characterized by a series of indications of age, sex, occupation or social status. This signalling function of costume is relayed by a two-edged process, both within the staging system as a series of signs interconnected by a more or less coherent system of costumes; and off stage as a reference to our world where costume also has meaning.

Within the staging, a costume is defined by its resemblance to and contrast with the form, material, cut and colour of other costumes. The important thing is how costumes develop in the course of the performance, the meaning of contrasts, complementarity of form and colour. The internal system of these relationships is (or should be) highly coherent, to enable the audience to interpret the *fabula**. But their relationship with the outside is equally important, if the performance is intended to involve us and permit comparison with a historical context. Choice of costume always proceeds from a compromise and tension between internal logic and external reference; the variations are infinite. The spectator's eye must register everything the costume has to say about action, character, situation and atmosphere, as a bearer of signs, a projection of systems onto a sign/object.

In this sense, costume has only followed the evolution of staging (as the actor's and character's "calling card") from naturalistic imitation to realistic abstraction (for example, Brechtian), to the symbolism of effects of atmosphere and surrealist or absurd deconstruction. Today all of these effects are used syncretically; everything is possible and nothing is simple. Once again, developments in costume move between dress used as mere character identification and the autonomous, aesthetic function of a sartorial creation that is answerable only to itself. The difficulty is to make costume dynamic and multifaceted. Its possibilities should not be exhausted by a few minutes' initial inspection; it should "give off" signs at the appropriate moments according to how the action and the actantial relationships are developing.

3. Costume and Mise-en-scène

It is sometimes forgotten that costume is meaningful only for and on a living organism. It is not only an ornament and an external wrapping for the actor, it is a link to the body. Sometimes it serves the body by adapting to the actor's gestures, movements and attitudes; sometimes it restricts the body by subjecting it to the weight of material and form, enclosing it in a restraint as fixed as rhetoric or the alexandrine.

Costume partakes alternatively, and sometimes simultaneously, of the living being and the inanimate object. It ensures the transition between the interiority of the speaker and the exteriority of the objective world since, as G. BANU says, "it is not only costume that speaks, but also its historical relationship with the body" (1981b, 28). Costume designers today ensure that costume is both sensuous material for the actor and perceptible sign for the spectator.

The perceptible sign of costume is its integration into the performance, its ability to function as a mobile piece of scenery connected to life and speech. All variations are relevant – approximate period, homogeneity or intentional discrepancies, diversity, rich or poor materials. For the attentive spectator, discourse on action and character is communicated through the development of the system of costumes. Also communicated thereby, as much as through gesture, movement or intonation, is the *gestus* of the play: "Hence everything in the costume that blurs the clarity of this relation, that contradicts, obscures, or falsifies the social *gestus* of the spectacle, is bad; on the contrary, everything in the forms, the colors, the substances, and their articulation that helps us to read this *gestus* is good (BARTHES 1964b, 53–54; Eng. 1972a, 42).

This principle applies above all to realistic stage work. However, it does not preclude extravagance or excess in costume – anything is possible, so long as a costume remains systematic, coherent and accessible (so that the audience can decipher it according to their frame of reference, and provided it produces the appropriate meanings). Costume in contemporary theatre is a paradox – it has multiple functions and goes beyond mimetism and signalling, questioning fixed traditional categories (scenery, props, makeup, masks, gesture, etc.). A "good" costume reinterprets the entire performance through its shifts in meaning.

It is easier to diagnose the "illnesses" of theatrical costume (according to BARTHES, the hypertrophy of the historical, aesthetic or sumptuary functions) than to propose a course of therapy or simply a practice for costume effects. Costume always oscillates between over-use and under-use, between a confining shell and a spontaneous metamorphosis.

The last word on costume has yet to be said: fascinating research is being done which could renew stage work. Research into a minimal costume with multiple meanings "of variable geometry" that redivides and represents the human body in a different way, a "phoenix" costume that would be a true intermediary between the body and the object is, in fact, the focus of current experiments in staging. Like a mobile mini-staging, costume restores scenery to its lost glory by emphasizing it and integrating it with the actor's body. It was right for the actors of the sixties and seventies to get undressed, but now they must get dressed again in a way that will show their bodies to advantage, while appearing to conceal them, and enter the kingdom of costume.

Further reading: Laver 1964; Louys 1967; Bogatyrev in Matejka and Titunic 1976, 15–19.

COUNTERPLOT

Fr.: *contre-intrigue*; Ger.: *Nebenhandlung, Gegenhandlung*; Sp.: *contra-intriga*.
See SUBPLOT

COUNTERPOINT

Fr.: *contrepoint*; Ger.: *Kontrapunkt*; Sp.: *contrapunto*.

1. Counterpoint, a musical term, refers to a combination of two or more vocal or instrumental melodies superimposed on each other to form a coherent structure.

2. By analogy, a counterpoint dramatic *structure** presents a series of parallel thematic lines or *plots** that correspond according to a principle of contrast. For instance, in the comedies of MARIVAUX, the double plots of valets and masters, the parallelism of the situations (mutatis mutandi) form a counterpoint dramatic structure (*subplot**).

Counterpoint may be thematic or metaphorical as well, when two or more series of images are placed on parallel or converging lines and are comprehensible only in relation to each other (cf. the tragic theme of the pistols, death in *Hedda Gabler* or the apparently chaotic dialogue in Chekhov) when characters and themes answer each other from one act to another rather than one sentence to another, creating an impression of polyphony (PAVIS 1985c).

Counterpoint in timing or gesture is often established between an individual and a group (chorus). Through his *timing** and *attitude** toward the group, an actor must suggest his exact place on stage. The agitation of the group may be offset by the immobility of a character or, conversely, the character may take up a position in relation to a group that occupies and structures most of the space on stage.

The use of counterpoint requires the playwright and the spectator to be able to "compose spatially" and regroup according to theme or place elements which seemed unrelated, to consider staging as a very precise orchestration of voices and instruments.

See also: play and counterplay, paradoxical composition.

COUP DE THÉÂTRE

Fr.: *coup de théâtre;* Ger.: *Theatercoup, coup de théâtre;* Sp.: *golpe de efecto.*

A totally unexpected action that suddenly changes the situation, development or outcome of the action. It is used by playwrights in classical tragedy (after carefully preparing the audience), in bourgeois drama and in melodrama. In *Entretiens sur le fils naturel* (1757), DIDEROT defines it as "an unexpected incident that occurs in the course of an action, and which suddenly changes the status of the characters," as opposed to a *tableau**, which describes a typical state or a pathetic situation.

A dramatic device *par excellence*, the coup de théâtre speculates on the effect of surprise and sometimes allows a *conflict** to be resolved through outside intervention (*deus ex machina**).

Further reading: Szondi 1972b; Valdin 1973.

COURT BALLET

Fr.: *ballet de cour;* Ger.: *Hofballet;* Sp.: *comedia-ballet.*

See BALLET COMEDY

CRISIS

(From the Greek *crisis*, decision.)

Fr.: *crise;* Ger.: *Krise;* Sp. : *crisis.*

1. A point in the *fabula** that announces and prepares the *complication** and the *conflict** (corresponds to the epitasis in Greek tragedy). The crisis immediately precedes the moment of *catastrophe** and *dénouement**.

2. The classical playwright always chooses to show the particularly intense moment of a psychological or moral crisis of the characters, focusing the action on the hours or days of that crisis and sketching in its main phases. The *epic** or naturalistic playwright, however, refuses to give priority to moments of crisis at the expense of humdrum everyday existence.

See also: obstacle, classical dramaturgy, dramatic and epic.

CRITICISM

See THEATRE CRITICISM

CROSS-CULTURAL THEATRE

Fr.: *théâtre interculturel;* Ger.: ; Sp.: *teatro intercultural.*

Cross-cultural theatre cannot be said to be an established genre or clear-cut category. At most it is a style or practice that is open to different cultural sources. It is a nascent trend or movement that has to do with staging or acting practices, in the West or elsewhere, as opposed to writing, where ethnic or cultural influences are much more difficult to trace.

1. Cross-cultural Dramaturgy

Nevertheless, even contemporary writing bears the marks of this cultural exchange issue. Francophone authors come to mind, like A. CÉSAIRE (*La Tragédie du Roi Christophe*, 1963), S. SCHWARTZ-BART (*Ton beau Capitaine*, 1987), K. YACINE (*L'Homme aux sandales de caoutchouc*, 1970), É. GLISSANT (*Monsieur Toussaint*, 1962), S. LABOU TANSI (*Moi, Veuve de l'Empire*, 1987), D. PAQUET (*Congo-Océan*, 1990), and many others, such as the authors invited by G. GARRAN to the Théâtre International de Langue Française. An author like KOLTÈS is constantly exploring values, times and different lifestyles, embodying the trends and tensions of his time.

2. Cross-cultural Staging: Historical Background

Cross-cultural stage practice, even more than dramaturgy, appeared about one hundred years ago, in other words following the beginnings of the conscious practice of staging.

In Europe, as if to renew the heritage of European theatre – to give it a blood transfusion as it lies dying in the throes of psychology – directors often draw on Eastern acting traditions: MEYERHOLD and Japanese theatre, BRECHT and classical Chinese theatre, ARTAUD and Balinese dance. These artists found in the East the kind of vitality, precision and intense focus on the body that they were seeking according to their own aesthetics.

During the 1960s and 1970s, the avant-garde harboured a similar fascination for the formal perfection and spirituality of the East (early WILSON, GROTOWSKI, BARBA, SCHECHNER, MNOUCHKINE) and the "spontaneity" of Africa (BROOK). Unlike the pioneers at the turn of the century, these artists reflected on how to use concretely, in acting much more than in thematics or exotic decor, the techniques of these traditions that inspired them. BROOK made them the source of his direct, raw theatre. BARBA saw in Eurasian theatre the "meticulous artificiality" whereby artists could "give birth to the actor in life." MNOUCHKINE's interpretations of Shakespeare's tragedies, featuring a high degree of formal perfection, were inspired by Kabuki. At the same time, Japanese artists like T. SUZUKI, HIJIKATA and K. OHNO, creators of Butoh, borrowed from Western dramaturgy and expressionist dance. Japan and China opened up to Western influence around 1980 and 1911, respectively. They also see the other culture as enriching and inflecting their cultural and aesthetic path.

During the 1980s and 1990s, with the acceleration and trivialization of travel and cultural exchange, cross-cultural theatre entered a period at once euphoric (in the many joint projects under way) and sceptical (the levelling and interchangeability of cultures with all cultural practices placed at the same level: Gregorian chant and rap, conceptual minimalism and graffiti).

The label of cross-cultural staging – though easily removable – has the merit of finding a place for itself within the system of contemporary creation. It stands in contrast, for instance, to *art theatre*, generally unicultural and grounded in a single national tradition, which pursues homogeneity and stylization and tends to conserve traditional forms. It also differs from post-modern theatre, which does welcome the most diverse cultures and artistic practices, but effects a confrontation, an exchange or a hybridization of those cultures in a stated desire to present a patchwork that can be called a one world culture, i.e. an agglutination of cultural debris or bric-à-brac without complications. There is also a distinction between cross-cultural and multicultural theatre. The latter is created and received by several communities in pursuit, not of a hybrid, but the coexistence of forms and identities.

3. Difficulties at the Theoretical Level

A solid theory is therefore still far off, perhaps because there are many cultural parameters and confronting them means dealing with a series of simulations or covert strategies. This is true, for instance, of the prefix *cross*: does it refer to an exchange, a mixture, a levelling out, a dialogue among the deaf or indifferent?

Exchange theory cannot help taking into account the economic and political relationships among the parties concerned. Exchanges are often unequal or plagued with ulterior motives: those between West and East (Europe importing Noh theatre) have nothing in common with those between North and South (the city of Limoges inviting an African author to write a play in French as writer in residence).

We also need to establish a few major categories of cross-cultural exchange, ranging from quotation of the foreign culture to wholesale assimilation, from absolute strangeness to perfect familiarity (CARLSON, in PAVIS 1996b).

Cultural transfer theory distinguishes among several major mechanisms:

- Identification of foreign formal and thematic elements in the staging.
- The adapters' aims: their strategy in making the other culture accessible to the public.
- Preparatory work by artists involved in the transfer and spectators required to "adapt."
- Selection of a form to hold the foreign materials and traditions.
- Theatrical representation of culture: mimetic by imitation or as the performance of a ritual action.

These observations are merely an outline of the kinds of cross-cultural experimentation now under way. The spectator, as theoretician, is forced to question the certainty of his gaze. This aesthetic and intellectual relativism may come as a shock to those who believe their art to be accessible and their theory universal.

Perhaps we are at a crossroads, forced to choose between the sacred but inaccessible and a democratic but insipid syncretism. We are enjoined to decide between a search for identity that quickly leads to a kind of fundamentalism, and a postmodern patchwork that no longer has any sense or taste. Cross-cultural theatre, in the image of Büchner's revolution, may well end up devouring its own children.

Further reading: Pavis 1990, 1992, 1996b.

CROWD SCENE

Fr.: *scène de foule*; Ger.: *Massenszene*; Sp.: *escena de masas*.

See MASS THEATRE

CRUELTY

See THEATRE OF CRUELTY

CURTAIN

Fr.: *rideau*; Ger.: *Vorhang*; Sp.: *cortina*.

1. The function of the curtain – rather than its forms and variants, which cannot be studied here – can be very instructive for the student of theatre.

First used systematically by the Romans, then forgotten in the Middle Ages and Elizabethan age, the curtain became a mandatory mark of theatricality in the Renaissance and the classical era. Not until the eighteenth century was it lowered during the performance at the end of each act. Today it is used as an ironic quote of theatricality and sometimes occupies half the stage (VITEZ, MESGUICH, LIOUBIMOV, LIVCHINE).

2. First of all, the curtain is used to conceal the scenery or stage temporarily to allow the property people and stagehands to do their work unseen, in a theatre based on illusion.

3. The curtain is the tangible sign of the separation between stage and auditorium, the line between the watched and the watcher, the border between what can be semiotized (and thus become a sign) and what cannot (the audience). Like an eyelid, the curtain protects the stage from the gaze. When open, it gives access to a hidden world composed of both what is actually visible on stage *and* what can be imagined in the wings "in the mind's eye," as Hamlet says, and thus on *another stage* (that of the imagination). Every curtain opens onto a second curtain which is all the more difficult to open for being invisible, not so much the boundary of the wings, as the frontier of what is off stage, of the *other stage**.

4. By its *presence**, the curtain speaks of *absence*, the absence of all desire and all representation (theatrical or otherwise). Like the spool that the child described by FREUD made to disappear and reappear as if to evoke its mother's presence before making her disappear again, the curtain summons theatre up and then revokes it, becomes a *denial**: it shows that it is concealing something, is a *larvatus prodeo*, excites curiosity and the desire to unveil. Hence the pleasure of watching the curtain rise, then fall heavily, punctuating the performance and defining its boundaries by "sandwich-

ing" the theatrical world: "Some theoreticians, no doubt taking things to extremes, hold that performances are given in theatre solely to justify the movements of the curtain. They sleep through the play and experience pleasure when the curtain is raised before the show and lowered at the end" (G. LASCAUT, *Journal du Théâtre national de Chaillot*, no. 9, Dec. 1982). Such pleasures may be more widespread than one might think, but they are beset by the risk of too brutally cutting off the stage of the imagination and all that goes beyond. BRECHT, not without some ulterior motives, challenged the traditional heavy barrier, and proposed that such a dangerous instrument be eliminated altogether.

5. There are many other, softer forms of curtain: the use of darkness and light or musical interludes between scenes, alternating speech and silence; in short, any binary semantic system that sets up a presence/absence opposition. In theatre, one curtain may hide another.

See also: frame, space.

Further reading: Radke-Stegh 1978; Malpurgo 1984; Banu 1989.

CURTAIN RAISER

Fr.: *lever de rideau*; Ger.: *Vorspiel*; Sp.: *loa*.

A curtain raiser is a play (generally a *one-act play**) performed along with the main performance, from which it may differ substantially as to theme (a farce before a tragedy, for instance). Curtain raisers, quite common in the nineteenth century, are rarely seen today. They are still performed at the Comédie-Française when the main play is too short to fill an evening. In Spain, the *loa* serves as a *prologue** to an *auto sacramental* or a comedy.

D

DANCE THEATRE

Fr.: *danse-théâtre*; Ger.: *Tanztheater*; Sp.: *teatro bailado*

Dance theatre (an expression calqued on the German *Tanztheater*) is known mainly through the works of P. BAUSCH, but dates back to 1928, when the Folkwang Tanztheater was founded by K. JOOS, BAUSCH's mentor and a proponent of *Ausdruckstanz*, German expressionist dance. This line of contemporary choreography also includes J. KRESNIK (and his "choreographic theatre"), R. HOFFMANN, G. BOHNER and, in France, M. MARIN, J.-C. GALOTTA, J. NADJ and K. SAPORTA. The latter, however, do not use the term but take an approach to choreography that is open to theatricality and favors decompartmentalizing stage arts.

1. Background

The 1970s saw a return to a more figurative art that was more engaged and anchored in history, more concerned with telling stories well. This was a reaction to the radical avant-garde, the search for the specificity of art and, in choreography, pure dance. P. BAUSCH, for instance, casts a sympathetic but critical eye on day-to-day life, relations between the sexes, customary ways of talking; KRESNIK deals more radically with alienation in all its forms (*Ulrike Meinhof*); M. MARIN creates characters inspired by BECKETT's depressing universe (*May B.*); K. SAPORTA places the electrified bodies of arsonists in a disused metal factory (*La Brûlure*). In all these experiments, the stage tells a story without reverting to the idealized plot of classical dance, far from the abstraction and formalism of postmodern dance (for example, of CUNNINGHAM).

2. A Vital Oxymoron

Having emerged in reaction to formalism, dance theatre moves beyond what it deems the sterile tendency to oppose body and language, pure movement and words, formal experimentation and realism. It aims to reconcile *kinesis* and *mimesis*, sets up the *fiction* of a character embodied and imitated by an actor against the *friction* of a dancer whose value lies in the ability to kindle the imagination through technical prowess, athletic performance and *kinesthetics**.

Dance theatre rediscovers the eternal dilemma of dance, torn between the art of pure movement and a pantomime that tells a simple story.

3. The Aesthetics of Dance Theatre

More than theatre leading to dance, movement and choreography, dance theatre is dance that produces the effect of theatre:

A. THE THEATRICALITY

The theatricality is apparent when the dance-actors are representing a character through recourse to a mimetic representation of situations, when the stage appears both realistic and exaggerated. By way of an example, the torture inflicted on U. MEINHOF is so spectacular, systematic and sophisticated that it constitutes an accusation of the apparatus used to repress young German democrats (KRESNIK). By repeating an ordinary action an infinite number of times, P. BAUSCH proposes an outrageous, caustic theatricality, laying bare power games and daily ways of speaking or behaving.

B. REALITY EFFECTS

One has the impression that dance theatre conjures and cites moments and aspects of reality. Dance theatre explores reality rather than abstracting from it like pure dance; it brings reality closer rather than distancing itself from it; hence many reality effects in which the work of art appears to have been taken over and replaced by surrounding reality.

C. STAGING EFFECTS

Dance theatre has available to it all the ingredients of a theatre staging: texts or speeches which are recited, read or spoken using a voice-off; drawing attention to scene design, props and costumes; careful coordination of all stage materials. What results is a plot and dramatic writing that tells a story using symbolic actions by characters who "stay in character" and convey the dramaturgy. It is the social *gestus* rather than individual or psychological gestures that counts: movement is never pure or isolated, but rather linked to psychological or sociological motivations. In 1933, J. MARTIN wrote, in connection with literary dance or pantomime and anticipating the Tanztheater of WIGMANN or JOOS: "In this kind of dance spatial and temporal designs are less important. The composition process develops through a series of incidents that are often related to external factors. Form is governed by dramaturgical laws and movement plays only a secondary role" (1991, 71). This dramaturgy outside movement in dance theatre always indicates a return to theatre in dance, a return to theatrical *fiction* within the choreographic *friction* which, through virtuosity and kinesthetics, was intended to win over and delight the spectator. This is how dance theatre is made: dance obeys a particular dramaturgy and staging to rediscover theatre without necessarily understanding or experiencing the (often obscure and unreadable) cause it intends to serve by entering into such an alliance. Of this unnatural union between dance and theatre have come the most beautiful productions of our times.

DEBATE

Fr.: *débat*; Ger.: *Debatte*; Sp.: *debate*.
See DILEMMA

DECLAMATION

(From the Latin *declamatio*, exercise of speech.)
Fr.: *déclamation*; Ger.: *Deklamation*; Sp.: *declamación*.

1. The art of *diction** of a text spoken by an actor, or (pejoratively) a "theatrical" and rather singsong delivery of a text in verse. MARMONTEL (1787) remarked that this notion is related to music and dance. "Natural declamation gave rise to music, music to poetry; music and poetry in turn made declamation an art [...] In order to give music more expression and truth, people wanted to articulate the sounds used in the melody; melody thus required words to be adapted to the same numbers; hence the art of verse. The numbers given by the music and observed by the poetry invited the voice to mark them off; hence the art of *eurythmics*. Gesture naturally followed expression and movement of voice; hence the *hypocritical* art or theatrical action, which the Greeks called *Orchesis*, the Latins *Saltatio*, and which we have taken for dance" (1787, "Déclamation"). Although the lineage MARMONTEL established through declamation, music, *eurythmics** and physical elements is suspect, he grasped the relationship among these elements of vocal and body movement remarkably well. That relationship is at the centre of the most avant-garde research today (BERNARD 1976; MESCHONNIC 1982).

In the eighteenth century, declamation was contrasted with a simple recitation and song, as a recitation "accompanied by movements of the body" (DU BOS *Réflexions critiques sur la poésie et la peinture* 1719) and approached the recitative: each actor had to give the text a rhythm based on its punctuation and segmentation, on its syntactic sense and on the "stressed words" isolated in the sentence and foregrounded.

The delivery of the text – slow, tragic diction or comic vivacity – depends on the actor (and may depend on the director's instructions as well) and determines how the unspoken aspect of text or discourse will be perceived.

2. Since the end of the eighteenth century, declamation has been seen as an emphatic and pompous way of saying the text, whereas in the classical period it was considered the *natural** acting style. The actor TALMA noted that both the term and the acting style it designated were out of date: "This may be the appropriate place to stress the impropriety of using the word *declamation* to denote the actor's art. This term, which appears to refer to something other than natural delivery, carries the notion of a certain conventional pronunciation, and was probably used at the time when tragedy was in fact sung, has often sent young actors off in the wrong direction. To declaim is to speak with emphasis; therefore, the art of declamation is to speak as one does not speak" (TALMA 1856).

3. The term very quickly took on a pejorative connotation. In his first preface to *Britannicus*, RACINE defines it as "discourse marked by affectation," as opposed to so-called naturalness. But every school proclaims itself to be "natural" and considers its competitors to be too "declamatory." RICCOBONI, in his *Pensées sur la déclamation*, mocks the "exaggerated expression of tragic declamation" (1738, 36). And today, STREHLER can write: "Every actor in every era is opposed to the actors who preceded him and 'reforms' them on the basis of truth. What was or seemed simple twenty years earlier becomes rhetorical, emphatic, twenty years later" (1980, 154).

The issue of declamation should not be relegated to history, as is often the case. If current theatre practice no longer reflects on the question of proper declamation, it is because, except for a few directors (among them K.M. GRÜBER, J.-M. VILLEGIER and A. VITEZ), declamation is once again considered to be a shameful disability, useful only for playing classical tragedies at the Comédie-Française or impressing schoolchildren.

Declamation is nevertheless one of the modes of *diction**, which is one of the modes of *rhythm**, on the agenda of present-day studies on gesture, *voice**, *rhetoric** (MESCHONNIC 1982). In this sense, the issue is wider than the debate about what is natural or artificial, and is at the centre of a reflection on orality and voice. Like the concept of the rhythm of mise-en-scène, it is a construction, a system of conventions advocated by MEYERHOLD in opposition to STANISLAVSKY: "The entire essence of stage rhythm is contrary to that of reality, of everyday life" (1973, 1:129).

Some directors, such as VILLÉGIER, VITEZ or REGY, tend to stress the artificiality of theatrical declamation, to distance verse from the banality of everyday language, and to give a verbal and gestural sense of rhythm and rhetoric, by articulating all twelve syllables of the alexandrine, dieresis, alternate feminine and masculine rhymes, unequal length of metric feet. Paradoxically, once this mechanism has been established, the director can afford to put in some natural-sounding lines to shock the audience's ears, now reaccustomed to declamation (in a line such as RACINE's *Bérénice*, III,2: "Non, ne la voyons point, respectons sa douleur"). This alternation between the natural and the musical can overcome the banal style of recitation that is often found at the Comédie-Française. The entire process of reflection about literary *devices**, theatrical *conventions**, *theatricality** and the coercive value of discourse is thus linked to a rediscovery of declamation.

Further reading: Dorat 1766; Engel 1797; Chancerel 1954; Aslan 1963, 1974; Klein 1984;

Bernard 1986; Bernardy 1988; Milner and Regnault 1987; Regnault 1996; J. Martin 1991.

DECONSTRUCTION EFFECT

Fr.: *effet de déconstruction*; Ger.: *Dekonstruktionseffekt*; Sp.: *efecto de deconstrucción*.

The term "deconstruction," borrowed from DERRIDA by American post-structuralist criticism, is used most often in a trivial sense whereby the contemporary staging dismantles and challenges any claim to shape a stable, unequivocal meaning. The spectator, accustomed to seeking meaning everywhere, cannot manage to reconstruct the performance out of the ruins of its fragments or contradictions. A deconstruction effect is not merely an *alienation* effect or estrangement that always works out, nor is it a foregrounding effect that lays bare its own devices. Deconstruction mounts a radical attack (though "in play") upon the overall workings of the performance. An actor may disassemble the set and reassemble it for a different staging, or the scene design may take elements from the surrounding reality visible to the audience: the view of the Trocadéro and the Eiffel Tower used by Y. KOKKOS for A. Vitez's staging of *Ubu Roi* in Chaillot in 1985.

DECORUM

Fr.: *bienséance*; Ger.: *Anstand*; Sp.: *decoro*.

1. A term from classical dramaturgy meaning compliance with the literary, artistic and moral *conventions** of an era or an audience. Decorum is one of the rules of classicism. It originated with ARISTOTLE, who stressed moral propriety: the hero's conduct must be acceptable, the actions moral, the historical events reported with verisimilitude; vulgar or everyday aspects of reality must not be shown. Sexuality, violence and death were also frowned upon. Decorum also imposes coherence in construction of the plot and sequencing of actions.

J. SCHERER makes a distinction between decorum and *verisimilitude**: "Verisimilitude is an intellectual requirement; it calls for a certain coherence among the elements of the play; it condemns the absurd and the arbitrary, or at least what the audience considers as such. Decorum is a moral requirement; it demands that the play not offend the audience's tastes, morals or, if you like, prejudices" (1950, 383).

The notion of decorum, as it was developed between 1630 and 1640 by scholars such as CHAPELAIN or LA MESNARDIERE, often comes into conflict with that of verisimilitude (or *appropriateness*, cf. MARMONTEL on "Decorum"). Historical truth is often shocking, and the playwright is required to sweeten it out of respect for decorum. Thus appropriateness is "character-related," whereas decorum is "more specifically spectator-related." Whereas appropriateness "governs the customs and values of the time and place of the action, decorum has to do with the opinions and manners of the country and century in which the action is represented" (MARMONTEL, 1763–1787).

Generally speaking, respecting decorum means adapting a play to the audience's tastes and conceptions of reality. CORNEILLE justifies his allusion to the marriage between Chimène and le Cid, a marriage that might have "shocked" the spectators, in this way: "In order not to contradict history, I decided I could not avoid alluding to it, but I was uncertain of the effect of doing so; and only in this way could I reconcile the decorum of theatre with the truth of the event" (*Examen du Cid*). (See also R. RAPIN, *Réflexion sur la Poétique d'Aristote*, 1674.)

2. The rule of decorum is thus an implicit *code** of ideological and moral precepts. In this sense, it is present in any era and is difficult to distinguish from *ideology**. Any school of thought or society, even as it rejects the rules of the preceding era, dictates guidelines for conduct. Decorum is the image an era has of itself, an image it looks for in artistic productions. It is naturally subject to the "upset of all values" (NIETZSCHE). Right now, in Paris or New York, decorum leads many directors to

show an actress undressing in the course of the play, whether it is MARIVAUX, BRECHT or R. FOREMAN who is being staged.
Further reading: D'Aubignac 1927; Bray 1927.

DEDICATION
Fr.: *dédicace;* Ger.: *Widmung;* Sp.: *dedicatoria.*

A text, often printed along with the play, in which the *playwright** symbolically gives his work to a person or an institution. In the classical period, when writers needed the material protection and moral backing of powerful figures, the dedication became an essential formality to secure a living and avoid trouble. CORNEILLE did this particularly obsequiously (cf. his dedication of *Cinna* to Montoron), but it was the general rule of the genre. Today, playwrights sometimes dedicate a play to the director of the initial production (*preface**).

DEFAMILIARIZATION
See ALIENATION-EFFECT

DEIXIS

The Greek word for showing or pointing at. In linguistics, deixis is an expression that draws its meaning from the *situation of enunciation**: time and place, the speaker and listener, exist only in relation to the message transmitted. The deictics include personal pronouns (I and you), adverbs of time and place, proper names and all mimetic, gestural or prosodic means of indicating the spatial and temporal co-ordinates of the situation of enunciation (BENVENISTE 1966, 225–285).

1. Deixis plays such an important part in theatre as to be one of its specific characteristics. Everything that occurs on stage is closely linked to its place of *ostension** and becomes meaningful only because it is shown and put on display. The extra-linguistic situation clarifies the linguistic text according to the director's interpretation. On this basis, each speaker (being a character or any other instance of verbal or iconic discourse) organizes his space and time around himself, enters into communication with the others to varying degrees, and turns his discourse (ideas about the world, ideology) back upon himself and his direct interlocutors: he is, by definition and of necessity, egocentric. This "showing" activity has been considered since ARISTOTLE as fundamental to the theatrical act: theatre shows (imitates) characters in the process of *communication**; it exhibits the "word on stage."

2. There are innumerable deictics (or actual forms of deixis) in theatre. First there is the concrete *presence** of the actor, and the aura of that physical presence in front of the audience prevents him from being annihilated and reduced to a univocal and definitively coded representation. Through his gestures (*facial expression**, *gaze** and *attitude**), he always reminds the spectator of the situation. Finally, the stage itself exists only as a space which is continuously experienced in the present and subjected to the audience's act of perception; what happens (what is "performed") only exists through the simple action of enunciation. By implicit convention, a character's speech means and represents (shows/resembles) what he is speaking of. Like a performative (for example, "I swear"), theatrical discourse is "spoken action" (PIRANDELLO).

3. The stage acts as a speaker addressing an audience and establishing his meaning according to the rules of verbal exchange. Once place and time have been clearly defined for the spectator, the frame of action is sketched out and then all the conventions and substitutions in representing the dramatic world are possible.

Deixis is also that which situates the various elements of the stage in relation to each other, which points (indicates, shows) in the direction of the aesthetic message to be received (*index**).

The actor is a deictic element *par excellence* in the performance. *Space** and *time** are structured in relation to him, as a kind of aura that never leaves him. This explains why theatre can easily do without scenery as long as the speaker indicates where he is speaking from with a word or a gesture. Theatre may use all the epic means it likes (narratives, commentaries), but it still remains linked to its deictic utterances, which give the stage its emotional colour. Rather than summing up the dramatic text as a *fabula* or an imitation of reality, then, we would do better to see it as a space where different discourses come together, "a dynamic crossing of discursive instances" (SERPIERI 1981). There is no need for a narrator to describe the deictic situation, since it is shown (*ostension**) and the stage "lives" in a permanent present. Legitimate attempts have been made to segment the dramatic text on the basis of the directions of discourse, of the relationships woven between the characters, and of the general orientation of the dialogue toward a peak, a plateau or cyclical time.

4. Identifying the deictics in a text, however, cannot give a satisfactory account of the performance, which uses many other deictics, such as:

A. STAGE DESIGN

Stage design orients (with reference to the audience) the various signs issued by the stage. The best theatre company in the world cannot be effective if it is playing in a place that is contrary to what the play's dramatic situation requires.

B. GESTURE AND FACIAL EXPRESSION

The text is not only said; it can be spat out or let drop in passing. Facial expression modulates it, *modalizes** it and directs it as desired.

C. TRANSITION FROM THE REAL TO THE FIGURATIVE OR FANTASTIC

The discourse moves continuously from a concrete situation linked to the stage to an imaginary plane whose deictic orientations are entirely directed towards fantasy and change. We can therefore distinguish between concrete and figurative deitics and then observe the transition from one to the other.

D. MISE-EN-SCÈNE

The mise-en-scène groups all of the movements on stage in a metadeixis and places them in relation to each other. This is what BRECHT calls the *gestus** of delivery to the spectator.

See also: presence, segmentation, semiology, pragmatics.

Further reading: Honzl 1940, Jakobson 1963: 176–196; Veltruský 1977: Serpieri 1981; Serpieri (et al.) 1978.

DELIBERATION

Fr.: *délibération*; Ger.: *Überlegung*; Sp.: *deliberación*.

A term from classical dramaturgy, originally borrowed from rhetoric. A scene in which the character evokes an agonizing inner conflict (often of a political nature) in a *monologue** or *stances**, in an attempt to reach a decision, sometimes with the help of his advisers. The orator expounds on his motivations and arguments, hesitates at great length or prepares to choose the least objectionable solution.

Further reading: Fumaroli 1972; Pavis 1980d.

DEMONSTRATION

Fr.: *démonstration de travail*; Ger.: *Arbeitsvorführung*, Sp.: *demostración de trabajo*.

Presentation by an actor of a few moments of training or preparation for a role or staging, and basic experimentation with voice, gesture, memory, etc. This is not a rehearsal, a show at reduced price, or a one-(wo)man show, but a way of getting across how an individual artist prepares. Such demonstrations are often given repeatedly during courses, festivals or conferences so that they become a mini-show, although this would appear to contradict their primary purpose as an *acting exercise**.

DENIAL

(Translation of the German *Verneinung*.)
Fr.: *dénégation*; Ger.: *Verneinung*; Sp.: *denegación*.

A term from psychoanalysis that refers to the process which brings to consciousness repressed elements that are denied at the same time (for example, "Don't think I'm angry with you").

The experience of theatrical *illusion**, accompanied by the feeling that what one is observing does not really exist, is an instance of denial. Denial turns the stage into a place where *imitation** and illusion (and thus *identification**) appear, but questions the deception and the imaginary, refusing to recognize the character as a fictitious being by considering him to be a person similar to the spectator. Denying identification enables the spectator to free himself from the painful elements of a mental representation by attributing them to a previous, infantile and long-repressed self. Like the child (described by FREUD) who enjoys being both actor and spectator as he plays at throwing away the spool and then recovering it, denial makes the stage oscillate between *reality-effect** and *theatrical effect**, eliciting identification and *alienation** by turns. This dialectical process probably holds the key to one of the pleasures of theatrical performance (*theatrical pleasure**).

Further reading: Freud 1976, 10:161–68; Mannoni 1969; Orlando 1971; Ubersfeld 1977a, 46–54, 260–61 and 1981, 311–18.

DÉNOUEMENT

Fr.: *dénouement*; Ger.: *Lösung, Enthüllung*; Sp.: *desenlace*.

In classical dramaturgy, the dénouement (literally, "unknotting") is situated at the end of the play, just after the peripeteia and the climax, when the contradictions are resolved and the threads of the plot unraveled. The dénouement is the episode of comedy or tragedy that finally eliminates the conflicts and obstacles. The normative poetics of ARISTOTLE, VOSSIUS, d'AUBIGNAC or CORNEILLE requires that it conclude the drama in a realistic, focused and natural way, employing a *deus ex machina** only occasionally, when nothing but the intervention of the gods can resolve a dead-end situation. The dénouement must provide the spectator with all the answers to his questions about the fate of the protagonists and the conclusion of the action. An open dramaturgy (*epic** or *absurd**, for instance), on the other hand, would refuse to have the action appear as a final, resolved schema. The classical dénouement, as opposed to that of a Romantic drama or melodrama, often takes the form of a narrative, in order to respect decorum. To avoid the tragic dénouement of catastrophe, playwrights tried to soften the ending, avoiding death, arranging reconcilations or lightening the tragic aspects with an absurd or tragicomic world view.

DESCRIPTION

Fr.: *description*; Ger.: *Beschreibung*; Sp.: *descripción*.

Theatre has already taken place when one begins to talk about it. A performance can be described only on the basis of the spectator's memory or documents which are necessarily fragmentary – production notes (which are not the same as the production), sketches or photographs (which reify the event), audiovisual recordings (which impose their own segmentation of the performance).

1. Vagueness of Notions and Objectives
The "analysis," "description" or "interpretation" of the performance or mise-en-scène: the vagueness of the terms betrays an equal vagueness as to one of the major tasks of theatre semiology – giving meaning to a body of heterogeneous materials brought together at a specific time and place for a given audience. Clearly, the work cannot begin until a minimal set of data about the performance has been collected, but how does one organize and establish the process of collection? Is it a preparation for a second stage, which would be the interpretation, or should the organization of meaning be grasped immediately in the act of descrip-

tion? Should we make a distinction between description and notation? Must description necessarily be expressed in articulate language? Is an "objective" method not linked to verbal description possible?

2. Description and Notation
If the subtle differences in meaning between "analysis," "description" and "notation" are unclear, it is because the activities are very similar. We cannot analyze without doing a notation and, inversely, notation is never a neutral operation that precedes or excludes interpretation and meaning. Whether description or notation, the analysis is often presented as an impoverishment of the performance, a reduction of a complex reality to a simplistic formula. Transformation does of course take place. This transformation, however, is not necessarily a reduction, but rather the only way of grasping the meaning of the performance, by effecting a modelling and a reduced-scale model of it. The reduction of the performance in the act of analysis or notation is not a technical, but a theoretical issue. It is not because recording equipment or notation techniques are still too primitive and deficient to record the staging that there is reduction – it is because notation changes the object analyzed. Notation means making a selection, moving from the concrete to the abstract, proposing a theoretical choice on the basis of the empirical object that is the performance before reflecting on it.

Could we admit the principle of a general methodology of description, i.e. a system of notation or a method of analysis and reading adaptable to any theatre object whatsoever? To answer this question, we must first distinguish between an analysis intended to make a notation of the performance and an anlysis intended to describe it in order to comment on and interpret it verbally. In so doing, we reintroduce the distinction between notation and interpretation, which should in fact be questioned. To make a notation of a performance always implies selecting what is noteworthy within an overall project of meaning, in the context of a synthetic grasp of the performance or at least some part of it. In other words, we note and describe only what is perceived as being notable, i.e. what is already and immediately noted; what already has a function and meaning within a much larger, already organized whole; what makes sense within a mise-en-scène.

3. Description and Mise-en-scène
If the analysis is not to flounder in a description of isolated signs or an unstructured list of codes, the procedure of noting down the smallest item must be done within an already organized whole in a semiotic system having its own rules and perceived as being coherent. The notion of mise-en-scène is therefore essential, provided it is understood not as the individual work of the director or, still less, as the translation of the text into performance, but as the structural system of a stage utterance, i.e. as the way in which the signifying systems are put together and contrasted, and placed in perspective according to their reception by an audience which is itself an active and variable factor. Description or notation is possible only as an analysis that presupposes a synthesis, in itself changeable and "deconstructible." The mise-en-scène provides a convenient theoretical *framework** for this framing and analysis of meaning, this work of analysis and synthesis.

4. Establishing the Performance Text
An attempt may be made to relate the description of the performance to the actantial and/or narratological analysis by identifying microsequences. Within these microsequences, series of signs are identified both vertically (i.e. according to the density of the various systems in a short lapse of time) and horizontally (in the context of a narrative unit). The idea is to group together various sets with different rhythms, taking care to pick out the redundancies, changes of pace, transitions from quantitative to qualitative. Little by little, the *performance text** begins to take shape.

Rather than describing every detail, like conscientious scribes, we should explain the principles on which the performance text is constructed, what constitutes its *coherence**, its productivity, its dynamism. In the series of signs and signifying systems, we search for a minimal coherence in order to grasp the direction of the series and assess redundancies and new information. Description never implies clarifying all of the signs, but rather includes a reflection on the areas of indeterminacy in the performance text and on the answer the performance may have supplied to the areas of indeterminacy in the dramatic text. Reception is therefore guided, at least in part, by certain pertinent signals in text and performance, along a *parcours** (trajectory) through the ambiguities, which may be either resolved or maintained. Possible *parcours** are thus proposed by description – we are very far from a positivistic and technical view of description. Describing means taking into account stage enunciation, defined as the activation in space and time of all the scenic and dramaturgical elements deemed pertinent to the production of meaning and its reception by the audience.

Further reading: Bouchard 1982; *Theaterarbeit* 1961; Bowman and Ball 1961; Mehlin 1969; *Voies de la création théâtrale* 1970, 1985; Ivanov 1977; Pavis 1979b, 1981a, 1985e; McAuley 1984; Kowzan 1985; Gomez 1986; Sauter 1986, 1988; Hiss 1993.

DEUS EX MACHINA

Fr.: *deus ex machina*; Ger.: *Deus ex machina*; Sp.: *deus ex machina*.

The *deus ex machina* (literally, the god from a machine) is a dramaturgical notion that accounts for an ending through the appearance of an unexpected character.

1. In some productions of Greek tragedies (notably EURIPIDES), a machine was suspended from a crane that brought to the stage a god who could solve all the unresolvable issues in the twinkling of an eye. By extension and figuratively speaking, the *deus ex machina* represents the unforeseen and providential intervention of any kind of character or force capable of resolving a dead-end situation. According to ARISTOTLE (*Poetics*), this technique should be used only "for matters lying outside the drama, either antecedents of the action which a human being cannot know, or things subsequent to the action that have to be prophesied and announced" (1454b). This kind of ending must come as a total surprise.

2. The *deus ex machina* is often used when the playwright is hard put to find a logical conclusion and seeks an effective way of settling all the conflicts and contradictions at one stroke. It does not necessarily have to seem artificial and unrealistic, if the spectator believes in a philosophy in which divine or irrational intervention is considered possible (*verisimilitude**).

3. Comedy uses subterfuge similar to the *deus ex machina*: the recognition or return of a character, discovery of a letter, sudden inheritance, etc. In this case, an element of chance is admitted in human action. In tragedy, however, the *deus ex machina* is not the result of chance but the instrument of a superior will. It is motivated to a greater or lesser degree, and is artificial and unexpected only on the face of it.

4. The deus ex machina is sometimes an ironic way of ending a play without any illusion about verisimilitude or logical necessity. It becomes a way of questioning the effectiveness of divine or political solutions. Thus, the arrival of the police in *Tartuffe* is both an acknowledgement by MOLIÈRE of monarchical power and a way of demonstrating the power and danger of the falsely pious in seventeenth-century society. In the *Threepenny Opera* and *The Good Person of Setzwan*, BRECHT used this technique to "conclude without concluding," to help the audience toward an awareness of their power to act on social reality. Today, the *deus ex machina* is frequently a character who serves as an ironic double of the playwright.

See also: motivation, epilogue, recognition.

Further reading: Spira 1957.

DEUTERAGONIST

Fr.: *deutéragoniste;* Ger.: *Deuteragonist;* Sp.: *deuteragonista.*
See PROTAGONIST

DEVICE

Fr.: *procédé;* Ger.: *Verfahren;* Sp.: *procedimiento.*

1. A theatrical device is a staging, acting or writing technique used by the artist to create the aesthetic object, which retains its artificial, constructed nature in our perception of it. The Russian formalists (SHKLOVSKY, TYNIANOV, EIKHENBAUM) stressed the importance of the artistic device in the symbolization of the work of art: "We will call aesthetic objects, in the proper sense of the word, objects that are created with the help of particular devices whose goal is to ensure an aesthetic perception through those objects" (SHKLOVSKY 1965b, 8).

2. An approach to dramaturgy and staging that does not conceal devices of theatrical construction and their functioning avoids illusion and identification with the characters on stage. It re-establishes "the reality of theatre as theatre," which for BRECHT is "the precondition for the existence of realistic reproductions of the shared life of human beings" (1972, 246). The device then takes on the status of a signifying practice, a practice involving stage systems, which are not a reflection of reality but a place where artistic and social processes are produced. Foregrounding the device and breaking the illusion occur whenever theatre is presented as a material production of signs by the creative team. In this kind of materialist theatre (popular forms, circus, Brechtian *realism**, etc.), preparatory work for the production of illusion and the workings of textual and stage machinery will always be clearly visible to the spectator.

The rhythmic *declamation** of the alexandrine, visible set changes, the actor's gradual "entry" into his role; these are all accepted theatrical devices.

See also: alienation-effect, theatricality, theatricalization.

Further reading: Meyerhold 1963; Erlich 1969; Matejka 1976; Matejka and Titunik 1976; Mukarovsky 1977, 1978.

DIALOGISM

Fr.: *dialogisme;* Ger.: *Dialogismus;* Sp.: *dialogismo.*
See DISCOURSE

DIALOGUE

(From the Greek *dialogos*, or discourse between two people.)
Fr.: *dialogue;* Ger.: *Dialog;* Sp.: *diálogo.*

Conversation between two or more characters. Dramatic dialogue is generally a verbal exchange between characters. Other dialogical communications are possible, however: between a visible and an invisible character (*teichoscopy**), between a man and a god or spirit (cf. *Hamlet*), between an animate being and an inanimate object (for example, dialogue with or between machines, telephone conversation). The essential criterion of dialogue is the exchange and reversibility of the *communication**.

1. Dialogue and Dramatic Form

Dialogue between characters is often considered to be the fundamental and exemplary form of drama ("The complete dramatic form is the dialogue," HEGEL). When theatre is conceived as a presentation of characters in action, dialogue "naturally" becomes the most important form of expression. By the same token, a *monologue** becomes an arbitrary and annoying ornament that does not meet the requirements of verisimilitude in interpersonal relationships. Dialogue would seem to be the best way of showing how the speakers communicate – the *reality effect** is stronger because the spectators perceive it as being a familiar form of communication between people.

2. From Monologue to Dialogue

Although it is useful to distinguish between these two forms of the dramatic text, it would be dangerous to set up a systematic opposition between them. Dialogue and *monologue** never exist in an absolute form; moreover, there is a fluid transition between them, and there are several degrees of dialogism or monologism (MUKAROVSKÝ 1941). Dialogue in classical drama, for instance, is more akin to a series of independently structured monologues than to an exchange of short speeches resembling a lively conversation (as in everyday dialogue). Conversely, many monologues, although they may be displayed typographically as a single unit and have only one enunciating subject, are actually a character's dialogues with a part of himself, another (imagined) character, or the world as his witness.

3. A Typology of Dialogues

It would be impossible to identify all potential variants of theatrical dialogue; all we can do is differentiate between them on the basis of various criteria.

A. NUMBER OF CHARACTERS

A knowledge of the respective *dramatic situations** of the protagonists will enable us to identify several types of communication (equality, subordination, class relations, psychological connections).

B. VOLUME

There is dialogue when the characters' speeches follow each other at a sufficiently rapid pace; otherwise, the dramatic text resembles a succession of monologues that are only distantly related. The most obvious and spectacular form of dialogue is the verbal duel or *stichomythia**. The length of the speeches depends on the dramaturgical style of the play. As classical French tragedy did not seek to render the characters' speeches in a naturalistic way, they are composed according to solid rhetoric. The character sets out his argument, often very logically, and his/her interlocutor can then reply point by point. In naturalistic theatre, dialogue is meant to reproduce everyday speech in all its violent, elliptical and inexpressible aspects; accordingly, it appears spontaneous and disorganized and may be reduced to an exchange of shouts or silences (HAUPTMANN, CHEKHOV).

C. DIALOGUE AND ACTION

In the theatre, by tacit convention, dialogue (and any discourse of the characters) is "spoken action" (PIRANDELLO). As soon as the protagonists exercise a language activity, the audience can imagine the transformation of the dramatic world, changes in the actantial model, and the dynamics of action. The relationship between dialogue and action varies widely, however, depending on the type of theatre.

In classical tragedy, dialogue symbolically sets off the action – it is both cause and consequence.

In naturalistic drama, dialogue is only the visible and secondary part of the action; it is the situation and the characters' psychosocial state that advance the plot; dialogue merely reveals or serves as a barometer.

Dialogue and discourse are the only actions in the play. The act of speaking, of uttering sentences, is what constitutes a performative action (cf. MARIVAUX, BECKETT, ADAMOV, IONESCO).

4. Interchangeability of Persons

Dialogue presents an exchange between a speaking "I" and a listening "you" in alternating roles. What is said is meaningful only in the context of this social link between speaker and listener. This explains the sometimes allusive form of dialogue that makes more use of the situation of enunciation than of the information conveyed by the words. Conversely, the monologue must begin by naming the characters or things to which it is addressed; it refers primarily to the world about which it speaks (the *it*). The *I* of dialogue, on the other hand, speaks to another *I*, thus stressing its metalinguistic or phatic function. It situates the speeches spatially and, in this cross-fire of utterances, abolishes any fixed centre of gravity or precise ideological subject – hence the difficulty, in theatre, of tracing the origin of the word and identifying the ideological subject from among the multitude of speakers.

Dialogue is by definiton unfinished, and necessarily elicits a response from the listener. Each speaker imprisons the other in the speech he has just uttered, forcing him to reply within the proposed context. Any dialogue is therefore a tactical struggle between two manipulators of discourse. Each tries to impose his own logical and ideological presuppositions by forcing the other to fight on the ground the speaker has chosen for the interlocutor (DUCROT 1972).

5. Dialogue within a Semantic Theory of Discourse
The overall context of a character's speeches, and the way in which the different contexts relate to each other, ultimately determine whether the text is dialogic or monologic in nature. Based on the way in which these two contexts interact, we can define three kinds of dialogue:

A. Normal dialogue. The subjects of the dialogue share part of their context, are more or less talking "about the same thing," and are able to exchange some information.

B. The contexts are totally foreign to each other. Even when the text is structured externally in the form of a dialogue, it is actually two monologues superimposed on each other in a "dialogue of the deaf." The characters speak at cross purposes (*Aneinandervorbeisprechen*, as the Germans say). This form of false dialogue is found in post-classical dramaturgy, where dialectical exchanges between characters and their discourses no longer exist (CHEKHOV, BECKETT).

C. The contexts are almost identical. The speeches are no longer in opposition, but spring from the same mouth. This is true of lyrical drama, in which the text does not belong to any one character, but is distributed "poetically" among all of them. This kind of multi-voice monologue is reminiscent of certain musical forms in which each instrument or voice contributes to the whole.

6. Divergent or Coherent Dialogue
It is the coherence of a very "tight" kind of dialogue that creates the impression of a true dialogue between characters (and not a monologue chopped into different dialogues attributed at random). The dialogue appears to be coherent and unified when (1) its *theme** is more or less the same for the speakers or (2) the *situation of enunciation** (the extra-linguistic reality of the characters) is shared by the speakers.

A. When the characters are talking about the same thing, their dialogues are generally understandable and dialectical, even if the speakers are very different otherwise. It is easy to imagine a man having a dialogue with a machine, for example, provided the subject matter is clearly identifiable.

B. When the characters are placed in the same stage situation and are felt to be very close emotionally or intellectually, their discourses are understandable and coherent even when they are talking about totally different things. Regardless of the subject of their conversation or "dialogue of the deaf," they are always "on the same wavelength" (for example, CHEKHOV's characters).

7. Origin of Dialogic Discourse
Dialogue may sometimes seem to be the individual or specific property of a character. Every speech by a character has its own rhythm, vocabulary and syntax. This type of believable dialogue, which seems to come from real life, is used by naturalistic playwrights. Changes in tone and semantic breaks between the speeches are very noticeable. Dialogue is as meaningful through *silences**, interruptions, and what is left unsaid, as it is through the content of the words (*spoken and unspoken**).

In the classical text, however, dialogues are unified and homogenized by suprasegmental traits that characterize the dramatist's style as a whole. Discrepancies in point of view and psychology between the characters are smoothed out in the interests of the coherence and monologism of the dramatic poem.

See also: monologue, discourse, speech, pragmatics.

Further reading: Szondi 1956; Todorov 1967; Klotz 1969; Rastier 1971; Ducrot 1972; Benveniste 1974; Turk 1976; Veltrusky 1977, 10–26; Pfister

1977; Runcan 1974; Avigal 1980; Wirth 1981; Todorov 1981; Dodd 1981; Klöpfer 1982; Kennedy 1983; Jaques 1985; Kerbrat-Orrechioni 1980, 1984, 1990, 1996.

DICTION

(From the Latin *dictio*, from *dicere*, say).
Fr.: *diction*; Ger.: *Diktion*; Sp.: *dicción*.

1. From Rhetoric to Declamation

A. In the archaic, eighteenth-century sense, diction refers to a way of wording and phrasing a text through a certain arrangement of the ideas or words. Good poetic diction then presupposes a specifically poetic choice of words and style. Diction possesses two major modes: narrative (narrative poetry) and the *imitation** of dramatic speech.

B. Diction refers to the way a text in prose or in verse is uttered – the art of reciting a text with the proper delivery, intonation and rhythm (*declamation**). The form of diction varies with the period, the most widespread criterion being whether it is realistic (*verisimilitude**) or artistic (modified *prosodic** or *rhythmic** diction). In fact, the diction of a text always moves between sound and sense, that is, between spontaneous cry (psychology) and rhetorical construction (literary *device**).

2. Two Kinds of Diction

A distinction can be drawn between two opposing types of diction. Naturalistic diction smooths out the melodic rhythms, favouring a "natural," down-to-earth, everyday mode of expression. This occurs when the actor seeks to play a character by showing the linguistic effects of the character's emotions. R. BARTHES has criticized this approach in the bourgeois interpretation of tragedy: "the bourgeois actor ceaselessly intervenes in the flow of the language, 'brings out' a word, suspends an effect, constantly signifies that what he is saying now is important, has a certain hidden meaning. This is what is called *speaking* a text" (1963, 136; Eng. 1964b, 142).

Artistic diction adapts to the rhythmic structure of the text to be spoken, this kind of diction does not conceal its artistic origins. Everyday emotional language and the prosodic scheme are kept at a distance. The actor does not mimic a realistic series of emotions through the rhythms of his speech, but structures his acting according to the rhetorical framework, displaying the verbal construction of the text, always contrasting "discursive" and "psychological."

This type of diction is quite difficult to carry off, as it needs to be supported by the style of the performance as a whole – a rejection of mimicry, theatricality, the defamiliarization of certain devices, a definitely artificial (though not parodic) atmosphere. Many productions (for example, those of VITEZ, MESGUICH, GRUBER, VILLEGIER) opt for this approach, keeping naturalism at arm's length. In this way, they achieve a certain authenticity in the way the text is approached and "spoken," while saying what they think about it. By separating certain words or phrases from the text, the actor gives an indication of which meaning is preferred, what physical relationship he has established with his discourse and character. Thus he reveals the architecture of the sentence and his subjective view of the spatial propositions of the text.

3. Diction and Interpretation

Being much more than simply a technical mode of presentation that may or may not be convincing, the actor's diction emerges at the junction of the text as it is offered physically and the text as it is interpreted intellectually. It gives voice and body to one of the possible meanings of the text. From this perspective, the actor is the ultimate spokesman of the dramatist and director, since he speaks the text by incarnating it on stage and conveying it through his body. L. JOUVET described this phenomenon in *le Comédien désincarné*: "The playwright's text is, for the actor, a physical transcription. It ceases to be a literary text" (1954, 153). Diction gives life to the sentence and, according to JOUVET, the sentence should come alive through diction rather than emotion (1968, 257).

As the ultimate spokesman of the text, the actor necessarily takes a stand on what he is saying, which may or may not coincide with the playwright's presumed meaning. Just as, in the sentence, the act of enunciation always has the "last word" over the utterance, diction is a *hermeneutic** act that imposes a certain volume, vocal colouring, corporality and modalization on the text that are responsible for its meaning. It necessarily assigns a meaning for the listener and spectator. By giving the text a certain *rhythm**, a continuous or interrupted flow, by lending it the stresses and accidents of his body, the actor constructs the *fabula** and takes a position on the events. This gestural and vocal enunciation gives the mise-en-scène its dynamics and its tone.
Further reading: Becq de Fouquières 1881; Barthes 1982, 236–245.

DIDACTIC PLAY

Fr.: *pièce didactique*; Ger.: *Lehrstück*; Sp.: *obra didáctica*.

In endeavouring to instruct the audience, the didactic play militates in favour of a philosophical or political thesis. The members of the audience are expected to draw a lesson for application to their private and public lives. Sometimes, instead of being meant for an audience, didactic theatre is made to be appreciated by the actors, who experiment with the text and their interpretations and swap roles (cf. BRECHT's *Lehrstücke*: *The Exception and the Rule*, *The Decision*)
See also: thesis drama, didactic theatre.

DIDACTIC THEATRE

Fr.: *théâtre didactique*; Ger.: *Lehrtheater*; Sp.: *teatro didáctico*.

1. Didactic theatre is any theatre that aims to instruct its audience by inviting them to reflect on a problem, understand a situation, or adopt a certain moral or political attitude.

In the sense that theatre does not normally present gratuitous or meaningless action, there is an element of didacticism in all theatre work. What varies is the clarity and force of the message, the desire to change the audience and to subordinate art to an ethical or ideological design. Didactic theatre in the strict sense is moralizing (the *morality plays** of the late Middle Ages), political (*agit-prop** and Brechtian *Lehrstücke*) or pedagogical (*thesis drama**, *parables**, philosophical fables such as *Quisaitout et Grobêta* or *Lapin-Lapin* by C. SERREAU). In the nineteenth century in Europe there were many experiments in exposing an underprivileged audience (workers and peasants, but also children), who often lacked a specific form of expression, to an often difficult art that was expected by artists and intellectuals to contribute to social change.

2. The call for didactic art dates back to antiquity. In HORACE's *Ars poetica* (14 B.C.) the useful is allied with the agreeable, in an attempt to edify the audience. The Middle Ages conceived of this edification as a religious education, while Renaissance poetics tended to moralize literature. The classical age in France yielded to this principle, at least in its prefaces and theoretical treatises, often restricting the moralism to an exordium, a prologue or an epilogue, to a compact form such as the *maxim**: "The only rule that can be set is that [maxims] must be placed judiciously, and particularly that they should be put into the mouths of clear-thinking people who do not get carried away in the heat of the action." (CORNEILLE, Discours du poème dramatique).

In the eighteenth century, bourgeois moralism led theoreticians like VOLTAIRE, DIDEROT and LESSING to organize their stories in such a way as to enable the moral message to appear clearly. LESSING tells the poet "to organize his story material such that it may serve as the explanation and the confirmation of a great moral truth." SCHILLER calls the stage a "moral institution."

3. Our own time is less open to this kind of didactic discourse, since politics have compromised art permanently, whether in the form of Nazism, Stalinism, or the official art of the former so-called peoples' democracies or many developing countries. On the other hand, it has become clear that meaning and message are never given directly but lie in structure and form, in the ideological unspoken. So the expression "didactic art" lends itself poorly to a serious and truly pedagogical reflection on art and politics.

DIDASCALIA

(From the Greek *didascalia*, teaching.)
Fr.: *didascalies*; Ger.: *Didaskalien, Bühnenanweisungen*; Sp.: *didascalias*.

Instructions given by the playwright to the performers (in Greek theatre, for example) to guide them in interpreting the dramatic text. By extension, in the modern age, *stage directions**.

1. In Greek theatre, the playwright was often his own director and actor, so that acting instructions are rarely found in manuscripts. Rather, the didascalia include information about the play's composition and performance dates and locations, results of dramatic competitions, etc. So little is given by way of acting directions that it is not always clear who is saying the lines.

In Roman theatre, the didascalia consisted of brief notes on the play and a list of *dramatis personae** and musicians.

2. The term *stage directions*, which is more frequently used today, would seem more suited to describe the metalinguistic role of this secondary text (see *main text and side text**) (INGARDEN 1971).

Further reading: Levitt 1971; Larthomas 1972; Ubersfeld 1977a; Ruffini 1978; Thomasseau 1984a.

DIEGESIS

(From the Greek *diegesis*, narrative.)

*Imitation** of an event in words, by telling the story rather than by presenting the characters in action.

1. Diegesis and Mimesis

ARISTOTLE (*Poetics*, 1448a), opposes imitation (*mimesis**) to narrative. The term *diegesis* is used to designate the narrative material, *fabula**, the "pure" narrative unmodalized by discourse. This notion is used mainly in film *semiology** (PERCHERON 1977).

The notion of diegesis as it is used in literary theory (Genette, 1969) and film studies subscribes to the same opposition between *narrative** as material, as *fabula** to be transmitted (story), and *discourse* as the individual use of that narrative, a construction that always reveals the traces of the enunciating instance – the dramatist, director, actor, etc. (BENVENISTE 1966, 237–250).

2. Presentation of Diegesis

The dramatic construction and the establishment of *fiction** and *illusion** may be visible or concealed to a varying degree. We could say that diegesis is presented as being "natural" when all of the fictionalizing and staging devices are concealed and when the stage gives the impression of a total illusion that has no need of being "manufactured" with various enunciation *devices**.

A style of dramaturgy that claims to be an artificial system and signifying practice, on the other hand, will show how the fiction is produced, how the *fabula* is elaborated, and will not rely on *identification** with the actor (BRECHT), but rather underscore the narrative effects of diegesis.

3. The Diegetization of Enunciation

The narrative (novel, short story, etc.) is familiar with the technique of "diegetizing" the text it produces, and often attempts to render the act of production more believable. This may be done, for instance, with an editor's note about a "found" manuscript, a "true" story told by an "I," or an "objective" scientific presentation of the facts. Theatre may do the same by using first lines *in medias res*, suggesting that the action began before the curtain was lifted, through an epic *narrator** who uses the prologue to introduce the story, or a *play within a play** in which a character states his desire to stage a theatrical performance. All these techniques are designed to mask literary construction; they are conventions and tricks used to produce the illusion. In this way the process of enunciation and literary or stage production of the performance is at once recovered and effaced.

Further reading: J. Scherer 1950; Pavis 1980a.

DILEMMA

(From the Greek *dilemma*, double choice.)

1. Situation in which the hero is forced to choose between two contradictory and equally unacceptable solutions. *Classical dramaturgy**, which seeks to illustrate the *conflict** in the most concentrated and visible way possible, is particularly fond of the dilemma, called *situation* in the seventeenth and eighteenth centuries in France. "Situation is that violent state in which one finds oneself between two pressing and diametrically opposed interests, between two imperious passions that tear us apart and do not permit us to decide, or at least only very painfully" (MORVAN DE BELLEGARDE 1702, on *le Cid*).

2. A dilemma confronts duty and love, moral principle and political necessity, obedience to two persons in opposition. The hero sets out the terms of the contradiction and finally takes a decision which resolves the dramatic conflict in any one of many possible ways. The dilemma is one of the dramaturgical forms of the *tragic**, and includes both terms of the contradiction. In dilemma, as in the tragic conflict between characters, "each of the opposed sides, if taken by itself, has *justification*; while each can establish the true and positive content of its own aim and character only by denying and infringing the equally justified power of the other. The consequence is that in its moral life, and because of it, each is nevertheless involved in *guilt*" (HEGEL 1832, 322; Eng. 1975, 1196).

See also: stances, conflict, monologue, dialectics, discourse, deliberation.

DIONYSIAC

Fr.: *dionysiaque;* Ger.: *das Dionysische;* Sp.: *dionisiaco.*

See APOLLONIAN

DIRECTING OF ACTORS

Fr.: *direction d'acteur;* Ger.: *Anleitung des Schauspielers, Schauspielerführung;* Sp.: *dirección de actores.*

Taken from cinema, where work by and on actors is often concealed by the technical apparatus, the directing of actors is a process whereby the director (who may be called a "coach") advises and guides the actors from early rehearsals to final adjustments during a play's run. This notion, at once fluid and crucial, has to do with the individual personal as well as artistic relationship established between the director and the artist. This is a personal, often ambiguous relationship that arises in Western theatre, particularly its realistic and psychological forms, where the actor seeks the identity of his character within himself, as "an actor's work on himself." In order to understand the basis of this notion and its importance in the staging, one must take care not to reduce it to a psychological and anecdotal relationship, but rather try to grasp its method and come up with a general theory.

1. The Director and the Staging

Apart from situations where directors spend years working with the same group — like BROOK, BARBA or MNOUCHKINE, a director does not have the time to offer his actors training to learn, or unlearn, the profession in a process where he would reexamine the actors' physical and psychic foundations (relaxation, sense perception, affective memory, concentration). Directors do not have the time to take actors marred by charlatans or mediocre working conditions and put them on the right track. There is, however, a widespread use of preparatory courses (for example, AFDAS) during which the future director of a play tests distribution, verifies the actors' skills, and invents basic exercises that subtly introduce the play. This effects a smooth introduction to creation.

2. Directing during Preparation of the Staging

A. READING THE SCRIPT

This covers various different areas. The director organizes long days of reading around the table, in which he explains the possible interpretations, prepares the diction, reflects on the characters' motivations to find personal keys to behavior ("What would I do if...?"). Sometimes, on the other hand, a director may impose a neutral voice and intonation in reading so as not to limit interpretation. A director may even do "screen tests," as does Vitez: "with no preliminary explanation, thought must be developed by examining the choice between such and such a gesture, such and such a place – sometimes a dramatic choice and subject of commentary–by means of an ongoing conversation on stage" (VITEZ 25; from *Théâtre/Public* no. 64–65, 1985, "La direction d'acteur").

B. BRINGING THE CHARACTER TO LIFE

The director's advice – almost like that of a spiritual counsellor – is needed in order for the actor to enter the character, grasp his motivations, use the features of his outer and inner persona to suggest and build up the role. This mammoth undertaking can fortunately be broken down into smaller tasks: holding onto the overall aim of the scene or the play, finding the right voice, gestures and behavior, establishing distance from or closeness to the character, ensuring that gestures are readable and beautiful to watch, deciding on an outer rhythm for visible physical actions and an inner rhythm connected to the subtext, helping the actor find his "score" and subscore, etc.

During this process, the relationship between director and actor may become fraught with conflict: the actor is more or less "pushed off balance, placed at ease and made uneasy" (RYNGAERT, "La direction d'acteur," 37); the director must "sustain, reassure, understand and contain him" (GUIGNON, "La direction d'acteur," 34). The director always knows tricks and can tell stories to the group or to each individual to establish a basic trust and commence collective work or "unblock the actor with a few words," "make his keen gaze felt" (MAYOR, "La direction d'acteur," 50). As in any interpersonal relationship, what is left unsaid and understood speaks eloquently. Not everything can or should be said; everyone lets little secrets out, everyone is like those ideal actors according to MARIVAUX who "know not the value of what they say." It is up to the director to give back all or part of the value of what they say, the image of what they do, to make them aware (or not) of the value they are expressing or the image they are giving. A director also discovers within the actor a complex individual with many tasks and unsuspected powers, with an individual view of the character but an understanding of the play as a whole, an individual contribution of relevant traits subordinate to the overall staging. An actor is necessarily an actor/creator, an "actor who is part of a project but brings elements to it that only he can contribute" (KNAPP 1993, 19).

3. Getting Instructions Across

Apart from secrets that cannot be told, there are well-established ways of conveying instructions to actors:

A. SHOWING

The director shows the actor what is expected. This approach has not had good press, and risks emasculating the actor, but when done by a STREHLER it is always a show in itself, an invitation to go beyond imitation, and a blessing for the actor.

B. DEMONSTRATION

CHEKHOV and VAKHTANGOV invented a way of wordlessly miming a few key moments in the role to give it the right attitude, rhythm, *psychological gesture**.

C. INSTRUCTION

The director gives verbal or mimed instructions concerning an aspect of acting or the character, though avoiding an imitation of what he expects from the actor.

D. DIRECTING TO ORDER
The actor is directed and corrected while acting. This avoids too-frequent interruptions and makes for dynamic open rehearsals (VITEZ 1994, 135).

E. INNER MIME BY DIRECTOR
This may be more useful to the director than the actor, but can also be transmitted from one to the other; it is an "internal, intimate, inner mime of what the other is going to do, what the other must do" (VITEZ, 25). It is up to the actor, of course, to decipher the mime.

F. BACK AND FORTH BETWEEN SCORE AND SUBSCORE
The actor is encouraged to establish movements, actions, thoughts and images by means of a subscore that helps him place himself in space and time and on the "continuous line of the action" (STANISLAVSKY). The sum total of the visible scores of the different actors becomes the master score for the staging. The director uses it as an organization chart, always in flux but lending some stability to the nascent show. By expressing the master score bit by bit, the director invites the actors to refine it and add their individual subscores to it.

G. CONTINUING THE RELATIONSHIP
This is possible, and often crucial, after the first stage. The director/manager often needs to tighten up the staging by making adjustments and leaving out scenes or moments that don't work, and a special touch is needed. The results of this work are difficult to register, but may be kept for the next show or role, used to shape an acting style, a school of thought, an aesthetic that will facilitate future directing work.

Directing actors is ultimately the very heart of the staging in its day-to-day, human dimension, and determines its human and artistic success. It would be misguided to make this the focus of a new science (like the Russians, from STANISLAVSKY and MEYERHOLD to CHEKHOV and VASSILIEV), but there are certainly grounds for examining what is at stake here, epistemologically speaking, as the key to any theatrical venture.

DIRECTOR

Fr.: *metteur en scène;* Ger.: *Regisseur;* Sp.: *director de teatro.*

Person in charge of putting on (i.e. staging) a play, who assumes aesthetic and organizational responsibility for the production by choosing the actors, interpreting the text and using available stage potential.

1. The term *metteur en scène* (or producer, director) appeared in the first half of the nineteenth century. Although the notion and systematic practice of *mise-en-scène* date back to this time, the director has many more or less legitimate ancestors in the history of theatre (VEINSTEIN 1955, 116–171).

2. In Greek theatre, the *didascale* (from *didaskalos,* instructor) was sometimes the author, who acted as organizer. In the Middle Ages, the pageant master had both ideological and aesthetic responsibility for the mystery plays. During the Renaissance and Baroque periods, it was often the architect or stage designer who organized the performance according to his own perspective. In the eighteenth century, major actors took over, with IFFLAND and SCHRÖDER becoming, in Germany, the first great *Regisseure* (directors). Not until the emergence of naturalism, however, did the function become a discipline and an art in itself, particularly with Duke George II of SAXE-MEININGEN, A. ANTOINE and K. STANISLAVSKY.

3. It is difficult to make a definitive statement about how appropriate and important the director is in theatre creation for, in the last analysis, the arguments always come down to a question of taste and ideology, and not an objective aesthetic debate. We will simply say that the director exists and makes his presence felt (particularly when he is not equal to the task) in the stage pro-

duction. During the 1960s and 1970s the director was challenged periodically by his "colleagues" – actors feeling hemmed in by overly – tyrannical instructions, stage designers wishing to catch the artistic team and the audience in the trap of their machinery, "collectives" rejecting any distinctions within the group and proposing a *collective creation** and, most recently, cultural *animators** acting as an intermediary between art and its marketing, between artists and city – an uncomfortable position, perhaps, but a strategic one.

4. The director's function in the 1990s is rarely challenged but has been trivialized considerably. The question is not even whether the director does too much or not enough, whether the mise-en-scène is a "mise-en-trop" (VINAVER 1988); rather, along with VINAVER, we "wager on a return towards more modesty and a lightness of hand, towards less art and more craftsmanship" (VINAVER in FLOECK 1989, 254). True, one still hears it said, somewhat ingenuously, that the best director should be content to let the text speak for itself (S. SEIDE, C. RÉGY, P. CHÉREAU, J. LASSALLE, quoted in *L'Art du Théâtre*, no. 6, 1986). M. DURAS makes an appeal for a staging that does as little as possible: "Acting takes away from the text. It doesn't add anything; on the contrary, it takes away from the text's presence, depth, muscle, blood" ("Le théâtre," in *La Vie matérielle*).

The younger generation of directors no longer relies on a deconstructive model – whether psychoanalytic, Marxist or linguistic – and no longer refers to models or schools, much less movements or "isms." They advance step by step, sometimes without the protection of institutions. Some directors go on to writing (A. HAKIM, H. COLAS, C. ANNE, P. RAMBERT, P. MINYANA, J. JOUANNEAU, D. LEMAHIEU, J. ROUSSEAU); others retain the memory of their "formal" education with VITEZ (B. JAQUES, C. SCHIARETTI, S. LOUCASHEVSKY, S. BRAUNSCHWEIG); some have opened up to cross-cultural production (C. VÉRICEL, G. ISAÏ, X. DURRINGER, E. SOLA); some feature a new relationship with the text, seen as plastic (E. DA SILVA, O. PY) or resistant (S. NORDEY, P. PRADINAS, C. ALLOUCHERIE, E. LACASCADE).

Further reading: Allevy 1938; Borgal 1963; Bergman 1964, 1966; Brook 1968; Dullin 1969; Vitez 1974, 1984; Wills 1976; Hays 1977; Temkine 1977, 1979, 1987; *Pratiques*, 1979; Godard 1980; Strehler 1980; Braun 1982; *L'Art du théâtre*, no.6, 1986; *Art Press* 1989.

DIRECTOR'S THEATRE

Fr.: *théâtre de metteur en scène*; Ger.: *Regietheater*; Sp.: *teatro de director*.

Theatre that employs the services of a *director** and therfore attaches great importance to the interpretation of text and the originality of *staging** options. The artist's mark and signature upon the play are discernable.

DISCOURSE

Fr.: *discours*; Ger.: *Diskurs*; Sp.: *discurso*.

1. The Concept of Discourse in Linguistics
Having borrowed a methodology (or, in some cases, just a vocabulary) from linguistics, theatre criticism is now overwhelmingly concerned with the concept of discourse and related issues. Critics speak of the "discourse of mise-en-scène" or the "discourse of the characters." The question remains, however, to what extent discourse analysis is applicable to theatre without being simply a mechanical application of linguistics and what it can bring to the analysis of text or performance.

The notion of discourse comes from SAUSSURE and then BENVENISTE (1966, 1974). The sentence belongs to discourse, rather than language (*langue*). Discourse is also opposed to the narrative (GENETTE 1969). In narrative, the "zero degree of enunciation," "events appear to tell themselves"; discourse, however, presupposes a speaker and a listener and is structured by the correlation of personal pronouns. Discourse is originally oral, but it may be conceptualized in written form, since "discourse is also the mass of writings reproducing spoken discourse or borrowing its style or purposes: correspondence, memoirs, theatre, didactic works – in short, all those genres in which someone addresses someone else, announces himself as a speaker and organizes what he says in the category of the person" (BENVENISTE 1966, 242). Therefore, we can speak of theatre discourse as performance and as dramatic text (awaiting enunciation on stage). "The theatre script," remarks ISSACHAROFF [we would prefer the term *dramatic text*], "is not an instance of spoken discourse in the strict sense. It is a conventionalized written form that represents the spoken discourse" (1985, 11). In accordance with this usage, we concur with ISSACHAROFF that discourse means "the specifically theatrical use of language in the broadest sense, from verbal utterance to nonverbal uses comprising the visual elements, including gesture, facial expression, movement, costume, players' bodies, properties, and decor" (1985, 9; 1989, 3, 5).

2. Discourse Analysis and Discourse of Mise-en-scène

If by *discourse* we mean "the utterance considered from the point of view of the discursive mechanism that conditions it" (GUESPIN 1971, 10), the discourse of mise-en-scène is the organization of the textual and stage materials according to a rhythm and a system of interdependence that are proper to the performance being staged. In order to define the discursive mechanism of the mise-en-scène, it must be seen in relation to its conditions of production, which are determined by the particular use made by the "authors" (playwright, director, stage designer) of the various artistic systems (stage materials) available to them at a given historical time. In linguistics, we have known since SAUSSURE that *parole* (and the discourses it produces) is a particular use and activation of *langue* (the phonological, syntactical and semantic systems). Similarly, theatre discourse, both textual and scenic, is an appropriation of the stage systems, an individual use of stage potential, even when the individual (the subject of discourse) is in fact the entire creative team. Naturally, these subjects of theatre discourse must be distinguished from the actual persons on the theatre team. They are defined at a theoretical (not a real) level as subjects in constant flux who leave their mark on the stage utterance. To capture these subjects in the making, or their discursive mechanisms, we will seek their traces in the theatre enunciation(s) and the logical presuppositions that are surreptitiously introduced by the discourse.

A. THEATRE ENUNCIATION

Central discourse and discourse of characters

Enunciation is assumed at two fundamental levels – that of the individual discourse of the characters and that of the overall discourse of the *playwright** and staging team. This first "split" conceals the origin of the word in theatre and sees discourse as a field of tensions between two opposing tendencies – one a tendency to present autonomous, mimetic discourses that define each character in his or her individual situation; the other a tendency to homogenize the characters' lines through the hallmarks of the playwright found throughout, which lend a certain rhythmic, lexical and poetic uniformity to the whole. Hence the obsolete term *dramatic poem**, in which the various roles were clearly subject to the "centralizing" and unifying enunciation of the poet.

Dialogism and the dialectics of utterance (énoncé) and enunciation (énonciation)

By multiplying the sources of speech (*parole*), by making scenery, gesture, facial expression or intonation "speak" as much as the text itself, the staging creates a space for all of the subjects of discourse and establishes a dialogue among all sources of speech (*parole*) (BAKHTIN 1973). Theatre is often a place where ideology appears fragmented, deconstructed, both absent and omnipresent: "Theatre discourse is by nature a questioning about the status of speech: who is speaking to whom, and under what conditions?" (UBERSFELD 1977a, 265). More than any other art or literary system, it lends itself to a dissociation of the utterance (what is said) and the enunciation (the way in which it is said). The mise-en-scène makes the textual utterances (that were believed to be clear and univocal) say a multitude of things. The actor/character can show the audience both the fiction (illusion) and the discursive, constructed form of this fiction: "story" and "discourse" (as established by BENVENISTE 1966, 237–250) coincide in the acting of the character.

B. LOGICAL PRESUPPOSITIONS

Not everything that is said on stage (through text or performance) is expressed directly. As in the case of linguistic presuppositions, the stage constantly sets up implications that go beyond the visible utterances alone and may be deduced by convention or association from what is visible or uttered. Thus, the presence of an object on stage can evoke a certain milieu, can prompt the spectator to wonder why and by whom it was brought to the stage, and what previous situation it presupposes. Things are said that are never expressly verbalized, which increases the effectiveness and *action** of the discourse. How the presuppositions are handled is left up to the director, who must, however, observe certain rules – once evoked, the presuppositions become an integral part of the utterance; they are maintained and they determine how the dramatic situation evolves; they have no need to be repeated and must not be contradicted or eliminated if the discourse is to be believable; finally, they are a tactical tool that may be manipulated skilfully to imprison the audience, forcing the spectators to accept a particular state of things and providing a guide for their ideological and aesthetic judgment (DUCROT 1972).

3. Discourse as Spoken Aaction

Theatre discourse differs from literary or "everyday" discourse through its performative force, its ability to carry out actions symbolically. By tacit convention, "saying is doing" in theatre (AUSTIN 1962). This has always been stressed by theoreticians, particularly in the classical era when it was unthinkable to stage violent actions or even actions that were difficult to represent. D'AUBIGNAC remarked, for instance, that the characters' speeches "must be like the actions of those who are made to appear, since here to speak is to act," and that "every tragedy, in the performance, consists only of discourse" (1927, 282–283). Theatre discourse produces meaning at the level of its rhetoric, its assumptions and its enunciation. It is not only intended, therefore, to represent the stage, but contributes to representing itself as a way in which *fabula*, character and text are constructed (PAVIS 1978a).

4. Discursive Formations

Discourse analysis, which studies the discursive formations of a text, gives promising results in theatre. This theory postulates that "a sequence or an utterance has 'meaning' for a subject only to the extent that the subject conceives it as belonging to a given discursive formation, but the subject represses this idea in favour of the illusion that he is the origin of meaning" (MAINGUENEAU 1976, 83). In analyzing dramatic texts, two or more discursive formations are often observable in the speeches of antagonistic characters, or even within the text of the same character. According to Marxist theory, these discursive formations are articulated on ideological formations that correspond to different material conditions. When practicing textual analysis, it is often very tricky to identify the various ideological and discursive formations, but theatre has the advantage (and the deception) of placing in conflict different points of view and making visible the heterogeneous nature of discourse.

5. General Features of Theatre Discourse

It is not possible to speak of theatre discourse in general, contrary to customary usage. Following, however, is a brief list of some of its more frequently observed characteristics:

A. The subject(s) need to be discovered, often in unexpected places. Ideological subject and psychoanalytical subject often appear to be decentred, and the staging gives only an approximate, illusory image of them.

B. The discourse is unstable. The actor and director can distance themselves from the text, *modalize** it and construct it according to the *situation of enunciation**.

C. It is "stagy" and gestural to a greater or lesser degree. Its "translatability" to the stage depends on its *rhythm**, rhetoric and phonic quality.

D. A contextualization, depending on the degree of precision and explanation involved, reveals elements that would otherwise remain hidden in the text (process of concretization) (*dramatic text**).

E. The discourse is *dialectical** to a greater or lesser degree, and tied to changes in the dramatic situation. It may unfold according to the dramatic conflicts or their resolution, or it may be shaped at random, by witty words, sudden ideas or "conceits" (DÜRRENMATT 1970, 57; Eng. 1982, 254).

F. Dramatic discourse is a form of conversation which, according to WIRTH (1981), tends to replace conversation-dialogue (dramatic exchange): "In dialogue-conversation, word space becomes confused with stage space. In non-conversational forms of discourse (for example, address to the audience), word space includes the house as well as the stage" (1981, 10).

See also: semiology, verbal and non-verbal, materialization, pragmatics.

Further reading: Fontanier 1977; Foucault 1969, 1971; Schmid 1973; Jaffré 1974; Van Dijk 1976; Pavis 1978a, 1983a, 1985e; Kerbrat-Orecchioni 1980, 1984; Wirth 1981; Elam 1984; U. Jung 1994; Danan 1995.

DISCOVERY

Fr.: *découverte*; Ger.: *Entdeckung*; Sp.: *descubrimiento*.

See ANALYTICAL DRAMA

DISGUISE

Fr.: *déguisement*; Ger.: *Verkleidung*; Sp.: *disfraz*.

1. The Potential of Disguise

The use of a costume or *mask** to change a character's identity, in a manner that may be concealed from the other characters or from the audience or disclosed to some of the characters or to the audience. The change may be individual (one person as opposed to another), social (a particular status for another, as in MARIVAUX), political (for example, *Measure for Measure*), or of gender (BEAUMARCHAIS).

Disguise is often used, particularly in comedy, to produce all kinds of dramatically interesting situations – mistaken identity, *coup de théâtre**, *play within a play**, voyeurism. It "overtheatricalizes" the acting, which is based on the notion of *role** and *character**, already a disguise for the actor, by pointing not only to the stage but also to the spectator's gaze. Disguise is presented as being believable (in realistic acting) or as a dramatic *convention** and dramaturgical technique necessary for the playwright to have information pass from one character to another, to facilitate the progression of the plot and to resolve it at the end of the play (MARIVAUX, MOLIÈRE).

2. The Basic Situation of Theatre

Disguise is nothing exceptional in theatre; rather, it is the basic situation as an actor plays another and his character, "as in life," appears to others behind various masks depending on his desires and projects. Disguise is a mark of theatricality, of the play within a play and *mise-en-abyme**. It cannot do without the complicity of the audience, who must accept this convention. "Truth in theatre is not the truth of reality. Disguise in theatre, as it should be employed, takes the whole theatrical performance toward a general, almost inevitable transposition" (DULLIN 1969, 195).

3. Forms of Disguise

Disguise most often takes the form of a change of costume or mask (i.e. of a convention specific to a character), but it is followed by a change of language or style, a modification of behaviour or a concealment of true thoughts or feelings. "Disguise as a signal" indicates to the spectator or another character that a temporary masking is taking place. "Disguise as vertigo" disorients observers: reference points are lost and the characters mislead each other, as in masked balls.

The ideological and dramaturgical function of disguise is infinitely varied, but it usually leads to a reflection on reality and appearance (MARIVAUX), man's identity (PIRANDELLO, GENET), the unveiling of the truth. As for plot, disguise causes conflicts, accelerates revelations, permits exchanges of information and "direct" confrontations between the sexes or classes. As an enlightener and as a short cut, disguise is an ideal dramatic convention to reveal the identity and evolution of the characters. It plays the role of a Platonic, hermeneutic unveiling of hidden reality, of the action to come and the conclusion of the play. It is frequently subversive, as it authorizes the playwright to expound on sexual ambiguity or the interchangeability of individuals and social classes (SHAKESPEARE, BRECHT).

Further reading: FORESTIER 1988.

DISTANCE

Fr.: *distance;* Ger.: *Distanz, Entfernung;* Sp.: *distancia.*

The spectator (and, more generally, the receiver of a work of art) takes distance when he sees the performance as entirely external to him, when he does not get emotionally involved and never forgets that he is faced with a *fiction**. By extension, distance is the faculty of using critical judgment, of resisting the theatrical *illusion** and detecting the *devices** used in performance.

The concept of distance is used in the theory of the novel to indicate where the narrator stands in relation to his enunciation or his utterances and to the characters.

1. The Spatial Metaphor in Theatre

Since the spectator is located in front of the stage in a kind of symbiosis with the event, the notion of his psychic distance toward the performance has become widespread, particularly since the famous Brechtian *Verfremdungseffekt* (*alienation-effect**), sometimes translated as "distantiation."

A. Distance is, first of all, the *stage-audience relationship**, or the audience's *perspective** and degree of physical participation (or involvement) in the performance. The *stage design** is both the effect and the cause of a given dramaturgy, and it reinforces the dramaturgical effect if it is adapted to the requirements of a world view and writing mode.

B. By extension, distance becomes the attitude of the ego toward the aesthetic object, somewhere between two theoretical poles:

- "zero distance" or total *identification** and merging with the character;
- maximum distance, or total lack of interest in the action as soon as the spectator leaves the theatre and directs his attention at something else. This kind of distance is measured in *breaks* in the illusion, which occur when some element of the stage appears improbable. Distance is therefore an approximate, subjective and difficult-to-measure (i.e. metaphorical) notion.

2. Critical Distance

In our culture, to take one's distance has a positive and critical connotation. There is a certain amount of shame attached to falling into the trap of the illusion and losing one's judgment; it is deemed better to keep one's distance. This is the cognitive context of BRECHT's critique of *identification**.

A denial of distance, on the other hand, leads directors to activate audience *participation** by tying the audience emotionally to the stage, by trying to break down the boundary between stage and audience and, in extreme cases, by having actors and spectators participate in the same ceremony or political action by unifying them in one community (*happening**).

Establishing distance from the play is not simply a question of how the stage is arranged or how the text is staged. It is

determined above all by: (a) the values and cultural codes of the theatre community; (b) the acting style and the genre of the production – tragedy (and any other form dominated by death and destiny) tends to weld the audience together and make them identify *en masse* with what is being presented. Comedy, on the other hand, does not have to keep the audience riveted to the event; it elicits a critical smile through its inventiveness in developing the plot – its devices always appear artificial and self-conscious.
See also: theatrical relationship, reception, communication.
Further reading: Brecht 1963, 1970; Starobinksi 1970; Booth 1977; Pavis 1980c.

DITHYRAMB

Fr.: *dithyrambe;* Ger.: *Dithyrambus;* Sp.: *ditirambo.*

Originally a lyrical song of praise for Dionysius performed and danced by the chorus under the leadership of the coryphaeus, the dithyramb evolved into a dialogue, for example with SIMONIDE OF CEOS (556–468) and, according to Aristotle, led to the tragedy.

DIVERTISSEMENT

Fr.: *divertissement;* Ger.: *Unterhaltung, Balletein-lage;* Sp.: *entretenimiento.*
See INTERLUDE, INTERMEZZO

DOCUMENTARY THEATRE

Fr.: *théâtre documentaire;* Ger.: *Dokumentartheater;* Sp.: *teatro documental.*

Plays composed of nothing but documents and authentic sources, selected and assembled according to the playwright's sociopolitical thesis.

1. Reusing Sources

In that dramatists never create *ex nihilo* but always use sources (myths, historical events), any dramatic composition carries an element of the documentary. As early as the nineteenth century, certain historical dramas used sources, often extensively. BÜCHNER, for instance, in *Danton's Death,* quoted from minutes of meetings and historical works. During the 1920s and 1930s, in Germany and then in the United States, E. PISCATOR (1893–1963) adopted this approach to give an account of current political events. But it was mainly in the 1950s and 1960s, up until the 1970s, that the documentary became a genre in the novel, in *cinéma verité,* in poetry, radio plays and theatre. No doubt this occurred in response to the current taste for reportage and the ascendancy of the *media**, which inundate us with contradictory and manipulative information, and to a desire to replicate with a similar technique. Documentary theatre is heir to *historical drama**. It is the opposite of theatre of pure fiction, which it deems too idealistic and apolitical, and rejects the manipulation of events by in turn manipulating documents for partisan ends. It often employs the form of a trial or inquiry in order to quote proceedings: R. KIPPHARDT in *In der Sache J. Robert Oppenheimer* (1964); P. WEISS in *Die Ermittlung* (1965) and *Vietnam-Diskurs* (1968); H.M. ENZENSBERGER in *Das Verhör von Habanna.* It often combines documents with fiction, as in *Der Stellvertreter* (1963) or *Soldaten* (1969), by R. HOCHHUT; *US* by P. BROOK (1969); *Front Page* by R. NICHOLS; *Trotzki im Exil* (1970) and *Hölderlin* (1971) by P. WEISS.

2. A Combative Montage

In the place of *fabula** and fiction, materials are arranged according to their contrastive and explanatory value. The use of fragments assembled according to an overall system and socioeconomic model conveys a critique of the customary view of society imposed by a group or a class and illustrates the thesis proposed.

The montage and theatrical adaptation of political events keep theatre in its role of aesthetic, indirect intervention in reality. The resulting perspective throws light on the deep causes of the event described and suggests alternative solutions (WEISS, 1968).
See also: collage, montage, history, agit-prop, thesis drama.

Further reading: Piscator 1980; Marx and Engels 1967, 1:166–217; Weiss 1968; Hilzinger 1976.

DOCUMENTATION

Fr.: *documentation;* Ger.: *Dokumentation;* Sp.: *documentación.*

In order to write the history of a production, a theatre, or a theatre artist, a researcher needs a certain amount of documentation, in his notes and in archives or works published on related fields. Theatre libraries and *museums** furnish information that is not always easy to process. What is documentation? Recorded or transcribed texts are only a thin (both literally and figuratively) relic of the production. On the other hand, a staging encompasses all of surrounding reality through its reflection in the stage, and is not easy to store: raw documents (costumes, stage design, props) are appreciated more by fetishists than by researchers and computers. Related documents such as pictoral, architectural or acting sources of a production belong to the unlimited domain of art and culture and can only be consulted if the spectator already knows about them and has the time to review them. Often programs and press reviews are kept in uncatalogued (and therefore inaccessible) archives or deposited at random in public buildings. Poorly kept documentation is a researcher's nightmare. Truly valuable objects (sketches or models of stage designs) may have been mislaid or sold by the artist upon completion of preparations for the production. Only a systematic computer-based medium such as CD-ROMs can solve the problem of keeping and conserving documents. This means seeking out the *monuments* left after the performance to turn them into *documents* that can be easily used. In short, the documentation process calls for a clear theoretical awareness of what information processing will allow to be taken and used. It depends on the entire *research** process and the gaze it fixes on the object to be documented. Documentation has the best chance of being used properly if it is associated with a (selective) exhibit, a research project (in process), an ongoing theoretical discussion. Files that are up to date and easy to handle, an ideal library, a provisional inventory of places and theories will certainly help in structuring undefined documentation materials.

See also: Theatre studies, didascalia, staging book.

Further reading: Veinstein 1983; Hiss 1993.

DOMESTIC (BOURGEOIS) TRAGEDY

Fr.: *tragédie domestique (bourgeoise);* Ger.: *bürgerliche Tragödie;* Sp.: *tragedia doméstica.*

Name used in the eighteenth century, mainly by DIDEROT, for *bourgeois drama**.

DOUBLE

Fr.: *double;* Ger.: *Doppel, Doppelgänger;* Sp.: *doble.*

The double is an infinitely varied literary and philosophical theme. Theatre draws widely on this theme because, as a representational art, it always shows the actor and its character, the word represented and its representations, signs which are both referential (in that they "imitate" or "speak" the world) and self-referential (in that they refer to themselves, like any aesthetic object).

The perfect double appears in the figure of Sosie (MOLIÈRE or PLAUTUS), with all the imaginable misunderstandings. The double is often a brother-enemy (RACINE's *la Thébaïde*, SCHILLER's *die Räuber*), an alter ego (Faust's Mephisto), someone who does the protagonist's dirty work (Oenone for Phèdre, Dubois for Dorante in MARIVAUX's *les Fausses Confidences*), an accomplice (Sganarelle for Don Juan), a partner of self-projection in dialogue (Rodrigue, son and lover in *le Cid*). Between identity and difference, both unachievable, the character (like theatre) is always in search of its double.

See also: mise-en-abyme, play within a play, disguise, valet.

Further reading: O. Rank 1971; Artaud 1938; Mauron 1963; Ferroni 1981.

DRAMA

Fr.: *drame*; Ger.: *Schauspiel*; Sp.: *drama.*

Although the Greek word *drama* (action) gave rise to similar terms in many European languages which are used in referring to theatrical or dramatic work, *drame* in French refers only to a specific genre – bourgeois drama in the eighteenth century and then Romantic lyrical drama in the nineteenth.

1. In the eighteenth century, through DIDEROT, *bourgeois drama** became a "serious genre" somewhere between comedy and (bourgeois) tragedy.

2. Victor HUGO became an advocate of Romantic drama in prose, attempting to evade the rules and unities (except for unity of action), presenting many spectacular actions, mixing genres, and aiming for a synthesis between extremes and periods, claiming to be Shakespearian drama: "Shakespeare is drama, and drama that merges in one breath the grotesque and the sublime, the terrible and the ridiculous, tragedy and comedy; drama is the very nature of the third period of poetry in today's literature" (Preface to *Cromwell*).

3. Poetic (or lyrical) drama culminated at the end of the nineteenth century with MALLARMÉ, RÉGNIER, MAETERLINCK and HOFMANNSTHAL. It proceeded from the musical forms of the opera, the oratorio, the cantata and the Italian *dramma lirico*, but it left music with "fin de siècle" drama composed in reaction to naturalist plays. Action in lyrical drama was limited in scope, and plot had no function other than to handle moments of lyrical stasis. The lyrical and the dramatic came together in a destructuring of the tragic or dramatic form. Music was only an external component added to the text; the text "musicalizes" itself in a series of motifs, words and poems that are valuable in themselves rather than in relation to a clearly defined dramatic structure.
Further reading: Szondi 1975a; Sarrazac 1981, 1989; Hubert 1988.

DRAMATIC AND EPIC

Fr.: *dramatique et épique*; Ger.: *dramatisch und episch*; Sp.: *dramático y épico.*

1. Epic/Dramatic

A. The dramatic is a principle of construction of text and performance which accounts for the *tension** in the scenes and episodes of the *fabula** toward a dénouement (catastrophe or comic resolution) and suggests that the spectator is captivated by the action. *Dramatic* theatre (which BRECHT opposes to the epic form) is the theatre of classical dramaturgy, of realism and naturalism and the *well-made play**: it has been the conventional form of Western theatre since the famous definition of tragedy in Aristotle's *Poetics*: "Tragedy is an imitation of an action that is serious, complete, and possessing magnitude; [...] in the mode of action and not narrated; and effecting through pity and fear [what we call] the *catharsis* of such emotions (1449b).

B. The epic also has its place in the theory and practice of theatre, as it is not confined to a particular genre (novel, short story, epic poem) and plays a fundamental role in certain forms of theatre (see *epic theatre**). Even within dramatic theatre the epic can play a role, for instance through the use of narratives, descriptions, character *narrators**. The following comparison, cutting back and forth from epic to dramatic, may throw some light on the dialectics between them.

2. Dramatic and Epic according to Brecht

This double attitude of the spectator toward the performance is examined by BRECHT in his comparison between carousel theatre and planetarium theatre (BRECHT 1967, 16:538–597).

3. Aesthetic and Ideological Criteria of the Epic

A. Epic elements are found in drama well before BRECHT's theatre. Medieval mystery plays, classical Asian theatre, even narratives within classical European theatre are epic elements inserted in the dramatic weave of the play. But these are always technical and formal devices that do not question the overall direction of the play or the function of theatre in society.

B. For BRECHT, however, the transition from dramatic to epic form is not motivated by a question of style but by a new analysis of society. Dramatic theatre is no longer able to account for the conflicts of mankind in the world; the individual is no longer opposed to another individual but to an economic system: "Simply to comprehend the new areas of subject-matter imposes a new dramatic and theatrical form. [...] Petroleum resists the five-act form; today's catastrophes do not progress in a straight line but in cyclical crises; the 'heroes' change with the different phases, are interchangeable, etc.; the graph of people's actions is complicated by abortive actions; fate is no longer a single coherent power; rather there are fields of force which can be seen radiating in opposite directions; the power groups themselves comprise movements not only against one another but within themselves, etc., etc. Even to dramatize a simple newspaper report one needs something much more than the dramatic technique of a Hebbel or an Ibsen" (1967, 15:197; Eng. 1964, 30).

The *Brechtian** system, which is not really a closed philosophical system, was set out the first time in "Notes to the opera *Aufstieg und Fall der Stadt Mahagonny*" and then more definitively in *A Short Organum for the Theatre* (1948), *The Purchase of Copper* (1937–1951) and *Dialectics in the Theatre* (1951–1956).

C. Experimental theatre today gives theoretical and practical consideration to dramatic and epic principles. According to BRECHT's indications toward the end of his theoretical work (cf. Appendices to the *Short Organum*, 1954), however, epic and dramatic are not arrived at individually or exclusively but complement each other dialectically – epic showing and total actor/spectator involvement often coexist in the same performance.

The principle of the narrator who tells the story of another narrator who himself tells a story, and so on, appears to be used very frequently, even though it may not always respond clearly to the need to interpret social reality in a realistic way (MONOD 1977b).

Finally, the love of epic play-acting is often accompanied by an emphasis on the play-related and theatrical aspects of performance. The epic then serves more to explore the possibilities and limits of theatre than to provide a pertinent interpretation of reality. In the 1970s and 1980s, the epic has lost ground in theatre creation because of the scepticism with which many directors regard the Brechtian approach.

See also: closed form and open form; dramaturgy; reality represented, fabula, plot, Aristotelian theatre, epic treatment of drama.

Further reading: Kesting 1959; Dort 1960; Lukács 1963; Szondi 1972a; Sartre 1973; Todorov 1976; Pavis 1978b; Knopf 1980; De Toro 1984; Segre 1984.

DRAMATIC ART

Fr.: *art dramatique*; Ger.: *dramatische Kunst*; Sp.: *arte dramático*.

The expression is often used in the very general sense of "theatre" to mean both the artistic practice and the corpus of plays, texts and dramatic literature on which performance or mise-en-scène is based. Dramatic art is therefore a genre within literature and a practice related to the work of an actor who incarnates or shows a character for an audience.

See also: essence of the theatre, specificity, theatricality.

Further reading: Arnold 1951; Villiers 1951; Aslan 1963; Mrlian 1981.

Dramatic Theatre	Epic Theatre
I. The Stage	
The stage is where the action takes place.	The stage is not "transfigured" by the place of the action; it displays its materiality, its ostensive and demonstrative nature (the podium). It does not incarnate the action, but keeps it at a distance.
1. Present/past Event	
The event unfolds before us, in an immediate present. – We are supposed to relive it. – It is confined to exceptional moments of human activity (crises, passions).	*The past event is "reconstructed" by the act of narration.* – The event is to be expounded quietly. – It constitutes a "totality," and may be made up of a significant whole of facts.
2. Point of View of the Performance	
– The action and its reconstruction coincide exactly in time and space; they are presented in the form of an exchange between an "I" and a "you."	The narrator disappears behind the fictional "he" of the characters. He takes his distance from the actions of the characters, whom he presents as external voices.
II. The Action of the Fabula	
It unfolds before me, forms a whole that could not be broken up without losing all substance: "A dramatic plot will move before my eyes" (SCHILLER-GOETHE correspondence, 26 December 1797; Eng. in BRECHT, 1964, 210).	The narrator is not caught up in the action, but retains full freedom of manoeuvre to observe and comment on it: "an epic [plot] seems to stand still while I move around it." (Ibid.)
III. Attitude of Reader-spectator	
Submission "[...] I am bound strictly to what is present to the senses; my imagination loses all freedom; I feel a continual restlessness develop and persist in me; I have to stick to the subject; any reflection or looking back is forbidden me, for I am drawn by an outside force" (Ibid.).	*Freedom* "[...] my pace can be irregular; I can linger or hurry according to my own subjective needs, can take a step backwards or leap ahead, and so forth" (Ibid.).
IV. The Acting	
The acting is direct, as the illusion of real action.	The actor through his epic acting, must, it not prevent, at least make it difficult for continual identification to take place between the spectator and his character. He keeps the figure at a distance, does not embody it but shows it.

Carousel Theatre	Planetarium Theatre
The spectator is embarked upon a story (a carousel) over which he has no control; he has illusions about the animals and landscapes he believes he encounters.	In the planetarium, the movements of the stars are reconstructed schematically but faithfully in their trajectories.

DRAMATIC LANGUAGE

Fr.: *langage dramatique;* Ger.: *dramatische Sprache;* Sp.: *lenguaje dramático.*

If we consider dramatic writing overall, apart from period and genre, we can speak of a dramatic language that is distinguishable from other languages: filmic, literary, poetic, etc. According to LARTHOMAS: "we can speak [...] of dramatic language, presuming rightfully, that very different plays use the same language, one which, accordingly, has a series of universal characters despite differences in form, period and effect" (1972, 12). Based on *effectiveness*, this language possesses the features that LARTHOMAS seeks out in *dramatic texts** (not in productions) and VINAVER tracks in *Écritures dramatiques* as acting language (1993, 9).

The inverse tendency exists as well, whereby dramatic language becomes a stage language that includes, according to LEMAHIEU, the staging (directing) and even the spectator's reception: "Dramatic language is the composition of the text, from its directing, filled out and rewritten by the spectator's creative projection, decipherer of the art of theatre as he bends to the sophisticated task of decoding the signs deployed on stage" (in CORVIN 1995, 488).

We think it preferable to maintain a distinction between dramatic language (or *dramatic writing**), as we read it in the text, and stage language (or *stage writing**) as it is realized on stage by a director for a spectator.

DRAMATIC LITERATURE

Fr.: *littérature dramatique;* Ger.: *dramatische Literatur;* Sp.: *literatura dramática.*

See DRAMATIC ART

DRAMATIC PLAY

Fr.: *jeu dramatique;* Ger.: *Spielpädagogik;* Sp.: *juego dramático.*

A collective practice in which a group of "players" (rather than actors) improvise on a theme chosen in advance or indicated by the situation. The actor/spectator separation is eliminated, and an attempt is made to have each person participate in building up an activity (rather than an action), making sure that each individual improvisation is integrated into the common project. The aim is neither a *collective creation** for later presentation to an audience, nor a *cathartic* psychodrama** experience, nor a hoax as in the *happening**, nor a theatricalization of everyday life. Dramatic play is intended both to bring an awareness to participants (of all ages) of the basic mechanisms of theatre (character, convention, dialectics of dialogue and situation, group dynamics) and to promote a certain physical and emotional freedom in play and, eventually, in the private lives of individuals.

See also: improvisation, gesture, gaze, expression, body.

Further reading: Barret 1973; Barker 1977; Ryngaert 1977, 1985; Monod 1983; Spolin 1963, 1986; Beauchamp 1984; Boal 1990.

DRAMATIC POEM

Fr.: *poème dramatique;* Ger.: *dramatisches Gedicht;* Sp.: *poema dramático.*

1. The theory of literary genres, by tradition, speaks of epic, lyric and dramatic poems.

In the classical age, the dramatic poem was the *dramatic text**, considered apart from its realization in the stage performance, which tended to be rejected by scholars as external, secondary or at the very least less valid than the poem. The tragic poem is related to the arrangement of a *fabula;* up to the eighteenth century, it was most often written in alexandrines.

2. The expression *dramatic poem* appears contradictory today, since we consider the text to be only the first and incomplete stage of the performance. However, in the classical age, when the term *dramatic poetry** (or even *representational poetry*) was used, the poem was deemed to contain all the elements required for its comprehension, and speeches to represent action, so that "to act is to speak" (d'AUBIGNAC, 1927). This

poem may be read "in an armchair" (*closet drama**), but it is already "divided into" roles; the *poesis* or fabrication of the fiction does not prejudge the literary quality of the text but its harmonious composition as a story that is told rather than played by actors who express themselves in long, alternating monologues.

3. Aesthetics and genre classification often assign the dramatic poem a place in the development of literary forms. According to HEGEL, "because drama has been developed into the most perfect totality of content and form, it must be regarded as the highest stage of poetry and of art generally"; dramatic poetry is the only genre that "unites the objectivity of epic with the subjective character of lyric" (HEGEL, *Aesthetics*, Eng. 1975, 1158).

4. There is often a very fluid boundary between the *"dramatized" poem*, containing characters, conflicts and occasional dialogues, and the poetic drama, which is not really meant for the stage and is composed of a series of poetic texts.

5. Sometimes an opposition is set up (as in VILAR 1963, 140) between dramatic poet and playwright or dramatist: whereas the former does no more than put the text into verse, as a "master of prosody," the latter constructs actions and characters, which are beyond the absolute control of prosody. Sometimes the same author, for instance RACINE, is conceived either as a master of prosody (BARRAULT) or as an author of actions for the stage (VILAR, PLANCHON). This is a specious and dangerous opposition that arbitrarily dissociates form and content of the dramatic text.
See also: play, rhythm, stage writing.

DRAMATIC PROVERB

Fr.: *proverbe dramatique;* Ger.: *dramatisches Sprichwort;* Sp.: *proverbio dramático.*

Literary genre originating in a society game that consisted of using an improvised sketch to illustrate a proverb that the audience had to guess. A game played in the salons of seventeenth and eighteenth-century France, the "jeux des proverbes," involved carrying on a conversation consisting of nothing but proverbs. Mme. DE MAINTENON wrote them for her pupils at Saint-Cyr, CARMONTELLE published a whole collection in 1768. In the nineteenth century, Henri DE LATOUCHE, Octave FEUILLET and, above all, Alfred de MUSSET perfected the genre (*On ne badine pas avec l'amour, Il faut qu'une porte soit ouverte ou fermée*). The genre exists today only in a parodic play form. Many titles retain the form of a riddle or a moral or philosophical maxim: WILDE's *The Importance of Being Earnest*, BRECHT's *The Exception and the Rule*.

DRAMATIC SITUATION

Fr.: *situation dramatique;* Ger.: *dramatische Situation;* Sp.: *situación dramática.*

Set of textual and performance data required to understand the text and action at a particular point in the reading or performance. Just as the linguistic message means nothing unless the situation or context of *enunciation** is known, in theatre the meaning of a scene hinges on the presentation, clarification or knowledge of the situation. Describing the situation of a play is like taking a picture of all the relationships of the characters at a particular moment, like "freezing" the development of the events to take stock of the action.

The situation may be reconstructed from *stage directions, indications of time and place**, the *facial expression** and body language of the actors, the deep nature of the psychological and social relationships between the characters and, more generally, any indication that is important to the understanding of the characters' motivations and actions.

The expression "dramatic situation" at first gives the impression of being a contradiction in terms. The dramatic is linked to tension and expectation, a dialectic of actions; situation, however, may appear to be static and descriptive, like a genre painting. Dramatic form proceeds by a series of dialogues that alternate descriptive moments and dialectical changes of situation. Any situation, though apparently static, is the preparation of the ensuing episode, and contributes to building up the *fabula** and the action.

1. Situation and the Actantial Model

The reciprocal situation of characters engaged in the same undertaking can be "visualized" using various actantial models: the relationships among the *actants** of the play at a particular point of dramatic development furnish an image of their situation. None of the characters can be taken out of this actantial *configuration** without throwing the situation out of balance. Any action is only the transformation of successive situations. According to the structuralist approach, events and characters have meaning only within the overall context of a situation, are valid only through their status and their difference within the play's constellation of forces.

2. Situation and Mise-en-scène

To set the boundaries of a situation, for some scholars (JANSEN 1968, 1973), means correlating a segment of text with stage elements that remain unchanged over a period of time. The situation mediates between text and performance in that the text is always segmented on the basis of the stage business corresponding to a particular situation.

3. Situation and Subtext

Situation can exist without being spoken (described or made explicit) by the text; it belongs to the domain of the extralinguistic, of the stage, of what people do and know implicitly. For the actor or director, "playing the situation" (as opposed to "playing the text") is much more than just delivering the text; it means using pauses and stage business to recreate a particular atmosphere and situation. In such cases, the situation holds the key to the scene. The notion of situation is close to that of a *subtext**. The spectator needs it as an overall deep structure for understanding, as a point of reference and a relatively stable background against which the varied and changing points of view of the characters are seen in contrast.

4. Situation or Text?

Ultimately, the text may become accessory to a situation, losing its autonomy and depth to become an "epiphenomenon of situation" (VITEZ). In a theatre based entirely on naturalistic situations, character and situation become the only realities, relegating the text to the rank of a secondary manifestation. This inversion is not without risk, as it reduces the text to a scenario that cannot be consulted in itself, outside its actual situation and production. Some directors have reacted to this invasion of situation by claiming to "play the text" rather than the situation: "When an actor says a word, I am interested in that word and the associations of ideas it sets off, and instead of playing the situation, I play the dreams the situation suggests to me [...] the dreams that the words trigger in me and the actors" (VITEZ, l'Humanité, 12/11/71).

See also: situation of enunciation, language situation, dramatic text.

Further reading: Polti 1981; Propp 1929; Souriau 1950; Mauron 1963; Sartre 1973.

DRAMATIC SPACE

Fr.: *espace dramatique*; Ger.: *dramatischer Raum*; Sp.: *espacio dramático*.

Space represented, as opposed to stage space (or theatre space). Whereas the latter is visible and materializes in the staging, the former is constructed by the spectator or reader as a framework for the development of the action and the characters. It pertains to the dramatic text and can only be visualized when the spectator builds the dramatic space in his imagination.

1. Dramatic Space as Spatialization of Dramatic Structure

The dramatic space is constructed when we form a mental image of the dramatic structure of the world represented in the play – an image informed by the characters, their actions and the relationships between them as the action develops. If we spatialize (i.e. schematize on paper) the relationships between the characters, we obtain a projection of the *actantial** scheme of the dramatic world. The actantial scheme is structured around the relationship between a *subject* on a quest and the *object* of that quest. Around these two poles gravitate the remaining actants who together make up the dramatic structure, which may be visualized in a dramatic space. J. LOTMAN (1977) and A. UBERSFELD (1977a) note that this dramatic space is necessarily split into two "dramatic sub-spaces," representing the *conflict* between two characters or fictions, or between a desiring subject and the desired object. In fact, it comes down to a conflict between two *parts* or dramatic spaces, and any narrative is only the syntagmatic projection (i.e. the linear succession) of these two paradigms.

No staging need occur for this projection of the dramatic space to take place – a reading of the text suffices to give the reader a *spatial* image of the dramatic world. We build that space on the basis of the playwright's *stage directions** (a kind of *pre-performance**) and the *indications of time and place** included in the dialogues (*word scenery**).

Each spectator, therefore, has his own subjective image of the dramatic space and, not surprisingly, the director also chooses only *one* possibility for an actual stage location. So the "right" mise-en-scène is not, as is often believed, that which best reconciles dramatic space and stage space (*text and performance**).

2. Construction of Dramatic Space
The dramatic space is constantly changing. It depends on the actantial relationships, which must evolve if the play is to have any action. It becomes actual and visible only when a mise-en-scène illustrates some of the spatial relationships implied by the text. In this sense, it can be said that the stage space and the mise-en-scène are always, to some extent, dependent on the text's dramatic space and structure. No matter how inventive the director, no matter how much he tries to remove himself from the text, he cannot completely ignore the mental image of the dramatic space he formed as he read it (*text and performance**).

The dramatic space belongs to the *fiction** (as in a poem, novel or any other linguistic text). Its construction depends as much on indications given by the playwright as on our own imagination. We build and shape it as we please, and it is never shown or destroyed in an actual performance. This is both its strength and its weakness, for it "speaks less to the eye" than the actual stage space. On the other hand, (symbolized) dramatic space and (perceived) stage space become intertwined in our perception (each helps the other to take shape), so that soon we are unable to differentiate what is given to us from what we have created ourselves. At that precise instant, theatrical *illusion** comes into play. For that is the nature of illusion – to be convinced that we are not inventing, that the fancies before our eyes and mind are real (*denial**).

3. Dramatic Space and Stage Design
This configuration of dramatic space that we reconstruct upon reading the text in turn provides feedback on stage space and stage design. A given dramatic space requires a stage space that will serve it and enable it to exhibit its specificity. So, for dramatic space and structure based on conflict and confrontation, a space is required that will make the most of that opposition.

At this point we must ask ourselves the eternal question: which comes first, stage design or *dramaturgy** (dramatic structure)? Naturally, one determines the other, but it would appear that the dramaturgical conception comes first, i.e. the ideological issue concerning human conflict and the force that drives the action. Only then does theatre choose the type of stage space that best reflects the dramaturgical and philosophical vision. The stage is, after all, only a tool, not a yoke that is given once and for all and applies to the entire dramaturgical milieu. There is no doubt that there have been times in the history of theatre when a certain type of stage design blocked dramaturgical analysis, hence the representation of human beings on stage. But stage design is, finally, always abandoned when it no longer serves its purpose, and then adapted to the ideological or dramaturgical change.

Further reading: Hintze 1969; Moles and Rohmer 1972; Sami-Ali 1974; Issacharoff 1981; Jansen 1984.

DRAMATIC STRUCTURE

Fr.: *structure dramatique*; Ger.: *dramatische Struktur*; Sp.: *estructura dramática.*

The analysis of the dramatic structures of a play largely coincides with *dramaturgy**. Both disciplines study properties specific to the form of drama. The refinement of the structuralist method has been very helpful in formalizing the play's levels and in integrating everything into an overall project so that performance appeared as an organism constructed according to very strict rules (*closed form**).

The term *structure* indicates that the system's constituent parts are organized in a way that gives meaning to the *whole*. But there are several systems at work in any theatrical performance: *fabula* or action, characters, relationships of time and place, stage configuration, and even, in a large sense, *dramatic language** (in that we can speak of theatre as a specific *semiological** system).

1. Dramaturgy as the Study of Dramatic Structures

In examining the dramatic structures of a play, a model of action is often used which presents the dramatic curve visually.
The development of the *fabula** may be observed: distribution of episodes, continuity or discontinuity of action, introduction of epic moments in the dramatic structure, etc. (*open form**, *closed form**).

To speak of *a* dramatic structure is licit only in the historically preeminent but relatively limited case of classical Aristotelian dramaturgy (closed and dramatic, according to the criteria of ARISTOTLE's *Poetics* rather than being open to manipulation and epic duration). It is easy to characterize that structure with several pertinent features: the event happens in the present in front of the spectator, the "suspense" and uncertainty about its ending are usual; the text is distributed among the speakers, each actor has a role and it is the result of the speeches and roles that establishes the meaning. Preparation for the action is therefore "objective"; the poet does not speak in his own name but gives his characters the floor. Drama is always an "imitation of a certain duration" (sect. 1449), "such, however, that the memory can easily grasp it" (1450b). The events will therefore be concentrated, unified and organized teleologically according to a crisis, a development, a dénouement and a catastrophe.

2. Composition of the Dramatic Work: Immanent Analysis

The composition of the play (its structure) comes out in an analysis of the recurring images and themes: types of scenes, entrances and exits by the characters, correspondences, regularities and typical relationships. This would be an immanent study of the play based solely on the visible elements, the inner relations of the play, with no need to refer to the outside world described by the play and interpreted by the critic. This immanent structure has been called *external structure* by J. SCHERER, in opposition to the *internal structure* which is the study of the "basic problems facing the playwright when constructing the play, even before he writes it" (1950, 12). The *external structure* (called here *immanent structure*) is defined as "the various forms that may be taken, in accordance with theatrical traditions or stage needs, by the play as a whole, the act, the subdivision of the act or scene, and finally certain privileged aspects of theatre writing."

3. Form and Content

The search for structure comes up against the problem of finding an appropriate *form** for a specific *content**. There is no typical and universal dramatic structure (as HEGEL and the theoreticians of classical drama thought). Any change in the content or new knowlege of reality generates a form suited to transmitting the content. As shown by P. SZONDI (1956), the destruction of canonical dramatic form occurred in response to a change in ideological analysis in the late nineteenth century. Defining dramatic structures is a dialectical operation. One should neither seek to find how definite ideas (a content) are "placed" in an external, secondary form, nor believe that a new form necessarily says something new about the world.

4. Structure and Event
The discovery of dramatic forms and structures, of the principles of composition and dramaturgy of the play, no matter how precise, is insufficient. In effect, it geometrizes and visualizes the structure to the point of making it a *real* construction, an object that would be the quintessence of the play and reduce it to a fixed construction existing independently of the critic's interpretative work. Also, the play always maintains a relationship with the outside world that comments on it: "The structured structure of the work refers us to a structuring subject, just as it refers us to a cultural world to which it is added, most often bringing disturbance and challenge" (STAROBINSKI 1970, 23). Thus, the search for dramatic structures must be more of a method of structuring than a photography of structure. In theatre, particularly, it will always be determined by the *event**-aspect of stage performance and by the continuous *signifying practice** the spectator is obliged to carry out.

See also: hermeneutics, formalism, realism, sociocriticism.

Further reading: Slawinska 1959; Lepschy 1967; Barry 1970; Beckerman 1970; Levitt 1971; R. Durand 1975; M. Kirby 1976, 1987.

DRAMATIC TEXT

Fr.: *texte dramatique;* Ger.: *dramatischer Text;* Sp.: *texto dramático.*

1. Problems with a Restrictive Definition
Finding a definition of the dramatic text that will differentiate it from other types of texts poses a problem, as the current trend in dramatic writing is to claim that any kind of text is suitable for mise-en-scène. The ultimate consequence – staging the telephone book – hardly seems, at this point, a whimsical or impossible undertaking. Any text can be made into theatre, provided it is used on stage. What was considered *dramatic** up until the twentieth century – *dialogue**, *conflict**, *dramatic situation**, *character** – is no longer an essential condition for a text that is to be staged. We would simply describe several characteristics of the text in Western dramaturgy.

2. Possible Criteria for the Dramatic Text

A. MAIN TEXT (DIALOGUE), SIDE TEXT (STAGE DIRECTIONS)

The text to be spoken by the actors is often introduced by *stage directions** (or *didascalia**), a text composed by the playwright or, conceivably, the director. Even when there is no secondary text, its traces may be found in the *word scenery** or *gestus** of the character. The status of word scenery, however, is radically different from that of the secondary text. *Indications of time and place** are an integral part of the dramatic text and cannot be ignored by the reader or spectator, while stage directions may or may not be reflected in the staging.

B. A SCATTERED AND "OBJECTIVE" TEXT

Apart from monologues, the dramatic text is scattered among the various character-speakers. Dialogue gives an equal chance to each of them, and visualizes the sources of speech without reducing it to a hierarchically superior centre. The origins of speech are not clearly specified: the lines of each character are given independently by a narrator or central voice. Reading or receiving the dramatic text means performing a dramaturgical analysis that will clarify space, time, action and character.

C. FICTIONALITY

Structural poetics, born of structuralism and text theory, is no longer capable of describing in a homogeneous way all of the innumerable textual practices and materials. As for the distinction between literary dramatic text and ordinary language, it must contend with a methodological barrier: any "ordinary" text can become dramatic as soon as it is staged, so that the criterion for differentiation is not textual but pragmatic. As soon as a text is uttered on stage, it is read within a *framework** that vests it with fictionality and differentiates it from "ordinary" texts that claim to describe the "real" world. According to SEARLE, "there is no textual property, syntactical or semantic, that will identify a text as a work of fiction" (1975, 325).

D. RELATIONSHIPS BETWEEN CONTEXTS

In order for the characters to move within a single dramatic universe, they must share at least a portion of the universe of discourse. Otherwise, they will be engaged in a dialogue of the deaf or will be unable to exchange any information (theatre of the absurd). We must also look at the way the text switches from one character's lines to another's, one argument to another, one action to the next. In short, reading the text implies a concern with its cultural, historical and ideological context, so as not to approach it within a formal vacuum. There is no method, not even that of VINAVER (1993) – contrary to his assertions – that fails to "put [us] in contact directly and immediately with the very life of the text, without requiring prior knowledge" (1993, 893).

3. Construction of the Dramatic Text

A. CIRCUIT OF CONCRETIZATION

It would be wrong to consider the dramatic text a fixed entity that can be understood in a particular way once and for all. In fact, the text exists only upon completion of a reading, which is always situated in history. Such a reading depends on the reader's social context and knowledge of the context of the fictional text. INGARDEN (1973; 1949) and, particularly, MUKAROVSKY (1934) and VODICKA (1975) have spoken of a process of concretization of the text. Attempts have been made to define the circuit of concretization, through the perception of the textual signifiers and the social context, to arrive at the possible reading or readings of the text (PAVIS 1983a).

B. SPOTS OF INDETERMINACY

The various different readings and their concretizations point up the spots of indeterminacy in the text, which are neither universal nor fixed forever, but vary according to the reading level, particularly the elucidation of social context. The dramatic text is like shifting sand. On its surface we can see, periodically and variously, signals guiding its reception and signals maintaining indeterminacy or ambiguity. In theatre, a particular episode of the *fabula** or verbal exchange may take on very different meanings according to the situation of enunciation selected by the mise-en-scène. The text, and particularly the dramatic text, is both shifting sand and hourglass: the reader chooses to clarify one half of the hourglass by obscuring the other, and so on, indefinitely. The notion of indeterminacy/determinacy is a dialectical one. Readability, the guiding of reception, is identifiable only in relation to the process of guiding/antiguiding that "walks" the reader through the text, alternating reference points and erratic paths. This "up-and-down" reading of the dramatic text is paralleled by a constant oscillation, in the performance, of fictional status, an oscillation between illusion and dis-illusion, identification and distance, mimetic reality-effects and foregrounding of form and play.

C. KEEPING AND ELIMINATING AMBIGUITIES

This view of the instability of the dramatic text brings up the question of how it can be used and manipulated. It is up to the reader and director, as well as the spectator, to decide where the areas of uncertainty (certainty) are found and to decide on their mobility and the possibility of identifying them. It is essential, for example, to decide whether the ambiguity is structurally inscribed in the text or if it is the result of a lack of knowledge of or change in the socialcontext. By highlighting the verbal exchange and situation of enunciation, any mise-en-scène takes a position on how determinacy and ambiguity should be inscribed in the play.

See also: discourse, off-stage, non-textual.

Further reading: Styan 1963; Savona 1980, 1982; Manceva 1983; Prochazka 1984; general bibliography in Pavis 1985e, 1987, 1990, 1996a; Swiontek 1986; B. Martin 1993; Sallenave 1988; Thomasseau 1984a,b.

DRAMATIS PERSONAE

Fr.: *dramatis personae;* Ger.: *dramatis personae;* Sp.: *dramatis personae.*

1. In old editions of plays, the *dramatis personae* or list of characters is presented at the beginning of the play. The list names the characters and describes them in a few words, clarifying the dramatist's *perspective** on the characters and serving as a guideline for the spectator's judgment.

2. It is significant that the Latin word *persona* (mask) is a translation of the Greek word for dramatic character or role. The character was originally conceived as a narrative voice, a double of the "real" man. Grammarians then used the image of mask and drama to characterize relations among the three persons: the first person (I) plays the main role, the second (you) gives the reply, while the *he,* who is not defined in terms of person in the exchange between *I* and *you,* is the subject of dialogue.

3. In English-speaking and German criticism, the term *dramatis personae* is sometimes used in the sense of *protagonists** or characters. It is the broadest generic term to designate characters (*character*, figure*, type*, role*, hero**) and the technical term used for the list of characters.

DRAMATIST

Fr.: *auteur dramatique;* Ger.: *Bühnenautor, Dramatiker;* Sp.: *autor dramático.*
See PLAYWRIGHT

DRAMATIZATION

Fr.: *dramatisation;* Ger.: *Dramatisierung;* Sp.: *dramatización.*

Adaptation of an epic or poetic text to a dramatic text with dialogues, or to material for a theatre performance.

The mystery plays of the Middle Ages were dramatizations of the Bible. Elizabethan theatre was fond of adapting texts by historians (PLUTARCH) or chroniclers (HOLINSHED). In the eighteenth and nineteenth centuries, popular novels (by DICKENS, SCOTT, etc.) were dramatized. This was done by using dialogue to create a theatrical style.

The *adaptation** of novels for theatre is just as frequent in the twentieth century, particulary of works with a strong "dramatic" character: *Les Frères Karamazov* (COPEAU 1911), *les Possédés* (CAMUS or DODINE), KAFKA's novels (*The Trial,* adapted by GIDE and BARRAULT, 1947; *Das Schloss,* adapted by Max Brod, 1953), *Des petits cailloux dans les poches,* based on V. WOOLF's work, by A.-M. LAZARINI and M. FABRE, *Rêves de Franz Kafka* based on excerpts from KAFKA's diary, staged by E. CORMAN and P. ADRIEN in 1984. The influence of and coexistence with film and television, which also adapt novels, explains the many adaptations and the unwillingness to confine theatre to a text in dialogue written specifically for the stage.
See also: translation, theatralization.
Further reading: Patsch 1980; Caune 1981; B. Martin 1993.

DRAMATURG

(From the Greek *dramaturgos,* playwright.)
Fr.: *dramaturge;* Ger.: *Dramaturg;* Sp.: *dramaturguista.*

This term, from the German *Dramaturg,* is used to refer to the literay adviser associated with a theatre company: a director or person responsible for preparing for a performance.

1. Background

The first dramaturg was LESSING. His *Dramaturgy of Hamburg* (1767), a collection of theory and criticism, generated a German tradition of theory and practice that precedes and determines the staging of a play.

Like English, but unlike French, German makes a distinction between the *Dramatiker*, who writes the plays, and the *Dramaturg*, who prepares them for performance on stage. Both activities may be carried out by the same person (for example, BRECHT). The use of a dramaturg working continuously with the same director is widespread in Germany, and more and more common in France (and now in North America).

2. The Ambiguous Task of the Dramaturg
When the dramaturg is accepted in theatre – and acceptance is still not automatic in France – he is in charge of:

a. Selecting plays for a program on the basis of a particular issue or objective; combining and selecting text for a single mise-en-scène.
b. Carrying out documentary research on and about the play. At times, drawing up a documentary *program** (taking care not to give away everything in advance, as sometimes happens).
c. *Adapting** or modifying the text (*montage**, *collage**, deletion, repetition of passages); if necessary, translating the text (or adapting the translation) alone or in collaboration with the director.
d. Determining how meanings are linked and interpreting the play according to an overall social or political project.
e. Intervening from time to time at rehearsals as a critical observer with a "fresher" pair of eyes than the director, who works on the play every day. The dramaturg is therefore the first internal critic of the performance in progress.
f. Looking after relations with a potential audience (*animation**).

3. Does the Dramaturg Come Before or After the Director?
Long deemed useless or good only for preliminary *dramaturgical work**, "sandwiched" in between actors and directors, the dramaturg has finally joined the artistic team, even though directors today neglect Brechtian-type *dramaturgical analysis**. His imprint on the mise-en-scène is undeniable, both in the preparatory stages and in the actual realization, in aspects such as acting, consistency of performance, and the guiding of reception. For several years now, the dramaturg has no longer served as an ideological officer, but assisted the director in searching for possible meanings of the play.
Further reading: Tenschert 1960; Dort, 1960 1975.

DRAMATURGICAL ANALYSIS

Fr.: *analyse dramaturgique*; Ger.: *dramaturgische Analyse*; Sp.: *análisis dramatúrgico*.

1. From Text to Performance
Dramaturgical analysis is the task of the *dramaturg**, and of dramatic criticism (at least in the more in-depth branch of that activity), in order to define the specific characteristics of text and performance. It attempts to clarify the transition from *dramatic writing** to *stage writing**: "What is this dramaturgical work but a critical reflection on the transition from the literary to the theatrical fact?" (DORT 1971, 47). There is an opportunity for dramaturgical analysis both before the work is staged, by the dramaturg and director; and after the performance, when the spectator analyzes the staging options.

2. Work on Creating Meaning in Text or Performance
Dramaturgical analysis examines the reality represented in the play, and asks the following questions: How can the time, the space, the characters be described? How should the *fabula** be read? How does the play relate to the time when it was written, the time it represents and our own time? How do these different historical dimensions intervene?

Analysis identifies the "blank spots" and ambiguities in the play, clarifies aspects of the plot, takes a position as to its meaning or puts forward several possible interpretations. In an attempt to integrate the perspective and *reception** of the spectator, it establishes links between the *fiction** and the *reality** of our times.

Social analysis is often done using the Marxist model, or any of its variants applied to the study of literature (LUKÁCS

1963, 1964); it looks for the contradictions in the action and the ideologems involved (PAVIS 1983b), for the relationship between ideology and the literary text, the individual and social aspects of the characters, and how the performance can be fragmented into a series of social *gestus**.

3. Between Semiology and Sociology
Dramaturgical analysis goes beyond a semiological description of stage systems. It asks, pragmatically, what the spectator will get out of the performance, how theatre relates to the audience's ideological and aesthetic frame of reference. It integrates and reconciles a semiological (aesthetic) perspective on the performance signs with a sociological examination of the production and reception of these same signs (*sociocriticism**).

4. The Need for Reflection
A mise-en-scène necessarily involves dramaturgical work, even (and especially) if this is denied by the director in the name of "loyalty" to tradition or a desire to be faithful to the text "to the letter." Any *reading** and, even more so, any performance of a text presupposes a knowledge of the conditions of *enunciation**, of the situation and the acting, etc. This conception, even when it is embryonic or unimaginative, is in effect a dramaturgical analysis that involves a reading of the text.

5. The Decline of Dramaturgical Analysis
During the 1950s and 1960s, text analysis was widely political and critical, under the influence of Brechtian dramaturgy. The "crisis" of the 1970s and 1980s, however, has seen analysis stripped of its political dimension to some extent, and a refusal to reduce the play to its socioeconomic substratum by stressing its specific from and the *signifying practices** that may be applied to it. Directors such as VITEZ therefore forgo preliminary work on a text and endeavor to experiment as soon as possible with actors on the stage, not knowing what discourse will eventually emerge from the mise-en-scène. The same ideological "disengagement" can be felt in former Brechtians such as B. BESSON, B. SOBEL, J. JOURDHEUIL, R. PLANCHON, J.-F. PEYRET, M. MARÉCHAL, and in the new generation of the 1990s who have no ties to Brecht or a sociocritical reading of the classics.

Further reading: Brecht 1967, vol. 17; Girault 1973; Jourdheuil 1976; Klotz 1976; Pavis 1983a; Bataillon 1972.

DRAMATURGY

(From the Greek *dramaturgia,* to compose a drama.)

Fr.: *dramaturgie*; Ger.: *Dramaturgie*; Sp.: *dramaturgia.*

1. Evolution of the Concept

A. ORIGINAL AND CLASSICAL SENSE OF THE TERM

Dramaturgy is usually defined as "the art of composition of plays."

1. In its broadest sense, dramaturgy is the technique (or poetics) of dramatic art which seeks to establish the principles of play construction, either inductively on the basis of actual examples or deductively on the basis of a system of abstract principles. This notion presupposes a set of specifically theatrical rules that must be known in order to write a play and analyze it properly.

Until the classical period, dramaturgy, often developed by playwrights themselves (cf. CORNEILLE'S *Discours* and LESSING'S *Dramaturgy of Hamburg*), was intended to discover rules, or even recipes for composing a play and dictating rules of composition for other playwrights (for example, ARISTOTLE's *Poetics*, D'AUBIGNAC's *Pratique du théâtre*).

2. J. SCHERER, author of *Dramaturgie classique en France* (1950), distinguishes between the internal structure of the play (or dramaturgy in the strict sense) and the external (performance-related) structure: "The internal structure [...] is the set of elements which [...] constitute the basis of the play; it is what the play is about from the playwright's point of view, before staging

considerations come into it. In opposition to this internal structure we have the external structure: it is always a structure, but consists mainly of forms, and forms which put into play the modalities of writing and performance of the play" (SCHERER 1961).

*Classical dramaturgy** seeks to identify the constitutive elements of dramatic construction for any classical text – *exposition**, *knot**, *complication**, *conflict**, resolution, *epilogue**, etc.

Classical dramaturgy examines the playwright's work and the narrative structure of the play (text and performance) exclusively. It does not concern itself directly with the realization of the performance on stage, which explains a certain disaffection among critics today with this discipline, at least in its traditional sense.

B. BRECHTIAN AND POST-BRECHTIAN DRAMATURGY

Since BRECHT and his theorizing on dramatic and epic theatre, the notion of dramaturgy seems to have been expanded to become:

1. Simultaneously, the ideological and formal structure of the play.
2. The specific link between form and content in the sense of ROUSSET, who defines art as the "solidarity between a mental world and a tangible construction, a vision and a form." (1962, 1).
3. The all-encompassing work that produces the text staged, and is intended to produce a particular effect on the spectator. Thus, BRECHT considers "epic dramaturgy" to be a form of theatre that uses the devices of commentary and alienation-effects to better describe social reality and contribute to changing it.

In this sense, dramaturgy has to do with both the original text and the resources used to stage it. To analyze the dramaturgy of a performance, then, is to describe its *fabula* in three-dimensional reality, i.e. in its concrete performance, to specify the way in which an event is shown and narrated in theatre (cf. *questionnaire**, no. 9).

C. USE OF THE TERM "DRAMATURGY" TO MEAN THE WORK OF A "DRAMATURG"

Dramaturgy as the work done by a *dramaturg** consists of assembling textual and stage materials, bringing out complex meanings of the text by choosing a particular interpretation, and orienting the performance in the desired direction.

In this case, dramaturgy refers to the set of aesthetic and ideological choices made by the directing team, from director to actor. This work includes the development and *performance** of the *fabula**, the choice of stage location, the *montage**, acting, illusionist or distanced performance. Briefly, dramaturgy asks itself how, and according to what time sequence, the story materials are arranged in the text and on stage. In its most recent meaning, then, dramaturgy tends to go beyond the confines of a study of the dramatic text to include both text and performance.

2. Problems of Dramaturgy

A. LINKING AESTHETICS AND IDEOLOGY

To examine the links between world and stage, i.e. ideology and aesthetics, is the main task of dramaturgy. It tries to understand how ideas about human beings and the world are rendered in a form, i.e. in a text and on stage. This requires us to follow the process of modelling (abstraction, stylization and codification) of human reality that leads to a specific use of the theatre apparatus. Meaning in theatre is always a technical issue that has to do with materials, forms and structures.

Dramaturgy is based on an analysis of actions and their *actants** (the characters). This obliges us to determine the directional forces of the dramatic universe, the values of the actants and the sense (direction) of the *fabula*. By choosing to read and show the text according to one or several consistent points of view, the playwright clarifies the text's historicity, its roots in or detachment from the history of humankind, and any discrepancies between the dramatic situation and our frame of reference. When a play is interpreted according to various literary genres, very different *fabulae* and characters are created, so that the choice of a specific genre gives the text a particular configuration each time. All these choices enable us to identify, if not explain, structural and historical ambiguities, what is left unsaid (whether or not it is sayable), and blank spots (problems in reading that defy all hypotheses).

B. EVOLUTION OF DRAMATURGIES

The historical evolution of ideological content and formal research explain any discrepancies between form and content that may question their dialectical unity. SZONDI, for instance, speaks of the contradiction in European theatre at the end of the nineteenth century as it uses the outdated form of the dialogue for an exchange between human beings to speak of a world in which such exchange is no longer possible (SZONDI 1956, 76; Eng. 1987, 45). It is because mankind today has a scientific knowledge of social reality that BRECHT condemns the apparently illusionary and immutable dramatic form.

C. DRAMATURGY AS A THEORY OF REPRESENTABILITY OF THE WORLD

The ultimate goal of dramaturgy is to represent the world, whether it aims at mimetic realism or rejects mimesis to represent an autonomous world. In each case, it establishes the fictional status and level of reality of characters and actions; it represents the dramatic universe using audiovisual means and decides what will *seem real* to the audience (*verisimilitude**). As in music, it chooses a key to illusion/disillusion and maintains it throughout the stage fiction. One of the main options of this representation is to show actions and their protagonists as specific cases or as typical examples. Finally, the ultimate and major task will be to effect the adjustment between text and stage, to decide how the text should be *played*, how to give it a force on stage that will make it clear for a given time and a given audience.

The stage-audience relationship determines and specifies all others: deciding whether theatre should entertain or instruct, comfort or disturb, reproduce or denounce; such are the questions raised by dramaturgical analysis.

D. EXPLOSION AND PROLIFERATION OF DRAMATURGIES

For one who lacks an overall, unified image of the world, reproduction of reality in theatre must necessarily be fragmentary. The question is no longer one of developing a dramaturgy by artificially correlating a coherent ideology with an appropriate form, and a single performance often draws on several types of dramaturgical analysis. The performance is no longer based solely on identification or alienation effects; some productions may even try to divide up the dramaturgy by letting the actors organize their narratives according to their own world views. The notion of *dramaturgical choices* gives a better account of current trends than *dramaturgy* seen as a global and structured set of homogeneous aesthetic and ideological principles.

Further reading: Gouhier 1958; Dort 1960; Klotz 1969, 1976; Rousset 1962; Styan 1963; Calderwood 1968; Larthomas 1972; Jaffré 1974; Keller 1976; Monod 1977a; Moindrot 1993.

DRAWING-ROOM PLAY

Fr.: *comédie de salon*; Ger.: *Salonstück, Konversationsstück*; Sp.: *comedia de salón*.

The drawing-room play shows characters talking, often in a middle-class living room. Its comedy is verbal, subtle and witty, with *authorial interventions**. The action is confined to an exchange of agreeably formulated ideas, arguments or nasty remarks (for example, WILDE, MAUGHAM, SCHNITZLER).

DUPLICATION

Fr.: *dédoublement*; Ger.: *Verdoppelung*; Sp.: *desdoblamiento*.

See DOUBLE

E

EDIFICATION

Fr.: *édification;* Ger.: *Erbauungstheater;* Sp.: *teatro didáctico.*

See DIDACTIC THEATRE, THESIS THEATRE

ELECTRONIC ARTS

Fr.: *arts électroniques;* Ger.: *neue Medien;* Sp.: *artes electrónicos.*

This is a generic term encompassing all media, not only video but also tape recording, electronic sound creation, audiodrama, "cinema for the ear" as in W. RUTTMAN's *Week End* (1930), "a film without images, an orchestration of natural noises recorded by sound film using filmic techniques and means" (*Revue du Cinéma,* 1930). Video is rediscovering sound and is leaving overly directive static projects or visual virtuosity to plunge into an overall sensorial event, and electronic CDs use natural or electronic sounds in a montage to make "music without musicians" as in the mini-CDs of P. MION and M. CHION (1990).

Electronic acoustics attempt to give a new perception of sounds and images to a spectator-listener, an individual who is able to integrate sound and visual perceptions within himself by testing what they have in common and how they are linked in time and space: density, rhythm, intensity, location on the visual and sound score, all the parameters that bring together sight and hearing, music, text, dance and movement.

ELOCUTION

Fr.: *élocution;* Ger.: *Vortragskunst, Elocution;* Sp.: *elocución.*

A term from rhetoric meaning the choice and order of words in speech, the mode of expression through figures. According to ARISTOTLE (*Poetics,* 1450a), elocution (language) is one of the six elements of tragedy (the others being plot, character, thought, spectacle and melody). For CICERO, *elocutio* defines style according to correctness, decorum, ornamentation, clarity and *rhythm**.

In theatre, elocution or the art of *diction** and *declamation** involves the meaning of the text spoken by the actor in an act of *enunciation**. A clear distinction was made in the classical period between "ELOCUTION, DICTION and STYLE: the three terms are used to express the way in which ideas are conveyed. The style bears a closer relation to the author, diction to the work, and elocution to the art of oratory" (BEAUZÉE, Diderot's *Encyclopédie*).

EMPATHY

Fr.: *identification;* Ger.: *Einfühlung, Identifikation;* Sp.: *identificación.*

See IDENTIFICATION

ENCODING

Fr.: *codification;* Ger.: *Kodifizierung;* Sp.: *codificación.*

See CODES IN THEATRE

ENTANGLEMENT

Fr.: *imbroglio*; Ger.: *Verwicklung*; Sp.: *enredo*.
See IMBROGLIO

ENTR'ACTE

Fr.: *divertissement*; Ger.: *Unterhaltung*; *Balleteinlage*; Sp.: *entretenimiento*.

In the seventeenth and eighteenth centuries, performances were often interrupted or concluded with an entr'acte, or *interlude**, which was danced and sung. A mixed genre located both within the staged fiction and on the fringes of the social space, the entr'acte sometimes summarized the play, drawing moral conclusions while making jokes, eliciting the audience's goodwill and offering well-known popular airs to gild the message, ending with songs.

ENTREMÉS

(Spanish term meaning *intermezzo**.)
Fr.: *entremés*; Ger.: *Entremes*; Sp.: *entremés*.

Short comic play representing popular characters, presented at a feast or between the acts of a tragedy or comedy. LOPE DE RUEDA, BENAVENTE, CERVANTES and CALDERÓN were masters of the genre.
See also: entr'acte, sainete.

ENUNCIATION

Fr.: *énonciation*; Ger.: *die Aussage*; Sp.: *enunciación*.
See DISCOURSE, SITUATION OF ENUNCIATION

ENVIRONMENTAL THEATRE

Fr.: *théâtre de l'environnement*; Ger.: *environmental Theatre*; Sp.: *teatro ambiental*.

A contemporary term coined by SCHECHNER (1972, 1973b, 1977) to mean a practice intended to establish a new stage-audience relationship, to consider the audience in terms of distance or closeness, to minimize the distinction between stage and audience and to reduce the points of view and tension in the performance.

Environmental theatre transcends the separation between life and art, uses the space shared by actors and spectators, plays in found spaces and multiplies focalization points without privileging actors over space, words over performance.
Further reading: Schechner 1972, 1973b, 1977.

EPIC THEATRE

Fr.: *théâtre épique*; Ger.: *episches Theater*; Sp.: *teatro épico*.

In the 1920s, BRECHT, and before him, PISCATOR, gave this name to an approach to theatre that goes beyond classical, "Aristotelian" dramaturgy based on dramatic tension, conflict and a regular progression of action.

Epic theatre, or at least theatre containing epic elements, existed as early as the Middle Ages (in the mystery plays, with their simultaneous stages). The chorus of Greek tragedy, which gradually fell into disuse, reveals that action was originally recited and spoken in theatre rather than incarnated and represented through dialogues between two or more characters. In the same manner, prologues, interruptions, epilogues and messengers' narratives are remnants of the epic in the dramatic form which tell us who is speaking and to whom the words are addressed.

Many dramatists, even before the advent of Brechtian epic theatre, have tended to break down the dramatic tension into scenes containing narratives, narratorial interventions, messengers, the "announcer" (CLAUDEL) or the "theatre director" (GOETHE'S *Faust*). In *Woyzeck*, BÜCHNER uses several short tableaux to recount the alienated life of a man whom everything incites to crime. IBSEN, in *Peer Gynt*, describes the hero's poetic path through space and time. WILDER evokes the Christmas dinners that punctuate the lives of successive generations (*The Long Christmas Dinner*).

All these experiments choose to tell the event rather than show it. *Diegesis** replaces *mimesis**, and the characters expound on the facts instead of dramatizing them (like BRECHT's witness to a street accident who reproduces, in gesture and word, what has happened). The outcome of the drama is known in advance, and the frequent interruptions (sounds, commentaries, choruses) prevent tension from building. The acting accentuates the feeling of distance and of narrative neutrality.

Epic theatre appeared in reaction to the facile effects of the well-made play and the audience's cathartic fascination. It has not been established, however, that the Platonic opposition between *mimesis* and *diegesis* corresponds strictly to a theoretical one, since mimesis is never a direct representation of things – rather, it realizes many indexes and signs that must be read in a linear, temporal way in order for meaning to be produced. Direct dramatic imitation therefore cannot do without a mode of telling, and any mimetic dramatic presentation presupposes a "narrativization" of the stage.

Epic theatre undertakes to rediscover and underscore the intervention of a narrator, i.e. a *point of view* on the *fabula** and the staging. In order to do this, it calls upon the talents of the composer (dramatist), the story-teller, the builder of the stage fiction (director), the actor who builds up his role speech by speech, gesture by gesture.

There is no such thing as pure epic theatre, any more than there is purely dramatic and "emotional" theatre. BRECHT later introduced the term "*dialectical** theatre" to deal with the contradiction between acting (showing) and living (identifying with). Epic theatre, therefore, has lost its frankly anti-theatrical, revolutionary character to become a special, systematic instance of theatrical performance.

See also: open form.

Further reading: Kesting 1959; *Theaterarbeit*, 1961; Piscator 1980; Ruelicke-Weiler 1968; Klotz 1969, 1976; R. Grimm 1971; Sartre 1973; Knopf 1980.

EPIC TREATMENT OF DRAMA

Fr.: *épisation du théâtre*; Ger.: *Episierung des Dramas*; Sp.: *epización del teatro.*

The trend in theatre since the turn of the century has been to incorporate *epic** elements into its dramatic structure – elements such as narratives, the elimination of *tension**, breaking the *illusion** and interventions by the *narrator**, crowd scenes and the use of a *chorus**, documents (used as in a historical novel), projections of photographs and inscriptions, *songs**, visible scenery changes, and the foregrounding of a scene's *gestus**.

This movement toward the epic (and away from the dramatic), already apparent in certain scenes by SHAKESPEARE or GOETHE (*Goetz von Berlichingen, Faust II*), was accentuated in the nineteenth century with *closet drama** (MUSSET, HUGO) and historical frescos (GRABBE, BÜCHNER), and culminated with contemporary epic or documentary theatre (BRECHT). There are various possible explanations of this phenomenon, as explored by HEGEL (1832), SZONDI (1956) and LUKACS (1963), all having to do with the end of heroic individualism and single-handed combat. To replace them, the playwright, if he wishes to render social processes in a comprehensive way, must have a commentary voice intervene and arrange the *fabula** as a general overview, which requires more of a novelist's hand than a playwright's.

See also: history, Brechtian, conflict, narration.

EPILOGUE

(From the Greek *epilogos*, conclusion of a speech.)
Fr.: *épilogue*; Ger.: *Epilog*; Sp.: *epílogo.*

The epilogue is a summary speech that appears at the end of a play to draw conclusions from the story, thank the audience and encourage them to draw moral or political lessons from it, and win their indulgence. It differs from the *dénouement** in that it is outside the fiction and in that it welds together the fiction and the social reality of the production.

See also: prologue, address to the audience, discourse, raisonneur, fabula, announcer.

EPISODE

(From the Greek *epeisodion*, entrance)
Fr.: *épisode;* Ger.: *Episode;* Sp.: *episodio.*

1. Greek tragedy was segmented in *episodia*, parts situated between the songs of the *chorus**. The episodes are the parts in dialogue between the *prologue** and the *exodus* (exit of chorus), composed of long *tirades** or *stichomythia**.

2. In narratology, an episode is a secondary action that is indirectly linked to the main action and forms a whole (digression).

3. The episodes of the *fabula* or *plot** are the integral parts of a narrative.
See also: Romilly 1970; Scherer 1950.

EPISODIC COMEDY

Fr.: *comédie à tiroir;* Ger.: *Schubladenstück;* Sp.: *comedia de folla.*

Episodic comedy presents a series of sketches or short scenes that develop a single theme through variations on the same conflict structured in many, often autonomous episodes (episodic plot). MOLIÈRE's *les Fâcheux* is the most famous example of a gallery of portraits of the intruder in seventeenth-century society.
See also: epic, plot, dramatic structure.

EPITASIS

Fr.: *épitase;* Ger.: *Epitasis;* Sp.: *epítasis.*
See CRISIS

ESSENCE OF THE THEATRE

Fr.: *essence du théâtre;* Ger.: *Wesen des Theaters;* Sp.: *esencia del teatro.*

1. The rather mythical search for the essence or *specificity** of theatre has always been an obsessive feature of critical thought. H. GOUHIER, in an examination of many philosophies of *theatre art**, for instance, indicates that the inductive method based on the corpus of works attempts to determine "through the differences, a kind of essence that would pose the raison d'être and outline the basic structure of the theatrical work of art" (1972, 1063). As an "immanent rule of the theatrical work," he sees "a principle of economy and harmony" (1063).

2. Such an essentialist conception of the essence of theatre is only one aesthetic and ideological choice among many others. It glosses over historical and cultural relativity, being too preoccupied with discovering an eternally and universally human essence. Are the anthropological needs that are deeply anchored in man (love of *play**, of metamorphosis, of *ritual**) sufficient to explain the permanence and diversity of theatrical undertakings in human historical and cultural evolution? Similarly, the innumerable studies on the ritual or festive origins of theatre are more interesting from an anthropological than from an aesthetic point of view.

In seeking the essence of theatre, one soon tends to relativize Western European tradition and expand the notion of theatre to that of performance practice. This calls for an ethnoscenology that picks up the local conditions of all the cultural performances in which theatre, in the Western sense, is only one practice among many others.
See also: theory of theatre, staging, aesthetics of drama, theatre anthropology, poetics (bibliography).
Further reading: Nietzsche 1967; Appia 1921; Bentley 1957; Gouhier 1958, 1968, 1972; Artaud 1964a; Schechner 1977; Barba and Savarese 1985.

ESTRANGEMENT

Fr.: *effet d'étrangeté;* Ger.: *Verfremdungseffekt;* Sp.: *efecto de extrañamiento.*

Unlike the *reality effect**, estrangement shows, quotes and criticizes an element of the performance, "deconstructs" it, places it at a *distance** through its unusual appearance and an explicit reference to its artificial, artistic nature (*device**). In a manner analogous to the self-referential poetic sign (JAKOBSON 1963) that refers to its own codes, *theatricality** is heightened in producing this effect.

The strange, as an aesthetic category of *reception**, is not always easy to distinguish from other impressions such as the unusual, bizarre, marvellous or the untranslatable "Unheimliche" (disquieting strangeness). The Brechtian term *Verfremdungseffekt* (*alienation-effect**) is also sometimes rendered as "estrangement effect," a term that underlines the new perception involved in the acting and staging and is preferable to *distantiation*.

See also: alienation-effect, absurd, fantasy, fantastic.

Further reading: Brecht 1963; Vernois 1974; Knopf 1980.

ETHNODRAMA

Fr.: *ethnodrame*; Ger.: *Ethnodrama*; Sp.: *etnodrama*.

This is a term given by several ethnologists and *ethnoscenologists** to phenomena that relate to religion, ritual and theatre simultaneously. These see the origins of theatre in theatrical ceremony, whether Greek tragedy, Japanese Noh, or Haitian Voodoo. The term "ethnodrama" seems to have been coined by the psychiatrist L. MARS, who used it to baptize "this original phenomenon which is at once religion and drama [and] lies at the origins of the theatre and popular religion of many peoples" (*Revue de psychologie des peuples*, 1962, no.1, p. 21).

Further reading: Lorelle 1962, 1974, in Corvin 1995.

ETHNOSCENOLOGY

Fr.: *ethnoscénologie*; Ger.: *Ethnoszenologie*; Sp.: *etnoscenología*.

Neologism coined by J.-M. PRADIER (1996) to refer to a new discipline that broadens the study of Western theatre to include performance practices from all over the world, particularly those relating to the ritual and the ceremonial – cultural performances – without projecting a Eurocentric vision onto them. It is "the study, among different cultures, of organized human performance practices and behaviours" (1996, 47).

The main difficulty has to do with how to use ethnology and cultural anthropology in order to apply them flexibly to objects which are neither metaphors (such as the *theatricality* of everyday life or social life) nor infinitely open areas such as performances in games, sports, rituals, ceremonies, etc.

The notion of spectacle (*spectaculum*, that which is visible; and *speculum*, that which transmits an image) and of *performance* (action accomplished) belong to two worlds which are epistemologically incompatible, or two gazes upon the same object. Ethnoscenology should be able to reconcile them to undertake this study. To avoid having every possible kind of human activity come under the ethnoscenologist's gaze, we would focus on phenomena that meet the following criteria: aesthetic shaping of an event, fictionality, pleasure in acting, gratuitousness of action.

Further reading: Pronko 1967; Pavis 1990, 1992, 1996.

EURHYTHMICS

Fr.: *rythmique*; Ger.: *Eurhythmie*; Sp.: *eurítmica*.

Study of musical and poetical *rhythms**. A term invented by Rudolf Steiner (1861–1912) and revived by JAQUES-DALCROZE in 1919, the aim of eurhythmics is "the representation by the body of musical values with the aid of specific experiments to find within ourselves all of the elements required for such a figuration" (1965, 160). This discipline searches for an expression common to the rhythms of music and to those of the body that accompany it: "Magnificent, powerful music is that which animates and stylizes human gesture, and gesture is an eminently 'musical' emanation from our aspirations and desires" (1965, 18).

EVALUATION

Fr.: *évaluation*; Ger.: *Bewertung*; Sp.: *evaluación*.

See AESTHETICS, DESCRIPTIVE

EVENT

Fr.: *événement*; Ger.: *Ereignis*; Sp.: *acontecimiento*.

Theatrical performance when considered not with respect to the fictional aspect of its *fabula* but rather its reality as an artistic practice that effects an exchange between actor and spectator.

1. One of the specific hallmarks of theatricality is to present a human presence to the audience's gaze. It is this living relationship between actor and spectator that forms the basis of the exchange: "the essence of theatre is found neither in the narration of an event, nor in the discussion of a hypothesis with an audience, nor in the representation of life as it appears from the outside, nor even in a vision – but that the theatre is an act carried out *here and now* in the actors' organisms, in front of other men..." (GROTOWSKI 1971: 86–87; Eng. 1968, 118).

2. This peculiarity of the theatrical art explains why all stage systems, including the text, depend on this "event relationship" being established: "The meaning of a play is much further from the meaning of a purely linguistic message than it is from the meaning of an event" (MOUNIN 1970, 94).

3. The stage has powerful means at its disposal to produce narrative, visual and linguistic illusion, but the performance is also subject to the outside intervention of events at any time, in the form of a break in the illusion, an interruption of the performance, unforeseen effects, or spectator scepticism.

4. For some directors and theoreticians, the goal of the performance is no longer the magic of illusion but the audience's awareness of the reality of the event. The very idea of fiction causing the communication of the event to be forgotten is alien to them: "The illusion that we will seek to create will not have to do with the degree of verisimilitude of the action but with the communicative force and reality of that action. Each performance shall therefore become a kind of event." (ARTAUD) The stage is a "concrete language," a place where an experience takes place that does not reproduce something that went before.

5. Some current forms of theatre (such as the *happening**, the popular festival, the "invisible theatre" of BOAL, 1977, *performance art**) pursue the purest vision of the reality of events: the performance invents itself, eschewing any advance planning or symbolism.

See also: illusion, reception, specificity, hermeneutics, essence of theatre.

Further reading: Derrida 1967; Ricoeur 1969; Mounin 1970; Voltz 1974; D. Cole 1975; Boal 1979; Kantor 1977; Hinkle 1979; Wiles 1980; Barba and Savarese 1985.

EXPECTATION

Fr.: *attente*; Ger.: *Erwartung*; Sp.: *expectativa*.

1. As *dramatic** form, the theatre speculates as to the spectator's expectation of events, but this expectation has to do mainly with anticipating the conclusion and final resolution of the conflicts. It is the "anxious anticipation of the end" (DEMARCY 1973, 329). Certain *motifs** or scenes in the play are there exclusively to announce and prepare for what is to follow, by building up *suspense** and *tension**.

2. The *horizon of expectation* (JAUSS 1970) of a work is the set of the audience's expectations, based on their real-life situation, the play's place in literary tradition, contemporary tastes and the nature of the questions the text purports to answer.

To this horizon should be added the spectators' sociocultural models, including personal expectations, as well as what they know about the author, the *context** in which the performance takes place, the title and social acceptability of the play, the role of fashion and snob appeal in preparing for *reception**, etc. Directors are, to a large extent, aware of these expectations and take them into account in establishing their aesthetic/political line. Aesthetics are closely related to cultural politics.

EXPERIMENTAL THEATRE

Fr.: *théâtre expérimental*; Ger.: *Experimentelles Theater*; Sp.: *teatro experimental.*

The term *experimental theatre** must compete with terms such as avant-garde theatre, laboratory theatre, *performance art**, or even modern theatre, all in opposition to the traditional, commercial and *bourgeois theatre** whose primary aim is financial profit and which is based on time-tested artistic formulas, or to repertory theatre that stages only classics and already famous playwrights. More than a genre or historic movement, it refers to an artist's attitude toward tradition, institutions, and commercial operations.

1. The Time of the Innovators

It would be arbitrary to situate the beginnings of experimental theatre historically, for any new form necessarily experiments as soon as it is no longer content to reproduce existing forms and techniques and no longer considers the meaning of its production as self-evident. It is generally agreed, however, that the creation of ANTOINE's Théâtre libre (1887) and LUGNE-POE's Théâtre de l'Oeuvre represented the birth of a theatre founded on mise-en-scène. The time coincided with the institutionalization of the director and of mise-en-scène, which was henceforth to be considered artistic activity in its own right. Experimentation has often been much more than a formal reshuffling, since the high point of naturalism at the turn of the century (ZOLA, STANISLAVSKY, ANTOINE), the Russian avant-garde of the 1920s (VAKHTANGOV, MEYERHOLD, TAIROV), the pioneers of stage light and volume (APPIA, CRAIG), the French innovators (ARTAUD, COPEAU, BATY, JOUVET), the critical realists (PISCATOR, BRECHT, JESSNER), the Bauhaus project of MOHOLY-NAGY and W. GROPIUS. The time of the "innovators," in the words of J. COPEAU, has only half arrived, for they have not managed to match theory with practice and have "remained suspended and disconcerted between their unsatisfied spiritual aspirations and the vain mastery of their *métier*," have confined their experiments to technique and have let themselves be "turned off course and weakened by endless experiments, external refinements, aimless technical research" (COPEAU 1974, 198).

For many, in fact, the notion of experimental theatre evokes merely a theatre with new architectural, scenographic or acoustical techniques, whereas the experiment should have to do above all with the actor, the relationship with the audience, the conception of mise-en-scène or rereading of the text, the renewed reception of the stage event. Naturally, we should not ignore the influence of technological advances on the development of performance: new architecture in theatres, mobile and multipurpose stages, the use of lightweight materials that can be adapted to infinite applications, refinements in lighting and more sophisticated sound effects are all ways of facilitating the staging. What is still needed is for the audience to understand their dramaturgical function, so that these new effects do not become an end in themselves to impress the spectators but take part in elaborating the meaning of the production.

Experimenting implies a trial and error process in a search for something that does not yet exist, or a hidden truth. The trial and error has to do with choosing unpublished or "difficult" texts, with the acting style or the audience's situation of reception. The performance varies from one evening to another; the time required for rehearsals and theorizing is much longer than in commercial theatre. The right to try out new things, and therefore to make mistakes, encourages creators to take risks in connection with reception (sometimes to the point of not even intending to put on a public performance), to change the mise-en-scène constantly, to seek to transform the hide-bound gaze of the spectator – hence the frequent accusation that they are elitist or hermetic.

Examples of experimental directors today are Brook, Kantor, Monk, Wilson and Bausch.

2. An Indefinite Space

Rather than describing a fixed program of experimental theatre in its various manifestations, and rewriting a history of experimental practices that would have to include all contemporary theatre activity, it would seem more appropriate to describe some of the trends and obsessions, to give an idea of some of the directions of experimentation.

A. MARGINALITY

This theatre is located on the fringes of the mainstream theatre that attracts the public, creates stars, brings in funding and is part of the establishment. It occupies a place that is both highly visible (because of its eccentricities) and marginal (because of its budget and audience). Its marginality is often the bad conscience or counterweight of the official stage. BROOK, for instance, experimented under the auspices of the Royal Shakespeare Company in the 1960s before reconciling mise-en-scène and experiment at the Centre d'études et de recherches théâtrales in Paris. GROTOWSKI and, more recently, T. KANTOR have worked under the tacit protection of a highly conformist official theatre and constraining political authorities. M. KIRBY and R. SCHECHNER in the United States, J. LASSALLE, R. DEMARCY, J.-F. PEYRET, J. JOURDHEUL, G. BRUN, C. BUCHVALD, J.-P. SARRAZAC and F. REGNAULT in France are professor-creators. Frequently, the success of this kind of theatre, its expansion to the general public and the resulting demand and off-shoots, neutralize its original experimentality, eliminating the desire and the need for its very existence.

B. RECONQUERING STAGE SPACE

Experimental theatre has no one specific architecture or *stage design**. The theatre in the round and the total environment theatre are not (or not any more) synonymous with modernity. Inversely, the most striking achievements take place through a subversion or an overstatement of the principles of the proscenium-arch theatre. The use of an unconventional space (stadiums, factories, public transit vehicles and squares, apartments) disorients the audience. The crucial effect of pulling the rug out from under our feet is at its peak here – all is theatre, and nothing more is theatre.

C. RELATIONSHIP WITH THE AUDIENCE

The audience is the focus of experimentation, for theatre is no longer content with the dull-witted opposition between entertainment and didactics; it wishes to act on the gaze that is overly susceptible to narrative models and advertising myths, promote a questioning attitude, provoke uneasiness with the meaninglessness of the text or stage events. Changing the listening situation (a *physical* situation in the audience's arrangement in space or facilities where the spectators may rest their tired bodies, but above all a *psychic* situation, for it is the attitude toward the work of art that varies) causes the spectator to be conditioned by the work of art, rather than the opposite (cf. groups such as Il Carozonne, La Fura dels Baus, Brith GOF, le Théâtre de l'Unité).

D. THE ACTOR IN ABEYANCE

GROTOWSKI's laboratory theatre reminded us that theatre is what happens between an actor and a spectator. Most experiments consist in stretching the limits of the two domains. The spectator expands his ability to perceive the unusual and the unrepresentable. The actor organizes his body according to a dual requirement; to be readable in its expressiveness and unreadable as to its meaning or intentions. His body and voice are the relays between all the stage materials and the physical presence of the spectator.

E. PRODUCTION OF MEANING

There need not be one single univocal meaning, produced by addition and accumulation of the various signifying systems, because the performance is always in progress or off balance. The process of signification and vectorization is more important than the identification of isolated signs. Theatre often experiments with relationships between materials, sound and image, as in H. GOEBBELS (*Où le Débarquement désastreux*), APERGHIS (*Énumerations*), N. FRIZE (*La Voix des gens*).

F. TEXT VERSUS WORK

BARTHES's distinction (1971) between *work*, a closed, material system, and *text*, an operative, semiotic concept, establishes a single dividing line between the text to be interpreted (which the reader/spectator is invited to complete and close) and the text to be manipulated, where the meaning is no longer tied to the narrative structure and is scattered according to the way it is heard. The text is treated as raw material, as an assemblage of fragments, in resistance to a definitive and universal meaning.

G. SPECIFICITY

Contemporary practice casts doubt on the idea of an *essence** or *specificity** of theatrical art, questioning the borders erected in the eighteenth century between the visual arts, music, mime, dance, ceremony, poetry. It makes use of film and video, reflects on the relationships between the human and the inhuman, animate and inanimate, and calls itself post-modern, or removed from everything that constituted a certainty in the art and aesthetics of another age.

H. A MELTING POT OF GENRES AND TECHNIQUES

The performing tradition of a school or institution is thrown into question; it is no longer relevant to separate and rank genres by value. Forms and cultures from different contexts are brought together, searching for a possible metaphor for this confrontation.

Today, a theatre that doesn't view the spectator as a halfwit and refuses to sell its consumer products knows that it must be experimental, or not be at all.

Further reading: Brecht 1967, 15:285–305; Schlemmer 1978; Ginestier 1961; Pronko 1963; E.T. Kirby 1969; M. Kirby 1965, 1987; Kostelantz 1968; Veinstein 1968; Roose-Evans 1989; Artioli 1972; Corvin 1973; Bartolucci and Ursic 1977; Grimm 1982; *Raison présente* 1982; Brauneck 1982; Banu 1984; Javier 1984; Berg and Rischbieter 1985; Thomsen 1985; Rokem 1986; Piemme 1989; Finter 1990.

EXPOSITION

(From the Latin *expositio*, *exponere*, to put on view)

Fr.: *exposition*; Ger.: *Exposition*; Sp.: *exposición*.

In the exposition, the playwright provides the information required to evaluate the *dramatic situation** and to understand the action to be presented. It is particularly important that this background be known for plays with complex *plots**. It is indispensable to any dramatic text that imitates or suggests an outside reality and a human action.

1. Location of Exposition

The debate is still open as to whether the exposition is a component part of the play (like the *crisis* or *epilogue**) or whether it is scattered throughout the text. In classical dramaturgy, the exposition (or *protasis*) tends to be concentrated at the beginning of the play in the first act or opening scenes, and that it is often to be found in a *narrative** or "naive" exchange of information. As soon as the dramatic structure relaxes and is no longer confined to a crisis or conflict, however, the notations on the action are much more fragmented and scattered. In the extreme case of *analytical** drama, which does not show the conflict but rather presupposes it before proceeding to analyze its causes, the entire text becomes an extended exposition, and the concept loses its spatial and distinctive value (cf. HEBBEL, IBSEN).

Also, the exposition is not always placed where one might expect; for example, the stage in naturalistic theatre provides, in a hidden way, a great deal of information that is decoded by the audience, sometimes unconsciously, to explain the course of the action. The overall *framework** of the performance also provides detailed information: the location of the theatre, the origins and political tendencies of the group, the *program** and the proposed dramaturgical analysis have a profound influence on the spectator. It is becoming more and more difficult in modern theatre to pinpoint the exposition and reduce it to a stock of information (CORVIN 1978a).

2. Techniques of Exposition

A. EXPOSITION AS RECALL

Elements of the action may already be known to the audience and therefore not require explicit mention. Examples are *mythos* for Greek tragedy, the reference text for parodies of classics.

B. NATURALIZATION

As the exposition is often perceived as a necessary evil that precedes and sets off the action without being part of it, the playwright seeks to mask it or at least make it seem real. This is why a play may begin *in medias res*, plugging us into a story that has already begun and that we will receive piecemeal: "The art of dramatic exposition consists of rendering it so naturally that it contains not the slightest hint of art" (MARMONTEL 1787).

C. DRAMATIZATION

In order to appear natural, the exposition, which tends to be static and epic (an objective narrative of certain circumstances) may be turned into an animated dialogue that gives the impression that the main action is already under way. This is *exposition in action*: "The best dramatic subject is one in which the exposition is already part of the development" (letter from GOETHE to SCHILLER, 22 April 1797).

3. Forms of Exposition

In classical drama, the exposition, naturalized and dramatized through the use of all the techniques of verisimilitude, is often transmitted in a conversation between protagonists or between hero and confidant. It must be both short and effective, transmit information economically and clearly, avoid useless repetition, omit nothing that is important to understanding the characters' motivations, and prepare the way discreetly for the continuation and conclusion of the *fabula*.

When the performance does not strive for imitation and illusion, however, it is no longer important to justify new information. It can even be furnished "ironically" and directly by an announcer character or by a group of characters who may state their names and personal particulars (PIRANDELLO, BRECHT). For the sake of contradicting, absurd characters may announce a series of facts, as in *la Cantatrice chauve* (*The Bald Soprano*) or "philosophical" propositions that are unrelated to their situation. In these cases, the exposition paradoxically consists of exposing facts of no relevance to an understanding of the action. The exposition is nowhere and everywhere at the same time. The exposition is easily "dissolved" to reappear in other categories: *context**, *situation**, ideological presuppositions. This "dissolving" and "de-dramatizing" of the exposition is one of the most difficult aspects of dramatic structure to grasp, and also has to do with the questions raised below.

4. Questions Raised by the Exposition

A. ACTANTIAL MODEL*

Who are the protagonists? What divides them or brings them together? What is the purpose of their actions?

B. REALITY-EFFECT*

What effect does the play produce? What atmosphere and reality are simulated? For what purpose?

C. LOGIC OF REPRESENTED WORLD

If the logic of the possible world of the fiction differs from that of our own, what are the rules that govern it? How do we read the psychological, social or amorous motivations of the characters?

D. PURPOSE OF THE THEATRE PRACTICE

What is the aim of the staging? How can we draw a parallel with our own world? It is through the ideological *recognition effect** that the exposition is realized fully, thus giving the spectator information about the fictional world and building ideological and emotional bridges between the *fiction** and the spectator's own situation.

See also: horizon of expectation, prologue, dramatic and epic, classical dramaturgy, analytical drama.

Further reading: Freytag 1965; Scherer 1950; Bickert 1969 and in Keller 1976; Klotz 1969.

EXPRESSION

Fr.: *expression*; Ger.: *Ausdruck*; Sp.: *expresión*.

1. Dramatic or theatrical expression, like any artistic expression, is conceived, according to the classical view, as an externalization, as a foregrounding of deep meaning or hidden elements, and thus as a movement from inside out. Ultimately, the actor is responsible for this "revelation," "by explaining the author through bringing out into something present and alive, and making intelligible, all his secret intentions and the profundity of his master-strokes" (HEGEL 1832; Eng. 1975, 1189–1190).

This expression (or expulsion) of meaning is best achieved on stage (still according to classical dogma) in the actor's gestures and body language.

The classical theory of expression implicitly postulates that the meaning already exists in the text, that expression is only a secondary process of "extraction" based on a prior idea. Fundamental to it is the author's aesthetic experience, of which the actor affords a few glimpses; this position entails an overestimation of the value of the *idea* at the expense of the expressive *matter*, a belief in a meaning anterior to expression.

2. The tendency today is no longer to separate form and content; the modern work of art is considered a creation rather than an expression. The work of art does not reflect an anterior world but delivers a world according to its own particular view and form. Whether this process of giving form a content (and vice versa) is called *writing** (*écriture*) or *signifying practice** (*pratique signifiante*), it no longer separates thought and expression but makes them one. In theatre, this means that a particular production will experiment with all of the resources it has available to it, to produce a meaning that was not established in advance for all eternity. The director assembles his stage materials in such a way as to evoke a given reading by the spectator. Such a reading may be distorted, uninteresting or insignificant, but at least it raises questions about the text and the meaning of the performance. Similarly, the actor makes a conscious choice of signs to obtain a given effect, rather than incarnating an idea in a single right way (*reading**).

3. The actor is attentive to both expressing his emotions and giving shape to emotion through gesture. Expression does not only happen from the inside out, but also from the outside in, and as remarked by J. COPEAU, "emotional expression comes from the right expression [*expression juste*] (1974:211).

F

FABULA

Fr.: *fable*; Ger.: *Fabel, Handlung*; Sp.: *fábula (relato)*.

1. Contradictions of Basic Notion

A. ORIGINS

From the Latin *fabula* (tale, story, narrative); corresponds to the Greek *mythos*; refers to the series of events that make up the narrative element of a work, "the plot or story of a play or poem" (*Oxford English Dictionary*).

The Latin *fabula* is a mythical or invented narrative and, by extension, a play or tale. Here we will refer only to the *fabula* of the theatrical work of art. A study of the fables of Aesop or La Fontaine, however, shows that the theoretical problems related to the notion of *fabula* have to do as well with the short story, epic and drama (cf. LESSING, "On fable") (cf. VANDENDORPE, 1989). An overview of the innumerable uses of the word brings out two opposing conceptions of *fabula*: (1) as material anterior to the play's composition; and (2) as the narrative structure of the story. This double-edged definition supports the opposition of *inventio* and *dispositio* in rhetoric and of *story* and *plot* in Anglo-American criticism.

To compose the *fabula* (in the second sense) is, for the dramatist, to structure the actions – motivations, conflicts, resolution, dénouement – in a space and time that is "abstract" and constructed on the basis of the space/time and behaviour of human beings. The *fabula* textualizes actions that may have taken place before the play began or will follow the conclusion of the play. It effects a selection and ordering of episodes in a more or less pre-established way. That of classical dramaturgy, for instance, calls for respecting the chronological and logical order of the events: exposition, rising suspense, crisis, complication, catastrophe and dénouement: "The poet shall take care, when arranging a *fabula*, that all of the events depend on each other in such a way that one follows another as if by necessity; that everything in the action appears to have happened as it should after what has gone before; and so, that all things be so connected that one arise from the other as the proper outcome thereof" (LA MENARDIÈRE, *Poétique*, 1640, chap. 5).

According to this classical conception, the notion of *fabula* is very close to that of *story*, while the *plot* corresponds to the causal series of actions. "We have defined a story as a narrative of events arranged in their time-sequence. A plot is also a narrative of events, the emphasis falling on causality" (E.M. FORSTER, *Aspects of the Novel*, 1927).

B. *FABULA* AS MATERIAL

Fabula *vs szujet*

In Greek theatre, the *fabula* is often borrowed from a well-known myth that preexists the play. The *fabula* or myth is then the material, the source from which the poet draws the themes for his play. This sense persists in the classical era, and

RACINE, who himself uses Greek sources, still uses *fabula* as opposed to *subject*: "We should not quibble with poets over the few changes they may have made in the *fabula*; we should, however, make sure to consider the excellent use they have made of such changes and the ingenious manner in which they have made the *fabula* conform to their subject" (Second preface to *Andromache*).

In this sense, the *fabula* is the set of motifs that may be reconstructed in a system of events or logic at the playwright's disposal. "The cause of the events (notes MARMONTEL, 1787, in his entry on *intrigue*, or plot) is thus independent of the characters, anterior to the action itself or assumed to be outside of it." The *fabula* of any dramatic text may be reconstructed as a series of motifs or themes that are communicated to us in the course of the play in the specific form of the *sjuzet*. This distinction was formulated most precisely by the Russian formalists: "The *fabula* is opposed to the *sjuzet*, which, although it is made up of the same events, follows their order of appearance in the play and the series of data furnished by them. (...) In short, *fabula* is what actually happened; *sjuzet* is the way in which the reader is apprised of it" (TOMACHEVSKY 1965a, 67).

In this first sense, *fabula* is defined as the chronological and logical ordering of the events that constitute the framework of the story represented. The relationship between *fabula* and *szujet* gives us the key to the *dramaturgy** involved.

Fabula *as "the combination of the events" (ARISTOTLE) (translated into English as* plot)

In Aristotle's *Poetics*, *fabula* designates the imitation of action, "the organization of the events [...] Clearly, then, the first principle and, as it were, the soul of tragedy is the plot, and second in importance is character" (1450b). Here *fabula* is linked to its constitutive element: dramatic action. The point of view is therefore displaced slightly from the "raw" dramatic material of the sources to the level of the narration of actions and events. These actions are common to the sources and the play in which they appear: here we are in the territory of a logic of actions or narratology.

This analogy between *fabula*-as-material and *fabula*-as-action prepares the way for the conception of *fabula* as the narrative structure of the play.

C. *FABULA* AS THE STRUCTURE OF THE NARRATIVE

But *fabula* is often seen as the specific structure of the story told by the play, in which we may observe the poet's personal approach to his subject and arrangement of the episodes of the plot. "Any invention with which the poet associates a certain intention constitutes a fable" (LESSING, *Treatise on fable*, 1759). Thus the *fabula* is considered, beginning in the eighteenth century, as an element of the structure of the drama that must be distinguished from the sources of the story narrated. Clarification is necessary for the terms action, subject and *fabula*. MARMONTEL makes a clear distinction between them: "In epic and dramatic poems, *fabula*, action and subject are commonly taken to be synonyms; but in a narrower sense, the subject of the poem is the substantial idea of the action, the action is the development of the subject, and the *fabula* is the same arrangement considered from the point of view of the incidents that make up the plot and serve to complicate and unravel the action" (MARMONTEL 1787, *"Fable"*).

D. *FABULA* AS POINT OF VIEW ON (HI)STORY (BRECHTIAN STORY)

Reconstruction of fabula *(story, Fabel in German)*

Whereas pre-Brechtian conceptions of *fabula* saw it as an obvious, automatic fact apparent upon reading the play that attempted to identify the phases of the action, BRECHT, criticizing ARISTOTLE, considered the *fabula* not as an immediate fact but as something that must be reconstructed and sought by all, from *dramaturg** to actor: "The exposition of the story (*Fabel*) and its communication by suitable means of alienation constitute the main business of the theatre. [...] The 'story' is set out, brought forward and shown by the theatre as a whole, by actors, scene designers, mask-makers, costumiers, composers and choreographers. They unite their various arts for the joint operation, without of course sacrificing their independence in the process" (*A Short Organum for the Theatre*, sect. 70). Bringing forward the story (*Fabel*), for BRECHT, means having a point of view on both the *story* (narrative) and on *history* (events seen in a Marxist light).

Discontinuity of Brechtian fabula
The Brechtian *fabula* does not rest on a continuous, unified story but on the principle of discontinuity; rather than telling a coherent story it brings together autonomous episodes that the spectator is invited to compare with the real processes to which they correspond. In this sense, *fabula* is no longer, as in classical (i.e. non-epic) dramaturgy, an indivisible whole made up of episodes connected by relationships of temporality and causality, but a broken-up structure. Hence the ambiguity of the notion in BRECHT: the *fabula* must simultaneously "follow its course," reconstruct the narrative logic and be constantly interrupted by the appropriate alienation-effects.

Storytellers' point of view
Clearly, there is a misunderstanding that arises in connection with the Brechtian concept of *fabula*. One attempts to reconstruct it by making a narrative of the events, thus by disregarding the arrangement of the episodes in the play; but at the same time one wishes "to act out the *fabula*," which should become readable in the narration of events. Actually, the search for the *fabula*, or Brechtian story, is intended to permit a reconstruction of the logic of the represented reality (the signified of the narrative) while maintaining a certain logic and autonomy of the narrative. It is precisely the tension between the two projects and the contradictions between the world represented and the way of representing it that results in the *alienation-effect** and the proper perception of (hi)story.

To extract the *fabula* is not, for BRECHT, to discover a universally decipherable story inscribed in the text in a definitive form. In "seeking the *fabula*," reader and director expose their own points of view on the reality they wish to represent: "The story does not just correspond to an incident from men's life together as it might actually have taken place, but is composed of episodes rearranged so as to allow the story-teller's ideas about men's life to find expression" (Appendices to *Short Organum*, sect. 64; Eng. 1964, 278).

Every storyteller and every era has its own particular view of the *fabula*. BRECHT "reads" *Hamlet*, and thus "adapts" it according to an analysis of the society in which he lives. ("Given the dark and bloody period in which I am writing – the criminal ruling classes, the widespread doubt in the power of reason, continually being misused – I think that I can read the story thus ..." *A Short Organum for the Theatre*, sect. 68).

The *fabula* is in a constant process of development, not only through the writing of the play but also, and particularly, in the staging and acting: in the preliminary work by the *dramaturg**, choice of scenes, indication of the characters' motives, actor's criticism of the character, coordination of the various stage arts, questioning of the play by making prosaic queries (for example, "Why doesn't Faust marry Marguerite?"). To read the *fabula* is to give an interpretation (of the text for the director, of the performance for the spectator), is to choose a particular distribution of the significant stresses of the play. The *staging** is no longer a definitive updating of the meaning, but rather a choice in terms of dramaturgical and play elements, and therefore a hermeneutic choice.

Determining basic gestus
Apprehending the Brechtian *fabula* requires an understanding of the gestus ("gest" in Willet's translation), which tells us not about the characters themselves but about their interrelationships within society: "Splitting such material into one gest after another, the actor masters his character by

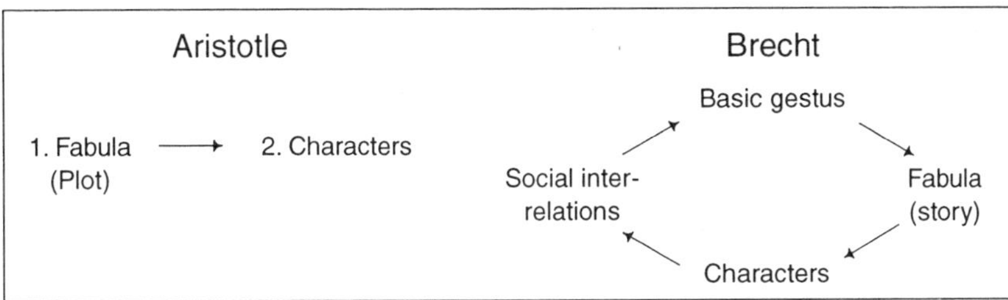

first mastering the 'story.' It is only after walking all round the entire episode that he can, as it were by a single leap, seize and fix his character, complete with all its individual features" (*A Short Organum for the Theatre*, sect. 64). The Brechtian *fabula* is thus closely linked to the constellation of characters within the microcosm of the play and the macrocosm of their original reality: "The 'story' is the theatre's great operation, the complete fitting together of all the gestic incidents, embracing the communications and impulses that must now go to make up the audience's entertainment" (ibid., sect. 65).

Determining the *fabula* in the Brechtian manner is done through a dialectical process that is never completely finished, as shown in the following comparison with the Aristotelian conception:

Search for contradictions
The *fabula* must not confine itself to reconstructing the general movement of the action, but lay bare the contradictions, indicating the reasons for them. In *Mother Courage*, for example, it will always stress the impossibility of opposite actions: living off the war *and* not sacrificing anything to it; loving one's children *and* using them for business purposes. Rather than masking the "inconsistencies of the story told" (1963, sect. 12), the lack of logic in the connections between the events, the Brechtian epic *fabula* makes us aware of them by disrupting the harmonious continuity of the action. The perspective on the events is always historical, affording a view of the ideological and social backdrop that often clarifies the supposedly individual motivations of the characters.

2. Importance and Difficulties of the Notion of *Fabula*

A. AMBIGUITY OF *FABULA*: INTERFERENCE OF THE NARRATIVE AND THE DISCURSIVE

The notion of *fabula*, with its dual definition as *material* (story narrated) and *story structure* (narrating discourse) indicates by its very ambiguity that a critic faced with a dramatic text should address himself simultaneously to signified (story narrated), signifier (way of narrating), and the relationship between the two.

The imprecision of the term (material or structure) reflects the junction within the notion between the actantial model reconstructed on the basis of the narrative materials (*narrative structure* or "deep" structure) on one hand, and the surface structure of the story (*discursive structure*) on the other. The *fabula* is drawn from both the actantial model (of the narrative) and the organization of the materials along the axis of the unfolding of the play (the discursive).

In the first case, the story narrated is examined in its systematic (paradigmatic) form before the materials of discourse are arranged. Inversely, in the second case, it is the connections between motifs that are observed. This opposition confirms that between *action** and *plot**: the action gives an account, at a general or even potential level, of the possible relationships between the different forces; the plot follows in detail the actual form taken by such action (on stage and in the text).

B. *FABULA* OR *FABULAE*

The Brechtian construction of several *fabulae* or stories based on the same text casts doubt on the idea of *fabula* as the sole denotative interpretation of the text. The *fabula* cannot play the role of a neutral, definitive "soul of the drama," and does not exist outside the text as an unalterable fixed system, but rather is constructed after each reading, each acting, each staging.

Accordingly, it is dangerous to conceive of the *fabula* as the invariant of the text or as the denotation common to all onto which the connotations of the performance may be grafted. The *fabula* is never an objective fact. Rather, in order to be reconstructed, it requires a critical perspective on the text and reality it conveys.

Through this problem of the productivity of the *fabula* we come back to the notion of *isotopy**, which enables us to centre the *fabula* around a unique reference plan and to eliminate ambiguities attributable to the interference of several readings of the *fabula*.

C. *FABULA* AND NARRATION OF TEXT

Moreover, the text does not have exclusive right of access to the *fabula*, which can be reconstructed on the basis of all the stage signs, even though in practice it is more difficult to decode the narration of gesture or music than that related through language. The notion of *fabula* must be extended to the whole set of stage systems which, together and concurrently, constitutes it.

D. GENERAL PROPERTIES OF *FABULA*

1. The *fabula* can be *summarized* in a few succinct phrases describing the events. "The summary of the narrative (if conducted according to structural criteria) maintains the individuality of the message. In other words, the narrative can be *translated* without undergoing any fundamental harm" (BARTHES 1966a, 25)

2. The *fabula* can be *transposed* by changing the substance of expression (film, short story, theatre, painting) while conserving the meaning. As a narrative "that governs the conservation and transformation of the meaning within a directed utterance" (HAMON 1974, 150), the *fabula* can accommodate any changes in use that the director may make of the stage media. What varies from one production to another may, of course, be the general interpretation of the *fabula*, but sometimes it is only the use of materials and does not question the meaning attributed to the *fabula*.

3. The *fabula* can be broken down into smaller units (see *narrative analysis**)

E. END OF *FABULA*, RETURN TO TEXT?

Cherchez la fable: that will be the watch-word of theatre people in future. The search has given rise to innumerable re-readings of classical texts hitherto considered to be closed. Directors of *fabula* have often thrown new light on plays (for example: PLANCHON on *Tartuffe* and *la Seconde Surprise de l'amour*; B. SOBEL and A. GIRAULT on *Dom Juan* and *Timon of Athens*). Sometimes the result has been a necessary simplification and popularization of the text as a signifying structure: the spectator could clearly see the curve of the plot and the fictional universe, but in the process lost his sensitivity to the form and the textual, dramaturgical and stage rhetoric. In addition, the play seemed distant in history and far removed from his situation as a spectator involved in the actual play (not only in the fiction narrated).

Another tendency, counterbalancing the first, then emerged – to show textuality, rhetoric and declamation (as in VITEZ), approach the text as a living, provocative organism (as in BROOK and recently in SOBEL). For the moment, the staging dilemma is whether to play the *fabula* or the text. Perhaps, as stated by A. GIRAULT, dramaturg to B. SOBEL, that is "the central contradiction in any performance of an old play – on the one hand, distance must be created to 'historicize' the play; on the other, a text has no chance of becoming a 'theatre text' unless it is projected directly toward the audience, and in this case 'mass (en-scène)' is not far off" (*Théâtre/Public*, 1975, "Deux *Timon d'Athènes*"). In short, *fabula*, having barely achieved its detachment from the text, tends today to return to it, but only after a detour through the bodies of actor and spectator.

Further reading: Tomachevsky 1965; Todorov 1966; Gouhier 1968; Olson 1968a; Hamon 1974;

Prince 1973; Brémond 1973; Kibédi-Varga 1976, 1981; Vandendorpe 1989.

FACIAL EXPRESSION

Fr.: *mimique*; Ger.: *Mimik*; Sp.: *mímica*.

1. In the classical era, facial expression was deemed to include both sign language and facial attitudes. The author of the article on gesture in DIDEROT's *Encyclopédie*, for example, defines gesture as "outward movement of the body and face, one of the primary means of expression given to man by nature." Current usage denotes above all the use of physionomy and *facial expression*, a practice that has a paraverbal function in underscoring or distancing a verbal utterance, noting a psychological reaction to a stimulus, communicating a message through a look, making "faces," contracting or relaxing one or more facial muscles, setting up a contradiction between the eyes and the mouth.

2. Facial expression, whose precise coding is immediately understood by the spectator (with a precision comparable to that of *intonation**), may appear particularly important in the naturalistic or psychological style of acting. The face is linked to psychology, to the inexpressible, to an entire metaphysics of the speaking body, that can be manipulated with the ease of "the machinery of opera" (MARIVAUX). Facial expression is, as well, "the place in theatre that expresses most clearly the *reflexivity* of the discourse produced by the actor, who not only says the speech act, but also says that he is saying it" (UBERSFELD 1981, 227).

To confine facial expression to a phatic and paraverbal accompaniment would be to underestimate its scope. Although it is used, as in everyday communication (mainly to modalize the linguistic message) to underline presence and the phatic function, it can also be an autonomous system unrelated to psychological reality-effects, a veritable staging of the face and the whole body (in *gestural theatre**, for instance). The classical era captured expressions and attitudes and their coded meanings in stereotyped poses that are reproduced in engravings, a procedure that cannot fail to lead to a rigid conventionality in acting and a "psychologization" of expressiveness. In reaction to this psychological tendency of facial expression, modern theory of mise-en-scène such as that of ARTAUD or GROTOWSKI, both influenced by Oriental traditions, seeks to codify and control the body plastically, and not as a psychological byproduct. According to ARTAUD, "the ten thousand and one expressions of the face caught in the form of masks can be labeled and catalogued, so they may eventually participate directly and symbolically in this concrete language of the stage, independently of their particular psychological use" (1964b, 143; Eng. 1958, 94). For GROTOWSKI, "the actor must himself compose an organic mask by means of his facial muscles and thus each character wears the same grimace throughout the whole play" (1971, 68, photos, 64; Eng. 1968, 77, photos, 71).

Certain forms of theatre, such as *commedia dell'arte** or farce, being less tied to psychology or the codification of facial expression, eschew precision in this area in favour of gestures by the rest of the body, using *masks** (COPEAU, DECROUX, LECOQ) or heavy *makeup** to neutralize facial expression, which is considered too precise and overwhelming. BRECHT admired in Karl VALENTIN and Charlie CHAPLIN "the almost complete renunciation of effects of physiognomy and cheap psychology" (BRECHT 1972, 44). Contemporary creation is characterized by the greater attention it pays to the face, the hands, the gaze, the whole body. The face becomes a walking set, whether it is controllable like a *puppet** or subject to effects that are difficult to control. Here, meaning draws signs in flesh.

See also: kinesics, body, expression.

Further reading: Engel 1979; Aubert 1901; Bouissac 1973; Birdwhistell 1973; Bernard 1976; Pavis 1981a, 1996a; Winkin 1981; Bruyer 1983; Roubine 1985; Paquet 1990.

FAIRYTALE PLAY

Fr.: *féerie;* Ger.: *Märchendrama;* Sp.: *comedia de magia.*

This is a play based on magical, marvellous and spectacular effects, featuring imaginary characters with supernatural powers (fairies, demons, natural elements, mythological creatures).

1. The marvellous

The fairytale play exists only through the creation of marvellous or *fantastic** effects that contrast the real, "realistic" world with a reference world governed by different physical laws. When the marvellous or the supernatural arises, "such incidents are most effective when they come unexpectedly and yet occur in a causal sequence in which one thing leads to another" (ARISTOTLE, *Poetics,* sect. 1452a), when "through a series of interconnected causes that are neither inevitable nor imposed from the outside, one sees events result which are either contrary to expectation or out of the ordinary" (CHAPELAIN, *Preface à l'Adonis*). It is the opposite of the real, of "all that goes against the ordinary course of nature" (P. RAPIN), but it is also, in classical doctrine, the necessary and dialectical complement to verisimilitude. It is not confined to themes but also affects form, language and how the story is told. The pleasure of the spectator who is "filled with wonder," is that of a child before a huge stage toy that he does not understand, a toy that captivates him with its unexpected quirks. The marvellous requires him to suspend his critical judgment and believe in the visual effects of the stage *machinery**: supernatural powers of mythological heros (flight, weightlessness, strength, divination), and a total illusionism in stage design which can be used in many ways. Here convention reigns supreme, demanding a temporary belief in phenomena that we well know are artifical effects. Pleasure in theatre is the pleasure of the marvellous and the supernatural, which "enhances and embellishes the fiction, supporting in spectators the sweet illusion that is pleasure in theatre, where it casts the marvellous" (LA BRUYÈRE). The stage, as an unreal place, is naturally an ideal place for the marvellous. The performance tends to repress text, literature and verisimilitude. Only the senses and the imagination are appealed to in this theatre that expresses the pleasure of regression. Sometimes, however, the marvellous can be a covert and carefully coded way of describing reality (*Gulliver's Travels*, the "island" plays by MARIVAUX and political parables masked in unreality). The fairytale play therefore effects a total inversion of these signs of reality, thus maintaining a veiled contact with it. It does not necessarily, as is often stated, reflect an idealistic and apolitical view of the world that escapes analysis; on the contrary, it is sometimes the inverted and "faithfully distorted" image of reality and thus the true source of realism. Most often, however, the sole aim of the marvellous is to evoke dreamlike euphoric states that banish everyday reality (operetta, musical comedy or full-scale opera). Classical theoreticians (such as P. RAPIN in *Réflexions sur la poétique*) advocate the use of the marvellous for divine characters, as in EURIPIDES and SOPHOCLES. They use it to create a simplified, popular or aristocratic mythology, accommodating it to verisimilitude and making it a borderline case of the human marvellous. In the divine (or Christian) supernatural, miracles and supernatural occurrences are justified by the extraordinary powers of the gods. In an attempt to limit its effects, classical theoreticians confine it to form and expression: "The marvellous exists when the story is supported by concepts and the wealth of language alone, so that the reader puts aside the subject-matter and concentrates on its embellishments" (CHAPELAIN, *Préface à l'Adonis*).

The marvellous on stage may take many different forms – appearances by superhuman beings, ghosts or dead people, supernatural actions (magical effects), objects on stage. It is not essential that the audience (today often a sceptical one) believe in the marvellous; they have only to appreciate it as a highly theatrical and poetic moment, as a symbol to be deciphered (as in theatre of the absurd).

2. Forms of the Fairytale Play
The fairytale play may take the form of an opera, a ballet, a pantomime or a play with a fanciful plot (SHAKESPEARE's *A Midsummer Night's Dream*), using all imaginable visual means (costumes, lighting, fireworks, water ballet). It enjoyed popularity in the baroque seventeenth century (productions by TORELLI, dramatizations of fairy tales by PERRAULT, creation of *l'Andromède* and *la Toison d'or* by CORNEILLE and *Psyché* by MOLIERE. In the eighteenth century, the Comédiens-Italiens, the Opéra and Théâtre de la Foire created a spectacular genre informed by theatre and opera. In Italy, *commedia dell'arte* and the *fiabesque** comedies of C. GOZZI staged by A. SACCHI use a stage display in which convention and fancy prevail. At the end of the eighteenth century, phantasmagoria could give the illusion of ghosts in dark rooms. In the nineteenth century, the fairytale genre is associated with melodrama, opera, pantomime (DEBUREAU, NESTROY), and then *vaudeville**, producing spectacles that mixed human heroes with supernatural forces in the midst of singing, dancing, music and staging effects. The fairytale play meets the popular play in the performances of Viennese *Volksstücke* in the nineteenth century (RAIMUND, WESTROY), in "Crime boulevard" theatres and, in our times, in the lavish spectacle of operettas and erotic (Casino de Paris) or sporting (Holiday on Ice) revues. Film is the direct heir to this form (special effects as in MÉLIÈS, cartoons, fantastic films), in which techniques are used to evoke the extraordinary and the unimaginable at great expense.
Further reading: Winter 1962; Christout 1965.

FALLING ACTION
Fr.: *chute*; Ger.: *Fall, fallende Handlung*; Sp.: *acción final*.
See CATASTROPHE

FANTASTIC
Fr.: *fantastique*; Ger.: *das Phantastische*; Sp.: *fantástico*.

The fantastic is not specific to theatre, but does find its place on stage since *illusion** and *denial** are always produced there. The alternatives are not only fiction and reality; the natural and supernatural are opposed as well: "The text must force the reader [...] to hesitate between a natural and a supernatural explanation of the events" (TODOROV, 1970, 37).

Probably because theatre is based on a visible unreality and therefore cannot easily contrast the natural with the supernatural, it has not generated a great body of fantastic dramatic literature, as have narrative and film. There are, however, *alienation-effects**, the theatre of the marvellous and *fairytale plays**, which have found their own stage devices on the fringes of the fantastic.
See also: fantasy, other-scene, verisimilitude.

FANTASY (IMAGINATION), THEATRE OF
Fr.: *théâtre du fantasme*; Ger.: *Phantasie*; Sp.: *teatro de fantasía*.

In psychoanalysis, a fantasy is a representation imagined by the subject in a daydream that reflects his unconscious desires: "A fantasy floats, so to speak, between three times, the three temporal moments of our representative faculty. The psychic work starts off with an actual impression, an opportunity by the present that is capable of awakening one of the great desires of the subject; from there it extends to the memory of an event of another time, most often from childhood, when that desire was realized; then it builds a situation in relation with the future which presents itself in the form of the realization of the desire, being the daydream or fantasy that bears the traces of its origins: present opportunity and memory. Thus past, present and future are strung along the continuous thread of desire" (FREUD 1976, 10:174).

Such dreamwork on stage is produced in the phenomenon of negation or *denial**: theatre, writes LE GALLIOT, "is a constant oscillation between the symbolic and the imaginary, the field of exchanges and metaphorical currents, the place where desire tends to go, though always to be deceived, the place where fantasy unfolds in the realm of the inaccessible, and where the 'real' self returns more alone and naked than before, with the nostalgic memory of this 'other stage' to which the true stage had swung" (1977, 121).

1. Theatre and Fantasy

Theatre performance shares with fantasy that confusion of temporalities and melding of the real and the imaginary stage. In order to assimilate the present event placed before them, the spectators must call on their past experience, while projecting themselves into a forthcoming world. The same is true of a director's activity: as soon as he frees himself from the compulsion to imitate and illustrate the text and begins to model the *stage space** by merging several "raw" images with it, he adds an element of fantasy to his vision. The stage is a fantasy for the spectator because it always melds the image (of the fiction represented) with the event (of reception in the present). In this respect the theatre stage can always be analyzed as another stage, that of the imagination. The dramaturgical work as a whole, involving *montage**, *collage**, use of metaphor and metonymy, is an operation based on the collective fantasies of the playwright, stage designer and actors. It enables us to sketch out a *rhetoric** of the major stage *figures**, trace their origins and aims, and seek out devices of condensation and displacement in the stage rhetoric.

2. Fantasy in Classical Theatre

Fantasy is at work in any dramatic text from the moment when the actor summons up a place external to the stage from which he is speaking, which HONZL (in MATEJKA and TITUNIK 1976, 124–126) calls fantasy-oriented dexis. In the classical *narrative**, the character reconstructs a scene experienced in the past, colouring it with his current vision and adding to it an extra-objective dimension. In RACINE, for instance, narrations of tragic actions have the clarity and distorted vision of dream (BARTHES 1963).

3. Temptations of a Theatre of Fantasy

Counterbalancing a theatre of imitation, a theatre of interiority – hence of fantasy – sometimes seeks to establish itself (as in IBSEN, WEDEKIND, MAETERLINCK, STRINDBERG, PIRANDELLO, O'CASEY, WILLIAMS, ALBEE, ADAMOV). This dramaturgy finds its best expression in mise-en-scène: it is "in search of a surreality that would denounce more strongly the real, in a theatre where performance (*représentation*), becoming a direct transcription of the imaginary in space, seeks, not without some uneasiness, to deny itself as representation" (BENMUSSA 1974, 29). Such is the paradoxical nature of the theatre of fantasy: it imitates nothing external, is not the image of a thing or an unconscious, but is the thing or the unconscious itself. This requirement of sincerity means, by the same token, that a direct staging of fantasy is impossible. Rather than *theatre of fantasy* (with its own laws, style, techniques), we should speak of the *fantasy of the theatre* as a *place of fantasy*, of a sort of Hamlet complex that would like to see represented on the stage what occurs in a confused way on the inner stage of its creators.

In the theatre of fantasy, spectators and creators necessarily meet, since each projects his own fantasies and unconscious desires onto the stage, and the mise-en-scène evolves within this same exchange. We know that the spectator's pleasure comes from projecting onto the hero: "The hero is the place of encounter between the power of the bard, who gives life to fantasy, and the desire of the spectator who sees his fantasy embodied and represented" (GREEN 1969, 38).

4. Theatre of Fantasy and Political Theatre

There has long been a radical separation – it must be BRECHT's fault again! – between theatre of political process and dramaturgy of intimate fantasy. The split has objective causes; the difficulty of reconciling an external, "objective" view with a lyrical inner sensitivity, the ideological and epistemological concurrence of Marxism and psychoanalysis, but also of unconfessed causes in themselves having to do with fantasy – the refusal to make a connection between individual neurosis and social oppression, to admit that the historical view may be one of fantasy and that fantasy itself is informed by history. A. ADAMOV was one of the first to make (and lose) the bet that there would be a necessary reunion of politics and fantasy. The *theatre of everyday life** and neonaturalism (KROETZ, WESKER, TILLY) have tried their hand by addressing ideological and linguistic stereotypes rather than the archetype of fantasy. Productions sometimes experiment with tying fantasy to realism, for instance in relation to CHEKHOV (VITEZ, KREJCA, PINTILIÉ, BROOK, BRAUNSCHWEIG, PY) or other presumably realistic playwrights.

See also: inner space, text and performance.

Further reading: Freud 1976, 10:161–68; Mauron 1963; Green 1969, 1982; Mannoni 1969; Vernois 1974; Ubersfeld 1975; Marranca 1977; Sarrazac 1989, 1995.

FARCE

Fr.: *farce*; Ger.: *Farce, Schwank*; Sp.: *farsa*.

1. A "Grab-bag" Genre

The etymology of the word *farce* – spicy food used to stuff meat – indicates the foreign-body aspect of this spiritual nourishment within dramatic art. Originally, medieval mystery plays were intercut with moments of laughter and release of tension. Farce was conceived as something to spice and "complete" the "cultural" meal of serious literature. Thus excluded from the realm of good taste, farce was at least successful in never permitting itself to be diminished or co-opted by order, society or the noble genres such as tragedy and high comedy. One usually associates farce with a grotesque, *comic** buffoonery, with coarse laughter and an unrefined style – all the more condescending adjectives establishing straight away, often wrongly, that farce is opposed to the mind and tied to the body, social reality and everyday life. (BAKHTIN's rediscovery of the comic and farcical perpetuated this view, even though it values them inversely: farce equals realism, body; comedy equals idealism.) Farce is always defined as a primitive and coarse form that does not attain the level of comedy. As to its coarseness, it is not always clear whether it has to do with the too-visible childish techniques of the comic or the scatological subject-matter.

2. An Indestructible Genre

Farces have been in existence since the Greeks (ARISTOPHANES) and Romans (PLAUTUS), but the genre did not arise until the Middle Ages (approximately one thousand were composed, of which only about one hundred remain – examples are la *Farce de maître Pathelin, le Pâté et la Tarte, le Chaudronnier, le Cuvier*) and continued to the beginning of the seventeenth century (with playwrights such as TURLUPIN, GROS-GUILLAUME, TABARIN, GAULTIER-GARGUILLE). In MOLIÈRE, it merged with comedy of intrigue. Vaudeville playwrights such as LABICHE, FEYDEAU and COURTELINE, and absurd dramatists such as IONESCO and BECKETT, have perpetuated the tradition of nonsensical comedy in our days. Farce owes its longlasting popularity to its intense theatricality, its attention to stage mechanisms and elaborate body techniques for actors.

3. Triumph of the Body

A genre both scorned and admired, but "popular" in every sense of the word, farce enhances the corporal aspect of character and actor. Within the comic genre, critics make a distinction between farce and comedy of language and of intrigue, in which wit, the intellect and subtlety prevail. "Farce, on the other hand, makes people laugh, a hearty and popular laughter; to this end, it uses proven means that each varies according to his particular style: typical characters, grotesque masks, clowning, comical expressions, grimaces, lazzi, puns, heavily comical situations, gestures and words, all with a copiously scatological or obscene colouring. The emotions are elementary, the plot cobbled together; gaiety and movement provide the impetus"

(MAURON 1963, 34–36) Such rapidity and force give farce a subversive nature – subversion against moral or political authorities, sexual taboos, rationalism and the rules of tragedy. Through farce the spectators have their revenge on the constraints of reality and reason; liberating laughter and drives win over tragic inhibition and anxiety, in the guise of buffoonery and "poetic license."

See also: juggler, parade, grotesque, intermezzo, commedia dell'arte.

Further reading: Bakhtin 1984; Aubailly 1976; Tissier 1976; J.M. Davis 1978; Rey-Flaud 1984; Issacharoff 1990.

FEAR AND PITY

Fr.: *terreur et pitié*; Ger.: *Furcht und Mitleid*; Sp.: *terror y piedad.*

ARISTOTLE believed that it was by provoking pity and fear in the spectator that tragedy achieved the purging (*catharsis**) of passions. Compassion, and therefore identification, exist "when we presume that we too, or one of our own, could be victims, and that the danger is close to us" (ARISTOTLE, Rhetoric II:3). In this case, according to classical dogma, characters should be neither "completely good" nor "completely bad"; they must "fall into misfortune by some fault that makes them complain but not hate" (RACINE, Preface to *Andromaque*).

FESTIVAL

Fr.: *festival*; Ger.: *Festspiel*; Sp.: *festival.*

1. We sometimes forget that *festival* is the adjectival form of the feast. In Athens in the fifth century, at religious feasts celebrating, for instance, Dionysius, comedies, tragedies and dithyrambs were performed. These annual ceremonies marked a favoured time of rejoicement and encounter. From such traditional events, the festival has retained a certain solemnity of celebration, an exceptional and periodic nature that is sometimes rendered meaningless by the proliferation and trivialization of modern festivals.

2. A similar kind of celebration is found in Western theatre in the passion of Christ at Oberammergau as early as 1033. The SHAKESPEARE "cult" was already being celebrated in 1769 by the actor GARRICK; that of WAGNER was self-organized in Bayreuth beginning in 1876. Europe has its prestigious cultural manifestations – Stratford, Salzburg, May in Florence, Prague spring. In France, the Avignon Festival created in 1947 by Jean VILAR draws a large audience in July. It features an enormous number of groups and experimental endeavours seeking critical and public recognition. Parallel, off-Avignon networks spring up in the city, theoretically on the fringes of the official festival, where sketchy shows ("open theatre") are organized.

3. There are other such cultural manifestations in France – the Autumn Festival in Paris that launches the season with music, theatre and dance; the Festival of Nancy, which since 1963 has welcomed more experimental, less mainstream theatre companies; and a number of summer festivals such as the one at Aix-en-Provence, in which theatre, opera and music join forces.

The primary interest of these festivals lies in the opportunity they provide to the public to watch new shows, discover little-known trends and experiments, and meet "animators" and theatre-lovers.

4. This modern resurgence of the sacred festival reflects a deep-seated need for a time and place in which an audience of "celebrants" can meet periodically to take the pulse of theatre life, sometimes to compensate for a dearth of performances seen during the winter months and, more importantly, to feel that they belong to an intellectual and spiritual community while recovering a kind of cult and ritual in modern form. Thus, the festival tends to accentuate the almost schizophrenic break between work – throughout the year – and vacation time, in which art is consumed in large doses, by way of compensation and to build up a reserve.

FIABESCO

Fr.: *fiabesque*; Ger.: *Fiabesco*; Sp.: *fiabesco*.

From the Italian *fiaba*, or fable. These are fairytale comedies taken from folktales, notably in the work of Carlo GOZZI (*l'Amour des trois oranges*, la *Princesse Turandot*).

FICTION

(From the Latin *fingo*, I fashion or shape.)
Fr.: *fiction*; Ger.: *Fiktion*; Sp.: *ficción*.

Type of discourse that refers to people and things that exist only in the imagination of their author, then in that of the reader/ spectator. Fictional discourse is a "non-serious" discourse, an unverifiable assertion that does not effect any commitment, and is set forth as such by its author: "There is no textual property, syntactical or semantic, that will identify a text as a work of fiction. What makes it a work of fiction is, so to speak, the illocutionary stance that the author takes toward it ..." (SEARLE 1975, 325).

1. An Illocutory Act that does not Involve a Commitment

In theatre *discourse**, text and performance are only fictional, since they are wholly invented and contain assertions having no truth value. According to SEARLE (1975), it is a language that is not "serious," in that it does not commit the person offering it as a judgment or proposition in everyday language would. The authors (enunciators) of this discourse – playwright, director, actors – pretend to utter sentences having the status of truth, of carrying out illocutory acts (performatives) bearing witness to verbal action, when in fact these phrases do not tie them to any criterion of truth or logic. SEARLE states that "the author of a work of fiction pretends to perform a series of illocutory acts, normally of the representative type" (1975, 325).

The discourse takes on exactly the same sense as if it were uttered in real life; it just does not bind its author, thanks to a convention that authorizes it to lie with impunity. But, and here lies the specificity of theatre, the fiction is built up of real actors' bodies. (For a critique of SEARLE's position, see the entry under *pragmatics**.)

2. Production of Theatrical Interest

Theatrical fiction is relayed by at least two "simulators" – author and actor. Others, the directors and technicians, frequently come between them. In theatre, the pretence is presented directly, apparently unmediated by a narrator. This explains the distinct impression of the "direct" and the "real" felt by the audience (*reality-effects**, *illusion**). But fiction should not be metaphysically opposed to reality (as in SEARLE). There is an interpenetration of both elements, which are all the more inextricable because textual fiction and stage fiction are there intermingled as well.

See also: represented reality, theatrical reality, pragmatics, text and performance, sign, situation of enunciation.

Further reading: Urmson 1972; Iser 1975; Pratt 1978; Guarino 1982a; Jansen 1984; Pavis 1980b, 1985d; Hrushovski 1985.

FIGURABILITY

(Translation of Freud's *Darstellbarkeit*.)
Fr.: figurabilité; Ger.: *Darstellbarkeit*; Sp.: *figurabilidad*.

The "change undergone by the subject-matter of the dream in order to become a dream" (FREUD 1969, 2:335; Eng. 1976, 29). In theatre, this term refers to the way of representing visually what was not originally visual; by showing a certain scenery, portraying a character, suggesting a psychological state, the staging makes choices on the interpretation of the play and the emergence of visual *fantasies**. Like dream, the stage "writes" in images: "The plastic arts, painting and sculpture, in comparison with poetry, which can make use of the word, are in an analogous position [to that of the dream and the theatre]: here too the lack of expression is attributable to the nature of the material used by these two arts in their efforts to express something. In the past, even though painting had not yet discovered its own laws of expression, it endeavoured to remedy that handicap. The painter placed streamers before the mouths of the individuals represented, on which he wrote the words he despaired of making understood" (FREUD 1969, 2:311; Eng. 1976, 249).

The staging represents or *figures* the dramatic text. This does not mean that it "translates" or expresses it, but that it provides a mechanism of stage *enunciation** in which it takes on meaning for a particular audience.

See also: text and performance, interpretation, inner space, fantasy.

Further reading: Schlemmer 1978; Francastel 1965, 1970; Metz 1977; Lyotard 1971; Galifret-Granjon 1971.

FIGURATION

Fr: *figuration*; Ger.: *Darstellen*; Sp.: *figuración*.

See FIGURABILITY

FIGURE

(From the Latin *figura*, configuration or structure.)

Fr.: *figure*; Ger.: *Figur*; Sp.: *figura*.

1. In classical French, *figure* described a person's appearance and behaviour. A similar meaning is evident in the English expressions "to cut a sorry figure," "to cut a figure in society." The term is sometimes found in phrases such as "the figure of the hero" or "the figure of Mother Courage." It describes a type of character without specifying the particular traits that make up that character. It is a vague form that signifies more through its structural position than by its inherent nature (as in the German word *Figur*, which means both "silhouette," "outline" and "character"). As *role** and *type**, the figure groups together a number of fairly general distinctive traits and manifests itself as a silhouette, a still-imprecise mass that acquires its value mainly through its place among the protagonists as "the form of a tragic function" (BARTHES 1963, 10).

The figure gains in syntactical coherence (in the *actantial** configuration) what it loses in semantic precision; it becomes a structural notion that formalizes the relationships between the characters and the logic of actions.

2. Viewed as a figure of style (or of *rhetoric**), the whole stage always presents an abstract, *figurative** meaning beyond its immediate reality on which the *fiction** and the *illusion** are based.

See also: *caractère*, character, characterization, figurability, configuration.

Further reading: Genette 1966, 1969; Francastel 1967; Fontanier 1977; Lyotard 1971; Bergez, Géraud and Robrieux 1944.

FINAL RESOLUTION

Fr.: *apaisement final*; Ger.: *Auflösung des Konflikts*; Sp.: *solución final*.

In *classical dramaturgy**, the drama may end only once the *conflicts** have been resolved (*dénouement**) and the spectator no longer wonders how the action will end. The sense of resolution proceeds from a narrative structure that clearly indicates that the hero has come to the end of his journey, reinforced by the impression that all has returned to the comic or tragic order that governed the world before the play began. The final resolution is thus related to either comic relief or the transcendental justice of the *tragic** universe: "Eternal justice, because of the rational nature of its power, brings us relief, even when it has us witness the loss of the individuals involved in the struggle" (HEGEL 1832).

When the playwright refuses to offer a harmonious ending, he sometimes opts for a *deus ex machina** (which has been more or less prepared for) or concludes on the impossibility of resolving the conflict properly and harmoniously (e.g. BRECHT at the end of the *The Good Person of Sichuan*, 1940).

FLASHBACK

Fr.: *flash-back*; Ger.: *Flashback*, *Rückblende*; Sp.: *flash-back*.

1. The term, borrowed from film, describes a scene or *motif** in a play that refers us to an earlier episode. The corresponding figure in rhetoric is the analepsis. This narrative technique recalls the opening of a play *in medias res*, which then refers to the antecedents of the action.

Although a "cinematic" technique, it pre-existed cinema in the novel. It has enjoyed a certain amount of popularity in theatre since experiments with the *narration** or *story** such as MILLER's *Death of a Salesman*. One of the first occurrences was in A. SALACROU's *l'Inconnue d'Arras* in 1935.

2. In theatre, the flashback may be indicated by a narrator or by a change in lighting or dreamlike music, or by a framing motif. It can be used in many ways, but certain precautions are in order. First of all, the confines of the flashback should be specified to indicate the *modality** and degree of reality of the action. The flashback operates according to simple dichotomies: here/there, now/then, truth/fiction. It must always be clearly defined by the spectator – a flashback within a flashback or series of them would be disorienting. On the other hand, all these devices become legitimate once the dramaturgy gives up linearity and objectivity of presentation and begins to interweave different realities (dreams, fantasies, poetics of the narrative, as in RESNAIS/ROBBE-GRILLET's *l'Année dernière à Marienbad*).

See also: time, narrative analysis, fabula.

FLAW

Fr.: *faute*; Ger.: *Schuld, Mangel, Fehler*; Sp.: *yerro*.

See HAMARTIA

FOCALIZATION

Fr.: *focalisation*; Ger.: *Fokalisierung, Fokuslenkung*; Sp.: *focalización*.

Stress placed by the author on an action according to a particular point of view, in order to underscore its relevance. This essentially epic device (GENETTE 1972; BERGEZ, GÉRARD and ROBRIEUX 1994) also applies to theatre, as the playwright, theoretically absent from the dramatic universe, actually intervenes in the development of the conflicts and individualization of the main characters, subordinating the rest to the focalized elements. Focalization influences the characters' *points of view** and thus, indirectly, those of the playwright and spectators.

On stage, focalization is often achieved by directing a spot-light on a character or place to draw attention to them "in close-up." The close-up, a technique borrowed from film, is not necessarily done with lighting. It may be produced through the way the actors look at another actor or an element of the stage, or through a *foregrounding** effect. The enunciation of the staging is what brings out (or "frames") a particular moment or space in the performance.

FOOL

Fr.: *bouffon*; Ger.: *Narr*; Sp.: *bufón* (*gracioso*).

The fool appears in most comic dramaturgies. The "vertigo of the absolute comic" (MAURON 1963, 26), he is the orgiastic principle of overflowing vitality, the unextinguishable word, the revenge of the body on the spirit (for example, Falstaff, Feste, Touchstone, the Fool in *King Lear*), the carnivalesque derision of the small for the power of the great (Harlequin), popular culture as opposed to learned culture (the Spanish *pícaro*).

Like the madman, the fool lives on the fringes of society. His outsider status allows him to comment on events with impunity, like a parodic form of the chorus in tragedy. His words, like those of the madman, are both forbidden and heeded: "Since the Middle Ages, the fool has been one whose speech is not allowed to circulate like that of others: sometimes his words are considered to be null and void [...]; sometimes, however, he is vested with strange powers; the power to speak a hidden truth, to predict the future, to see in naïveté what all the wisdom of the others cannot perceive" (FOUCAULT 1971, 12–13).

His power of deconstruction attracts the powerful and the wise: the king has his jester, the young lover his valet, the noble gentleman of Spanish *comedia* his *gracioso*, Don Quijote his Sancho Panza, Faust his Mephisto, Vladimir his Estragon. The fool is out of place no matter where he goes. Considered common at court, coarse by decent people, cowardly by the soldier, gross by the aesthete, vulgar by the affected, he goes his merry way.

The fool is as puncture-proof as a Michelin tire. It is impossible to pin the blame on him or make him a scapegoat, because he is the very incarnation of physical vitality, a creature who refuses to pay for collective sins and never tries to pass himself off for someone else. Always masked, he serves as a foil for others and never speaks in his own name, never taking a serious role like the others except to his own detriment. Like Harlequin, the fool retains a memory of his childish and simian origins. This we are told by the very serious philosopher ADORNO: "Likeness to animals, however, is a human characteristic which is never entirely repressed by consciousness. There are instances of a sudden rediscovery of that likeness, instances which spell happiness for the individual. The language of little children and of animals seems to be the same. The similarity between man and ape is thrown into sharp relief by the animal-likeness of clowns. The constellation of animal, fool and clown constitutes one of the most basic dimensions of art" (1970, 182; Eng. 1984, 175).

See also: comic, *commedia dell'arte*, character, raisonneur.

Further reading: Bakhtin 1984; Ubersfeld 1974; Gobin 1978; Pavis 1986; *Bouffonneries*, especially no. 13–14.

FOOTLIGHTS

Fr.: *rampe*; Ger.: *Rampenlicht*; Sp.: *rampa*.

See FRAME, CURTAIN

FOREGROUNDING EFFECT

Fr.: *effet de mise en évidence*; Ger.: *Aktualisierungseffekt*; Sp. *efecto de actualización*.

Device baptized *aktualisace* by the Prague School theorists: "actualization," i.e. to bring a phenomenon to the fore.

Foregrounding of the aesthetic *device** (whether in language, on stage, or in acting) brings out the artistic structure of the message and frees the subject from an automatic perception of an object that is seen suddenly as unusual. The Brechtian *alienation-effect** is just one example, as foregrounding is a much broader phenomenon that applies to art in general.

In theatre, foregrounding may consist in the emphatic declamation of certain lines and words, the unnatural acting style of an actor who stresses the theatricality of a character, the highlighting of a principle or detail of the visual aspects of the stage (colour, place, lighting). One of the basic tasks of dramaturgical analysis is to bring out or downplay certain aspects and meanings of the play, to distribute the stress according to a very definite aesthetic and ideological plan. To foreground is simply to stage in a balanced way – too little foregrounding precludes a structured conception; too much trivializes and defuses the performance for lack of ambiguity.

See also: estrangement, coherence, theatrical effect.

Further reading: Knopf 1980; Matejka 1976; Matejka and Titunik 1976; Deák 1976.

FORM

Fr.: *forme*; Ger.: *Form*; Sp.: *forma*.

1. Form in Theatre

Form exists in theatrical performance at all levels: (1) at a tangible level in stage location, the sign systems used, acting and body language; (2) at an abstract level in the *dramaturgy** and *composition** of the fabula, the *segmentation** of the action in space and time, the elements of *discourse** (sound, words, rhythm, metrics, rhetoric).

2. Form and Content

Form comes about only through the formalization of a particular content and a precise signified. A theatrical form does not exist in itself; it has meaning only within an overall stage project, that is when it is associated with a content transmitted and yet to be transmitted. For instance, it is nonsense to say that there is such a thing as an epic form; one must specify how such a (fragmented, discontinuous, narrator-assumed) form relates to a particular content – whether it is Brechtian epic form intended to break with *identification** and the *illusion** of an organic development of the *fabula**, or whether it is *epic form of classical narrative* inserted as an objective narration in third person within the dramatic weave and used for reasons of verisimilitude (and not, as in BRECHT, as a critical break with illusion).

3. Hegelian Problematics of Form and Content

According to HEGEL, form and content are in a dialectical relationship in the work of art. They can be separated only for the purpose of theorizing – form is a content made manifest in a form. This is why, according to Hegelian aesthetics, "the only true works of art are those whose content and form prove to be completely identical" (HEGEL, quoted in SZONDI 1956, 10; 1983, 8; Eng. 1987, 4). Such an aesthetic values harmony between form and content and postulates content as anterior to form. One might say, for instance, that classical dramaturgy is the most appropriate form to "express" the essentialist and idealist conceptions of man. Changes in form, particularly the destruction of dramatic form to favour epic elements, are viewed as decadent and as a deviation from the canonic form of drama (*epic treatment of drama**). As demonstrated by SZONDI (1956), this is to misjudge the new knowledge of man and the evolution of society, to misjudge the novelty of ideological contents that can no longer use the closed classical form without doing it violence, emptying it of its content and introducing epic critical elements that destroy the overly-classical dramaturgy of the well-made play. Thus, it was the emergence of new contents (man's isolation and alienation, the impossibility of individual conflict) that exploded dramatic form at the end of the nineteenth century and made it necessary to use epic *devices**.

4. Levels of Form

Theatre does not use forms created *ex nihilo* but borrows them from social structures: "Painting, art and theatre in all their forms – and I would prefer the term spectacle – visualize for a period of time not only the literary terms and legends but the structures of society. It is not form that creates thought and expression, but thought, as an expression of the common social content of an era, that creates form" (FRANCASTEL 1965, 237–238).

Any unit, no matter how *minimal**, will have meaning in a semiological analysis only if one is able to draw an analogy between the unit and an overall aesthetic and ideological project (being the production of meaning and its inner workings within the performance as well as the spectator).

See also: semiology, formalism, closed form, open form, represented reality, dramaturgy.

Further reading: Langer 1953; Rousset 1962; Heffner 1965; Lukács 1963, 1964; Klotz 1969; Todorov 1965; Calderwood 1968; Fowler 1982; Tynianov 1969; Erlich 1969; Witkiewicz 1970; Kirby 1987.

FORMALISM

Fr.: *formalisme;* Ger.: *Formalismus;* Sp.: *formalismo.*

1. Formalism was originally a method of literary criticism developed by the Russian Formalists between 1915 and 1930. They examined the formal aspects of the work of art, highlighting its techniques and devices (composition, images, rhetoric, metrics, estrangement, etc.). Biographical, psychological, sociological and ideological factors are not wholly ruled out, but are subordinate to formal structure.

2. The debate surrounding *realism** and formalism sprang up in the thirties, between

LUKACS and BRECHT, in relation to the question of socialist realism. In this context, the term formalist quickly became an insult used to write off one's adversaries on the grounds of a lack of social commitment and complacency with respect to aesthetic experimentation.

Formalism exists whenever form is totally separate from social function. According to BRECHT, for example, "any formal element that prevents us from grasping social causality ought to disappear; any formal element that helps us understand social causality ought to be used" (1967, 19:291).

Formal experimentation is essential in theatre if one considers that a production always throws a new light on the text and that nothing is carved in stone as to a play's meaning and staging potential. Today we are far from the debate on the entitlement of forms, which are the only place where an artist can be true to himself.

See also: figurability, function, theatricality, dramaturgy, aestheticism, history, represented reality, structure.

Further reading: Mukarovský 1934, 1941; Jakobson 1963, 1977; Shklovsky 1965; Todorov 1965; Brecht 1967, 19:286, 382; Tynianov 1969; Gisselbrecht 1971; Jameson 1972; Bennet 1979; Frow 1986; M. Kirby 1987.

FORMALIZATION

Fr.: *formalisation;* Ger.: *Formalisierung;* Sp.: *formalización.*

See DESCRIPTION, NOTATION.

FORMS OF THEATRE

Fr.: *formes théâtrales;* Ger.: *Theaterformen;* Sp.: *formas teatrales.*

This term is often used today, probably in an attempt to replace the over-used term *genre** and to distinguish between types of plays and performances that are more specific than the major genres (*tragedy**, *comedy**, *drama**). The current mixing of genres (and even the lack of interest in a typology of forms and clear separation of the various types of performance) greatly facilitates the use of the term. *Form* indicates immediately the eminently mobile and changeable aspect of the types of performance, based on new circumstances and goals that make it impossible to come up with a canonical, fixed definition of *genre**. One may speak of theatrical forms in reference to the most heterogeneous things: harlequinade, ballet, interlude, melodrama, parody, tragedy, and so on. The term is also used for the components of dramatic structure or performance (dialogue, monologue, prologue, montage, blocking).

FOURTH WALL

Fr.: *quatrième mur;* Ger.: *vierte Wand;* Sp.: *cuarta pared.*

Imaginary wall separating stage from audience. In *illusionist** (or *naturalistic**) theatre, the spectators watch an action that is supposed to be unfolding independently of them, behind a transparent barrier. They are invited, as voyeurs, to observe the actors, who behave as if they were protected by a fourth wall and the audience were not there. (ANTOINE actually placed furniture against the fourth wall and had his actors play with their backs to the audience.) In *l'Impromptu de Versailles*, MOLIERE wondered "whether this invisible fourth wall does not conceal a crowd observing us," and DIDEROT recognized the reality of it: "Whether you are composing or acting, think of the spectator as if he did not exist. Imagine, at the edge of the stage, a great wall that separates you from the stalls; act as though the curtain would never rise" (*De la poésie dramatique*, 1758, XI:66). Realism and naturalism stressed the requirement that the stage be separated from the audience, while contemporary theatre is fond of breaking the illusion, *(re)theatricalizing** the stage, or forcing the audience to *participate**. A more dialectical attitude would seem to be in order; there is in fact a boundary between stage and audience, but also constant crossings in both directions, and it is within this *denial** that theatre exists.

See also: epic and dramatic, space, illusion.

Further reading: Zola 1881; Antoine 1903; Deldime 1990.

FRAME

Fr.: *cadre;* Ger.: *Rahmen;* Sp.: *marco.*

The frame or framework of the theatre performance is not only the type of stage or space in which the play is performed. More broadly, it also refers to the set of the spectators' experiences and *expectations**, the contextualization of the fiction represented. *Frame* is to be taken both literally (as a "boxing-in" of the *performance*) and abstractly (as a contextualization and foregrounding of the action).

1. Stage Frame

The theatre event (acting, "spatialization" of the text, arrangement of the house, etc.), is presented to the audience in a manner appropriate to each production. From the proscenium-arch theatre, in which nothing is presumed to leave the picture frame of the stage conceived as a living tableau, to fragmented stage space, there have been many attempts to redefine the frame of action. Obviously, it is crucial that we know how the stage reality is being presented to the spectator. The places where the actors enter and exit mark the boundary between the stage and the outside, hence the real and symbolic importance of the door in theatre. From the Racinian open space of the antechamber that makes the transition between the outside and the tragic place, to the actual massive door of the naturalists, the door links the stage and the outside world as it favours or prevents the appearance of that world on stage (*teichoscopy**).

2. Frame of the Action

Text and performance situate the action more or less concretely by explaining or suggesting it (*milieu**). The stage design may enclose the actors in a particular space or let them generate the space using acting conventions and movements.

3. Framing

The spectator's involvement with what he sees and critical distance toward the stage may vary considerably. By changing the distance to the stage (*identification** or *distance**) and by deciding from what angle the *performance* should be viewed, the mise-en-scène constantly modifies the framing. As in the zoom technique in film, the action is brought closer or moved farther away and details are hidden or foregrounded.

Playwrights sometime use the same motif at the beginning and the end of a play, giving the impression of a circle closing in on itself. (CHEKHOV, PIRANDELLO, all forms of the *play within a play**). In other cases of *mise-en-abyme**, we can distinguish a framing action that presents a framed action within itself (for instance, in embedded narrative). Any performance consists of framing a part of the world for a certain length of time, while declaring the tableau meaningful and artificial (fictional). Everything within the frame appears as a model sign offered to the spectator for deciphering.

The staging frames an event by displaying certain signs and excluding others. This process of *semiotization** defines the line between the visible and the hidden, sense and nonsense.

4. Fiction and Function of the Frame

The modern work of art is often characterized by imprecise boundaries. It is sometimes difficult to establish, for instance, exactly where a modern sculpture or *installation** begins and ends in its display environment. Similarly, some productions (influenced by Pirandello) sow confusion and tend to erase the boundaries between stage and the real world. Theatre then "surrounds itself," as a "precaution," with ever-smaller frames through which we enter, step by step, into the heart of the fiction. Among these frames are the neighbourhood where the theatre is located, the immediate surroundings of the theatre, the entrance hall with its exhibition of documents and its atmosphere, an auditorium arranged like scenery that is part of the play, a program introducing the world represented, "narrator" characters who announce the beginning of the play, characters who introduce themselves, etc. All of these frames introduce the story to be told, serving as a transition between the outside world and the reported play, modalizing and filtering the fictional material to render it believable and to gradually introduce the audience to the situation.

5. Breaking the Frame

In wishing to give the impression that there is no division between art and life, contemporary art has often endeavoured to invent forms in which the frame is eliminated: *Six Characters in Search of an Author*, by PIRANDELLO, *Offending the Audience* by P. HANDKE, *The Price of Revolt on the Black Market* by D. DIMITRIADIS, *Paradise Now* by the Living Theatre, *happenings**, street theatre, etc.

See also: event, narrative, perspective, play within a play, closure, segmentation.

Further reading: Goffman 1959, 1974; Uspensky 1972; Bougnoux 1982; Swiontek 1990.

FUNCTION

Fr.: *fonction*; Ger.: *Funktion*; Sp.: *función*.

The dramatic function of a character consists in all of that character's actions considered from the point of view of his role in the development of the plot.

1. Narrative Function

The narrative function is drawn from V. PROPP's functionalist narrative theory, which defines this notion as "the act of a character defined from the point of view of its significance for the course of the action" (1968, 21). According to this theory, the dramatic text and the performance (viewed as a narrative structure) can be broken down into a finite number of *motifs** and *actants**, which are interconnected by the *actantial** system (*narrative analysis**).

PROPP distinguished between thirty-one functions or "spheres of action" with seven *actants**: hero, false hero, villain, donor, helper, princess, dispatcher. BARTHES (1966a) speaks of *cardinal functions*, which are "the true pivots of the narrative," and of catalysts which are "subsidiary notations." For a function to be cardinal, the action to which it refers must open up an alternative that is of consequence to the rest of the story. Certain series of functions, according to PROPP, form obligatory sequences or, according to BRÉMOND (1973), triads (eventuality/act/completion).

2. Dramatic Function

E. SOURIAU (1950) applied this functional view of actions to Western dramaturgy in distinguishing six functions and defining "mathematically" (in spirit if not in reality) the 210,141 *dramatic situations** generated by the dramatic functions. The situations designate both the groups of actions actually observable in a play or a dramaturgy and the models that could theoretically be realized.

The permutability of the actants (in the role of subject, for example) entails variations in point of view within the play: any character or function can organize the other functions-characters according to its own *point of view**.

3. Function of Communication

JAKOBSON's model of the six functions of communication ("Linguistics and Poetics," *Style in Language*, T.A. Sebeok, ed., New York, 1960) has been applied to theatre on occasion. It could be assumed that, like poetic language, *theatre language* (*mutatis mutandis*) represents a particular use of the six-function scheme. Still, representation should not be reduced to a mechanical application of these six functions of communication, since a staging is not intended to communicate a message clearly formulated in advance.

Further reading: Polti 1981; Slawinska 1959; Ingarden 1971; Jansen 1973; Marin 1985.

G

GAG

Fr.: *gag*; Ger.: *Gag*; Sp.: *gag*.

In film, a gag is a comical effect or *sketch** that appears to be improvised or is produced visually using objects and unusual situations. It is, "in studio slang, an irresistible stroke of inspiration that makes a comic film rebound" (CENDRARS in *l'Homme foudroyé*). In film, as in theatre, the comic actor may invent stage business or *lazzi** that contradict the speech and upset the normal perception of reality.

Further reading: Bergson 1940; F. Mars 1964; Freud 1969, vol. 4; Eng. 1985, vol. 6 (*Jokes and their Relation to the Unconscious*); Collet et al., 1977.

GAZE

Fr.: *regard*; Ger.: *Blick*; Sp.: *mirada*.

1. Psychology of the Gaze

The actor's gaze is an inexhaustible source of information, not only for its psychological characterization and the relationships it reveals with the other actors, but also for its structuring of space, enunciation of the text and production of meaning.

*Kinesics** and *proxemics** analyze the face and spatial relations, but the study of the gaze has yet to make much progress in either psychology or in theatre semiology.

Psychologists know that the direction and movement of the gaze provide invaluable information on the interaction between two persons, and that an exchange of glances is the most immediate and quickest of all exchanges. The gaze structures the meeting of two faces and regulates the conversation, particularly the alternation of speakers.

2. The Gaze of Mime and Actor

Most discoveries in psychology and neurolinguistics are directly applicable to the study of the actor's gaze. A very declamatory and rhetorical aesthetical approach, such as that of the eighteenth century treatises on eloquence and acting, even uses an entire vocabulary of the gaze that sets up correspondences between facial expressions and particular situations or feelings (ENGEL, 1979).

On stage, the gaze connects words to situations (*deictic** function), anchors the discourse to an element of the stage, and acts as a relay system for words and verbal and gestural interaction. The gaze introduces a duration into space thanks to the possibility of "sweeping," of connecting disperse spatial elements, of telling a story with nothing but glances. The actor's gaze attracts the spectator's attention (and gaze) either frontally and directly (as if the spectator identified with the actor) or laterally and indirectly, when we see one actor look at another. The actor "takes us by the eyes," in a way, somewhat as in the movies, to force us to watch the rest of the scene through his eyes. In this way, glance by glance, we penetrate the fictional universe of the stage.

Mimes in particular have developed this kind of communication. A focused gaze indicates that the mime is seeing and perceiving the world, is concentrated and present; an unfocused gaze lets him see without seeing. An upward gaze connotes reflection and high ideas; a downward one, details and the beginnings of a gesture. Gazing ahead into space means the realization of a concrete project. Curiously, this aesthetic system matches up with the results of neurolinguistic research, which analyzes eye movement and gaze direction to identify a limited number of recurring mental attitudes.

If the eyes are "windows onto the soul," the gaze is the underpinning of the body, movement and the entire stage *enunciation**, and is quite often used to organize theatre performance. In the words of JAQUES-DALCROZE: "The mastery of bodily movement is nothing but empty virtuosity if the movements are not given meaning by the expression and gaze. A single gesture can express ten different emotions depending on the expression in the eyes. Special training should therefore be given on the relationship between body movements and the direction of the gaze" (1965, 108).

GENRE

Fr.: *genre*; Ger.: *Genre, Dramengattung*; Sp.: *género*.

1. A Confusion of Terminology

Such expressions as "dramatic or theatrical genre," "comic and tragic genres," or "comedy of manners genre," are often heard. Such excessive usage of the term dilutes any exact meaning and ruins attempts at classifying literary and theatrical forms.

Literary theory, unlike criticism, is not confined to a study of existing works. It goes beyond the narrow framework of a description of individual works to establish a typology of *forms**, of literary *categories**, of types of discourse, thus going back to the old question of a *poetics* of genre. It is no longer content to classify historical works completed, but prefers to reflect on how to establish a typology of discourse, inferring those types from a general theory of the linguistic and literary fact. Thus, the determination of genre is no longer a matter of more or less subtle and consistent classification, but rather the key to an understanding of any text in relation to a set of conventions and norms that define each genre precisely. Any text is both a concretization and a deviation from the genre. As for any ideal model of a literary form, an examination of its conformity with and deviation from the model would clarify the originality of the work and how it functions.

2. Historical Approach and Structural System

There are two possible approaches to genre, depending on whether one considers genre as a historical form or a category of discourse. The distinction is sometimes explained by the genre/mode opposition: "Genres are strictly literary categories; modes are categories that depend on linguistics or, more precisely, on an anthropology of verbal expression" (GENETTE 1977, 418).

A. The historical approach identifies the various theatrical forms in literary evolution and attempts to discover criteria of similarity or difference between the genres.

B. The structural approach draws up a universal typology of discourse based on a theory that takes into account all possible variants, then attempting to match actually occurring genres with those categories, while allowing for genres that have not yet been invented but are theoretically imaginable.

In theatre, the question is whether it constitutes by itself a genre that is distinguished from epic poetry (the novel) and lyrical poetry. The division into three appears to date back to *The Republic* (III, 392), in which PLATO sets out a distinction based on the way in which past, present and future events are transmitted to the public; whether by exposition alone (dithyramb), by imitation (tragedy and comedy), or by both methods at once (epic poetry). The classification is based on the way reality is represented, on a semantic criterion of "imitation" of reality and on whether the poet intervenes directly or indirectly in the exposition of the facts. Theatre is the most "objective" genre, in which the characters appear to speak for themselves without the author speaking directly (though, exceptionally, he does so in the form of the spokesman, messenger, chorus, prologue, epilogue or stage directions).

3. Theatre within a Theory of Genres
Within the dramatic genre, it is quite difficult to draw boundaries based on discursive criteria. The weight of history and the norms imposed by poetics is considerable, and types are almost always defined within the comedy/tragedy opposition in relation to content and techniques of composition – hence the various types of comedy and tragedy that expand their possibilities without questioning the basic opposition between comedy and tragedy. This is why an intermediate genre such as tragicomedy or *drame* is so difficult to establish; sometimes it is only a tragedy that ends optimistically (CORNEILLE), sometimes a comedy with nothing comical about it. When domestic bourgeois tragedy was introduced by DIDEROT, the new genre, "lacking a ridiculous aspect of the character to laugh about, or a danger eliciting shivers" (*Troisième Entretien avec Dorval*), became a rather sinister form without much aesthetic value, having lost all the vitality of the two basic aesthetic categories of the tragic and the comic. Romantic drama and existentialist or absurd drama succeeded in overcoming this bourgeois middle-of-the-road approach only at the price of the excesses and vulgarities of the grotesque or the marvellous. As for contemporary writing for the theatre, it uses many forms, a mix of criteria and materials (all the visual arts, the performing arts and music), so that the categories inherited from previous eras are of little use in capturing their originality. Only a typology of discourse and of modes of functioning can provide a clear description.

Accordingly, we may wonder why we should determine the genre of theatre texts and performances. In addition to the norm established by poetics, genre consists of a set of codifications that provide information about the reality the text is supposed to represent, which informs the verisimilitude of the action. The genre – and, for the reader/spectator, the choice of reading the text according to the rules of a particular genre – gives an immediate indication about the reality represented, provides a grid for reading, establishes a contract between the text and its reader. Upon determining the genre of the text, the spectator sets up a series of expectations, of obligatory figures that codify and simplify reality, so that the author does not need to reiterate the rules of the game and the genre that are supposed to be known to everyone, and can meet, or short-circuit, those expectations by distinguishing the text from the canonical model.

To identify the genre involves reading the text while comparing it with other texts, particularly the social and ideological norms which for a given time and audience constitute the typical model of verisimilitude and ideology. Thus, the theory of genres examines much more than the internal laws governing plays or performances; it looks at how they are inscribed in the other kinds of texts and the social text, which is a fundamental reference to any kind of literature.

Further reading: Bray 1927; Staiger 1946; Frye 1957; Bentley 1964; Ruttkowski 1968; Genette 1969, 1977; Lockemann 1973; Todorov 1976; R. Grimm 1971; Fowler 1982.

GESAMTKUNSTWERK

Fr.: *Gesamtkunstwerk*, Ger.: *Gesamtkunstwerk*; Sp.: *Gesamtkunstwerk, obra total.*

A term introduced by R. WAGNER (1813–1883) around 1850, meaning, literally, "global (or whole) work of art," sometimes translated as *total theatre**. The aesthetics of Wagnerian opera aims for a work that is a synthesis of music, literature, painting, sculpture, architecture, stage design and other elements. That aim is itself symptomatic of the Symbolist movement and of a fundamental conception of theatre and mise-en-scène.

1. The Symbolist Ideal

For symbolism, the work of art, particularly in theatre, forms a meaningful, autonomous whole that is sufficient unto itself and does not imitate reality. The stage is a coherent scaled-down model, a kind of cybernetic (or semiological) system that incorporates all of the stage materials in a significant project. Baudelairean correspondences govern the various stage arts, forests of *symbols** bring together what would appear to be heterogeneous. For WAGNER, for instance, the word, or masculine element, inseminates the music or feminine element; mind and affections, sight and hearing are connected by synaesthesia. "Dance, music and poetry are three sisters born with the world. As soon as their rounds were formed, the conditions existed for art to appear. They are, by their very nature, inseparable" (WAGNER). This synthetic work of art postulates a harmony (already in existence or yet to be established) among the components of the performance, and even an equivalence between theatre and life, a kind of aesthetic and philosophical cult represented in MALLARMÉ's *Livre à venir*: "I believe that literature, taken back to its source, which is the art of science, will provide us with a theatre whose performances shall be the true modern cult; a book, an explanation of man sufficient for our most beautiful dreams [...] This work exists, everyone has tried it without realizing it; there is neither genius nor clown who has not discovered one of its features without being aware of it."

2. Staging: Merging or Separation of the Arts?

The *Gesamtkunstwerk* theory poses the problem of the *specificity** of theatre. Is it a hybrid, "impure" art made up of odds and ends (the various stage systems)? Or is it a harmonious whole in which everything that appears on stage passes through a kind of melting pot, as WAGNER seems to suggest?

A. AN IMPOSSIBLE FUSION

Even when such a fusion is the director's ultimate aim, total theatre cannot effect it, at least not in the non-metaphorical or non-mystical sense of the word. WAGNER himself, who wished for the transitions between tableaux to take place in a kind of dreamlike dissolve, was forced to give up on his attempt to achieve a sufficiently unrealistic symbolist staging. He gave in to the realistic representation of the stage designers, and the perfect union remained a dead letter.

For "Aristotelian" directors (i.e. those who consider the *fabula* and narrativity as the backbone of any play), action is a unifying factor. HONZL (1940) sees action as the electric current that passes through actors, costumes, scenery, music and text. The number and frequency of the materials matter little as long as the current is flowing toward a goal, thus generating the action.

B. LINKING SYSTEMS

If there is an effect of fusion, it will occur not in the production of signs, but in their reception by the spectator. By multiplying the sources of the performing arts and synchronizing their effect on the audience, an effect of fusion can be produced provided the spectator is inundated with converging impressions that appear to shift easily from one to the other. Here lies the paradox of the *Gesamtkunstwerk*: uniting the stage arts in a *unique* experience for the spectator *(Erlebnis)* while conserving the specific power of each. Rather than effecting a fusion, in which each element would lose its own qualities, the *Gesamtkunstwerk* integrates each art into a transcendental whole, i.e. into musical drama for WAGNER. Rather than undertaking a mythical search for a production with equal elements, it is more appropriate to distinguish various types of *Gesamtkunstwerk* according to the element that serves as foundation for the remaining arts. In WAGNER, of course, it is music that plays this role. In CLAUDEL (1983) and M. REINHARDT (1963), it is the poetic text. For the *Bauhaus*, it is architecture on which all the other arts rest. Similarly, by structuring the performance *codes**, one can determine the basic system that underlies the other codes, according to the spectacle or particular parts of it. This method precludes having to opt metaphysically for a hierarchy and specificity of the various arts.

C. THE ANTI-GESAMTKUNSTWERK OR MUTUAL ALIENATION OF SYSTEMS

In addition to the impossible fusion of systems, there is, theoretically, a third possibility: to show the different performing arts by contrasting them with one another and refusing to add them up to an integrated whole. This is the technique of *alienation** (which need not be Brechtian). The separateness of techniques is stressed, with music contradicting text, gesture betraying atmosphere or action. Each signifying system not only retains its autonomy but alienates the others: "So let us invite all the sister arts of the drama, not in order to create an 'integrated work of art' in which they all offer themselves up and are lost, but so that together with the drama they may further the common task in their different ways; and their relations with one another consist in this: that they lead to mutual alienation" (BRECHT, *A Short Organum for the Theatre*, sect. 74).

See also: staging, semiology.

Further reading: Wagner 1850, 1852; Baudelaire 1861, in 1951; Appia 1895, 1954; Craig 1905; Kesting 1965; Szeemann 1983.

GESTUALITY

Fr.: *gestualité*; Ger.: *Gestik*; Sp.: *gestualidad*.

A neologism introduced by studies in semiotics, probably created in the mould of literature/literarity, theatre/theatricality, and used to designate the properties specific to *gesture**, particularly those which make gestures similar and dissimilar to other communication systems.

Gestuality can be distinguished from individualized gesture in that it constitutes a more or less coherent system of corporal "ways of being," while gestures are single bodily actions.

Further reading: *Langages*, 1968; Stern 1973; *Versus*, 1979, no. 22; Pavis 1981a, 1996a.

GESTURAL SPACE

Fr.: *espace ludique (gestuel)*; Ger.: *gestischer Raum*; Sp.: *espacio lúdico (gestual)*.

This is the space created by the actors' movements. With their actions, their proximity to or distance from each other, their free movements or restriction to a minimal playing space, the actors define the exact limits of their individual and collective territories. Space is organized around them as around a pivot that changes position as required by the action.

This type of space is constructed on the basis of the acting. It is in perpetual motion, its boundaries expandable and unpredictable, while the stage space, although it may appear to be vast, is in fact limited by the structure of the building. Even more than stage space, gestural space lends itself to all kinds of conventions and manipulations – it is not a realistic space but a stage tool available to actor and director. Any performance is, in this sense, theatre with a dual movement of expansion and condensation: the stage space provides the general framework and tends to encompass and overshadow everything that appears upon it. Gestural space, on the other hand, dilates and fills the surrounding space, at least when it is used properly. The harmony of its contradictory spatial movements gives the impression of an acting style that makes the best possible use of the space in the house. Gestural space is also the way in which the actor's body behaves in space, whether it is drawn upward or downward, curled up or stretched out, expanding or folding in on itself.

See also: gesture, gestus, body.

GESTURAL THEATRE

Fr.: *théâtre gestuel*; Ger.: *gestisches Theater*; Sp.: *teatro gestual*.

A form of theatre that gives preference to gesture and body expression, without necessarily excluding the use of words, music and all possible scenic resources. This genre tends to avoid not only theatre tied to written texts but also *mime**, often enslaved to the codified and narrative language of classical *pantomime** à la Marcel Marceau; it makes the actor's *body** the origin of performance and even of speech, in that *rhythm**, phrasing and *voice** are seen as expressive gestures.

Further reading: Lecoq 1987.

GESTURE

(From the Latin *gestus*, attitude, body movement.)

Fr.: *geste;* Ger.: *Gebärde, Geste;* Sp.: *gesto.*

Movement of the *body**, most often voluntary and controlled by the actor, meant to produce a meaning that may or may not be dependent on the spoken text.

1. Status of Gesture in Theatre

A. GESTURE AS EXPRESSION

Every period has its own conception of gesture in theatre, which in turn influences acting and performance styles. The classical conception, which still largely prevails today, considers gesture a medium of *expression** and externalization of a pre-existing psychic content (emotion, reaction, meaning) that the body is intended to communicate to others. CAHUSAC's definition in the *Encyclopédie* is revealing of this current of thought; gesture is "an external movement of body and face, one of the first expressions of feeling given to man by nature [...] In order to speak about gesture in a useful manner for the arts, it must be considered from its various points of view. No matter how it is viewed, however, it must always be seen as expression: there lies its original function, and it is through this attribute, granted by the laws of nature, that it embellishes art, of which it is all and with which it unites, to become a major part of it." The expressive nature of gesture makes it particularly useful to the actor, who has no other resources than those of his body to convey his moods. "There are whole scenes in which it comes infinitely more naturally to the characters to move than to speak" (DIDEROT, *De la poésie dramatique*, 1758). There is a whole "primitive" psychology that sets up a series of equivalents between emotions and their gestural visual form. In this case, gesture acts as intermediary between interiority (consciousness) and exteriority (physical being). Again, this is the classical view of gesture in life as in theatre: "If gestures are the external, visible signs of our bodies, by which we know the internal manifestations of our souls, it follows that one may consider them in a dual perspective: first, as changes which are visible by themselves; and second, as means that indicate the inner operations of the soul" (ENGEL 1979, 62–63).

B. GESTURE AS PRODUCTION

In a reaction against that expressionist doctrine of gesture, there is a tendency at present to define gestuality as production rather than communication of a pre-existing meaning. Going beyond the dualism of impression/expression, this monist conception considers the actor's gestures (at least in an experimental form of acting and improvisation) as a production of signs and not merely as the communication of feelings "translated into gesture." For example, GROTOWSKI refuses to separate thought from bodily activity, intention from realization, idea from illustration. Gesture is for him the object of investigation, of a production/deciphering of ideograms: "New ideograms must constantly be sought and their composition appears immediate and spontaneous. The starting point for such gesticulatory forms is the stimulation of one's own imagination and the discovery in oneself of primitive human reactions. The final result is a living form possessing its own logic" (GROTOWSKI 1968, 142). Gesture in theatre, according to such a theory, is both source and goal of the actor's work. It cannot be described in terms of feelings, or even significant position-poses (MEYERHOLD). For GROTOWSKI, the image of the hieroglyph is synonymous with the untranslatable *iconic* sign that is as much symbolized object as symbol. For other directors, the "hieroglyphic" gesture is decipherable: "Every movement is a hieroglyph with its own peculiar meaning. The theatre should employ only those movements which are immediately decipherable; everything else is superfluous." (MEYERHOLD, 1969, 200).

C. GESTURE AS INNER BODY IMAGE OR EXTERNAL SYSTEM

One of the main difficulties in studying gesture in theatre is determining both its productive source and adequate description. A description obliges us to formalize certain key positions of gesture, and therefore to break it down into static moments and reduce it to a few oppositions (tension/relaxation, speed/slowness, discontinous/fluid, etc.). But such a description, besides being dependent on a verbal descriptive metalanguage that imposes its own segmentation, remains (like any description) external to the object and does not specify its relationship with speech or with the performance style; it is often poorly integrated into an overall meaningful dramaturgical and stage project.

As to capturing gesture through body image and body scheme, this depends on the actor or dancer's representations of the space in which he or she moves. This representation of the gestural figurative is, so far, perceptible only intuitively (GALIFRET-GRANJON 1971).

2. Toward a Typology and Code of Gesture

A. TYPOLOGY

1. No typology of gesture can be truly satisfactory, neither for gesture in reality nor in theatre. The following distinctions are usually made:

- innate gestures linked to an attitude or movement of the body;
- aesthetic gestures elaborated to produce a work of art (dance, pantomime, theatre, etc.);
- conventional gestures, which express a message understood by both sender and receiver.

2. Another distinction contrasts *imitative* with *original gesture*. The imitative gesture is that of the actor incarnating a character in a realistic or naturalistic manner by reconstructing his behaviour and gestural "tics" (in fact, stylization and characterization are inevitable and even condition this gestural reality-effect). On the other hand, gesture may refuse imitation, repetition and discursive rationalization. It manifests itself as a hieroglyph to be deciphered. "The actor," says GROTOWSKI, should not use his organism to illustrate 'a movement of the soul,' he should accomplish this movement with his organism" (1968, 123). The aim is to discover body ideograms or, as in ARTAUD, "a new physical language based on signs rather than words" (1964b, 81; 1958, 38).

3. Any typology of gesture should be reexamined in relation to the stage. Everything in the actor's gestural work is significant, nothing left to chance; everything takes on the value of a sign so that the gestures, no matter what category they belong to, enter into the aesthetic category. Inversely, however, the actor's body can never be totally reduced to a set of signs; it resists *semiotization**, as if gesture in theatre always retained the imprint of the person having produced it.

B. GESTURAL CODE

Rather than breaking down gestural movement into recurrent units (kinemes and allokinemes in BIRDWHISTELL), we will indicate some features of a gestural code (for a detailed discussion, see PAVIS 1981a):

- tension/relaxation of gesture;
- physical and temporal concentration of several gestures (cf. MEYERHOLD'S ideograms);
- perception of the aim and orientation of the sequence of gestures;
- aesthetic process of stylization, exaggeration, purification and distantiation of gesture;
- establishment of link between word and gesture (accompaniment , complementarity, substitution).

3. Problems with a Formalization of Gesture

Gestures occur in a continuum throughout the performance, which makes a *segmentation** into gestural units very difficult. The absence of movement is not sufficient criterion to define the beginning or end of the gesture; nor are there truly recurring elements in the "gestural phrase" such as subject, object, verb.

Any verbal description of an actor's gesture misses much of its specific qualities of movement and attitude; also, it segments the body according to linguistic semantic units, whereas it should in fact be examined according to its own units or laws, if they exist. The point is to find out what ideological function determines the need for a *notation** and grid applied to the study of movement. Is it to establish and codify gesture by reassuring actor and observer? Should we not accompany the external description with an intuitive view of the actor's body image and look behind gesture for the drives whose articulation at the border of the psychic and the physical were established by FREUD?

The study of gesture, if it is to go beyond a purely aesthetic commentary and discover the deeper dimensions of gesture, has a long road ahead of it.

Further reading: Bühler 1934; Laban 1960; Artaud 1958; K. Scherer 1970; Birdwhistell 1973; Bouissac 1973; Leroi-Gourhan 1974; Cosnier 1977; Hanna 1979, 1983; Krysinski 1981; Sarrazac et al. 1981; Marin 1985; Lecoq 1987, 1996; Pavis and Villeneuve 1993.

GESTUS

Fr.: *gestus;* Ger.: *Gestus;* Sp.: *gestus.*

1. Gesture and Gestus

The term comes from the Latin *gestus* (gesture), a form that persisted in German until the eighteenth century. LESSING, for example, speaks of "individualizing gestuses" (i.e. characteristics) and the "gestus of fatherly warning." As used here, the form means a *characteristic way* of using one's *body**, and has already been coloured by the social connotation of an *attitude* toward others, a concept taken up by BRECHT in his theory of gestus (translated by Willet as "gest"). MEYERHOLD identifies "pose positions" (*rakurz*) that indicate a character's fixed and fundamental position. One of the goals of his *biomechanical** exercises is to seek out these fixed attitudes, which are veritable "switch-blades" of gestural movement (*raccourci**).

2. Brechtian Gestus

A distinction must be made between gestus and individual gestures such as scratching oneself or sneezing. "The realm of attitudes adopted by the characters towards one another is what we call the realm of gest. Physical attitude, tone of voice and facial expression are all determined by a social gest: the characters are cursing, flattering, instructing one another, and so on." (*A Short Organum for the Theatre*, sect. 61) Gestus consists in a simple movement by one person when faced with another, in a particular social or corporal kind of behaviour. Any stage action presupposes a certain attitude on the part of the protagonists toward each other and within the social universe – the *social gestus*. The *basic gestus* of a play is the kind of basic relationship that governs social behaviour (servility, equality, violence, trickery). Gestus is situated between action and character type (an Aristotelian opposition in any theatre). As action, it shows the character engaged in a social *praxis*; as character type, it represents a group of traits peculiar to an individual. Gestus is perceptible both in the actor's body behaviour and in his speech. A text or a piece of music is indicative of a certain gestus when it incorporates a *rhythm** appropriate to the sense of what it is speaking of (e.g. the jerky, syncopated *gestus* of Brechtian song to give the impression of a discontinuous, unharmonious world). It is better for an actor to use gesture rather than word (*"non verbis, sed gestibus"*).

This notion deserves to be reconsidered in the light of theories of poetic language, of the *iconicity** of theatrical discourse and of theatre gestuality seen as a hieroglyph of the human and social bodies (ARTAUD 1964b; GROTOWSKI 1971).

See also: alienation-effect.

Further reading: Brecht 1967, 19:385–421; Pavis 1978b.

GIBBERISH

Fr.: *grommelots*; Ger.: *Gemurmel*; Sp.: *murmullo.*

Actors are using this technique when they murmur or mutter, not speaking a language but giving the impression that they are saying something or expressing themselves in the correct intonations. *Le Saperleau* by G. BOURDET is written in an imaginary language that is "muttered" by the actors. D. FO uses this approach to indicate a nation or imitate a group. Gibberish plays at the destruction of articulate language, the better to reconstruct it in a mixed system that includes music, gesture, narrative and vocal expression (FO 1991).

GRACIOSO

Fr.: *gracioso*; Ger.: *Gracioso*; Sp.: *gracioso.*
See BUFFOON

GROTESQUE

(From the Italian *grottesca*, derived from *grotta*.)
Fr.: *grotesque*; Ger.: *das Groteske*; Sp.: *grotesco.*

Name given to paintings brought to light during the Renaissance and containing fantastic motifs such as animals in vegetable form, chimeras and human figures.

1. Emergence of the Grotesque

A. The grotesque is comical in a caricaturesque, burlesque and bizarre way. It is something perceived as being a significant deviation from an accepted norm. Thus, T. GAUTIER, in *les Grotesques* (1844) undertakes to rehabilitate the "realistic" authors of the early seventeenth century by revealing "literary deformities" and "poetic deviations."

In the Romantic era, the grotesque appeared as a form capable of counterbalancing the aesthetics of the beautiful and sublime, of conveying an awareness of the relative and dialectical nature of aesthetic judgment: "The grotesque of ancient times is timid and seeks to hide itself away. [...] In the opinion of the Moderns, however, the grotesque plays a fundamental role. It is everywhere; on one hand it creates the deformed and horrible, on the other the comical and buffoon-like. [...] We believe that the grotesque is the richest source nature can open to art (HUGO, preface to *Cromwell*, 1827).

B. When it is applied to theatre – meaning both dramaturgy and stage production – the grotesque retains its essential function as a principle of deformation having, furthermore, a highly-developed sense of the concrete and of realistic detail. MEYERHOLD refers to it constantly, going so far as to make theatre, in the aesthetic tradition of RABELAIS, HUGO and later BAKHTIN (1973) the ideal form of expression of the grotesque: "A premeditated outrage, a disfiguration of nature, with emphasis on the sensible, material side of the forms."

2. Spirit of the Grotesque

A. The reasons for grotesque deformation are many, from the simple pleasure in gratuitous comic effects (as in *commedia dell'arte*) to political or philosophical satire (VOLTAIRE, SWIFT). Rather than one particular grotesque, there are many grotesque aesthetic and ideological projects (satirical, parabolic, comical, romantic, nihilistic, etc.). Like *distantiation**, the grotesque is not a mere stylistic device but affects the very understanding of the performance.

B. The grotesque is closely allied with the *tragicomic**, which becomes obvious historically with *Sturm und Drang*, *drama** and *melodrama**, and with Romantic (HUGO) and expressionist theatre (cf. BÜCHNER, NESTROY, KAISER, STERNHEIM, WEDEKIND), and in the Italian "teatro grottesco" (CHIARELLI, PIRANDELLO). As mixed genres, the grotesque and the tragicomic maintain a delicate balance between the laughable and the tragic, each genre presupposing its opposite so as not to be set in a definitive attitude. In the world of today, which is renowned for its deformity, i.e. its lack of identity and harmony, the grotesque declines to deliver a harmonious image of society. It represents the chaos "mimetically" at the same time as it gives a reworked image of it.

C. The result is a mixture of *genres** and styles. Its grimacing comic effect paralyzes the spectator, who can neither laugh nor cry freely. This constant movement between two opposite perspectives brings out the contradiction between the object actually perceived and the abstract, imagined object – concrete vision and intellectual abstraction always go hand in hand. Similarly, there is often a transformation of man into an animal, and vice versa. The bestiality of human nature and the humanity of animals leads to a questioning of traditional human ideals. This is not always a sign of degeneracy and contempt, but only a way of putting man in his rightful place, particularly concerning his instincts and corporality (BAKHTIN 1984).

D. In this sense, the grotesque is a realistic art, since the object, though intentionally deformed, is still recognizable (as in caricature). It affirms the existence of things while criticizing them. It is the antithesis of the *absurd**, at least of the kind of absurd that rejects all logic and denies the existence of social laws and principles. It is also far removed from nihilist or dadaist art, which rejects all values and believes only in the parodic or critical function of artistic activity. As DÜRRENMATT pointed out, "it is fascist art, supposedly positive and heroic, that is truly nihilistic and destructive of all humanist values. The grotesque, on the other hand, is one of the possibilities of being precise [...] It is an extreme stylization, a sudden concretization and, to that extent, it is able to grasp current issues and even our time, without being a thesis play or a news report" (1966, 136–137).

E. Grotesque derision makes us laugh, not *at* something in a detached way, but *with* something that we poke fun at. We are participating in the feast of mind and body: "Laughter caused by the grotesque contains something profound, axiomatic and primitive that comes much closer to the innocent life and absolute joy than does laughter caused by comedy of manners... I will call the grotesque the absolute comical... as the antithesis of the ordinary comical, which I will call the significant comical" (BAUDELAIRE, *L'essence du rire*, in 1951, 985).

F. The question is whether this absolute comical ravages every value and every absolute in its way, thus approaching the blind mechanism of the absurd, as – wrongly, it appears – held by J. KOTT: "The failure of the tragic actor is the absolute open to derision and having lost its sacred aura, its transformation into a blind mechanism, a sort of automaton" (1965, 137). "The grotesque opens to derision the absolute of history, just as it opened to derision the absolutes of the gods, of nature and of predestination" (144).

From the tragicomic grotesque to the absurd there is only a small step, and it is quickly taken in contemporary theatre. But the dividing line (even if it is only theoretical) is useful to distinguish between dramaturgies such as those of IONESCO or BECKETT and those of FRISCH, DÜRRENMATT or even BRECHT. For the three latter authors, the grotesque is a last attempt to give an account of today's tragicomic man, of the rending of his fabric but also of his vitality and regeneration through art.

Further reading: Kayser 1960; Dürrenmatt 1966; Heidsieck 1969; Ubersfeld 1974.

GROUPING OF CHARACTERS

Fr.: constellation des personnages; Ger.: *Figurenkonstellation*; Sp.: *constelación de personajes*.

See CONFIGURATION

GUERILLA THEATRE

Fr.: *théâtre de guérilla*; Ger.: *Guerillatheater*; Sp: *teatro guerrillero*.

Theatre that sees itself as militant and committed to political life or to the radical struggle for liberation of a people or group. Examples are VALDEZ's Teatro Campesino, the San Francisco Mime Troupe, the Living Theatre.

See also: agit-prop, theatre of participation, street theatre.

Further reading: R. Davis 1966.

H

HAM ACTING

Fr.: *cabotinage;* Ger.: *Komödiant, Schmierenkomödiant;* Sp.: *fanfarronada.*
See ACTING

HAMARTIA

(Greek word for "error.")
Fr.: *hamartia;* Ger.: *Hamartia;* Sp.: *hamartia.*

In Greek tragedy, error in judgment (i.e., miscalculation) and ignorance are the causes of the catastrophe. The hero "does not fall into misfortune through vice or depravity, but falls because of some mistake" (ARISTOTLE, *Poetics*, sect. 1453a).

Hamartia is conceived of as being ambiguous: "Tragic guilt is established between the ancient religious tragic conception of the stain of sin, of *hamartia* as an illness of the mind, a delirium sent by the gods that necessarily but involuntarily engenders the crime, and the new conception, in which the guilty one, the *hamartôn* and particularly the *adikôn*, is defined as he who has deliberately chosen to commit a crime without being constrained to do so" (VERNANT and VIDAL-NAQUET 1972, 38).
See also: hubris, conflict, tragic.
Further reading: Saïd 1978; Romilly 1961, 1970.

HAPPENING

Type of theatre activity that does not use a pre-established text or programme (at most a scenario or "directions for use"), proposing what has variously been called an *event* (George BRECHT), an *action* (BEUYS), a device, a movement, *performance art**. This is an activity proposed and carried out by performers and participants based on the random and the unexpected, with no attempt to imitate an outside action, tell a story or produce a meaning, using all imaginable arts and techniques as well as surrounding reality. It is not, as often thought, a disorganized, cathartic activism; rather, it proposes a process of theoretical reflection about the spectacular and the production of meaning within the strict limits of a pre-established environment. Michael KIRBY, one of the best theoreticians of the happening, writes that it is "a purposefully composed form of theatre in which diverse alogical elements, including nonmatrixed performing, are organized in a compartmented structure" (1965, 21).

The immediate origins of the happening are experiments by artists from different backgrounds. John CAGE (who "organized" a concert in 1952 with painter RAUSCHENBERG, choreographer Merce CUNNINGHAM, poet OLSEN and pianist TUDOR) led the way toward this federation of the arts. In Japan there is the group GUTAI, founded in 1955; in New York, in the 1960s, sculptors OLDENBURG, KIRBY and KAPROW (*18 Happenings in 6 Parts*, 1959); in Europe BEUYS and VORSTELL, proponents of *body art* G. PANE, M. JOURNIAC, H. NITSCH. The happening lives on in *invisible theatre** and performance art,

though the enthusiasm it generated during the 1960s has waned.
See also: improvisation, installation, environmental theatre, agit-prop theatre.
Further reading: Lebel 1966; Rischbieter and Storch 1968; Tarrab 1968; Suvin 1970.

HARLEQUINADE

Fr.: *arlequinade;* Ger.: *Harlekinade, Hanswurstiade;* Sp.: *arlequinada, pantomima.*
See PANTOMIME

HERMENEUTICS

Fr.: *herméneutique;* Ger.: *Hermeneutik;* Sp.: *hermenéutica.*

Method of *interpreting** text or performance that consists in proposing a *meaning** for them, taking into account the situation of enunciation and evaluation of the interpreting subject. Hermeneutical methodology owes much to biblical exegesis and law, both of which look for the hidden meaning of texts. Its other source is Greek: in the fifth century B.C., the rhapsodes recited HOMER's text to try to make it more accessible to a disconcerted audience. Generally speaking, the purpose of hermeneutics is "to make signs talk and discover their meaning" (FOUCAULT 1966, 44). It is a given in dramatic criticism that the interpretation of text and performance by the director, actor and audience is an essential aspect of theatre work, since the performance includes a series of interpretations at every level and at every moment.

Broadly speaking, hermeneutics aims to:
- Determine how the director and spectator put the work of art into practice;
- Clearly identify the historical situation of the exegete;
- Show the dialectics between the critic's present and the play's past, by stressing the heterogeneity of their historicities.

Accordingly, there is no final, conclusive meaning of the play and the staging, but a relatively wide range of interpretations. The play, over the course of history, acquires a series of concretizations. We could speak of a "hermeneutical circle" in the interpretation of the staging, as the isolated stage elements can be understood only if one has already grasped the "overall discourse" of the mise-en-scène. In addition, hypotheses need to be formulated constantly about the signs, and then confirmed or invalidated in the course of the performance.

2. The performance, then, is not a closed system of stage systems; it "overflows" into the outside world and summons up the sense and *meaning** of the stage. It requires the critical intervention of the spectator, who interprets it in the light of previous experiences.

3. This opening up of the work into the outside world leads us to take the text as a pretext for successive, non-definitive interpretations, to facilitate all imaginable interactions between *text and performance**.

4. As a particular arrangement of stage systems that are more or less integrated into an overall project, the performance is constantly being manipulated and reworked by the creator and the spectator in connection with possible ways of structuring the different components of the stage systems.

5. In the end, it is the precision of the subjective, as well as the social and ideological conditions of the interpreting subject that will determine how relevant the interpretation is. To avoid becoming ineffective, the hermeneutical method should include a concrete knowledge of the historicity of the object of study and of the interpreter's own situation of enunciation. This historicity will lend a more complete and flexible aspect to a semiology that may be too concerned with mechanically decoding signs – better a little hermeneutics today than a semiotic catastrophe tomorrow.
See also: event, theatrical relationship, reading, reception, semiology, anthropology, history.
Further reading: Ricoeur 1969; Jauss 1982a, b; Warning 1975; Fischer-Lichte 1979; Borie 1981; Postlewait and McConachie 1989.

HERO

(From the Greek *hérôs*, demi-god and divine man.)
Fr.: *héros*; Ger.: *Held*; Sp.: *héroe*.

1. The Origins of the Concept

The hero of Greek mythology was a character elevated to the rank of a demi-god. In theatre, the hero is a type of *character** endowed with extraordinary powers. His attributes and faculties are of a higher order than those of mortals, but "the appearance of the hero stabilizes the image of man" (M. AUGÉ, *Génie du paganisme*). Even when the hero does not perform extraordinary tasks or compel the spectator's admiration through catharsis, he is at least recognizable as "the character who receives the most vivid and noticeable emotional colour" (TOMACHEVSKI 1965b, 89). In tragedy, this emotional colour consists in *fear** and *pity**, through which we identify best with the character. Therefore, it is impossible to come up with an exhaustive definition of the hero, since *identification** depends on the audience's attitude toward the character – the hero is he who is said to be the hero.

2. The Classical Hero

The hero in the strict sense exists only in a dramaturgy that represents the tragic actions of kings or princes, so that the spectator's *identification** is directed toward a mythical or inaccessible being. His actions must appear to be exemplary and his destiny as freely chosen. The hero is, however, tragically caught between blind but inevitable divine law and unhappy but free consciousness *(tragic*)*.

The classical hero coincides perfectly with his actions. He poses and opposes himself through his struggle and moral conflict, answers for his fault and finds reconciliation with society or with himself after his tragic fall. A heroic character can exist only when the social, psychological and moral contradictions of the play are fully contained in the consciousness of the hero. He is a microcosm of the dramatic universe.

HEGEL, in his *Aesthetics* (1832), distinguishes between three types of hero, corresponding to three historical and aesthetic phases:
1. The *epic hero* is crushed by his destiny in his struggle with the forces of nature (HOMER).
2. The *tragic hero* carries within himself a passion and desire for action that will be fatal (SHAKESPEARE).
3. The *dramatic hero* reconciles his passions with the necessity imposed by the outside world, thus avoiding annihilation. In this category, the title of hero applies to the illustrious man whose exploits are related, as well as to the character in theatre.

One of the precepts of tragedy has been that the author recruits his heros from among high-ranking characters. This has arisen from a confusion between two different things: first, pleasing a noble audience by offering a flattering portrait (political motive); and second, presenting characters who in real life already enjoy a capital role in historical development and deserve to be called heroes. The second requirement (of a historical hero) is quite legitimate for a dramaturgy that must function on the basis of already "dramatized" material; i.e. using individuals "of world-historical significance" (HEGEL) who embody social forces and conflicts. These real-life heroes and their conflicts then need only be expressed in a naturally dramatic form.

3. Outgrowths of the Hero

In the nineteenth century, *hero* meant both "tragic character" and "comic figure." Then the word lost its exemplary and mythical value and retained only the meaning of the main character in an epic or dramatic text. The hero might be negative, collective (the people, as in some nineteenth-century dramas), unidentifiable (in the theatre of the *absurd**, DÜRRENMATT), or self-assured and linked to a new social order (the positive hero of social realism). The hero has continually fallen in status throughout literary history. Classical tragedy showed him in splendid isolation. The *drame bourgeois* made him a representative of the bourgeoisie, attempting to take the individualistic values of his class to victory. Naturalism and realism showed us a pitiful, fallen hero at the mercy of social determinism. The theatre of the absurd completed his fall by making him a metaphysically disoriented being with no aspirations (IONESCO, BECKETT). BRECHT had already signed the hero's death warrant by renouncing the representation of an individual hero in favour of the collective "set up by capitalist production or taken over by the working class" [...] "one can no longer understand the decisive events of our time from the point of view of individual personalities, and these events can no longer be influenced by individual personalities" (1967, 15:274). The contemporary hero no longer has the power to influence events, has no point of view on reality. He gives way to the masses, whether organized or amorphous. "The individual personality must give up his place to the great collective" (DÜRRENMATT 1970, 244).

The absence of a hero opens the way to generalized derision, for "there are no true representatives, and the tragic heroes are nameless [...] Creon's secretaries close Antigone's case" (1970, 63; Eng. 1982, 253).

4. The Antihero

Since the late nineteenth century, especially in contemporary theatre, the hero exists only as his ironic or grotesque *double**, the antihero. With all of the values associated with the classical hero in decline, the antihero appears to be the only option to describe human actions (DÜRRENMATT, 1970). In BRECHT, man is systematically taken apart (cf. *Man for Man*), reduced to an individual made of contradictions and integrated into a *(hi)story** that determines him more than he imagines. The hero does not survive the reversal of values and dismantling of his consciousness. Or else, in order to survive, he must disguise himself as a *fool** or a pathetic creature as in BECKETT.

See also: classical dramaturgy, protagonist, hamartia.

Further reading: Aristotle 330 B.C.; Scherer 1950; Frye 1957; Lukács 1963; Vernant and Vidal-Naquet 1972; Hamon 1977; Abirached 1978.

HEROIC COMEDY

Fr.: *comédie héroïque*; Ger.: *heroische Komödie*; Sp.: *comedia heroica*.

1. An intermediate genre between tragedy and comedy, heroic comedy throws high-ranking characters into an action with a happy ending in which there is "no peril through which we may be transported to pity or fear" and in which "all the characters [...] are kings or grandees from Spain" (CORNEILLE, Preface to *Don Sanche d'Aragon*, 1649).

Imported from Spain (LOPE DE VEGA) by ROTROU and CORNEILLE, it became a new genre in France with CORNEILLE, in England around 1660–1680 with DRYDEN (*The Conquest of Granada*, 1669).

Tragedy becomes heroic when the sacred and tragic give way to the psychological and bourgeois compromise. *Le Cid*, for instance, attempts to reconcile psychology, individualism and reasons of state.

2. The *heroic* in comedy or tragedy is expressed in an elevated tone or style, in noble actions, a series of violent conflicts (war, kidnapping, usurpation), exotic places and characters, an illustrious subject and admirable heroes: "The illustrious aspect of the heroic is based on the highest virtues of war" (T. TASSO, *Discorsi del poema eroico*, 1594).

3. The *mock heroic* is a parody of the heroic tone, a description in prosaic terms of noble and serious actions. It is very close to the *burlesque** or the *grotesque**.

HEROIC TRAGEDY

Fr.: *tragédie héroique*; Ger.: *heroische Tragödie*; Sp.: *tragedia heroica*.

Heroic tragedy arose in England after restoration of the monarchy, in particular with John DRYDEN (*The Conquest of Granada*, 1870). It is an imitation of French classical tragedy, played in an elevated, pathetic style, with romantic, idealist themes. Heroic tragedy never recovered from its parody by BUCKINGHAM in *The Rehearsal* (1671).

HISTORICAL DRAMA

See HISTORY

HISTORICIZATION

Fr.: *historicisation*; Ger.: *Historisierung*; Sp.: historización.

A term introduced by BRECHT, historicizing means showing an event or character in a social, historical light, as relative and changeable. It is "to show events and men in their ephemeral, historical aspect" (BRECHT 1967, 15:302), which leads the spectators to think that their own reality is historical and can therefore be criticized and changed as well (see *history**).

In Brechtian *dramaturgy**, as in a staging inspired by critical *Brechtian** *realism**, to historicize is to refuse to show human beings in an individual, anecdotic light; to reveal the underlying sociohistorical infrastructure beneath the individual conflicts. In this sense, the individual drama of the *hero** is recontextualized socially and politically, and any theatre is historical and political.

Historicization brings out two historicities: the play in its own context, and the spectator in the circumstances of his attendance: "Historicization leads to considering a given social system from the point of view of another social system. The evolution of society provides the points of view" (BRECHT 1976, 109).

The fundamental medium of historicization is the *alienation effect**, in which the spectator alienates the theatrical performance as well as his own reference reality.

See also: epic and dramatic, history.

Further reading: Dort 1975, 1977a; Pavis 1978b; Ubersfeld 1978b; Banu 1981; Knopf 1980.

HISTORY

Fr.: *histoire*; Ger.: *Geschichte*; Sp.: *historia*.

1. Dramaturgy and History

Theatre shows human actions that may be invented or refer to historical events. Dramaturgy takes on history whenever the play reconstructs a past episode that actually took place (or, as in science fiction, imagines a future situation). Any dramatic work, whether or not it is labelled a historical play, takes place within a temporality and represents a historical moment in social evolution. In this sense, theatre's relationship with history is a constant element of any dramaturgy.

The playwright who speaks of history works with two subjectivities: (a) that of the historian who judges various discourses on the events and takes a particular point of view in explaining them, and (b) that of the writer who selects and arranges the materials of his *fabula**. Through his text, the playwright restores a certain coherence to (hi)story: "To think of history objectively, such is the silent task of the playwright; that is, to think of everything in a series, weave isolated elements into a whole; and always to presuppose that one unit of the scheme must be placed in things, if it is not already there" (NIETZSCHE).

2. The General and the Particular

According to ARISTOTLE, "Poetry [...] is a more philosophical and a higher thing than history, in that poetry tends rather to express the universal, history rather the particular fact." (*Poetics*, 1451b). It is impossible to restore all the wealth of the historical facts, in text or performance. A systematic screening of the materials must be carried out, on the basis of the poet's evaluation of the reality to be represented and of his own reality. The writing of history, which imposes these choices, can only be *epic**, and the presence of the narrator/historian is always perceptible. That is why historical dramas favour the epic form, with many descriptions of events and objectives and authorial intervention. It is always tricky to show this history "in action," in a dramatic form, since epic and historical accuracy stand to suffer.

3. Totality of Objects and Totality of Movement
In the historical novel, as shown by G. LUKÁCS (1963), epic accuracy applies to the objects, which are described and accumulated by the narrator in a "totality of objects." The essential thing in drama is to give the illusion of movement ("totality of movement") by placing the conflicts on the shoulders of typical characters who represent "world-historical individuals [whose] own particular purposes contain the substantial, which is the will of the world spirit" (HEGEL, quoted in LUKÁCS 1965, 131; Eng. 1963, 119).

4. Historicity and the "Eternally Human"
As a painter of history, the playwright is caught between two contradictory requirements and temptations:

A. The first is to provide a historically accurate representation of the events, to trace them back through all their details and show the discrepancy that effects a radical separation between two historical situations (his own and that of the period evoked). Such concern for accuracy implies doing many preliminary studies and presenting authentic documents. It leads to two diametrically opposed results. One possibility is that the heroes are too well particularized, too photographically precise, and the principle of their meaning has been lost; or the playwright makes historical abstractions, what MARX called "mouthpieces of the spirit of the ages" (MARX and ENGELS 1859, in 1967, l:181). In this case, the characters become lifeless and the spectator does not recognize himself in them, for a philosophical abstraction is not credible when it takes the place of a flesh-and-blood character.

B. The second temptation is to generalize the action, purifying and simplifying it in order to bring the protagonists closer to a general type, to generalize the action into an abstract and identifiable parable. The character is then divested of historicity and becomes a *character type** that belongs to no period or milieu. This kind of character resembles everybody and nobody; is only an ideal with which we hasten to identify, as we perceive only that which brings us together. The *conflict** is no longer one of social forces embodied by characters but of very subjective individuals with a rich inner life. The "privatization" of the conflict leads to the conversation play or a "dialogue" of silent characters, whose traits and inner lives are finely drawn, to the point of being inexpressible (CHEKHOV, PIRANDELLO and psychologist drama).

5. Historical Truth and Dramatic Truth
Historical truth and dramatic truth have nothing in common, and their confusion by playwrights engenders all kinds of misunderstandings about *realism** in theatre performance. A "good" playwright has a talent for taking liberties with history. A certain amount of inaccuracy in characterization or chronology is harmless provided the overall processes, the social movements, and the motivations of the groups are correct. A sociological analysis with Marxist affinities will endeavour to situate the conflict at the point where deeper historical movements converge (for instance, the opposition between Antigone and Creon at a time of transition from a primitive form of society to the centralized power of the city). To use the Brechtian phrase, the important thing is to highlight the relationships of social causality.

On the other hand, a truth of detail that neglects to give the underlying causes of conflicts can lead only to a derivative kind of naturalism.

Sometimes a compromise is found between historical truth and dramatic truth, through the way in which the hero's actions are motivated and justified. Private motivations such as character traits or passion should never let us lose sight of the objective and historical motivations of the action. The hero's fate is at once unique and exemplary, particular and general.

All of these principles, which must be respected if the playwright is to express historical processes clearly, are valid above all in the classical form of drama as perceived by HEGEL and then LUKÁCS in historical drama and tragedy until the first half of the nineteenth century. In his theory of the tragic and dramatic model *par excellence*, HEGEL noted the growing difficulty of presenting a "totality of movement" and a conflict between individualized heroes (cf. SZONDI 1956).

6. History in Post-Classical Dramaturgy

A. AN ALIENATED HISTORY
BRECHT (whom LUKÁCS addresses without naming) took over this dramaturgical conception of history. He also sought to identify social processes, to fabricate "heroes" borne along by the deeper movements of society, and to restore a complete, though fragmented, image of human evolution *(represented reality)**.

B. THE HISTORY OF EVERYDAY LIFE
History also means the insignificant details of every day, the repetition of alienating work and ideological stereotypes. The *theatre of everyday life** explores this avenue on the basis of a minimalist and voluntarily mutilated view of history to arrive at a few furtive glimpses of reality, giving the illusion of photographs of everyday language and gestures.

C. HISTORY OF THE ABSURD
The dramaturgy of the *absurd** gives a cyclical, irrational, fatalistic, uncontrollable or playful picture of history. It is as if only the second part of MARX's aphorism, parodying HEGEL, had been retained: "HEGEL remarks somewhere that all of the great events and persons in world history occur twice, in one way or another. He forgot to add the following: the first time as tragedy, the second time as farce" (*The Eighteenth Brumaire*). Absurd dramaturgy has its sources in SCHOPENHAUER'S pessimism at the fact that history and tragedy no longer have any meaning, are nothing but "the representation of the terrible side of life, [...] the nameless pain, the anguish of humanity, the triumph of evil, the mocking rule of chance and the irremediable fall of the just and the innocent [...] here paraded before us" (quoted in LUKÁCS 1956, 135; Eng. 1983, 122). There is a thematic line in this conception of history that unites dramaturgies as diverse as those of BÜCHNER (and his "dreadful fatalism of history"), GRABBE (history as indifferent nature), MUSSET (history as carnival), JARRY and IONESCO (grotesque or absurd history).

D. POST-HISTORY
At present, playwrights appear hesitant to accept an overall explanation of the world, showing a tendency to throw the baby out with the historic bathwater in which all are compromised if not guilty. Political, even historical explanations are on the decline. Even the members of the Théâtre du Soleil, once masters of the particular and general evocation of man, are arriving at a conception of history in which great individuals, like peoples, no longer appear to obey a foreseeable logic, as in productions of SHAKESPEARE, *Sihanouk*, *l'Ondiade* or *La Ville parjure* (CIXOUS). The question remains, however, whether one can in fact leave history behind.

See also: time, represented reality, chronicle play, documentary theatre.

Further reading: Althusser 1965; Hays 1977, 1981; Lindenberger 1975; Jameson 1981; Pavis 1983c; Frow 1986; Postlewait and McConachie 1989.

HORSE SHOW

Fr.: *théâtre équestre*; Ger.: *Reitkunsttheater*; Sp.: *teatro ecuestre*.

Originally employed above all in the circus (dressage, trick riding) and reproductions of historical periods, horses have become the protagonists of shows devoted entirely to them. They are no longer the rider's servants, but have become true partners. For example, the Zingaro horse show directed by BARTABAS evokes civilizations in which horses were at the centre of social life (M.-C. PAVIS).

HUMOUR

Fr. *humeur*; Ger.: *Humor*; Sp.: *humor*.
See COMIC, COMEDY OF HUMOURS

HUBRIS

Fr.: *hybris*; Ger.: *Hybris*; Sp.: *hybris*.

Greek word meaning "tragic pride or arrogance." Hubris is what drives the hero to act and provoke the gods in spite of their warnings, what leads to their vengeance and his fall. This feeling is the hallmark of the actions of the *tragic hero**, who is always ready to assume his own destiny.

See also: hamartia, tragic.
Further reading: Saïd 1978.

I

ICON

Fr.: *icône*; Ger.: *Ikone*; Sp.: *ícono*.

1. Similarity

In PEIRCE's typology of signs, the icon is "a sign which would possess the character which renders it significant, even though its object had no existence" (PEIRCE, sect. 2247; Eng. in LYONS 1977, 102). Icons may be conventional, like portraits, in that an icon is a "sign which refers to the Object which it denotes simply by its own features, and everything may be an Icon of something: it has only to be similar to the something, and to be used as a sign of it" (ibid.; Eng. in SEBEOK 1986, 1:328). The icon maintains a relationship of resemblance with its model, which may be visual (the actor "resembles" his character), auditory (a broken voice expressing emotion) or gestural (one behaviour imitating another).

2. Iconicity and Mimesis

Theatre is sometimes defined as an iconic art because of its ability to imitate on stage, through actors, a referential reality that we are invited to consider as real. As it is the art of *mimesis** or *imitation** *par excellence*, it is not surprising that theatre is also considered the domain of iconic signs. Still, the notion of iconicity poses as many theoretical problems as it solves (see *theatrical sign**). A reevaluation of the Saussurian branch of *semiology** and Peircian semiotics would enable us to pose the problem of the referent of the *sign** and of the status of stage reality. The triadic Peircian model (sign, object, interpretant) takes into account the relationship between sign and referent and the pragmatic use of signs. The Saussurian dichotomy (signified/signifier) excludes the thing designated by the sign and retains only the concept to which the materiality of the signifier is associated.

Because of its complexity and a certain distrust of some metaphysical traits of its philosophy, PEIRCE's model has been little used. A notable exception is the semiotic research group in Perpignan (MARTY et al. 1980; DELEDALLE in PEIRCE 1978). But the usefulness of the Peircian model for theatre *semiology** remains to be demonstrated.

3. Use and Difficulty of the Notion of Iconicity

A. Rather than setting up oppositions of signs on the basis of a typology (icon, index, symbol), it is more useful to speak of signs having a *dominant function* that can be iconic, indexical or symbolic, and to determine the respective roles of the functions in a sequence, thus retracing the circuit of symbolization (PAVIS 1976a; ECO 1978).

B. Although we can establish a scale of iconicity, it is difficult to quantify a quality as imprecise and subjective as the notion of resemblance or *realism**. By opposing iconicity and symbolism as two dialectical mechanisms, we are able to describe the stage as a place that is coded to a certain extent and reduced to an abstraction and symbolization.

C. No analysis of visual elements can avoid breaking them down into units, and this process is necessarily coloured by the grid of language, falsifying a purely iconic apprehension of the stage phenomenon.

D. The iconic can thus be resymbolized in two fundamental ways:

– *Diagrammatic iconicity*: Encoding is done by maintaining the proportions and general configuration common to the object and its sign. Brechtian *realism**, when it reconstructs an environment using a few basic signs, is proceeding diagrammatically (cf. BRECHT 1967, 15:455–458).

– *Metaphorical* and *metonymic iconicity*: Encoding is effected according to a parallelism between object and sign; so, cramped space may mean a prison or straw a dungeon (in the case of metonymy), abstract scenery a town, etc.

E. The icon/symbol opposition has now been replaced by a theory of sign *vectorization** based on the opposition between metonymic displacement and metaphoric condensation (PAVIS 1996a).

4. Non-visual Iconicity: Theatre Discourse
A. The dramatic text is situated in space, so that the *discourse** is modulated according to its place of enunciation, rather like calligrams, in which the visual presentation of the text has a considerable influence on its meaning.

B. Prosodic phenomena (*rhythm**, *intonation**, foregrounding of rhetorical devices) are very perceptible, and leave their mark on interpretation. The text is received and experienced in its rhetorical aspect.
See also: index, symbol.
Further reading: La Borderie 1973; Ertel 1977; Ubersfeld 1977a; Pavis 1978c; Marty 1982; Kowzan 1985; Boussac 1976.

IDENTIFICATION
Fr.: *identification*; Ger.: *Einfühlung, Identifikation*; Sp.: *identificación*.

Process of *illusion** whereby the spectator imagines himself to be the character represented and the actor gets right "into the skin" of the character. Identification with the hero has deep roots in the unconscious. According to FREUD, pleasure in identification comes from the *cathartic** recognition of the other's ego, from the desire to appropriate it but also to distinguish oneself from it (*denial**).

1. Identification with the Character
The pleasure of identifying with a character is, according to NIETZSCHE, the fundamental dramatic phenomenon: "to see oneself transformed before one's own eyes and to begin to act as if one had actually entered into another body, another character" (*Birth of Tragedy*, 1872, sect. 8; Eng. 1967, 64). This process implies that the dramatic text or the staging enables the spectator to judge the character. If we judge the hero to be "better" than ourselves, identification occurs through admiration and at a certain inaccessible "distance." If we consider him worse, but not totally to blame, identification occurs through compassion (*fear and pity**).

The spectator's pleasure is linked to the pleasures of *illusion**, *imitation** and *denial**. FREUD described the spectator's pleasure as the satisfaction of "feeling the different parts of myself moving freely on stage" (FREUD 1976, X:167–168).

2. Process of Identification
Given the lack of a scientific theory of emotion to distinguish between the various levels of reception (affectivity, intellection, ideological recognition), it is impossible to propose a definitive typology of the interactions of identification with the hero. The one below drawn up by H.R. JAUSS, however, deserves credit for its clear definition of criteria: associative, admiring, sympathetic, cathartic, ironic (JAUSS 1982a, 159).

Interaction Patterns of Identification with the Hero

Modality of Identification	Reference	Receptive Disposition	Norms of Behavior or Attitude (+ = progressive) (– = regressive)
associative	game/competition (celebration)	placing oneself into roles of all other participants	+ pleasure of free existence (pure sociability) – permitted access (regression into archaic rituals)
admiring	the perfect hero (saint, sage)	admiration	+ *aemulatio* (emulation) – *imitatio* (imitation) + exemplariness – edification/entertainment by the extraordinary (need for escape
sympathetic	the imperfect hero	compassion	+ moral interest (readiness to act) – sentimentality (enjoyment of pain) + solidarity for specific action – self-confirmation (tranquilization)
cathartic	the suffering hero	tragic emotion, liberation of heart and mind	+ disinterested interest/free reflection
	the beset hero	mockery, comic relief for heart and mind	– fascination (bewitchment) + free moral judgment – mocking laughter (ritual of laughter)
ironic	the vanished or anti-hero	astonishment (provocation)	+ responding creativity – solipsism + refinement of perception – cultivated boredom + critical reflection – indifference

Source : from H.R. Jauss, 1977 : 220.

3. Criticism of Identification

Among these patterns of identification, catharsis and boundless admiration have always been criticized severely. A moralizing attitude often condemns catharsis because it hardens the spectator to evil. Brechtian criticism of the theatre of identification is much more radical: identifying with the hero is thought to imply a lack of critical spirit and assume a conception of human nature as being eternal and placed above history and class.

When it is taken to the extreme (not to say the absurd, as in the younger BRECHT), however, this radical criticism of spectator identification threatens to throw off balance the identification/*alienation** opposition. In any case, one always identifies with the hero by differentiating oneself slightly, thus through a certain denial, in order to affirm one's superiority or difference; inversely, any criticism of the hero requires a certain perception of his "psychology." Thus, to play (show) and to live (identify with) are "two antagonistic processes that join together in the actor's work" (BRECHT 1979, 47).

4. Identification and Ideology
Some critics of Marxist and Brechtian inspiration, such as L. ALTHUSSER (1965), have tried to overcome the narrow psychological conception of identification by expanding the spectator's consciousness to an entity that is also recognizable in the ideological content of the play or production. Through the characters and the *fabula**, the spectator adheres to the myths and beliefs of his everyday ideology. To identify with something is always to be impressed by the misleading "obviousness" of an ideology or psychology.
See also: recognition, represented reality, spectator, hero, fear and pity, irony.
Further reading: Schoenmakers, in Sauter 1988.

ILLUSION
(From the Latin *illusio*; *ludere*, to play, *illudere*, to deceive.)
Fr.: *illusion*; Ger.: *Illusion*; Sp.: *ilusión*.

Illusion exists in theatre when we accept as real and true what is only *fiction**, the artistic creation of a reference world that is presented as a possible world that could be our own. Illusion is related to the *reality-effect** produced on stage, and is based on the psychological and ideological recognition of phenomena already familiar to the spectator.

Theatre of illusion (*Illusionstheater* in German) refers, in BRECHT's terminology, to a naturalistic theatre, a theatre of special effects (Baroque theatre or melodrama), the "bourgeois theatre" (1750–1880) to which BRECHT opposed his epic theatre.

1. Objects of Illusion
Illusion involves all the components of the performance, to various degrees and in various ways.

A. WORLD REPRESENTED
The naturalistic stage, in which signified reality is reconstructed exactly, provides the framework for illusionist representation/performance. The audience see this framework as being "transplanted" from its own reality to the stage. It contains objects typical of a particular environment, producing the effect of reality for the spectator and thereby following in the footsteps of the classical certainty that "the only way to produce and entertain illusion is by resembling what one is imitating" (MARMONTEL 1787).

B. STAGE DESIGN
Some styles of stage design are better than others at producing illusion. The frontal stage (proscenium-arch theatre), for example, which places events in a frame, is particularly apt for producing the illusionist effects of *trompe-l'oeil*.

C. FABULA
In order to produce illusion, the *fabula** is arranged in such a way that its logic and direction are clear, without the conclusion being totally predictable. The spectator is caught up by the "suspense" and cannot escape the path traced out for him, but believes in the story told.

D. CHARACTER
The spectator has the illusion of seeing the actual character before him, and everything contributes to his *identification** with that character.

2. The "Double Game" of Illusion
True to their nature, illusion and disillusion never appear alone, always as a pair. Illusion presupposes the knowledge that what we see in theatre is only a performance. If we were completely taken in, our pleasure would be diminished. Hypernaturalistic aesthetics that aim at perfect illusion have sometimes misunderstood this need for the ambivalent pleasure of illusion/disillusion. Conversely, classical theatre and, generally, any theatre that does not seek to deny itself, has a much more balanced and "pragmatic" and subtle approach than presenting exclusively the effects of reality or unreality. Thus, MARMONTEL recommends that the illusion not be pushed to the limit, and that

the spectator be left with the impression of glimpsing an image of reality, rather than reality itself. There must be "two simultaneous thoughts," that one has "come to see a story performed" and that one is witnessing a real event; but the first thought must prevail, as illusion should not win over reflection: "... the more vivid and intense is the illusion, the more strongly it acts on the soul, and consequently the less it leaves room for freedom, reflection, and a grasp of truth" (MARMONTEL 1787, on *Illusion*). This thoughtful control of illusion is not unlike the Brechtian requirement to "re-establish theatrical reality [as the] necessary condition for realistic representations of the shared life of human beings" (1972, 247 – see *(re)theatricalization**). What is being described here by MARMONTEL (for classical theory) and BRECHT (for epic theory) is none other than the phenomenon of *denial**.

3. Producing Illusion

There is nothing mysterious about the illusion; it is based on a series of artistic *conventions**.

An examination of the *image** and of *iconic** signs shows that figurative reality is not a passive imitation; it obeys a set of *codes**: "Generally speaking, every period comes up with its own recipes for illusion. [...] Painting, like theatre and like the other arts, is illusionism, and both its means and its ends are linked to a certain stage of society, and more specifically to a certain stage of theoretical and technical knowledge, adapted to the reactions that a way of life inferred from a certain understanding of the universe imposes on a collectivity" (FRANCASTEL 1965, 224).

For illusion, as for imitation, there is no definitive formula for a true and natural representation of the world. Illusion and mimesis are only the result of theatrical *conventions**.

4. Illusion and Unconscious

As FREUD has demonstrated, the search for illusion is linked to the search for pleasure and a double denial: I know that this character is not me, but what if he were! (MANNONI, 1969). Theatre, as Hamlet well knew, is the place where the repressed returns.

Illusion and identification draw their pleasure from the feeling that the actor we see on stage is only another, and that we do not believe in a present illusion, but at the most in the illusion that a former self (that of the child) might have felt at another time and in another place. It becomes pleasant to witness with impunity events that in real life would be painful: "Accordingly, [the spectator's] pleasure is based on an illusion; that is to say, his suffering is mitigated by the certainty that, firstly, it is someone other than himself who is acting and suffering on the stage, and, secondly, that after all it is only a game, which can threaten no damage to his personal security" (FREUD 1969, 10:163; Eng. 1976, 14:122).

The *cathartic** experience makes the subject relive all that he has repressed: the child's desires and expectations, the Proustian madeleines, and all the rest.

See also: fourth wall, naturalism, represented reality, theatrical reality.

Further reading: Calderwood 1968; Trott 1970; *Nouvelle Revue de psychanalyse*, 1971; Reiss 1971; Gombrich 1977; Rivière 1978.

IMAGE

Fr.: *image;* Ger.: *Bild;* Sp.: *imagen.*

1. The image is playing an ever greater role in contemporary theatre practice. It has become the expression and the notion opposed to those of text, *fabula** or action. Having fully recovered its visual representational nature, the *theatre og images** appears at times in the form of a series of stage images, and may even deal with its linguistic and actantial materials as images or tableaux, as, for example, in the productions of R. WILSON, R. FOREMAN, C. REGY, P. CHEREAU, K.-M. GRÜBER, P. ADRIEN, R. DEMARCY and, more recently, R. PLANCHON, S. BRAUNSCHWEIG, G. LAVAUDANT, P. GENTY, R. LEPAGE.

2. A staging (mise-en-scène) is always an "imaging" ("mise-en-image"), but the image is more or less figurative and "imaginary": rather than mimetic figuration or symbolic abstraction, today one often sees scenes made of a series of beautiful images. The stage is closer to a mental landscape or picture, as if the aim were to go beyond the imitation of a thing or its "mise-en-signes" (rendering into signs). After being an "acting machine," the stage, according to A. PIERRON, has become a "dreaming machine." "It is time for the scenery to be de-intellectualized. The white surface of the abstract scenery, in its limpidity or its hermeticism, puts forward the best detoxification cure for a stage design that is overly inclined to illustration and sign" (PIERRON 1980, 137).

3. This search for the fantasy-like and dematerialized dimension of the image renews the status of performance and dramatic text. As soon as it is rendered into images on stage, the text lends itself to being reread in new ways. In spite of its desire to break the linearity or logic of the text, the image does not become unreadable and intangible, but remains a construction of the theatrical machinery with its own formal structure that is easily travelled by an experienced eye.

Further reading: Lindekens 1976; Marranca 1977; Barthes 1978b; Rivière 1978; *Théâtre public*, 1980; Gauthier 1982; Dubois 1983; Simhandl 1993.

IMBROGLIO

Fr.: *imbroglio*; Ger.: *Verwicklung*; Sp.: *enredo*.

This Italian word (meaning "entanglement") refers to a complex and confusing situation or *plot** that prevents the characters (or spectators) from clearly perceiving their respective positions on the strategic chessboard of the play. This is usually the case in *vaudeville** or *comedy of intrigue**.

The spectator's pleasure in following the imbroglio is mixed with the exasperation of never being sure of understanding completely or quickly enough, and of being blocked in the desire to get to the final point. Conversely, it is the pleasure of solving the imbroglio, thanks to a shortcut or anticipatory clue, that makes the comedy of intrigue so interesting.

IMITATION

(From the Latin *imitatio*, corresponding to *mimesis** in Greek.)

Fr.: *imitation*; Ger.: *Nachahmung*; Sp.: *imitación*.

1. The Universal Call

The call for imitation has recurred constantly in the history of theatre, from ARISTOTLE to Socialist realism. For essentially ideological reasons, it is meant to give the spectator the *illusion** of reality and the reassurance of *verisimilitude**. "The perfection of a spectacle consists in an imitation of an action that is so accurate that the spectator, deceived uninterruptedly, imagines that he is witnessing the action itself" (DIDEROT 1962, 142). This aesthetic of imitation culminates with *naturalistic** theatre, which claims to substitute for reality.

2. The Goal of Imitation

Imitation, however, is a very vague process that applies to all kinds of things – gesture and human behaviour, a character's speeches, the stage *milieu**, a historic *event**, a literary model. In theatre *practice**, the watchwords are many. There is little in common, for instance, between a classical text that "imitates" a Greek model in *fabula** or theme, and a naturalistic stage that reconstructs a bourgeois interior down to the last detail. Its very vastness and vagueness renders the concept of imitation inoperative. It is always confined to an example of rules deemed to be essential to good taste, to verisimilitude or to deeper reality. In the specific case of classicism, the imitation of the Ancients is tied to the imitation of nature, a touchstone of classical doctrine. It requires a mastery of devices and rules. Classical imitation imposes a description not of society as a whole but of outstanding traits of human psychology. As to the terms nature and *natural**, which are even more loaded than those of imitation or *mimesis**, every aesthetics refers to them systematically in a call for a new relationship with reality.

3. Imitation and Codification

Present-day literary theory is loath to use the notion of imitation, for studies on artistic and literary *devices** have revealed what was concealed behind it: *conventions** and *codification**. The stage shows nothing that does not require the spectator to accept tacit conventions. The stage is presented as the world, the actor *represents* a character, the lighting *clarifies* reality, etc. Imitation is based on a system of codification that produces illusion. "What is rather thoughtlessly called imitation of reality in theatre has always been merely a matter of conventions, even when there was no awareness of them. Whether the scenery or the costumes are eliminated, whether the text is recited or performed, makes little difference. When ANTOINE wanted to make it 'more' real, he was introducing a style, even a fashion, that was transitory and of no importance" (MANNONI 1969, 166). Imitation and illusion exist only dialectically, in contrast to an effect of "disillusion" and *denial** of reality.

See also: mimesis, sign, represented reality, denial, realistic staging.

Further reading: *Princeton Encyclopedia of Poetry and Poetics*, 1974; Culler 1975; Genette 1976; Barthes et al. 1982.

IMPROMPTU

Fr.: *impromptu*; Ger.: *Stegreifspiel*; Sp.: *madrigal*.

An impromptu play is improvised, or at least presented as such by simulating improvised theatre creation, in the same manner as a musician improvising on a theme. The actors behave as if they were inventing a story and representing their characters, i.e., as if they were really improvising. One of the first and most famous plays in this genre was MOLIÈRE's *L'Impromptu de Versailles*, written at the king's command in response to the polemical attacks on *la Critique de l'Ecole des femmes* (1663).

The genre of the impromptu reappeared in the twentieth century with *Questa era si recita a soggeto* (1930) by PIRANDELLO and the series of *Impromptus de Paris* (GIRAUDOUX 1937), *Impromptus de l'Alma* (IONESCO 1956), *Impromptus du Palais-Royal* (COCTEAU 1962). A self-referential genre that refers to itself and creates itself in the very act of enunciation, the impromptu stages the playwright, involves him in the action and *embeds** his creation, introducing a kind of *play within a play**. Attentive to the conditions of creation and its hazards and difficulties, he reveals at the same time the aesthetic and socioeconomic fators of the theatre enterprise.

See also: commedia dell'arte, improvisation.

Further reading: Kowzan 1980.

IMPROVISATION

Fr.: *improvisation*; Ger.: *Improvisation*; *Stegreifspiel*; Sp.: *improvisación*.

Technique in which the actor plays something unplanned, unexpected and invented in the heat of the moment.

Improvisation exists to varying degrees, ranging from inventing a text on the basis of a very precise, well-known scenario (as in *commedia dell'arte**), to *dramatic play** based on a theme or slogan, to total gestural and verbal invention in *body expression**, to verbal deconstruction and the search for a new "physical language" (ARTAUD).

All the different philosophies of creativity refer to this theme of improvisation. This practice is in vogue because of the rejection of the text and of passive imitation, as well as the liberating power of the *body** and spontaneous creativity. The influence of GROTOWSKI's exercises, of the Living Theatre, of the improvisational work on characters done by the Théâtre du Soleil, and other non-academic stage practices, made a powerful contribution to forging – during the 1960s and 1970s – a myth of improvisation as a key to collective theatre creation, a formula properly denounced by

M. BERNARD (1976, 1977) as a resurgence of the expressionist theory of body and art.
See also: collective creation, expression, body expression, gesture.
Further reading: Spolin 1963, 1986; Hodgson and Richards 1974; Benmussa, Bernard and Aslan in *Revue d'esthétique*, 1977, 1–2; Barker 1977; Ryngaert 1977, 1985; Sarrazac et al. 1981; Monod 1983.

INCIDENT

Fr.: *incident;* Ger.: *Vorfall, Episode;* Sp.: *incidente.*

A term from classical *dramaturgy** that is little used today. It constitutes part of the plot, and may be a secondary event in the main action: "The plot is a chain in which each incident is a link" (MARMONTEL 1787.) Current usage prefers the terms *motif**,*peripetia**, *episode** or *event** of the action.
See also: fabula, narrative, narrative analysis.
Further reading: Olson 1968a; Forestier 1988.

INCIDENTAL MUSIC

Fr.: *musique de scène;* Ger.: *Bühnenmusik, Begleitmusik;* Sp.: *música incidental.*

Music used in a performance, whether it is composed specially for the play or borrowed from existing compositions, and whether it is an autonomous work of art or exists only in reference to a particular production. The music may be so important that it becomes a musical form in its own right as the text is relegated to second place (opera, musical interlude, overture, finale), as in BEETHOVEN's *Egmont Overture* for GOETHE's play, MENDELSSOHN's *Midsummer Night's Dream* for SHAKESPEARE, GRIEG's symphonic pieces for IBSEN's *Peer Gynt.*

1. Status of Musical Accompaniment

A. Music produced or motivated by the fiction: a character sings or plays an instrument.

B. Music produced outside the dramatic universe (to open or close an act, for example), as in the musical entrances and exits composed by M. JARRE for the TNP.

- Invisible source: pit orchestra, tape recording. The music produces an atmosphere, creates a milieu, a situation or a mood; it adds a lyrical and euphoric quality that removes the dialogue and stage from reality and suggests "lyrical" meanings. Sometimes it is composed specially, but it is most often a recording of existing muisic.
- Visible source: musicians are on stage, sometimes disguised as characters (chorus), actors are able to play an instrument. The mise-en-scène and music do not seek to create any illusion about their origins and production.
- Music that is as much (or as little) fiction as external illustrative reality (e.g. the musicians in the "Orientalist" productions of the Théâtre du Soleil). This is the case with current experiments in musical theatre (APERGHIS, GOEBBELS, KUHN, FRIZE). Verbal and musical elements do not contradict each other but form an integral part of the overall stage production.

2. Function of Stage Music

- Illustration and creation of an atmosphere consistent with the dramatic situation, which it echoes and reinforces (as in musical accompaniment).
- Structuring of the staging: while the text and acting are often fragmented, the music links up the scattered elements and forms a continuum. Music can punctuate the strong beats of the staging.
- Contrapuntal effect: as in EISENSTEIN, BRECHT, WEILL, DESSAU and RESNAIS, the music underscores, sometimes ironically, a particular moment in the text or play (*alienation-effect** of Brechtian *songs**).
- Recognition effect: by creating a melody or refrain, the composer sets up a structure of *leitmotifs**, creates expectations of the melody and signals thematic or dramaturgical progression.
- Substitution for the text, as in popular music between 1930 and 1980 (*Le Bal*, dance theatre).

- Film technique using music to create ambiance and a series of sequences with corresponding changes in the melody.

Stage music or music *on* stage has become quite important over the past years, to the point of becoming a structure that lends a certain *rhythm** to the entire production. In the Théâtre du Soleil's productions of *Richard II*, *Twelfth Night*, *Sihanouk* and *l'Indiade*, the percussionists create the dynamics of the play rather than accompanying the actors.

Further reading: Appia 1963; Craig 1905.

INDEX

Fr.: *index*; Ger.: *Index*; Sp.: *índice.*

1. Index According to Peirce

In PEIRCE's typology (1931–58, 2:233–71), the index is a sign "in a dynamic (including spatial) connection with the individual object, on the one hand, and with the senses or the memory of the person for whom it serves as a sign, on the other hand." It maintains a relationship of contiguity with external reality.

Smoke is an index of fire. A man with a rolling gait probably indicates a sailor. A finger pointing at something is an index that designates the object. The index contextualizes elements that, without it, would have no spatial or temporal anchor. This type of sign is frequent in theatre because the stage generates situations that have meaning only at the moment of enunciation and in relation to the characters. *Ostension** is the primary form of theatrical *communication** (OSOLSOBE 1980). It is this aspect of *semiology** that the theory of theatre could develop, in the tradition of *mimesis**, rather than automatically reproducing PEIRCE's typology.

2. Forms of the Index in Theatre

When a linguistic text is used, the apparatus of *enunciation** (personal pronouns, indications of time and space, verb system) functions as a concrete contextualization of the text.

There are also other indexical forms specific to the stage: gestuality, the *proxemic** relationships between the characters, exchanges of glances. These signs are linked to the actor's stage presence, to the general rhythm of the performance, to the direct or distanced reading of the *fabula**. The index is essential to the linkages between the various moments of the action. It ensures the contiguity and continuity between the episodes of the action and thereby the coherence of the *fabula*.

See also: icon, symbol, deixis, sign, vectorization.

Further reading: Barthes 1966a; Pavis 1976a; Eco 1978.

INDICATIONS OF TIME AND PLACE

Fr.: *indications spatio-temporelles;* Ger.: *Information über Raum und Zeit;* Sp.: *indicaciones espacio-temporales.*

To differentiate them from *stage directions**, we could use this term to refer to explicit mentions, in the dramatic text, of a place or time, an action, an attitude or an action by a character. These mentions are "heard" by the reader-spectator and help establish the fiction. They need not necessarily be translated in the staging, but the failure to take them into account in the mise-en-scène is never innocent, and an alert spectator will notice. Conversely, the director is not obliged to actually use the stage directions in his production. Stage directions are not heard by the spectator and have quite a different status than the *dramatic text** to which the indications of place and time belong.

INGÉNUE

Fr.: *ingénue;* Ger.: *Ingenue, die Naive;* Sp.: *ingenua.*

*Character type** of the naive, inexperienced and innocent young girl (or, less frequently, young man) with little experience of life (e.g. Agnès in *l'Ecole des femmes* or VOLTAIRE's Candide).

INNER SPACE

Fr.: *espace intérieur*; Ger.: *innerer Raum*; Sp.: *espacio interior.*

1. The Spectator

At first sight, the theatre is a "place of exteriority" where one contemplates a stage with impunity from a certain distance. According to HEGEL, it is the place of objectivity and of confrontation between stage and audience, and therefore apparently an exterior, visible and objective space.

But the theatre is also a place of projection for the spectator *(catharsis*, identification*)*. It therefore becomes an interior space as if by osmosis, an "extension of the ego with all its possibilities" (MANNONI 1969, 181). For theatre to exist there must be at least a beginning of identification and catharsis: "The true enjoyment of the poetic work is derived from the release of tensions within our own souls" (FREUD 1969, 10:179). In the character we discover a part of our own repressed ego, and "perhaps even the fact that the creator enables us to enjoy our own fantasies henceforth without reproach and without shame contributes greatly to its success" (179).

In this way, the stage space takes on the shape and form of the spectator's self. In current trends, its features are sketched out only lightly, and it takes shape through the projection of an external ego.

2. The Director

The themes of the play or the particular bias of the production may call for a stage arrangement that is intended to represent an inner space, as in a character's dreams, images and *fantasies**.

The character's inner space is, naturally, determined largely by that of the director, who is in the same reassuring position with respect to his character as the spectators who with delight contemplate their own egos and the ghosts of the characters on stage. In this way they can manipulate and contemplate part of their intimate selves in the guise of another. A large part of the visual aspect of the stage, therefore, proceeds directly from the director's unconscious, through the fictional unconscious of the character. Dream sequences are for the most part parentheses in the performance, played in a different mode than scenes of reality (with "unreal" music and atmosphere). For instance, PLANCHON sprinkles his saucy descriptions of the *Folies bourgeoises* with dreamlike passages in which surrealistic imagery prevails (collage, juxtaposition of dissimular objects, gestures unrelated to subjects). These dream "parentheses" come at a point when established verbal thought is incapable of rendering the work of the imagination and in which the oneiric image gives an approximation and a stage "idea" of the work of the subconscious. The latter (mainly displacement and condensation) revolves around a play of images that cannot be verbalized (*rhetoric**). This use of unconscious dream elements or ghosts is frequent in a theatre of images that lacks an overly dominant text that would require minute detail. It is employed deliberately by the director to lend a certain virtuosity and *aestheticism** to the play at the expense of an ingenuous intuitive approach. But it is present in any production, since nothing in the text can impoase a specific kind of visualization *a priori*, and since the director and the stage designer are free to make up whatever imagery they please. In a way, it is in realistic and naturalistic performances that it is most revealing to observe this involuntary escape of the creative fantasy. For it is precisely when he is careful not to betray himself, not to show anything of his own vision, that the director most risks allowing this to occur as his unconscious takes over. Paradoxically, theatre of fantasy exists only where one least expects it, because those stagings that are richest in this respect give out subtle doses of reality and fantasy. The plays of CHEKHOV, IBSEN, STRINDBERG, GORKY and even BRECHT (when staged by LAVAUDANT – *Puntila* or ADRIEN – *Man for Man*) vacillate between the two styles (realistic and fantastic) and lend themselves marvellously well to the undamming of repressed inner spaces on stage.

3. The Actor

In the last analysis, all of these spaces revealed on stage are filtered through the actor's *body**. In projecting images of his character and exhibiting the invisible aspects of his consciousness, the actor cannot help revealing the innermost depths of his being. GROTOWSKI (1968) and BROOK (1968) have taken advantage of this "denuding" of the actor before the audience to enrich the theatrical relationship and the process of self-knowledge. This externalization of inner space, a veritable obsession of current research on the actor, goes hand in hand with research on *stage space**.

Further reading: Jamati 1952; Langer 1953; Derrida 1967, 253–340; Green 1969; Dorfles 1974; Benmussa 1974, 1977; Le Galliot 1977; Pierron 1980; Finter 1990.

INSTALLATION

Fr.: *installation*; Ger.: *Installation*; Sp.: *instalación*.

The concept of installation contradicts the uninterrupted flow of a living theatre performance, the constant renewal of signs upon the stage. But it is precisely this apparently static nature that fascinates directors in their search to provoke and alter the spectator's gaze: once things are installed and the installers have left, come the visitors who can undo everything with a single glance.

1. Installation Strategy

An installation puts in place visual elements alongside elements from the media, words or music, itineraries through a scene design, but excluding living actors or performers. The media – video, film, slide projections, computer screens – are incorporated in a scene design that facilitates the spectator's *path**, route or trajectory as the spectator embarks upon an open or guided tour more as a walker than as a watcher. By providing a path in time for those who walk through the installation space, the temporality of the spectator's experience is better reflected. Walkers are free to stop and examine a detail, come at the installation from different directions, including the rear, and influence the time and space of the play.

2. Types of Installation

- The visual and stage objects in a production take a participatory role.
- Sound installation: several speakers scattered throughout the space provide strands of words or music, and the listener is free to choose his own path.
- Musical installation: As long ago as 1920, Eric Satie, with his *Musique d'ameublement*, proposed a sound installation in his own furniture.
- Film installation: A. Warhol's hours-long filming of the *Empire State Building* (1964) or a sleeper (*Sleep*, 1963), in which the tiniest involuntary movement by the sleeper seems like shameless overacting.

3. Why the Fascination with Installation?

Why does the theatre, by its very definition always on the go, opt for installation?

- Theatre people have always dreamed of an alliance with the other arts through a common project in which all could preserve their nature. Some directors boast that they do not use a stage designer or stage musician but a visual artist or composer, and ensure that they are not subordinated to the overall concept.
- Having tired of deciding on the chronology and tempo of the story told, theatre prefers to put the visitor in the actor's place, in a different frame of mind: that of a stroller who happens upon the act.
- The other arts keep their eye on theatre: we hear of "architectural gesture" (1992:343), of theatricality in painting, of orality in traditional poetry, of theatricality in music. Theatre is tempted by the arrival of conceptual art in an area of theatre customarily inhabited by real actors, and impressed by a minimalist art that runs counter to the mimetic habits of representation.
- In a time of large-scale art exhibitions and museography, directors and stage designers are inclined to think that they can dispose of plays, so to speak: "switch" them on or off, put up and take down the stage and house, and still

remain masters of the spectator's fleeting gaze.

INTEREST

Fr.: *intérêt;* Ger.: *Interesse;* Sp.: *interés.*

Term from classical dramaturgy meaning the quality of a play that is capable of inducing strong emotions in the audience – "all that touches human beings deeply" (FONTENELLE, *Réflexion sur la poétique*), "the true source of constant emotion" (HOUDAR DE LA MOTTE, *Premier Discours sur la tragédie*). According to MARIVAUX, the interest of a great tragedy "proceeds less from the facts than from the way they are dealt with, which results in an interest that is more widely distributed and scattered than confined to a few places" (1969, 226).

INTERLUDE

(From the Latin *interludere,* to play by intervals.)
Fr.: *interlude;* Ger.: *Zwischenspiel;* Sp.: *interludio.*

Musical composition played between the acts of a performance to illustrate or vary it in tone and to facilitate scene and costume changes. By extension, any verbal or mimed presentation that interrupts the action on stage (*intermezzo**).

INTERMEDIALITY

Fr.: *intermédialité;* Ger.: *Intermedialität;* Sp.: *intermedialidad.*

This term, patterned after *intertextuality,* refers to exchanges between different media, particularly with respect to their specific properties and their impact on theatrical performance. This involves a systematic examination of how one medium influences another. Examples include how a particular type of film lighting is used on stage or the film techniques of fade-in, fade-out, slow motion, or jerky movement are taken up by DECROUX in his body mime; or how a narrative montage of short sequences of film shots can become a technique of dramatic writing. Thanks to technological advances, man has become – according to FREUD in his *Civilization and its Discontents* (1929), a "prosthetic god." The bodies and minds of the actors and spectators have been moulded by the new media, and these interactions as a whole are the subject of study of intermediality.
Further reading: Pavis 1996a.

INTERMEZZO

Fr.: *intermède;* Ger.: *Intermezzo, Zwischenspiel;* Sp.: *intermedio.*

Acrobatic, dramatic, musical or pantomimic entertainment provided between the intermissions of a play, consisting of a chorus, a ballet or a playlet (*sainete*). Medieval mystery plays were divided into scenes or acts between which songs or commentaries were performed in which God or the Devil commented on the preceding actions. In Renaissance Italy, *intermedii* were made up of scenes with mythological subjects, performed between the acts of the main play. The French and Spanish terms, respectively *entremets* and *entremés,* reflect the practice of presenting dramatic or musical *interludes** between the courses of royal feasts. In seventeenth century France, ballets enlivened intermissions (as in MOLIÈRE's *le Bourgeois gentilhomme* and *le Malade imaginaire*). As the intermezzo became longer and more elaborate, it gradually became a brief independent show such as a play in one act or a *curtain raiser**.

INTERMISSION

Fr.: *entracte;* Ger.: *Pause;* Sp.: *intermedio.*

Lapse of time between acts in which the play is interrupted and the audience leaves the house temporarily; a break that marks a return to social time, dis-illusion and reflection.

The intermission is used to change the scenery during a long pause or blackouts; also, changes may be made in full view of the audience. Its primary function, however, is a social one. The custom became widespread in Renaissance court theatre, as it allows spectators to meet and show off their outfits (hence the ritual in the foyer of the Opera or the Comédie-Française in the nineteenth century).

Classical dramaturgy took over the intermission and tried to motivate it to serve the illusion: "During the interval, the stage remains vacant; but the action continues off stage"; "The intermission is a rest only for the spectators, not for the action. The characters are deemed to continue acting during the interval from one act to another" (MARMONTEL, 1763). It matters little how long the intermission lasts, as long as it is motivated by the action that continues off-stage: "Since action never stops, when movement ceases upon the stage it continues behind. No rest, no interruption." (DIDEROT, *Discours de la poésie dramatique*, chap.15).

There are many other reasons for having an intermission, however, besides this illusory verisimilitude. First of all, it is a psychological necessity for the audience, whose attention is difficult to hold for more than two hours at a stretch. Actors also need to rest. The return to reality invites the spectators, like it or not, to think about what they have just seen, to judge the work, to put together their impressions in a structured way. The intermission signals an awakening of the critical faculties, and it is not surprising that epic dramaturgy favours many such pauses, forcing the audience to intervene in these moments of "dis-illusion." Productions that are based on fascination and have their own specific rhythm, on the other hand, often do away with these precious minutes of respite. Riveted to his place, mute, his back aching from seats designed with no consideration for human anatomy, the present-day spectator cannot even express his bad temper – he is compelled to take part in the religious ceremony of "mass-en-scène" and not break the continuity of the performance. In this test of endurance, it is a *coup* to prevent the "brain-drain" of the spectators from the theatre spece.

See also: segmentation, time, silence, act.

INTERPLAY

Fr.: interlucidité; Ger.: *Spiel und Gegenspiel;* Sp.: *interacción.*

See PLAY AND COUNTERPLAY

INTERPRETATION

Fr.: *interprétation;* Ger.: *Interpretation;* Sp.: *interpretación.*

Critical approach by the reader or spectator of text and stage. Interpretation is concerned with determining *meaning** (*hermeneutics**). It deals with the process of production by the "authors" of the performance as well as reception by the audience.

1. Interpretation of Mise-en-scène

The dramatic text cannot be acted "directly," without a previous process of *dramaturgical** analysis intended to determine the meaningful aspects of the play that should be enhanced by the stage. Once a reading has been chosen, the concretization of the play depends as much on the times and circumstances of the *production** as on the audience to which the performance is addressed.

2. Interpretation by Actor

The actor's interpretation may be anything from an interpretation planned by the author and director to a personal transposition of the play, a total re-creation by the actor using the materials available to him. In the first case, the interpretation tends to take second place to the intentions of an author or director; the actor does not use and transform the message to be transmitted, but is only a puppet. In the second case, the interpretation generates all of the meaning, and *signs** are elaborated not as a result of a pre-existing system but as the way the system is structured and produced. Since the advent of the mise-en-scène that refuses to be subordinated to an all-powerful text and fixed in a single meaning, interpretation is no longer a second language – it is the very substance of the performance.

3. Interpretation by Reader/Spectator

A. HERMENEUTICAL APPROACH

"To interpret a text [...] is not to seek out an intention *hidden behind* it; it is to follow the movement of meaning toward reference; that is, toward the kind of world, or rather of being-in-the-world, *open before* the text. To interpret is to deploy the new mediations that *discourse** establishes between man and the world" (RICOEUR 1972, 1014).

We cannot do without the notion of *hermeneutics** and interpretation, in spite of a certain branch of semiology of *communication** that is applied mechanically to literature and art, which would have us think so. Interpretation organizes the many possible readings of a single play, invites us to evaluate the spectator's productive and receptive work, his hermeneutical link with the performance: "The spectator's relationship with the performance is, by nature, hazy, uncertain, equivocal. He has the task, not of pursuing the meaning, but of attending at its birth, producing it in a relationship of communication with the performance that is so random that it no longer warrants the name of communication, but, entirely, that of interpretation" (CORVIN 1978b, 15).

B. THE SEMIOTIC AND SEMANTIC DIMENSIONS

BENVENISTE's distinction (1974:43–67) between the semiotic dimension (the closed system of differences between the signs) and the semantic dimension (which opens the system onto world and discourse, situation and interpreter) enables us to distinguish between the *sense** of the performance and its *meaning**. If sense is the immanent functioning of the work of art (its structure), interpretation encompasses the performance in the external systems of a given time, a history and the subjective approach of the spectator.

C. PLURALITY OF INTERPRETATIONS

Critical work on text and performance can choose between the problematical search for a centre of gravity (i.e. a static interpretation) and the multiplication of various interpretative paths and possible vectorizations within the performance. The latter choice seems to be the favourite option of practitioners, many of whom are adept at pluralism, thus echoing BARTHES' words: "To interpret a text is not to give it a (more or less justified, more or less free) meaning, but on the contrary to appreciate what *plural* constitutes it" (1970, 11; Eng. 1974, 5).

See also: dramatic text, text and stage, textual and visual.

Further reading: Ricoeur 1965; Barthes 1966b; Jauss 1982a; Pavis 1980c, 1983a; Postlewait and McConachie 1989.

INTERTEXT

Fr.: *intertexte*; Ger.: *Intertext*; Sp.: *intertexto*.

See INTERTEXTUALITY

INTERTEXTUALITY

Fr.: *intertextualité*; Ger.: *Intertextualität*; Sp.: *intertextualidad*.

The theory of intertextuality (KRISTEVA 1969; BARTHES 1973a) postulates that a text is comprehensible only through the interplay of texts that precede it, and that, by different transformation, influence and change it in turn.

Similarly, *dramatic text** and *performance text** are situated within a series of dramaturgies and stage devices. Some directors do not hesitate to insert foreign texts whose only link to the play is thematic, parodic or explicative (VITEZ, PLANCHON, MESGUICH). This sets up a dialogue between the quoted text and the original text (for example, VITEZ quotes *Aragon* in *Andromaque*). This technique is different from the simple social or political contextualization done in many productions: the search for an intertext transforms the original text on the level of both signifier and signified; it explodes the linear *fabula** and theatrical illusion, contrasts two often opposing rhythms and writings, and places the text at a distance by stressing its materiality.

Intertextuality also exists when the director stages two echoing texts using the same scenery, often with the same actors, as, for example, in VITEZ' Molieresque tetralogy, A. DELBEE's three "Racine," the Théâtre de l'Aquarium's production of MAETERLINCK's *l'Intruse*, FEYDEAU's *Léonie est en avance*, O. PY's *La Servante*. This phenomenon forces us to seek links between two texts, to make thematic comparisons, and to expand the horizons of our reading.

See also: quote, play and counterplay, discourse.

Further reading: Bakhtin 1973; *Texte*, 1983 (bibliography); Ruprecht 1983; Pavis 1983a, 1986; Lehmann in Thomsen 1985.

INTONATION

Fr.: *intonation*; Ger.: *Betonung, Intonation, Tonfall*; Sp.: *entonación*.

See VOICE, DECLAMATION

INVISIBLE THEATRE

Fr.: *théâtre invisible*; Ger.: *unsichtbares Theater*; Sp.: *teatro invisible*.

A term from BOAL (1977, 37), meaning improvised acting in the midst of a group of people who must be oblivious that they are taking part in theatre so that they do not fall back into the "spectator" mode.

IRONY

(From the Greek *euronia*, dissimulation.)
Fr.: *ironie*; Ger.: *Ironie*; Sp.: *ironía*.

An utterance is ironic when, in addition to its primary, obvious sense, it reveals a deeper, different, perhaps even opposite meaning (antiphrasis). Certain signals (intonation, situation, knowledge of the represented reality) indicate, directly or indirectly, that the obvious meaning should be passed over in favour of its opposite. There is a real pleasure to be found in identifying irony, because one is able to extrapolate and feel superior to the commonsense level.

1. Irony in Characters

Characters, as language users, are able to resort to verbal irony. They can mock one another or demonstrate their superiority to a partner or a situation (for example, "Brutus is an honourable man"; Antony in *Julius Caesar*). There is nothing specifically dramatic in this kind of irony (*pragmatics**), but it lends itself well to the stage, as the situation must make it clear who is in the wrong, or contradict with a gesture, intonation or facial expression what the text is *apparently* saying. SOCRATES "makes theatre" when he uses his diabolical irony to make his interlocutors reveal what they cannot formulate. The *eiron*, for instance, though weak and feigning ignorance, always achieves his ends, often at the expense of the grotesque *buffoon** (*alazon*; see *braggart**).

2. Dramatic Irony

Dramatic irony is often connected to the *dramatic situation*. It is perceived by the spectators when they are able to perceive elements of the plot that remain hidden to the characters and prevent them from acting with full knowledge of the facts. Dramatic irony is always perceptible to the spectactors to the extent that the *egos* of the characters, who appear to be autonomous and free, are in fact subjected to the central ego of the playwright. In this sense, irony is the dramatic situation *par excellence*, since the spectators are always in a position of superiority to what is shown on stage. The inclusion of internal *communication** (among the characters) in external communication (between stage and auditorium) allows for all possible ironic commentary on the situations and protagonists. In spite of the *fourth wall** that is supposed to protect the fiction from the outside world, the playwright is often tempted to address his accomplices, the audience, directly by appealing to their knowledge of the ideological code and his own *hermeneutic** activity to make them grasp the true meaning of the situation. Irony acts as an *alienation effect** that breaks the theatrical illusion and invites the audience not to take what they hear to the letter. Irony indicates that the play's "narrators" (actor, dramatist, author) may only be telling stories after all. It invites the spectator to see the unusual aspects of a situation, not to swallow anything without examining it carefully. Everything shown in theatrical fiction seems to be preceded by the warning, "use at your own risk," to be subject to an ironical judgment. Irony is present and visible in the text to a varying degree, is only recognizable as such by the outside intervention of the spectator, and remains always ambiguous (*denial**).

The dramatic structure is sometimes built on the opposition between main plot and comic subplot (*comic relief**), with one relativizing the other. In more modern authors, such as CHEKHOV, irony determines the structure of the dialogues: it is based on the constant production of ambiguities that cannot be solved without creating new ones, on the demotivation of characters, and on the reading strategy that will make both a particular interpretation and its opposite possible, refusing to take sides explicitly.

3. Tragic Irony

*Tragic** irony (or the irony of fate) is a case of dramatic irony in which the hero is completely deceived about his situation and runs toward his end, thinking he will be able to escape. The most famous example is that of Oedipus, who leads the enquiry to discover, finally, that he himself is the guilty one. Tragic irony can come very close to black humour, as when Wallenstein (in SCHILLER's play) declares, moments before his death, that he intends to "take a long rest," or when Othello speaks of "honest Iago." Beyond the character, it is the whole audience that gains an awareness of the ambiguity of language and of moral and political values. The hero makes a mistake out of over-confidence (*hubris**) and because of an error in the use of words and the semantic ambiguity of speech: "Tragic irony may consist in showing how, in the course of the drama, the hero finds himself literally 'taken at his word,' a word that strikes back, bringing with it the bitter experience of the meaning that he refused to acknowledge" (VERNANT VIDAL-NAQUET 1972, 35).

This discovery of irony at the very heart of the *tragic* conflict is a relatively recent one in the history of literary criticism. *New Criticism* even saw in irony the origins of any poetics or reading process. It dates back to the Romantic era, when irony was considered to be a principle of the work of art, of the author's consciousness in the work, and of the irreducible contrast between the subjectivity of the individual and the objectivity of blind, implacable fate, of "the clear conscience of eternal agitation, of infinite total chaos," in the words of SCHLEGEL (1814), theoreticians of Romantic irony along with SOLGER (1829).

Further reading: S. Kierkesgaard, *The Concept of Irony*, in 1865; Sharpe 1959; Knox 1961, *The Word Irony and its Context: 1500–1755*, 1961; Behler 1970; Muecke 1982; States 1971; Booth 1974; *Linguistique et sémiologie*, 1976; *Poétique*, 1978; Rozik 1986.

ISOTOPY

Fr.: *isotopie*; Ger.: *Isotopie*; Sp.: *isotopía*.

1. Semantic Isotopy

The concept was introduced by A. GREIMAS, who defined it as "a redundant set of semantic categories that make possible a uniform reading of the narrative, as it results from partial readings of the utterances and from the resolution of their ambiguity, which is guided by the search for a single reading" (1970, 188). In a nutshell, the isotopy is the through-line that guides the reader or spectator in his search for meaning by helping to group various signifying systems according to a given perspective.

This definition, rightly criticized by CORVIN (1985, 234), at least accounts for the *coherence** of a theatrical text or performance, in spite of the diversity of the different materials and reading paths, mainly by showing how the reader moves from one level of the text to another using isotopy connection devices. The concept may be extended from the level of content to that of expression (RASTIER 1972) in order to observe, in the theatrical performance, the regularities, recurrences and signifying practices of all the stage systems.

2. Isotopy of Action

There is no single fundamental isotopy of a given production. In order to define isotopy, we need to look at the stage production, look for recurring traits that unify the performance and provide the spectator with a path for interpretation. One immediately thinks of the integrating role of *fabula** and *action**, which regroup and rework the stage systems within a narrative scheme. For a whole dramaturgy that dates back to ARISTOTLE, action channels the rest of the performance: "Action, understood as the essence of dramatic art, unifies word, actor, costume, scenery and music in the sense that we can identify them as different conductors of a single current that may pass from one to the other or through several at the same time" (HONZL 1971, 19). The image of the multiform current (or the through-line) is one way of visualizing the isotopy. But contemporary productions, no longer based on narrativity or continuous action, are read according to quite different types of isotopies, usually linked to the signifiers of the performance.

3. Isotopy of performance

The isotopy may appear in the form of a kind of lighting, a verbal or musical refrain, a long drawn-out metaphor, a series of images in the same register; in short, anything that lends a certain coherence to the play. Our reception and vectorization of the performance depend on our ability to recognize and establish connections among the bits of information furnished by all the performance materials. This notion takes us back to that of the textual strategy (or reading strategy) or discourse of mise-en-scène.

See also: redundancy, reception, discourse, hermeneutics, dramatic text, semiology, performance text.

Further reading: Rastier 1972; Arrivé 1973.

J

JUGGLER

Fr.: *bateleur;* Ger.: *Gaukler;* Sp.: *malabarista.*

The juggler was a travelling popular artist who appeared in public places, most often on a trestle stage, to perform tricks, acrobatics or improvised theatre as a preface to selling merchandise such as pomades or medicines to the audience.

In the Middle Ages, jugglers gathered in well-travelled places: Pont-Neuf in Paris and Plaza San Marco in Venice. They represented a non-literary, popular brand of theatre with satirical or political tendencies. These shows were free and provided a meeting place for the lower classes and slumming aristocrats.

Jugglers' shows were most often based on physical prowess rather than on the production of textual or symbolic meaning. The techniques generally involved physical or burlesque expertise, but sometimes more elaborate forms were developed that included satirical text, comic dialogue, or *parades**. Between 1619 and 1625, TABARIN (1584–1633) and MONTDOR performed "Tabarinic fantasies," monologues which were at once popular and learned, farces performed in the open air on a *trestle stage**.

With the current revival of popular theatre, jugglers, as animators and agitators, orators, vendors and leaders, are all the rage in *street theatre**. Artists like Dario FO are renewing an old tradition in addressing an audience avid for social or political satire in factories, public places, or even suburban theatres.

K

KINESICS

Fr.: kinésique; Ger.: *Kinesik*; Sp.: kinésica.

Science of communication by *gesture** and facial expression. The basic hypothesis is that body *expression** obeys a coded system that is learned by the individual and varies according to the culture. The study of movement encompasses several areas: the study of the forms and functions of individual communication, the nature of the interaction between movement and verbal language, and the observation of gestural interaction between two or more individuals.

Kinesics should enable us to analyze stage interactions among actors, to determine the conscious and unconscious system that governs their configuration on stage, the blocking and the distances between them. It is clearly necessary to keep in mind the discrepancies between so-called "normal" behaviour and stage behaviour, particularly by calculating the effect of the *proxemic** arrangement of the actors on the spectators' view.

A kinesics of theatre gestuality would have to formalize the process of this gestural "subconversation": the influence of the social milieu described, of the kind of aesthetic *stylization**, of the individual involuntary factors involved in the actor's *gestuality** and their use by the director. There are many factors involved in gestural encoding as it appears to the audience, and they are not easy to identify. On the other hand, the stage obliges the gestures to be encoded consciously; it simplifies for the sake of legibility, which makes it a valuable research laboratory for the kinesist.

Even more important than the distances between actors (*proxemics**), in reality as well as in theatre, would seem to be the *gaze** and point of view of the actors and spectators. In this sense, a study of the *perspectives** of *reception** and their emotional or simply physical value is indispensable. The intuitive experiments of *mimes** and some theatre practitioners (BRECHT, MEYERHOLD) with *attitudes**, postures and *gestuses** were the first steps toward a kinesic approach to the phenomenon of gesture, before the term existed.

See also: expression, mime, body.

Further reading: Goffman 1967; *Langages*, 1968; K. Scherer 1970; Schechner 1973a; Stern 1973; Birdwhistell 1973; Sarles 1977; Sebeok in Helbo 1979; Pavis 1981a; Sarrazac et al. 1981.

KINESTHETICS

(From the Greek *kinesi-* and *aisthesis*, sensation of movement.)

Fr.: *kinesthésie*; Ger.: *Kinästhetik*; Sp.: *kinestesia*.

Kinesthetics is the conscious perception of own's own body position or movements through the muscles and the inner ear. Kinesthetic elements have to do with communication between actors and spectators, as for instance the tension in an actor's body or the impression that a scene may make "physically" upon the audience. According to BARBA's theatre anthropology (1995), a spectator is affected physically by the pre-expressive level of the actor's body and the performance. Dance is very aware of this kinesthetic impact: "There is a kinesthetic response in the spectator's body that reproduces the dancer's experience within him in part" (John MARTIN 1966, 48). MARTIN even gives the name *metakinesis* to the correlation between "the physical and the psychic as the two aspects of a single fundamental reality" (ibid, 29).

Kinesthetics allows us to appreciate body movement through a "muscular sense that regulates the many nuances of force and speed of body movements in a manner appropriate to the emotions that inspire such movements, to allow the mechanism of the human body the possibility of stylizing these emotions and thus make dance a full and essentially human art" (JAQUES-DALCROZE 1965, 141).

KNOT

Fr.: *noeud*; Ger.: *Knoten, Verflechtung*; Sp.: *nudo*.

The knot or complication is a device that blocks the thread of the plot, causing a conflict between the desire of the subject *actant** and the obstacle of the object actant. Once this complication or blockage exists, the actants struggle to unblock the plot. Narratology looks at how the *fabula* is set in motion by "dynamic motifs that upset the balance of the initial situation. The set of motifs that violate the immobility of the initial situation and initiate the action is called the knot" (TOMACHEVSKY 1965, 274).

1. Knot and Dénouement

The *knot*, or set of conflicts blocking the action, is opposed to the *dénouement* or unraveling, which unblocks it: "The knot of plays being an unexpected accident that checks the course of the action represented, and the dénouement another unforeseen accident that facilitates that action, we find that these two parts of the dramatic poem are apparent in the poem on le Cid" (*Sentiments de l'Académie sur "le Cid"*).

The unraveling consists in taking the action from happiness to misfortune, or vice versa. The dramaturgy of the *well-wrought play** handles this with virtuosity, to excess in the view of some, like ZOLA, who complains about those who "knot up complicated threads only to have the pleasure of unraveling them afterwards" (ZOLA 1881).

2. Presentation of the Knot

The knot is an integral part of any dramaturgy that includes conflict, but it may be "visible" to a varying degree. In classical dramaturgy, contradiction and the tightening of the knot take place in a continuous but concealed manner. In Brechtian epic dramaturgy, on the other hand, attention is drawn to the sensitive nodal points of the action; to show the way the story is "stitched together," the causality and collision of the contradictions: "The individual episodes have to be knotted together in such a way that the knots are easily noticed" (BRECHT, *A Short Organum for the Theatre*: sect. 67). The action is often interrupted "from the outside" at a moment that might be tragic.

3. Nature of Knot and Dénouement

Things can become knotted for many reasons, all of which are reducible to the same basic scheme: an insoluble contradiction between two consciousnesses, two equally justified aspirations or requirements (in classical tragedy) or, on the contrary, a *conflict** that refers back to social contradictions that are man-made and therefore can be changed (according to BRECHT). In the first case, the knot is eliminated finally through the intervention of that "sense of reconciliation which the tragedy affords by the glimpse of eternal justice. In its absolute sway this justice overrides the relative justification of one-sided aims and passions" (HEGEL 1832, 379; Eng. 1975, 1198). In the second case, the knot calls on the outside intervention of the spectator, who is the only one capable of eliminating the social contradictions entangling the characters. Whether it is disentangled or cut, the knot always leaves its mark.

L

LABORATORY THEATRE

Fr.: *théâtre laboratoire;* Ger.: *Labortheater;* Sp.: *teatro laboratorio.*

*Experimental theatre** in which experiments on acting and staging are carried out with no concern for commercial profitability, and without even considering it essential to present a finished play to the general public (for example, E. AUTANT and L. LARA's Art and Action Laboratory, GROTOWSKI's Laboratory Theatre, 1971).

Further reading: Corvin 1973; Jomaron 1981.

LANGUAGE, THEATRICAL (STAGE LANGUAGE, DRAMATIC LANGUAGE)

Fr.: *langage dramatique, scénique, théâtral;* Ger.: *dramatische Sprache, szenische Sprache, Theatersprache;* Sp.: *lenguaje dramático, escénico, teatral.*

See WRITING

LANGUAGE GAME

Fr.: *jeu de langage;* Ger.: *Sprachspiel;* Sp.: *juego de lenguaje.*

According to WITTGENSTEIN, language games should "bring out here that to speak a language is part of an activity, of a way of life" (1961, sect. 23). As applied to the theatre, this notion describes quite well how a dramatic text acts and provides an example of verbal action. Unlike the *dramatic situation**, in which the action results from a conflict between characters, the term language game could be used for a dramatic structure in which *fabula** and action are replaced by a strategy of discourse and a progression of the enunciations (apart from their content). In MARIVAUX, for instance, in parallel to the visible plot, the play is constructed according to the (hi)story of the enunciating consciousness, from "I'm about to tell you" to "all has been told" at the end of the play. The main characters are constantly setting word traps for each other, confessions of love constituting the failure or victory of the verbal ruse.

A whole trend in contemporary theatre (PIRANDELLO, BECKETT, T. BERNHARD, HANDKE, PINGET, SARRAUTE, TARDIEU) builds the *fabula* around assonance, word associations or references to communication or enunciation. As soon as language is no longer used primarily for its meaning but rather for its texture and volume, it becomes a set of building blocks to be handled as things, not as signs.

See also: language situation, textual space, rhetoric, spoken action.

Further reading: Barthes 1957, 88–91; Pavis 1980c, 1983c; Elam 1984; Spolin 1985.

LANGUAGE SITUATION

Fr.: *situation de langage;* Ger.: *Sprechsituation;* Sp.: *situación de lenguaje.*

1. The term *language situation* is to be distinguished from *dramatic situation**. While the latter contrasts the situation experienced with the text spoken, the *language situation* is generated by a discourse that does not refer to a reality outside itself but to its own fabrication, like poetic language, which also is intransitive and self-reflexive. It is a "configuration of words appropriate for engendering relationships which at first appear psychological, not so much false as fixed in the very compromise of an anterior language" (BARTHES 1957, 89).

2. Any text that does not attempt to appear clear and "transparent" and to translate itself into a situation and an action, but relies on its own materiality, produces language situations. The text stresses its constructed, artificial nature, refusing to pass for the natural expression of a particular psychology. All *devices** of literariness and theatricality are openly shown. Such a text cannot be reduced to a referent or a system of ideas. As examples of texts supported by language situations, BARTHES (1957) mentions the theatre of MARIVAUX and ADAMOV. We could add all those dramatic texts which reflect (on) the idea of the play within a play and point to their own rhetorical devices. In the same spirit, stagings of classics (such as those of A. VITEZ, J.-C. FALL, J.-M. VILLÉGIER and C. REGY) attempt to discover the rhetorical and linguistic dimension of the text.
See also: stereotype, discourse, semiology.
Further reading: Segre 1973; Helbo 1975; Pavis 1980a,c, 1986.

LAUGHTER

Fr.: *rire*; Ger.: *Lachen*; Sp.: *risa*.
See COMIC

LAZZI

(From the Italian *lazzi*, meaning buffoonery, comical stage business.)

Term from *commedia dell'arte**. An element improvised by the actor, used for comic characterization (originally of Harlequin). Contorsions, grimaces, burlesque and clownish behaviour and endless stage business are its basic ingredients. *Lazzi* quickly become *bravura pieces** that are expected of the actor by the audience. The best or most effective are often set out in the *scenario** or text (plays on words, political or sexual allusions). With the development of the *commedia*, and particularly its influence on French theatre in the seventeenth and eighteenth centuries (MOLIERE, MARIVAUX), lazzi tended to be included in the text and became a more refined (but always play) way of conducting dialogue, a mise-en-scène of all the paraverbal components of the acting.

In contemporary performances, which are often very theatrical and parodic, lazzi play an essential role as visual aids (STREHLER's productions of the Italian classics, popular forms and techniques, etc.).
See also: scenario, improvisation, acting.
Further reading: Mic 1927; Pavis 1986a; Fo 1991.

LEITMOTIF

(German word meaning "leading motive.")
Fr.: *leitmotiv*; Ger.: *Leitmotiv*; Sp.: *leitmotiv*.

A term introduced by Hans VON WOLZOGEN in connection with the music of Richard WAGNER, who himself used the term *Grundthema* (basic theme).

1. In music, a leitmotif is a recurring musical theme, a sort of melodic refrain that punctuates the piece (for example, the Grail leitmotif in *Parsifal*). In literature, it is a group of words, an image or a form that recurs periodically to announce a theme or indicate a formal repetition or obsession. It is a musical device, as it is mainly the effect of repetition and familiarity that is essential; the meaning of the expression is secondary. This explains why the theme does not necessarily have a central value for the text as a whole but acts rather as an emotional signal and structural element. The linking of leitmotifs forms a kind of long drawn-out metaphor that sets the tone for the entire work. A signal is sufficient to characterize a character or situation imme-

diately; leitmotifs function as a rallying code and orient the spectator. In this way the work sets out its temporal structure, punctuation and pace (BERLIOZ speaks of the *idée fixe* of a work).

2. In theatre, the technique is frequently used. In comedy the leitmotif appears as comical repetition (MOLIERE's "and Tartuffe?" and "no dowry?"); in poetic theatre, as the repetition of a line or a rhetorical figure. More generally, any repetition of terms, any assonance, any conversation that goes around in circles (CHEKHOV) constitutes a leitmotif.

The playwright may make dramaturgical use of the leitmotif when the theme marks the inevitable passage of time (the reference to the cherry tree in the play of the same name) or a slow progression toward catastrophe (the pistols in *Hedda Gabler*). The chorus of tragedy also fulfills this function of warning and fate.

The necessarily subterranean nature of this subconversation makes it difficult to formalize all the thematic networks. At the same time, however, it impregnates the text and communicates it to the spectator in the infralinguistic and suggestive mode of music. The playwright and director are quite free to produce almost imperceptible leitmotifs directed at subconscious perception (sound effects, rhythms, parallel expressions, thematic refrains).

3. Some productions operate on the basis of stage leitmotifs, using gestuality, repetition of entire sequences (R. WILSON), reduplicated performance or surrealist imagery as poetic interludes (cf. PLANCHON in *Folies bourgeoises*), or repetition of a short piece of music (in stagings of RACINE by MESGUICH). The system of mise-en-scène often imbues the performance with a theme or a recurring commentary that acts as a leitmotif.

See also: composition, dramatic structure.

LIFE ARTS

Fr.: *arts de la vie*; Ger.: *Lebenskünste*; Sp.: *artes de la vida*.

This term is patterned after the "life sciences" (BARBA 1993 and his "body-in-life"; PRADIER and his "organized human performance behaviours") and applied to stage arts that use the living body – spoken theatre, dance, mime, dance theatre, opera – as opposed to mechanical arts that limit themselves to reproducing an image of the body (cinema, video, installation art).

LIGHT COMEDY

Fr.: *comédie légère*; Ger.: *leichte Komödie*; Sp.: *comedia ligera*.

See VAUDEVILLE

LIGHTING

Fr.: *éclairage*; Ger.: *Beleuchtung*; Sp.: *iluminación*.

1. We have seen the successive reigns of the actor-king, the director, the stage designer; now it is the light designer's turn to hold the key to the performance. As early as the turn of the century, APPIA spoke of the importance of light to the actor: "The flexibility of light is something almost miraculous. Light contains all degrees of brightness and movement; like a palette, it contains all possibilities for color. It can create shadows, and it can spread the harmony of its vibrations out in space exactly as music would. With it, we control all the expressive power that is in space – if space is put in the actor's service" (1954, 39; Eng. 1982, 58).

2. Light is not simply a decorative element; it participates in the meaning-producing efforts of the performance. Its dramaturgical and semiological potential is infinite. It can clarify or comment on an action, isolate an actor or an element of the stage, create an atmosphere, pace the performance, help interpret the development of arguments and emotions, and so on. Situated at the junction of space and time, light is one of the principal "enunciators" of the mise-en-scène, as it comments on the entire performance, and may even *be* the performance, by defining its path (*parcours**). A marvellous material of unsurpassed fluidity and

flexibility, light gives a tone to the stage, modalizes the action, controls the timing, ensures the transition from one dramatic *moment** to another, and co-ordinates the remaining stage systems by establishing relationships between them or isolating them.

3. Lighting technique has shown its versatility and its "musical" force. Light is "the only external means that can act upon the spectator's imagination without distracting. Light has a power similar to that of music; it touches different senses but acts in the same way. Light is a living element, one of the fluids of imagination. Scenery is a dead thing" (DULLIN 1969, 80). As it breathes life into space and actors, light takes on an almost metaphysical quality, controlling and lending modality and nuance to meaning. It can be infinitely modulated and is the opposite of a discrete sign (yes/no, true/false, white/black, sign/non-sign). It is an element of atmosphere that links and infiltrates elements which are scattered and separate, a life-giving substance.

Further reading: Bablet 1973; Bergman 1977; *Travail théâtral*, 1978; Bonnat 1982; *Oxford Companion*, 1993 (history); Pavis 1996a.

LINES

Fr.: *réplique*; Ger.: *Stichwort, Replik*; Sp.: *réplica*.

The lines spoken by a character in the course of dialogue have value only in relation to the lines preceding and following them. The *minimal unit** of meaning and situation consists in the reply/counter-reply, action/reaction pairs. The spectator does not follow the path of a coherent and monologic text, but interprets each line in the changing context of the situation of enunciation. The way in which the text is structured as a whole furnishes indications on the rhythm of the play and the outcome of the forces in conflict. The interplay of the characters' lines is not situated only at the level of the semantic oppositions between characters, but takes place at the level of intonation, acting style and rhythm of mise-en-scène. For BRECHT, this process is like a game of tennis: "An actor needs to take the lines served him like a tennis player taking a ball. This is done by catching the tone and passing it on, so that rhythms and cadences develop which run through entire scenes. (*Theaterarbeit*, 1961, 385; Eng. 1964, 244). However, there are playwrights who do not use lines in this way but as a series of speech events that only the listener can put together and draw meaning from (CHEKHOV, BECKETT, VINAVER, CHARTREUX, DRAGUTIN).

See also: text and countertext, intertextuality, dialogue, monologue.

LINKING OF SCENES

Fr.: *liaison des scènes*; Ger.: *Szenenverflechtung*; Sp.: *enlace de escenas*.

In classical dramaturgy, a principle whereby two consecutive scenes are to be connected by the continuous presence of a character, so that the stage is never empty. D'AUBIGNAC makes a distinction between *linkage by presence*, involving a character, and *linkage by sound*, when a sound is made on stage and a character who could probably have made it comes to find out the cause, or for another reason, and finds that there is no longer anyone there (1927, 245). A *linkage by flight* takes place when "a character leaves the stage just as another character is entering, because the first doesn't want the second to see or speak to him" (SCHERER 1950, 437).

LIST OF CHARACTERS

Fr.: *liste des personnages*; Ger.: *Liste der Personen*; Sp.: *lista de personajes*.

The list of characters, generally placed before the play's title and the beginning of the dialogues, is an element of the *didascalia** (or *stage directions** or *paratext**), and is not therefore addressed to the reader or the director. From the Renaissance until the early nineteenth century, the Latin term *dramatis personae* was often used, which stressed a resemblance with real people involved in an action. The list is almost always reproduced in the *programme** made available to the audience. In this way both readers and spectators are able to familiarize themselves, before and during the performance, with the constellation of characters, to check on their family and social relationships, and so on – sometimes a very necessary exercise. The list may be organized in various ways but generally reflects an attempt to mention all the characters, at least those who are individualized. The order of the names, particularly in the classical period, often corresponds to the social hierarchy: first comes the king or the character with the highest social status; then, in decreasing order of merit, the other characters. Sometimes couples, parents and children are listed together.

Following classicism, and in parallel to the mushrooming of stage directions, names were sometimes followed by identifying information indicating age, character, physical appearance (e.g. BEAUMARCHAIS' *le Barbier de Séville*), even hidden motives. Many a playwright has been tempted to turn the list into an essay or short story on each character.

The list was sometimes organized in such a way as to clarify conflicts and factions, oppose men and women (cf. *Cyrano de Bergerac*), schematize large families and alliances. The editor frequently added the names of the actors who performed in the first production.

A similar device is to list at the beginning of each scene all the characters present on stage, so that the reader will know who is on stage but remaining silent, and when the characters enter or exit.

Naming the characters is a decisive factor in how they are defined and perceived throughout the play, regardless of what they say or do. It is the dramatist's first word, and often also his last.

Further reading: Thomasseau 1984a.

LITERARY ADVISER

Fr.: *conseiller littéraire;* Ger.: *Dramaturg;* Sp.: *consejero literario.*

See DRAMATURG

LITURGICAL DRAMA

Fr.: *drama liturgique;* Ger.: *geistliches Spiel;* Sp.: *drama litúurgico.*

Liturgical drama appeared in France between the tenth and the twelfth centuries with the staging of holy texts. In the course of the Mass, the faithful participate in the chanting and speaking of psalms and commentaries on the Bible (the Easter cycle being concerned with themes of the Resurrection, the Christmas cycle with the Nativity). Gradually scenes from the Old and New Testaments were added, gestures were added to the singing, French replaced Latin (in semi-liturgical drama) for the *sainetes** played under the aegis of the church (1175, *Sainte Résurrection* in the vulgate). Liturgical drama produced *miracle plays** and *mystery plays**.

LOA

(From the Spanish word for "praise.")

Fr.: *loa;* Ger.: *Loa;* Sp.: *loa.*

See CURTAIN RAISER

M

MACHINERY

Fr.: *machine théâtrale*; Ger.: *Theatermaschinerie*; Sp.: *maquinaria teatral.*
See STAGE MACHINERY

MAGIC

Fr.: *magie*; Ger.: *Magie*; Sp.: *magia.*
See FAIRYTALE PLAY

MAINSPRING OF THE ACTION

Fr.: *ressort dramatique*; Ger.: *Handlungspotential*; Sp.: *recurso dramático.*

1. This is a mechanism which, effective though often concealed, directs the action, organizes the play's meaning and provides the key to motivations and plot. It may be found in the motivations of characters, the organization of the *fabula*, the *suspense** and all those stage devices that contribute to creating a theatrical and dramatic atmosphere that captivates the spectator: "The secret is to please and to move: to invent mainsprings that can hold me" (BOILEAU). The use of such devices, though permitted and even advised by classical dramaturgy, always presupposes a taste for easy motivations and effects, hidden motives for behaviour: "The modern system of tragedy brings into play all of the mainsprings of the human heart," writes MARMONTEL.

2. The string, a favourite figure of the mainspring, is in fact an ironic and pejorative term used to refer to something that ties together and keeps the episodes and characters in one piece, and enables their creator to manipulate them like puppets according to the whimsical needs of the plot. When these structural elements and dramaturgical devices are too automatic and visible, the play becomes a *well-made play** but the playwright is only a "Mr. Strings," to use SCRIBE's nickname, whose virtuosity is reduced to a mechanical and repetitive technique.

MAIN TEXT, SIDE TEXT

Fr.: *texte principal, texte secondaire*; Ger.: *Haupttext, Nebentext, Bühnenanweisungen*; Sp.: *texto principal, texto secundario.*

This distinction was introduced by R. INGARDEN (1931, 1973), who saw the "written" drama as containing two parallel texts: that of the side text and that of the main text (characters' speeches).

1. The two texts are in a dialectical relationship. The speeches themselves give indications of how the text should be spoken, and complement the stage directions; conversely, the stage directions clarify the characters' situations or motivations and therefore the meaning of their speeches.

INGARDEN (1973, 221) believes that the two texts necessarily come together through the mediation of the objects shown on stage, which are also echoed in the speeches. In fact, this coming together takes place only in a realistic staging in which the stage designer is careful to follow the stage directions. This very dated conception is based on the principle that the playwright had a certain vision of the stage in mind that the staging absolutely must reconstruct.

2. Today, many productions take a course opposite to the stage directions and clarify the speeches using critical (sociological, psychoanalytical) illustration. This kind of interpretation clearly transforms the text to be played, or at least fixes and concretizes it in one of its potential directions.

Current theatre *practice** reveals that the side text is not an obligatory aid indispensable to the construction of meaning, and that it does not control and supervise the main text of the characters' speeches. We would add that this conception runs counter to many commonly held ideas, particularly that of a single "right" mise-en-scène or one that is "faithful to the text."

See also: dramatic text, text and performance, visual and textual.

Further reading: J. Steiner 1968; Pavis 1983b, 1987.

MAKEUP

Fr.: *maquillage;* Ger.: *Schminke;* Sp.: *maquillaje.*

1. A Changing Art

Makeup is particularly important in theatre, as it adds the finishing touches to the actor's face and conveys a great deal of information. Some theatres, such as Kabuki and Kathakali, practise makeup as a ritual ceremony, a phenomenon reflected in the habit of the Théâtre du Soleil of exposing its rather smug-faced actors to the audience as they make up.

If we look at makeup as the simple fact of embellishing natural features, we might expect the art to be as old as the world of theatre itself. The Greeks, however, used it not to make the actors more beautiful (they wore masks anyway), but to give ritual colouring to the face with animal blood and ashes. Beauty makeup, which by definition should be invisible, has been in use since the sixteenth century. As the technique was developed, the paint gradually covered the face. In the eighteenth century, actors painted themselves outrageously, causing a contemporary to remark, "All the actors to be seen on the stage are as many damsels. The queens and heroines wear so much paint that their complexions look fresh and rosy, like young dairymaids." Whatever the techniques used (and some, based on arsenic, were extremely dangerous), makeup adapted skin colour to stage lighting, and thus underwent changes with the introduction of gas and then electric lighting.

2. Functions

A. BEAUTIFICATION

This everyday use of makeup is magnified on stage, the art lying not so much in ageing characters as in making them more youthful. Character *roles** have the makeup artist doing all kinds of repairs and improvements: erasing bags under eyes, eliminating double chins, getting rid of spots – only a plastic surgeon could do better.

B. ENCODING THE FACE

Certain theatrical traditions, such as the Chinese, are based on a purely symbolic system of correspondences between colours and social characteristics. White is for intellectuals, red for the loyal hero, dark blue for the proud, silver for the gods, etc.

C. THEATRICALIZING THE BODY

As the actor's living costume, makeup can render the face inanimate or become a more or less opaque and supple mask that takes advantage of the face's mobility. The actor sometimes makes and holds grimaces (GROTOWSKI 1968, 71). Actors at the Serapions Theater, or an actress like Roberta Carreri in *Judith*, staged by Eugenio BARBA, practise facial sculpture with the aid of posturings that use their hands. In the art of the face, makeup can simultaneously underscore theatricality and facial machinery – "the machinery of the Opera," as MARIVAUX put it – and give an impression of life, renaturalize and "interiorize" facial expression. It plays on the inherent ambiguity of theatre performance, the mixture of natural and artifical, of thing and sign.

D. EXTENDING MAKEUP

No longer limited to the face, makeup may be applied to the whole body. In his production of *Britannicus*, VITEZ painted the actors' hair, reshaped the line of their legs, and made their faces unnatural, without resorting to caricature. Makeup becomes a walking set, strangely symbolic; it no longer characterizes in a psychological fashion but contributes to the elaboration of theatrical forms along with the other *objects** of performance (*mask**, *lighting**, *costumes**). By renouncing its psychological effects, it takes on a quality as one of the *stage systems** and an aesthetic element of the production.

See also: gaze, body.

Further reading: *Traverses*, nos. 7, 10, 14–15, 17, 18, 21–22, 29; Paquet 1990.

MASK

Fr.: *masque*; Ger.: *Maske*; Sp.: *máscara*.

Contemporary Western theatre has revived the use of the mask. This rediscovery (it had already been used in classical Greek theatre and *commedia dell'arte*) coincides with the *retheatricalization* of theatre and the promotion of body expression.

Beyond the anthropological motivations for the use of masks (imitation of the elements, belief in transsubstantiation), there are several indications for their use in theatre, particularly the ability to observe others while being protected from observation oneself. The masked ball liberates participants from their identity and from restrictions based on class and gender.

By hiding one's face one voluntarily renounces psychological expression, which generally provides the greatest amount of information, often very detailed, to the spectator. The actor is forced to make a considerable physical effort to compensate for this loss of meaning and identification. The body translates and amplifies the character's inner self by exaggerating each gesture. This reinforces the theatricality and makes the actor's use of space considerably more important. The opposition between a neutral face and a body in perpetual motion is one of the essential aesthetic consequences of wearing a mask. The mask does not have to represent a face; a neutral mask or a half-mask is enough to immobilize facial expression and concentrate attention on the actor's body.

The mask denaturalizes the character by introducing a foreign body into the relationship of identification between spectator and actor. It is therefore often used when the mise-en-scène seeks to avoid emotional transference and defamiliarizes the character.

The mask can easily deform human physionomy, caricaturing and recasting the contours of the face. Grotesque expression or stylization, sketch or accentuation; all is possible with modern materials, which have an amazing range of forms and mobility.

Masks are meaningful only within the mise-en-scène as a whole. They are no longer confined to the face, and retain close links with facial expression, the actor's overall appearance and even the scenery.

See also: makeup, body.

Further reading: Bernard 1980; Gauvreau 1981; Aslan and Bablet 1985; Roubine 1985; Bernard in Corvin 1995.

MASQUE

Fr.: *masque*; Ger.: *Maskenspiel*; Sp.: *máscara*.

An English dramatic genre of the sixteenth and seventeenth centuries, of French and Italian origins. The actors wore masks and performed programs of dance, music, poetry, allegory and pageantry. The masque is comparable to the *court ballet** and the early operas. Action, when there is any, is confined to a few mythological or allegorical elements or a sketchy debate. The masque is dominated by two major trends, one poetic and literary (BEN JONSON, *The Twelfth Night*, 1606; *The Masque of Queens*, 1610), and one spectacular with an emphasis on special visual effects (JONES and his architectural and stage experiments inspired by the Italian stage).

The *antimasque*, invented by BEN JONSON, is a grotesque and pantomimic version of the masque. It was played before or during the masque as a comic interlude.

See also: ballet comedy

Further reading: Orgel 1965; Jacquot 1972; Daugherty 1984; Lindley 1984.

MASQUERADE

Fr.: *mascarade;* Ger.: *Maskerade;* Sp.: *mascarada.*

See MASQUE

MASS THEATRE

Fr.: *théâtre de masse;* Ger.: *Massentheater;* Sp.: *teatro de masas.*

Terms such as this, as well as "people's" or "popular theatre" and so many others, are slogans rather than clearly defined concepts. The era of mass arts began with the invention of the technical means to reproduce works or art and to reach large numbers of people through the *media** (BENJAMIN). Originally, theatre did not even think about the issue of reproduction, being born of ritual and the ceremonial gatherings of primitive societies. Only after losing that direct relationship with the group – through its move towards literature, its appropriation by a group of scholars or specialists – did it begin to miss contact with the people, until that became one of its main nostalgic aspirations with ROUSSEAU in the eighteenth century and then again in the late nineteenth century. The ambiguity of the term has to do with the concept of mass art: is it art made *by* the masses, like a craft, or is it art made *for* the masses by a minority or using modern technology (radio, television)?

1. Theatre by the Masses

Aside from the *ritual**, whose artistic status is questionable in any case, and the festival, "where the spectators become the spectacle," becoming "actors themselves" (ROUSSEAU), there are few experiences in which the masses are invited to act and participate "in person" in theatrical activity (cf. theatre reformers such as APPIA, FUCHS, ROLLAND, GEMIER). Only in major political upheavals and their commemoration or representation are people called on to participate *en masse*. Federation day (1790) celebrated the first anniversary of the storming of the Bastille; the Russian director EVREINOFF organized the taking of the Winter Palace in Leningrad on 7 November 1920, and the palace became the scene of a festival, a celebration, a happening and a gigantic film studio in which 8,000 actors were shot in a mass film. Only military parades and Fascist and Stalinist parades come close to this highly-organized theatre in which the audience is reduced to a few handicapped generalissimos and decorated dictators. This kind of pathetic spectacle is clearly the antithesis of that celebrated by prophets of popular theatre like R. ROLLAND (1903) and F. GEMIER (*Cahiers du théâtre*, 1926–1938), since they believe theatre should above all be made *for* the people.

2. Theatre for the Masses

"Dramatic art," writes F. GEMIER, "should be addressed to all people. By people I mean not only the popular classes but the members of all social categories; scholars and craftsmen, poets and merchants, leaders and subjects; the whole vast family of the powerful and the meek." (*Le Théâtre*, 1925). This demand, later taken up by VILAR and many advocates of popular theatre, became the rallying cry for a theatre *for* the masses. It was not, however, followed by the creation of a specifically "mass" dramaturgy and repertory. (There are some exceptions, such as the university theatre *cum* soccer festival held yearly in Santiago, Chile, cf. OBREGON, 1983). At the most, we could speak of the side effects: the use of easily readable and repetitive signs, flashy melodramatic devices, a simplified *fabula* and clear, obvious messages. No new genre was created, apart from *agit-prop** or *street theatre** or *guerilla theatre**, and the tendency has been rather to reactivate proven popular techniques (*commedia dell'arte* for the San Francisco Mime Troupe and the Théâtre du Soleil, *parades** and mime plays). Not even industrial techniques of reproduction such as radio and television have created a convincing mass art, if by that we mean a more original genre than sentimental soap operas or broadcasts of *Au théâtre ce soir*. It would appear that theatre is neither an art that can be reproduced mechanically nor one that can be multiplied infinitely, since the live "theatrical relationship" cannot be reconstructed electronically, and since the forms of television neo-tribalism described by MCLUHAN do not entail a theatrical participation that only the happening can muster. "Theatre for the masses" continues to be a political rather than an aesthetic aim: the idea is to create social conditions such that the largest social classes are assured access to culture, before and instead of creating a mass art that will magically transform all those who watch it. The formula expressed by T. MANN, as utopic as it is skeptical, reflects the difficulties and ambitions of an art of the masses: "Theatre, that sublime and childlike pastime, realizes its most beautiful task when it crowns the masses 'the people'" (1974, 105).

MATERIALIST THEATRE

Fr.: *théâtre matérialiste;* Ger.: *materialistisches Theater;* Sp.: *teatro materialista.*

When the production of materials and their inclusion in the performance is visible and is supposed to be an essential part of the performance, we can speak of materialist theatre (BRECHT). Here the stage is a place where human beings can act, thereby functioning as prolegomena for a model of the transformation of the world. The materiality of the performance goes well beyond the stage object, and extends to the critical manipulation of the *fabula**, the actors' role and the meaning of the play. BRECHT and MEYERHOLD, for instance, tried to base the staging "on an exact system, above all deeply materialist and [...] built upon the method of dialectical materialism" (1980, III:88).

See also: code, represented reality, semiology, aesthetics.
Further reading: Althusser 1965; Macherey 1966; Voltz 1974.

See STAGE MATERIALS

MATHEMATICAL APPROACH

Fr.: *approche mathématique;* Ger.: *mathematische Methode;*
Sp.: *acercamiento matemático.*

The common denominator of mathematical approaches to drama consists in a process of reflection on the various combinations of dramatic situations based on the possible relationships (i.e. those which are probable and can be realized effectively) among the characters.

There is a tradition of studies on situations that dates back to POLTI (1895) through PROPP (1929) and, particularly, SOURIAU (1950). The latter's work has inspired many narratological and cybernetic studies (CUBE 1965; MARCUS 1974, 1975; DINU 1977). Here, the narrative (as a series of actions and actantial configurations) is conceived as a movement from a point of relative balance between protagonists to an imbalance (conflict, hubris, catastrophe) that is finally stabilized in an even more profound balance.

The process of formalization is possible only on the basis of objectively observable data; namely, the number of people, scenes, entrances and exits, the length of the various speeches, the existence of recurring themes or images, actantial configurations. These calculations simultaneously validate the scientific nature of the procedure but necessarily neglects the qualitative changes in action and the irrational factors contained in the plot. Although mathematical thinking is, by definition, unassailable, actual *segmentation** into sequences of actions, characters and pertinent moments of scene changes (entrances/exits, set, psychological and moral changes) is clearly quite tricky and open to discussion. Here a dramaturgical or *semiological** analysis becomes indispensable to clarify the basic units of the dramatic universe and to ensure that the resulting formalization takes into account basic intuitions and the overall aesthetic project. Cohabitation between poetry and mathematics is necessary, but painful.

Further reading: Ginestier 1961; Brainerd and Neufeldt 1974; Alter 1975; *Poetics*, 1977; Dinu, in Schmid and Van Kesteren 1984; Schoenmakers 1986; Lafon 1991.

MAXIM

(From the Latin *propositio maxima*, greatest theme.)

Fr.: *sentence, maxime;* Ger.: *Sentenz;* Sp.: *sentencia, máxima.*

The maxim (or *sententia*) is a form of *discourse** that expresses a general truth and transcends the narrow framework of the *dramatic situation**. Sententia may be uttered within a linguistic context of a different kind (novel, dialogue, play), whereas a maxim needs a context (for example, *Maximes* by LA ROCHEFOUCAULD, 1664 or VAUVENARGUES, 1746). The maxim's connection with the text is established only at the price of an abstraction and generalization of the dialogue. Maxims are "general assertions that contain common truths and are connected with the action only by application and consequence" (D'AUBIGNAC, *Pratique du théâtre*, IV,5:1657). They are particularly frequent in classical dramaturgy and in genres that claim to edify the audience through lessons drawn from the play. They are hardly ever seen in the naturalistic play, which seeks to characterize the speech of an individual or group and eschews general authorial forms as being too prescriptive.

1. Status and Function

The maxim is an absolute, autonomous and concise discourse that is not subordinated to the text in which it is embedded. It passes for a truth, a kind of pearl set in the "normal" discourse of the play. It absolutely must be identified as a discourse of *another*, universal and metatextual level.

The spectator has the impression that this discourse does not really belong to the character, that it is only put in his mouth by the author as a higher moralist and stylist. It is therefore a form of direct communication between author and spectator, like the *authorial intervention** or the *address to the audience**. Its *modality** is (wrongly) given as a "serious" discourse that is true, rather than fictional like the rest of the play. It is this privileged status that sets up the maxim as "the gospel truth."

2. Form

Grammatically, a maxim may often appear in an impersonal form ("Triumph without peril brings no glory," *le Cid*, II.2.V:434), without any connection to the character in the play or the "historical" present. It is sometimes only a false (I-you) dialogue disguised as an exchange of lines hidden behind an ideological code or external wisdom ("No matter how great the men, they are made of the same stuff as we," *le Cid*, I.3.V:157). A classical speech often begins with a series of general assertions and then goes on, as in a syllogism, to a minor premise suited to the hero's situation.

See also: dramatic proverb, stichomythia.

Further reading: Scherer 1950; Meleuc 1969; Pavis 1986.

MECHANICAL THEATRE

Fr.: *théâtre mécanique;* Ger.: *mechanisches Theater;* Sp.: *teatro mecánico.*

This is a kind of puppet theatre, or theatre of objects, in which actors are replaced by animated figures, automatons or machines. From the automatic theatre invented by HERON OF ALEXANDRIA in the first century to the *multimedia** theatre of today, including Torelli's experiments in the sixteenth century and the fairs of the eighteenth and nineteenth centuries, mechanical theatre has tried to short circuit the living actor as if he wished to cancel himself out or play the (often misunderstood) paradox of the Übermarionette (CRAIG).

The most aesthetically beautiful experiments in mechanical theatre have taken place in the twentieth century. According to the futurist E. PRAMPOLINI, "the colours and scenery should elicit from the spectator emotional values that cannot be rendered by the poet's words or the actor's gestures" (*Manifeste de la scénographie futuriste*, 1915), and the aim is to seek out a "luminous expression that will illuminate, with all its emotional power, the colours required by the theatrical action." In *Vengono*, MARINETTI staged a drama of objects with eight chairs and a sofa. In his *Ballet Triadique* (1922), Oskar SCHLEMMER conceals the actors under costume-scenery that gives the impression of moving with mechanical precision, and MOHOLY-NAGY imagines an *eccentric mechanics*, while Fernand LÉGER creates a mechanical ballet. The objects made to move are sometimes paintings, as in KANDINSKY and his *Tableaux d'une exposition* (1928), or moving sculptures, as in CALDER and his *Work in Progress* (1968). Theatre people's fascination with stage machinery may stem from the taboo of the presence of the living, which they take pleasure in breaking as if to better reaffirm their technical expertise.

MEDIA

Fr.: *médias*; Ger.: *Medien*; Sp.: *medios de comunicación*.

1. Is Theatre One of the Media?

To propose the inclusion of theatre in a theory of the media is to assume, perhaps rather hastily, that it is comparable to artistic and technological processes such as film, *television**, *radio** and video. This means comparing theatre to phenomena that are ordinarily contrasted with it: the (mass) media, the mechanical and *electronic** arts, the techniques of the cultural industry. In a way, we do theatre a disservice by denying its specificity when we measure it against media that are supported by precisely the kind of technological infrastructure that theatre has so long done without. On the other hand, theatre practice blithely encroaches on other domains; it uses video, television and audio taping within theatrical performance, and is constantly in demand for taping and broadcasting on television, radio, film and video, subsequently to be filed away for posterity. The process of exchange between theatre and the media is so constant and so diverse that we must take into account the network of influences and interferences in which it results. There is not much sense in defining theatre as a "pure art," or even in postulating a theory of theatre that neglects media practices, because the media accompany and influence theatre production. The question is simply whether theatre can be integrated into a theory of the media and whether it can be compared to mechanical arts or practices (*intermediality**).

The notion of media is not easy to pin down. The media seem to define themselves essentially according to a sum of technical characteristics (both possible and potential) and the technological means by which they are produced, transmitted and received and can be reproduced an infinite number of times. Consequently, the media are not tied to a particular content or theme, but to an apparatus and the prevailing state of technology. Still, the technology of mechanical reproduction and production of works of art implies a certain aesthetic, and is useful only when it materializes in a particular, unique work or is evaluated in an aesthetic or ethical judgment. As SARTRE said, any technique of the novel leads to a particular metaphysics. The same could be said of media technology: it is comprehensible only in the context of a process of aesthetic, even metaphysical, reflection on the transition from (reproductive) quantity to (interpretative) quality. It is not enough to describe the technological properties of a particular branch of the media such as radio or television; we must appreciate the dramaturgy visible (or *seeable*) in a radio or television broadcast and *foreseeable* for a future production in those media. We need an ideological theory of the media that goes beyond MacLuhan-like slogans ("the medium is the message") and can take us farther than the "TV novel" or computerized dating services. Is that too much to ask?

2. Media and Theatre

We could write an anecdotal history of inventions in the media, showing how the various branches are related to each other and indicating the chronological series of technical improvements. It would then be easy to place theatre in relation to these technical phases, before and after the appearance of the media, in reaction to technological progress. The task would be an arduous one, however, and we will note only that theatre and the media tend to move in opposite directions. Theatre tends toward simplification, minimalism, the fundamental reduction of a direct exchange between actor and spectator. The media, on the other hand, tend to become more complicated and sophisticated through technological advances and are, by definition, reproducible and multipliable *ad infinitum*. Being part of technological, but also cultural and ideological practices, of a process of information or disinformation, the media can easily expand their audience to become accessible to a potentially infinite number of spectators. In order for the *theatrical relationship** to be established in a theatre, there must be a limited number of spectators and performances, for theatre too often repeated deteriorates or, at best, changes. In this way, theatre is "in essence" (based on its optimal mode of reception) an art of limited scope.

3. Quantification and Massification

Mass media productions, given the possibility of repeating and diversifying them indefinitely, have a much more active influence on audience expectations and tastes than does (often infrequent) theatregoing. Here we could draw a distinction between media and arts that must be sought out and constructed actively, such as theatre or video (to the extent that a performance is attended or a taping requested), and media that are *immediate*, served up ready-made and as a matter of course without really being ordered (we turn on the television or radio as automatically as we switch on the light). This active/passive criterion is, however, quite tenuous and does not explain the spectator's reception and interpretation activity, which is always necessary whether we are watching a Western or a production of SHAKESPEARE. It is not the media themselves – that is, their technological potential – that favour the active or passive attitude; it is the way in which they structure information and use it in accordance with a dramaturgical and strategical approach that stimulates spectator activity to a varying degree.

4. The Double Game of Media and Theatre

What distinguishes the media from theatre, at least at first sight, is their double fictional status. A television or radio broadcast over the same airwaves can be presented either as true (transmitting information) or as fictional (telling a story), even though we generally make a clear distinction between truth and fiction. The spectator needs to know at all times what status to assign to what he perceives on the screen or what he hears: information or fiction? Each branch of the media has its own way of indicating fictional status. Theatre also plays both sides, as it supports its *fabula* with "reality-effects" and remarks that make it believable. Inversely, however, television news and so-called objective reports have their own *fabula*, narrative structure, rhetoric and areas of invention and pure fiction. In this sense, theatre and the media are closely akin to each other in their ability to mix fiction and reality-effects, invention and information.

In order to come up with a theory of the media loose enough to include theatre practice, we would have to contrast certain specific features of several branches of the media with a minimal definition of theatre. Such a process would be fundamental to establishing a general theory of performance and the media (PAVIS/HELBO 1987).

See also: photography.

Further reading: Moles 1973; Adorno 1984; Quéré 1982; Ertel 1983; Pavis 1996a.

MEDIEVAL PLAY

Fr.: *jeu*; Ger.: *mittelalterliches Theater*; Sp.: *obra medieval*.

The French *jeu* was prevalent in the twelfth and thirteenth centuries. The term corresponds to the Latin *ludus*, which refers to liturgical performances, and *ordo*, a text arranged in monologues or speeches. These plays usually dramatized episodes from the Bible, but also had profane themes beginning in the thirteenth century (*Le Jeu de la Feuillée* by ADAM DE LA HALLE), appearing in such diverse forms as the fairytale play, the parable, satirical revue, and the pastoral (*Le Garçon et l'aveugle*).
See also: farce, morality play, *sotie*, mystery play.

MELODRAMA

Fr.: *mélodrame*; Ger.: *Melodrama*; Sp.: *melodrama*.

Melodrama (meaning, literally and according to Greek etymology, drama performed with songs) appeared in the eighteenth century as a genre in which, as in an operetta, music was played at the most dramatic moments to express the emotions of a silent person. It is "a kind of drama in which words and music, instead of accompanying each other, are heard successively, and in which the spoken phrase is somehow announced and prepared by the musical one" (J.J.ROUSSEAU, *Fragments d'observation sur l'"Alceste" de Gluck*, 1766).

At the end of the eighteenth century, melodrama, this "bastard son of Melpomère" (GEOFFROY) became a new genre of popular plays that, by showing the "good guys" and the "bad guys" in terrifying or touching situations, set out to move the audience at little textual cost but with much effort on stage. Melodrama emerged at the end of the Revolution (around 1797) and held sway until the early 1820s. *L'Auberge des Adrets* marked both its high point and its parodic subversion through the acting of F.LEMAITRE (immortalized in the film *Les Enfants du Paradis*). It was a new genre, with a dramatic structure that was rooted in family tragedy (EURIPIDES: *Alcestis*, *Iphigenia in Tauris*, *Medea*; SHAKESPEARE, MARLOWE) and in the *bourgeois drama** (DIDEROT).

Melodrama was the unknowing parodic offspring of classical tragedy, whose heroic, sentimental and tragic side was played to the hilt by using multiple *coups de théâtre**, events of recognition and tragic commentaries by the hero. The narrative structure is invariable: love, unhappiness caused by betrayal, the triumph of virtue, punishment and reward, persecution as the "axis of the plot" (THOMASSEAU). This form developed just as the stage began to be taken over by spectacular visual effects, edging out the elegant text in favour of impressive *coups de théâtre**. Melodrama triumphed in theatres such as the Ambigu-Comique, the Gaité and the Porte-Saint-Martin, with plays such as those of PIXERECOURT, the "CORNEILLE of the boulevards" (*Coelina ou l'Enfant du mystère*, 1800).

The emergence of melodrama is related to the ideological ascendancy of the bourgeoisie, which affirmed its new-found power at the beginning of the nineteenth century after the Revolution, substituting itself for the egalitarian aspirations of a people represented as infantile, asexual and historically marginal (cf. UBERSFELD in the special issue of *Revue des sciences humaines*, 1976, no. 162).

There is no tragic choice possible for the characters, who are clearly labelled as either good or bad. They are steeped in good or bad sentiment, certitudes and beliefs that leave no room for contradiction. Their feelings and their speeches, taken just short of parody, promote easy identification and cheap catharsis in the spectator. The situations lack verisimilitude but are clearly drawn: extreme unhappiness or unspeakable joy; cruel fate that sorts itself out in the end, in the optimistic version, or remains dark and tense, as in the Gothic novel; social injustice or reward for virtue and public-spiritedness. Generally situated in totally unreal and fanciful places (in the wild, a castle, an island, the bottom of the sea), the melodrama conveys social abstractions, conceals the social conflicts of its time, and reduces contradictions to an atmosphere of ancestral fear or utopic happiness. The melodramatic genre, betraying the class to which it would appear to be addressed (the people), seals the newly-established bourgeois order by universalizing conflicts and values and by promoting a process of "social catharsis" in the spectator that discourages any kind of reflection and criticism, though it is at least within the reach of the people: "Melodrama will always be a means of instruction for the people, for at least this genre is within their reach" (PIXERÉCOURT).

The melodrama survives and prospers today in *boulevard theatre**, in television soap operas and in popular romances. It has left behind the garish trappings of the Gothic novel and facile melodrama and taken shelter in the new bourgeois myths of the marriage in crisis or unrequited love. In a parodic form, that is in its own negation, it is seen today in a derisory style of theatre with special visual effects, in Dadaism, Surrealism, and theatre of the absurd. Many performers, such as J.SAVARY and the Magic Circus and many popular television announcers, are fascinated by that heady broth of bourgeois culture, the melodrama, and by the repulsion and fascination it continues to evoke from our contemporaries. Here, melodrama reasserts its complicity with theatricality and the spectacular.

Further reading: Brooks 1974; *Revue des sciences humaines*, no. 162, 1976; Thomasseau 1984b; Przybos 1987; Ubersfeld in Corvin 1995.

MELODRAMATIC

Fr.: *mélodramatique;* Ger.: *melodramatisch;* Sp.: *melodramático.*

An adjective corresponding to *melodrama** (melodramatic play), meaning something that produces an effect of exaggerated and excessive emotion in style, acting or mise-en-scène. The melodramatic text is full of complex rhetorical constructions, affected speech, and phrases that reflect the emotionalism and structural disorganization of the sentence. The acting prolongs and accentuates gestures and aims to insinuate much more than is expressed. The mise-en-scène freezes pathetic moments in *tableaux vivants**, promotes identification by evoking emotion, and contributes to the spectator's fascination with an illusionist stage through an action-packed story line.

See also: *drame,* boulevard theatre, stereotype.

MESSAGE

Fr.: *message;* Ger.: *Botschaft;* Sp.: *mensaje.*

1. Message as Thesis

In the traditional sense of the term, which has gradually fallen into disuse, the message of a play or performance was what was supposedly meant by its creators, the summary of their philosophical or moral theses. Such a conception of literature is somewhat suspect, as it implies that the creators, even before doing the dramaturgical and staging work, have a prior message to convey, and that the theatre is only a subsidiary, second-hand medium used to transmit it. But even if the author and director have a certain artistic project in mind at the outset of their work, their work takes on form and meaning only in the concrete work of *writing**, of *dramaturgy** and of the *mise-en-scène**, and not in some abstract intentionality that may be applied secondarily to the stage. In addition, aside from the *didactic play** (and perhaps even there), there is not one single message but a whole set of questions and signifying systems that the spectator must interpret and combine, with a varying degree of freedom and imagination.

Expressions such as *thesis drama** or philosophical theatre, then, are felt to be pejorative. The audience would rather not be presented with a system of ideas poorly disguised with dramaturgy and rendered into the dramatic form purely for the sake of form. It is much more challenging for the audience to arrive at a "message" after a process of reflection on the ways in which theatre produces meaning. Experimental theatre people are well aware of this, and are careful not to display their theses too prominently but to rely on the audience's intelligence and sensitivity.

2. Message and Information Theory

Message here contrasts with *code**. The message is deciphered with the help of a code that in turn produces new messages. In theatre, the scheme of *communication** seeks to set up codes (narrative, gestural, musical, ideological and so on) that will break down the information conveyed by the performance (*function**). BARTHES was the first to suggest this theory: "What is theater? A kind of cybernetic machine. When it is not working, this machine is hidden behind a curtain. But as soon as it is revealed, it begins emitting a certain number of messages. These messages have this peculiarity, that they are simultaneous and yet of different rhythm; at a certain point in the performance, you receive at the same time six or seven items of information (proceeding from the set, the costumes, the lighting, the placing of the actors, their gestures, their speech), but some of these remain (the set, for example) while others change (speech, gestures); what we have, then, is a real informational polyphony, which is what theatricality is: *a density of signs* [...]" (1964, 258; Eng. 1972, 261–262). Unfortunately, it turned out to be impossible to identify the *units** of the various codes, and particularly to go further than simply describing the channels of transmission and the signs emitted. So much the better for the theatre, perhaps. Actually, the spectator "practises" the performance by building up meaning from signs or sets of signs that form so many *vectorizations** within the performance and are chosen according to how useful they are for description and how productive they are in clarifying the meaning(s) of the performance.

See also: spoken and unspoken, silence, signifying practice, reception, communication.

Further reading: Jakobson 1963; Moles 1973; Eco 1976.

MESSENGER

Fr.: *messager;* Ger.: *Bote;* Sp.: *mensajero.*
See NARRATIVE

METALANGUAGE

Fr.: *metalangage;* Ger.: *Metasprache;* Sp.: *metalenguaje.*
See DESCRIPTION

METAPHOR, METONYMY

Fr.: *métaphore, métonymie;* Ger.: *Metapher;* Sp.: *metáfora, metonimia.*
See RHETORIC

METATHEATRE

(Term introduced by L.ABEL in 1963.)
Fr.: *métathéâtre;* Ger.: *Metatheater;* Sp.: *metateatro.*

Theatre which is centred around theatre and therefore "speaks" about itself, "represents" itself.

1. Theatre within Theatre

This phenomenon does not necessarily involve an autonomous play contained within another, as in the "play within a play." All that is required is that the represented reality appear to be one that is already theatrical, as in plays in which the main theme is life as theatre (for example, CALDERON, SHAKESPEARE and, more recently, PIRANDELLO, BECKETT and GENET). Metatheatre, thus defined, becomes a form of *antitheatre**, where the dividing line between play and real life is erased.

This hypothesis, developed by L.ABEL (1963), who seems to have coined the term, is simply an extension of the old theory of the play within a play. It continues to be too closely tied to a thematic study of life as a stage and is not sufficiently supported by a structural description of dramaturgical forms and theatre discourse.

2. Image of Reception* of the Play

J.CALDERWOOD's (1971) study of SHAKESPEARE is founded on the hypothesis that "Shakespeare's plays are not only about the various moral, social, political, and other thematic issues with which critics have so long and quite properly been busy but also about Shakespeare's plays" (1971, 5). More generally, any play can be analyzed according to its author's attitude toward language and toward his own production, an attitude that can always be glimpsed in the text, and often the author is so aware of the problem that he *thematizes** it and makes it one of the main driving forces of his writing, structuring the play around this metacritical and metatheatrical tension (SHAKESPEARE, MARIVAUX, PIRANDELLO, GENET, PINGET, SARRAUTE).

3. Self-consciousness of Enunciation
This theory that a metaplay is at work in any dramatic text, as its commentary, its inverted image and its enunciation, is still only a hypothesis in the making. It is founded above all on forms of the play within a play. We can expect it to be developed, however, through research on performatives and on *discourse**.

If theatre can be said to be metacommunication (OSOLSOBE, 1981) (i.e. communication to an audience about communication among actors), we should be able to find conceptions common to both internal and external types of communication – the character is necessarily made of the same communicative matter as the playwright has (though vaguely) in mind. The formula for any speech act in the dramatic text is, in fact, "I(1) say that I(2) say...." The first *I* is theoretically an objective *it*, that of the playwright, but it is still it which *narrates*, in its own way, what appeared to be merely shown mimetically. The second *I*, that of the character, is deemed to be the subject of action verbs and not to reflect on his situation as speaker; however, the character may show himself to be the producer of the word, an enunciator whose only utterance is that of a speaking being (MARIVAUX, BECKETT, PINGET). Between these two changing *Is*, a play of identification and exchange is established. Metatheatricality is a fundamental property of all theatrical communication. "Operation Meta" in theatre consists in taking the stage and everything on it – actor, scenery, text – as objects equipped with a demonstrative sign of *denial** ("it is not an object, but a meaning of the object"). Just as poetic language designates itself as an artistic *device**, theatre designates itself as a world already tainted by illusion.

4. Staging of the Theatrical Work of the Staging
There is a marked tendency in contemporary stage *practice** not to separate the process of preliminary work (on text, character, gestuality) and finished product. Thus, the staging (mise-en-scène) presented to the audience should give an account not only of the text to be staged, but also of the attitude and *modality** of its creators with respect to the text and the acting. In this way, the staging is not confined to telling a story but reflects on theatre and puts forward its reflection on theatre by integrating it, more or less organically, into the performance. It is no longer only the actor who verbalizes his relationship with his role, as in the Brechtian alienation-effect, but the whole team that is staged "to the second degree." In this way theatre work becomes an activity of reflection and play, blithely mixing the utterance (the text to be spoken, the performance to be produced) with the enunciation (the reflection on the act of saying). This practice speaks of a metacritical attitude on theatre and enriches contemporary theatre (exercises for actors in productions by VITEZ, the Living Theatre, the Schaubühne, etc.).

See also: communication, ostension, mise-en-abyme, alienation-effect.

Further reading: A. Righter 1972; Dort 1977b, 1979; Pfister 1978; Dodd 1979; Swiontek 1980, 1990; Schmeling 1982.

MILIEU

Fr.: *milieu*; Ger.: *Milieu*; Sp.: *medio*.

Milieu is the set of external conditions in which beings live. This concept is fundamental to *naturalistic** theories according to which man cannot be seen apart from his environment.

Milieu in theatre, for the naturalistic or any aesthetics of photographic illusion, is the place where man may be observed. In the *action*/character** pair, it takes the place of character and suppresses action in favour of a detailed description of the human condition, often seen as elemental and unchanging. It is always "the milieu that determines the movement of the characters and not the movements of the characters that determine the milieu" (ANTOINE 1903) (see also ZOLA 1881).

A descriptive *epic dramaturgy** proceeds by static moments (*tableaux**); it eschews any dramatic tension between scenes, and concentrates on evoking man's gradual deterioration. The stage is a well-worked substance imbued with the often morbid atmosphere of a family, an enterprise, a social class or a weary humanity. Contrary to the *practicable** that can be manipulated along with the action or a "theatre machine," it exerts all of its weight, like the destiny of matter, on the protagonists in the drama.

See also: represented reality, history, realism.

MIME

(From the Greek *mimos*, or imitation.)
Fr.: *mime*; Ger.: *Mimus, Mimenspiel, Mime*; Sp.: *mimo*.

Art of body movement.

1. Mime and Rhapsody

Narrative has two basic means of expression: direct imitation through *mime* and verbal description through the *rhapsodist*. A mime artist tells a story in gestures, words being absent altogether or used only to introduce and connect the numbers. The tradition dates back to Greek antiquity (SOPHRON of Syracuse, in the fifth century B.C., composed the first mime plays.) In Greek and Latin translation, mime became a popular form. It survived the Middle Ages thanks to wandering troupes. Mime underwent a renaissance in the fifteenth century in Italy in the form of *commedia dell'arte**, and flourishes today in the art of DECROUX (1963), MARCEAU (1974), LECOQ (1987) (cf. *gestural theatre**).

2. Mime and Pantomime

Current usage distinguishes between the two terms as follows: the *mime* is an original, inspired creation while the *pantomime** is an imitation of a verbal story that it tells with "explanatory gestures." Mime tends towards dance and body expression free of figurative content; pantomime seeks to evaluate through imitations of social situations or types: "Like life itself, theatre appears to be bounded by two silences, by a mime of the beginning consisting of cries, inspiration and identification and a mime of the end that is a last cabriole into virtuosity and pantomime" (LECOQ 1967). The *mime/pantomime* opposition is founded on a question of stylization and abstraction. Mime tends to the poetic, expands its means of expression, proposes gestural connotations that each spectator can interpret freely. Pantomime presents a series of gestures, often intended to amuse, that replaces a series of sentences; it denotes faithfully the meaning of the story shown.

3. Forms of Mime

Mime varies with each performer, so that it is more appropriate to speak of trends rather than *genres*:

A *mime play* builds up a story around a series of gestural episodes, linking up with the narrative structures of comedy or tragedy (for example, MARCEAU).

Danced mime uses stylized, abstract, bare gestures reminiscent of ballet. It is accompanied by music and is often confused with dance (for example, TOMASZEWSKY).

Pure mime corresponds to a gesture that does not imitate a situation or aim for the effect of recognition; it is very abstract and spare (PAVIS 1980d).

Body mime comes from COPEAU's experiments, in which actor, masked face, body "as naked as decency will permit" (DECROUX 1963, 17) practised a "dramatic art made exclusively with the body," the ancestor of all contemporary gestural theatre.

4. Mime, Gesture and Word

Mime can produce a constant dynamism of movement; it is an "art in movement in which attitude is only punctuation" (DECROUX, 1963, 124). The gesture restores the rhythm of a kind of phrasing, by highlighting its key moments, stopping just before the beginning or end of an action, drawing attention to the unfolding of gestural action rather than its outcome (*epic* technique): "In mime, the spectator grasps the gesture only if he is prepared for

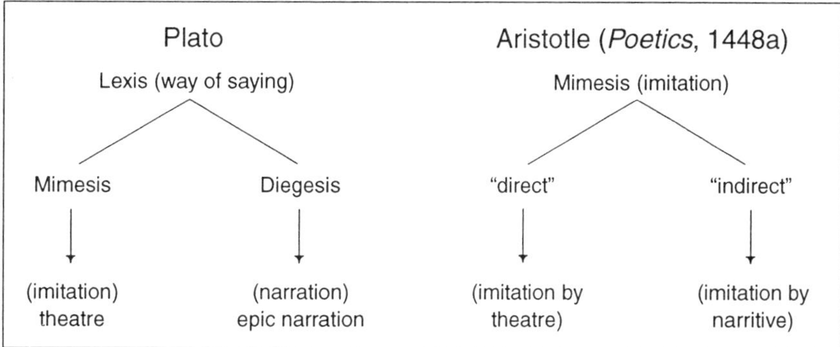

it. So, when I am going to pick up a wallet, first I raise my hand, the audience looks at my hand, and then I move towards the wallet. There is a moment of preparation, then one of action" (MARCEAU 1974, 47). The mime artist structures time in his own way; decides when to introduce pauses and "punctuation" marked by the actors' attitudes. In this way, he detaches himself from the rhythm of the verbal sentence and avoids the effect of redundance.

Further reading: Dorcy 1958, 1962; Lecoq 1987; Mounin 1970, 169–180; Marceau 1974; Kipsis 1974; Lorelle 1974; de Marinis 1980, 1993; Leabhart 1989.

MIME PLAY

Fr.: *mimodrame;* Ger.: *Mimusspiel;* Sp.: *mimodrama.*

Play that uses only the body language of mime. It is, however, to be distinguished from pantomime: "Their starting point was the same, but not their point of arrival: in pantomime, the body was not sufficient in itself, and other elements of the performance were called for; in the mime play, the body is all there is" (DORCY 1962, 89). Today, parts of a spoken drama can become a mime play (BECKETT, HANDKE, IONESCO).

MIMESIS

(From the Greek *mimeistkai,* to imitate.)
Fr.: *mimésis;* Ger.: *Mimesis;* Sp.: *mímesis.*

Mimesis is the imitation or representation of something. Originally, mimesis was the imitation of a person using physical and linguistic means, but the "person" could be a thing, an idea, a hero or a god. In ARISTOTLE's *Poetics,* artistic production (*poiesis*) is defined as *imitation** (*mimesis*) of action (*praxis*).

1. Place of Mimesis

A. IN PLATO

In Books 3 and 10 of *The Republic,* mimesis is conceived of as the copy of a copy (of the idea, which is inaccessible to the artist). Imitation (essentially dramatic imitation) is prohibited in education, because it could lead men to imitate things that are unworthy of art, and because it takes account of the outside appearance of things only. Imitation, particularly in the Neo-Platonics (PLAUTUS, CICERO), is the image of an outside world that is contrasted with the world of ideas. Hence, perhaps, the condemnation over the centuries of theatre, and specifically of spectacle, because of its external, physical nature, as opposed to the divine idea.

B. IN ARISTOTLE

In *Poetics* (section 1447a), mimesis is the fundamental mode of art; it appears in various forms (poem, tragedy, epic narrative). The imitation is not of an ideal world, but of human action (not of character). The important thing for the poet is to reconstruct the *fabula**, that is the structure of events: "Tragedy is an imitation of an action that is serious, complete, and possessing magnitude; in embellished language, each kind of which is used separately in the different parts; in the mode of action and not narrated; and effecting through pity and fear (what we call) the *catharsis* of such emotions" (section 1449b). "The imitation of the action is the plot. By plot I here mean the combination of the events" (section 1450a). The distinction is still valid, and corresponds to the *showing/telling* distinction of Anglo-American criticism (BOOTH, 1961).

2. Object of Mimesis
Mimesis has to do with the representation of men and particularly of their actions: "The imitation of the action is the plot. By plot I here mean the combination of the events" (1450a).

Mimesis is the imitation of a thing and the observation of narrative logic. It has to do with the action/character opposition:

A. IMITATION OF ACTION
ARISTOTLE's *mythos* is defined as the mimesis of action (praxis).

B. MITATION OF CHARACTER (ETHOS)
This is imitation in the pictoral sense – figurative representation.

C. MITATION OF THE ANCIENTS
We should add this category to the two above (SCALIGER,1561; BOILEAU, 1674). Sometimes, as in classicism, the poet is enjoined to "imitate nature," which can mean anything from writing in a simple, clear style to observing a detailed *naturalism**.

See also: represented reality, theatrical reality, fiction, realism, diegesis.
Further reading: Plato, *Republic*; Else 1957; Francastel 1965; Auerbach 1953; Genette 1969; Ricoeur 1983, 1984, 1985.

MINIMAL UNIT

Fr.: *unité minimale*; Ger.: *minimale Einheit*; Sp.: *unidad mínima.*

The search for minimal units of performance is not merely that of a semiologist concerned with identifying units and their syntax within the performance and, on that basis, mapping out the unknown territory of how theatre works. It is a step that becomes necessary as soon as the performance is conceived as a set of *materials** brought together by the mise-en-scène, with an arrangement and vectorization that produces the *meaning** of the performance.

1. Existence of the Minimal Unit

With the aim of tracing the origins of theatrical "matter," attempts have been made to distinguish "atoms" of meaning by defining the unit as the smallest *sign** transmitted in time (BARTHES 1964, 258). Despite KOWZAN's clear warning (1968), this approach has led to descriptions of the performance as a whole consisting of very small signs. Neither the ranking nor the relationships between signs have been elucidated thereby, given the lack of a project or structure capable of "attracting" various systems to participate in the same ensemble (signified). In a concern with the distinctiveness of signs, it was forgotten that the minimal unit depends on the overall meaning, and that segmentation is never innocent but is always determined by the meaning that the observer attributes to the performance.

That "atomizing" analysis of the performance has now been abandoned, or at least complemented by the dimension called the semantic (*le sémantique*) by BENVENISTE, who reintroduced the general impression of the spectator and overall meaning.

2. Semiotics and Semantics
A second method, then, would be to stop looking for semiotic units at any price, as we do for langauge, i.e. "to identify the units, describe their distinctive marks and discover finer and finer criteria of distinction" (BENVENISTE, 1974:64). This method starts with overall meaning, with the intended sense ("what it means") and thus with the semantic aspect of theatrical discourse.

Henceforth, every unit is seen as part of a larger project, a *dramaturgical** project, a *situation** or a *gestus**. Only afterwards do we worry about whether the semantics (the overall meaning) can be articulated and particularized in semiotic units. In fact, we could say of theatre semiology what BENVENISTE says of semiology of language: it has "been obstructed, paradoxically, by the very instrument that created it, the sign" (1974, 66). The fact that theatre, unlike language, does not have minimal units such as words, which cover both a semiotic and a semantic dimension, obliges us to begin with the semantic dimension of theatre. This semantic dimension of artistic experience includes the notions of theatre *event**, *reception** and *signifying practice** by the spectator. The units of theatrical meaning, then, are no longer minimal, but synthetic and global. (See the entry under *segmentation** for a presentation of a few global units.)

Further reading: Propp 1968; Jansen 1968, 1973; Greimas 1970, 1973; Caune 1978; de Marinis 1978, 1979; Pavis 1978d; Ruffini 1978.

MINIMALIST THEATRE

Fr.: *théâtre minimal*; Ger.: *Minimaltheater*; Sp.: *teatro mínimo*.

Like minimalist visual arts, theatre may seek to reduce its effects, representations and actions to a minimum, as if what is essential lay in the *unspoken**, whether it be ontologically unsayable (BECKETT), impossible for the alienated character to formulate (*theatre of everyday life**) or written/shown in the montage, the spaces in between, silence, the unspoken (VINAVER and his chamber theatre). This kind of theatre shows the influence of Minimal Dance (Cunningham, Rainer, Monk, Childs).

MIRACLE PLAY

Fr.: *miracle*; Ger.: *Legendenspiel, Mirakelspiel*; Sp.: *milagro*.

Medieval theatrical genre (eleventh and fourteenth centuries) that tells the life of a saint in narrative and dramatic form (*Miracle de Théophile* by RUTEBOEUF). The Virgin saves a repentant sinner, giving rise to scenes of everyday life and miraculous interventions. The most famous collection is the *Miracles de Notre-Dame* by GAUTIER de COINCY (1177–1236); it consists of thirty tales making up a narrative body of 30,000 lines. Some miracle plays were staged by schoolchildren, novices or guilds. They were gradually supplanted by *mystery plays**, *morality plays** and *passion plays**.

MISE EN ABYME

Fr.: *mise en abyme*, Ger.: *mise en abyme*, Sp.: *mise en abyme*.

1. The expression *mise-en-abyme* derives from the heraldry term *abîme*, which refers to the fess point, the central point of the coat of arms. By analogy, the mise en *abîme* (or *abyme*, a term introduced by GIDE) is a device in which an enclave is embedded in the work (which may be pictoral, literary or theatrical), reproducing certain of its structural similarities or properties (specular reduplication). It is a common practice in painting (VAN EYCK, MAGRITTE), in the novel (CERVANTES, DIDEROT, STERNE, the *nouveau roman*) and in theatre (ROTROU, CORNEILLE, MARIVAUX, PIRANDELLO). The reflection of the external work in the internal enclave may be presented in the form of an identical, reverse, multiple or approximate image.

A *mise-en-abyme* is "any mirror that reflects the entire narrative by simple, repeated or specious duplication," "any enclave that bears a relation of similarity to the work that contains it" (DÄLLENBACH, 1977:71,18). In theatre, this device features a structural and thematic doubling, "i.e., a close correspondence between the content of the embedding piece and the content of the embedded piece" (FORESTIER 1981, 13).

2. *The play within a play** is the most common form of mise-en-abyme in theatre. The internal play takes up the theme of theatrical acting, the link between the two structures being provided by analogy or parody. The device is generally used to *frame** or relativize the performance, as in the use of puppets miming the action of the play and representing the theatre of the world (in GOETHE's *Faust* or CORNEILLE's *l'Illusion*

comique); a framing device that uses the same motif to announce and conclude the *fabula*; an actor playing an actor playing a role; the repetition of words or scenes summarizing the main action; or a stage placed on the stage of the theatre to underscore the illusion and how it is produced *(Hamlet, The Seagull)*.

3. Some contemporary texts attempt to embed (and reduplicate) their own writing practice and make the problem of creation and enunciation the centre of their concerns and utterances (HANDKE, PINGET, SARRAUTE).

4. Self-representation (also called self-referentiality when a text refers to itself rather than the world), is a specific case of *mise-en-abyme*; it is one of "those mirror effects whereby the text quotes, quotes itself, sets itself in motion" (DERRIDA 1972, 351). It is therefore a case of intertextuality that refers to the text itself. Self-representation in theatre appears most often in the form of a duplicated performance, bringing us back to the well-known device of the play within a play.

Reflexivity in theatre is expressed on many other levels than the textual. The scene design may mirror an element considered to be pertinent, by placing a stage on stage *(Hamlet* by MESGUICH, VITEZ' *Bérénice*). The actor may "quote" his own acting or reduplicate his partner's, thus establishing an "interplay" that refers only to itself. Reflexivity is often only a rather banal hallmark of the self-referential poetic function that, according to JAKOBSON (1963), characterizes the aesthetic sign. It is very difficult for the theatre to speak of theatre in theatrical terms, i.e. not in literary or linguistic terms but in terms of stage or play elements – even PIRANDELLO is a rather long-winded theoretician.

See also: metatheatre, alienation effect, fantasy.
Further reading: Kowzan 1976; Dällenbach 1977; *Texte*, 1982; Pavis 1985c; Corvin in Scherer 1986; Jung 1994.

MISE-EN-SCÈNE

See STAGING

MISTAKEN IDENTITY

Fr.: *quiproquo, méprise;* Ger.: *Verwechslung;* Sp.: *quiproquo.*

This occurs when one *character** or thing is mistaken for another. It may be internal to the play (we see that X takes Y for Z), external (we confuse X with Y) or a combination (like one of the characters, we take X for Y). This device is an inexhaustible source of comic, sometimes tragic, situations (*Oedipus Rex*, CAMUS's *le Malentendu*). Mistaken identity is "a situation that presents two different meanings at once, [...] one that the actors give it [...] one that the audience gives it" (BERGSON).

MODALITY

Fr.: *modalité;* Ger.: *Modalität;* Sp.: *modalidad.*

Modality (or modalization) is, in linguistics, the mark of the speaker's attitude toward his utterances (i.e. the *dictum*). Specifically, it translates his attachment to or *distance** from his own speech, expressing affirmation, questioning, negation, doubt, the modes of capability, duty, probability, etc.

This discursive notion of modality is crucial in mise-en-scène. Its is essential role is to *say* the text according to a particular mode, translating its interpretation of the play, its dramaturgical choices, the overall tone of the performance and the actor's attitude toward his role. Unlike modality in language, the modality of a mise-en-scène cannot be found in definite expressions or techniques added to the text staged (the *dictum*), but is integrated into the interpretation itself and clarifies the text from within. There is no need, then, for an external (indirect) commentary to express it; it is based on the discourse of mise-en-scène and its enunciation.

See also: diction, alienation-effect, pragmatics, situation of enunciation.

Further reading: Hughes and Cresswell 1968; Benveniste 1974; Greimas and Courtès 1979; Kerbrat-Orecchioni 1980.

MODALIZATION

Fr.: *modalisation;* Ger.: *Modalisierung;* Sp.: *modalización.*

See MODALITY, DISCOURSE

MODELLING

Fr.: *modélisation;* Ger.: *Modellierung;* Sp.: *modelización.*

Operation that consists in organizing, and reducing to a more or less coherent model, the ideological and aesthetic reality of the play being staged and of the spectator attending the performance. In the first case, the playwright and director come up with a performance that enables the audience to "read" the theatrical universe symbolized and to recognize some of its organizational principles. In the second case, the spectator must be able to construct a model of his own ideological universe and gain an awareness of the ideological system in which he moves.

Only once these two processes of abstraction (of the fictional world of the play and of the real world of the spectator) have taken place do productive exchange and understanding become possible. The ideological codes of the aesthetic object and the perceiving subject are then sufficiently "in agreement" for the proper aesthetic and ideological decoding to occur. Psychological, and particularly ideological, *identification** cannot truly exist unless the spectator is helped (by the staging and dramaturgical work and the mise-en-scène) to understand the ideological workings of the represented world by comparing (or replacing) them with those of his own ideological practice (ALTHUSSER 1965). This modelling process is particularly applicable to BRECHT's plays and to productions in the Brechtian style (WEKWERTH 1974). But it is fundamental to all *theatrical communication** to varying degrees. LOTMAN (1977) has developed a theory of "secondary languages (secondary modeling systems) – communication structures built as superstructures upon a natural linguistic plane [...] *Art is a secondary modeling system*" (1977, 9).

See also: reception, semiotization, represented reality, sign, model representation.

Further reading: Badiou 1969; Lotman 1977; Pavis 1985d.

MODEL REPRESENTATION

Fr.: *représentation modèle;* Ger.: *Modellaufführung;* Sp.: *representación modelo.*

The "model" representation of the Brechtian *Modellbuch* is by no means an *exemplary* model to be imitated; it is a *reduced* model to scale of a *staging**, a dossier consisting of photographs, acting instructions, dramaturgical analysis and *characterizations**. It sets out the phases in which the performance is to be developed, notes problems with the text and suggests a general framework for *interpretation**. As introduced by BRECHT at the Berliner Ensemble, these models were to serve as a basis from which future directors could work, without however being used as is in subsequent productions. In the same spirit, the volumes of the *Voies de la création théatrale* (CNRS) reconstruct productions through dramaturgical analysis and are an invaluable source of documentation.

See also: adaptation, description, pre-performance.

Further reading: *Theaterarbeit* (1952), 1961; Pavis 1981b, 1996.

MONODRAMA

Fr.: *monodrame;* Ger.: *monodrama;* Sp.: *monodrama.*

1. In the everyday sense, this is a play with a single character, or at least a single actor (who may take on several roles). The play is centred around one person and explores his innermost motivations, subjectivity or lyricism. Plays with a single character were in fashion at the end of the eighteenth century (ROUSSEAU's *Pygmalion*) and in the early

twentieth century, particularly with Expressionism.

2. In the beginning of the twentieth century, monodrama became a genre that endeavoured to reduce everything to the vision of one character, even within a play with several characters. STANISLAVSKY, when inviting CRAIG to put on *Hamlet*, suggested that he "make the audience understand that they are looking at the play through Hamlet's eyes; that the king, the queen and the court are not shown on stage as they are in reality but as they appear to Hamlet" (quoted in D. BABLET 1962, 175).

EVREINOFF, in his *Introduction au monodrame* (1909) and his monodrama *Les Coulisses de l'âme*, established the pedigree of this genre. For him it was "a type of dramatic performance in which the world surrounding the character appears just as the character perceives it at every moment of his stage existence." It is the audience who is supposed to become the protagonist's partner through this world.

3. One type of monodrama where everything is conveyed by representation of an *inner space** is *cerebral drama*, following Maurice BEAUBOURG's term for his play *L'Image* (1894), "a play in which all human interest, all action, all emotion derive from a mental crisis."

4. The contemporary staging often draws inspiration from this point of view on reality and drama to give up an image from inside the character, whether his actions are visible (*Concert à la carte* by F.-X. KROETZ, 1972) or take place in his imagination (R. WILSON's staging of V. WOOLF's *Orlando*, 1989, 1993; EVREINOFF, 1930; DANAN, 1995).

MONOLOGUE

(From the Greek *monologos*, speech by a single person.)

Fr.: *monologue*; Ger.: *Monolog*; Sp.: *monólogo*.

A monologue is a speech by a character to himself, while a *soliloquy** is addressed directly to an interlocutor who does not speak.

The monologue differs from the *dialogue** in the lack of verbal exchange and in that it is of substantial length and can be taken out of the context of conflict and dialogue. The *context** remains the same from beginning to end and changes in semantic direction (proper to dialogue) are kept to a minimum to ensure the unity of the subject of *enunciation**.

1. Lack of Verisimilitude

Because the monologue is felt to be antidramatic, it is often condemned or restricted to a few indispensable instances. Besides the fact that it is static, even boring, it is seen as improbable. A man alone is not expected to talk aloud, so that showing a character confiding his feelings to himself is easy to ridicule as being unrealistic and improbable. Consequently, realistic or naturalistic theatre accepts the monologue only when warranted by exceptional circumstances (a dream, sleepwalking, inebriation, lyrical outbursts). In other cases, the monologue reveals the artificiality of theatre and acting conventions. Certain periods that were not concerned with producing a naturalistic rendering of the world could easily accommodate the monologue (SHAKESPEARE, *Sturm und Drang*, Romantic or Symbolist drama). In *intimate theatre** (STRINDBERG, but before him in MUSSET and MAETERLINCK), monologue becomes a kind of writing that approaches lyrical poetry.

2. Dialogic Traits of Monologue

There is no such thing as a dialogue so naturalistic that it erases all traces of its author-enunciator. Similarly, the monologue tends to exhibit certain dialogic traits. This occurs particularly when the hero evaluates his situation, addresses an imaginary interlocutor (Hamlet, Macbeth) or externalizes an inner conflict. According to BENVENISTE, the "monologue" is an internalized dialogue, formulated in "inner language," between a speaking I and a listening I: "Sometimes the speaking self is the only one to speak, but the listening self remains present nevertheless; its presence is necessary and sufficient to render significant the enunciation of the speaking self. Sometimes, as well, the listening self intervenes with an objection, a question, a doubt, an insult" (1974, 85–86).

3. Typology of monologues

A. BY DRAMATURGICAL FUNCTION

a. *Technical monologue* (*narrative**): a character's version of events that are past or cannot be shown directly.
b. *Lyrical monologue*: a moment of reflection and emotion in a character who gives away confidences.
c. *Monologue of reflection or decision*: given a difficult choice, the character outlines to himself the pros and cons of a certain course of behaviour (*dilemma**, *deliberation**).

B. BY LITERARY FORM

a. *Aside**: a few words suffice to indicate the character's mood.
b. *Stanza**: a very elaborate form similar to a ballad or song.
c. *Dialectics of reasoning*: the logical argument is presented systematically in a series of rhythmic semantic oppositions, as in CORNEILLE (PAVIS 1980a).
d. *Interior monologue*, i.e. *stream of consciousness*: the speaker delivers whatever snatches of thought come into his head, with no concern for logic or censorship. The main effect is one of the emotional or cognitive chaos of consciousness (BÜCHNER, BECKETT).
e. *Authorial intervention**, hit song: the author addresses the audience directly to seduce or provoke, bypassing the fiction of the *fabula* or musical universe (OSOLSOBE 1974).
f. *Solitary dialogue*: "The hero's dialogue with the divinity, a paradoxical one in which only one of the interlocutors speaks, addressing the other who never replies, and might not even be listening" (GOLDMANN 1970, 26).
g. *Play as monologue*: This is a play that has a single character (for example, A. MAILLET's *La Sagouine*) or is made up of a series of very long speeches (*Inventaires* by P. MINAYA, *Le Faiseur de théâtre* by T. BERNHARD, *Vous qui habitez le temps* by NOVARINA).

4. Deep Structure of Monologue

All discourse tends to establish a relationship of communication between the speaker and the person to whom the message is addressed, and dialogue lends itself best to this exchange. The monologue, which does not depend structurally on a reply from an interlocutor, establishes a direct relationship between the speaker and the *it* of the world of which he speaks. As a "projection of the exclamatory form" (TODOROV 1967, 277), the monologue communicates directly with all of society; in theatre, the whole stage becomes the monologuist's discursive partner. In fact, the monologue addresses the spectator directly as an accomplice and a watcher-hearer. In this direct communication lies both the strength and the improbability and weakness of the monologue.

5. Dramaturgy of Discourse

In Brechtian and particularly post-Brechtian dramaturgy, it is the speeches of the play as a whole that are important, not the isolated consciousness of individual characters. The "monologue" has made a forceful comeback in contemporary writing (M. DURAS, P. HANDKE, B. STRAUSS, H. MÜLLER, B-M KOLTÈS), and the literature of the interior monologue and stream of consciousness has much to do with it. The idea of an ordered conversation between two individuals having coffee and talking calmly about the world is anachronistic, even absurd. In contemporary texts it is the text as a whole that is addressed, or rather thrown, at the audience (HANDKE, BERNHARD). Dialogue is possible only between the text as a whole and the spectator. This kind of writing is characterized by a "destruction of dialogic dramaturgy," a "suicidal plunge into the soliloquy": "If the characters in this dialogueless theatre speak, it is only for appearance's sake. It would be more correct to say that they are spoken by their creator or that the audience lends them their inner voice" (WIRTH 1981, 11 and 14). In this "dramaturgy of discourse" (WIRTH 1981), the discourse is neither monologic nor dialogic; it is both monolithic and fragmented. The entire stage arrangement depends on it and its structure; it is no longer the linguistic code inscribed in the image and the stage language, but the organizing principle of all theatricality. According to P. HANDKE, "the figure of discourse determines the figure of movement."

Further reading: Mukarovský 1941; Szondi 1956; Klotz 1969; von Matt in Keller 1976; Sarrazac 1989, *Alternatives Théâtrales*, 1994.

MONTAGE

Fr.: *montage*; Ger.: *Montage*; Sp.: *montaje*.

Term originating in film (EISENSTEIN) but used since the thirties (PISCATOR, BRECHT) to describe a dramaturgical form in which the textual or stage sequences are assembled in a series of autonomous moments.

1. Montage in Film

Montage was "discovered" by filmmakers (GRIFFITH, EISENSTEIN, PUDOVKIN) to cut the sequence shots already filmed into bits of film that, once placed end to end, would give the film its final shape. The film's narrative structure and rhythm are governed by the work done at the editing table (MARIE 1977).

2. Montage in Theatre

A priori, such an operation would appear to be difficult to achieve in theatre, as the stage seems less able to transform it as effectively as film. But montage in theatre is not a slavish imitation of montage in film; it is an epic narrative technique that has had such practitioners as DOS PASSOS, DÖBLIN and JOYCE. It is apparent in BRECHT and, particularly, EISENSTEIN and his "montage of attractions" (1929). Playing on the double meaning of the word, the montage of attractions is one of popular performances (circus, music hall, fair or *Balagan*), and of free association between visual motifs (or *intellectual montage*) through "the collision, the conflict between two contradictory fragments" (EISENSTEIN, 1976:29).

A. DRAMATURGICAL MONTAGE

Instead of presenting a unified, constant action, a "natural, organic work constructed like a developing body" (BRECHT 1967, 19:314), the *fabula* is broken down into autonomous units. By renouncing dramatic tension and the integration of every action into an overall project, the playwright cannot take advantage of the thrust of each scene to "launch" the plot and make the fiction hang together. Cut and contrast become the basic structural principles. The various types of montage are characterized by discontinuity, a syncopated *rhythm**, collision, *alienation-effects** or fragmentation. Montage is the art of recycling old materials; it creates nothing *ex nihilo*, but organizes the narrative material by ensuring that it is cut in a meaningful way. Here we see the difference between montage and *collage**: montage is structured around a particular movement or direction to be given to the action, while collage effects selective juxtapositions.

Examples of dramatic montage are as follows:

- composition in *tableaux**, in which each image forms a scene that does not develop into another scene (SHAKESPEARE, BÜCHNER, BRECHT);
- the chronicle or biography of a character when presented as separate stages of a progression;
- a series of *sketches** or variety show or music hall revue;
- *documentary theatre**, which may use only authentic sources, selecting and organizing them according to its thesis;
- *theatre of everyday life**, examining commonplaces and the phraseology of a certain milieu.

Like film, theatre may intersperse short repetitive sequences that bring out the meaning of the fragment framed by contrast: a refrain, a musical theme, a particular kind of lighting can be enough to set off the "edited" scene and act as a visual *counterpart**.

B. MONTAGE OF CHARACTER

As a consequence of this dramaturgy of fragments, the character also is the result of a montage/démontage or assembly/disassembly (theme of BRECHT's *Man for Man*. Each property is chosen according to an action or kind of behaviour to be illustrated. We go from one figure to the other by addition/subtraction of these properties, and their place within the *actantial** scheme determines their composition logically. As for role preparation, when it is based on improvisations or research into sources (*commedia dell'arte*, Théâtre du Soleil), it also consists of a patient montage of character traits and acting sequences.

C. MONTAGE OF STAGE

The whole set is like a building set, as props from the outside are brought onto the stage to constantly transform the signs of the scenery. One tableau gives way "openly" to another with no thematic transition or justification through the story or the characters' speeches. Montage has had a considerable influence on contemporary theatre writing.

Further reading: *Change*, 1968; Eisenstein 1976; Bablet 1978; Ruffini 1986.

MORALITY PLAY

Fr.: *moralité*; Ger.: *Moralität*; Sp.: *moralidad*.

Medieval play (first appearing around 1400) of religious inspiration and didactic or moralizing intention. There are between five and eight characters, who are abstractions and allegorical personifications of vice and virtue. The plot is insignificant, but always pathetic and touching. The morality play has affinities with both *farce** and the *mystery play**. The action is an *allegory** that compares the human condition to a journey, an unceasing struggle between good and evil; hence the edifying pedagogical nature of the plays. The subjects may be Biblical (*l'Enfant prodigue*) or contemporary (*le Concile de Bâle*, 1432, *Métier, Marchandise et le temps qui court, Bien avisé, mal avisé*) with farcical and buffoonesque elements as in a *sotie**. The *psychomachia* stages the conflicts between the seven deadly sins, virtues and vices, while man, the eternal sinner, is invited to repent and seek divine mercy. The "path of the spiritual combatant" is full of pitfalls, but divine guidance delivers him from temptation. This was already a theatrical form since the text, which was quite literary and often the work of a known author, was written in dialogue and outlined an action. *Everyman*, published in 1509, is considered to be one of the oldest and purest morality plays. There have been a few attempts to revive this form in recent times (HOFMANNSTHAL, ELIOT, YEATS, and BRECHT in his parodic *Seven Deadly Sins*).

See also: miracle play, auto sacramental, mystery play, masque, entr'acte.

Further reading: Compendium of morality plays in Helmich 1980.

MOTIF

Fr.: *motif*; Ger.: *Motiv*; Sp.: *motivo*.

A unit of the plot that cannot be broken down into smaller units. According to TOMACHEVSKY (1965), the motif is an autonomous unit of action, a functional unit of the narrative. This term is not specific to theatre, but is frequently used by theatre critics.

1. Analysis of Motifs

Narrative analysis, particularly that of PROPP (1929), turned to simple *stereotyped** forms such as the folk tale in order to formalize a number of recurring motifs, define their respective spheres of action and determine their syntax. It would appear difficult to apply the same procedure to complex theatrical forms, although some simple, codified genres (farce, *commedia dell'arte*, popular theatre) lend themselves to drawing up an inventory of motifs and a syntactical outline. Still, within a single play we can make out certain basic, sometimes repetitive themes (*leitmotif**); such *themes** form a chain that is both poetic and narrative (for example, the pistol motif in

IBSEN's *Hedda Gabler* or the cherry orchard and the seagull in CHEKHOV's plays).

2. A Typology of Motifs

A. BY GENRE

In theatre, the motifs most frequently found are rivalry between two people, conflict and dilemma, struggle against fate, love or desire thwarted by society, and so on. The most common trait of these motifs is that they are dialectical: rivalry, *conflict**, exchange, *mistaken identity** (*motivation**).

B. BY DIMENSION

A motif may be closely connected with a certain character *type** (the miser, the misanthropist), but it always pertains to the thematic content and is not the property of a type of character, figure or narrative episode. It may take on the most diverse dimensions, from the general motif of the play (the main theme summarizing the general idea, such as the motif of vengeance in *Hamlet*) to the individual motif of a scene or dialogue. Generally speaking, a motif should be broken down into a serie of individual motifs in order to show how they are linked together in the *fabula** or *plot**.

C. BY INTEGRATION INTO THE ACTION

- Dynamic motif: *episode** that moves the action forward;
- Static motif: episode used for characterization that neutralizes the action temporarily;
- Retarding motif: prevents a project from being realized and provides suspense. This is an essential phase of classical tragedy before the catastrophe, intended to build suspense and give the hero a last opportunity to make a different decision or retreat before the obstacle;
- *Flashback** or anticipating motif;
- Central motif and framing motif (*frame**).

D. BY INTEGRATION INTO PLOT

TOMACHEVSKY (in TODOROV 1965) distinguishes between *free motifs* and *bound motifs*. While the first may be omitted without affecting comprehension, eliminating the second type would prejudice the causal succession of events.

E. BY INCLUSION WITHIN A CORPUS

- Motif proper to a single work;
- Obsessive motif or theme of an author;
- Motif observable within a literary tradition (the theme of *Faust*, seduction);
- Anthropological motif or *archetype**.

Further reading: Frenzel 1963; Mauron 1963; Propp 1968; G.Durand 1969; Trousson 1981.

MOTIVATION

Fr.: *motivation*; Ger.: *Motivation*; Sp.: *motivación*.

1. Motivation of Characters

Statement or suggestion of (psychological, intellectual, metaphysical) reasons that lead a character to behave in a certain way.

Motivation is an essential part of *characterization**. It tells the spectators about the *mainsprings of the action** and the (often obscure) reasons for the characters' actions. In literary theory, according to TOMACHEVSKY (1965, 282), it is the "justification immanent in the logic of the narrative for the introduction of a particular motif."

The "objectivity" of drama, i.e. the external presentation of characters in action, obliges the playwright to allow each character's vision and project to show through his speeches and actions, to make those actions plausible and to give, or at least to appear to give, an equal chance to all in the general conflict. Characterization varies according to the type of dramaturgy: it is general, universal and elliptic in classical drama; precise and socioeconomic in naturalism. The playwright sometimes creates mystery around the *hero*'s motives, leaving it up to the audience to discover his true intentions. One of the actor's principal tasks is to clarify his character's motivations and to find ways to act as if he himself were in the character's situation (STANISLAVSKY 1963, 1966).

2. Motivation of Action

In classical dramaturgy and any theatrical form resting on *imitation** and the production of *illusion**, the action appears necessary and logical. Chance, the irrational, and the illogical are therefore excluded from the outset, or at least, when they do appear, their presence is duly explained and justified. The spectator must be able to accept the changes of action and recognize in them the logic of his own world. Taking the opposing view, the theatre of the *absurd** has characters acting in ways that are impossible to predict for the average speaker, to the point that the latter, like Polonius, realizes that "though this be madness, yet there is method in it."

Motivation also has to do with the dénouement, which leaves no doubt about the state of things and the final outcome of the conflicts. In classical dramaturgy, all conflict and action must be motivated, whereas other dramaturgies refuse to give motives for the conclusion and to have the *fabula* end on a stable, definitive note and provide the key to physical actions.

MOUTHPIECE

Fr.: *porte-parole;* Ger.: *Sprachrohr;* Sp.: *portavoz.*

1. Playwright's Mouthpiece

1. The playwright's mouthpiece is the character deemed to represent the playwright's *point of view**. The kind of theatre that represents characters "objectively" (HEGEL) with their own points of view does not need a narrator or mouthpiece. Only in *thesis drama** or in short, particularly thorny bits of the dramatic text is the mouthpiece clearly discernable. This thankless job often falls to the *raisonneur**, who is responsible for the proper *reception** of the speeches by the spectator, and for correcting *perspective** as required. It is always difficult, not to say tedious, to hunt down the tracks of an "authorial" voice, and moreover goes against the grain of the theatrical work of art, which is characterized by the lack of a central subject and is the result of the entanglement of the *actantial** and discursive contradictions.

2. When the play is more of an intellectual debate or philosophical dialogue than a fiction with several voices, one may detect the ideology or philosophy concealed by the actor's mask. Here the character functions solely as a teaching aid for the exchange of ideas (*didactic play**). He is reduced to the role of what MARX (1967, 187) called the "mouthpiece of the spirit of the times," an allusion to SCHILLER's characters, meaning a completely idealized and abstract kind of character that represents a historical and philosophical trend and has nothing in common with a tangible, individualized character. This kind of idealization contrasts with the Shakespearean character of realistic construction that gives the impression of being an indefinable living person who exists only through his drives and contradictions (Hamlet, Lear, Othello).

See also: confidant, parabasis.

MOVEMENT

Fr.: *mouvement;* Ger.: *Bewegung;* Sp.: *movimiento.*

This is a neutral and frequently used way of referring to an actor's activity or training (movement classes). Movement provides a first overall approach to acting analysis and brings together most questions about body, gesture and acting, which we will simply outline here.

1. Study of movement

The analysis of movement that dates back to the end of the last century, with MAREY's experiments, MUYBRIDGE's chronophotography and DELSARTE's classifications, provides a better understanding of how to organize a study of acting. The categories put forward by the study of movement are edifying. According to LABAN, "the movements of the body can basically be divided into steps, arm and hand gestures, and facial expressions" (1994, 46). These three sets of movements are sometimes called differently or grouped differently:

- *Instinctive impulses or movements.* These may be *triggers* (as in STANISLAVSKY) or, in GROTOWSKI, something that overcomes an actor's block and opens up the whole act which engages all his psychophysical resources, the *determined body* of the actor who, according to BARBA, "does not study physiology but creates a network of external stimuli to which he reacts with physical actions" (1993, 55).

- *Postures*, characterized by a way of standing on the ground, according to weight and gravity.
- *Attitudes**, described in terms of somatic, segmentary positions.
- *Movements in space*, as a way of using the stage space and the path taken by the actor or dancer.
- *Walking* is particularly important for most directors directing actors: STANISLAVSKY, VAKHTANGOV and DECROUX make walking one of the pillars of actor training, for "Not one beginner knows how to walk on stage" (DULLIN, 1946:115), and "To have a role 'in your legs', as the [French] expression goes, sometimes takes much experimentation."
- *Gait* has been the subject of philosophical reflection and gives mimes infinite room for experimentation. BALZAC, in his *Théorie de la démarche*, saw gait as "the countenance of the body." "Gaze, voice, breathing and gait are identical, but since it has not been given to man to be able to see to all four of these different and simultaneous expressions of his thinking at the same time, look for the one that tells the truth, and you will know the whole man" (BALZAC, quoted in LECOQ 1987, 24). LECOQ made a hilarious moment out of this during his presentation-demonstration "Everything moves," and in experiments at his movement study laboratory. The theatre of movement practised by C. HEGGEN and Y. MARC created a show, *Attention à la marche*, that compared different ways of walking and concluded that "the actor's designs on the ground express the character's 'designs'" (quoted in ASLAN 1993, 365).
- LABAN's *body actions* are defined on the basis of the following four questions: "(a) which part of the body is moving; (b) what direction it is moving in; (c) how fast it is; (d) how much muscular energy is being used" (1994, 53).
- *STANISLAVSKY's physical actions* are executed by the actor on the basis of a logic of movement and an aim of the stage action.

2. Relationship Between Physical and Mental

A study of movement cannot be done convincingly unless it is accompanied by a reflection on the interior of the moving person, whether we call it emotion, mental pictures or inner life. This leads to a continuous back and forth between motion and emotion. The various theories and acting exercises consist of clarifying this back and forth action, which may examine the difference (duality) or the merging and organic relationship between body and mind. Most of the time, the place between motion and emotion is reaffirmed, as in LABAN: "Every phrase of a movement, the least transfer of weight, any gesture by one of the parts of the body, reveals some feature of our inner lives" (1994, 46). M. Cechov has used the notion of *psychological gesture** to influence the actor's physical and mental state by engraving more and more deeply these two sides of the same coin. FELDENKRAIS made this the basis of his practice, considering that each emotion is association and linked in the cortex to a muscular configuration and attitude that has the same power to recreate the overall situation as sensory, vegetative or imaginary activity. Rather than giving in to mysterious analyses of the character's psychology, JOUVET believes it is preferable to seek the rhythm and breathing of the text and character and to gradually reconstruct the character's feelings in the way the text is spoken.

This is how we understand the work of the mime, dancer or actor, as what J. LECOQ calls "re-acting": "to re-act the real world in our bodies." A real world in perpetual motion...

MULTIMEDIA THEATRE

A multimedia performance is not simply a performance that uses audiovisual means and many different sources of information, but one that introduces a whole different dimension into the live performance as customarily defined: the place where an actor meets a spectator.

All available media – visual technologies (slides, films, videos), HF mikes, vocalizers (voice modelling) – can be used in one way or another as part of the theatre event, which can easily be submerged in a deluge of new technologies. Is the whole still a work of art? The media must at least be used according to certain criteria: formal beauty, authentic experience, free acting, communication addressed to a spectator.

Still, communication can takes unexpected forms. It is not discursive, linear or hierarchical. The text is treated more as noise or music, as a malleable substance, than as a place that produces meaning. The actor's human body is consecutively experienced live in real time, then blurred by a series of masks, then seen as a shadow through electronic media; its supports change constantly, making even the distinction between real and virtual problematic at times. The spectator is faced with a "synthetic" actor made up of bits and pieces by means of an art of simulation that pushes back the line between the authentic and the fabricated. This redefines the roles of the author, spectator and protagonists, whether they be "synthetic" or "flesh and blood."

During the 1960s in the United States, visual artists and dancers attempted to incorporate cutting-edge technologies into live performances (CAGE, RAINER). The Wooster Group specialized in ineraction between audiovisual technology and live actors (*Fish Story*, 1993); LEPAGE uses stage transformations and live recorded images, somewhat blurred and indistinct but very present and alive (*Les Sept Branches de la rivière Ota*, 1994; *Elseneur*, 1996). In a "dialogue" with his own filmed image, the actor questions the identity of the human being, suggests the *intermediality** of stage arts and persons.

Further reading: Kostelanetz 1968; Battcock and Nickas 1984; Norman 1993; Couchot and Tramus 1993; Carlson 1996.

MUSEUM, THEATRE

Fr.: *musée de théâtre*; Ger.: *Theatermuseum*; Sp.: *museo de teatro.*

The recent tendency to create museums for any reason whatsoever has not extended to theatre, at least in France, where there is not a single theatre museum. Although there are invaluable archives and collections in existence, there is no place where theatre objects – dramatic texts, programs, posters, stage design sketches and models, costumes, props, press documentation – are exhibited either permanently or temporarily. A library or archives only becomes a museum when it is allowed to be exposed to our critical gaze, when we are invited to go and spend time there rather than burying ourselves there like bookworms or anemic erudites.

What can be shown of the theatre? Basically, nothing at all except for a few pitiful relics (texts of dialogues, costumes or props, fragments of stage design, recorded voices as in N. FRIZE's voice library), like still lifes, which are somewhat depressing for yesterday's artists and today's researchers alike. What to do with this trivia? Often, it accumulates mutely in layers that accumulate over the years on top of an event that can no longer be grasped, a series of relics and indications of its past splendor that bear witness to its genesis and reception, systematically decontextualizing the setting in which the performance took place and placing a body whose previous life is unimaginable in the coffin.

Museographic art will consist of finding the right scene design for displaying a past theatre event, not a replica of the theatre but a new device it invents for itself; otherwise the museum will become a garage where a production is reconstructed. Taking things out of boxes and giving them an aesthetically pleasing presentation may be a double-edged sword: it facilitates presentation and improves perception, but takes a position as to the object's meaning and aesthetics, often lending it an intention or function that did not belong to it. The temptation to be a theatre of objects can quickly become a new staging of objects from the past or a pedagogical initiation to theatre (Bern Museum), which is one of the most beautiful ways of celebrating its perennial nature.

Access to documents, their classification system and ranking, valuing their material or abstract nature: all of this is revealing and decisive for a methodological reflection on performance analysis. Researchers include hoarders, pollsters, illustrators, samplers, fetishists, scavengers, even deserters.

The most beautiful theatre museums are in central and eastern Europe, in Switzerland, Germany, Austria, Poland (the Grotowski center of theatre studies in Warsaw), Hungary (Gizi Bajor acting museum) and Russia, where they are often devoted to a particular author or director. The Arsenal library, the Maison Jean Vilar in Avignon, the Centre National du Théâtre, the SACD, the Kwok-On Museum, the National Library on Richelieu all hold treasures that could easily be used in exhibits and talks. Further reading: Veinstein, 1984.

MUSIC AND THEATRE

Fr.: *musique et théâtre;* Ger.: *Musik und Theater;* Sp.: *música y teatro.*

Leaving aside the question of *incidental music**, *opera** and *music theatre**, a look at the complex and thorny relationship between music and theatre is warranted.

1. Musical metaphor

A staging is often compared to a composition in space and time, a score that uses different materials, an individual interpretation by actors. Musical notation and composition provide the master plan for the performance, allowing both spectators and actors to feel the beat on stage just as musicians do. "A musically organized performance is not a performance in which one makes music or sings constantly from off stage, but a performance with a precise rhythmic score, a performance in which time is strictly ordered" (MEYERHOLD 1992, IV:325).

2. New alliances

The relationship between music and stage are in the process of changing. One is no longer exclusively at the service of the other, and even keeps an autonomy that also benefits its partner. Music is not merely a servant or accompanist of the stage. It no longer, as in Romantic opera, engulfs the text and theatricality. For many years (historically) systematically (in theory) separate in the search for *specificity**, music and theatre are now much more in agreement on their complementarity. The musicality of texts is being rediscovered, and the theatricality of music (for example, APERGHIS' musical theatre) is being updated. As perceived in the theatre, music takes on a completely different resonance for the spectator than in the aseptic setting of the concert hall. What remains to be established – and this is much more difficult than in film, where they were created separately – is how the visual and the auditory work together. The tendency in current theory on stage music (N. FRIZE) or opera (MOINDROT 1993) is rather to underscore the integration of visual and auditory perception, following a vectorization and marking of sight and hearing, a filtering of all materials by the listener-spectator: "our spectator's perception requires things to be organized, not composed" (N. FRIZE). We would then need to evaluate these (re)organizations based on the various components of the performance, considering what each component is able to convey:

- music alone creates virtual worlds, emotional frameworks for the rest of the performance;
- architecture provides concrete evidence of a receptacle to be filled;
- literature and the dramatic text provide a rhythmic mould that can be altered slightly by the acting, while the musical structure is much too rigid for this; hence the need for a compromise in opera between the (flexibly inclined) director and the (rigidly inclined) conductor.

Among the components of these (re)organizations, each element influences the others, sometimes in unexpected ways. Music provides an emotional atmosphere that sheds light on the actor's gestures and movements; inversely, gesture and dance can "open up" the music: "Dance can reveal all the mystery that music harbours, and also has the merit of being human and tangible" (BAUDELAIRE, *La Fanfarlot*).

MUSICAL THEATRE

Fr.: *théâtre musical*; Ger.: *Musiktheater*; Sp.: *teatro musical*.

This contemporary form of theatre (to be distinguished from opera, operetta and musical comedy) endeavors to bring together text, music and visual staging without integrating them, merging them, or reducing them to a common denominator (as in Wagnerian opera) and without distancing them from one another (as in the didactic operas of Kurt WEILL and B. BRECHT).

The early experiences of musical theatre took place with pocket operas such as *L'Histoire du soldat* by STRAVINSKY and RAMUZ (1918) and BRECHT's didactic operas (*Mahoganny, Celui que dit oui, celui qui dit non* (1930). The genre took hold during the 1950s, when composers such as SCHNEBEL, KAGEL and STOCKHAUSEN viewed their concerts as theatrical performances rather than renderings of a score or libretto. The theatricality of vocal or musical production is underscored by G. APERGHIS. In *Énumérations*, for instance, the performers — who are singers, actors and musicians as well as sound effects engineers and tricksters — make noise by striking everyday objects or materials, varying the rhythm and evoking voice and text. They reconstruct in music an entire physical and visual environment, not without a certain desire to hoax. Diametrically opposed cultures and musical traditions can rub shoulders, as in H. GOEBBELS's *Ou bien le débarquement désastreux* (1993): Western electrical/acoustic or rock music with kora and African chants. Musical theatre is a huge building site where every imaginable relationship between the materials of stage arts and musical arts are tried out and tested.

MYSTERY PLAY

(From the Latin *ministerium*, office, act. Or, according to another etymology, from the Latin *mysterium*, secret truth.)
Fr.: *mystère*; Ger.: *Mysterium, Mysterienspiel*; Sp.: *misterio*.

Medieval religious play (from the fourteenth to the sixteen centuries) that dramatizes episodes from the Bible (Old and New Testaments) and the lives of saints, performed at religious holidays by amateur actors (mainly mimes and jugglers), under the direction of a conductor, in *mansions* or simultaneous sets. A mystery play lasts several days and has a narrator to make connections between episodes and places and a master of ceremonies. Such plays were commissioned by municipalities (text and conductor) and performed in all styles in a series of tableaux. The actors belonged to brotherhood groups. In 1548, shocked by the mystery play's development toward the burlesque and the vulgar, the Church banned religious shows on Ile-de-France, but the tradition persisted, both in France and throughout Europe (*autos sacramentales** in Spain and Portugal, *miracle plays** in England, *laudi* in Italy and *Mysterienspiele* in Germany). Its influence on playwrights both Elizabethan (MARLOWE, SHAKESPEARE) and Spanish (CALDERON) was considerable.

Le Mystère de la Passion recounts the life of Christ, combining grotesque comedy with theological discussion and theatricalizing the entire town with spectacular effects.

See also: auto sacramental, miracle play, liturgical drama.

Further reading: Konigson 1969, 1975; Rey-Flaud 1973.

MYTHOS

Fr.: *mythos*; Ger.: *Mythos*; Sp.: *mythos*.

Term from ARISTOTLE's *Poetics*, most often translated as *plot* in English, *fable* in French and *Handlung* in German (here also as *fabula*). It is the combination of the actions (1450a), the selection and ordering of the narrated *events**.

Originally, *mythos* referred to the literary or artistic source, the mythical story upon which dramatists build their tragedies. The myths were constantly being changed and combined, forming *motifs** and *themes** that Greek dramatists used over and over in their tragedies. Then, beginning with ARISTOTLE, *mythos* was used to mean the organized structure of the action. It is characterized by (a) the temporal order of the events: beginning, middle, end (1450b); (b) the perceptible structure of a whole (1450b); (c) the *unity** of action. Thus, from being a mere imitation of a previous source, the *mythos* is elevated to the rank of the *unity** of action, the narrative ordering of scattered elements and the closed (*Aristotelian**) form.

Further reading: Mauron 1963; Vernant 1965, 1974; Vernant and Vidal-Naquet 1972; Szondi 1972a; Ricoeur 1983, 1984, 1985; Delmas 1985; Schechner 1985; Barba and Savarese 1985.

N

NAMES OF CHARACTERS

Fr.: *noms des personnages;* Ger.: *Figurennamen;* Sp.: *nombres de los personajes.*

See ANTONOMASIA

NARRATIVE

Fr.: *récit;* Ger.: *Bericht, Erzählung;* Sp.: *relato.*

Strictly speaking, as used in theatre criticism, a narrative is the speech of a character relating an event that occurred *off stage**. Although in principle it is proscribed, since theatre shows action mimetically rather than alluding to it in speech, the narrative is frequently included in the dramatic text (spoken by the messenger or *confidant** in classical dramaturgy). In contemporary epic theatre as well, characters are frequently called on to give their points of view on the development of the drama. When the narration takes place at the same time as an action occurring out of the spectator's sight, it is called *teichoscopy** (seeing through walls). Generally speaking, a narrative exists when the action itself is difficult to stage: "One of the rules of theatre is to make a narrative only of those things that cannot occur in action" (RACINE, Preface to *Britannicus*).

In the classical period, the narrative was considered to be less effective than real action, for "what is exposed to view is much more moving than what is learned only through a narrative" (CORNEILLE, "Examen du *Cid*").

1. The Narrative: Definition and Boundaries

As defined by narratology (*narrative analysis**), the narrative is a very loose category that includes all narrative forms. It is "precisely what Aristotle called *mythos*, i.e., the arrangement of facts" (RICOEUR 1983, 62).

We speak of a narrative in the strict sense when the character takes the floor to relate to the other characters events that only he witnessed (for example, Théramène's speech in *Phèdre* and the narrative of the battle of Maures in *Le Cid*).

It is difficult to establish the boundaries of a narrative, since a play (particularly a classical one) presents a series of often long exchanges within which characters organize their speeches by alluding to events outside the stage. The very term *dramatic poem**, as plays were called in the seventeenth century, indicates that the dramatic text was conceived more as a series of connected dialogues than as an actual verbal exchange in the heat of the action. Each character played a (clearly fictional) role as an organizer of dramatic material, and his speeches were structured very rhetorically according to the logic of a narrative: presentation of facts, description of feelings, indication of intentions, moral conclusions, etc. This structure is also found in the narrative monologues of classical heroes. The narrative tends to become detached from the stage situation in structure and sometimes takes the form of formulas or general *maxims** (*rhetoric**).

2. Functions of the Narrative

In classical dramaturgy, the narrative was used when the reported action could not be performed on stage for reasons of decorum or *verisimilitude**, or because of technical difficulties. The narrative most often related violent scenes (duels, battles, catastrophes), peripety that prepared the action or followed upon catastrophe or conflict resolved: "What ought not be seen should be described in a narrative" (BOILEAU, *Art poétique*, chap. III).

The narrative's function, however, is not only to help out a playwright who would have had no choice but to summarize an action verbally. It streamlines the play by skimming lightly over events that would otherwise require a profusion of sets, gestures and dialogues. It filters the events through the consciousness of the narrator, who interprets the facts freely and adds appropriate remarks. To the utterance, then, is added the speaker's *modalization** when reporting the event.

For Rodrigue, for instance, the battle narrative also serves as a political argument in his personal situation: events are told so as to make his services appear indispensable.

Finally, by "distancing" the action in a narrative, by having a *narrator** intervene, the playwright allows the spectator to judge more objectively. This technique was frequently employed by BRECHT when critical reflection was deemed preferable to emotional identification. By making the performance unreal and dematerialized, the narrative prevents illusion and "de-psychologizes" the stage by stressing the production of the character's words and, through him, the playwright and actors.

Unlike the dramatic narrative, the Brechtian narrative does not seek to justify a situation that requires a monologue by a main character. It appears entirely artificial; the character states his personal particulars and takes up a position outside the fiction to emphasize its falsity and summarize the action from the point of view of a director supervising the performance. The narrator often plays a didactic role in indicating the problems of characters or the need to appeal to the audience to change the "scenario of reality" (as at the end of BRECHT's *The Good Person of Sichuan*). The narrative, particularly the classical narrative, is always an ornament, a bravura piece, a poem that is especially well crafted in its form.

3. "Dramatization" of Narrative

The narrative cannot, however, take on too much importance in the body of the play without running the risk of destroying its theatrical quality. It is most often confined to the *monologues** of the *exposition** and the funeral or wedding speeches of the epilogue. Moreover, the narrative is integrated into the action and must occur at points of intensity to retard information (technique of *suspense**), or at the major linkages of the action. It is often divided up between the hero and his *alter ego* (*confidant**), who describe the situation in a false dialogue, or in an artificially animated discussion (as when Alceste and Philinte relate their conception of social life at the beginning of *le Misanthrope*). The narrative is also broken up by the monosyllabic remarks of the listeners. In short, the narrative quickly returns to the status of dramatic scene and action; *diegesis** and *mimesis** are not easily separated.

4. The Play of Embedded Narratives

Current productions (adaptations of novels or non-"dramatic" texts, for example) are particularly fond of staging narrators who make use of other narrators in their narrated stories, and so on. More than a fad, this is obviously a play on the relativity of speech and the *modalization** of utterances. From the fortuitous and guilty role it played in classical dramaturgy, the narrative has come to be central to all narratological practices and a way of rewriting for the stage "the great narrative of the life of the world."

See also: fabula, dramatic and epic, Brechtian, flashback, diegesis, narration.

Further reading: Scherer 1950; Szondi 1956; Genette, in *Communications*, 1966; Wirth 1981; Mathieu 1974.

NARRATIVE ANALYSIS

Fr.: *analyse du récit*; Ger.: *Handlungsanalyse*; Sp.: *análisis del relato*.

1. The Notion of Narrative in Theatre

A. STATE OF RESEARCH

Narrative analysis (which must be carefully distinguished from the construction of the *fabula**) dealt first with simple narrative forms (folktale, legend, novella), then with the novel and multiple-code systems such as comic strips or motion pictures. Theatre has not yet been analyzed systematically, no doubt because of its extremely complex nature (given the number and variety of its different signifying systems), but perhaps also because it is associated by critics with *mimesis** (imitation of an action) rather than with *diegesis** (*narration** by a narrator). The main reason may be that theatrical narrative is only one specific case of a narrative system whose laws are independent of the kind of semiological system used. By *narrative analysis* we understand not the analysis of the characters' narratives, but rather the study of narrativity in theatre.

B. MIMESIS AND DIEGESIS

Traditionally defined (since ARTISTOTLE's *Poetics*) as the *imitation** of an action, theatre does not tell a story from the point of view of a narrator. The events reported are not unified by the consciousness of an author who structures them into a series of episodes; they are always transmitted in the heat of a communicative situation that depends on the here and now of the stage (*deixis**).

From the point of view of the spectator who unifies the subjective views of the various characters, however, theatre does in most cases present a *fabula** that can be summed up in a narrative. This *fabula* has all the features of a series of motifs, each with its own logic, so that a narrative analysis is perfectly possible provided one works on a narrative that has been reconstituted in a theoretical narrative model (*narration**, *narrator**.

The narrative is therefore located within the deep structure, at the level of the *actantial** code. Many of the problems encountered in narrative analysis arise when it is not clearly specified on what level one is working; whether the surface level (series of visible motifs of the *plot**), or the deep level (configuration of the *actantial model**). The narrative may be formalized at two levels: by following the winding path of the plot broken down into its smallest elements (as it appears in all situations on stage) or, alternatively, within a very general code of human action (actantial code), a code which is reconstituted on the basis of the text and conceived of in its general form as a logic of action.

C. GENERAL DEFINITION OF NARRATIVE

The most general definition of a narrative is applicable to narrative in theatre. A narrative is always a "monosemiological system (for example, a novel) or a polysemiological system (comic strip or movie), which may or may not be anthropomorphic, that regulates the conservation and transformation of meaning within a directed utterance" (HAMON 1974, 150).

2. Methods of Narrative Analysis in Theatre

A. ANALYSIS OF FUNCTIONS OR MOTIFS

It is difficult, if not impossible (except perhaps in strictly coded forms of theatre such as farce, popular theatre or medieval mysteries), to identify a fixed number of recurring functions (narrative motifs) as did PROPP (1929) for the folktale in his *Morphology of the Folktale*. The action is never as codified or subject to a fixed order of appearance of the functions.

B. TEXTUAL GRAMMARS OF THEATRE

Textual grammar presupposes the existence of two textual levels: the *deep narrative structure*, which examines the possible relationships between the actants at a logical, non-anthropomorphical level (*actantial model**);

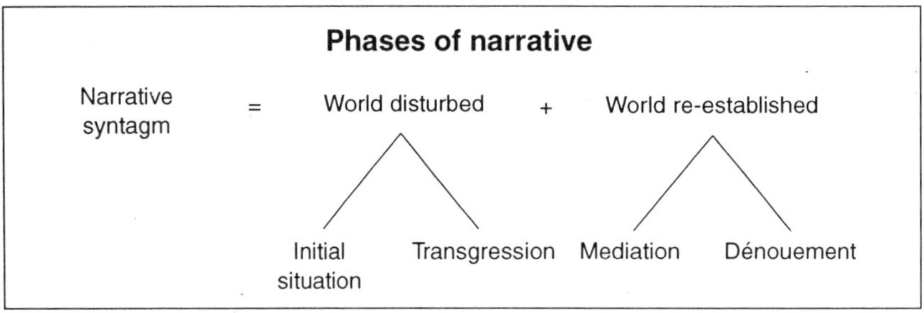

(*from* T. Pavel 1976, 18)

the *surface discursive structure,* which defines the way in which the characters are actually realized and how they appear at the level of discourse. The difficulty lies in establishing rules that will explain the transition of actantial macrostructures to the surface of the text and the performance, in linking the logic of the events reported to the reporting discourse. We will therefore analyze the transition:

- from actant to actor, from narrative to discursive (actantial model, *character**),
- from reported story to reporting discourse.

C. NARRATIVE STRUCTURE

In the absence of a precise number of functions or rules governing the organization of the discursive surface, several narrative structures can be identified:

1. Obviously we must be content with a very general description of the phases that must be included in any narrative. Every analysis revolves around the notion of an *obstacle** imposed on the hero, who accepts or turns down the challenge of a conflict to become the victor or the vanquished. When he accepts the challenge, the hero is "invested" by the sender (who assigns moral, religious, human and other values) and becomes the actual *subject* of the action (HAMON 1974,: 139).

2. For instance, the rules that govern Racinian narrative, as described by T. PAVEL, are as follows: the characters "(1) fall in love at first sight, (2) feel the effects of the ban, try to overcome their passion and sometimes think they have succeeded, (3) realize the futility of the struggle and abandon themselves to their passion" (PAVEL 1976, 8).

3. The narrative has at its centre the sore point of a conflict (of values or between persons) in which the subject is led to transgress the values of his world. Through mediation (outside intervention or free choice of the hero), this world, after a temporary disturbance, is finally re-established. The minimal narrative can therefore be represented as in the table below.

4. Mediation is the key moment of the narrative because it allows the conflictual situation to be resolved just as the actantial scheme (i.e. the paradigmatic deep structure of the relations of force) "emerges" and appears at the syntagmatic level of the story being told. The mediation, that is the response to the test or resolution of the conflict, is therefore the link between the deep (actantial) narrative structures and the surface of the discourse where the chain of events (*plot**) is located.

D. MINIMAL SENTENCE OF NARRATIVE

In practice, we will seek to reduce the *fabula* to a minimal sentence that sums up the action while discovering its articulations or contradictions. This brings to mind the Brechtian method of indicating the play's *gestus** (translated as "gest" by WILLET) in a short utterance: "Each single incident has its basic gest: Richard Gloster courts his victim's widow. The child's true mother is found by means of a chalk circle. God has a bet with the Devil for Dr. Faustus' soul. Woyzeck buys a cheap knife in order to do his wife in, etc." (BRECHT, *A Short Organum for the Theatre*, sect. 66).

In seeking out the gestus of the action, we are obliged to centre the narrative around the main action and the conflict/ mediation that enables the protagonist's contract to be terminated.

The minimal sentence of the narrative is descriptive to a varying degree. It may give a precise account of the episodes or summarize the movement "metalinguistically." For *Mother Courage*, for instance, we would have: Mother Courage wants to make a profit on the war, but loses everything. This proposition is repeated three times in three variations of loss/gain, each of which can be summarized in the sequence "prospects of material gain/loss of a child."

The narrative of *Mother Courage*, therefore, consists of the following series: desire for gain/loss // desire for gain/loss // desire for gain/loss.

E. PERSPECTIVE OF NARRATIVE ANALYSIS

Narrative analysis cannot make any real progress in theatre until several theoretical problems have been resolved:

1. *The transition from deep narrative structures to surface discursive structures* is currently being studied (GREIMAS 1970; BREMOND 1973; PAVEL 1976). Both ends of the chain are now fairly well known. What remains is to discover appropriate rules of transformation and identify their nature for each genre and, finally, for each specific play. As to the old question posed by ARTISTOTLE about whether action or characters should prevail (*Poetics*, section 1450a), GREIMAS' research has shown how there is a progressive movement from an elementary structure of meaning to the actants, then to the actors, then to roles and finally to actual characters. Far from eliminating one of the two terms of the action/character pair, the analysis should examine how such and such a feature of the character acts on the action, and, inversely, how the action changes the character's identity.

2. *Segmentation of the dramatic narrative*: Theorists have not succeeded in isolating relevant units of narration other than artificial ones based on the division of a play into scenes or acts. The distinction between a play in *acts** and a play in *tableaux** is of course essential to describe two ways of presenting reality (the *dramatic** stresses the indivisible whole of the curve that leads inevitably to the conflict while the epic, for example, Brechtian, implies that the real is constructed and therefore subject to change). But this distinction between acts and tableaux does not tell us anything about the progression of the narrative, the arrangement of the sequences or functions, or the actantial logic.

3. *"Narratization" of theatricality*: Despite the postulate that a semiotic theory of narrative can exist independently of its object (short story, novel, gesture), it may be that theatre, because of its ability to represent, escapes the tyranny of a narrative logic to some extent. Perhaps in reaction to the insistence of BRECHT and his followers on delivering the *fabula** (story) and determining the meaning of the text without concerning themselves sufficiently with the tangible aspects and meaningful interplay of stage writing (*écriture scénique*), some experimental theatre today, such as that of Robert WILSON or Bread and Puppet, is based precisely on the desire to deliver images "in bulk" with no necessary, univocal link between them. Even if we succeeded in constructing a mini-narrative for each stage image, the manifold and contradictory nature of those narratives would prevent us from establishing a macro-narrative that could account for a logic of events. In any case, identifying the narrative structures would not reflect the rich visual side of the performance.

Thus, narrative analysis represents only a small part of *theatre studies**.

See also: narrative, narrator.

Further reading: Brémond 1973; Chabrol 1973; Mathieu 1974; *Communications*, 1966; Prince 1973; Greimas and Courtès 1979; Kibédi-Varga 1981; Segre in Amossy (ed.) 1981; Segre 1984; Mathieu-Colas 1986.

NARRATION

Fr.: *narration*; Ger.: *Erzählung*; Sp.: *narración*.

1. In the sense of *narrative**, the way in which facts are related by a system, usually linguistic but occasionally a series of gestures or stage images. Like the narrative, narration uses one or more stage systems and orients the meaning in a linear manner according to a logic of actions toward a final goal: the *dénouement** and the resolution of *conflicts**. Narration makes us "see" the *fabula** in its particular temporality and establishes a succession of images and actions.

According to the distinction made by BENVENISTE (1966) and GENETTE (1966), narration can be either the *story* told (the narrative content as a whole) or the narrating *discourse* or *narrative* (the discourse that relates the events). The story or *fabula* is what is narrated; the narrative is the narrating discourse; the narrration is the fictive or real acte that produces the narrative.

2. In classical dramaturgy, the characters narrate past events in long speeches. CORNEILLE refers to Cinna's speech about the conspiracy as an *ornate narration*.

3. *Narration* and *description* are often contrasted (particularly in *epic** forms) according to the purpose of their discourse: "Narration is an exposition of facts, whereas description is an exposition of things" (MARMONTEL, 1787). In the theatre, *description** is provided by visual events, while narration takes place "in the making" in the linking of the different motifs of the *fabula*. Because it is performed on stage, this kind of narration necessarily uses the discursive instance that structures the *fabula* according to its own modes and techniques. A distinction must be made between the (deep) narrative structures and the (surface) discursive structures. The former are visible only in the form of a theoretical system of actions presented by *actants** according to a universal logic (PROPP 1968; GREIMAS 1970, 1973). The latter constitute the concrete arrangement of speeches and dialogues, all of the *actors** (in the semiotic sense) in the narrative.

See also: narrator, discourse, narrative analysis, focalization, storyteller, diegesis.

Further reading: Savona 1980, 1982.

NARRATIVITY (NARRATOLOGY)

Fr.: *narrativité, narratologie*; Ger.: *Erzählweise, Narrativität*; Sp: *narratividad, narratología*.

See NARRATIVE ANALYSIS, NARRATION

NARRATOR

Fr.: *narrateur*; Ger.: *Erzähler*; Sp.: *narrador*.

Although in principle there is no narrator in *dramatic** theatre, in which the playwright never speaks in his own name, a narrator appears in certain forms of theatre, particularly epic theatre. Some popular traditions in Africa and the Orient frequently use a narrator as a mediator between audience and characters (*storyteller**). We could also say that the director acts as a narrator toward the text and the stage, in choosing a point of view and telling a *fabula**, like a subject of enunciation directing all textual and stage utterances.

The narrator does not intervene in the text of the play (except sometimes in the *prologue**, *epilogue** or *stage directions** when they are spoken or shown). The narrator can only exist in the form of a character who gives information to the other characters or the audience by telling and commenting on the events directly. The most frequent case is that of a character-narrator who, as in the classical narrative, relates what cannot be shown directly onstage for reasons of decorum or verisimilitude. A *narrative* exists (and therefore a narrator and not simply a character acting) whenever the information provided is not concretely related to the stage situation, when the discourse appeals to the spectator's mental representations rather than the actual stage representation of the event. It is sometimes hard to draw a dividing line between narrative and dramatic action, since the narrator's enunciation remains tied to the stage, so that a narrative is always "dramatized" to a varying degree.

2. The Narrator in the Epic System

A. SHATTERING ILLUSION
The dramatic *illusion** of an acting style that addresses the audience directly without going through the playwright is shattered in epic theatre (BRECHT), and the characters take their author's place to play an identical role to that of the narrator of a novel. Commentary, summary, transition, song – these are forms specific to the narrator-character. It becomes impossible to distinguish what pertains to the character's role (i.e. what the character is likely to narrate) and what is a direct transposition of the author's discourse. There is a constant movement from the internal fiction to the play (in which the narrator's presence is motivated and justified by the fiction) to a shattering of the illusion (in *addresses** to the audience).

B. AUTHOR'S DOUBLE
A character or group of characters (*chorus**) appears as different from the usual acting style and "steps out of" the fictional universe or at least creates another level of fiction in order to comment on the play and provide an interpretation of the performance that could be the author's. This is the case of narrators in BRECHT, GIRAUDOUX, WILDER (SZONDI 1956, 1972a).

C. DIRECTOR
The narrator takes charge of the performance, as master of ceremonies, as the one who arranges the story materials (for example, the beggar in GIRAUDOUX'S *la Guerre de Troie n'aura pas lieu* anticipates the ending. In M. FRISCH's *Biografie*, the commentator lets the characters speak and suggests various solutions to their problems).

D. MEDIATOR BETWEEN FABULA AND ACTOR
In collective creations based on novels, or in groups working with improvisations before finalizing a text, the actor-narrator explains how he understands his character, what he might say, what he is incapable of expressing, and so on. With no fear of putting narrators on stage, narrative texts are staged that are not "meant" for the stage, such as poems, novels or press notices. The emphasis on the narrator is often attributable to a desire to take into account the actor's enunciation and critical attitude toward what he is playing, his desire to play that he plays, perhaps in the hope of recovering a lost authenticity.

See also: narrative analysis, epic and dramatic, dramaturgy, narration.

NATURAL

Fr.: *naturel*; Ger.: *natürlich, Natürlichkeit*; Sp.: *natural.*

A notion as old as it is vague, the natural is just as metaphysical and as difficult to define as naturalism. Every acting style sees itself as natural and claims to have invented the "truly natural" style of performance. The natural, though man-made, denies that it is an artificial production and refers to "artificial objects that are presented to us as if there were no art involved in them and they were productions of nature. A painting that strikes the eye as if it were the very object it represents; a dramatic action that makes one forget it is only a performance [...], all this is called *natural* [...]" (Article on *Natural*, in *l'Encyclopédie*).

The actor's *diction** and gestures are felt to be either natural or codified, particularly when the text is written in a very strict rhetorical form such as the classical alexandrine. The actor is required to choose to make the alexandrine commonplace, neutralizing it with a petit-bourgeois naturalness, or, conversely, to attempt to create the formal distance given the rhetoric and signifying material, to accept or even amplify the power of convention on the creation of fiction.

See also: Barthes 1963; Vitez and Meschonnic 1982.

NATURALISTIC STAGING

Fr.: *représentation naturaliste*; Ger.: *naturalistischer Aufführungsstil*; Sp.: *representación naturalista.*

A naturalistic performance passes itself off as actual reality, and not as an artistic transposition on stage. B. DORT defines it as "an attempt to set up the stage in a coherent and concrete milieu that, given its materiality and closure, incorporates the actor (actor as instrument or actor as creator) and presents itself to the spectator as reality itself" (1984, 11).

1. Origins
Historically, naturalism is an artistic movement that, around 1880–1890, advocated a total reproduction of unstylized, unembellished reality, stressing the material aspects of human existence. By extension, it refers to a style or technique that claims to reproduce reality photographically.

Naturalism appeared in an era of postivistic and scientific euphoria, along with a desire to apply the scientific method to observe society as would a clinician or physiologist, while confining it to a non-dialectical determinism. In spite of ZOLA's exhortation for theatre to show "the dual influence of characters on facts and of facts on characters," in naturalistic performance, man is caught up in an unchangeable *milieu** and illustrates the "inevitable laws of heredity and environment."

Naturalism in theatre represents the culmination of an aesthetics that calls, moderately in the seventeenth century and more insistently in the eighteenth (DIDEROT and the *drame**), for the production of an illusion. It is not, however, confined to the work of ZOLA, IBSEN, BECQUE, STRINDBERG, HAUPTMANN and GORKY, but has developed into a style characteristic of a major tendency of contemporary mise-en-scène (*boulevard theatre**, television soap operas) and a "natural" conception of theatre.

2. The Naturalist Aesthetic
We will concentrate on three features of naturalistic performance, although we are quite aware, as non-naive spectators of this non-naive aesthetic, that reality is much more complex.

A. The *milieu** is conveyed by scenery that is true to nature and acts as a "continuous description" (ZOLA), often made of actual objects (real doors, bloody quarters of beef on ANTOINE's stage). Naturalistic mise-en-scène is fond of accumulation, detail, uniqueness and surprise.

B. The *language* reproduces unchanged the various levels of style, dialects and ways of speaking specific to each social class. By saying the text in a highly psychological way, the actor creates the impression that the words and literary structure are made of the same material as the character's psychology and ideology. In this way, the text's literary or poetic construction is trivialized and denied. The bourgeois aesthetic of art as psychological expression endeavours to camouflage the signifying work of mise-en-scène, the work to produce meaning, discourse and unconscious mechanisms of the stage (*signifying practice**, *reality-effects**).

C. The *acting* style aims at producing *illusion** by reinforcing the impression of mimetic reality and by inducing the actor to identify wholly with the character, all of which is supposed to occur behind an invisible *fourth wall** that separates the audience from the stage.

3. A Critique of Naturalism
The main ideological reservation concerning naturalistic mise-en-scène has to do with its metaphysical, static view of social processes, which are presented as natural phenomena. BRECHT criticized G. HAUPTMANN's *Die Weber*, a leading naturalistic play, for implying that class struggle is inherent to human nature. So naturalism took over from the classical conception, also based on a misleading view of man as an intellectual abstraction. This "idealism" has simply been inverted in a narrow materialism that saw man as a "thinking animal that is part of nature at large" (ZOLA 1881).

The critique also has to do with the naïvety of an aesthetic that claims to evade *convention** and the shattering of *illusion** when it is subject to them throughout, and when the spectator requires the dual play of illusion/disillusion in order to derive pleasure from and identify with the play. In fact, naturalistic acting calls on precisely the convention and artificiality it set out to avoid. It is never very far from its opposite, *stylization** and *symbolism**. The most realistic or naturalistic text is the one that best masters the artistic conventions governing its production.

4. Prolongation and Renewal of Naturalism

In addition to the assured success of a dramaturgy based on *reality-effects** (*bourgeois** or *boulevard theatre**, soap operas), naturalism has inspired interesting attempts at neo-naturalism that are characterized by an always-perceptible underlying critique of the naturalizing ideology. The "kitchen-sink drama" of the 1950s in England (WESKER, OWEN) was a return to the description of less favoured milieus. In Germany, KROETZ's theatre represents and gives voice to the "language-less." The vogue for *theatre of everyday life** was also seen in France during the 1970s (DEUTSCH, WENZEL, LASSALLE, VINAVER) in various forms, from a photographic rendering to a critical lyricism that imparted a subjective view of reality.

See also: realism, represented reality, history, theatre of everyday life.

Further reading: Zola 1881; Antoine 1903; *Drama Review*, 1969; Sanders 1974, 1978; Amiard-Chevrel 1979; Chevrel 1982; Grimm 1982.

NECESSARY

Fr.: *nécessaire*; Ger.: *das Notwendige*; Sp.: *necesario*.

See VERISIMILITUDE

NEGATION

Fr.: *dénégation*; Ger.: *Verneinung*; Sp.: *denegación*.

See DENIAL

NEW COMEDY

Fr.: *comédie nouvelle*; Ger.: *neue Komödie*; Sp.: *nueva comedia*.

Greek comic theatre in the fourth century B.C. that represented everyday life and made use of types and stereotyped situations (MENANDER, DIPHILUS). It influenced Latin authors (PLAUTUS, TERENCE) and extended into *commedia dell'arte**, *comedy of situation** and *comedy of manners** in the classical period.

NON-TEXTUAL

Fr.: *hors-texte*; Ger.: *Kontext*; Sp.: *extra-texto*.

The non-textual is both the ideological, historical *context** and the intertext, i.e. the series of previous texts that influence the dramatic text through any number of mediations and transformations.

In theatre, the non-textual is essential to understand the characters' lines, as the stage directions and descriptive text of the mise-en-scène are omitted in the performance. All of these "author's notes" [...] "the resulting gaps in the unity of the text are filled in by other than linguistic signs" (VELTRUSKY 1941, 134; 1976, 96). In this way, the non-textual (and off-stage) elements appear on stage through the contextualization effected by the mise-en-scène. The "visualized" dramatic text, the text "uttered on stage," although it appears not to be, is pre-shaped and *modalized** by the non-textual, rendered physically perceptible in the stage *situation**. All that is said on stage therefore has meaning only according to what is suppressed or presupposed in the pre- or extra-text. Theatre, like literature, summons up external reality not by imitating it, as was long believed, but by using it as an assumption common to playwright and spectator and as a referential illusion (a reality-effect) that makes it possible to read the dramatic text.

See also: intertextuality, sociosemiotics.

Further reading: Althusser 1965; Lotman 1977; Ubersfeld 1979a; Pavis 1978a, 1983a, 1985d.

NON-VERBAL COMMUNICATION

Fr.: *communication non verbale*; Ger.: *non-verbale Kommunikation*; Sp.: *comunicación no verbal*.

See KINESICS

NOTATION

Fr.: *notation*; Ger.: *Notation*; Sp.: *anotación*.
See DESCRIPTION, SCORE

NOUVEAU THÉÂTRE

This is a term used in France for theatre in the 1950s, including IONESCO, BECKETT, ADAMOV, the *Absurd* playwrights, novelist playwrights such as PINGET, DURAS, SARRAUTE, poets WEINGARTEN, TARDIEU, VAUTHIER.

Further reading: Jacquot 1965b; Serreau 1966; Corvin 1969; Jacquart 1974; Mignon 1986; Rykner 1988; Corvin in Jomaron 1989.

NUDITY

Fr.: *nudité*; Ger.: *Nackheit*; Sp.: *desnudez*.

A naked body on stage reintroduces the spectator's gaze and private *body** as he or she is wrested from the fiction into the reality of exhibition and desire. Nudity is therefore a semiological scandal: it reminds us that the stage is not just a representation and a sign of reality but a summoning and showing of that reality.

We can make no generalizations about the functions and effects of nudity. All we can do is distinguish between certain uses of nudity and certain ways of reacting. A first distinction must be drawn between erotic theatre or shows that systematically use nudity – chiefly of women – as a voyeuristic genre, and fictional theatre where the act of disrobing is required by the dramatic situation (even if the nudity and the emotion unleashed in the watchers breaks the protective framework of the fictional "as if").

It is therefore difficult to judge nudity without being either moralistic or emotional, simply by listing its aesthetic qualities. Unlike nudity in painting, sculpture, and even film, in theatre there is really a flesh-and-blood person that the spectator is seeing. Hence its "inevitable" eroticism, but also discomfort, as the pleasure is attenuated by the fear of being caught in the act of voyeurism.

The naked body is not always erotic or pornographic, as when it is shown indulgently; sometimes it is related to destruction and death, to Thanatos rather than Eros, like the pallid, sepulchral bodies of Butoh dancers; the violated, suffering bodies of the half-ritual, half-aesthetic actions of the Fura dels Baus group.

Although nudity no longer poses an ethical problem, at least in the West, it always sparks an existential crisis as the testing ground and resonator of a display of life and death, delight and terror.

O

OBJECT

Fr.: *objet;* Ger.: *Gegenstand;* Sp.: *objeto.*

In critical writing the term *object* often replaces *prop** or *scenery**. The neutral or empty nature of the expression explains its success in describing the contemporary stage, which uses in equal parts figurative scenery, modern sculpture or *installation** and the living sculpture of the actors. The difficulty of drawing a definite boundary between the actor and the surrounding world, the desire to comprehend the stage as a whole according to its way of producing meaning – these factors have promoted the object to the rank of the primordial *actant** of the modern *performance**. A typology of stage objects drawn up on the basis of their form, their materials or their degree of realism would not be very meaningful, for the object varies with the dramaturgy followed and, provided it is used properly, is incorporated into the performance as a visual aid and an essential signifier.

1. Functions of the Object

A. MIMESIS OF THE FRAMEWORK OF ACTION

As soon as it is identified by the spectator, the object situates the scenery. When it is important for the play to characterize the stage milieu, the object must show some distinctive traits. The naturalistic object is authentic, like a real object. The realistic object, however, represents only a few features and functions of the object imitated. The symbolist object establishes a counter-reality that functions autonomously.

B. USE IN ACTING

The theatre object is used for certain operations or manipulations. This pragmatic function is particularly important when the stage shows human beings in their daily occupations. When the scenery is not figurative, certain elements may be used as stage machinery (*practicables**, slopes, mobiles, constructivist machines, etc.). Here the object is less functional than playful: it "produces" stage meanings that are grafted onto the text.

C. ABSTRACTION AND NON-FIGURATION

When the mise-en-scène is structured around the acting alone, without calling for a specific location, the objects are often abstract. They are not used for social purposes, and take on a value as an aesthetic (or poetic) object (SCHLEMMER 1927).

D. MENTAL LANDSCAPE OR MOOD

The scenery gives a subjective image of the play's mental or emotional universe; objects are rarely figurative, but fantastic, oneiric or "moonlike." The goal is a visual familiarization with the imaginations of the characters (see *image**) (for example, FRIEDRICH's painting, *Schiffsbruch* [*Shipwreck*], for GRÜBER's *Empedokles, Hölderlinlesen* in 1975 in Berlin or LANGHOFF's production of *La Danse de mort* at the Comédie-Française in 1996).

2. Polymorphism of the Object

A. DIVERSION OF MEANING

The non-mimetic object lends itself to any use, particularly one that may seem farthest away (as in the surrealist technique of the found, decontextualized or defamiliarized object). Thanks to a series of *conventions**, the object can become a sign of the most diverse things (technique used in popular theatre and in theatre based on the presence of the actors, as for example the bricks and the wheel in the *Ubu roi* staged by P. BROOK in 1978 in Paris.

B. LEVELS OF APPREHENSION

The object is not reduced to a single meaning or level of apprehension. The same object is often utilitarian, symbolic or playful at different times in the performance and seen from different perspectives of aesthetic apprehension. It functions as a projectional Rorscharch test and encourages the audience's creativity.

C. REDUCTION OF SIGNS

There is no such thing as a raw object without a social meaning or a place within a value system. The object is consumed as much by its connotation as by its primary function. Moreover, in theatre the object is always a sign of something, so that it is caught in a circuit of meanings (of equivalences) and referred back by connotation to a host of meanings that the spectator tries out one by one (BAUDRILLARD 1968).

D. ARTIFICIALIZATION/MATERIALIZATION

Because of this circuit of meanings, the object functions as a signified; its materiality (or signifier) and its identity (or referent) are rendered useless and become part of the overall process of symbolization. Any staged object undergoes this effect of artificialization/abstraction (of *semiotization**), which cuts it off from the real world and intellectualizes it. This is especially true of non-utilitarian symbolic objects that refer to their referents in an abstract or even mythical way (religious symbols and idealizations of reality).

But the opposite tendency – that of the material object that cannot be translated into abstract categories – is also present in current staging practice. The scenery selects one or two basic materials (wood, leather, metal, tapestry) according to the material atmosphere of the play and its basic tone. These materials have a rough look and do not have any fixed signified but act as raw material that will generate meaning based on the stage situation. The material objects, like "gadgets," do not convey an imitated reality; they exist as autonomous bodies and participate more in action than in characterization. The object is elevated to the status of an element of visual art, playing for and with the stage, its poetic, theatrical and playful dimensions combining to produce a myriad of mental associations in the spectator.

See also: represented reality, sign, stage machinery, stage boards, stage design.

Further reading: Veltruský 1940 (Eng. 1964); Hoppe 1971; Saison 1974; Bablet 1975; Pavis 1976a, 1996a; Ubersfeld 1978a.

OBLIGATORY SCENE

Fr.: *scène à faire*; Ger.: *obligatorische Szene*; Sp.: *escena obligatoria*.

This is a scene that the audience has anticipated, is expecting, and demands, and so must be written into the play by the playwright. According to SARCEY, it is a "scene that necessarily ensues from the interests or passions that motivate the characters," a scene that is often seen in a *well-made play** or *boulevard theatre**. According to ARCHER (*Play-Making*, 1912), there are five major circumstances that render a scene obligatory:

- the internal logic of the theme requires it;
- the obvious requirements of a specifically dramatic effect make it necessary;
- the playwright appears to be leading up to it inexorably;
- it is needed to justify character development or a change in determination;
- history or legend requires it.

OBSTACLE

Fr.: *obstacle*; Ger.: *Hindernis*; Sp.: *obstáculo*.

An obstacle or hindrance is something that opposes the character's action, thwarts his projects and frustrates his desires. In order for *conflict** and therefore *dramatic** development to exist, "one individual's aim encounters hindrances from other individuals, because an opposite aim, seeking commensurate realization, stands in the way" (HEGEL Eng. 1975, 267).

1. In the *actantial** model, the obstacle is the *opponent**, who prevents the subject from reaching the desired object.

In classical dramaturgy, the *outside obstacle* is materialized through a force beyond the character's control and opposing him. The *inner obstacle* is a psychological or moral opposition self-imposed by the character. The dividing line, however, is quite fluid and depends on the type of dramaturgy: the classical character tends to internalize external conflicts, make them his own, and then act according to his own freely consented-to rules (SCHERER 1950).

The specificity of characters and action depends on the precision and explanation of the obstacle. The obstacle is sometimes real, sometimes purely subjective and imaginary; sometimes surmountable, sometimes artificially eliminated (*deus ex machina**).

2. Narrative analysis and semiology use the notion of obstacle (or test) to describe the necessary phases of any narrative (obstacle, trial, mediation). The obstacle is placed at the junction of the linear narrative and the actantial model (that is, the logical system of oppositions at a given point in the action). After having traced a model of these oppositions and obstacles, we can observe the changes in the model in the course of the play. The characters' obstacles and the changes in them (in which they are eliminated or restructured) provide the key to the *plot**. The obstacle is the structural element that serves as an exchanger between the system of characters and the dynamics of the action.

OFF STAGE

Fr.: *hors-scène;* Ger.: *ausserhalb der Bühne;* Sp.: *extra-escena.*

1. This term refers to the reality that unfolds outside the spectator's field of vision. It can be the area that is theoretically visible to the characters on stage but concealed from the audience (*teichoscopy**) or the area that is invisible to both audience and stage (the *wings*).

2. The status of the off-stage area varies according to how realistic the stage environment claims to be. In naturalistic performance, it seems to exist with as much right as the stage; it is truncated and seems to be an extension of the stage, so is both visible and invisible. For a performance that is limited to the playing area (as in the Brechtian epic stage), or a self-enclosed stage (as the Symbolist stage), however, the area off stage is not an extension of the stage but another distinct reality, the place where our real reference world begins.

3. Sound is often used to suggest the area off stage, echoing in hidden rooms or producing noises in the wings. As, for instance, in G. BOURDET's production of *Britannicus*, the stage may be lit from the wings through invisible windows that supposedly look onto another room or a park. Such techniques try to give us the impression of an adjoining real *space** that had to be arbitrarily excluded from the stage.

See also: framework, non-textual, represented reality.

ONE-ACT PLAY

Fr.: *pièce en un acte;* Ger.: *Einakter;* Sp.: *obra en un acto.*

A short play lasting an average of twenty to forty minutes, this genre has developed mainly since the late nineteenth century. Like the short story as opposed to the novel, the one-act play concentrates all its dramatic material on one crisis or significant episode. The pace is very quick, as the playwright proceeds by allusions to the situa-

tion and rapid realistic touches to represent the milieu. Major writers are SYNGE, SHAW, O'CASEY, WILDER, STRINDBERG, WEDEKIND, SCHNITZLER, CHEKHOV, MAETERLINCK, TINTER, IONESCO.
See also: entr'acte, curtainraiser.
Further reading: Szondi 1956.

ONE-(WO)MAN SHOW

A one-man (or one-woman) show is a performance by a single person playing one or more characters. It lasts for a limited time and is frequently centred around one character. The term, borrowed from music hall, is often somewhat negative when applied to theatre, since it is associated not with a complete process of theatre work but rather a recital of song or variety show. This explains why the notion is sometimes rejected by theatre artists, like P. CAUBÈRE, whose *Le Roman d'un acteur* resembles a theatrical staging than a comic number, *sketch** or acting number.

OPEN FORM

Fr.: *forme ouverte*; Ger.: *offene Form*; Sp.: *forma abierta*.

Whereas the *closed form** draws most of its characteristics from classical European theatre, the open form defines itself in reaction against that dramaturgy. There are many variants and particular instances of this form. The opening of form practically leads to a total destruction of the preceding model, although works as diverse as those of SHAKESPEARE, BÜCHNER, BRECHT and BECKETT have been given the loose label of open works (ECO 1989).

The open/closed criterion comes from the study of artistic forms, specifically the representational arts. According to WÖLFFLIN's *Principles of Art History*, the closed composition "is a style of composition which, with more or less tectonic means, makes of the picture a self-contained entity, pointing everywhere back to itself, while, conversely, the style of open form everywhere points out beyond itself and purposely looks limitless" (1915, 145; Eng. 1950, 124).

V. KLOTZ (1969) took up this distinction and applied it to theatre history, thus establishing the existence of two styles of dramatic construction corresponding to two modes of stage performance. His model accounts perfectly well for the formal and ideological differences between the two dramaturgies, provided the necessary adjustments are made to the generic mould to facilitate a specific analysis of the play in question.

ECO's book on the open work, *Opera aperta* (1965), inaugurated a new approach to the literary text, which is seen as the depositary of many meanings, while several signifieds may coexist with a single signifier. The "opening" takes place on the level of *interpretation** and *signifying practice** projected by the critic onto the object studied.

1. Fabula

The *fabula* is an assemblage of motifs that are not structured in a coherent whole but presented in a fragmentary, discontinuous way. The scenes or *tableaux** are the basic units that accumulate to produce an epic series of motifs. The playwright is not obliged to organize his materials in a logical order that excludes randomness; he alternates scenes according to the principle of contradiction or even *alienation** (BRECHT). He does not integrate the various *plots** in one main action, but plays on the thematic variations or repetitions (*leitmotif**) and on the parallel actions. Sometimes, however, the latter may, though freely arranged, come together at a "*point of integration**."

2. Structures of Time and Place

Time is fragmented and does not elapse in a continuous fashion. It may stretch over an entire human lifetime or a whole period. In certain playwrights it is no longer simply a medium of action but becomes a character in its own right (BÜCHNER, IONESCO, BECKETT).

The stage space opens onto the audience (disappearance of the *fourth wall**); the stage design bursts its traditional confines and encourages direct *addresses** to the audience. The location and meaning of objects on the stage changes constantly, and the spectator is asked to accept their conventions.

3. Characters
Characters suffer the worst outrages at the hands of playwright and actor. They cannot be reduced to a consciousness or a finite set of characteristics – they are dramaturgical tools that may be used in various ways, with no thought for *verisimilitude** or *realism**.

See also: dramaturgy, dramatic structures, dramatic and epic, collage, montage.

Further reading: Szondi 1956; Barry 1970; Levitt 1971; Pfister 1977.

OPERA

Although they belong to different genres and are quite different in terms of stage practices, funding, operations and audience, opera and theatre are closer today than ever before. They have discovered each other, to their mutual fascination. Opera exerts a great influence on contemporary staging, even though they have evolved very differently.

1. Theatre *par excellence*
Using all the means available to theatre, as well as the prestige of voice and music, opera is theatre *par excellence* and takes pleasure in underscoring conventionality and theatricality. A naturally excessive kind of art based on vocal feats and heightened by the pathos of music and the prestige of the stage, opera "speaks" more to the theatre people who give it the systematic nature of mise-en-scène and the committed virtuosity of actors. The physical virtuosity of performers who are emotional athletes as well as singers has enabled theatre to renew opera productions that were once static, unimaginative and merely slaves to music. CHÉREAU with WAGNER's *Ring*, BROOK with *Carmen*, LAVELLI with *Madame Butterfly* have pushed their singers to their physical limits and freed the staging of outdated conventions. In doing so, they have only respected "one of the particularities of opera in musical repertoire: the singer is exhibited on stage as an actor" (MOINDROT 1993, 72).

2. Is Theatre Becoming More Like Opera?
It is said that theatre is becoming more like opera, in the somewhat trivial sense that theatre resorts to all the resources of theatricality and artificiality embodied best by a singing voice. Moreover, theatre staging has become an overall composition noted very precisely on a score. Theatre and music are forming close and unexpected relationships. Theatre staging compares theatricality (the visuality of the stage) and musicality (vocal and textual). It receives the performance like a score that filters and joins text, music and image, that vectorizes the whole set of stimuli in a certain direction, addressed to a spectator who can no longer distinguish among the products of vision, hearing and *kinesthetics**.

However, theatre no longer seeks in opera only the paradigm of total theatre or the Wagnerian illusion of correspondences between the arts or between space, text and music. It renegotiates these relations differently, bit by bit, seeking out new alliances between a vocal-musical element and a scenic-visual element. Thus, *music theatre** (OHANA, MALEC, APERGHIS, GOEBBELS) reduces relations to a noise that is as much "musical" as textual; the *Lehrstück* – BRECHT and WEILL's opera *He who says yes, he who says no* or RAMUZ/STRAVINKSY's *L'histoire du soldat* put forward a pocket opera in which the music endeavours to be as simple as the story is simplistic. Then we have the recent "rediscovery" of Mozart's *opera seria*, attempting to reconstruct apparently codified gesture and mise-en-scène that seems repetitive and conventional. GROTOWSKI and BARBA have experimented with a voice score grafted onto a gestural trajectory. Redefining the notion of opera, renegotiating the relationship between text and music, reactivating the transition from text to music and from music to text: all this radically changes the basis of theatrical opera

or operatic theatre, and forces us to question old categories and traditional oppositions.
Further reading: Appia 1963; Regnault 1980.

OPSIS

(Greek term meaning *vision.*)
Fr.: *opsis;* Ger.: *Opsis;* Sp.: *opsis.*

The *opsis* is that which is visible, offered to the gaze, hence its connection with the notions of *spectacle** and *performance**. In ARISTOTLE's *Poetics, spectacle** is one of the six constituent parts of tragedy, but ranks below others considered to be more essential (*fabula**, *character**, song). The place in theatre history assigned subsequently to the *opsis,* to what we would now call the mise-en-scène, determined the mode of transmission and the overall meaning of the performance. *Opsis* is a specific feature of the performing arts.

ORCHESIS

(From the Greek *orkhêstikê.*)

The art of dance and knowledge of positions and expressive movements, especially codified gesturs and their conventional meanings.

ORCHESTRA

(Term from Greek theatre meaning "place of dance.")
Fr.: *orchestra;* Ger.: *Orchester;* Sp.: *orquesta.*

A circular, and later a semi-circular, space in the centre of the theatre, between the stage and the audience, occupied by the chorus in Greek tragedy. During the Renaissance, the orchestra was below the stage, and court society could dance there during the intermissions. In proscenium theatres today, the orchestra is the part of the auditorium located almost at the same level as the stage and across from it.

OSTENSION

(From the Latin *ostendere,* to show.)
Fr.: *ostension;* Ger.: *Zeigen;* Sp.: *ostensión.*

Communication by the simple fact of showing or exhibiting something.

1. Ostensive Communication
This "putting something at the cognitive disposal of someone" (OSOLSOBE 1980) is always done in the here and now of communication. Partly intentional and partly unintentional, this kind of communication takes place outside the systems of linguistic and gestural signs and is extrasemiotic, or presemiotic according to OSOLSOBE.

Ostension shows objects and people to the observer directly, without the intermediary of a sign system. Not all communication is necessarily ostensive (language, symbols, alphabets), but it does always imply placing on view at least one element of the thing communicated: letters, a map, a portrait. The sign is always necessarily shown and proposed for cognitive activity. Any aesthetic object, even when it is made up of a sign system (which may be linguistic, pictoral, visual), shows these signs (and not only the reality to which the signs refer). This emphasis on the message and on its production characterizes all aesthetic works (JAKOBSON 1963; MUKAROVSKÝ 1977, 1978).

2. De-monstration of Ostension
Ostension is one of the essential principles of theatrical representation. The stage is always something to look at, regardless of its form or function. This "showing" aspect (*Monstratio*) of theatre has always been considered the feature that distinguishes it from the epic or the poetic, which do not show things directly but describe them through a narrator. Whereas in the novel the act of showing occurs within the fiction, in theatre it bursts the bounds of the play and addresses the audience directly through the actor's gestures and the "*gestus** of delivery" of the mise-en-scène, breaking the *framework** of *performance**.

In theatre as well as in life, ostension rarely exists in the pure state: it is accompanied by words or music or any other semiological system. Contrary to OSOLSOBE's thesis, we would be tempted to say that ostension needs to be contextualized and therefore requires a framework and semiological systems that can do this. In theatre, ostension takes place successively in a series of conventions: come at such and such a time, to such and such a place, sit here, look over there, etc. Like J. MARTIN (1984), we would stress the relational aspect of theatre.

3. Forms of Ostension

There can never be complete ostension, as we perceive only signs or fragments of stage or gestures in the course of a performance. Ostension also applies to elements that are not shown but only suggested. It may take the form of a synecdoche, in which a part refers to the whole; the director need only suggest a complex reality with a characteristic detail: a crown for the king, a ball and chain for captivity. The mise-en-scène often proceeds by metonymy or by metaphor. One element shown calls up another; a single object takes on a thousand figurations according to the needs of the performance (*symbol**).

One would have to draw up an entire stylistics or rhetoric of ostension according to the mode of de-monstration, of showing. Three basic types could serve as points of reference:

A. *Mimetic ostension* shows the object and suggests that it is identical to its referent. For instance, the door on stage is a real door (*naturalism**).

B. *Symbolic ostension* isolates properties of the object that suggest a different existence (ideal, religious or moral). What is shown implies the existence of a veiled aspect of things: the seagull is murdered innocence, for instance.

C. *Abstract ostension* shows only the principal features and overall structure.

D. *Demonstrative ostension* shows an object as able to be reconstructed or taken apart. There is no secret behind it, but the figure of its maker and the commentary of whoever is showing or distancing this reality. We know that BRECHT, to "de-monstrate" his epic theatre, compared theatrical performance to a traffic accident. All that we see is reconstructed by witnesses of the accident, who act out the scene and comment on all levels, technical, social and political. The actor reconstructing the accident "never forgets, nor does he allow it to be forgotten, that he is not the subject but the demonstrator. That is to say, what the audience sees is not a fusion between demonstrator and subject [...] such as the orthodox theatre puts before us in its productions" (BRECHT 1972, 522–523; Eng. 1964, 125). Demonstrative ostension as practised by BRECHT appears to be a synthesis of the first two categories. It goes beyond mere naturalism and poetic subjectivism while using the two methods successively: that of a direct rendering and that of a commentary determined by a critical *perspective**. It brings together pure ostension and a socio-aesthetic commentary on ostension.

4. The Limits of Ostension

Theatrical ostension is often limited to the scenery, the choreography, and the organization and representation of the characters. As soon as the actor comes on stage he is the one who will be watched uninterruptedly and whose *presence** fascinates us. But to this ostension of visual elements we must add *verbal ostension**; that of the characters' words. As soon as the discourse is transmitted in a theatre, and therefore within a fictional and aesthetic situation, the spectator receives it as a poetic sign, is attentive to its hidden meanings, its rhetorical structure and its stylistic *devices**. This highlighting of the texture of the discourse is a way of showing and *iconizing** language and the text and its rhetoric. Although it is true that theatre shows things, it is no less true that it shows only what it wishes to show of them, using an unnoticeable technique. The playwright, the director and the dramaturg participate as commentators in their exposition of actions and protagonists. As BRECHT intuited, objective representation and subjective commentary by a narrator are only complementary aspects of the same artistic activity. *Showing* does not work without a metacritical arrangement by a narrator, i.e. without *telling*. And, inversely, *telling* is not exclusive of the attempts to convey the reality of the language and the universe represented in an iconic manner.

Jacky MARTIN, who unfortunately does not refer to OSOLSOBE's pioneering work, puts forward a theory of ostension that takes into account the *theatrical relationship** and describes the elements shown as "a tool used by the sender to establish a significant link with the audience" (1984, 125). MARTIN's theory misrepresents the original notion of ostension – which according to OSOLSOBE is self-sufficient – and above all fails to distinguish between what is based on a semiotics and what is given as pure showing, so that the notion of ostension loses its specificity and gives up the ghost.

See also: epic, index, icon, communication, textual and visual, deixis.

Further reading: Goffman 1959; Booth 1961; Jakobson 1963; Eco 1976b, 1977, 1985; de Marinis 1979.

OTHER-STAGE

Fr.: *autre scène*; Ger.: *ein anderer Schauplatz*; Sp.: *intra-escena*.

See INTERIOR SPACE, FANTASY

P

PANTOMIME

(From the Greek *pantomimos*, "one who imitates everything.")

Fr.: *pantomime*; Ger.: *Pantomime*; Sp.: *pantomima*.

The pantomime of the Ancients was "the representation and hearing of all that can be imitated, by voice as well as gesture: nautical, acrobatic and equestrian pantomime, processions, carnivals, etc." (DORCY 1962, 99). In Rome at the end of the first century B.C., text and gesture were separated, with the actor miming scenes commented on by the chorus and musicians. The *commedia dell'arte** uses popular stock characters who talk and express themselves using *lazzi**. The heyday of pantomime was in the eighteenth and nineteenth centuries (DEBUREAU), with harlequinades and *parades** and dumb show by entertainers who introduced speech with comic subterfuge. Today pantomime no longer uses words, but is composed entirely of the actor's *gestures**. Closely related to the anecdote or story told through the medium of theatre, pantomime is not only an independent art but also a component of any theatrical performance, particularly those which tend to externalize the acting and favour the production of *stage business** or *tableaux vivants**. The mute pantomime of the Foire actors used signs to circumvent the ban on words. With DIDEROT and his call for realism on stage, a call arose from the second half of the eighteenth century for "a man of genius who knows how to combine pantomime with speech, intersperse spoken scenes with silent scenes [...] Pantomime is a part of drama."

In the nineteenth century pantomime-harlequinade, as in DEBUREAU, settled in on the boulevard du Temple. Its blank mime was immortalized in CARNÉ's film *Les Enfants du Paradis* (1943) and PRÉVERT's pantomime *Baptiste* (1946). The best examples in the twentieth century are to be found in the burlesque films of B. KEATON and C. CHAPLIN.

See also: mime, gesture, mime play, body, atellan farce.

Further reading: Diderot 1975; Decroux 1963; Lecoq 1987; Marceau 1974; de Marinis 1980, 1993; Lorelle 1974.

PARABASIS

(Greek word meaning "to go sideways.")

Fr.: *parabase*; Ger.: *Parabase*; Sp.: *parábasis*.

Part of ancient Greek comedy, notably in ARISTOPHANES, in which the chorus came toward the audience to set out the dramatist's views and claims through the coryphaeus and to proffer advice.

See also: address to the audience.

PARABLE

(From the Greek *parabolé*, comparison; *parabollein*, stand aside.)

Fr.: *parabole*; Ger.: *Parabel, Parabelstück*; Sp.: *parábola*.

1. Duality and Ambiguity

In the proper sense of the word, the (Biblical) parable is a narrative that conceals a moral or religious precept or truth (e.g. the parable of the prodigal son).

A parabolic play can be read at two levels, like the *allegory** or parable in rhetoric: the immediate narrative, which is a perceptible exterior, and the hidden narrative whose "soul" must be discovered by the listener. Plays often contain parable scenes (e.g., the ring scene in LESSING's *Nathan der Weise* or the three caskets in SHAKESPEARS's *The Merchant of Venice*). Historically, the parable in theatre emerges in times of great ideological debate, when literature is used for pedagogical purposes: the Reformation and Counter-Reformation, the philosophical eighteenth century, and our own modern period (BRECHT, CLAUDEL, FRISCH, DÜRRENMATT, B. STRAUSS).

2. Structure and Function

A. The parable is a "false-bottom" genre with two levels: (1) that of the anecdote, or *fabula*, an easily understandable and amusingly told narrative that is situated in a specific place and time and evokes a fictitious or real milieu in which the events are supposed to have occurred; and (2) that of the "moral" or lesson, to which the story is transposed intellectually, morally and theoretically. It is at the deep, "serious" level that we grasp the didactic scope of the play and can draw parallels with our own situations.

B. The parable is a scale model of our own world, with all the proportions being faithfully respected. All of the actual events are related to a theoretical principle that is given as an example. Paradoxically, the parable is a means of talking about the present, putting it into perspective and dressing it up in an imaginary story and framework. Often the dramatist rejects the immediate solution, describing the present with naturalistic details, for that would mean running the risk of masking the essential, of not foregrounding the ideological mechanism that lies under the appearance of truth.

C. The parable, by its very make-up, demands a translation into an ideological subtext that will relate the appearance of the *fabula* to our own situation. Normally this is easily done; for example, behind BRECHT's *The Good Person of Sichuan* we can read the impossibility of being human in the world of economic exploitation. It may be, however, that the lesson cannot be deciphered, particularly in contemporary absurd or grotesque theatre. M. FRISCH gave his *The Fire-Raisers* (*Biedermann und die Brandstifter*) the subtitle *Didactic play with no moral*. The dramaturgy of the *absurd** refuses to seek out any symbolic meaning, but often gives the illusion that it is only the playful wrapping of essential truths about the human condition, though it perversely thwarts any interpretative hypothesis.

However, we should not think of the parable as a simple dressing-up of a univocal message, word for word. It must always retain some measure of autonomy and opacity in order to signify on its own; never be fully translatable into a lesson, but lend itself to a signifying practice and the reflections of theatricality.

Further reading: Dürrenmatt 1955, 1966; Hildesheimer 1960; Brecht 1967: vol. 17; Müller in Keller 1976.

PARADE

Fr.: *parade*; Ger.: *Parade*; Sp.: *parada*.

The *parade* was originally a group of tightrope walkers and artists, often on a balcony or raised area, who drew an audience to invite them to a show. The term was sometimes used to mean "a bad piece of theatre" (*Littré*). The *Oxford English Dictionary* notes the meaning of an "ostentatious display."

The word expresses the desire to display the acrobatic and comic talents of the actors. The parade is a traditional form of theatrical participation that experienced a boom in the seventeenth and eighteenth centuries. At the beginning of the seventeenth century at the Hotel de Bourgogne there were already farces being shown (GROS-GUILLAUME, GAULTIER-GARGOUILLE, TURLUPIN). The popular tradition of farce and *commedia dell'arte** was perpetuated in the Théâtre de la Foire (cf. Ch. GUEULLETTE's *Parades inédites* from the Saint-Germain Fair, published 1885).

Parades are deliberately vulgar and provocative; the language is coarse, even scatalogical. They are presented as a popular parlance with questionable connections. They showed great verbal inventiveness in parodying noble genres and the higher classes and sparked a crisis of noble, serious theatre.

Parades were sometimes written by playwrights like COLLÉ and VADÉ or BEAUMARCHAIS for society theatres and actors from high society who found slumming and writing occasional plays a good way to unwind.

The tradition was maintained in the nineteenth century with the "Boulevard du Crime" and wandering actors (like BOBECHE and GALIMAFRE). Today the *parade* is a favourite form of *agit-prop** theatre or popular tale (as in DARIO FO). It was rediscovered by MEYERHOLD, who was fascinated by its theatricality (cf. his staging of A. BLOK's *Balagan* (*La Baraque de foire*).

Further reading: Fo 1991.

PARALINGUISTIC ELEMENTS

Fr.: *éléments paralinguistiques;* Ger.: *paralinguistische Elemente;* Sp.: *elementos paralinguísticos.*

See KINESICS

PARATEXT

Fr.: *paratexte;* Ger.: *Parasprache;* Sp.: *paratexto.*

J.M. THOMASSEAU (1984a) proposed this term to avoid the *main text/side text** distinction between dialogue and stage directions, which he considered to be too normative. The paratext is "this printed text (in italics or a different type to differentiate it *visually* from the other part of the play) that envelops the text in dialogue of a play" (1984a, 79). The paratext includes the *title**, the *list of characters**, indications of time and space on stage, descriptions of scenery and didascalia concerning acting (*kinesics**, *proxemics**), but also an accompanying text such as the *dedication** or *preface**.

Further reading: Thomasseau 1984a, 1996.

PARATHEATRE

Fr.: *parathéâtre;* Ger.: *Paratheater;* Sp.: *parateatro.*

This term refers to a dramatic activity – theatrical in a loose sense – that makes use of devices borrowed from theatre but is not intended to produce an aesthetic creation, and happens outside of the mainstream.

Events on the fringe of theatre are infinite:

1. GROTOWSKI uses the term *paratheatre* in the early 1970s to denote his transition from staging to theatre anthropology: "that is to say participatory theatre (with *active* participation by outside people" (RICHARDS 1995, 182). The theatre of sources (1970 to 1979) is interested in an anthropological approach that seeks "the source of different traditional techniques, of what precedes the differences" (182). In an attempt to find the common denominator of all these types of performance, BARBA seeks the *pre-expressive* and the major universal principles that are shared by all acting and dancing traditions.

2. Theatre may be used in therapy as an awareness activity that is interested in *stage expression* (DARS and BENOIT, 1964), in which exercises that come close to *psychodrama* are carried out in the presence of a psychiatrist and an actor.

3. The mentally handicapped are sometimes invited to play with actors, where the acting is not a kind of therapy but a means towards an aesthetic end (cf. the experience recounted by Mike PEARSON in *Internationale de l'Imaginaire*, 1996, no. 4).

4. The *third theatre*, as defined by BARBA (International Journal Information, 1976), also "exists on the margins, often outside or on the periphery of cultural centres and capitals. It is a theatre by people who define themselves as actors and directors although

they only rarely have a traditional background in theatre, so that they are not recognized as professionals." As much a sociological phenomenon as an aesthetic statement, the third theatre consists of networks for exchanges, support and mutual encouragement (WATSON 1993). It is unlike commercial, subsidized or militant theatre and is organized within a parallel network and economy with its own production and publishing facilities (cf. the publication *Bouffonneries* edited by P. PEZIN and BARBA's Odin Theatre.

PARODY

(From the Greek *parodia*, counter-ode, counter-song.)
Fr.: *parodie*; Ger.: *Parodie*; Sp.: *parodia*.

Play or fragment of text that transforms an earlier text ironically by mocking it, using all kinds of comic effects. The *Littré* defines it as a "play of burlesque genre that travesties a play of noble genre." ARISTOTLE attributed its invention to HEGEMON OF THASOS, while ARISTOPHANES parodied works by AESCHYLUS and EURIPIDES in *The Frogs*. The seventeenth-century *Parodie du Cid* and *Le Chapelain décoiffé* of 1665, and R. PLANCHON's *la Mise en pièce(s) du Cid*, mocked *le Cid*, while *Harnali ou la contrainte par cor* "paid homage" to *Hernani*, and *Ruy Blag* to *Ruy Blas*. OFFENBACH's comic operas (*La Belle Hélène*, *Orphée aux enfers*) deconstruct the mythological and tragic universe.

1. Split Structure

A parody consists of both a parodying text and the text parodied, the two levels being separated by an ironical critical distance. The parodying discourse should never let us forget the object of the parody, or it will lose its critical force. It quotes the original by distorting it, and constantly calls on the reader or spectator to reconstruct it. Both *quotation** and original creation, it maintains close *intertextual** ties with the earlier text. More than the pastiche or travesty, the parody displays the object of parody and pays it homage in its own way. The act of comparison is part of the phenomenon of *reception**. For the one parodying, then for the spectator, it consists in inverting all the signs; replacing noble with vulgar, respect with disrespect, seriousness with mockery. This inversion of signs most often, but not always, takes place in a negative direction. However, a vulgar genre or dismal tale can be replaced with a noble style or princely story; the contrast and effect will only be more striking (this technique of travesty is employed by the heroic-comic).

2. Automation

According to the Russian Formalists, genres evolve mainly through successive parodies, with the parodying element attacking the automated and stereotyped devices: "The essence of parody lies in the automation of a well-defined device [...] Thus the parody achieves a dual objective: (1) automation of a well-defined device; (2) organization of new material which is none other than the old device automated" (TYNIANOV 1969, 74). Parody tends to become an autonomous genre and a technique that lays bare the artistic devices. In theatre, this is achieved by stressing theatricality and breaking the illusion by overemphasizing the features of acting (exaggerated declamation, pathos, tragic elements, stage effects). Like irony, parody can be a structural principle proper to the dramatic work that comes into play as soon as the mise-en-scène makes its "strings" a little too visible and subordinates internal *communication** (on stage) to external communication (between stage and audience).

3. Purpose and Content

Parodying a play is not only a comic technique. It initiates a play of comparisons with a commentary on both the play being parodied and on literary or theatrical tradition. It is a critical metadiscourse on the original play. Sometimes, on the other hand, it rewrites and changes the dramaturgical basis of the play imitated (IONESCO's *Macbett* and SHAKESPEARE's *Macbeth*).

Parody has to do with a style, a tone, a character, genre or simply dramatic situations. When it is done for a didactic or moralizing purpose, it comes close to social, philosophical or political satire. Its scope, then, is fundamentally serious, as it sets up a coherent system of counter-values in opposition to the values criticized. Like *irony**, parody or pastiche, satire is not confined to a superficial treatment of its object for the sake of play. It sees itself as a reformer (see BOILEAU, *Satire IX*). It is virulent and tends to attack what man holds most sacred. In this sense, it is close to *mockery*, which according to LA BRUYÈRE is "[...] of all the insults the least pardonable; it is the language of scorn [...] it drives man into a corner and attacks his own opinion of himself, attempts to make him appear ridiculous in his own eyes [...]" (1934:86).

When it lays no claim to reform, parody is often formal (destroying to break a style or form) or *grotesque** and *absurd**, denying all aesthetic and philosophical values in one great massacre.

See also: comic, intertextuality.

Further reading: *Cahiers du XXe siècle*, 1976; Hutcheon 1985; Genette 1982; Pavis 1986.

PAROXYSM

(From the Greek *paroxusmos*, to sharpen or excite.)

Fr.: *paroxysme*; Ger.: *Höhepunkt*; Sp.: *paroxismo (punto culminante)*.

The turning point in the play, when the dramatic intensity is at its peak, generally after a gradual rise in the action and just before the falling action and the catastrophe, at the *culminating point** of the dramatic curve. The paroxysm (often called the *climax*) can be the high point of excitement in the play or the turning point of the *fabula**.

PARTICIPATION

Fr.: *participation*; Ger.: *Beteiligung, Teilnahme*; Sp.: *participación*.

See THEATRE OF PARTICIPATION

PASSION

Fr.: *passion*; Ger.: *Leidenschaft*; Sp.: *pasión*.

There has always been a concern with knowing how to express passion in theatre, how to signify it by voice and gesture. During the classical era, with DESCARTES and his *Traité des Passions* and LE BRUN and his *Conférence sur l'expression générale et particulière* (1668), an attempt was made to codify facial expressions and body attitudes. Passion is "a movement in the most sensitive part of the soul that takes place to follow what the soul thinks is good for it, or to flee what it thinks is bad for it, and as a general rule what causes passion in the soul induces some action in the body" (LE BRUN 1668). Treatises by LE BRUN, CORNEILLE and LE FAUCHEUR (*Traité de l'action de l'orateur*) put forward an inventory of the soul's passions and of the facial expressions and body attitudes that express them. According to LE BRUN, the eyes are particularly eloquent and the eyebrows express passion best.

Voice is often employed to convey passion along with highly codified facial expressions, the left hand beating time while the right underscores effects, nuances and allusions. Hence a kind of declamation that owes more to the recitative and chant than a pantomime of action, as called for by DIDEROT and ENGEL (1788). The latter undertook a collection of expressive gestures, an inventory of all codification. That undertaking was still apparent in ARTAUD when he said that "the ten thousand and one facial expressions in masks could be labelled and catalogued" (1964, 143).

PASSION PLAY

Fr.: *passion*; Ger.: *Passionsspiel*; Sp.: *pasión*.

Medieval form of drama in the vernacular that reenacted the Passion of Christ in *mystery plays**, inspired by the Gospels and performed in Germany and France. These performances involved spectacular tableaux, lasted several days and employed hundreds of actors, taking over the whole town. Passion plays are still performed at Oberammergau, Tefelen, Nancy, and Ligny.

PASTORAL PLAY

Fr.: *comédie pastorale*; Ger.: *Schäferspiel*; Sp.: *comedia pastoral.*

A play that sings the praises of the simple life led by shepherds as the prototypes of an innocent, utopian existence, expressing nostalgia for the good old days. Mainly in the sixteenth and seventeenth centuries (for example, RACAN's *Bergeries*, 1625).

Further reading: Effe, *Das Schäferspiel*, 1977.

PATH

Fr.: *parcours*; Ger.: *Parcours*; Sp.: *itinerario.*

In reaction against a tradition that turned the spectators into passive beings anchored to their seats facing the stage, the mise-en-scène sometimes encourages the audience to take a particular *parcours* or path through the performance and the scenery: the set is no longer a constraint on actor and audience but an object travelled by the deconstructing gaze and, most often, by the physical movement of the audience toward a playing area, stage, showcase, place or object on display. This is a rite of movement that is also sometimes done as a journey of initiation. Examples are the *Orlando Furioso* staged in 1969 by Luca RONCONI, the Théâtre du Soleil's *1789* and *1793*, *Shakespeare's Memory* by Peter STEIN (1976) and *le Désamour* by la Comédie de Caen (1980).

This path within the stage invites the spectator to discover its sensitive points, not to consider the scenery as fixed and finished but as a place where the gaze is vested differently depending on the particular point in the performance, changes in lighting, and the movements of the actors. The spectators design the scenery and (in part) the performance using these pauses and changes: they are no longer overwhelmed by the scenery, but shape it according to the action and acting. In this process, the spectators size up the performance, take their distance or vest themselves within it, pay attention to the sensitive points of the stage. Mise-en-scène (or the placing of an object confronted with a gaze) becomes a meditation on the spectator's gaze and what it produces, based on what the set proposes.

The *parcours* is the materialization of a freedom of movement, of a reconciliation with the visual arts (installations) or play (promenade or *happening**). It engenders many visions and images adapted to the theatrical, textual and stage object, which is no longer linear and monotonous but fragmented and scattered.

See also: Site-specific performance.

PATHOS

(Greek word for emotion or suffering.)

Fr.: *pathos*; Ger.: *Pathos, falsches Pathos*; Sp.: *pathos.*

1. The quality of a play that arouses emotion (pity, tenderness, compassion) in the spectator.

In rhetoric, *pathos* is a technique used to move the listener (as opposed to *ithos*, the moral impression left by the orator). It must be distinguished from the dramatic and the tragic.

The *dramatic** is a literary category that describes the action, its progressions and its rebounding.

The *tragic** is tied to the idea of the necessity and fatality of a dire fate, which is however freely caused and accepted by the hero.

The *pathetic** is a mode of *reception** of a spectacle that invites compassion. The innocent victims are defenseless and left to their own fate.

The pathetic had its apogee in the tragedies of the seventeenth and eighteenth centuries and in bourgeois drama, but it is always one of the ingredients of emotional and/or commercial success.

2. Theatre, particularly tragedy, invokes the pathetic when it invites the audience to identify with a situation or cause that overwhelms the listener.

In ARISTOTLE's *Poetics*, pathos is that part of tragedy which, because of the death of or tragic events occurring to the characters, incites feelings of *pity** (*eleos*) and *fear** (*phobos*), leading to *catharsis**.

HEGEL (1832, 327–340; Eng. 1162–1170) makes a distinction between subjective pathos and objective pathos. Subjective pathos is the feeling of suffering, despondency and passivity that takes possession of the audience, while objective pathos consists in "addressing rather to the audience a development of the substance of affairs, aims, and characters" (340; Eng. 1170) "this driving 'pathos' may indeed, in each of the actors, derive from spiritual, moral, and divine powers, such as law, patriotism, love of parents, relations, spouses, etc." (327; Eng. 1162).

3. Today pathos often has a pejorative sense, as in an overly-affected pathetic. Certain actors (particularly in the eighteenth century) and styles of writing made too much use of pathos, overexaggerating its effects and tugging a bit too hard at our heartstrings. The parodies of Schillerian pathos by BÜCHNER and BRECHT are indicative of how close this stylized emotion comes to the ridiculous.

4. Pathos is not only apparent in a text full of exclamations, repetitions and terms conveying the speaker's psychological state. It is also evident in an unrealistic gestuality that accentuates expression, plays on the visual effects of the blocking of the actors, reconstructs *tableaux vivants** (cf. DIDEROT 1975, describing the death of SOCRATES and the terrified reactions of his peers).

Being an element that can be grasped in production as well as *reception**, pathos varies with the times. For instance, it may be not jarring but natural for its time. Only a few years later, listening to a recording or watching a film, will it appear exaggerated and artificial. This is a measure of the importance of the ideological codes of reception in gauging its presence and its quality (*natural**).

Further reading: Diderot 1975; Schiller 1793; Hegel 1832; Kommerell 1940; Romilly 1961; Eisenstein 1976, 1978.

PERCEPTION

Fr.: *perception*; Ger.: *Wahrnehmung*; Sp.: *percepción*.

This is a concept to be distinguished from *reception**, which concerns the whole cognitive, intellectual and hermeneutic process that unfolds in the spectator's mind. Perception is the concrete use of the five senses, beyond sight and hearing which tend to be associated with performance exclusively.

1. *Touch*. Apparently banned from the experience of the Western spectator, who is kept at a respectable distance from the stage and invited only to listen and watch without taking part, the sense of touch plays a role through the perception of movement and activation of the senses, as through the use of natural elements such as earth, water and fire (BROOK). The sense of touch, according to BARRAULT, makes dramatic art "a fundamentally carnal, sensual art. Representation in theatre is a collective free-for-all, an act of love, a sensual communion between two groups of human beings" (1961, 13).

In short, there are two kinds of theatre: a dry theatre in which the stage is only a place of symbolization and only the "clean" image and abstraction of the text is important; and a wet theatre in which aesthetic experience consists of getting one's hands dirty in everyday reality.

The *corporal memory* that dance gives rise to through changes in stability, balance, tone reminds us of our own personal history recorded in our bodies, which the performance constantly affects.

2. *Smell and taste*, senses appealed to by forms of popular theatre in which feasting combines with the performance, are normally neutralized in the West, though there are notable exceptions: olfactory theatre (PAQUET 1995), performances in which food is prepared and consumed on stage (SCHECHNER's *Faust gastronome*, *Risotto* by the Rome Politechnico) before being offered to the audience at the play's end.

A phenomenological approach to the performance tends to centre everything around the spectator, making him the director of the mass of stimuli, signs and materials that cannot be reduced to a single sense.

It integrates heterogeneous perceptions, linking the visual to the auditory, the cognitive to the sensory, gesture to psychology. Whether in the form of the thinking body or body in the mind (JOHNSON 1987), the spectator's perception is located at the strategic place where the theatre experience takes place, in all its complexity and irreducibility.

PERFORMANCE

Fr: *spectacle; Vorstellung, Aufführung;* Sp.: *espectáculo.*
See SPECTACLE

PERFORMANCE ANALYSIS

1. The Status of Performance Analysis

A. ANALYSIS AND SEMIOLOGY

Given the many different methods used in performance analysis, one might legitimately wonder whether such a thing as an overall method or general epistemology still exists. Beyond the "spontaneous" remarks of spectators, specialized critiques, questionnaires, descriptions of the staging, recordings and descriptions of sign systems, it is difficult even to choose an approach, much less identify shared elements. During the seventies, semiology brought about a certain homogeneity of point of view and a reflection on the conditions of analysis, of which it became the prevailing method in spite of minor differences of approach (KOWZAN 1968, 1975; CORVIN 1973; UBERSFELD 1977, 1981; PAVIS 1975, 1985, 1992) and beyond its various affinities with hermeneutics or phenomenology. Analysis as practised today, however, is not confined to semiology; it takes forms that have nothing "scientific" about them but often emerge from a deep understanding of the play: verbal descriptions, journalistic accounts, diagrams of acting movements and rhythms, etc. The important thing is not so much the nature or form of various discourses on performance as their methodological and ideological implications, which slip equally easily into an ordinary conversation, a newspaper review or a formal semiological examination.

B. TWO TYPES OF ANALYSIS

All of these different discourses can be grouped under two main approaches to analysis: reportage and reconstitution.

a. *Reportage analysis*, patterned after live sports broadcasting, gives a blow-by-blow description of the performance, examines how it affects us (what its *punctum* is, following BARTHES's distinction) and how the waves of meaning are generated through the multiplicity and simultaneity of signs. Ideally, a survey, like a live report, should be done during the performance, to allow the spectator to react immediately and take stock of his reactions. Being impractical during the performance (except to measure the spectator's physiological changes or give a very brief account of his reactions), reportage requires the analyst to examine in depth the cognitive and emotional mechanisms of reception.

b. *Reconstitution analysis* restores the performance *post festum* with the help of all possible and imaginable documents, based on a systematic desire for *studium*. It accumulates indexes, relics and documents, without always knowing how to use them or how to take them to clear and simple conclusions as to staging options and organizing principles. The documents used are either "statements of intent" (VILLENEUVE 1989, 33) or audiovisual recordings, i.e. traces left after the event. We must be careful not to equate a statement of intent with the event itself, which alone is of interest to the analyst. It is advisable also to take into account the way in which recordings impose their own mode of transcription and transformation on the performance object. Whether in the description of a staging by someone who has seen it and in the historical analysis of a performance in the distant past, all that can be reconstructed in fact are a few "major principles" of the staging, not the whole event. Once those guiding principles have been determined, the *performance text* becomes the object of knowledge, the theoretical model that opportunely replaces the illusory whole of the empirical object that was the performance.

By identifying these major principles of the performance text, by reconstructing the staging discourse, the analysis overcomes certain dogmatic prejudices that marked the beginnings of semiology, which we will outline here to remind ourselves not to succumb to them again.

C. WHAT HAS BEEN OVERCOME

a. The analysis is no longer concerned with discovering a *repertory* of signs or signifying systems (KOWZAN, 1968) or a typology of signs (PAVIS, 1975). As early as 1941, MUKAROVSKY remarked that "the enumeration of components in itself is a lifeless list" (1977, 64). Lists of signs or sets of signs are meaningful only if their structure, and therefore the signifying strategy, is specified within them. An understanding of this strategy is, in turn, essential to the listing and description of these same signs.

b. Therefore, the *minimal unit* is no longer the philosopher's stone that is expected to unlock the performance as if by magic. It is best to avoid breaking down the performance into micro-units whose overall arrangement thereby loses relevance.

c. In renouncing a *microscopic analysis* of the performance based on spatial and temporal fragmentation, one is rid of the illusion of a scientific analysis that attempts to reconstruct the performance on the basis of incontrovertible units, from the simplest to the most complex.

d. The old nostalgia of German *Theaterwissenschaft* – that of Max Herrmann, for instance, with his *reconstruction* of performance – can no longer be satisfied. "The intention was," G. HISS remarks, "to assemble and keep what remained of historical performances, in order to reconstruct from scattered details what had originally formed a whole" (1993, 65). Such a reconstruction, however – such an incomplete empirical object - could never be more than an unsatisfying mirage, precisely because it lacked a "soul," i.e. the object of knowledge which would have reconstructed in theory the major guiding principles of the performance, its "staging discourse."

e. Theoreticians have attempted in the more recent past to distinguish their work from taxonomic semiology by exploring German hermeneutic and pragmatic traditions (WEKWERTH 1974; PAUL 1981) or phenomenology (INGARDEN 1931; STATES 1983; CARLSON 1984). LYOTARD's essay (1973), and project of "general de-semiotics," a theatre of energies, did certainly conjure up many dreams for poststructuralists (and for postmodernists, always in a hurry to get to the point), without however inspiring them to discover a vehicle for comprehensible description other than the sign that could account properly for the "energies" released.

States provides a useful definition of the task of semiology in recalling Merleau-Ponty's reservations about dissecting impressions: "The problem with semiotics is that in addressing theater as a system of codes it necessarily dissects the perceptual impression theater makes on the spectator. And, as MERLEAU-PONTY has said, 'it is impossible... to decompose a perception, to make it into a collection of sensations, because in it the whole is prior to the parts' " (STATES 1987, 7). The analysis must therefore account for the performance as a whole, and not seek to reduce it to its constituent parts.

D. THE GLOBALIZING PHASE

These attempts to go beyond classical semiotics led, in the 1980s, to a "globalizing" stage in which *analysis*, paradoxically, consisted of a series of *syntheses*. Thus, the staging became a key concept of the "new semiology," capable of synthesizing the acting and scenographic choices (cf. *questionnaire**, question 1d). This globalization is not devoid of risk, however, since the aim at present is to avoid fragmenting the staging by identifying its "cipher," its condensed, unified form, which rules out at once studies based on decentring and constant contradiction. There is no such thing as a "turnkey" staging, only dramaturgical guidelines, general staging options, and then a whole series of practical decisions having to do with stagework which may deviate from the general direction. Vector theory serves as a means of regrouping various sign systems which are like so many nets holding together the staging and keeping it from breaking apart at any moment.

Since an exhaustive account would be impossible, tedious and finally irrelevant, the wholeness of the staging discourse leads us to resituate things in the context of a master plan to avoid getting bogged down in insignificant details. Better a reconstruction of the performance text (and therefore the staging choices) than a disorganized mass of tangible remains and unrelated documentary records. Still, the object of the exercise is not to discover a global, systematic, complete structure within the staging at any price, thereby eliminating inconsistencies, gaps and the tangible nature of the performance in an obsessive search for the intentionality and final aim of the artistic work.

E. WHICH QUESTIONNAIRE?

Since the performance cannot be reconstructed fully, but at most evoked in a statement of its major principles, its dramaturgical choices or staging options, one is sometimes tempted – as I was between 1976 and 1987 when faced with groups of fifty students who were to analyze in class a performance seen by all – to come up with a very precise questionnaire to be answered immediately after the performance, to serve as a basis or outline for discussion.

This question-and-answer exercise is unquestionably useful as a teaching aid (it distracts the student spectators from devouring the tamer), but it can also lead to a narrow perspective, with answers formulated exclusively within the categories defined. The students may feel they must adhere to the categories outlined by the instructor, and conform their thinking to the same headings and the same internal divisions of the work. This approach soon becomes normative and schoolish – which may be welcomed (Anne UBERSFELD, 1987, 169–201) or derided (LEHMANN 1989, 43). It favours the act of verbalization (for oral commentary) or rewriting, which rules out anything that cannot be broken down or translated into signs or reduced to words; in short, everything that surrounds the actors' words on stage. This forced verbalization, this movement from the subconscious to the conscious, appropriates elements that would have been better off in the half-light, not of nonsense, but of that which cannot be represented or verbalized. In being too anxious to do and say the right thing, one might say, semiologists deprive themselves of inexpressible pleasures... But they must be excused for doing so, for they, too, "know not what they do." And it is not easy to distinguish between *analysis* and *description*, *interpretation* and *evaluation*: any description analyzes, dissects and fragments the performance, which must then be reconstructed *synthetically*. Description as a differentiation of units is already an interpretation, as the segmentation it proposes is based on a reading of the signifieds for which the corresponding signifiers are verified. Further semantic confusion arises when one seeks to determine the exact object of analysis. Is it the performance or the staging? The concepts vary irreconcilably from one language to another, as we can see if we compare French and English usage:

French	English
spectacle	*Performance*: the generic notion of "spectacle" and "spectacularity" is missing in the English *performance*.
représentation	The French term has no real equivalent; the double meaning of theFrench is not paralleled in an English term.
mise en scène	*Production* refers mainly to the process of manufacturing the performance. The expression *mise-en-scène* when used in English tends to be confined to spatial organization and blocking.

These semantic discrepancies make it difficult to transfer a methodology from one language to another. In addition, there are special ways of conceiving and categorizing genres, of identifying what one is actually analyzing: how to distinguish, for instance, between *theatre, gestural theatre, mime, dance* and *dance theatre* (*Tanztheater*)? Perhaps a specific method should be tailored to each category – but would we not then risk an irremediable loss of universality and scientificity? The desire to adapt the method to the object of analysis is a laudable one, but risks ruling out the possibility of verifying it or comparing it with other examples.

Such is the current state of analysis: considerable progress has been made, but we are still faced with methodological obstacles that must at least be clarified, if they cannot be overcome completely.

2. Methodological Obstacles

However annoying and pervasive they may be, there is nothing shameful or inexplicable about such impediments; they reflect the difficulties of adapting one's approach to changing practices that defy analysis and invite one continually to come up with new strategies. Our stated intention here, to compare the analysis of theatre performance with the textual analysis of film, represents an attempt to free dramaturgical and theatrical analysis from its complacency and to confront it with other kinds of analysis.

A. SEGMENTATION OF PERFORMANCE

The segmentation of performance continues to be the key question of the analysis, and although it is clear that nothing much will be gained by fragmenting the performance into minimal units, one hesitates over the macro-units called for. Regrettably, the segmentation of performance is all too often done on the basis of the text and its dramaturgical arrangement in speeches, scenes and acts, rather than using the segmentation of the staging as a starting point. This structure does not necessarily correspond to the dynamics of the performance, which has its own rhythm and continually provides breaks and caesuras that could provide reference points for segmentation.

Logically, then, one must seek out the system of the performance events that constitute the performance. In doing so, researchers are not always able to resist the philological (or textocentric) temptation of reducing the performance to units marked by those points in the text where one can (and, according to them, one must) note movement by the actors. According to Gay MCAULEY, for instance, "it is evident both from watching the rehearsal process and from analysing performance, that the fractioners divide the action into units and that the performance units (consisting of both speech and physical action) are signalled by the major moves" (1991, 10–11). This kind of segmentation, which insists on making movements and dramaturgical units coincide on the basis of very precise moments anchored in the text, gives priority to one of the signifying systems (visible, sweeping movements) and imposes text-based divisions on the rest of the performance. We, on the other hand, would suggest that the differences between *speech acts* and *performance events* be taken into account and that the performance be divided up on the basis of its overall rhythm as established by physical actions and the "musical" composition of the staging; in other words, that the discrepancies between text and performance be observed.

B. CONCRETIZATION OF A TEXT

In the same logocentric way, there has often been a tendency to equate the staging with the concretization on stage of a dramatic text. For frequently staged classics, there may in fact be a need to refer to the text to compare the series of stage concretizations it has generated. But this is still a philological, even a "schoolish" approach, according to the implacable LEHMANN (1989, 43). In analyzing the staging, we should think of it as an autonomous preserve that has no need to concretize, carry out or invalidate a pre-existing dramatic text or project of meaning, i.e. as "an artistic practice that is strictly unpredictable from the point of view of the text" (LEHMANN 1989, 44).

C. THE STATUS OF THE TEXT

It is in fact the status of the text in the staging that is at stake here. The words spoken by the actor (or by another source of enunciation on stage) must be analyzed as being located and uttered concretely in the text, and not according to what we expect in advance from the dramatic text. We can observe what the diction, voice and pace of enunciation imprint upon it as energy, what they bring out or tone down. Text and performance are not seen in a causal relationship but as two wholes that do not always meet for the sake of illustration or redundancy.

D. THE NARRATOLOGICAL MODEL

Performance analysis cannot do without a narratological approach that distinguishes among its components and clarifies the dynamics of the story and the performance events. Here too, the narratological model should not be based solely on the text, but on the staging as well; it should neither be too universal nor patterned too closely after each particular case.

The way in which the different rhythms of the stage systems are put together and the resulting perception of the overall rhythm will provide a preliminary outline. For performances that tell a story figuratively, in which the action may be followed in its sensory-motor sequence by the spectator, one stands to gain by applying the Stanislavskian notions of "physical action," the "through-line of the action" and the "superobjective." We would propose the use of vector theory to regroup and vitalize whole moments of the stage or film performance. These vectoral configurations must be seen, however, in the context of frames which constrain the directed action, the *fabula* and its chronological presentation in the *szujet* (two notions of the Russian Formalists that we would do well to take out of the prop room).

E. THE QUESTION OF SUBJECTIVITY

Theatre semiology was born of a desire to avoid impressionistic discourse on performance. In its taxonomic and positivistic version, however, it rejected the authority of the subjective, never neutral, gaze of the spectator, held by the object of analysis in accordance with an entire conceptual and methodological apparatus. This tenuous gaze should not be eliminated altogether; on the contrary, it must be taken into account in the spectator's relationship with the stage, and particularly with the actor, if only to try to grasp intuitively "the indefinable nature of acting, the obscure emergence of emotion" (BENHAMOU 1988, 10). True, it is not an easy task to clearly grasp such "emergences." At the very most one might imagine – in considering film's gaze upon reality, particularly theatrical reality – that the analyst's gaze is comparable, though metaphorically, to that of the filmic apparatus: point of view, distance and scale of shots, framing, connections with other perceptions through editing, free association of editing within the shot, etc.

F. THE UNPERFORMABLE

The signs of acting are often, in current practice, minuscule, barely perceptible, and always ambiguous, even unreadable: intonations, glances and gestures, more latent than apparent, are so many fleeting moments in which the meaning is written, but in a way that is impossible either to read or externalize. The question is how such signs, barely materialized, can be read if not by intuition and through a "corps-à-corps" [body-to-body] relationship whereby the spectator enjoys a sensory-motor perception of the performance. The rather unscientific and unsemiological term of *energy* is of use in conveying an idea of the phenomenon in question here: the actor or dancer, through his or her presence, movements and phrasing, gives off an energy that strikes the spectator forcefully. One "feels" that it is this quality that makes all the difference and contributes to the whole aesthetic experience and the elaboration of meaning. We seek to identify the unperformable, i.e. the essentially invisible, in reaction against the hegemony of an audiovisual culture; we seek it in what we hear, in the text, the rhythm, beyond the all-too-obvious visual signs and overly visible units. We read the body, as we do with dancers: "Literacy in dance begins with seeing, hearing, and feeling how the body moves. The reader of dances must learn to see and feel rhythm in movement, to comprehend the three-dimensionality of the body, to sense its anatomical capabilities and its relation to gravity, to identify the gestures and shapes made by the body, and even to reidentify them when they are performed by different dancers. The reader must also notice changes in the tensile qualities of movement - the dynamics and effort with which it is performed - and be able to trace the path of dancers from one part of the performance area to another" (FOSTER 1988, 58).

G. DESUBLIMATION

The "corps-à-corps" relationship with the performance is to be taken literally: the analyst is to make a "desublimated" return toward the body of the performance (VILLENEUVE 1989, 25) and not confine the aesthetic experience to a decoding of signifieds. Thus the analyst reproduces the experience and materiality of the performance, overcoming that "blindness of many semiologists to the material force of aesthetic signifiers" and accounting for the "phenomenon of unintentionality, the investment of events with libido, the sensuous materiality of signifiers, which force us to take note of the corporality of the things, structures and living beings through which signifiers are produced in theatre" (LEHMANN 1989, 48).

The phenomenology of Bert STATES shows a similar concern about semiotics looking for nothing else in a thing than its signified: "What is disturbing, if anything, about semiotics is not its narrowness but its almost imperialistic confidence in its product: that of its implicit belief that you have exhausted a thing's interest, when you have explained how it works as a sign" (1987, 7).

There is a trend now to return to the concrete realities of the stage, a desublimated return to the body of the performance, instead of seeing the *mise-en-signes* as a sublimation of the stage body. This return, this desire for the body, prompts us to follow the path and perceive the energy of a particular movement or utterance, to zero in on the breathing, rhythm and voice of the text "uttered on stage." This "logic of sensation" (DELEUZE), this motion that moves the text and moves the spectator, can be grasped (i.e. described, interpreted, assessed) only if we avoid resublimating it in an unequivocal written record or reducing it to a signifier or a secret cipher.

In spite of everything, this desublimation, desemiotics, or poetic insistence on the material aspect of signs always occurs within the context of an event within the performance analyzed which is organized, structured, systematic, and therefore predictable. Desemiotization and semiotization are therefore antithetical but inalienable operations of the work of art and its aesthetic experience.

H. A SEMIOLOGICAL BLOCK

We have seen how theory, in trying to break the deadlock, has moved further and further away from a semiotics of communication and codes; how the semantic model of the sign and levels of meaning adapts poorly to the staging, particularly in today's experimental theatre. Models copied directly from information theory and JAKOBSON's functions of communication or a typology of codes (specific and non-specific) have been abandoned almost completely. The stage-audience relationship is no longer seen as a simple exchange or as communication between spectacle and spectators through intermediary signs or codes. And a more flexible model of the way signs function can be glimpsed once we respect their materiality and the guidelines of the vectors that carry and organize them.

In order for the idea of such a model to become a reality, we need to determine the conditions of analysis and theoretical areas to which it is best suited.

3. Conditions of Analysis and Key Areas

The fundamental question of analysis is for whom and to what end it is being done. Whereas a newspaper or television report is addressed to a broad audience that wishes above all to receive information and advice, the semiological report, which calls for a longer time for reflection and a more sophisticated conceptual apparatus, is nearly always addressed to other theoreticians and analysts, to colleagues caught in the same studious and fetishistic relationship to theatre. Theatre people are rarely users of analysis, whether out of a fear of discovery, a vague distrust of analysis, or a lack of interest and time. Studies are almost always done, then, in a controlled environment by a group of specialists within a single critical tradition. We know only too well that there is very little dialogue between French semiology, Dutch empiricism, Swedish studies of audience and German hermeneutics. Alas, poor Erasmus!

Despite the dismal list of hindrances, it does appear that analysis could start off on a sounder foundation if we are careful to bring into it highly sophisticated disciplines such as sociology and anthropology, which are usually elaborated far from actual texts and performances.

As a memory aid, then, below are three areas of research in which specific analyses could best be effected.

A. PRODUCTION-RECEPTION THEORY

We have put forward a model elsewhere (PAVIS 1985, 281–297) that combines production aesthetics with reception aesthetics. The tension between production and reception helps to avoid a unilateral view of the way text and performance function. It studies both the part of reception that is anticipated in the process of artistic production and the part that is tied to spectator activity.

B. SOCIOSEMIOTICS

Empirical studies on audiences have recently shown an understanding that they cannot neglect an examination of the cognitive, emotional and semiological devices employed by the spectator in building up meaning (SCHOENMAKERS 1986, SAUTER 1988). Can the semiocognitive approach and the sociological and ideological approach be used in conjunction with each other? That is the crucial question asked explicitly by a discipline such as sociosemiotics (PAVIS 1987). In so doing, it contradicts the reception theory born of German *Rezeptionsästhetik* or American *reader response criticism*, both of which theories neglect the ideological plurality of the reader or audience.

C. BETWEEN SOCIOSEMIOTICS AND CULTURAL ANTHROPOLOGY

The development of a cross-cultural theatre over the past few years has hastened the process of questioning purely linguistic and semiotic instruments of analysis. A cross-cultural semiotics encourages us to relativize our choices, our priorities in performance analysis. It protects us, for instance, against our obsession to describe a visible and readable space, to seek out and process information and redundancy quantitatively, to value what deviates from the norm and shows originality. Such a semiotics may heal us of our deafness to the phenomena of hearing, time and rhythm, of our inability to follow several parallel actions and assess the energy of an actor. Without repudiating our Western cultural habits, we must simply note how our ethno- or Eurocentrist gaze determines and often mortgages our perceptions, and how much we would gain by changing our perspective and tools of analysis from time to time (PAVIS 1992).

Further reading: Fitzpatrick 1986, 1989; Issacharoff 1986, 1989; Ouaknine 1970, Schechner 1988.

PERFORMANCE ART

Fr.: *performance*; Ger.: *Performance*; Sp.: *espectáculo*.

This phenomenon emerged in the 1960s, alongside the *happening** (it was influenced by the works of composer John CAGE, choreographer Merce CUNNINGHAM, videomaker Name JUNE PARK, sculptor Allan KAPROW), but did not come to maturity until the 1980s.

Performance art brings together visual arts, theatre, dance, music, video, poetry and film, with no preconceived ideas. It takes place, not in theatres, but in museums or art galleries. It is a "kaleidoscopic multithematic discourse" (A. WIRTH).

The accent is on the ephemeral and unfinished nature of the production rather than a completed work of art. Rather than an actor playing a role, the performer is in turn a narrator, painter and dancer and, because of the emphasis on physical presence, a stage autobiographer who has a direct relationship with the objects and situation of enunciation. "Performance art is perpetually restimulated by artists who have a hybrid definition of their work, shamelssly letting their ideas drift in the direction of theatre on the one hand, of sculpture on the other, with more regard for the vitality and the impact of the performance than for the accuracy of the theoretical definition of what they are in the process of doing. Performance art, properly speaking, means nothing" (Jeff NUTTAL).

Andrea NOURYEH, in an unpublished article, identifies five trends in performance art:

1. Body art uses the performer's body to put him or her at risk (V. ACCONCI, Ch. BURDEN, G. PANE); to expose the performer, test his or her image.
2. The exploration of space and time using slow motion or figures, as in RINKE's *Walking in an Exaggerated Manner Around the Perimeter of a Square* (1968).
3. Autobiographical presentation, in which the artist tells the actual events of his life (L. MONTANO's *Mitchell Death* or Spalding GRAY's *A Personal History of the American Theatre* in 1980).
4. Ritual and mythical ceremony, e.g. NITSCH's *Orgies and Mysteries*.
5. Social commentary, e.g. videomaker Bob ASHLEY telling about modern mythologies or Laurie ANDERSON in *United States* I and II (1979–1982), combining poetry, electronic music, film and slides in a multimedia performance.

See also: media, experimental theatre.

Further reading: Marranca 1977; Goldberg 1979; Wiles 1980; Battcock and Nickas 1984; Thomsen 1985; Carlson 1996. See also the following periodicals: *ArTitudes international, Performing Arts Journal, Parachute, The Drama Review*.

PERFORMANCE TEXT

Fr.: *texte spectaculaire*; Ger.: *Aufführungstext*; Sp.: *texto espectacular*.

The semiological notion of *text* has given us the notion of *performance* (or *stage*) *text*: this is the relationship of all the *signifying systems** used in performance, whose arrangement and interaction constitute the mise-en-scène. The notion of performance text is therefore an abstract and theoretical one, not an empirical and practical one. It considers the performance as a scale *model* in which the production of meaning may be observed. The performance text may be recorded in a *production book**, a *Modellbuch** or another metatext that presents a *notation** (necessarily an incomplete one) of the staging, and in particular of its aesthetic and ideological options.

See also: text and performance, semiology, description, visual and textual.

Further reading: *Theaterarbeit*, 1961; Ruffini 1978; de Marinis 1978, 1979, 1982; Lehmann 1989.

PERFORMER

1. A term that goes beyond the concept of actor, which is confined to spoken theatre, to include singers, dancers and mimes – in

other words, everything that a Western or oriental artist can *perform* on a stage. The performer always accomplishes a vocal, gestural or instrumental feat, as opposed to the interpretaton and mimetic representation of a role by an actor.

2. More specifically, a performer is someone who speaks and acts on his own behalf (as an artist and as a person) and thus addresses the audience, while the actor represents his character and pretends not to know he is only a theatre actor. The performer stages his own self, while the actor plays the role of another.

PERFORMING ARTS

Fr.: *arts de la scène;* Ger.: *Bühnenkünste;* Sp.: *artes de la escena.*

1. This generic term covers all arts based on the performance (representation) or re-presentation of their raw materials (stage, actor, image, voice, etc.). There must be an image (a representation) that functions as a signifier (audiovisual material) for a signified that is both the result and the goal of the *performance**, a signified that is neither fixed nor final. This category includes spoken, musical or gestural theatre, dance, opera and operetta, circus and puppet shows, as well as media arts such as cinema, television and radio.

2. The performing arts are characterized by their dual structure – the representing (stage, etc.) and the represented (figurative or symbolized reality). Representation is always a recreation of something – a past event, a historical figure or a real object; hence the impression that it reveals only a secondary reality. Theatre, however, is the only representational art that is "presented" to the spectator only once, even though it borrows its means of expression from a multitude of outside systems.

See also: theatre arts, theatricality, media, staging, ethnoscenology.

PERIPETEIA, PERIPETY

(Greek word meaning "unexpected reversal," "sudden change.")
Fr.: *péripétie;* Ger.: *Peripetie;* Sp.: *peripecia.*

Sudden and unforeseen change, *turning point** or "reversal in the action" (ARISTOTLE).

The peripeteia occurs when the hero's fate takes an unexpected turn, when there is "a change of fortune in the action of the play to the opposite state of affairs." According to ARISTOTLE, things can go from good to bad or vice versa. For FREYTAG, it is "the tragic moment that occurs because of an unexpected event that, though believable in the context of the action previously set out, shifts the hero's quest and the main action to a new direction" (1965).

PERSPECTIVE

(From the Latin *perspicere,* to see clearly through.)
Fr.: *perspective;* Ger.: *Aussichtspunkt, Perspektive;* Sp.: *perspectiva.*

1. Visual Perspective

Since theatre presents things to the spectator's view, perspective is, in concrete terms, the angle from which the stage is seen and the way the stage action appears: "Theatre is precisely that practice which calculates the place of things *as they are observed*: if I place the spectacle here, the spectator will see this; if I place it elsewhere he will not, and I can avail myself of this masking effect and play on the illusion it provides" (BARTHES 1973b, 185; 1977, 69).

The director arranges the scenery and the actors according to both the logic of their interrelations at a particular moment and the way their image will appear to the audience. According to the conception of the stage as a cube and a slice of life that is "showcased" (*Guckkastenbühne* in German), the spectator is immobilized at the vanishing point of the stage lines; he becomes a passive and voyeuristic being who is easily taken in by the illusion. Everything seems to be concentrated and played out within the spectator's optic beam. Inversely, a circular playing area, or one that is split up into several spaces surrounding an audience, is not perceived from a single perspective. Perspective is a dynamic dramaturgical element that forces the audience to "accommodate," i.e. to relativize different views of things and therefore to situate them in relation to each other. We should not, however, carry over this concept of actual vision directly as an objective and measurable indication of the onlooker's intellectual and emotional involvement, as involvement depends on many other factors of *reception**: the structure of action and presentation of events, illusionist or "distanced" acting, identification with a particular side or a hero. These elements already belong to the characters' inner perspective, to their *point of view** within the world of fiction.

2. Perspective of Characters

This is the character's point of view on the world and the other characters, his views, opinions, knowledge, value systems, etc. Since different perspectives can only be compared on the basis of a single fixed object, the characters' perspectives are meaningful only in relation to the same issue, most often a conflict of interests or of values, a judgment on reality. It is up to the playwright who allocates the speeches to the characters, then to the spectator who perceives their worldviews, to carry out this comparison.

The examination of points of view is based on the assumption that each character is an autonomous consciousness equipped by the playwright with the ability to judge and expose his differences with the others. This assumption is reinforced in theatre by the presence of the actors/characters in the process of exchanging words that appear to belong to them. When speaking of perspective, there is a risk of treating it as a psychological notion, making it the prerogative of a consciousness that does not exist in fact, and not associating it with a form or a specific discursive instance. It is impossible to carry out an objective comparison of all the points of view, simply because the characters' speeches are not modelled exactly after those of real people and dramatic writing is not an imitation of dialogues taken from daily life; it is the author's dramaturgical work that builds the perspectives. The playwright alone constitutes a central perspective (even if it is vague, contradictory and unknown to the playwright). The perspective of each character is therefore determined by the "authorial" perspective.

This warning aside, it continues to be very important for dramaturgical purposes to analyze individual perspectives, particularly the individual perspective of reception "intended" or suggested by the playwright. This is what enables us to judge the characters and therefore to *identify** with them or take a critical backwards step.

3. Determining Individual Perspectives

Apart from the *monologue** or *aside** in which the character describes what he is thinking directly, we must always reconstruct the protagonists' points of view. In order to judge the action shown on stage, we need to put ourselves in the shoes of each character and guess his point of view on the action. This point of view is like a file in which we note all characteristics. All information is valid, indirectly, for all the other characters, for we may assume that each character says only that which makes him original and different from the others. We gradually become able to bring together the *contexts** of the figures and to establish our own system of values, in order to decide where our sympathies lie. After a certain period of time (often once the exposition has taken place), the *characterization** is so precise and the territory so well mapped out that we form a definitive opinion and the characters can no longer surprise us, except if the playwright's technique consists in turning the "good guy" into a "bad guy" all of a sudden, or if the murderer turns out to be someone we never suspected, etc.

The treatment of these points of view can be classified as follows:

- Grouping together by identity or by opposition;
- Relativization of all points of view; subordinating one point of view to another;
- Construction of an *actantial** system; determining each one's share of the truth;
- Relative importance of views;
- *Focusing** of interest and ruling out what is secondary.

All these questions raised by the characters help us arrive at a meaning and, finally, to look for a *central perspective* resulting from the individual perspectives, i.e. for the ideological centre of the play.

4. Central Perspective

The central perspective cannot always be deduced from the overall structure of the individual points of view. The theory of reception is currently attempting to find, in the play, the image of an implicit spectator, i.e. an ideal super-spectator on whom all the meanings of the play would converge, who would be the ideal receiver the author had in mind.

A. CONVERGENT PERSPECTIVES

This occurs when our sympathies have been unambiguously manipulated in the direction of a hero. For example, there is no doubt that the perspective of the pharisee Tartuffe is wrong; although we may not be told which is the right one, at least we know in which direction MOLIÈRE leans. Often it is the middle way between two extremes that is presented as the right solution (as in classical comedy).

B. DIVERGENT PERSPECTIVES

Sometimes the playwright refuses to draw conclusions (Who is right, Alceste or Philinte?) or confuses the issue (it matters little, in *Waiting for Godot*, whether it is Vladimir or Estragon who is right). It is up to each individual or social group to choose its own perspective (that of the masters or the valets in MARIVAUX, for instance).

C. THE "UNDECIDABLE" PLACE OF IDEOLOGY

It is precisely the spectator who, in the last analysis, is required to take a position on the confusion of points of view. This undecided and undecidable aspect of the dramatic text is the territory of ideology. The ideology appears as a representation of ideas and as a provocation of reaction/reception on the part of the spectator. If the work is constructed in such a way as to question and provoke an implicit receiver, its overall perspective is found at that point of indeterminacy where artistic and ideological meaning find themselves in a perpetual process of elaboration.

Further reading: Uspensky 1972; Pfister 1977, 225–264; Fieguth 1979; Pavis 1980c; Francastel 1965, 1967, 1970.

PHOTOGRAPHY IN THEATRE

Fr.: *photographie de théâtre*, Ger.: *Theaterphotographie*; Sp.: *fotografía en teatro.*

1. A Photogenic Art

Theatre is photogenic. Some photographers specialize in theatre photography, and their art goes far beyond that of a documentalist or reporter. Photography is abundantly used, whether to provide documentation on productions for theatre archives or research, or to provide newspapers or periodicals with pictures of the production for immediate or later publication.

Photographs may be taken for all kinds of reasons and in all kinds of ways. There is a substantial difference between photos taken in the course of rehearsals or at the final dress rehearsal and photos taken live of a performance for an audience. The question arises of the authenticity of the photographic document, where it fits into the mise-en-scène or is left outside for technical reasons to get a better shot or a different angle. By photographing the performance – with all the problems, risks and imperfections that it implies – one seeks access to the actual situation of enunciation; by posing the actor or the set, on the other hand, one attempts to highlight a detail, to stage the predatory act of the photographic shot. The following step, as described by

R. BARTHES in "L'acteur d'Harcourt," is studio photography, the logical outcome of this technique of reconstruction.

2. Focusing the Portrait

That the actor attracts the gaze of the camera is no surprise. Is he not the focus of any performance, irradiating the entire stage, attaching the words to the stage image? The anthropomorphism that comes naturally to photography is reinforced in theatre, which can easily be reduced to a face and a voice. The photograph is a voice with the ability to prolong its life by fixing itself on the surface of the paper. Setting its limits, however, is no easy matter: it is not only the face (including hair, eyes, perhaps the shoulders) that carries meaning in contemporary performance; the attitude of the whole body, the relationship with objects, the proxemics of the actors are also elements that the camera could capture to good advantage, but they are not part of the photograph of the actor, at least not in the "classic" version, and the tendency is to use close-ups, even if the actor's face is only one small piece of the performance.

3. Specificity of the Theatre Photograph

It is not an easy task to define a photographic genre by its subject (portrait, landscape, news reporting), because the subject itself is variable and ill-disposed to keep to an autonomous category. It is even more difficult to define theatre photography by the sole criterion of where it is taken, since there no longer appear to be any rules about what to photograph, where or when, or about the specificity of theatre work. Some pictures taken in the theatre succeed in making us forget that their subject was a theatre event; their aesthetic function suppresses their communicative function. Without falling into a false debate between "documentary, objective photography" as opposed to "artistic photography that is independent of its subject," we must agree that theatre photography is first of all photography *per se*, and that it should be judged as an aesthetic object and form, independently of the theatrical subject it wishes to record.

Nevertheless, this type of photography is an image of an image, and that is another specific feature. It must capture a reality that is already a representation and an image of something: a character, situation or mood. Its referent (its subject) is already rendered into forms and signs, and it cannot ignore this first semiotization. It is necessarily a mise-en-scène (on paper) of a theatrical mise-en-scène, and therefore it will choose either to make explicit and complement the mise-en-scène or to take its distance and comment on it by deconstructing it. But in doing so, whether or not it takes into account the staged reality that it is photographing, it also records the a-signifying materiality of the theatre event – the accidental body of the actor, the random use of space, the (non-fictional) rhythm of theatrical machinery, everything that cannot be semiotized, i.e. reduced to an organized and intentional system of meaning. The eye of the lens is not much different from that of the semiologist viewing the play: semiology cannot maintain a neutral scientific discourse on a pre-existing object but organizes a process of construction of meaning; similarly, photography constitutes a possible, not the final meaning of the theatre object, and is only the (fictional and real) mise-en-scène of a (fictional and real) mise-en-scène. Here we are far from the positivism of the photographs in BRECHT's *Modellbuch*, which claimed in all good (positivistic) faith to capture the mise-en-scène or the gestus in order to keep them for future reproduction in another staging.

4. Functions of Photography in Theatre

In order to understand the potential of theatre photography, we might ask ourselves about the goals pursued by the artist and by the institution behind him. Very often the photographer works for an agency from which the press will order, either now or later, one or more negatives for the sole purpose of identifying famous actors appearing in the production. The function is purely communicative. For the specialized press (theatre periodicals), it will attempt to capture the originality of the scenery, to find a way to frame and handle the image that will somehow evoke some of the mood of the mise-en-scène. Sometimes photographers follow a director's career and publish a book on the subject (TREATT/CHEREAU; D'URSO/BARBA). The aesthetic that emerges is that of the subject of the photographs, but above all that of the photographer.

In the past, more than at present, the function of photography of actors was promotional rather than intended to impart knowledge of the role or the production: "In the nineteenth century, theatre photography served essentially to promote actors, with the help of sophisticated lighting and skillful retouching. Sarah Bernhardt very soon realized how to take advantage of this instrument of worship that is inseparable from the audience's need to idealize. Leopold Reutlinger, when photographing Yvette Guilbert or Cécile Sorel, responds to the same concern with beautification and the creation of myths" (BORHAN, *Clichés*, no. 11, 1985). The development of photography is tied to the development of the press and the star system: "It was the reproduction of the first photo in a magazine in 1880 that created a real market for theatre photography. Specialty periodicals such as *l'Illustration* and *le Théâtre* and monthly and weekly newspapers became the principal consumers, reinforcing the cult of the stars" (MEYER-PLANTUREAUX 1984, 22).

5. Portraits of Actors

The industrial development of photography in "the age of mechanical reproduction" (W. BENJAMIN) took over the tradition of portraiture and engravings of actors. Photography's contribution was, first of all, imprinting reality on film, recording a piece of the performance and the actor, a shadow of the person captured forever. What theatre fan could resist such a fetishistic relationship with the actor? Photography creates multiple points of view on the performance and selects a number of them, accepting the lens's surprises in advance, while a painting or engraving can only be the result of concerted activity; in theatre, more than elsewhere, the exact moment when the button is pressed can be left to chance. When photographing an actor on the wing, so to speak, a fraction of a second can change everything, and one would have to be very clever to know in advance exactly how a shot will come out.

A. CHOOSING A POSE

Whether or not the moment when the shutter clicks is left to chance, the choice of pose is never accidental. Every discourse on theatre, every aesthetic or prevailing norm guides this choice as a way of making its point. Long considered to be the realm of the dramatic, theatre insists on providing itself with dramatic representations of the actors. This "dramaticity" is often evoked by a concentrated, inward-looking gaze (in individual portraits) or by the "designed" circuit of expression of all the actors in a group (as in Agnès VARDA's portraits of the actors of the Théâtre National Populaire).

B. THE LEGEND

This kind of portrait is meant for *writing* a legend below the picture, as if there were only one text possible, provided by the photo. But such portraits, inferring a univocal legend, are built on a prior editing of the meaning of the character and the play which the photograph only clarifies and embodies. Consequently, the photograph is only a foil for the mise-en-scène, a clarification; it has no hermeneutical power over the performance, as one might expect today. This kind of "portrait-interpretation of text" is only possible, at least to a certain degree of perfection, in a studio with carefully planned lighting and posing. The photograph then becomes the mise-en-scène of the image of the role: as a "mood-photograph" (or "character- photograph"), it accumulates a duration and a series of redundant signs that characterize the part. Conversely, the "event-photograph" (or "action-photograph") is tied to a fleeting situation, and so it is taken "life-size" on stage instead of being reconstructed in the studio or on stage with no connection to the rest of the performance. There was something in the former practice of having the actors pose for press agencies after the dress rehearsal and shooting them with the most flattering lighting and from the most attractive angle, even though this photographic mise-en-scène obviously falsified the theatrical mise-en-scène. At least it allowed the long list of traits pertinent to the part to be reconstructed and grafted onto the portrait, recording a whole dramaturgical analysis on the actor's body (cf. BARTHES, "L'acteur d'Harcourt," 1957).

6. What the Patch of Shadow Says
But what do the photograph and the actor say through the portrait? In the "classical period" of theatre photography, which continued right up to the Brechtian method set out in the *Modellbuch* (*model**), the idea was to look for the "moral intelligence of the subject," "the intimate resemblance" (NADAR), so that "the outside man could be a picture of the inside man, and the face an expression that reveals the character as a whole" (SCHOPENHAUER). This kind of portrait seeks out the ideal essence of both the actor-subject and his part, as if the photograph could guide him in discovering how he should really be cast, the aim of the classical theory of the portrait as stated by DIDEROT: "Man comes in angry, he is attentive, he is curious; he loves, he hates, he scorns, he disdains, he admires; and each movement of his soul is painted on his face in clear, obvious characters about which we are never mistaken [...] For the painter, an expression is weak or false if it leaves any doubt about the feeling." With BRECHT, the aim is to make readable, not the character's physical interiority, but his social *gestus*. The actor's portrait should record the signs of the contradiction on his body, hence the photographer's preference for the group of actors (*Theaterarbeit*, 1961).

We have come a long way since that search for readability. The photographer endeavours to create multiple images of the actor and the roles he wishes to present. The actor lets himself be surprised by the photograph and becomes a gaze at the performance. The photographer stages him (or even "hands him over") by trying to bring out what he does not wish to show of his character or himself. It is the process of the production of meaning, learning and rehearsing the role that is in the spotlight. So the portrait has been decentred – it no longer aims for the face as expressive of an inner being, but for an accidental movement, the creation of an instant that is as much of the actor as of the photographer, a unique rapport between the actor and his environment. The portrait is no longer psychological and thus limited to the face and hands; it extends to the entire stage enunciation. The purpose of the photograph (or portrait) is no longer thought to be to discover the reality of its subject; the photograph will give an image, a representation that is just as valid – no more and no less – as what we think we know about the actor or character. In semiological terms, it could be said that photography no longer has to do with the referent of the actor or the character, but with its signifier: it does not claim to have access to a referent, either imaginary (that of the character) or real (that of the actor), but plays with the signifier of an actor/role complex that is no longer divided up in the customary way (actor = signifier/role = signified).

These are some of the powers of theatre photography. It already has a long tradition, and we should not expect a photograph to have a documentary value. It is one of the possible testimonies on theatre, and in this respect it is invaluable: an aesthetic, but also a somewhat false testimony. It is the impossibility of describing theatre and fixing its fleeting meaning that the camera deceptively records on film.
Further reading: *Théâtre/Public*, 1980; Girault 1982; Dubois 1973; *Jeu*, 1985; Aliverti 1985; Rogiers 1986; Meyer-Plantureux 1992; Meyer-Plantureux and Pic 1995.

PHYSIOGNOMY
Fr.: *physionomie;* Ger.: *Physiognomie;* Sp.: *fisionomía.*
See FACIAL EXPRESSION

PITY

Fr.: *pitié;* Ger.: *Mitleid;* Sp.: *piedad.*
See FEAR

PLAY

Fr.: *jeu;* Ger.: *Spiel;* Sp.: *juego, actuación.*

The English and German languages accentuate the playful aspect of theatre in the words *to play, a play* ("a play is a play," BROOK 1968, 157; "The play's the thing," *Hamlet,* II,2) and *spielen, Schauspiel.* The same is true of the French only in terms such as *jeu du comédien* and *jouer un rôle.* The recent concept of *dramatic play** underscores the spontaneous and improvised tradition of play.

2. The Play Aspect of Theatre

A. RULES AND CONVENTIONS

Theatre has many things in common with play in its principles and rules, if not in its forms. HUIZINGA gives the following overall definition of play: "Summing up the formal characteristics of play we might call it a free activity standing quite consciously outside 'ordinary' life as being 'not serious,' but at the same time absorbing the player intensely and utterly. It is an activity connected with no material interest, and no profit can be gained by it. It proceeds within its own proper boundaries of time and space according to fixed rules and in an orderly manner. It promotes the formation of social groupings which tend to surround themselves with secrecy and to stress their difference from the common world by disguise or other means" (1950, 13). This description of the play principle could be one of theatre, as it includes fiction, masks, a defined stage and conventions. Of course, there is a stage/audience division that effects a radical separation of players from spectators and appears to run counter to the spirit of play. And it is true, as well, that only the *happening** or *dramatic play** brings everyone together in a kind of community of play. But theatrical performance cannot exist without the audience's complicity, and the play can only be "successful" if the spectators play the game by its own rules.

B. PLAY ASPECTS OF THEATRE

Rather than looking for a relationship of identity between play and the theatrical, we should examine what characteristics theatre shares with certain kinds of play. The typology drawn up by R. CAILLOIS (1958) appears to cover what we intuitively understand by play, at least from our Western perspective.

a. *Mimicry* (simulacrum): Since ARISTOTLE, theatre has been considered an imitation of men's actions. This continues to be fundamentally true even if we conceive of *mimesis* not as a photographic reproduction of the real but as a transposition (abstraction and reconstruction) of human events. The actor always uses a *persona,* a mask, even when he draws attention to it.

b. *Agon** (competition): Competition, in the form of rivalry and comic or tragic conflict, is one of the basic mechanisms of the dramatic genre. By analogy, the actor-audience relationship also has the effect of a kind of rivalry. In classical dramaturgy, the intention is to wring support from the audience as a whole, to have the stage become an autonomous universe under its gaze. In Brechtian epic theatre, the aim is to move the contradiction from stage to audience, so that the audience becomes divided on the narrative and political issues. Although this desire for radical division may appear somewhat in the guise of a naive fantasy of political activism, there is no doubt that such a dramaturgy underscores contradictions by presenting opposite ideologies and solutions.

c. *Alea* (chance): Many kinds of dramaturgy have tried experimenting with chance. It has long been thought that the outcome of drama must be decided in advance, and that chance has little place in the performance event. Some daring playwrights, however, have used it for their dramatic construction. For instance, the theatre of the *absurd** and experiments with an alogical narrative (DÜRRENMATT) surprise the audience with an unpredictable story in which the action is meant to take the "worst possible path," one that "happens by chance." (DÜRRENMATT 1991) Sometimes the actors draw lots to decide what ending to give the play. But only *psychodrama**, *dramatic play** and the *happening** incorporate chance fully into their performance.

d. *Illinx* (vertigo): Theatre does not (usually) manipulate the spectators' bodies so as to produce vertigo, but it does effectively simulate the most vertiginous psychological situations. In this sense, *identification** and *catharsis** can be seen as a slide into the undefined areas of fantasy or, as ROBBE-GRILLET would say, as "the gradual glidings of pleasure."

If the main task of theatre is to please, as playwrights are wont to say, the rules of the dramatic game call for the spectator's vision to be adapted to certain basic principles of play. From *ludus* (conventional play) to *paida* (spontaneous, anarchic play), there is a vast range of emotions and combinations.

3. Toward a Semiotic Theory of Play?
To leave the metaphysical soil in which these considerations on the universality of play are rooted, to avoid repeating the humanist discourse about the playful nature of man or the psychological view that rightly stresses the importance of play in the child's psychological and social development, it would be advisable to look for a semiotic theory of play considered as a *modelling** system and a "mise-en-signes" of reality. Guided by the director and his reading of the text or scenario, the actor asks himself a few questions according to the future reception by the audience: Which movements are visible and relevant? Should the text be contradicted by facial expression? How should interaction among actors be placed in context? Should the character's existence be simulated or suggested by convention? The acting takes shape in the course of the rehearsals, and then in the staging choices made to solve technical problems. Each of the actors' speeches involves the production of gestural sequences that attempt to reconcile all these requirements, to establish the fictional status of the performance, and to deliver to the audience something that will both satisfy its expectations and surprise it.

See also: pleasure, reception, spectator, *theatrum mundi*.

Further reading: Caillois 1958; Winnicott 1971; Schechner 1977; Dort 1979; Sarrazac 1981; Ryngaert 1985.

PLAY AND COUNTERPLAY

Fr.: *jeu et contre-jeu*; Ger.: *Spiel und Gegenspiel*; Sp.: *juego y contra-juego*.

If we acknowledge that any text borrows as much from earlier texts as it contributes to them in new information (*intertextuality**), we may assume that the same holds true for acting: it borrows from other acting techniques and other styles and, above all, it functions within the context of the other characters in the play. Voluntarily or not, it "quotes" from different acting techniques. Therefore, a full understanding of acting rests on the notion of "inter-playfulness."

Such a phenomenon is sometimes visible in the dramaturgical structure, as in *parody**; it can be understood only with reference to the object of parody and the motifs and techniques used in the parody. Certain passages in BÜCHNER (*Danton's Death*) and BRECHT (*St. Joan of the Stockyards*), for example, are difficult to decipher if one does not notice the parodic quotation of Schillerian *pathos**.

Generally speaking, interludicity permeates acting (and not only in the alienating Brechtian style). The actor is necessarily involved in the acting of his partners. He is talking about the same things, moving within the same situation, and cannot help reproducing certain *attitudes** and behaviours of other actors. This interaction is reflected in a "homogenization" and constant borrowing back and forth of acting techniques. To act according to the cue will consist of using the impetus of his partner's preceding lines. To oppose with gestures a character with whom one is in conflict obliges one to take from his gestures certain attitudes that will help counter him.

PLAYING AREA

Fr.: *aire de jeu, lieu scénique;* Ger.: *Spielfläche;* Sp.: *lugar escénico.*

A term of contemporary usage meaning the *stage** or *performance** area. Any performance defines its playing area, which forms a symbolic space that is inviolable by and inaccessible to the audience, even if the latter is invited to come on stage. As soon as the actors take physical possession of the playing area, the space becomes "sacred," as symbolic of a represented place. The gestural activity of the actors structure this "empty space" (BROOK 1968) which they furnish by moving upon it and fill symbolically. The playing area is thus structured by the actor's gestures or even his gaze. This structuring process may even extend to a coded and defined occupation of the stage through the creation of fields and squares on the chequer board of human relationships, representing "houses," territories or clans.

PLAY WITHIN A PLAY

Fr.: *théâtre dans le théâtre;* Ger.: *Theater im Theater;* Sp.: *teatro en el teatro.*

Play or performance whose subject is the performance of a play. The external audience watches a performance within which an audience of actors is also watching a performance.

1. Origins

This aesthetic has its origins in the sixteenth century (*Fulgence et Lucrèce* by Medwall was the first instance, in 1497, followed by T. KYD's *The Spanish Tragedy* in 1589 and Shakespeare's *Hamlet* in 1601). It is associated with a baroque worldview according to which "all the world's a stage, and all the men and women on it merely players" (SHAKESPEARE), and life is but a dream (CALDERON). God is the playwright, director and main actor. From being a theological metaphor, the play-within-a-play went to being the form of play *par excellence*, in which the performance is self-conscious and represents itself, with a taste for irony and for enhanced illusion. It culminates in the forms of theatre of our everyday reality, where it is no longer possible to separate life from art and where playacting is the general model of our everyday and aesthetic behaviour (GOFFMAN 1959, 1974).

Among the many playwrights who have developed the form are SHAKESPEARE, T. KYD, ROTROU, CORNEILLE, MARIVAUX, PIRANDELLO, GENET, ANOUILH, BRECHT.

2. A Game of Superillusion

The use of this form may be a response to many different needs, but it always implies reflection on and manipulation of *illusion**. By showing actors on stage who are engaged in performing a play, the playwright involves the "outside" spectator as a spectator of the inner play, thus reinforcing his actual situation as someone who is in a theatre watching a fiction. Through this double theatricality the external level acquires a heightened reality – the illusion of illusion becomes reality.

3. An Epistemological Tool

The universality of the play within a play over the centuries and in various styles can be explained by the epistemological property of the technique. Theatre is "meta-communication" or communication about communication between the characters (OSOLSOBE 1980). In an identical (and meta-critical) way, the play within a play treats theatre theatrically, therefore using the artistic devices of the genre. It becomes impossible to dissociate what the author says about the stage from what the stage itself says. (Is not *Six Characters in Search of an Author* the staging of 25 centuries of theatre poetics?) So the play within a play is only a systematic and self-conscious way of making theatre. On the basis of this hypothesis, we can examine the metatheatrical elements inherent in any kind of theatricality, make generalizations about the ability of any theatrical performance to reproduce

itself spontaneously in a fiction and a reflection on that fiction. We would then arrive at a very loose but valid definition of the notion: a play within a play exists "when one element of theatre is isolated from the rest and appears as the object of attention of the spectators located on the stage, when both the watcher and the watched are on stage, when the spectator sees actors watching a performance that he also is watching" (UBERSFELD, in COUTY and REY 1980, 100). There is a distinction to be made between a play within a play in the strict sense and theatricality effects.
See also: metatheatre, denial, mise-en-abyme.
Further reading: Nelson 1958; Reiss 1971; *Revue des sciences humaines*, 1972; Kowzan 1976; Sawecka 1980; Swiontek 1990; Forestier 1981, 1988; Schmeling 1982; Jung 1994.

PLAYWRIGHT

Fr.: *auteur dramatique*; Ger.: *Bühnenautor, Dramatiker*; Sp.: *autor dramático.*

1. The playwright's status has varied considerably over the years. Until the beginning of the seventeenth century in France, the playwright was still only a supplier of texts. Not until P. CORNEILLE did the playwright attain true social status, becoming a person acknowledged as being essential to the preparation of the performance. In the ensuing evolution of theatre, the playwright took on an importance that may appear disproportionate as compared to that of the director (who didn't appear in a conscious form until the end of the nineteenth century), and particularly the actor, who is, in HEGEL's words, "only the instrument on which the dramatist plays, a sponge that absorbs the colours and gives them back unchanged."

2. Theatre theory tends to replace the playwright with a collective subject of enunciation, somewhat like the narrator in the novel. This "authorial" subject is difficult to identify, however, except in *stage directions**, the *chorus**, or the *raisonneur**. Even these instances are only a literary and sometimes deceptive substitute for the dramatist. It might best be seen in the organization of the *fabula*, the way the actions are put together, the resultant (though it is difficult to trace) of the points of view and semantic contexts of the speakers (VELTRUSKY 1941; SCHMID 1973). The classical text, when it is formally homogenous and possesses suprasegmental prosodic and lexical features which are proper to all texts, always reveals the playwright's stamp, although it may be be scattered through several different roles.

3. The playwright is only the first link (though an essential one, as language is the most accurate and stable system involved) in a production line that "flattens," but also enriches, the text through the mise-en-scène, the acting, the actual presentation on stage, and reception by the audience.
See also: play, discourse.
Further reading: Vinaver 1987, 1993; Corvin and Lemahieu in Corvin 1995, 73–75.

PLOT

Fr.: *intrigue*; Ger.: *Handlung, Intrigue*; Sp.: *intriga.*

1. The plot is the series of *actions** *(incidents**) that form the *knot** or complication of the play (or novel or film). "In the action of a poem, we mean by *plot* a combination of circumstances and incidents, of interests and characters which, in anticipation of the event, produces uncertainty, curiosity, impatience, concern, etc.) [...] The plot of a poem should therefore be a chain in which each incident is a link" (MARMONTEL 1787). The terms action and plot are used rather anarchically by critics, whereas we would draw a clear distinction between the two.

2. *Plot* refers to the causality of events, whereas *story* considers the same events according to their temporal succession. Unlike action, plot is the detailed series of developments of the *fabula**, the interlacing series of *conflicts** and *obstacles** and the ways taken by the characters to overcome them. It describes the external, visible aspect of dramatic progression, not the basic movements of the (internal) action.

Table of current terminology

	Theory of literary discourse	Aristotelian and anti-Aristotelian (Brechtian) conception	Anglo-American criticism	Russian formalists (Tomachev sky (1965)	G. Genette (1966)
A	Story narrated or action (sense 2)	*Fabula* (sense 1.B)	Story	*Fabula*	Story (narrated)
B	Narrating discourse or plot	*Fabula* (senses 1.C and 1.D)	Plot	*Szujet*	Narration (discursive presentation of Story, act of narrating)

"Plot is the subject of the work, the play of circumstance, the complication of events. Action is the deeper dynamism of that subject" (SIMON 1970, on "Plot").

3. *Actantial model**, *action* and *plot* are three different levels of abstraction that demonstrate the transition between a system of characters and action and the concrete materialization of the play in the plot.

4. A comedy of intrigue (with an "intrigue plot") is a play with multiple reboundings in which the comic is linked to repetition and a variety of effects and *coups de théâtre* (Ex.: MOLIÈRE's *les Fourberies de Scapin*, SHAKESPEARE's *The Comedy of Errors*, BEAUMARCHAIS' *Mariage de Figaro*).
See also: narrative analysis, dramturgy.
Further reading: Gouhier 1958; Reichert 1966; Olson 1968a.

PLOT OUTLINE

Fr.: *argument*; Ger.: *Inhaltsangabe*; Sp.: *argumento*.

1. A summary of the story told by the play, the plot outline (or *expositio argumenti*) is given before the play begins, to provide the audience with information about the story to be told. For instance, in the Middle Ages in France, a French summary was supplied for plays in Latin. CORNEILLE, in the 1660 edition of his drama, preceded each of his plays with a plot outline.

ARTISTOTLE suggests that the playwright make the plot outline the starting point and general idea of the drama: "As for the story, whether the poet takes it ready made or constructs it for himself, he should first sketch its general outline, and then fill in the episodes and amplify in detail" (*Poetics*, Section 1455b). The poet may then structure the plot in episodes, specifying names and places. Reflecting on the plot outline at the very beginning, according to Aristotle, forces the author to talk about universal truths and conflicts, and to stress the philosophical and the general rather than the anecdotic and the particular (Section 1451b).

2. As a synonym of *fabula**, *mythos** or *sjuzet**, the plot outline is the story reported, reconstructed in a logical sequence of events; the signified of the plot outline (story narrated) as opposed to its signifier (narrating *discourse**). Some genres, such as *farce** or *commedia dell'arte** use the plot outline (the *scenario**) as a basic text for improvisation by the actors. Sometimes the plot outline is presented in the form of a pantomime. In *Hamlet*, for instance, pantomime precedes dialogue in the poisoning scene.
3. Like *fabula*, *plot outline* is sometimes found in the two meanings of (1) *story narrated* (fabula as material) and (2) *narrating discourse* (fabula as structure of the narrative). Usage would appear to give preference to *plot outline* as *story narrated*,

independently of and prior to the order of presentation (e.g. the plot outline of *Bérénice* as told by RACINE in the preface).

PLOT THREAD

Fr.: *ficelle;* Ger.: *Handlungsfaden;* Sp.: *hilo.*
See MAINSPRING OF THE ACTION

POETICS (THEATRE)

Fr.: *poétique théâtrale;* Ger.: *Theaterpoetik;* Sp.: *poética teatral.*

1. The most famous poetics, that of ARISTOTLE (330 B.C.), is based primarily on theatre: the definition of tragedy, the causes and consequences of *catharsis**, and many other prescriptions that are commonly found in poetics. Still, poetics extends far beyond theatre and addresses itself to many other genres (poetry in general). Although there are more and stricter rules and regulations in theatre, which, as a necessarily public art, is closely regulated, such guidelines conceal or discourage an overall descriptive and structural reflection on how text and stage function. That is why the science of literature and *semiology** have today undertaken that universal and titanic enterprise, taking care to meet two requirements: first, to transcend the idiosyncracies of authors or schools and not to dictate rules to decide what theatre should be; and second, to grasp theatre as stage art (whereas poetics before ARTAUD and BRECHT gave priority to the text).

2. Although minds of the best calibre have applies themselves to poetics as applied to theatre, it must be said that its methodological assumptions today appear outdated and anachronistic. Theatre poetics is based on a comparison of story, plot or character with the object represented, making *mimesis** the yardstick of truth and therefore of the success of the performance. The result is a secular aesthetic of verisimilitude, a distinction between the popular genres, which are disparaged (satire and comedy, with "ordinary people" as protagonists), and the noble and serious genres (tragedy and the epic, presenting persons who are noble by birth or in spirit). Not until the age of Romanticism and bourgeois individualism did poetics bring up the issue of different forms and examine the connection between a work and its author. And it was not until the late eighteenth century, and above all in the twentieth, that theatre poetics became less normative and more descriptive, even structuralist, and began to look at plays and the stage as autonomous artistic systems (so that the relationship between the play and its referent and receiver was quickly lost from view).

3. Theatre poetics, then, has failed in its claim to elucidate two essential relationships: that of the performance with the spectator and that of theatrical work with the actor. This is attributable, paradoxically, to the *theoretical* universalization (by innumerable poetics) of the Greek model based on emotion and catharsis. Other poetics belong to other traditions: the treatise on classical Indian theatre (*Natya-Sastra*) or Zéami's treatise on Nô would have led to quite a different view of conflict, drama and theatrical reception. Similarly, a survey on the theatricalized ceremonies of Africa would call into doubt the rules of unity and tension and the boundary between art and life. It may be that the semiology of the actor, begun by J. DUVIGNAUD (1965), J. MUKAROVSKÝ (1941, 1977) and Anne UBERSFELD (1981), will show the way to finally overcoming the banal but recurring questions of the natural, of emotion and of distance in acting. Then the poetician will be free to clarify the exchange that takes place between actor and spectator in psychological, as well as social and historical terms.

4. A list of some poetics based on theatre follows:

ARISTOTLE, *Poetics*, 330 B.C.
HORACE, *Ars poetica*, 14 B.C.
ST. AUGUSTINE, *On music*, 386–389.
VIDA, *La Poetica*, 1527.
DU BELLAY, *Défense et illustration de la langue française*
PELETIER DU MANS, *Art poétique*, 1555.

SCALIGER, *Poetices libri septem*, 1561.
CASTELVETRO, *Poetica d'Aristotele vulgarizzata e sposta*, 1570.
Jean DE LA TAILLE, *De l'art de la tragédie*, 1572.
LAUDUN D'AIGALIERS, *Art poétique*, 1598.
VAUGUELIN DE LA FRESNAYE, *Art poétique*, 1605.
LOPE DE VEGA, *Arte nuevo de hacer comedias en este tiempo*, 1609.
HENSIUS, *Poétique*, 1611.
OPITZ, *Buch von der deutschen Poeterei*, 1624.
CHAPELAIN, *Lettre sur les vingt-quatre heures*, 1630.
MAIRET, Preface to *Silvanire*, 1631.
CHAPELAIN, *De la poésie représentative*, 1635.
GUEZ DE BALZAC, *Lettre à M. Scudéry sur ses observations du "Cid,"* 1637.
SARASIN, *Discours sur la tragédie*, 1639.
SCUDÉRY, *Apologie du théâtre*, 1639.
LA MESNARDIERE, *Poétique*, 1640.
VOSSIUS, *Poétique*, 1647.
D'AUBIGNAC, *La Pratique du théâtre*, 1657.
CORNEILLE, *Discours sur les unités*, 1657.
CORNEILLE, *Discours sur le poème dramatique*, 1660.
MOLIÈRE, *La Critique de "l'École des femmes,"* 1663.
ABBÉ DE PURE, *Idée des spectacles*, 1668.
BOILEAU, *Art poétique*, 1674.
DRYDEN, *Essay of Dramatic Poetry*, 1688.
LA BRUYERE, "Tragédie," in *Caractères*, 1691.
FONTENELLE, *Réflexions*, 1691–1699.
DACIER, translation of ARISTOTLE's *Poetics*.
BOSSUET, *Maximes et réflexions sur la comédie*, 1694.
DU BOS, *Réflexions critiques sur la poésie et la peinture*, 1719.
HOUDAR DE LA MOTTE, *Discours et réflexions*, 1721–1730.
BAILLET, *Jugements des savants sur les principaux ouvrages des auteurs*, 1722.
VOLTAIRE, *Discours sur la tragédie*, 1730.
RICCOBONI, *Histoire du théâtre italien*, 1731.
LUZAN, *Poetica*, 1737.
RICCOBONI, *La Réformation du théâtre*, 1743.
DIDEROT, *Entretiens sur le fils naturel*, 1757.
DIDEROT, *De la poésie dramatique*, 1758.
ROUSSEAU, *Lettre à d'Alembert sur les spectacles*, 1758.
NOVERRE, *Lettre sur la danse et sur les ballets*, 1760.
JOHNSON, *Preface to Shakespeare's works*, 1765.
BEAUMARCHAIS, *Essai sur le genre dramatique sérieux*, 1767.
LESSING, *Dramaturgie de Hambourg*, 1767–1769.
DIDEROT, *Paradoxe sur le comédien*, 1773–1780.
MERCIER, *Du théâtre*, 1773.
MARMONTEL, *Éléments de littérature*, 1787.
GOETHE, *Traité sur la poésie épique et la poésie dramatique*, 1797.
GOETHE, *Règles pour les acteurs*, 1803.
SCHILLER, Preface to *The Brigands*, 1781.
SCHILLER, Preface to *The Fiancée of Messina*, 1803.
CONSTANT, *Réflexion sur la tragédie de Wallstein et sur le théâtre allemand*, 1809.
KLEIST, *Über das Marionettentheater*, 1810.
SCHLEGEL, *Cours de littérature dramatique*, 1814.
STENDHAL, *Racine et Shakespeare*, 1823'1825.
HUGO, *Preface to Cromwell*, 1827.
MUSSET, *Un spectacle dans un fauteuil*, 1834.
HEGEL, *Esthétique*, 1832.
WAGNER, *L'Oeuvre d'art de l'avenir*, 1848.
FREYTAG, *Die Technik des Dramas*, 1863.
NIETZSCHE, *The Birth of Tragedy*, 1871.
MEREDITH, *Essay on Comedy*, 1879.
ZOLA, *Le Naturalisme au théâtre*, 1881.
APPIA, *La Mise en scène du drame wagnérien*, 1895.
JARRY, *De l'inutilité du théâtre au théâtre*, 1896.
MAETERLINCK, *Le Trésor des humbles*, 1896.
ANTOINE, *Causerie sur la mise en scène*, 1903.
ROLLAND, *Le Théâtre du peuple*, 1903.
CRAIG, *The Art of Theatre*, 1905.
APPIA, *L'Oeuvre d'art vivant*, 1921.
PISCATOR, *Le Théâtre politique*, 1929.
ARTAUD, *Le Théâtre et son double*, 1938.
STANISLAVSKI, *La Formation de l'acteur*, 1938.
SARTRE, *Un théâtre de situations*, 1947–1973.

BRECHT, *A Short Organum for the Theatre*, 1948.
CLAUDEL, *Mes idées sur le théâtre*, 1894–1954.
DÜRRENMATT, *Problèmes de théâtre*, 1955.
IONESCO, *Notes et Contre-Notes*, 1962.
GROTOWSKI, *Toward a Poor Theatre*, 1968.
SASTRE, *Anatomía del realismo*, 1974.
Further reading: See entry for "Theory of theatre."

POETRY IN THEATRE

Fr.: *poésie au théâtre*; Ger.: *Dichtung im Theater*; Sp.: *poesía en el teatro.*

This refers, rather than to essential or historical relations between poetry and theatre, to poetry's place in the contemporary writing and staging of plays. Poetry has played an important role in theatre creation in the twentieth century, as if it were seeking to reconquer lost territory.

1. Poetic Language

Without going into the debate on the specificity of poetic language or the difference between prose and poetry, we would simply note that poetry is normally read or heard outside the theatrical situation, i.e. with no concrete indications as to its enunciation. Moreover, what differentiates it from a philosophical, novelesque or pragmatic text is its emphasis on form, condensation and systematization of literary devices, distance from everyday language and communication, and the reader or listener's awareness of being seized by an enigma that speaks to him personally.

It is not versification that makes a text a poetic text: RACINE wrote his tragedies in verse, but never to the detriment of dramatic tension, and the poetic language, regardless of its force and autonomy, is at the service of the dramatic situation.

It is advisable to distinguish between the poetic text (poem) and the poetic nature of a text (its "poetic" character, in the current and broadest sense of the term). As to poetry in theatre, what is important is not whether a poem is being performed, but whether the text performed is highly poetic, and what consequences this poetic charge has on the theatrical performance.

2. Poetic Situation, Theatrical Situation

It is the strategy of poetry and theatre that differs, forcing us to rethink their relationship as problematic by definition. Poetry is sufficient unto itself and contains its own images, while the dramatic text is subject to a staging and interpretation. Even more than a dramatic text destined for actors, the poetic (or philosophical) text is at the mercy of the staging.

Poetry read or transmitted by voice by the poet or a performer is received as a mental space that opens up in the reader or listener, which makes the text resonate without the need to illustrate or represent a situation or action (as in theatre). It is like a blank page within us, an empty screen, an echo that has no need of being externalized. In this sense, the static nature (subtlety) of poetry contrasts with and contradicts the dynamic nature (brutality) of drama, even if, as CELAN holds (*Discours de Brême*, 1968), the poem is essentially dialogic.

It is not incompatibility but peril that dogs the attempt to reconstruct this blank page and make it materialize on stage, for the reader–listener will be disturbed to see elements from his mental space on stage. As soon as a poetic text is dis-posed upon a concrete space, as soon as the characters-speakers take on a body, poetry is shifted from protected mental space to a public space open to all. Thus suddenly taking shape, the poetic text that presented no more than a combination of voices to the reader begins to represent speakers, and it is not clear whether they are direct representatives of the poet, his voice centralized in them and speaking in the first person, or characters expressing themselves in their own right. Normally, in the dramatic form of theatre (SZONDI 1956), the characters' voices are not identical to the playwright's, for drama is objective. In poetry recited on stage by actor-speakers, however, it is the poet's ego that returns, breaking the law of objectivity. We no longer know how to take it: is it the voice of the characters reciting the poems or of the poet speaking to us directly, with the actor being only a translucent package.

3. Difficulties of Poetic Utterance

The poetic text, by its very nature, is sufficient unto itself, asks only to be read, and calls for no illustration external to itself. It is sometimes even "self-sufficient," refusing any other support besides its resonance in the head of the reader-listener. Everything that the stage and the staging invent to handle it will appear to be superfluous, wordy and disruptive. And in fact poetic stagings are often reproached for just this; the actors move about too much and interfere with the listening process through their excessive gesturings. DECROUX made this a fundamental law of the apportionment of word and gesture: "Words and gestures can be combined provided they are meagre" (1963, 49). "The richer the text, the poorer the actor's music should be; the poorer a text, the richer should be the actor's music" (54).

The accompanying voices and gestures are often overly inflected and disruptive, but also overly repetitive, in the form of an address to the audience, a taking of sides, a violence done to the spectator to attract his attention by any possible extra-verbal means.

In order to make himself heard, the poet-delegate on stage tends to scream and impose himself rather than allowing the listener to enjoy a floating, concentrated but selective reading. Since the text is often extremely rich and dense, and difficult to understand, the risk is that the listener, appealed to through his verbal imagination and distracted by oral and physical gesturing, will quickly become disengaged and not do justice to the text. If, in addition, the text is a montage of several texts or authors, it will only be more disorienting and difficult to concentrate on, making it more likely that the spectator will give up and direct his attention to the stage props. And if the poetry is a translation besides, if the verbal signifier is no longer accessible in its original vocal body, the weakening of the text and diversion of attention are almost guaranteed.

4. Reasons for Success when Poetry Comes into Theatre

Why, then, does theatre persist in its attempts to stage poetry?

First of all, because poetry forces the spectator to undertake a different kind of listening, which is of benefit to both poetry and theatre. Poetry reclaims the orality, corporality and humanity of texts that are too often reduced to the secret of paper and inner voice. Interior monologue, combined voices and polyphony are exhibited in a stage performance. Theatre thus opens up another *path* to poetry. By becoming theatricalized and being uttered in public, poetry recovers its origins in oral poetry and story in certain surviving oral cultures, giving the poet an opportunity to read their own texts in front of large crowds, audiences accustomed to listening to their poets (as in Russia or Indonesia).

Mise-en-scène, determined to "make theatre out of everything" (VITEZ), extends its empire to other domains, making transitions by staging texts considered poetic or philosophical (BLANCHOT, HANDKE, KAFKA, by P. A. VILLEMAINE, for instance) or written in an invented language (NOVARINA's *Vous qui habitez le temps* in the staging by C. BUCHVALD and G. BRUN). Seeking not to explicate or illustrate the poetic intention, being not a staging but an "acting of a writing" (DERRIDA on VILLEMAINE's work), the staging has freedom to play and forces the spectator to renounce his natural laziness, his taste for tempting identification or protective distance, to reflect on what is happening within him during utterance of the text, and to favor inner mediation, free association based on listening to the poems.

POINT OF ATTACK

Fr.: *point d'attaque;* Ger.: *Einsatzpunkt der Handlung;* Sp.: *punto de ataque.*

1. In the *narrative**, whether in theatre, the novel, or elsewhere, the point of attack is the moment when the action is engaged and the story is set in motion (often in the first and second acts). The dramaturgical

point of attack is determined by the more or less explicit presentation of the *actantial** scheme specific to the play and, above all, of the beginning of the action.
2. As well as the actantial point of attack there is a stage point of attack when, after several seconds or minutes used to create atmosphere and establish communication (phatic function), the acting begins. The timing of the mise-en-scène often extends this pause as long as possible to evoke a certain expectation. In introductions in *medias res*, however, in which something is happening as soon as the curtain rises, the point of attack seems to occur right away, even before the play begins, suggesting that the performance is a slice of life.
Further reading: Levitt 1971; Pfister 1977.

POINT OF INTEGRATION

Fr.: *point d'intégration*; Ger.: *Integrationspunkt*; Sp.: *punto de integración*.

Point at which the various lines of the action – those of the different destinies of the characters and of the subplots – converge in a single scene at the end of the play. It is the "vanishing point at which the many perspectives of the drama fall into place" (KLOTZ 1969, 112).

POINT OF VIEW

Fr.: *point de vue*; Ger.: *Gesichtspunkt, Perspektive*; Sp.: *punto de vista*.

View that the playwright, then the reader or spectator, has of the event narrated or shown. The term ties up with *perspective**, but might better be reserved for the perspective of the playwright, as opposed to the individual perspective of each character.

1. Objectivity of the Dramatic Genre
The narrator's point of view characterizes the playwright's attitude toward the story told. Normally, the *dramatic** genre does not use the narrator's point of view, or at least it does not change throughout the play but remains invisible behind the *dramatis personae**.

Generally speaking, the spectator's point of view closely follows that of the playwright, as they have no access to the play other than in the dramatic construction imposed by the playwright. When epic elements are employed, the overall point of view changes as well: the intervention of a narrator (in the form of a character, a placard, a song or a substitute for the playwright) breaks the illusion and destroys the fiction of an objective and external presentation of the facts (objective vision).

2. The Playwright's Point of View
Since the playwright does not copy dialogues taken from life but puts together a *montage** of speeches according to a structure that is his own, clearly he intervenes directly in the text as an arranger of material, i.e. as a kind of narrator. This narrator role is also played by the director, who arranges the stage materials, thus adding to the montage of the dramatic text a second montage of the visual elements and their connection with the text. Finally, the actor, to some extent, has a role to play not as a performer but as a kind of orchestra conductor and organizer of all the stage systems (linguistic, proxemic, spatial). In short, the final theatre product is "filtered" through a series of points of view – dramaturgy, mise-en-scène, acting – each of which determines the subsequent one and has repercussions on the final performance.
See also: discourse, narrative analysis, narrator, attitude, gestus.

POLITICAL THEATRE

Fr.: *théâtre politique*; Ger.: *politisches Theater*; Sp.: *teatro político*.

Etymologically speaking, all theatre is political, as it presents protagonists within a town or group. The expression more properly refers to *agit-prop** theatre, *popular theatre**, Brechtian and post-Brechtian *epic theatre**, *documentary theatre**, *mass theatre**, BOAL's theatre of political therapy (1979). All of these share a desire to impose a theory, social belief or philosophical project. Aesthetics is thus subordinated to political struggle, to the point where the theatrical form may simply break down into a debate of ideas.

Further reading: Piscator 1980; Fiebach 1975; Miller 1977; Brauneck 1982, Abirached 1992.

POLITICAL TRAGEDY

Fr.: *tragédie politique;* Ger.: *politische Tragödie;* Sp.: *tragedia política.*

Tragedy covering authentic (or supposedly authentic) historical events. Its tragic nature proceeds from the decisions imposed by the hero by opposing groups. Examples are *Horace* and *Cinna* by CORNEILLE, *Britannicus* by RACINE, BÜCHNER's *Dantons Tod.*

POOR THEATRE

Fr.: *théâtre pauvre;* Ger.: *armes Theater;* Sp.: *teatro pobre.*

A term coined by GROTOWSKI (1968) to describe his performing style, founded on an extreme economy of stage resources (sets, props, costumes) and filling the remaining void with high-intensity acting and a heightened actor/spectator relationship. "It is no mere coincidence that our own theatre laboratory has developed from a theatre rich in resources – in which the plastic arts, lighting and music, were constantly exploited – into the ascetic theatre we have become in recent years: an ascetic theatre in which the actors and audience are all that is left. All the other visual elements – e.g. plastic, etc. – are constructed by means of the actor's body, the acoustic and musical effects by his voice" (Eng. 1968, 33).

This same trend is very marked in contemporary mise-en-scène (P. BROOK, 1968), the Théâtre de l'Aquarium, BARBA, the Living Theatre), for aesthetic rather than economic reasons. The performance is organized entirely around a few basic signs, through a series of gestures that, with the help of a few conventions, quickly establish the framework of the acting and characterization. Anything that is not strictly necessary tends to be eliminated from the performance; only the suggestive power of the text and the inalienable presence of the body are important.

POPULAR THEATRE

Fr.: *théâtre populaire;* Ger.: *Volkstheater;* Sp.: *teatro popular.*

1. The notion of popular theatre, so often invoked today, is more a sociological than an aesthetic category. This is how the sociology of culture defines an art that is addressed to and/or proceeds from the popular classes, an ambiguous approach in that it does not specify whether this is theatre made by the people or for the people. In any case, how are we to define people; and, as BRECHT asked, are the people still popular?

The first step in disentangling this complicated problem is to determine what notions are contrasted to that of popular theatre, as the term is used in a polemical and discriminatory way:

- elitist, academic theatre, the theatre of learned people who dictate rules;
- literary theatre based on an inalienable text;
- court theatre, whose repertory was addressed, in the seventeenth century, to leading citizens and to the aristocratic and financial elite;
- bourgeois theatre (boulevard, opera, private-sector theatre, melodrama);
- the proscenium-arch theatre, with its hierarchical and immutable architecture that keeps the audience at a distance;
- political theatre aimed at transmitting a specific, univocal political message, even if it is not associated with a particular ideology or party.

2. Confronted with all these doubles, popular theatre has a hard time finding its own identity. Although it has always existed alongside literary theatre (just as the *commedia dell'arte** existed alongside the *commedia erudita*), it was not until the late nineteenth century that attempts were made to institutionalize it: for instance the Freie

Volksbühne in Berlin (1889), Maurice POTTECHER's Théâtre du peuple at Bussang, the Vienna Volkstheater, Romain ROLLAND in his essay *Le Théâtre du peuple* (1903) and his plays, *Danton, Le 14 Juillet*. In France, the project of a popular theatre reappeared after the second World War with the impetus given it by high-ranking cultural officials like Jeanne LAURENT and directors like Jean VILAR and Roger PLANCHON, as well as the theoreticians of the periodical *Théâtre populaire* (1953–1964). Its creators aimed for a style, an audience and a repertory accessible to the greatest possible number of people. In fact, such a popular audience understands little of workers and peasants and is recruited from among the intellectual middle class, executives and teachers.

Is there such a thing as a popular repertory? The plays performed by villagers, the scenarios that inspired the players of the *commedia dell'arte** do not together make up a repertory that has been conserved to the present day. In the twentieth century the great classics are employed to assemble the public, as if those were the plays that could speak directly to the greatest numbers. It is an ambiguous issue for, like SARTRE, we could see repertory theatre both as a traditional popular theatre and a bourgeois cultural fact (SARTRE 1973, 69–80).

It seems there is no longer a consensus about popular theatre. VITEZ speaks of a theatre that would be "elitist for all," and says "the popular public is just that, the expanding public, and not necessarily very popular" (*Loisir*, Nov. 1967, 17). One speaks more often of "intercultural theatre" (BROOK) or *theatre of participation** (BOAL), a return to theatrical traditions (*commedia dell'arte**, Nô) or, in a different connection, of boulevard theatre, television broadcasts such as the very "popular" *Au théâtre ce soir*, or of pop culture (television and video). Such mass culture may have closed off any possibility of promoting the creativity of popular forces. Popularity is no longer proof of anything much in these media-filled times.

Further reading: Rolland 1903; T. Mann 1974; Copeau 1959; Brecht 1967; Vilar 1975. See also the periodical *Théâtre Populaire* (1954–1964).

PORTRAIT

Fr.: *portrait d'acteur*; Ger.: *Porträt*; Sp.: *retrato del actor*.
See PHOTOGRAPHY

POSSIBLE, PLAUSIBLE

Fr.: *possible*; Ger.: *das Mögliche*; Sp.: *posible, plausible*.
See VERISMILITUDE

POSSIBLE WORLD

Fr.: *monde possible*; Ger.: *mögliche Welt*; Sp.: *mundo posible*.
See FICTION

POST-MODERN THEATRE

Fr.: *théâtre post-moderne*; Ger.: *postmodernes Theater*; Sp.: *teatro postmoderno*.

The term is little used by French theatre critics, perhaps because of its lack of theoretical rigour, for neither modernism ("modern drama," SZONDI 1956) nor what comes afterwards appears to correspond to specific historic moments or distinct genres or aesthetics (PAVIS 1990, 65–87). More than a rigorous instrument for characterizing dramaturgy and staging, the term *post-modern* is a rallying cry (particularly in the United States and Latin America, a convenient label used to describe an acting style, an approach to production and reception, a "current" way of making theatre (*grosso modo*, since the 1960s, after the theatre of the *absurd** and existentialist theatre, with the emergence of *performance art**, the *happening**, so-called post-modern dance and *dance-theatre**). The post-modern philosophy (of LYOTARD 1971, 1973 and DERRIDA) remains foreign to the creators of theatre, or else poorly assimilated and adapted to their needs (with the exception, perhaps, of R. FOREMAN 1992). All we can do, then, is list some very general characteristics without much theoretical value that are generally associated with the notion of post-modern mise-en-scène. We will leave aside the question of post-modern (or, in LEHMANN's words, *post-dramatic*) writing for theatre, for literature obeys quite different criteria in determining whether a work is post-modern.

1. The post-modern staging is less radical, less systematic, than the historical avant-garde movements of the first third of the twentieth century. It frequently obeys several different and contradictory principles, is not afraid to combine disparate styles or present collages of heterogeneous acting styles. A similar fragmentation makes it possible to centre the staging around any principle, tradition, heritage, style or performer. It conceals moments and devices in which everything seems to be *deconstructed** and undone under the fingers of anyone who takes up the threads and clues to the performance.

2. Instead of *representing* a story and a character, the actor and director, as chief operators of the structure, *present* themselves as artists and private individuals presenting a *performance**, which no longer consists of signs but of "a wandering of flows to a displaceability and a kind of efficacy by affect: those of libidinal economy" (LYOTARD 1973, 99).

3. Accordingly, they deny their work the title of a staging as a closed, centred work, and prefer the notion of an event-based mechanism or *installation**.

4. Thus the pole of reception and perception is overvalued: the spectator is considered to organize divergent and convergent impressions and restore a certain coherence to the play through the logic of sensations (DELEUZE) and his own aesthetic experience. Since everything is delivered up in the same space and time, without no hierarchy among the components and no discursive logic assumed by a reference text, the post-modern play refers to nothing but itself. It is only a drifting of signs that place the spectator before an "emancipated performance" (DORT 1988): "The many and varied signs that succeed each other [on stage] never constitute a closed system of meanings. They endanger one another" (1988, 164). Post-modern theatre is already an endangered species.

PRACTICABLE

Fr.: *praticable;* Ger.: *Podest, Pratikabel;* Sp.: *practicable.*

Part of set made up of real, solid objects that are used in their everyday function, particularly for leaning on, walking on and moving about on, as on a fixed stage.

Nowadays the practicable is quite frequently used not as a decorative but as a functional object. It becomes an active element of the scenery as a *stage machine**.

See also: stage arrangement, playing area, scenery, stage design.

PRACTITIONER

Fr.: *praticien;* Ger.: *Theaterpraktiker;* Sp.: *teatrista.*

See THEATRE PRACTICE, STAGING.

PRAGMATICS

Fr.: *pragmatique;* Ger.: *Pragmatik;* Sp.: *pragmática.*

1. Branches of Pragmatics

The pragmatic dimension of language, "that is, the consideration of the speakers and the context" (ARMENGAUD 1985, 4), is also of interest to theatre, which sets up relationships between actants and actions and is a place where saying is always doing (*speech act**). In linguistics, pragmatics has developed recently to the point where it sometimes appears to be taking over from semantics to become one of the major branches of semiotics, which, since PEIRCE or MORRIS, has been divided into semantics, syntax and pragmatics. This uncontrolled growth has occurred in many directions and has used many different methodologies and epistemologies, and pragmatics has become (in the rough but accurate words of an Italian researcher) the "garbage can of linguistics" (quoted by KERBRAT-ORECCHIONI 1984, 46). Sorting out this garbage can of history can make one feel, if not nauseated, at least dizzy, so complex are the often overlapping issues involved. We will mention just a few of them here:

- American pragmatism and the philosophy of action (PEIRCE, MORRIS). For MORRIS, pragmatics is "that part of semiotics that deals with the relationships between signs and users of signs."
- Speech act theory (AUSTIN 1962; SEARLE 1969, 1980).
- Conversational theory (GOFFMAN 1959);
- The theory of the effects of discourse (DILLER, RECANATI 1979): "Pragmatics studies the use of language in discourse, and the specific marks in language that attest to its discursive vocation" (DILLER and RECANATI in *Langue française*, 1979, 3);
- F. JAQUES' interlocutory pragmatics that "approaches language as a phenomenon that is at once discursive, communicative and social";
- The problem of enunciation (BENVENISTE 1966, 1974; *Langages* no. 17; KERBRAT-ORECCHIONI 1980, 1984; MAINGUENEAU 1976, 1981), which distinguishes between the *utterance* (*énoncé*, i.e. what is said) and *enunciation* (*énonciation*, i.e. how it is said);
- "Semantic pragmatics" or "linguistic pragmatics" (DUCROT 1972, 1984), which deals with "human action accomplished through language, by specifying its circumstances and its scope" (1984, 173). DUCROT's basic hypothesis is that one must understand the argumentation and enunciation of an utterance in order to understand its meaning.

For our purposes, in seeking out the most practical use within a theory of theatre of all the area covered by pragmatics, we will select (not without serious methodological reservations) the following approaches:

- Study of the mechanisms of dialogue and language games and the comparison of "ordinary language" with dramatic language (ASTON et al. 1983; ELAM 1980, 1984);
- Study of action (*Poetica*, 1976), of the *fabula* and how it is formed by the reading and the staging;
- Empirical study of reception by the audience (GOURDON 1982; SCHOENMAKERS 1986; SAUTER 1986, 1988);
- Comparison of the various "concretizations" of a play in the course of history (VODICKA 1975);
- Study of the markers of theatrical enunciation and of production/reception by the spectator (PAVIS 1983a; UBERSFELD 1981).

In this preliminary research (these are more research projects than established methodologies), we can clearly see what pragmatics attempts to overcome: a solely narratological model that analyzes the *fabula* using narrative analysis, without accounting for the specificity of the theatrical performance; a *semiology** still centred too closely around the text.

Properly speaking, pragmatics is not really a new methodology; rather, it is the systematic examination of devices used, in dialogue analysis, to determine their role in setting up dramatic situations, in the progression of the action and development of the *fabula*. Although there are many linguistic and often literary studies that claim to be founded on pragmatics, we should not underestimate the difficulties involved in this area, particularly in theatre pragmatics.

2. Difficulties in Pragmatics

A. OBJECT OF ANALYSIS

Linguistic pragmatics tends to take into consideration only the dramatic text, reducing the performance to the text. It is certainly easy to transpose to the dramatic text pragmatic studies of argumentation in ordinary speech (logical connectors like *but*, *since* and *if*, for instance, in DUCROT 1984). The conclusions, of course, continue to be valid for that specific text, but not for performance as a whole. Thus, the performance situation is excluded, even though the concrete use of stage enunciation is what determines the pragmatic meaning of the *text in performance*. It would be better to examine which logical connectors (in what form) are used by the actor and the stage and how they modify those of the text.

B. EPISTEMOLOGICAL UNCERTAINTY

The diversity of the pragmatic approaches indicated above explains why they are frequently incompatible epistemologically. That is true, for instance, of linguistic pragmatics (such as that of DUCROT) and of approaches that seek to account for the opening of the subject through psychoanalysis or the Marxist theory of conflicting discourse (following BAKHTIN). For a long time DUCROT sought to confine his investigation to an ideal, abstract subject, but under pressure from researchers such as AUTHIER (*Langages*, no. 73, 1984) or FUCHS (DRLAV, no. 25, 1981, 50) and a whole branch of political and psychological discourse analysis, he finally resorted to calling on BAKHTIN for assistance (1984, 171). This was in fact a purely tactical move, since DUCROT, in spite of his "sketch for a polyphonic theory of enunciation" (1984), continues to argue, always quite impeccably, for an ideal speaking subject observable in the orientation of his argumentation, battling against a dialogism in theatre ("within the framework of polyphony and the 'theatrical' conception of speech acts," 1984, 231).

His "theatrical" conception of speech acts does not, however, generate a model that can be used to analyze dialogue in theatre, for it is based on a very naive view of theatrical enunciation. According to DUCROT, there are two kinds of words; "original" words that "the playwright addresses to the audience by identifying with the character" (1984, 225), and "derived" words that "the playwright addresses, not through the characters, but by the very fact of representing those characters, by choosing them" (226). This distinction between two types of enunciation may appear obvious, and it is often cited by researchers as the specific mark of theatrical discourse, as its "double enunciation" (UBERSFELD 1977a, 129) or as the opposition (made by INGARDEN 1931, 1971 and then H. SCHMID 1973) between the "direct speech of characters" and the themes not stated but present in the receiver's consciousness, those themes that are suggested by the current situation but not actualized in the direct speech of characters (202). Such an opposition is only superficially relevant, since it is in fact very difficult to establish where to draw the line between the words of the playwright and of the actors, and this is only a last-ditch attempt to save the subject. The dividing line does not hold, for it is the playwright who organizes his characters' words and one never knows where to read *the* authorial discourse: it is neither in the stage directions nor in the margins of the text, but in the structural outcome of the conflicts and speeches in dialogue. It would appear to be more satisfying to examine each word, whether it comes from a character or from the "author" (but where, in the theatre, is the author, particularly in the mise-en-scène?) in its ability, clearly identified by BAKHTIN, to quote the speech of the other, to rework it, to build it like an arena for a struggle between discursive and ideological formations. The mechanism of enunciation is, in any case, much more complex than a clear separation between the voice of the author and that of the characters. It is to the credit of discourse and enunciation linguistics that it has made voices heard within the voices and shown the intertextuality, even the polyphony, of the text. It is all the more true of theatre that it quickly becomes impossible to distinguish the specific hallmarks of enunciation by each practician (stage designer, playwright, lighting designer, musician, actor, etc.).

Having expressed the above epistemological reservations, it would be wrong to neglect the importance to the study of the dramatic text of methods of textual analysis developed by pragmatics, particularly that of DUCROT (1972, 1984).

3. Applicability to a Study of Dialogue

Such an application is still at the experimental stages.

A. THE DIRECTION OF DIALOGUE
The argumentation and direction are determined and the utterances have meaning only if one has perceived their direction, for "all the utterances of a language are given, and derive their meaning from the fact that they are given, as imposing a particular kind of conclusion on the interlocutor" (DUCROT 1984, 12). One should therefore attempt to establish the underlying logic of the dialogues, no matter how loosely constructed.

B. THE MISSING CONNECTION
Reading the text forces us to establish a relationship of causality or thematic similarity between apparently unrelated utterances, to fill in the blanks.

C. REESTABLISHED ORIENTATION
In the text in open dialogue, we make possible connections among the speeches. Beyond the logic of the dialogue we can sometimes see a meta-enunciatory orientation that organizes scattered fragments or a network of images or sounds (CHEKHOV, VINAVER).

D. QUOTING THE OTHER'S DISCOURSE
One identifies repetitions from one character to another of terms, ideologems, themes and discursive formations, establishing certain laws of intertextual exchange.

4. Pragmatics of Enunciation
The theory of enunciation, although it is sometimes confused with pragmatics, is not identical to that discipline, which was developed on the basis of speech act theory (AUSTIN 1962; SEARLE 1969, 1980) and has a methodology that would appear to be much more difficult to transfer to theatre. The theory of enunciation, on the other hand (BENVENISTE 1966; MAINGUENEAU 1986; KERBRAT-ORECCHIONI 1980; PAVIS 1983a, 1986a), is crucial to clarify both the reading and the "concretization" of the dramatic text and the use of space in the production.

A. TEXTUAL MECHANISMS OF ENUNCIATION
Some of the observations made by DUCROT's "semantic pragmatics" or "linguistic pragmatics" (1984, 173) are applicable. We note the following, and their possible use in theatre:

- Shifters (how the dramatic situation is marked by the play of personal pronouns, indications of time and place, deictics);
- Modalities (what attitude toward the utterances can be read in the text; according to what mode of existence the action is set out);
- Structure of reported narrations (how the author indicates a quote from another text or style of performance);
- Discursive strategies (references to enunciation and their influence on the meaning of utterances; acceptance or refusal of the adversary's presuppositions, the fact that in dialogue "attacking the adversary's assumptions is, much more than denying what he proposes, attacking the adversary himself" (DUCROT 1972:92);
- Determining the orientation of the discourse in a character's argumentation;
- Insinuations, play of speaker and enunciator(s) in irony (DUCROT 1984, 210–213).

B. STAGE ENUNCIATION
As has been noted by epistemologists and linguists such as DUCROT (1984, 179) or CULIOLI (*Matérialités discursives*, 1981, 184), we tend to consider the situation of enunciation as "a situation that would be historically describable. Therefore, the term 'situation of enunciation' is a way of trying to recover everything in the empirical domain, experience, what has been lived ..." (1981, 184). There is a distortion involved in likening stage enunciation to the actual, real live situation of the performance at a given moment. But this notion would appear to be crucial in theatre, where stage enunciation means bringing into play, in space and time and using actors, all the scenic and dramaturgical elements deemed useful to the production of meaning and to reception by the audience situated in the situation of reception. Describing the stage enunciation invites us to show how the mise-en-scène organizes the fictional world of the text (its characters and actions) in the space and

time of the stage, by making use of a series of enunciators: the actor, his voice and intonations, but also the entire stage in which it is anchored in the present of the enunciation of all the stage materials. It also requires us to organize and rank the various sources of enunciation. To utter the text through the actor and the mise-en-scène is, very concretely, to vocalize it (see *diction**) by determining the actor's timbre, delivery, *rhythm** and paralinguistic (kinesic and proxemic) elements; in other words, to give it meaning and direction.

Further reading: Van Dijk 1976; Eschbach 1979; Pagnini 1980; Jaques 1979, 1985; Kerbrat-Orecchioni 1984; Savona 1980, 1982; Pfister 1985.

PRAXIS

Fr.: *praxis;* Ger.: *praxis;* Sp.: *praxis.*

In ARISTOTLE's *Poetics*, praxis is *action** by the characters, action that arises in the chain of events or *fabula**. Drama is defined as the *imitation** of that action (*mimesis** of praxis).

PRE-ACTING

Fr.: *jeu et préjeu;* Ger.: *Spiel und Vorspiel;* Sp.: *juego y juego previo.*

Pre-acting (*Predygra*) is a term from MEYERHOLD meaning that the actor plays a pantomime before portraying the character and reconstructing the dramatic situation. "Pre-acting prepares the spectator's perception in such a way that he comprehends the scenic situation fully resolved in advance and so has no need to make any effort to grasp the underlying message of the scene" (1975, 129; Eng. 1969, 206).

This technique, used in the 1925 production of *Bubus le professeur*, is characeristic of a marked and deliberately theatrical physical style of acting. "The actor-tribune needs to convey to the spectator his attitude to the lines he is speaking and the situations he is enacting; he wants to force the spectator to respond in a particular way to the action which is unfolding before him" (1975, 129; Eng. 1969, 206).

PREFACE

Fr.: *préface, avertissement;* Ger.: *Vorwort;* Sp.: *prefacio.*

Preamble in which the playwright addresses the readers directly, advising them of his intentions, describing the circumstances of his work, analyzing his play, and anticipating any objections. Belonging to the *paratext**, and therefore external to the *dramatic text**, the preface often attempts to orient the play's future audience, and in this respect guides reception by the spectator. The preface is used by CORNEILLE to justify himself, by RACINE to assure the reader that he has not taken too much liberty with the story, and, on the contrary, by BEAUMARCHAIS in his *Essai sur le genre dramatique sérieux* (1767) to suggest the novelty of a genre, and by HUGO in his preface to *Cromwell* to launch the Romantic movement in 1827.

PRE-PERFORMANCE

Fr.: *pré-mise en scène;* Ger.: *Vorinszenierung;* Sp.: *pre-puesta en escena.*

1. Hypothesis that the dramatic text contains more or less explicit instructions for an "optimal" staging (mise-en-scène). Those instructions, however, vary considerably in nature and importance, according to the playwright. It is clear that the way the text is structured in dialogues gives an immediate view that is both *dramatic** (conflict of speeches) and *theatrical** (opposition and visualization of the sources of discourse), one that any staging will have to take into account. But the pre-performance can often be read in "the rhythm of speech or movement, or through changes in or an intensification of their tone or manner" (STYAN 1967, 3). These rhythmic elements of the text are "the measure of the play's stage value" (Ibid.: 3). The entire Brechtian theory of *gestus** is based on the notion of a gestural attitude of the playwright that is already contained in the text, an attitude that translates into a particular kind of reading and staging.

2. Other theorists go so far as to presuppose the existence in the text of "textual matrices of representativeness" and of "kernels of theatricality" (UBERSFELD 1977a, 20), or even of a "stage virtuality connoted in the text," then taken over by the "metalanguage of the director, actor, etc. (SERPIERI 1978; GULLI-PUGLIATI 1976). Such a conception assumes that the dramatic text differs radically from other texts such as poems or novels because its enunciators are multiple and present. Unfortunately, these theories rarely specify how or where theatricality fits into the text. Does the absence of an ideological subject provide unity? What is the role of the *stage directions**, of *word scenery** or the notations of proxemics between characters suggested by the text? Only J. VELTRUSKÝ speaks of stage movements that are "transpositions of the meanings conveyed by the author's notes, remarks, and comments," which are "directly called for, therefore predetermined, by the dialogue" (1941, 139 and 1976, 100). Such a logocentrist conception is indeed quite debatable, but is typical of most of the theories that appear to confuse the dramatic text with the performance text (theatricality).

3. Rather than look to the text and its pre-performance for the source and guarantee of the "one right" staging – a position that tends to treat the text as a fetish and make it answerable for its supposedly valid mise-en-scènes – it is preferable to try out several stage options and find out which reading or rereading of the text will ensue. The text will not tolerate one particular staging better than another; texts are not inherently stageable or unstageable, theatrical or untheatrical. The actual dramaturgical and scenic hypotheses pose questions and, challenging the text, make it profess the most unsuspected things.

See also: text and performance, scenario, dramatic text.

Further reading: Swiontek 1990, 1993; Vinaver 1993; Hornby 1977.

PRESENCE

Fr.: *présence*; Ger.: *Präsenz*; Sp.: *presencia*.

"To have presence," in theatre jargon, means knowing how to captivate the audience, being endowed with an indefinable quality that immediately arouses the spectators' *identification**, giving them the impression of being elsewhere, in an eternal present.

1. Body Presence

According to an opinion often expressed by people in the profession, presence is the actor's greatest asset and the audience's greatest experience. It is thought to be related to a "direct" physical communication with the actor. Thus, according to J.-L. BARRAULT, "the final aim of mime is not the visual, but presence itself, namely the moment of the theatrical present. The visual is only a means, not an end" (1959, 73); in the words of E. DECROUX, "mime produces only presences that are not conventional signs" (1963, 144). According to J. GROTOWSKI (1968), experiments with improvisation must aim at discovering in gestuality the traces of universal drives and archetypes, of mythical roots comparable to Jungian archetypes. Presence is what theoreticians fall back on when confronted with an inexplicable mystery. According to J.-P. RYNGAERT, "It is not always to be found in the individual's physical features, but in a radiant energy whose effects are felt even before the actor has acted or spoken, in the vigour of his being-there" (1985, 29).

This presence is unsettling. Eugenio BARBA and Moriaki WATANABE see it as the actor's contradiction and oxymoron: "To be strongly present but to present nothing is, for an actor, an oxymoron, a true contradiction [...] the actor of pure presence [is an] actor representing his own absence" (*Bouffonneries*, 1982, 4:11).

2. Stage Presence

All of these approximations share an idealistic, even mystical, conception of the actor's work. They perpetuate the myth that acting is sacred, ritualistic and indefinable.

But they also touch upon a fundamental aspect of the theatrical experience.

Without entirely explaining the "mystery" of the actor endowed with presence, a semiological grasp of the problem does place things in the proper perspective, leaving aside any trace of mysticism. Presence could be defined as a collision between the social *event** of theatre and the fiction of the character and the *fabula*. The conjunction of event and fiction, which is the very characteristic of theatre, produces a kind of double vision; we have before us an *actor* X playing Y and *this* Y, a fictional character (*denial**).

Rather than the actor's *presence*, we could speak of the continual *present* of the stage and its enunciation. Everything is represented on stage in relation to the speakers' actual situation (*deixis**, *ostension**). Each actor animates the *I* of his character, who is faced with others (the *you*). The *I* can only be created in relation to a *you*, to whom one lends one's own *ego* through identification (i.e. by identical vision). What we see in the *body** of the actor *present* is none other than our own bodies, hence our uneasiness and fascination with this strange and familiar presence.

Further reading: Bazin 1959, 2:90–92; Strasberg 1969; Chaikin 1972; Cole 1975; Bernard 1976; States 1983; Barba 1993.

PRESUPPOSITION

Fr.: *présupposé*; Ger.: *Voraussetzung, Präsupposition*; Sp.: *presupuesto*.
See DISCOURSE, PRAGMATICS

PRE-THEATRE

Fr.: *pré-théâtre*; Ger.: *Urtheater*; Sp.: *preteatro*.

This is a term used by André SCHAEFFNER (in DUMUR 1965, 53) to cover performance practices in all cultural contexts, notably in societies once called "primitive." SCHAEFFNER notes that this is "not theatre before theatre, historically speaking" (27), but his notion risks suggesting that these forms have not yet achieved the perfection of Greek or European tradition or are at an incomplete stage. *Ethnoscenology** prefers today to speak of *cultural performances*, being cultural and/or performance practices. It looks at these practices with the relativizing eye of an ethnologist, who would agree here with SCHAEFFNER, who says that "the most direct path from one theatre to another will be easier to find for an ethnologist than for a historian" (in DUMUR 1965, 27).

Further reading: Theatre anthropology.

PROBLEM PLAY

Fr.: *pièce à problème*; Ger.: *Problemstück*; Sp.: *obra de problema*.

Like the *thesis play** and the discussion drama, the problem play uses the stage to expound on current moral or political issues. The dialectics of characters and their points of view provides an ideal instrument for embodying controversial ideas. The playwright may not designate a spokesman to convey his own position, or even a character close to him. Most of the time the story and the relative importance of the characters provide information about the possible solution to the problem. Every dramaturgy can potentially produce problem plays, but the genre did not actually emerge until the nineteenth and twentieth centuries (SCRIBE, IBSEN, SHAW, SARTRE in *L'Engrenage*, BRECHT in his didactic plays and the trend toward *documentary theatre** with P. WEISS, R. HOCHHUT and others).

PRODUCTION, THEATRE

Fr.: *production théâtrale*; Ger.: *Theaterproduktion*; Sp.: *producción teatral*.

This term, appropriately, suggests the constructed, concrete nature of the work that precedes any performance. Sometimes we speak of the production of meaning or the productivity of the stage in referring to the joint activity of theatre practitioners (ranging from playwright to actor) and of the audience (*reception**). The production of meaning does not in fact end with the play but continues in the spectator's consciousness, undergoing the changes and interpretations imposed by the development of his point of view within social reality.

PRODUCTION BOOK

Fr.: *Livre de régie*; Ger.: *Regiebuch*; Sp.: *Libro de producción*.

The production book contains the *description** of a mise-en-scène, often drawn up by the *stage manager** on the basis of the director's notes; it covers specifically the actors' movements, pauses, sound effects, lighting effects and any system of notation used, whether manual or computerized, to commit the performance to memory. It is an essential document for the revival of a mise-en-scène and for researchers, although it is not the mise-en-scène itself but only a more or less exhaustive notation that does not necessarily reconstruct the whole system.

See also: model, photography, media and theatre.
Further reading: Passow 1971; Pavis 1981b; Mathers 1985.

PROGRAM

Fr.: *programme*; Ger.: *Programmheft*; Sp.: *programa*.

1. Variations on a Program

The program as we know it is a relatively recent invention. Beginning in the sixteenth century, playbills were sometimes distributed, often to the public at large, to provide information about a production. Actual programs handed out or sold to the audience before a show date back to the late nineteenth century. They vary widely in form and content from one country to another. Even over the past thirty years their function has changed constantly, and current examples are as diverse as theatres themselves.

Essentially, a program is intended to give the audience the names of the actors and director, and sometimes includes a synopsis of the play. The advertising inserts provide the theatre with additional income, if only to cover the printing costs of the program ... Who can resist those glossy programs with perfume ads and pictures of the stars in street dress, and all the fashionable ceremony of bourgeois theatre?

2. Programming the Gaze

The programs of national theatres or experimental groups have quite a different image to offer. They include remarks by the director or playwright and long quotations from critical or literary texts that are meant to throw light on the staging options. An entire discourse on the production is furnished in addition to the performance, including the text of the play, the production notes and a paraphrase of the stage work. However interesting such a critical apparatus may be, there is a great risk of over-directing the spectator's vision, and of expressing verbally what the audience should sense through the mise-en-scène alone. This can cause distortions and spoil the viewer's pleasure.

Should such things be read before the performance? Perception will be altered thereby, even impoverished, but it is also possible that without an accompanying text the audience may miss the point of the mise-en-scène. The quotations or texts provided may add up to an intertext that is crucial to an understanding of the production. Anyone who did not read the quote from Giscard d'Estaing that headed the program for La Salamandre's staging of *Britannicus* might not have grasped the ironic, mocking tone of the performance. This kind of program comes somewhere between the dramaturgical analysis and the mise-en-scène, and goes beyond the bounds of the dramatic text and its staging. The (generally excellent) programs of certain theatres, such as those of Bochum, Stuttgart, Strasburg or Berlin (Schaubühne), are so complete as to be veritable books on the play. Sometimes they are actually special editions of periodicals, and some theatres publish a house periodical containing a wealth of illustrations and commentaries on the performance. Some directors, conscious of the risk of accumulating too much material, only quote other texts by the same playwright or other texts that clarify their work intertextually and indicate the path taken by practitioners during rehearsal (e.g. VITEZ, LASSALLE, STEIN).

This discourse is always very revealing of a strategy, a hermeneutic desire or a self-image, but it should not be considered part of the staging discourse as received by the spectator and the product itself. The program is not a gospel. A playwright who, like Daniel BESNEHARD, claimed on paper "to respect the ambiguities of MARIVAUX," introduced a production (of Michel DUBOIS's *La Double Inconstance*) that was hardly finely-drawn. Having gone from invitation to information, then advertising, the program runs the risk of reverbalizing theatre, of distracting the spectator from his scopic drive and putting him back in the position of a reader who refuses to be taken in by the stage.

PROJECTION

Fr.: *projection;* Ger.: *Übertragung;* Sp.: *proyección.*

When we project texts, fixed images, films or videos on stage, we inject materials in the form of images into the living and present body of the performance. The result is a blurring of the system of representation, since body presence and media reproduction are diametrically opposed. Since the beginnings of cinema, excerpts from films have been projected on stage. The first instances of this happening, with a clearly dramaturgical function, are CLAUDEL's *Livre de Christophe Colomb* mounted in 1927 and the socially engaged productions of PISCATOR, BRECHT and NEHER during the 1920s. But in 1891 APPIA was already using the projected shadow of a cypress on an abstract set.

Projections perform all imaginable dramaturgical functions: providing ambiance, using words, pictures or illustrations to create distance; confronting the living with the imaginary; visualizing a detail of the acting filmed live, enlarged and shown on video screens; or simply a technological bluff that is somewhat naive (colour TV doesn't necessarily make something post-modern ...).

PROLOGUE

(From the Greek *prologos,* previous speech.)
Fr.: *prologue;* Ger.: *Prolog;* Sp.: *prólogo.*

A opening section that comes before the play as such (and is therefore distinct from the *exposition**) in which an actor, or sometimes the theatre manager or the producer, addresses the audience directly to welcome them, announce a few major themes and introduce the play, mentioning points considered necessary for comprehension. It functions as a "preface to the play" that speaks to the audience of something outside the plot, in the author's and the play's interests.

1. History of the Prologue

The prologue was originally the first part of the action before the first appearance of the chorus: "The Prologue is the whole section preceding the entrance song (Parodos) of the chorus" (ARISTOTLE's *Poetics,* section 1452b). It was then changed (by EURIPIDES) to a monologue expounding on the origins of the action. In the Middle Ages it was spoken by the *praecursor,* who was a master of ceremonies and director in advance. Classical French and German theatre used the prologue to secure the favours of the monarch or to give a few hints about the mission of art or theatre (for example, MOLIÈRE in *L'Impromptu de Versailles*). As soon as the performance was presented as a realistic portrayal of a believable event the prologue began to disappear, as it was felt to detract from the theatrical fiction. It resurfaced with expressionist (WEDEKIND) and epic theatre (BRECHT). Current experimental theatre is particularly fond of using the prologue in its "illusion-less" productions as a means of modalizing "embedded" narratives.

2. Functions

The following is a non-exhaustive list of a few structural principles common to all prologues:

A. INTEGRATION WITH THE PLAY

The prologue is an integral part of the play, as its vanguard and presentation, or else a separate show, a kind of *interlude** or *curtain raiser**.

B. CHANGES IN PERSPECTIVE

The audience, having been briefed by the announcer, experiences the dramatic action on two levels; following the thread of the *fabula*, "skimming through" and anticipating the action; it is both in and above the play and, thanks to the change in perspective, identifies itself and takes the step backwards that is sometimes necessary. When the prologue announces how the action will end, the technique is said to be *analytical**. In this case, everything flows from the final proposition announced at the beginning, and the play is the reconstruction of a past *episode**.

C. INTERMEDIARY DISCOURSE

The prologue ensures a smooth transition from the social reality in the house to the fiction on stage. It introduces the spectator to the play gradually, either by authenticating the fictional world to be presented or by introducing the play in stages. Accordingly, its fiction is sometimes believable, sometimes playful (cf. the dialogues between director, author and actor in the "Prologue in Heaven" of GOETHE's *Faust*). It is a way of erasing the boundaries of the work of art and commenting ironically on its manufacture (*frame**).

D. MODALIZATION

The prologue sets the tone of the play by analogy or by contrast. It presents the various levels of text or performance, manipulates the spectator through direct influence, by proposing a fairly clear model for reception. As currently used, it contains an entire discourse on the group, its style, its commitment, the state of its finances, etc. The prologue is essentially a mixed discourse (reality/fiction, description/action, serious/playful, etc.). It always acts as a metalanguage, a critical instance *before* and *within* the performance.

See also: epilogue, exposition, discourse, address to the audience, chorus.

Further reading: *Enciclopedia dello spettacolo* (entry on "prologo"), 1954.

PROMPTER

Fr.: *souffleur*; Ger.: *Souffleur*; Sp.: *apuntador*.

The function of the prompter, instituted in the eighteenth century, is in the process of disappearing and exists as an institution only in the Comédie Française, perhaps because the system of alternating speeches and scenes played Italian style has been abandoned. The prompter helps actors in difficlty by whispering, articulating well but not shouting, from the wings or from a prompt box concealed with a little hood in the center front of the stage. He provides the word or, if the actor has muddled the sentence, the following sentence, taking care not to confuse variable pauses with memory lapses. A good prompter, just by observing the actors, can anticipate a mistake or problem and intervene at the right moment.

PROPERTIES

Fr.: *accessoires*; Ger.: *Requisiten*; Sp.: utillería.

Stage *objects** (not including *scenery** and *costumes**) used or handled by the actors in the course of the play. Very numerous in naturalistic theatre, which reconstructs a milieu down to the last detail, today they are used less to characterize and more as theatre machines or abstract *objects**. They may also become objectified metaphors for the invasion of the external world in the life of the individual, as in the theatre of the absurd (particularly IONESCO). They become characters in their own right and ultimately take over the stage.

See also: space, stage boards.

Further reading: Veltruský 1964, Bogatyrev 1971; Hoppe 1971; Saison 1974; Harris and Montgomery 1975; Adam 1976, 23–27; Ubersfeld 1978a; Pavis 1996a, 158–181.

PROSODY

(From the Greek *prosodia*, accent and quality of pronunciation.)

Fr.: *prosodie*; Ger.: *Prosodie*; Sp.: *prosodia*.

Vocalic accent in the diction of a line and the rhythmic structure used to enhance the text, rules on number of syllables, particularly alternating short and long ones, based on the metrics of the line. In linguistics, prosody is "the study of those phonic features which, in the various languages, affect sequences whose boundaries do not correspond to the division of the spoken flow into phonemes" (DUBOIS 1973, 398). The idea is to grasp phenomena that escape the phonemic framework, that are located beyond the phonemic structure, particularly the dynamic and tonic accent, the duration, level and timbre of sound.

The prosodic quality of the dramatic text depends on the melodic design perceptible upon reading it; i.e. on versification and metric constraints, but also on the way the actor uses his presence and body to give the lines rhythm, make them breathe, accompany them with gestures, stress or conceal parts of the text, bring out alliterations, echos and repetitions and a whole rhetoric of *declamation**. For the production, particularly that of a classical play in verse, the actor must try out the prosody and possible rhythms. To place the sounds is to establish the meanings the spectator will receive. *Diction** and *gestuality** are closely linked by the *rhythmic** structure, by the way in which verbal and gestural material is given form.

PROTAGONIST

(From the Greek *prôtos*, meaning first, and *agonizesthai*, to fight.)

Fr.: *protagoniste;* Ger.: *Protagonist;* Sp.: *protagonista.*

In Greek theatre, the protagonist was the actor playing the leading role. The actor playing the second role was called the deuteragonist, the actor playing the third role the tritagonist. In order of historical appearance were the chorus, then the protagonist (in THEPSIS), the deuteragonist (in AESCHYLUS), and the tritagonist (in SOPHOCLES) (*antagonist**).

In current usage, the term is used to mean the main characters of a play, who are at the heart of the *action** and the *conflicts**.

PROTASIS

Fr.: *protase;* Ger.: *Protasis;* Sp.: *prótasis.*
See EXPOSITION

PROXEMICS

Fr.: *proxémique;* Ger.: *Proxemik;* Sp.: *proxémica.*

1. A Measure of Space

A recent discipline of American origin (HALL 1959, 1966), proxemics studies the organization of human space: types of space, distances observed between people, organization of the habitat, organization of space in a building or room. HALL distinguishes between the following kinds of space: 1) fixed-feature or architectural space; 2) semi-fixed-feature space, or arrangement of objects in a place; 3) informal or interpersonal space. Relationships between individuals are defined in four major categories: intimate (under 50 cm), personal (50 cm to 1.50 m), social-consultative (1.50 to 3.50 m), public (as far as the voice will carry).

HALL proposes considering the proxemic behaviour of individuals according to the following eight variants:

1. Overall body attitude (based on gender);
2. Angle of orientation of partners;
3. Body distance defined by arms, etc.;
4. Body contact, by form and intensity;
5. Eye behaviour;
6. Sensation of warmth;
7. Olfactory perception;
8. Voice intensity.

2. Proxemics in Theatre

When applied to theatre, these categories would enable us to observe the kind of space (fixed/moveable) chosen by the mise-en-scène and how it codifies distances in terms of space between actants, between actors and objects or between stage and audience. As mimesis of social interaction, theatre reproduces these spatial laws, and any change in codes is significant. Rather than observing the spaces reproduced on stage, proxemics would be able to assess the (psychological/symbolic, and not purely geometrical) distance separating the stage from the audience, the way the mise-en-scène chooses to bring them together or pull them apart, and for what aesthetic and ideological reasons. We would see how gesture, voice and lighting can modulate this distance or create effects of meaning.

Theatrical mise-en-scène chooses a certain kind of spatial relationship between the characters/actors, according to their psychology, social status, gender, etc. Every stage aesthetics has its own implicit proxemic code, and the way it is visualized on the basis of spatial and rhythmic relationships between the actors has a bearing on the reading of the text (its *enunciation**) and its reception. The same playwright may thus be re-situated *proxemically* by several productions, as in the productions of RACINE's plays by A.VITEZ, M.HERMON, J.C.FALL and GRÜBER, each of whom invented a strict code of distances and movements. Theatre brings together on the stage people who would "normally" not meet, iconizing and showing their social relationships tangibly in the way they look at each other, listen and speak to each other, repel and manipulate each other. Their paths and trajectories are inscribed on the stage space. Sometimes the director uses this means to convey their private, social or unconscious itinerary. Their trajectory, their intentions, are inscribed on stage like a design, like a *score** that they are the only ones to write and decode properly. The path taken by a character (VITEZ) is inscribed in his movements and the design he traces on the ground.

3. Program for a Proxemics

By combining the methodology of proxemics with studies on *rhythm** and *stage enunciation**, we could propose the following program:

A. Measure and describe distances between speakers, trace their movements, evaluate their rhythms.

B. Note overlapping of spaces in which the actor moves (*space**, *questionnaire**).

C. Formalize situation of enunciation (gaze, distance, modality of speech, nonverbal communication, intonation, inscription of discourse on space and of space on discourse).

D. Effect a comparison of *parcours** of actor and spectator.

E. Analyze architecture of actor's *gaze** and *body*, production of overall stage enunciation based on individual enunciations of the various signifying systems, of what BRECHT called the *gestus of delivery*.

F. Examine how voice fits into space and its relationship with spectators (based on the places of actor and spectator within the stage space).

Further reading: *Langages*, 1968; K. Scherer 1970; Schechner 1973a, 1977; Cosnier 1977; Pavis 1981a; Sarrazac et al. 1981.

PSYCHOANALYSIS

Fr.: *psychanalyse*; Ger.: *Psychoanalyse*; Sp.: psicoan*álisis*.

See FANTASY

PSYCHODRAMA

Fr.: *psychodrame*; Ger.: *Psychodrama*; Sp.: *psicodrama*.

Technique developed by J.-L. MORENO (1892–1974) in the 1920s, based on theatrical improvisation (*Psychodrama Monographs*, 1944–1954). As a psychiatrist in Vienna, until 1925, and then in the United States, MORENO studied emotional relationships and group dynamics and created impromptu theatre (*Stegreiftheater*) in which each actor improvises a role. This attempt at theatre reform led him to discover psychodrama, "a science that explores truth through dramatic methods." Psychodrama is a psychological and psychoanalytical technique that seeks to analyze inner conflicts by having several protagonists act out an improvised scenario with a few instructions. The hypothesis is that it is in action and play, rather than in words, that repressed conflicts, problems with interpersonal relationships and errors in judgment are likely to be revealed most clearly.

Above all, psychodrama enables children to relive conflicts by giving them the opportunity to work with a team of two or three therapists and act out a play, assigning roles and improvising a story (cf. D. ANZIEU, *le Psychodrame affectif chez l'enfant*).

As a therapeutic technique, psychodrama differs from Aristotelian *catharsis** as well as from the psychological play or ARTAUD's *theatre of cruelty**. It does not have to imitate an action; the less mimetic a human relationship, the more authentic.

See also: dramatic play, identification, mimesis.

Further reading: Ancelin-Schützenberger 1970; Flashar 1974; Boal 1979, 1990.

PUBLIC, AUDIENCE

Fr.: *public*; Ger.: *Publikum*; Sp.: *público*.

See SPECTATOR, RECEPTION

PUBLIC READING

Fr.: *Lecture-spectacle*; Ger.: *Leseaufführung*; Sp.: *Lectura-espectáculo*.

As an intermediary genre between the reading of a text by one or more actors and the run-through or staging of a text, the public reading uses both methods in turn. Lucien ATTOUN employed this formula at his Théâtre Ouvert in Avignon and Paris and at *France-Culture*, bringing unpublished or unperformed texts to the attention of a small audience and actors who might wish to perform them in more "theatrical" conditions. We can distinguish between different types of public readings:

- A staged reading (*mise-en-espace*) is the "presentation of a new play [...] without sets or costumes" (*Europe*, 1983, 648:24).
- A voice reading (*mise-en-voix*) is the process during which the actors learn the text, especially at the beginning of rehearsals, before intonation, phrasing and blocking have been finalized.

PUPPET

Fr.: *marionnette*; Ger.: *Marionette*; Sp.: *marioneta*.

There is an old love-hate relationship between actor and puppet. Whenever the actor seeks perfection and difficulty in gesture, the metaphor of the disjointed puppet comes to his mind, the puppet that can be manipulated at will and responds to its handler's every command in gesture and voice. DIDEROT, in his *Paradoxe du comédien*, already saw the "great actor" as "another marvellous puppet whose strings are held by the poet and to whom he tells at every turn what form it should take" (1994, 1035). This conception of the human being as a puppet culminates in Gordon CRAIG's *Übermarionette*. It is because the actor cannot make a "work of art" of his body, but only "a series of accidental confessions," that CRAIG would like to replace him with a human puppet that would control all emotions and turn the stage into a purely symbolical place: "Do away with the actor, and you do away with the means by which a debased stage realism is produced and flourishes. No longer would there be a living figure to confuse us into connecting actuality and art; no longer a living figure in which the weakness and tremors of the flesh were perceptible" (1911, 66; Eng. in Cole and Chinoy, 1970, 383). Other utopias contemplate the same kind of remote control of human flesh with the mask, a special acting voice as if, according to A. JARRY, "the mask's mouth cavity could utter only what the mask would say if its lip muscles could move" (1962, 143); the actor's *biomechanical** body which, according to MEYERHOLD, should be a material "that is capable of executing instantaneously those tasks which are dictated externally (by the actor, the director)"; the mechanical ballet of SCHLEMMER in which it is possible "by making man wear constructed costumes, to effect every imaginable configuration, with unlimited variations" (1978, 67).

All these utopic experiments share a fascination with machinery, whether stage, gesture or voice. By repeating the same movement at will, the machine in effect breaks the strict rule of the uniqueness of theatre performance, of the uncodability of the human being, of the absolute extremist power of the actor. Machinery also means inertia, control, theatricality confident of its effects; it is the perverse outcome of a conception of theatre based on the absolute control of the director (the maker of signs) of the ceremony of the spectacle. It is no longer just the actor's emotions and body that are codified and reified; it is the performance as a whole. But such absolute power is hardly possible; at some point in the chain a human being must intervene to coordinate the machinery and to receive it as a spectator. Then the puppet becomes animate once again and makes mistakes, and it can all begin again. It has been said of semiology, not entirely without guile, that it necessarily leads to a "marionettization" of theatre performance, a "semaphorization" of actors, making mechanical the living reality of the performance. This is a very real danger indeed, but as long as the actors and spectators are seen as producers and receivers theory escapes this "marionettization," and the actor becomes the emblematic figure of the *grace* that KLEIST spoke of in connection with puppet theatre (1810), the grace of the animate and the inanimate, of knowledge and innocence, of the jointed puppet and the god.

Further reading: Kleist 1978; Bensky 1971; Dort in *Théâtre/Public*, no. 43, 1982; Fournel 1982; Plassard 1992; *Puck* magazine published by Institut International de la Marionnette.

PURE THEATRE

Fr.: *théâtre pur*; Ger.: *reines Theater*; Sp.: *teatro puro*.
See THEATRICALITY

Q

QUESTIONNAIRE

Fr.: *questionnaire;* Ger.: *Fragebogen;* Sp.: *cuestionario.*

Questionnaires are often used to survey the audience, but their methods, objectives and results vary considerably.

1. Sociological Questionnaires

The purpose of such questionnaires is to acquire knowledge about the audience's make-up, social and occupational origins, and ideological and cultural baggage. A. BOURASSA, in his survey on the social function of theatre (a study carried out at the Université de Québec), distributed a questionnaire to the audience before the performance. It begins with general questions about education, income and mother tongue, then seeks to determine theatre-going habits: frequency of attendance, knowledge of the troupe and the production in question; opinions on the program, the actors, the welcome received and various kinds of cultural activity. This information provides a fairly accurate image of the audience of a particular theatre or town.

2. Psychological and Ideological Questionnaires

Such questionnaires measure the perception of stage space, emotions felt by the audience during the performance, and spectator evaluations of the characters (cf. TAN and SCHOENMAKERS in KESTEREN and SCHMID 1984; TINDEMANNS in FISCHER-LICHTE 1985).

3. "Socio-Aesthetic" Questionnaires

These may be multiple-choice or open-answer questionnaires, or may be done in the form of more or less prepared interviews, sometimes videotaped. Often, as for Anne-Marie GOURDON, the idea is "to let the members of the audience speak in order to determine their motivations, aspirations and opinions concerning the theatrical phenomenon [...], to analyze the audience's reactions to particular productions and to obtain information to round out our knowledge about how theatre is created" (1982, 9). Revelations about how the production is deciphered are few, as the questions and statistical analysis elminate extraneous detail in responses. This approach lacks a hermeneutic and semiological theory of *reception**, but the image it gives of the contemporary audience is quite instructive.

4. Ideological-Aesthetic Questionnaires

These are drawn up on the basis of a particular production, and are meant to reconstruct the way in which spectators build meaning. The recognition of the nature of theatrical language and the sign systems used often obliges researchers to ask very general multiple-choice questions, without entering into the details of performance levels and non-verbal elements (e.g. AVIGAL and WEITZ 1985). It may be concluded that the audience, in this case an Israeli one, perceives only a limited number of the signs and that this quantitative limitation influences the quality of perception and interpretation. In particular, it is clear that the spectators see precisely what they wish to see in the play, as grist for their own political mills, so to speak.

5. Other Questionnaires
Other formulas may be used as well, whether quantitative or based on discourse. Here again, a prior knowledge of the audience would seem to be indispensable in order to draw up the most appropriate questionnaire. By way of example, below is one used in analyzing productions with students:

1. General features of the production

a. What holds the elements of the performance together? (relationships between stage systems)
b. Coherence or incoherence of the mise-en-scène: what is it founded on?
c. Where does the production stand within the cultural and aesthetic context?
d. What bothers you about this production: what are its strong, weak or boring moments? How does it measure up with other current productions?

2. Stage design

a. Forms of urban, architectural, stage, gestural space
b. Relationship between audience space and acting space
c. Principles of organization of space:
1. Dramaturgical function of stage space and its use
2. Relationship between what is on stage and what is off stage
3. Connection between space used and fiction of play staged
4. Relationship between what is shown and what is hidden
5. How does the stage design evolve, and what prompts the changes?

d. System of colours, forms and materials, and their connotations

3. Lighting system

Nature: its links to fiction, performance, actors
Effects on performance reception

4. Props

Nature, function, materials, relationship with space and body; system governing their use

5. Costumes, make-up, masks

Function, system, relationship to space and body, system governing their use

6. Actors' performances:

a. Physical description of actors (gestures, facial expressions, make-up); changes in their appearance
b. Presumed kinesthetics of actors, kinesthetics induced in observers
c. Building of character; actor/role
d. Actor's relationship with group: movements, links to whole, trajectory
e. Text/body relationships
f. Voice: quality, effect on hearer, relationship to diction and singing
g. Actor's status: past, status in the profession, etc.

7. Function of music, sound, silence
a. Nature and characteristics; relationship to *fabula*, to diction
b. When does it occur, and what effect does it have on the rest of the performance?

8. Rhythm and pace
a. Rhythm of signifying systems (exchange of dialogues, lighting, costumes, gestuality); relationship between actual duration and experienced duration
b. Overall rhythm of performance: continuous or discontinuous rhythm, changes, connections to mise-en-scène

9. Reading of the story (fabula) by this production
a. What story is being told? Summarize it. Does the staging tell the same story as the text?
b. What are the dramaturgical choices? Is the reading coherent or incoherent?
c. What ambiguities are there in the text, and how does the staging clarify them?
d. How is the *fabula* structured?
e. How is the story constructed by the actor and the performance?
f. What genre of dramatic text is this, according to this production?
g. Other possible staging options

10. Text in performance
a. Choices of stage version: what changes are made?
b. Characteristics of translation (if applicable): is it a translation, adaptation, rewriting, or recreation?
c. What place does the staging give to the dramatic text?
d. Relationship between text and image, between eye and ear

11. Spectator:
a. Within what theatrical institution does the production take place?
b. What were your expectations of the performance (text, director, actors)?
c. What are the prerequisites for appreciating this performance?
d. How did the audience react?
e. Spectator's role in the production of meaning: is there only one or several suggested readings?
f. What images, scenes, themes have you retained?
g. How is the spectator's attention manipulated by the staging?

12. How to record (photograph or film) this show
How to retain it in memory (what escapes recording)

13. What cannot be semiotized (i.e. rendered into signs):
a. What, in your reading of the staging, makes no sense?
b. What cannot be reduced to sign and sense (and why)?

14. Overall assessment
a. What special problems should be looked at?
b. Any other comments on this production or the questionnaire?

QUIPROQUO

(From the Latin *qui pro quo*, to take something for something else.)

Fr.: *quiproquo*; Ger.: *Verwechslung*; Sp.: *quiproquo*.

See MISTAKEN IDENTITY

QUOTATION

Fr.: *citation*; Ger.: *Zitat*; Sp.: *cita*.

1. In Dramaturgy

Quotations are normally inadmissible in plays, at least in the dramatic form of illusionist theatre. The actor plays his role to convey the impression that he is inventing his text as he speaks it; he does not quote the written text. The playwright gives the impression that he has extracted a fragment of reality, a milieu and words, and allows them to speak for themselves. The only apparent exception that classical dramaturgy would tolerate is the quotation of *maxims**, *authorial interventions** or general reflections attributed to a character. This gives the playwright the chance to express brilliant formulas or to raise the debate to a more general level. But this does not abolish the convention that the speech originates with the character.

On the contrary, epic dramaturgy shows the origins of the words and the process by which they have been formed by a playwright and actors. It is then clearly apparent that the performance is only a narrative, a quotation within the theatrical apparatus. To quote is to extract a piece of text and graft it onto a foreign tissue. The quotation is connected to both its former context and the new "host" text. The "friction" between these two discourses produces an effect of *estrangement**. The same holds true of "quotational" dramaturgy. We may conclude that:

1. The "host" text is the stage machinery, the actors, the playwright's composition;
2. The quote is the text to be spoken by the actors, the gestures adapted to the character and the *story** to be presented. The division between quoted and quoting is never masked for the sake of illusion. To quote is to take one's distance.

2. In Acting

An actor tags his text as a quotation mainly by gesture: "...the actor speaks his part not as if he were improvising it himself but like a quotation." (BRECHT, 1957:138). The quote is always achieved by a breaking-up effect, an interruption of the verbal and gestural flow, a destruction of the *coherence** of text and fiction.

In doing this, the actor quotes the character as he might exist in several versions or such as he, the actor, would play him if he were making theatre: "He narrates the story of his character by vivid portrayal, always knowing more than it does and treating its 'now' and 'here' not as a pretence made possible by the rules of the game but as something to be distinguished from yesterday and some other place, so as to make visible the knotting-together of the events." (BRECHT, *A Short Organum for the Theatre*, sect. 50).

3. In the Mise-en-scène

The quoting instance is the director, who proceeds by allusion (sometimes but not always decodable by all) to other productions, different styles, paintings (PLANCHON in *Tartuffe*, STREHLER in *Il Campiello*, GRÜBER in *Empedokles, Hölderlin lesen*). The quote (when it is not merely a game or a kind of namedropping), sets up a connection between the play and a different world and throws a new, often distanced light on it. It opens up a vast semantic field and *modalizes** the text in which it is introduced. It may produce a kind of mirroring effect if the play refers constantly to other meanings.

See also: parody, intertextuality.

Further reading: Brecht 1963; Benjamin 1969; Compagnon 1979.

R

RADIO AND THEATRE

Fr.: *radio et théâtre;* Ger.: *Rundfunk und Theater;* Sp.: *radio y teatro.*

1. Promises and Disappointments

A. Radio theatre, like television drama, depends on the development of recording and broadcasting technology as well as on the institutions backing and ensuring its dissemination. Though it was received enthusiastically in the 1920s by writers like BRECHT, DÖBLIN and COPEAU as an art of the future and of the masses, radio theatre does not appear to have lived up to its promises. The fault lies not in a lack of creativity on the part of the authors writing for it (though the tradition only really took hold in England and Germany, and to a lesser extent in France), but in the situation of production and reception, which does not favour radio. Competition from television, which is, in a way, radio in colour; the commercialization of radio and partial end to the state monopoly in France; the incessant and pointless debate about the legitimacy of radio free from government control; a cultural industry that promotes only standardized mass music; the changing tastes of a public mesmerized by television and video images – none of these factors has been favourable to the birth of a strong tradition in radio drama.

B. Nevertheless, radio theatre is a new creative sector, and potentially represents an important field of drama in general, particularly radio plays, a specific kind of creation that is more than just a recording or copy of theatrical performance. This has been understood in countries like Great Britain, where the BBC, often thought to be the best radio in the world, produces one thousand radio plays every year, brings dozens of writers to the public's attention, and pursues a policy of commissioning work, initiating dialogue, and even training authors for radio. In many cases radio has made a name for playwrights and broadcast their plays even before they were staged.

C. At the heart of this new genre (in which ultra-sophisticated experiments in electronic acoustics are currently taking place) is the desire to make literary texts heard; it is the art of reading with radiogenic voices. During the 1920s and 1930s, producers frequently called on poets (ARAGON, DESNOS, TARDIEU, ÉLUARD) to read or to write texts for radio. In Germany, the *Hörspiel* (audio play) has attracted authors like BRECHT, DÖBLIN, BACHMANN, BÖLL, DÜRRENMATT, GRASS, HEISSENBÜTTEL and HANDKE.

D. For a long time radio theatre did not see itself as an autonomous genre but as theatre freed from the contingencies of stage performance. That is the attitude of very literary theatre people such as Jacques COPEAU: "Released from the burden of memory, as he keeps the text in view; liberated from stage fright, as he works in isolation; dependent only on himself and his own inspiration, as the audience's reactions do not reach him; protected from those material accidents of set, costume and props that often dispossess an actor on stage; finally reduced to healthy nudity, purified by that tête-à-tête with the text that can only nourish his intelligence and sensitivity, condemned moreover to an immobility that should ensure his intense concentration, the proof of his sincerity dependent finally on a single instrument, his voice, the actor at the microphone, provided he has prepared intensively and with an appropriate number of rehearsals, should find his conditions ideal" ("Remarques sur la radio," in 1955, 57).

It is not by comparison with "real theatre" that the radio play is likely to become a new genre, however, but by concentrating on its own specific qualities, by not aping theatre. Halfway between the physical presence of theatre and the symbolic space of the novel, radio drama hesitates to formulate its own strategies.

2. Search for Specificity

A. THE WORD

The hearer is rarely concentrating only on listening to the play. The transistor has taken radio theatre to many new places. Radio rediscovers an intimate, almost religious source of the word, taking us back to an Eden-like state of exclusively oral literature. Without being so confined to his place as in television drama, the radio listener is in a daydream-like state. He can keep up an interior monologue through the radio. He is dematerialized and receives the amplified echo of his daydreams and drives.

B. FICTION

The radio play is tied to a fiction, even though the audience may not always perceive this to be so (cf. O. WELLES and his radio broadcast that unleashed panic in 1938). Unlike television reporting, newscasts and talkshows, radio fiction brings in voices that play characters and create an iaginary world. It gradually frees itself from journalism, linear information, dialogue, and realistic situations and voices.

C. STUDIO PRODUCTION

Unlike the stage, the studio is an intangible place not seen by the audience that provides support for the production of sound, voice montage and synchronization, sound effects and music. The listener has the impression that the sound performance is being made and transmitted as he hears it.

D. TYPES OF RADIO PLAY

1. Live broadcast from the theatre: In the early days of radio, plays were sometimes broadcast live from Parisian theatres. Sets and stage business were described by a commentator. Even today there are live broadcasts from the Comédie-Française. Neither theatre nor radio, such a broadcast is closer to documentary than original work.
2. Dramatized studio reading.
3. Dramatic radio play with the voices of recognizable characters, dialogues and conflicts, just as we would find them in a naturalistic play.
4. Epic radio play, dramatizing a character or voice.
5. Interior monologue.
6. Collage of voices, sounds, music.
7. Electronic simulation of human voice by synthesizer, musical work with voices and sounds.

3. Dramaturgy

A. CHARACTER

The character exists only in its voice, which must be very specific and distinguishable from those of the other characters. A good radio voice is unusual, inimitable. The voices of the various characters must be quite distinct, chosen according to the speaker's characteristic features. Casting is a fundamental element of broadcasting.

B. TIME AND PLACE

These are suggested by changes in voice intensity, echoes and distance effects. A sound "frame" is created by a sound or piece of music that opens and closes the sequence, establishing the stage and removing it at the end of the sequence – a kind of shooting and framing device. The location of the microphones, volume control, and a sequence of characteristic sounds creates an orientation in time and space that is easily identified by the listener. Raising or lowering the volume, or having the actor speak closer to or further from the microphone, signals a change of frame or a movement with a single frame.

A series of "shifters," or musical or sound leitmotifs between the squences help us identify the speakers and spot the various locations or temporalities. Often the editing erases the different time frames, composes an interior monologue, produces an effect of physical interiority through the interplay of rhythms, repetitions, almost musical variations, effecting exchanges between the visible and the audible. The pleasure in this perception lies in the hallucination of the listener who hears all and sees nothing. The actors' rendition of the text and its broadcast give the listener the impression that the scene was actually performed on another stage: one has the feeling both of seeing nothing and of seeing the scene performed in the "mind's eye."

More than any other, this is an art of metonymy, of convention and significant abstraction. It is up to the author to give the listeners the reference points they need to give the narrative a certain coherence and organize the fictional universe without any apparent effort of memory.

When the electronic and acoustical elements are used in addition to the strict rules of dramaturgy, the result is a very powerful and original play, proof that radio literature is an established and promising genre.

RAISONNEUR

Fr.: *raisonneur;* Ger.: *Raisonneur, Räsoneur;* Sp.: *raisonneur.*

Character representing the proper line of reasoning or morality, whose commentary is intended to give an "objective" or "authorial" view of the situation. It is never one of the main characters, but rather a neutral figure on the sidelines who gives informed advice and tries to synthesize or reconcile different points of view. The raisonneur is often considered to be the author's *mouthpiece**, but we should be aware of the playwright's deceptive manoeuvres in feeling it neccessary to reassure the audience that his intentions are pure. (For instance, the character Cléante in *Tartuffe* is meant to reassure true believers and praise a balanced religious attitude.) Sometimes the raisonneur gives only a superficial commentary on the action, and the overall *point of view** of the author or the play is to be found elsewhere, in the dialectics of each character's speeches. This type of character, heir to the *chorus** of Greek tragedy, is seen mainly in the classical period, in thesis drama and in *didactic theatre**. It appears – or resurfaces in a parodic form – in contemporary theatre, where it is simply a discursive manoeuvre that represents neither the playwright nor good sense nor the synthesis of various points of view; a norm the playwright can mock while at the same time keeping up appearances.

READABILITY

Fr.: *lisibilité;* Ger.: *Lesbarkeit;* Sp.: *legibilidad.*

Degree to which the performance can be read (i.e. deciphered). A performance is readable when the mise-en-scène allows the spectator to recognize certain signs, follow the narrative progression, understand how the various systems are organized and draw overall meanings from the whole. Some directors try to highlight the *fabula**, its logic and its contradictions *(historicized** readings of Brechtian influence). Others like to ensure that the associations of ideas and images produce a meaning that can be easily grasped. Still others try for a reading of the unconscious mechanisms of acting, of a performance or textual rhetoric that does not realize it is saying so much.

The notion of readability also depends largely on the spectator's *expectations** and ability to play with the signs offered and construct the meaning in a *linear* fashion (according to the logic of the narrative) and *visually* (according to the rhetoric of the images).

See also: reading, reception, semiology, performance text.

READING

Fr.: *lecture*; Ger.: *Lektüre*; Sp.: *lectura*.

To read the performance, in a metaphorical sense, is to decipher and interpret the various *stage systems** (including the *dramatic text**) offered to spectator perception (MOLINARI and OTTOLENGHI 1979). Critics today use the expression "to read theatre" (cf. UBERSFELD 1977a) in the sense of looking for all possible units of text and stage image, in order to "determine the reading modes that will enable us not only to clarify a very particular textual practice but also to show, if possible, how this textual practice is connected to another practice, that of performance" (1977a:8).

1. "Reading" the Text

To *read* a dramatic text is not simply to follow a text literally, as one reads a poem, a novel or a newspaper article, i.e. by fictionalizing or creating a fictional universe (or a possible world). The reading of a dramatic text presupposes a whole imaginary process that contextualizes the enunciators. Which characters? In what place or time? In what tone? These questions are all essential to an understanding of the characters' speeches. In addition, such a reading is inevitably accompanied by a *dramaturgical** analysis, which clarifies dramatic construction, the presentation of the *fabula** and the emergence and resolution of *conflicts**. Any reading takes place in the prospect of placing these dynamic elements of the drama in space, of bringing out the through-line of the action. This type of approach to text and performance through dramaturgy ties up with what has been called "horizontal reading" (DEMARCY, 1973).

2. Horizontal Reading, Vertical Reading

A. Horizontal (or syntagmatic) reading occurs within the fiction. It follows the action and the *fabula*, obeys the connections between episodes and concerns itself with the narrative logic and the final outcome of the *fabula*. Of the stage materials, it uses only those which are integrated into the narrative scheme and maintain the performance in the illusion of an inevitable progression.

B. Vertical (or paradigmatic) reading favours breaks in the flow of events and concentrates on stage signs and the paradigmatic equivalents of the themes they evoke by association. The "reader" is no longer interested in the series of events, but rather in the way they are arranged (*epic**). His constant concern is to have "his critical judgment inter-vene" (BRECHT).

Both kinds of reading, linear and paradigmatic, are essential to a proper decoding that reconstructs "plastically" (vertically) what it apprehends linearly (in the *fabula**). The appropriate reading mode is, however, strongly suggested by the dramaturgy and the corresponding attitude of *reception**. Horizontal reading, for instance, lends itself to identification and the abdication of critical judgment; vertical reading, on the other hand, keeps all "senses" alert and favours taking a certain distance (*alienation**).

Strictly speaking, the notion of *reading* should be reserved for the dramatic text, since theatre is read very differently from a linguistic text, through exposure to all the non-verbal languages (gesture, music, scene design, rhythm) that go beyond language to confront the spectator with a stage event rather than a text made of linguistic signs (LYOTARD 1971).

3. Slow Reading, Reading at Normal Speed

VINAVER and his colleagues (1993) distinguish between two kinds of reading. "A slowed-down reading" of a passage is "done by stopping at each line and beginning with the question 'What is the starting point'? Having defined this, along the way one picks up: (a) events, (b) information, (c) themes [...] in such a way as to isolate, in the text, what is action per se" (1993, 896). During "a reading at normal speed' of the whole play, "one verifies, completes, adjusts and corrects, if necessary, the results of the analysis of the passage" (898). We would suggest, contrary to VINAVER, not waiting until the end of such readings to take into account historical, socioeconomic or cultural information, which determine the way we read from the outset.

See also: communication, code, interpretation, semiology, text and performance.

Further reading: Ingarden 1931, 1971; Eco 1980, 1989; Iser 1972; Hogendoorn 1976; Charles 1977; Collet et al. 1977; Biagini 1979; Pavis 1980c, 1983a; Barthes 1984, 33–47; Avigal and Weitz 1985; Schoenmakers 1990.

REALISTIC PERFORMANCE

Fr.: *représentation réaliste;* Ger.: *realistischer Aufführungsstil;* Sp.: *representación realista.*

1. Points of Reference

Realism is an aesthetic movement that emerged between 1830 and 1880. It is also a technique to give an objective account of human psychological and social reality.

The word *realism* appeared in 1826 in the *Mercure français* in connection with an aesthetic that rejected classicism, Romanticism and art for art's sake and advocated a faithful imitation of "nature." In painting, COURBET grouped several of his canvases at an exhibition in a room entitled "On Realism." In literature, the realist movement includes novelists concerned with giving an accurate representation of society, such as STENDHAL, BALZAC, CHAMPFLEURY, DUMAS and the GONCOURTs. In all arts that portray man or society, realistic representation seeks to convey an image of its subject that is judged to be appropriate, without idealizing or interpreting reality subjectively or incompletely. Realistic art presents iconic signs of the reality that inspires it.

2. Imitative Realism, Illusionism, Naturalism

Realism in theatre is not always clearly distinguished from *illusion**, *naturalism** or *representationalism*. These labels indicate a shared desire to represent and imitate reality on stage as faithfully as possible. The stage *milieu** is a deceitful reconstruction of reality. Dialogues are drawn from the speech patterns of a period or of a social or occupational category. The acting makes the text appear natural, downplaying literary and rhetorical effects, by stressing its spontaneous and psychological aspects. So, paradoxically, to be real and true one must know how to handle artifice: "To look real is to give a complete illusion of the real [...] I conclude from this that talented realists should actually be called illusionists" (MAUPASSANT).

Often, however, naturalism does not go beyond realism because of its belief in scientificity and determinism (*milieu**). The reality described appears to be unchangeable, like an essence that is eternally hostile to man: "Naturalists show human beings as if they were showing a tree to a passerby. Realists show human beings as one shows a tree to a gardener" (BRECHT 1967, 16:797).

The literary theory that society is reflected in the work of art, as espoused by LUKÁCS, for instance, is quite unsatisfactory. History is not "deposited" directly in the work. It is illusory to expect to find, in a realistic work, a description of reality in "its diverse, agitated and changing totality." As for the intention to present a type that brings together the concrete elements and the law that governs them, what is in the domain of the "eternally human" and what is historically determined, that is a criterion of realism that is also very narrow and difficult to apply (LUKÁCS 1965, 98–153).

3. Critical Realism

Unlike naturalism, realism is not content to produce appearances and a copy of reality. Its intention is not to make reality and its representation coincide, but to give an image of the *fabula* and the stage through which the spectators can understand the social mechanisms of reality, thanks to their symbolic and play activity. This is very similar to the Brechtian approach, which is not confined to a particular aesthetic but creates a critical method of analyzing reality and the stage, based on the Marxist theory of knowledge. This method is quite relevant to current experiments in realistic performance, and should be outlined here in the context of its aesthetic and ideological system.

A. EXPRESS/SIGNIFY

The stage does not need to "ex-press," to externalize a reality that is first contained in an idea; it does not give us a photographic reproduction or the quintessence of reality. The stage "signifies" the world by offering up its relevant signs and moving away from a mechanical reproduction of "nature." This staging of the stage ensures the proper distance between signifier (the stage material used) and signified (the message to convey).

Accordingly, a realistic reproduction will not necessarily use a tangible property of the object imitated; it will simply ensure that the spectator is capable of identifying it: "The sign should be partly arbitrary, otherwise we fall into an art of expression, an art of essentialist illusion" (BARTHES 1963, 55).

B. MODELLING* REALITY

To signify reality is a means of proposing a *model** of coherent functioning; to clarify the causality of social phenomena, identify the fundamental relationship (the Brechtian *gestus**) between character and class, indicate clearly from what point of view the representation is done, to lay bare the "complex causality of social relationships" (BRECHT). In the final analysis, modelling consists in contrasting and comparing the scheme of reality (its perspective and historicity) with that of the audience (its present ideological and historical situation). Realism, said BRECHT, consists not in reproducing real things but in showing how things really are.

C. ABSTRACTION

Realism, then, is accompanied by a search for abstraction, *stylization** and formalization to simplify the perception of the *fabula* and scenic details. This stylization, which is inherent in any artistic performance, brings reality closer rather than distancing it. According to MEYERHOLD, it is the hallmark of all deep realism: "It is a mistake to contrast stylized theatre with realistic theatre. Our formula is stylized realistic theatre" (1963).

D. REALISM/FORMALISM

Realism is not tied to a canonical form. Not even the consummate realism of BALZAC can claim to be the only form of realism, *pace* LUKÁCS. Since human reality, in its psychological and social aspects, is in a process of constant change, the representation of man in theatre should evolve along with it. It is absurd, then, to put a formalist label on experiments with forms of theatre that reflect a new perspective on things, just as it is absurd to believe that content has remained invariable throughout literary history (*formalism**). Being realistic is also, and perhaps only, being aware of the aesthetic *devices** used to decipher the real. That is why "re-establishing theater in its reality as theatre" (BRECHT) and not having any illusions about the power of illusion are the first commandments of realism (*theatricalization**). BRECHT and his scene designers (NEHER, APPEN) kept this in mind in their "epic realism."

4. The Devices of Realism

"Formalist" criticism, preoccupied with a description of the discursive devices used to signal the real, must be credited with having demystified the notion of realism as a direct representation of the real. Realism is not tied to specific themes or contents but to a set of techniques: "Realism may be no more than a set of technical responses to narrative constraints, both formulated to some extent according to the times and the pressures of social control. These techniques must ensure the transitivity and therefore the *readability** of a text for a given audience; their dual role is to ensure the veracity of an utterance – its consistency with the reality to which it refers – and their own verisimilitude, i.e. that they are relatively invisible or 'natural'" (DUCHET 1973, 448).

In theatre, all these techniques are intended to legitimize communication and the referent of the discourse. The presence of what is *off stage**, always visible in its invisibility, gives the first illusion of being a world that is talked about, where the characters come from. The most "unrealistic" speeches and actions are made to appear natural by the presence of the stage and offstage area. It is, finally, ideology as the discourse of the obvious and the familiar that takes on this role as referential illusion and as the "guarantor" of realistic authenticity. Thus, it is not so much the *reality effect** that produces illusion and identification as the identification with an already familiar ideological content that produces realistic illusion (ALTHUSSER 1965).

See also: imitation, represented reality, theatrical reality, performance, verism, history.

Further reading: Marx and Engels, "Sickingen Debatte," 1859; Ingarden 1949; Jacquot 1960; Lukács 1962; Brecht 1967; Chiarini 1970, 1971; Gombrich 1977; *Poétique*, 1973; Amiard-Chevrel 1979; Styan 1981; Chevrel 1982; Barthes et al. 1982; Frow 1986.

REALITY EFFECT

Fr.: *effet de réel*; Ger.: *Wirklichkeitseffekt*; Sp.: *efecto de realidad*.

This expression, borrowed from R. BARTHES (*Communication*, no. 11, 1968), applies to literature, film or theatre when the spectator has the feeling of actually witnessing the event represented, the feeling of being transported into symbolic reality and faced, not with an artistic *fiction** or aesthetic representation, but a real event.

A naturalistic production, relying as it does on *illusion** and *identification**, produces reality effects by covering up the traces of the production of meaning, through the use of the various stage materials in accordance with the Hegelian requirement that a work should not reveal anything of its construction. The signifiers are then confused with the referents of those signs. The play is no longer perceived as a *discourse** and as a piece of writing about reality, but as a direct reflection of reality.

In addition to the spectator's pleasure in *identification**, the reality effect provides reassurance that the represented world corresponds to our ideological constructs of it, which are thus perceived as being natural and universal.

See also: theatrical effect, denial, alienation-effect, reception, naturalistic performance.

REBOUNDING OF THE ACTION

Fr.: *rebondissement de l'action*; Ger.: *Wiederaufleben der Handlung*; Sp.: *resurgimiento de la acción*.

This term, from classical dramaturgy, refers to the point at which, after a kind of "lull" (temporary effacing of *conflicts** and contradictions), the *fabula** progresses again toward its conclusion. An unexpected event (*coup de théâtre**) turns the course of action and relaunches the plot.

RECEPTION

Fr.: *réception*; Ger.: *Aufnahme, Rezeption*; Sp.: *recepción*.

The spectators' attitude and activity when faced with the performance; the way they use the materials provided by the stage to make an aesthetic experience. A distinction must be made between:

1. The reception of a particular play (by a particular audience, period or group), or historical study of the way a play has been received, how it has been interpreted by each group and period.
2. The reception or interpretation of a play by the spectator, i.e. the analysis of the mental, intellectual and emotional processes whereby the performance is understood. It is mainly the latter aspect that concerns us here.

1. A Spectator Art

A. When faced directly with the aesthetic object, the spectator is literally plunged into a sea of images and sounds. Whether the performance remains external or encompasses him, involves or attacks him, reception poses a problem of aesthetics and warrants the term, coined by BRECHT, of "spectator art."

This inverts the traditional perspective of aesthetics, which seeks out the structures of meaning in the play and on stage, neglecting the audience's mental and sociological structures and its role in establishing meaning: "If one wishes to achieve artistic enjoyment, it is never enough to want to consume comfortably and at little cost the result of an artistic production; it is necessary to take part in the production itself, to be productive onself to a certain extent, to incur a certain expense of imagination, to associate one's own experience with or oppose it to that of the artist" (BRECHT 1972–1979).

B. Etymologically speaking, *aesthetics** is the study of the sensations and marks left on the perceiving subject by the work of art. Some *theatrical categories** (such as the *tragic*, the strange or the *comic**) can be grasped only in relation to the subject with the aesthetic object. One must establish how perception is already an *interpretation**, even a re-creation of meaning, particularly in texts or performances where everything depends on the profusion or ambiguity of the significant structures and stimuli, where the spectator must necessarily follow his own *hermeneutic** trail.

C. The difficulty in formalizing modes of reception lies in the heterogeneity of the mechanisms involved (aesthetic, ethical, political, psychological, linguistic, etc.). It is also inherent in the spectator's own situation of reception. The spectator is "immersed" in a theatrical event in a performance that calls on his faculty for *identification**. He has the impression of being faced with actions similar to those of his own experience. He receives the *fiction** mixed with the impression of a direct address; there are few mediations between the work and the world, and the scenic codes act directly on him without seeming to be manipulated by a team or announced by a narrator; in this way the artistic *device** is masked. Finally, and above all, in witnessing an action that is transmitted directly, the spectator uses theoretical models of action already known to him to bring the diverse events together in a unifying scheme that is both logical and capable of organizing external reality.

D. We do not know much about the mechanisms governing the dynamics of a group of *spectators** assembled to watch an artistic event. Without even going into cultural presuppositions, we can say that the audience as a group is affected by how they are seated in the house. Light or darkness, overcrowding, the comfort of the seating: these factors weave a subtle fabric that influences the quality of the listening and the aesthetic experience.

2. Reception Codes

Without falling into the trap of postulating a *semiology** of *communication** (rather than of signification) or an information theory – disciplines that would make theatre a set of signals transmitted to the audience intentionally and directly – we can usefully identify some of the *codes** of reception (even if they exist only in a theoretical or hypothetical form):

A. PSYCHOLOGICAL CODES

1. Perceptions of space: how the stage presents artistic reality; how perspective is used; what distortions of vision are possible; how the performance is arranged according to spectator point of view.
2. Phenomenon of *identification**: what pleasure is drawn from it by the spectator; how illusion and fantasy are produced; what unconscious mechanisms are involved.
3. Structuring of previous perceptional experience (aesthetic and psychosocial): the subjects' horizon of *expectation**. There is no one universal way of receiving a work of art (*cross-cultural**).

B. IDEOLOGICAL CODES

1. Knowledge of *represented reality**, of the audience's reality.
2. Ideological conditioning mechanisms through ideology, the media, education.

C. AESTHETIC-IDEOLOGICAL CODES

1. Specifically theatrical codes of a period, a type of stage, a genre, a particular style of acting.
2. General codes of *narrative**.
3. Codes of *theatrical categories**.

4. Codes linking aesthetics with ideology:
- What does the spectator expect from theatre?
- What aspect of social reality does the spectator look for in the play?
- What connection is there between a mode of reception and the internal structure of the work; between, for instance, the Brechtian requirement of non-identification and a discontinuous, distanced *fabula*?
- How can the dramaturgical work and staging be used to find an ideological code that will enable today's audiences to read past plays?
- How can *historicization** be used to enable the audience to consider a given social system from the point of view of another social system?
- Why does one period prefer tragedy while another creates an ideal environment for the comic, the absurd, etc.?
- Can one distinguish between several different modes of theatre communication?

3. Fiction and Event

In the optimal hypothesis that such codes could be reconstructed, the final step would consist in giving an account of all the possible interactions between narrative fiction and the *event** of the actual performance. One would have to consider the nature of theatre practice as simultaneously *semiological* (structural, systematic) and bound to a given event (unique, uncodable, subject to the time of perception). Between the tangible event on stage viewed by the spectators and the fiction that appeals to their cognitive constructions, there are innumerable comings and goings.

4. Toward an Aesthetics of Reception

Relatively recent works by the Konstanz School (JAUSS 1970, 1977; Eng. 1982a, b) have moved toward a deeper understanding of the mechanisms of reception. The ideas of the Prague Circle (MUKAROVSKÝ 1977, 1978; VODICKA 1975) could be of even greater benefit if revived.

A. HORIZON OF EXPECTATION

A reconstruction of the audience's (aesthetic and ideological) expectations and of the work's situation in literary development leads to viewing the performance as a response to a set of questions at every phase in the staging.

B. THE PERCEIVING SUBJECT

The perceiving subject participates actively in establishing the work: his work is similar to that of the critic and the writer.

Reception, then, would appear to be a process that encompasses all critical and stage practices: "On the one hand, of course, theatrical activity takes place in performance, but on the other hand it begins before, continues during and extends after it, as one reads articles, talks about the performance, sees the actors, and so on. It is a circuit of exchanges that affects our lives as a whole" (VOLTZ 1974, 78).

The spectators possess varying degrees of *competence*, or knowledge of the rules of the game. Those rules can be learned and may help improve perception, but they are sometimes irrevocably damaged by bad reception habits or *media** "hype."

C. THEORY OF CONCRETIZATION, FICTIONALIZATION AND IDEOLOGY

An overall theory of the dramatic and performance texts attempts to determine how the work is concretized historically according to changes in "the total context of social phenomena" (MUKAROVSKÝ 1931, 389), which is that of the work at a given point of historical development. It examines the processes of fictionalization as a comparison of *text and performance**, as mediation in dramaturgical analysis and as a meeting place for the text and/or performance with the texts of ideology and *history** (PAVIS 1985e, 233–296).

See also: dramatic text, pragmatics, sociocriticism.

Further reading: Descotes 1964; Dort 1967; Lagrave 1975; Warning 1975; Turk 1976; *Das Theater und sein Publikum*, 1977; Caune 1978; Fieguth 1979; Klöpfer 1979; Beckerman 1979; Hinckle 1979; Eco 1980; Coppieters 1981; Gourdon 1982; Guarino 1982a; Heistein 1983, 1986; Avigal and Weitz, 1985; general bibliography in Pavis 1985e,

330–340; Versus 1985; Schoenmakers 1986, 1990; Sauter 1986, 1988; Fitzpatrick 1989.

RECITATION

Fr.: *récitation*; Ger.: *Rezitation*; Sp.: *recitación*.
See DICTION, DECLAMATION

RECITATIVE

(From the Italian *recitativo*.)
Fr.: récitatif; Ger.: *Rezitativ*; Sp.: *recitativo*.

1. In an opera or cantata, the part declaimed rather than sung. The rhythm and metrics differ widely from the music preceding and following it in that it observes the inflections and stresses of spoken speech. The recitative adapts to changes in emotion, narrative and rhetoric. It is as much a musical way of saying a spoken text as a verbal form of music. It serves as a transition between two airs or becomes a *Sprechgesang* or "singing chant" in SCHÖNBERG and in Brechtian *songs**.

2. In spoken theatre, passages which are declaimed in a different tone than the rest of the text. This includes *leitmotifs** and thematic refrains (CHEKHOV), certain "constructed" parts of classical narrative, monologues delivered as confidences or passages marking transitions in the action (e.g. epic commentary) or indications of the links betwen lyrical and musical moments. The recitative flourished in France in the seventeenth century in lyrical tragedy, with its changes in rhythm, orchestral support, artificial diction.

The recitative is an effective way of indicating changes in the texture of the dramatic text and performance.

RECOGNITION

Fr.: *reconnaissance*; Ger.: *Wiedererkennen*; Sp.: *reconocimiento*.

In classical dramaturgy, a character is frequently recognized by another, which *unties** the conflict by defusing it (in comedy) or by concluding it tragically or by magic (*deus ex machina*). For ARISTOTLE (*Poetics*), recognition or discovery (*anagnorisis*) is one of three possible itineraries of the plot; it follows the tragic error of the hero (*hamartia**). The most famous example is SOPHOCLES's *Oedipus Rex*.

Beyond the type of recognition (of a character, for instance), the performance systematically plays on the spectatorial faculty of ideological, psychological or literary recognition. This is how it produces the *illusion** required for the fiction to develop. The drama is complete only once the characters have become aware of their situation and have acknowledged the power of fate or moral law and their role in the dramatic or tragic universe.

In criticizing the illusionary effect of the naturalistic stage, BRECHT attempted to replace recognition-acceptance with recognition-criticism, by distancing, or alienating, the object presented: "A representation that alienates is one which allows us to recognize its subject, but at the same time makes it unfamiliar" (*A Short Organum for the Theatre*, sect. 42). In this case it matters little whether or not the character has become aware of its contradictions and their solution, as long as the spectator has done so and understands the ideological workings of both the represented world and his own.

See also: recognition effect, catharsis, mimesis, imitation, realism, disguise, reversal.
Further reading: Althusser 1965; Forestier 1988.

RECOGNITION EFFECT

Fr.: *effet de reconnaissance*; Ger.: *Wiedererkennungseffekt*; Sp.: *efecto de reconocimiento*.

More or less synonymous with *reality effect**. A recognition-effect occurs when the spectator recognizes on stage a reality, a feeling or an attitude that he believes he has already experienced. The impression of *recognition** varies according to what is being recognized: *identification** with a character occurs with a feeling or impression of déjà-vu. An ideological recognition effect comes about when the spectator feels part of a familiar milieu whose legitimacy is unquestioned: "Before being an occasion for identification (with oneself in the guise of another), performance is fundamentally the occasion for cultural and ideological recognition" (ALTHUSSER 1965, 150).

Psychoanalytical theory explains the spectator's pleasure in this recognition-effect by the need for aesthetic sublimation, which leads the spectator to appropriate a character's self, thus rediscovering a repressed or complementary part of a former (essentially infantile) self.
See also: illusion, denial, realism.

RECONCILIATION

Fr.: *reconciliation;* Ger.: *Versöhnung; Auflösung;* Sp.: *conciliación.*
See CONFLICT

REFERENT

Fr.: *référent;* Ger.: *Referent;* Sp.: *referente.*
See SIGN, REPRESENTED REALITY

REFLEXIVITY

Fr.: *réflexivité;* Ger.: *Autoreflexivität;* Sp.: *reflexibilidad.*
See MISE-EN-ABYME

REHEARSAL

Fr.: *répétition;* Ger.: *Probe;* Sp.: *ensayo.*

Work by the *actors**, supervised by the director, in which they learn their lines and prepare the performance. Such preparation for performance occupies the entire troupe and may take very different forms (mise-en-scène). P. BROOK (1968, 154) notes that the French word *répétition* evokes a mechanical kind of work, while rehearsals are always different and sometimes creative. Otherwise, if they become mired down in infinite repetition, it is soon clear that the theatre has gone out of them. The German *Probe* ("testing") gives a much better idea of the experimentation and the trial-and-error process involved before a final solution is adopted.
See also: theatre work, acting, casting.
Further reading: Spolin 1985; Cole 1992; Shomit 1992.

REPERTORY

Fr.: *répertoire;* Ger.: *Repertoire;* Sp.: *repertorio.*

1. Body of plays performed by a theatre in the course of a season or over a period of time (as in "the repertory of the Comédie-Française" or "adding a play to the repertory").

2. Body of plays in the same style or from the same period ("the modern repertory"). Repertory theatre is sometimes contrasted with "experimental theatre." Since COPEAU and his "attempt to renew the theatre" (1913), repertory includes the classics, contemporary creations, and everything that a director deems useful for drawing up a quality program structured over several years.

3. Body of *roles** that an actor has or can perform; his acting range.

4. The characters of repertory are fixed, characteristic *types** (for example, the treacherous valet, the noble father).
See also: distance, communication, reception, hermeneutics.
Further reading: Goffman 1967; Reiss 1971; Caune 1978; Chambers 1980; Pavis 1980c; Durand 1980a; Helbo 1983a; J. Martin 1984.

REPLY

Fr.: *réplique;* Ger.: *Stichwort, Replik;* Sp.: *Replik.*
See LINES

REPRESENTABILITY

Fr.: *figurabilité;* Ger.: *Darstellbarkeit;* Sp.: *figurabilidad.*
See FIGURABILITY

REPRESENTED REALITY

Fr.: *réalité représentée;* Ger.: *dargestellte Wirklichkeit;* Sp.: *realidad representada.*

As soon as we examine the link between represented reality and dramaturgical or stage form, we assume that there is a dialectical relationship between them: the nature and analysis of reality influence the dramatic form selected and, inversely, the dramatic form used clarifies and influences the knowledge of that reality. But the connection between reality and the aesthetic universe is far from being obvious. It was long thought that it could only be direct and *mimetic**, that is that the work of art was a reflection (however unfaithful) of the external world. If this is true, it is possible to observe the processes of representation and stylization, even distortion, of the represented world. If, however, we believe that dramaturgical and stage writing is not directly and mimetically subject to reality, that it models reality in its own way, it is much more difficult to determine its relationship with reality. To do so requires a grasp of the processes of fictionalization and ideologization that mark the transition from the dramatic or performance text and the intertext (PAVIS 1985d).

1. Mimetic Dramaturgy

A. THE HERO

G. LUKÁCS (1956), on the basis of his comparative analysis of the novel and the historical drama, sets out a series of criteria for a proper grasp of reality. At the same time, he elevates those criteria to the rank of absolute norms to balance out the growing practice of the *epic treatment of drama**, a process that has been "threatening" to explode the dramatic form since the middle of the nineteenth century (SZONDI 1956). He believes that the hero need not shine for his exceptional moral or social qualities but should have a *dramatic** existence in himself, an existence rich in significant moments and full of the contradictions of an era or a milieu, situated at a time of deep internal and political crisis. Only "world-historical figures" (HEGEL), in whom original individual traits coexist with the social framework of historical conflicts, make good dramatic subjects. The art of drama is to find individuals who by their actions (and not by the abstract, epic system whereby they are characterized) are involved personally in historical processes (unity of action and character, of the individual and the social).

B. "TOTALITY OF MOVEMENT"

Tragedy and epic literature "both lay claim to portraying the totality of the life-process" (LUKÁCS, 1963, 91). In theatre, "this totality, however, is concentrated round a firm centre, round the dramatic collision" (93), and has to do with the "totality of movement," not of objects, as in the novel.

C. STYLIZATION

Having little time to identify itself, the dramatic universe concentrates, and thus distorts, the social processes it describes. The *unity** of time and place forces the playwright to show the hero in action and in crisis. The drama thereby gains in simplification, distance and perspective. The natural consequence is a *stylization** and *modelling** of reality. This schematization permits a comparison of the hero's personal motivations and the social processes of the play, which in turn makes it possible to relate the historical aspects of the spectator with what is shown (*historicization**, *abstraction**).

2. Non-mimetic Dramaturgies

Lukácsian analysis does justice to classical, realist and naturalist theatre but rejects epic trends in modern drama, on the grounds that they are a perversion of the specifically theatrical (canonical) form. Nor does it take into account new forms of dramatic texts and stage practice.

A. EPIC INTERVENTION

However, an epic approach is not necessarily less realistic than the purely dramatic method. It may even be more capable of reflecting the current complexity of social processes and "the totality of movements" of classes and groups. In an epic commentary, the narrator can easily summarize a situation, present a political or financial report, draw attention to the salient points of a particular development. It is simply a question of giving the playwright the right to present his own version of social analysis and to intervene at will in the play with as much authority as a character, a universal representative or just a witness.

There are no longer any "world-historical individuals," and in any case, individuals can no longer influence the course of the world on their own. DÜRRENMATT remarked, in this vein, that Napoleon was the last modern hero: "Hitler and Stalin cannot be made into Wallensteins. Their power was so enormous that they themselves were no more than incidental, corporeal, and easily replaceable expressions of this power. [...] Creon's secretaries close Antigone's case" (1970, 63; Eng. 1982, 253). Tragedy is no longer able to represent the conflicts of our times. The worn-out *Aristotelian** form must give way to new dramaturgies. To DÜRRENMATT, that meant comedy, which derives its life from strokes of inspiration or "conceits" (1970, 64) and is therefore not subject to deeper necessity. For many other contemporary writers, only epic intervention or the narrative voice of a lyrical stream of consciousness can still touch upon a bit of reality.

B. TRANSFORMATION AND REPRESENTATION OF REALITY

In short, playwrights eschew a coherent and global representation of the world. Even BRECHT shows signs of being somewhat intimidated by reality: "Today's world can be reconstructed in theatre, but only if it is conceived as being changeable" (1967, 16:931). Hence the difficulties of post-Brechtian playwrights (DÜRRENMATT, WEISS) in representing reality, their declared intention to begin with artistic and fictional representations and then, perhaps, say something about a reality with which they claim to have lost touch.

C. NON-MIMETIC AND NON-EPIC IMITATION OF EVERYDAY REALITY

Without renouncing the Brechtian call for a realistic theatre showing human beings battling with social determinism, other dramaturgies probe reality while abandoning the idea of rendering it fully or reducing it to an autonomous cybernetic model. Among them, the *theatre of everyday life** attempts to liberate fragments of language that have been solidifed by ideology. This kind of theatre does not place the characters in a particular situation within the overall workings of society, but shows them in the everyday images that produce them and are reproduced by them. The only chance of elucidating this shrunken reality is to be found in the effect of recognition and in certain stereotypes of language and ideology of which neither the character nor the spectator had been aware.

D. SEMIOTIZATION

Recent attempts have gone beyond the often sterile Brechtian opposition between the dramatic and the epic, by altering the reality/fiction relationship, using a lyrical or narrative voice, varying the devices of fictionalization within the performance (representation) itself. Theatre has become more "modest" and "realistic" in its claims to represent reality: both terms are disappearing from the critical vocabulary and neither practice nor theory today claims to present a naturalistic or realistic imitation of reality but at most a version of it in the form of signs and acting.

See also: fiction, imitation, reproduction, theatrical sign, dramaturgy, form, formalism.

Further reading: Szondi 1956; Lukács 1963, 1964, 1975; Lotman 1977; Eisenstein 1976, 1978; Hays 1977, 1981.

REPRESENTATIONALISM

See REALISTIC PERFORMANCE

REPRODUCTION

Fr.: *reproduction*; Ger.: *Abbildung*; Sp. *reproducción*.

Brechtian term (*Abbildung* or *Abbild*) that refers to the images produced by theatre to represent extra-theatrical reality: " 'Theatre' consists in this: in making live representations [reproductions] of reported invented happenings between human beings and doing so with a view to entertainment."

(1967, 16:663; Eng. 1964, 180). Reproduction is an imitation/transformation of the world by theatre. It forms the basis of the theory of *realism**, but is not yet sufficiently free of that of art as a mimetic reflection of reality. For BRECHT, reproduction must be distanced and "alienate," that is, it must be one that "allows us to recognize its subject, but at the same time makes it seem unfamiliar" (1967, 16:680; Eng. 1964, 192). The spectator's part in this re-production is essential, so that stage reproduction only really takes shape after its re-creation, in Brechtian aesthetics and, more generally, in all *theatrical practice**.
See also: represented reality, theatrical reality, reception, sign.

RESOLUTION
Fr.: *conciliation*; Ger.: *Versöhnung*; *Auflösung*; Sp.: *conciliación*.
See CONFLICT

RETARDMENT
Fr.: *retardement*; Ger.: *Verzögerung*; Sp.: *retardo*.
See MOTIF, PERIPETEIA

RETHEATRICALIZATION
Fr.: *rethéâtralisation*; Ger.: *Retheatralisierung*; Sp.: *reteatralización*.
See THEATRICALIZATION

REVIVAL
Fr.: *reprise*; Ger.: *Wiederaufnahme*; Sp.: *reposición*.

1. To revive a performance is to redo it after an interruption of varying length (a few weeks to a number of years), usually as faithfully to the original as possible.

Revivals are tricky, for there will necessarily be shifts in emphasis and meaning from the first version, if only because the audience and its expectations will have changed. This is one of the reasons why directors sometimes choose to put on a totally different version, showing that any interpretation is relative and provisional. Revivals are often located in between as faithful a repeat as possible of the older performance and a new version that takes its distance from that earlier model. That is the case for the third version of *Dans la solitude des champs de coton* staged by CHÉREAU with different partners. The speech situation is identical, the characters have the same motivations, but their relationship to the text – and that of CHÉREAU, the director – has changed so that suddenly an entirely different tone emerges from the KOLTÈS play.

2. The revival of a role by a different actor oses the same problems to the staging, since an actor cannot be changed like a part in a motor. His arrival will alter the balance of the interpretations, the reactions of the other players, and therefore the entire performance. Any revival is a new production to some extent.

RHETORIC
Fr.: *rhétorique*; Ger.: *Rhetorik*; Sp.: *retórica*.

Rhetoric, the art of persuasive or impressive speaking or writing, has a role to play in theatre, as it constitutes a body of rules intended to transmit a textual and scenic message to the spectator as effectively as possible.

Treatises on rhetoric (by QUINTILIAN and CICERO, for example) often compare the orator's art with that of the actor. The doctrine of physical eloquence and presentation ("*sermo corporis, eloquentia corporis*") is directly applicable to the persuasive art of the actor (QUINTILIAN, *Institutio oratoria*, 11.3). The treatises on gesture often took up this theme in the eighteenth century. Both the orator's and the actor's voice are subject to the principles of clarity and expressiveness; eye movements, carriage and hand gestures are all codified. The gestures are meant to emphasize words rather than things. The actor's art reflects such counsel.

1. Rhetoric of the Classical Text
The classical text of the seventeenth and eighteenth centuries makes massive use of speeches that borrow numerous stylistic

devices. There are three main types of rhetoric: demonstrative, deliberative and judiciary.

A. DEMONSTRATIVE

Demonstrative rhetoric sets out the facts by describing the events. The exposition, narrative and demonstration of classical speeches belong to this category.

B. DELIBERATIVE

In *deliberative* rhetoric, the characters or parties in conflict endeavour to persuade the opposite camp, to defend their point of view, and thus to make the action progress in their favour. The stage is often conceived as a tribunal in which disputes are heard and judged by an audience.

C. JUDICIARY

Judiciary rhetoric takes the final decisions, establishes the roles of prosecution and defense, distinguishes between driving force (subject), opponent and arbiter (*actantial model**).

Other rhetorics of the classical text break the play down into: (1) pathetic exposition (epic); (2) dialectical debate (*dramatic**); (3) pathetic catastrophe (lyric).

2. Rhetoric of the Modern Text and Performance

From the nineteenth century on it became much more difficult to deduce universal rhetorical devices from the text. The speeches no longer obey a single clearly defined model or ideological project; they constantly violate the norms of earlier texts, creating a new, constantly changing rhetoric.

Current productions (particularly those of the classics) are rediscovering a rhetorical presentation of the text and acting. Instead of giving the discourse a psychological dimension in order to make it believable, they stress the constructed, literary nature of the text, revealing its inner workings: the rhythmical declamation of the alexandrine, the emphasis on the literary construction of the sentence (in VILLÉGIER), the artificially created gulf between textual signifier and signified (in MESGUICH), the foregrounding of artistic *devices**, the stage visualization of relationships between the characters, those figures who are "the form of a tragic function" (BARTHES 1963, 10), the search for an antinaturalistic diction (VITEZ). The actor gives the impression of quoting the text and aims not for psychological verisimilitude but for its codes. It is therefore the exact opposite of a rhetoric of persuasion in which the actor seeks by all possible means to maintain communication with the spectator (internalized acting, significant silences, false starts at the beginning of a monologue, etc.). Rhetoric provides a model for the metaphor/metonymy model, which is essential to understand the operation of the major figures on stage (JAKOBSON 1963, 1971; PAVIS 1996a).

See also: poetics, stage writing, stage space, genre, gestus, declamation.

Further reading: Engel 1979; Fontanier 1977; Lausberg 1960; Levin 1962; Jakobson 1963; Kibédi-Varga 1970; de Man 1971; Fumaroli 1972; Larthomas 1972; Kennedy 1983.

RHYTHM

Fr.: *rythme*; Ger.: *Rhythmus*; Sp.: *ritmo*.

Every actor and director intuitively senses the importance of rhythm and pace when working with words or gestures and developing a performance. This is not a new semiological notion invented to make a reading of the dramatic text or a description of the performance. It is part of the very fabric of the performance.

Still, the theoretical implications of rhythm are of paramount importance as soon as it becomes a determining factor in establishing the *fabula*, in the unfolding of events and stage signs and in the production of meaning, as is the case in contemporary theatre practice. Theoretical and practical research into rhythm appear at a point of epistemological break: following the imperialism of the visual, of space, of the stage sign within a mise-en-scène conceived as visualized meaning, there has been a search in both theory and practice (VINAVER, VITEZ) for quite a different paradigm of theatre performance, that of the auditory, the temporal, the significant sequence; in short, the paradigm of rhythmic structure.

1. Traditional Theories of Rhythm

A. The ornamental theory of rhythm is usually extended from the poetic text to the theatre. According to this view, rhythm is only a prosodic and superficial ornament of the text superimposed upon the syntactic and semantic structure, itself considered as fundamental and invariable. Rhythm is seen as a melodic and expressive way of saying the text and unfolding the *fabula*.

Henri MESCHONNIC, in his *Critique du rythme* (1982), distinguishes between three categories of rhythm: linguistic (specific to each language), rhetorical (dependent on cultural tradition) and poetic (tied to an individual writing). He speaks of the two risks involved in rhythm: "Either it is broken down like an object, a form alongside the meaning, when it is said to redo what was said: redundancy, expressiveness; or it is understood in psychological terms that eliminate it and see in it an ineffable something, absorbed in the meaning or the emotion" (1982a, 55). In theatre, as in poetry, rhythm is not an external ornament added onto the meaning, an expressiveness of the text. The rhythm constitutes the meaning of the text, as VALÉRY observed in his "Cantiques spirituels" (Variétés): "It is necessary and sufficient, for poetry to exist, that a mere adjustment of the words, which we were reading as one speaks, obliges our voice, even our inner voice, to free itself from the tone and the air of ordinary speech, and places it in a quite different world and time. This close constraint on impulse and *rhythmic* action transforms all the values of the text that imposes it upon us."

B. The theory of versification is most often content to examine how the verse is made technically and normatively and how it conforms to an established model. It may hold emotional speeches about the musicality of RACINE's verse or the pace of dialogue in comedy. Here rhythm appears to be no more than conformity to a model whose origins and effects on the meaning of the performance are not questioned. To MESCHONNIC's credit is his radical critic of rhythm, too long included "in metrics, identifying, particularly in France, prose with the absence of rhythm and with ordinary speech. That is the traditional theory of rhythm as an alternation of strong and weak beats, enclosed in metrics, outside meaning, a subcategory of form" (MESCHONNIC 1982b, 3).

C. Brechtian theory (with its *gestus**, its gestural music, its "rhymed poetry with irregular rhythms") brings us much closer to contemporary approaches. It sees itself more as a way of grasping social relationships in the individual gesture than as a method of demonstrating the influence of a movement or cadence in the production of the meaning of utterances or actions. This theory paved the way for current reflection on rhythm, which attempts to relate the production and perception of the rhythm to that of the meaning of the interpreted text and its mise-en-scène.

2. Rhythm and Meaning

A. EMERGENCE OF MEANING

What is the meaning of rhythm and where can it be heard and seen? MESCHONNIC, in his *Critique du rhythme* (1982), showed that the rhythm of the poetic text is not "above" the syntactical/semantic meaning but *is* that meaning. It is the rhythm that animates the parts of speech. The arrangement of the masses of dialogue, the figurability of conflicts, the distribution of strong and weak beats, the acceleration or slackening of exchanges – all this constitutes a dramaturgical operation that rhythm imposes on the whole performance (KLEIN, 1984). To seek or find a rhythm for the play is always to seek or find a meaning.

B. RHYTHM AND SEGMENTATION

The perception of rhythm obliges the text to be structured and destructured, particularly to highlight certain syntactical elements and thereby mask others. The syntactical segmentation of the sentence and resulting decrease in semantic ambiguity is closely related to the diction and to the perception of an inner rhythm of the sentence. It cannot be said, therefore, that the text has a primary, denotative, fixed and obvious meaning, as a different enunciation immediately deflects it from the "straight path."

C. RHYTHM AND VISUAL OR GESTURAL SUPPORT

The rhythm of the actor's reading and diction is also perceptible when part of the discourse is received against the backdrop of the stage business, so that the literal meaning of the verbal utterance is diverted by that stage business.

D. ORIGINS OF RHYTHM IN THEATRE

The theory of rhythm goes beyond the framework of literature and theatre. In most studies, it is shown to have a physiological basis: heart rate, breathing or muscular rhythm, influence of seasons and lunar cycles, etc. Without attempting to explore the maze of those rhythms, one might merely recall that they often have a two-beat tempo: inhalation/exhalation, strong (marked) beat/weak (unmarked) beat. The same is true of action in theatre, at least in classical dramaturgy: rising/descending action, complication/resolution, passion/catharsis. The practice of directors like MNOUCHKINE (in *Richard II* or *Henry IV*) often consist in rediscovering, in the actors' breathing and in the alternation of vocal and gestural pauses and explosions, that duality of biological rhythms, and in imbuing the text transmitted with a rhyme scheme that breaks the bounds of its linearity and prevents the text from being identified with a psychological individuality.

For the text to be read and/or spoken, the question is to decide whether the rhythm is given "from within," as an intonational and syntactical scheme inscribed in the text, or whether it is brought in from the outside by the enunciator (the actor, director and, finally, the spectator).

Contemporary mise-en-scène, whether by the Théâtre du Soleil (MNOUCHKINE), by VITEZ or by DELBÉE, seems fascinated by the possibility of changing the perception of a text through experiments with rhythm. In the Shakespearean productions of the Théâtre du Soleil, voice work (changing locations, intonation) is seen as similar to the stylization of gesture and the treatment of a text as masses of sound and rhetorical forms. VITEZ appears to instruct actresses (more than actors) to play false, to remain outside their roles, to theatricalize their vocal delivery. Looking for the flaw is the latest obsession of directors.

E. RHYTHM, NEGATION OF MEANING AND EXPRESSIVENESS

It should come as no surprise, then, that actors or directors concerned with the *reading* of the text, like Louis JOUVET, endeavour to "reject and contain emotion, the effect that the lines communicate at first sight, upon the first reading" (1954, 143). Restoring the physicality of the text, as described by JOUVET and in the spirit of ARTAUD, appears to be an experiment with rhythm that begins by de-semanticizing the text, de-familiarizing it for the listener, showing its rhetorical devices, its meaning and drives. This delaying of meaning opens the text to various readings, tries out different hypotheses, takes into account the different situations of reception.

3. Rhythm in Mise-en-scène

Rhythm is present at every level of the production, not just in the way the performance unfolds in time and its duration.

A. ENUNCIATION OF READING

Even when a text is given a "flat" and "expressionless" reading in a neutral voice, rhythm is already at work, as soon as the speaker takes a position on his utterances.

B. RHYTHMIC OPPOSITIONS

In the performance, the rhythm can be felt in the perception of binary effects: silence/speech, fast/slow, meaningful/meaningless, stressed/unstressed, foregrounded/backgrounded, determinacy/indeterminacy. Rhythm is not confined to the enunciation of a text, but applies to the visual arts as well; APPIA, for instance, speaks of "rhythmic space" in relation to stage design. CRAIG makes rhythm an essential component of theatre art, "the very essence of dance."

C. GESTUS AND TRAJECTORY

The search for the gestus and the basic *arrangement** and blocking of the actors on stage, the composition of groups in tableaux or subgroups – such are some of the actors' gestural and proxemic effects. Their movements on stage become a physical representation of the rhythm of the production. Rhythm is the visualization of time in space, a writing of the body and its contextualization in the stage and fictional space.

D. BREAKS

The practice of using *breaks**, discontinuity, alienation-effects – all devices that are frequently employed in contemporary art – favours the perception of pauses in the performance; this makes the syncopated rhythm all the more apparent.

E. VOICE

Voice has become the extreme modalizer of the entire text; the intonational coloration and its ability to relate verbal and nonverbal, explicit and implicit aspects make it "the phonic expression of social evaluation" (BAKHTIN in TODOROV, 1981: 74).

F. NARRATIVE RHYTHM

All the various rhythms of the stage systems of performance (the result of which forms the mise-en-scène) can be read only within the framework of the *fabula*. The rhythm recovers its function in structuring time in episodes, speeches, series of monologues or *stichomythia**, scene changes.

G. OVERALL RHYTHM OF MISE-EN-SCÈNE

Within the narrative framework that gives rhythm to the *fabula*, that "electric current" that connects the various materials of performance as described by J. HONZL (1940), arise the specific rhythms of all the stage systems (lighting, gestuality, music, costumes, etc.). Each stage system evolves according to its own rhythm; the perception of differences in synchronization, the different shifters, the hierarchies between signifying systems; all this is part of the (logical and narrative) ordering of the mise-en-scène by the spectator.

This classical conception of rhythm as an order that establishes relationships between the movements, as a *meta-rhythm*, is similar to those of the mise-en-scène or stage enunciation. Rhythm, in the sense in which speaking bodies are seen moving over a stage in time and space, enables us to understand the dialectics of time and space in theatre.

Rhythm is located in a hermeneutical circle, as the mise-en-scène's choice of rhythm gives the text a particular meaning, just as a given enunciation imprints a particular meaning on its utterances. What are the origins of the choice or choices of rhythm in the mise-en-scène? It is precisely the search for the signifier, the visualization of meaning, the more or less successful and productive project to animate a text and a performance.

Dramaturgical and semiological analysis necessarily pose questions about the meaning of a dramatic text by trying out various rhythmical schemes on it, at the same time making the notion of textual signified a relative one, decentring the text, casting doubt on the logocentrism of the dramatic text and on its claim to be able to find a rhythmical scheme previously inscribed in the text. The rhythm prevents a *semiology** from being founded on elements fixed once and for all in minimal units. It creates and undoes the units, effects reconciliations and distortions among the stage systems, injects dynamism into the relationships between the variable units of the performance, inscribes time in space and space in time.

Thus, in contemporary theory and practice, rhythm has been promoted to the rank of an overall global structure or stage enunciation. There is a real risk, though, that having been expanded to the overall structure of enunciation of and by the staging, it may become a category as general or vague as that of *structure*. But that would be to misjudge the desire to progress beyond a theory based on structure as a firm and final visualization of meaning, a desire also to make rhythm the place and time of a productive/receptive practice of mise-en-scène (PAVIS 1985e).

Further reading: Leroi-Gourhan 1974; Benveniste 1966; Mukarovský 1977, 116–134; Golomb 1979; George 1980; *Langue française*, 1982; Vitez 1982; Ryngaert 1984; García-Martínez 1995.

RIDICULOUS

Fr.: *ridicule*; Ger.: *lächerlich*; Sp.: *ridículo*.

See COMIC

RITUAL IN THEATRE

Fr.: *théâtre et rituel*; Ger.: *Theater und Ritual*; Sp.: *teatro y ritual*.

1. Ritual Origins

It is generally agreed that theatre originated in a religious ceremony that brought together a group of people to celebrate an agricultural or fertility rite, inventing stories in which a god died to be restored to life, a prisoner was put to death, or a procession, orgy or carnival was organized. In the Greeks, tragedy proceeded from the Dionysiac cult and the dithyramb. All such rituals already contain pre-theatrical elements: costumes for officiants and human or animal victims, choice of symbolic objects – the axe or sword that has been used for murders and is judged, then "eliminated," the symbolization of a sacred space and of a cosmic and mythical time different from those of the faithful.

The separation of the roles of actors and spectators, the establishment of a mythical narrative, the choice of a specific place for such encounters, all of these factors gradually institutionalized the rite as a theatrical event. The audience began to go to watch and be moved "from a distance" by a myth familiar to them and actors representing them.

Such rites, which are still found today in strangely similar forms in parts of Africa, Australia and South America, theatricalize the myth incarnated and related by officiants in an unchangeable way: opening rites of entrance to prepare the sacrifice and closing rites of exit to ensure the return to everyday life. Its means of expression are highly codified dance, facial expression and gesture, song, and then words. So, in Greece a long time ago, according to NIETZSCHE, occurred *The Birth of Tragedy* (title of his book published in 1871).

2. The Staging Ritual

In addition to the problematic parentage of rite and art, it should be pointed out that ritual imposes on the "actants" (players) words, gestures and physical actions whose proper syntagmatic organization is the measure of a successful performance. In this sense, all collective work on staging is a realization of a ritual as it is understood by Michel FOUCAULT, in the production and "the order of discourse": "Ritual defines the qualifications required of the speakers (and who in dialogue, interrogation or recitation, should occupy which position and formulate which type of utterance); it lays down gestures to be made, behaviour, circumstances and the whole range of signs that must accompany discourse; finally, it lays down the supposed, or imposed significance of the words used, their effect upon those to whom they are addressed, the limiations of their constraining validity" (1971, 41).

3. The Survival of Ritual in Theatre

Theatre today is nostalgic about its ceremonial origins, now that Western civilization has stopped considering itself unique and superior and has opened its horizons to non-European cultures in which ritual still plays an important part in social life. A. ARTAUD represents the most obvious example of this return to the roots of the theatrical *event**. Rejecting bourgeois theatre based on language, mechanical repetition and profitability, he revives the unchangeable order of ritual and ceremony; in fact he only focuses and expresses (like a shaman) a deep aspiration of theatre preoccupied with its roots: "The secret nostalgia, the ultimate ambition of theatre is to somehow rediscover the ritual that engendered it, in pagans as well as Christians" (MANN 1974, 144).

Ritual, then, finds its way into the sacred presentation of a unique event: action that by definition is inimitable, invisible or spontaneous theatre, but above all the sacrifical denuding of the actor (in GROTOWSKI or BROOK) before spectators who thereby exhibit their concerns and innermost depths to everyone's view, with the avowed hope of collective redemption. Mise-en-scène often becomes "messe-en-scène" (mass on stage): the rite of sacrifice of the actor, of the passage to a higher state of consciousness, submission to the same old repetition and serialism, obsession with immobility or unique performance, the desire to make the invisible visible, belief in political change as a result of the ritual death of the individual, obsession with audience participation in the stage ceremony. Whatever the manifestation, there is always this desire for a return to sources. GROTOWSKI, with the "Theatre of Sources," has become the emblem of that desire.

Alongside these conscious forms of ritualization, however, all theatre in every era shows traces of ritual (sometimes derisory ones, but none the less impossible to do away with): the three knocks that invariably precede the commencement of the play, the red curtain, the footlights and the greeting, not to mention the impatiently awaited themes of each genre – the traitor's deed, the fall of the innocent, redemption by a providential character, etc.

Everything seems to indicate that theatre, having barely disengaged itself from rite and ceremony, is seeking desperately to return to them, as if that matrix of a sacred theatre (BROOK's Holy Theatre) were its only chance of surviving its contact with the mass arts of the industrialized age within the electronic tribe of today.

See also: theatrical anthropology, theatricality, mass theatre, theatre of participation, ethnodrama, ethnoscenology.
Further reading: Artaud 1958; Girard 1974; Borie 1981, 1989; Innes 1981; Turner 1982; Grimes 1982; Slawinska 1985; Schechner 1985.

ROLE

(From the Latin *rotula*, or small wheel)
Fr.: *rôle*; Ger.: *Rolle*; Sp.: *papel*.

1. The Actor's Role

The actor's role, in Greek and Roman times, was a roll of wood wound with a parchment bearing the text and instructions for performance.

By analogy, the role refers to all the lines spoken and acting done by a single actor. The director generally distinguishes among the roles on the basis of the actors' characteristics and their potential use in the play (*casting**). The role then becomes synonymous with the character (the role of the traitor, the villain, etc.) built up by the actor. All plays have main roles and supporting roles. The actor's relationship with the role may be one of imitation and identification (when the actor "incarnates" the character) or one of difference and distance, or *alienation**. BRECHT rejects the myth of the possessed actor and attributes to the spectator the role of a critical connaisseur who closely monitors the construction of action and character.

The ancient image of the role as a coded score to be unrolled, a scrap of hide that exists before and after the performance from which the actor may distance or rid himself, resurfaces in our modern understanding that demystifies the vitalist notion of stage incarnation. This was not true until recently: actors confined themselves to a limited number of roles in their lifetimes (*typecasting**). They searched all their lives for the role that best suited them, developed (as in the masked actors of *commedia dell'arte*) the gestures and *lazzi** of their types, sometimes even imagined that their roles were based on their own lives (like Romantic actors such as KEAN).

The actor still experiences his relationship with the role as a kind of tension: he can either imitate and approach the role as if wearing someone else's clothing as close to the body as possible, or else tailor it to his personality, body and imagination. Trying out the role – its writing and reading – is a full-time occupation, but the actor today asks himself another question that determines his involvement and transformations: the question of his role in society and the role of theatre in the world, whether as a catalyst for change or to maintain the status quo.

2. Role as Type
As a *type**, the role is tied to a general situation or behaviour. It possesses no individual features but brings together several traditional and typical properties of a particular kind of behaviour or social class (the traitor or villain, for instance). It is in the latter sense that GREIMAS uses *role* as a technical term in the context of the three levels of the character (*actant**, *actor**, role). The role is at an intermediate level between the *actant*, the non-individualized general force of the action; and the *actor* (in the semiotic sense of the word), the anthropomorphic and figurative entity. It is an "animate, but anonymous and social, figurative entity" (GREIMAS 1970, 256). As a place of transition between the abstract actantial code and the character and the actor actually staged, it acts as an outline of the search for the final character (*gestus**).

3. Psychological Theory of Roles
GOFFMANN (1959) compares human behaviour to a mise-en-scène. The social text is determined by interpersonal relations. The director is played by parental or social authority, and the audience observes the player's behaviour.

This metaphorical theory of social interaction as *dramatic play** in turn clarifies the conception of theatrical role. Roles are built up by the actors on the basis of the whole group of characters and in the context of certain laws specific to a given dramatic universe. This process is never finished, as it both flows from and is the source of the *reading** of the text.

Further reading: Huizinga 1950; Goffman 1959, 1974; Stanislavsky 1977, 1989; Moreno 1924, 1965, 1973.

RULES
Fr.: *règles*; Ger.: *Regeln*; Sp.: *reglas*.

1. Normative Rules
Body of advice or precepts formulated by a theoretician or poetician. These rules are meant to guide the playwright in his dramatic *composition**.

A. The calm assurance of the normative theorists proceeded from their faith in ancient models and the conviction that dramatic art was a *techné* whose secrets were discoverable. The idea of a model to be imitated was more important than the contemporary notion of structural rules or textual functions.

B. The question of rules quickly went beyond technical advice to become a moral, even a political issue, couched in terms of freedom or harassment. It is difficult for an artist, particularly one successful with the audience, to accept legislation of every aspect of his work. LOPE DE VEGA, for example, in his *Nuevo Arte Dramático* (1609), showed a freedom of action and speech that was lacking in French tragedians 30 years later: "Such things are offensive to the connaisseurs? Well then, let those who take offence stay away from our comedies [...] If it is truly important to please the spectator, any means of doing so is fine."

The debate, once the heat is taken out of it, turns on the need for rules and unities: are they based on truth or are they only relative, tied to changing tastes and ideological/aesthetic tastes and standards? A difficult question to resolve, for although the rules, in their extreme codification, were indeed tied to an ephemeral order (who today would worry about observing the unity of time and place in writing a television soap opera?), the budding playwright clearly stands to benefit from the rules of dramatic construction or verisimilitude.

In Renaissance Italy, several poeticians (CINTHIO, GUARINI, CASTELVETRO) developed the rules that the French theoreticians of the next century (CHAPELAIN, LA MESNARDIERE, SCUDÉRY) sometimes held as dogma. Around 1630, the debate on rules reached its peak. The "Querelle du Cid" dispute marked the moment of most intense conflict between a brilliant practical success and a breach of the rules. The arguments exchanged ranged from the certainty of achieving perfection through the rules ("The closer the poem comes to the rules, the more a poem it is, that is the closer it is to perfection" – CHAPELAIN, Preface to *l'Adonis*) and the artist's scepticism of theoretical schemes ("How are we to establish general rules for an art in which practice and judgment call for new ones every day?" RACAN, letter of 25 October 1654).

The influence of norm and "regularity" on classical authors has, no doubt, been exaggerated. The watchword of the more prestigious of them is to please according to the rules. For CORNEILLE, the object of dramatic poetry is "to please, and the rules it prescribes us are only addresses to facilitate the poet's work, and not reasons that might persuade the spectators that something is pleasing when they don't like it" (Dedication of *Médée*, 1639). RACINE reminds us, in his preface to *Bérénice*, that "the main rule is to please and to move: all others are made only to achieve this." Such prudence concerning the critical doxa of the day is indicative, finally, of a certain scepticism as to the regulation of their art, but also of a desire not to collide head-on with taste and its growing jurisdiction. Imposing rules was also a way of being different from *machinery** plays, which were much more spectacular and popular, and not subject to the same jurisdiction.

C. The term *rules* covers two heterogeneous notions: the rules and techniques of literary construction that correspond to an analysis of theatrical devices; and the ideological rules of good taste, verisimilitude or consistency of tone. The latter are much more subjective, and vary according to the period and the society.

As we seek to determine the true nature of this legislative power, we can identify several criteria, though they would appear not to have much in common:

- the laws of a particular genre of theatre (comedy, tragedy), which obey certain constants as to *reception** by the audience (for example, distance versus emotion, imagination versus necessity);
- aesthetic tradition: the influence of ARISTOTLE's remarks was crucial, and the *Poetics* acquired the force of law;
- the rules of *decorum** and *verisimilitude** vary according to ideological norms and social structure; it is understandable that in the seventeenth century tragic heros had to be kings or princes, and not ridiculous individuals like most mortals represented in comedy;
- rules of the *unities** of time (the action is not to exceed the duration of the performance), place (the place of action does not change) and action (concentrated in a single event).

D. The history of the rules is as instructive for the sociological study of a group as for a solid understanding of literary structure. The aesthetic and political parallels are striking. It was in the seventeenth and eighteenth centuries that literary doctrine was formed and claimed to be universal, just as the power of the monarchy was at its peak and was attempting to legislate a "reasoned" maintenance of its power. The rules were relaxed in the eighteenth, and particularly the nineteenth centuries as ideological and political structures toppled. In the twentieth century, because of the proliferation of ideologies, systems and forms, we tend to consider poetic norms as out-and-out anachronisms.

2. Structural Rules

The notion of structural rules or structural regularity has quite a different meaning within a structuralist approach to the text. The rule is a property and a function of the dramaturgy employed; as, for instance, the rule of the opening and resolution of the *conflict** or of the convergence of main *plot** and subplots in the final *catastrophe** or *point of integration**.

This kind of rule is neither normative nor ornamental; it is the methodological consequence of a structure of the dramatic *narrative**. Seen in the light of literary development, there is nothing absolute about such a rule, and it varies with qualitative changes in dramaturgies. So the rule of conflict or the rule that calls for the integration of all actions at a nodal point is no longer valid for epic theatre or the happening. Other guidelines have taken its place, such as the autonomy of constituent elements, the defusing of conflicts in the first case, the continual invention of collective actions in the second. The structural rule is purely descriptive. It is valid only in the specific context of a particular play or dramaturgical mode; once it is established by induction through several texts, it is applied tentatively to texts, modified and refined on the basis of the facts. This dialectical circuit between play and structural rule refines the resulting rules and textual analysis. Normative rules set by theorists may sometimes leave their mark on the structural rule of the dramaturgy, on the one hand, because dogmas are sometimes based on a "pre-structural" rhetorical analysis of theatrical technique, and on the other, because playwrights must submit to at least some of the prescriptions of theorists. The essential thing is to discover the deep function of a dramatic rule and to observe how it contributes to shaping the dramaturgical model used.

When it is possible to group together several structural rules from a single school or author, we can reconstruct their thematic and narrative system. T. PAVEL proposes, as the operational rule of the tragic world of RACINE's characters, the following sequence: "(1) they experience love at first sight; (2) they feel the effects of the prohibition, try to fight their passion and sometimes think they have succeeded; (3) they realize it is useless to resist and abandon themselves to their passion" (1976, 8). There is no universal way of formalizing the actantial model. R. BARTHES proposes a double equation that is characteristic of both actions and characters: "A has complete power over B. A loves B, who does not love A" (1963, 34–35; Eng. 1964b, 24).

3. Rules of a Generative Grammar of Theatrical Narrative

The ultimate degree of generalization and, perhaps, of scientificity, is achieved in attempts to formalize a narrative grammar. Failing the reconstruction of an entire narration or dramaturgy on the basis of the rules governing deep structure, these grammars set out basic rules for "rewriting." T. PAVEL (1976) proposes, for CORNEILLE's tragedies, an adaptation of the models of PROPP and GREIMAS (see *narrative analysis**). This basic scheme is later supplemented and varied with a series of subrules that differentiate between the types of *fabula* and of *textualization** of conflict.

The use of rules for writing yields results that are, on the whole, disappointing. First of all, these rules apply only to narrative syntax and are therefore not specific even to dramaturgy, much less to performance. Also, the abstract semantics of conflict and action is only one aspect of theatre. Another aspect that needs examining is the ability of the performance to structure itself around constants analogous to narrative rules. Finally, the vast area of theatrical *conventions**, whether historical, aesthetic or specific to a particular acting style, has yet to be explored fully. It is too easy to confine oneself to speaking of reception conventions, without analyzing further the function and staging consequences of such conventional rules.

The quarrel between the Ancients and the Moderns has yet to be decided, and requires an evaluation of the rules of the game. It may not be a bad idea to keep in mind this skeptical remark, made by MATISSE: "Rules do not exist outside individuals; otherwise any professor would rival Racine in genius."

See also: units, conventions, dramatic structure, code, narrative analysis.

Further reading: d'Aubignac 1927; Bray 1927; Scherer 1950; Morel 1964; Viala 1985.

RUPTURE

Fr.: *rupture*; Ger.: *Bruch*; Sp.: *ruptura*.

See BREAK

S

SACRED

Fr.: *sacré;* Ger.: *heilig;* Sp.: *sagrado.*
See RITUAL

SAINETE

Fr.: *saynète;* Ger.: *Sainete;* Sp.: *sainete.*

1. The term in Spanish means "delicate morsel." Originally the *sainete* was a short comic or burlesque one-act play performed between the acts of full-length plays in classical Spanish theatre (*entremés*). At the end of the seventeenth century, replacing the *entremés*, they became autonomous compositions, notably those of Ramón DE LA CRUZ, who turned them into popular plays to entertain the audience. Written in the seventeenth and eighteenth centuries by QUIÑONES DE BENAVENTE (1589–1651) and, particularly, Ramón DE LA CRUZ (1731–1795), they remained in fashion until the late nineteenth century. The *sainete* uses modest means to paint an animated picture of popular society in large grotesque and critical strokes. The playwright stresses the comic characters and proposes an often virulent satire of their entourage. The *sainete* is fond of music and dance and has no intellectual pretensions.
See also: gag, sketch, agit-prop.

SATIRE

Fr.: *satire;* Ger.: *Satire;* Sp.: *sátira.*
See COMIC, PARODIC

SATIRICAL COMEDY

Fr.: *comédie satirique;* Ger.: *Satire;* Sp.: *comedia satírica.*

A play that exhibits a critical view of a social or political practice or human vice (for example, *Tartuffe, l'Avare*).

SCANSION

Fr.: *scansion;* Ger.: *Skanzion, Skandieren;* Sp.: *escansión.*
See DECLAMATION, VERSIFICATION

SCENARIO

Fr.: *scénario, canevas;* Ger.: *Szenarium, Kanevas, Handlungsschema;* Sp.: *guión, boceto.*

This Italian word, meaning "scenery," referred to the script for a play in the *commedia dell'arte* tradition. The scenario provided information on the *plot outline**, the succession of scenes, action and acting and, particularly, special effects or *lazzi**. The term is more often employed today in film, where it includes the same kind of information, except for technical instructions, as well as the actors' lines. When, infrequently, it is used in theatre, it is generally for productions that have no literary text and are based largely on improvisation and extralinguistic stage business. A scenario should not be read as a literary text but as a score comprised of reference points for use by the actor-improvisers. The mise-en-scène may treat the text of a play as a mere scenario – as a source of inspiration, as textual material that need not be taken literally but serves as a pretext for the performance. Hence the misunderstandings concerning the status of the text and the rights of directors.

See also: text and performance, script, dramatic text.

Further reading: Hornby 1977; Taviani and Schino 1984.

SCENE LINKING

Fr.: *enchaînement*; Ger.: *Szenenfolge*; Sp.: *encadenamiento*.

1. Connection between episodes of the *fabula*; how scenes follow each other in the play and how the mise-en-scène co-ordinates and times the various stage systems and the transition from one action to another. *Illusionist** dramaturgy (classical, Romantic or naturalist) sees the play as a thematic and *actantial** progression, ensuring that the linking is both efficient and discreet, giving an impression of seamlessness (*knot**).

2. A *motif** (text, lyrical or dance interlude, commentary) may be used to link two scenes (like the epic narrator or the master of ceremonies in the circus or music hall).

See also: epic and dramatic, narrative analysis.

SCENERY

Fr.: *décor*; Ger.: *Bühnenbild*; Sp.: *decorado*.

The scenery establishes the frame of action on stage, using pictorial, plastic, architectural and other means.

1. The Current Fragmentation of Scenery

A healthy trend has shaped up since the turn of the century, developing consciously and systematically over the last twenty or thirty years. Not only has the scenery been freed of its imitative role, it has taken charge of the performance as a whole, becoming its internal engine. It occupies the whole space because of its three-dimensional nature and the meaningful gaps it creates in the stage space. It becomes malleable (through *lighting**) and expandible and coexists with the actor's work and the audience's reception. All techniques of fragmented, simultaneous or contrapuntal theatre, for example, are fundamentally an application of the new principles of stage design, as can be seen in the selection of a basic form or material, in the search for a rhythmic tonality or structural principle, in the visual interpenetration of human beings and visual materials.

2. Non-scenery as Scenery

The aesthetics of poor theatre (GROTOWSKI, BROOK) and the desire for abstraction may lead the director to eliminate scenery entirely, insofar as this is possible, since even when empty the stage appears as "prepared" and "aesthetically denuded." Things become meaningful by their very absence – the absence of throne for king, of backdrop for castle, of precise place for myth. The scenery is perceptible only in *word scenery** or in the actors' gestures, their way of imitating or simply indicating the invisible element of the set. The notions of *stage arrangement**, *stage machinery** and stage *objects** are today preferred to that of décor, since rather than limiting the scenery to a static container for performance they turn the stage into a space for practice and rhetoric through directorial activity.

3. Dramaturgical Functions of Scenery

Rather than enumerating every type and form of scenery in existence from antiquity to modern day, we would organize the infinite variety of possibilities by naming a few dramaturgical functions:

A. *Illustration and representation* of elements that could exist in the dramatic world. The stage designer chooses objects and places suggested by the text; he "actualizes" it – or rather gives the illusion of mimetically representing the framework of the dramatic world. This representation always involves stylization and a pertinent choice of signs, but it may vary from a naturalistic rendering (in which the scenery is "a continuous description that may be much more accurate and gripping than the description in the novel" (ZOLA) to an evocation through certain relevant features (an element of the temple or the castle, a seat, the suggestion of two spaces).

B. *Construction and modification* presents the stage as performance machinery. The scenery no longer claims to give a mimetic representation but is reduced to a series of inclines, passages, constructions that provide the actors with a space for their movements. On the basis of their gestural space, the actors build the places and moments of the action. (Examples: constructivist scenery, *trestle stage**, *stage arrangement** of J. VILAR's Théâtre National Populaire.)

C. *Subjectivization* of the stage, which is broken down into lines and masses as well as colours, lighting, impressions of reality that play on the suggestion of dream-like or fantastic atmosphere on stage and in the relationship with the audience.

See also: parcours, image, stage space.

Further reading: Bablet 1960, 1965, 1968, 1975; Pierron 1980; Brauneck 1982; Rischsbieter and Storch 1968; Russell 1976; Bellmann 1977; "Scene," in Hartnoll 1983; Banu 1989.

SCENOLOGY

Fr.: *scénologie*; Ger.: *Szenologie*; Sp.: *escenología*.

MEYERHOLD uses this term (*scenovedenie*) to denote the stage science that studies dramaturgy, staging, acting, stage design – in short, all the constituent elements of stage production. The terms used today are *theatre studies** or, for non-European forms of theatre, *ethnoscenology**.

SCORE

Fr.: *partition*; Ger.: *Partitur*; Sp.: *partitura*.

1. The Impossible Stage Score

Although in music there is a very precise system available to note the instrumental parts of a piece, theatre does not have a similar metalanguage capable of drawing up a synchronic summary of all the stage arts, all the codes or signifying systems. Periodically, however, directors and theoreticians claim to have discovered a language for stage notation. The hieroglyphs of ARTAUD or GROTOWSKI, BRECHT's *gestus**, STANISLAVSKY's rhythmical waves and MEYERHOLD's biomechanical schemes are a few well-known examples of autonomous *stage writing**. The production books of STANISLAVSKY or BRECHT, for example, are veritable reconstructions of the performance. Choreographic notations, on the other hand (LABAN 1960, 1994), are difficult to transpose to the theatre. Is information technology being used to resolve the technical problems of *notation**? (MATHERS 1985; FRIEDLANDER 1989).

In its attempt to work from observable facts in the performance, semiology asks itself the same question, without however being able to establish a metalanguage that would be sufficiently flexible and precise. This is also attributable to the nature of theatre, and particularly to the very problematic relationship between *text and performance**. It is extremely difficult for this kind of stage score to avoid the grip of the metalanguage that determines how the stage will be divided up and its description.

2. Text as Score

For textual "purists," those who reject any mise-en-scène as necessarily distortions, the text is considered to be an end in itself (whereas no fan of music would dare to say that he preferred to read BEETHOVEN's score to going to a concert). There is nothing reprehensible *per se* in this philological attitude; after all, the text can also be read as literature, particularly the classical text; it always includes a minimum of stage directions, either external or incorporated within the play. And yet, the actual experience of performance is missing in reading alone and in the dramatic poem. We quickly forget that the dramatic text is only the impoverished trace of a past event: "Thanks to the terrorism of literature, which can be placed in the Western world around the end of the Middle Ages, a system of notation claims the right to be a work of art" (REY 1980, 187).

3. Score as Text

After the development of mise-en-scène and of a *theatre of images** that subordinate all to the use of space and the director's discourse, there is a return to the theatre of text and the requirement that a textual score be formulated, comparable in its precision and normativity (for a future production) to a musical score. Playwrights such as Jean VAUTHIER, Jean AUDUREAU or Michel VINAVER write texts by noting pauses and linkages, cadence, tied notes, staccato, rapid or slow tempo – in other words, they attempt to provide for the *rhythm** of the stage enunciation of the text. The question is where the rhythm comes from; whether the playwright owns or holds the key to it, or whether it is questioned and recreated for each new production and utterance by an actor.

4. The Actor's Sub-score

In place of the notion of *subtext**, which is confined to psychological and literary theatre, we would propose the sub-score, as a "kinesthetic and emotional master plan articulated around the actor's reference points and supports, created and represented by the actor with the help of the director, but able to be realized only in the body and mind of the spectator" (PAVIS 1996a, 94).

See also: production book, scenario, description, performance text, segmentation.

Further reading: Raszewski 1958; *Theaterarbeit*, 1961; Ivanov 1977; Pavis 1976a, 1981b.

SEGMENTATION

Fr.: *découpage*; Ger.: *Decoupage, Segmentierung*; Sp.: *segmentación*.

Segmentation takes place as soon as the spectator endeavours to analyze the overall impression left on him by the performance and to identify the units and how they function. Segmentation is not a perverse and useless theoretical activity that destroys the overall impression; rather it is an awareness of the way the play and its meaning is constructed. Segmentation is based on the structure of the narrative, stage and acting.

More than one segmentation of a performance is possible: the mode of segmentation and the determination of the *minimal units** have a considerable influence on the production of the meaning of the performance.

1. External Segmentation

The dramatic text is rarely presented as a compact block of dialogue. It is often divided into *scenes**, *acts** or *tableaux**. Signs of segmentation such as raising or lowering the curtain, the use of light and darkness, freezing the action, musical interludes or pantomines are objective ways of punctuating the action. This approach, however, may do little more than clarify (entrances and exits, locations, etc.). The organization of the text and the performance must comply with more objective criteria that are established on the basis of changes in the system of action or the use of stage materials.

2. Longitudinal or Cross Segmentation

Segmentation is done longitudinally along the temporal axis when a distinction is made between several sequences according to the development of the performance: this is an analysis of *fabula* or action.

When an attempt is made to identify and untie the innumerable *stage materials** by listing the different stage systems, cross cuts may be made to a given moment (scene or *situation**) of the performance. The first decision to be made is whether divisions will be based on the dramatic text or on the mise-en-scène.

3. Stage Systems

A. FRAMING

The *staging** operates the first and most basic segmentation. By rendering certain aspects visible and excluding others from the *frame** of the performance, it makes a choice that affects meaning. This framing organizes the stage hierarchically by focusing on those elements it wishes to emphasize, establishing a ranking order in the use of the stage materials (*focalization**).

B. ENUMERATING THE SIGNS OF THE PERFORMANCE

An account of all of the stimuli emanating from the stage points up several systems, such as music, text, facial expression, movement. Despite the pragmatic or teaching value of this list, however, it may be a rather positivistic description of the performance. For instance, it does not account for the relationships among the materials, their prevailing value or the choice which is more or less imposed on the audience. Neither does it take into account the fact that in contemporary staging the borders between actor and properties, music, sound, lighting, and scenery are ill-defined.

Similarly, segmentation based on auditory and visual signs depending on the channel of transmission or origin of the message (stage/character) unjustly reduce the staging to a set of signals emitted intentionally, like a mechanical system.

4. Dramaturgical Segmentation

A division of the performance on the basis of its dramatic units is much more satisfactory. It is determined by the indications of place and time scattered throughout the text which are used by the staging to distribute the narrative material in the place/time of the stage. This kind of division is always possible, as events and facts which are always situated in time and space (from the "narrated" story and the "narrating" staging) can be used. This narratological segmentation proposes a series of *functions** or *motifs** and extrapolates a logical/temporal model (*narrative analysis**) from the play (as from any other kind of discourse). Classical dramaturgy, for instance, calls for unity of action (ARISTOTLE) and breaking any *fabula* down into several stages; *exposition**, rising action, crisis, fall, *catastrophe**. From the point of view of the conflict, the series is the following: crisis and establishment of the complication, peripeteia, dénouement. This division links up with the analysis of dramatic situations – both group data from text and performance, defining situations through the entrances and exits of the characters. It is difficult, but important, to make the distinction between segmentation of the *story** (*fabula* narrated) and segmentation of the narrative (narrating *discourse**). The two kinds of division do not generally correspond to each other as the playwright is free to present his material in whatever order (discourse) he wishes.

Identifying the dramaturgical form is done somewhat intuitively, but always on the basis of a unified overall project of dramaturgical meaning. This unit or form groups a piece of stage business, a character's behaviour, a component of the *fabula*, etc.

The play may also be divided according to changes in situation, i.e. changes in the *actantial configurations**.

5. Segmentation According to Gestus

Dividing a play into units is analogous to the Brechtian method of identifying the various *gestuses** of a play. Each particular *gestus* corresponds to a stage action and groups the strong points of the actions on the basis of gesture and attitude. This kind of segmentation has the advantage of being based on concrete stage work and the actualization of the blocking and the *fabula**. The narrative segmented is that of the evolution and transformation of the various gestuses.

6. Other Possible Methods

The kinds of segmentation described above (except for gestus) are not always specifically theatrical. In particular, they do not properly account for the situation of enunciation and the *deictics** that are always linked to the present and the theatre event. The research of A. SERPIERI (1981), though too quickly abandoned, carefully segments a play according to dramatic utterance and the units belonging to the text and the performance. Instead of basing his divisions on *fabula*, logic of action, and so on, he identifies segments for any dramatic text which are characterized by their "indexical and performative orientation": beginning with a character speaking to an interlocutor (another character, the stage or the audience), a cluster of relationships is organized which links all of the stage elements to the same situation in time and space and an instance of discourse. It is the appearance of a new "performative-deictic orientation" – that is, the rooting of the discourse in a new situation and a "spoken action" – which segments the performance and channels the dynamics of the characters' speeches. (ELAM 1980).

See also: composition, minimal unit, dramaturgy, dramatic structure, semiology.

Further reading: Kowzan 1968; Jansen 1968, 1973; Pagnini 1970; Serpieri 1977, 1981 (in Amossy, 1981); Rutelli, Kemeny, in Serpieri 1978; Ruffini 1978; de Marinis 1979.

SELF-THEATRE

Fr.: *auto-théâtre;* Ger.: *Autotheater;* Sp.: *autoteatro.*

This term is used by ABIRACHED (1992) to denote the phenomenon of amateur theatre, which is often done by participants for themselves (regardless of their reasons for doing so) rather than for an outside audience. It would also apply to a kind of theatre that refers exclusively to itself by quoting acting, techniques or achievements, thereby avoiding a reproduction of the outside world: ("Dionysos cédant la place à un narcisse amoureux de son reflet" (Ph. IVERNEL, *Journal du TEP*, 1995).

SEMIOLOGY (SEMIOTICS) OF THEATRE

Fr.: *sémiologie théâtrale;* Ger.: *Theatersemiotik;* Sp.: *semiología teatral.*

Semiology is the science of signs. Theatre semiology is a method of analysis of text and/or performance that takes into account formal structure and the dynamics of the production of meaning by theatre practicians and audience.

According to M. FOUCAULT, semiology is "the totality of the learning and skills that enable one to distinguish the location of the signs, to define what constitutes them as signs, and to know how and by what laws they are linked" (1966, 44; Eng. 1970, 20). Semiology is concerned not with identifying *meaning**, that is the play's relationship with the world (a matter that pertains to *hermeneutics** and literary criticism), but with the way in which meaning is produced throughout the theatrical process from the time the director reads the play until it is interpreted by the spectator. It is at once an "ancient" and a "modern" discipline, for though all philosophy reflects on meaning and signs, semiological (or semiotic) studies strictly speaking date back only as far as PEIRCE and SAUSSURE. The latter, in his *Course in General Linguistics*, summarized semiology's vast task as follows: "It is therefore possible to conceive of a science *which studies the role of signs as part of social life*. [...] We shall call it *semiology*. [...] It would investigate the nature of signs and the laws governing them" (1915, 32–33; Eng. 1986, 15).

Its application to theatre studies dates back to the Prague Circle of the 1930s (ZICH 1931; MUKAROVSKÝ 1934; BOGATYREV 1938; HONZL 1940; VELTRUSKÝ 1941). On the history of the school, see MATEJKA and TITUNIK 1976; SLAWINSKA 1978; ELAM 1980.

1. Semiology or Semiotics?

The difference is not simply a quarrel over words, nor is it the result of a terminological battle between the PEIRCE-inspired American *semiotics* and the French *semiology* of SAUSSURE. It lies in an irreducible opposition between two models of the *sign**. Whereas SAUSSURE confines the sign to the alliance of a signifier and a signified, PEIRCE adds to those terms (which he called representanem and interpretant) the notion of *referent*, that is the reality denoted by the sign.

Curiously, in the usage that appears to have taken hold following the work of GREIMAS (1966, 1970, 1979), and according to him, *semiology* designates the *semiotics* of PEIRCE, while his own research, based on the work of SAUSSURE and HJELMSLEV, takes the name *semiotics*: "A gap therefore divides semiology (for which natural languages serve as instruments of paraphrase in the description of semiotic objects) and semiotics (the main task of which is the construction of an appropriate metalanguage) [...] semiotics more or less explicitly postulates the mediation of the natural languages in the process of reading signifieds belonging to the non-linguistic semiotic systems (pictures, paintings, architecture, etc.), whereas semiotics challenges this mediation" (1979, 338; Eng. 1982, 284).

One might have much to say about this disqualification *a priori* of semiology, theatre semiology for example, as merely a study of discourse on theatre. No doubt it is entirely legitimate in the perspective of GREIMAS, who is concerned solely with (deep) *semio-narrative* structures, leaving aside for the time being the examination of (surface) *discursive* structures. GREIMAS wishes to account for the emergence and elaboration of all meaning, to "identify the minimal semiotic forms (relations, units) common to the different visual domains" (1979:282). Theatre, as an external discursive manifestation, does not fall within the scope of his research. For the theatre theoretician cannot fail to describe what is visible on stage or to make the connection between signs and their referents (without, however, turning theatre into a more or less iconic imitation of reality, and *iconicity** the criterion of appreciation of theatrical signs).

It is therefore *semiology*, not *semiotics*, that we will discuss in this examination of the theoretical ground covered by and dead ends involved in this approach. But to speak of *theatre semiology* assumes that the theatrical phenomenon can be isolated and defined, not an easy feat in this age of burgeoning theatrical forms. It would not appear to be necessary, however, to resolve the aesthetic question of the *specificity** or lack thereof of theatrical art in order to postulate a theatre semiology. It is sufficient to conceive of that semiology as "syncretic," that is, as "implement[ing] several manifestation languages" (GREIMAS 1979, 375; Eng. 1982, 326) and to see it as a crossroads for other semiologies (space, text, gestuality, music, etc.).

2. Difficulties and Impasses in the First Phase of Semiology

A first and necessary phase, consisting in a reflection on the foundations of theatre semiology, encountered the methodological problems outlined below.

A. SEARCH FOR THE MINIMAL SIGN

Semiologists began by looking for the *minimal units** required to formalize performance, as proposed by linguists: "All semiotic study, in the strict sense, consists in identifying the units, describing their distinctive features and discovering finer and finer distinguishing criteria" (BENVENISTE 1974, 64). When it comes to theatre, however, as pointed out by KOWZAN (1975, 215), there is no point dividing up the continuum of performance into micro-units of time corresponding to the smallest *unit** of a single signifier. That would only fragment the staging, thereby neglecting the global nature of the stage project. A better idea would be to identify a body of *signs** making up a *Gestalt* that signifies as a whole, not merely through the accumulation of signs. As for the distinction between fixed and mobile signs (set vs. actor, stable vs. mobile elements), it is no longer relevant in contemporary practice.

Examining the sign as a minimal unit is therefore not a prerequisite for the creation of a theatre semiology; such an approach may even obstruct research if an attempt is made to define its limits at any price.

B. TYPOLOGY OF SIGNS

Similarly, a typology of signs (of Peirceian or other inspiration) is not a precondition for a description of performance. Not only because the degree of iconicity or symbolism is not germane to an account of the syntax and semantics of signs, but also because the typology is often too general to reflect the complexity of the performance. Rather than types of signs (such as *icon**, *index**, *symbol**, signal, symptom), we prefer to speak of *signifying function**. The term is from Umberto ECO, who sees the sign as the result of a semiosis, i.e. of a correlation and reciprocal presupposition between the plane of expression (Saussurian "signifier") and the plane of content (Saussurian "signified"). This correlation is not given at once but is established through the productive reading of the director and the receptive reading of the spectator. Such signifying functions at work in the performance give a dynamic image to the production of meaning. They replace a typology or inventory of signs and a mechanistic conception of substitutional codes between signified and signifier, and they permit a certain amount of leeway in the segmentation of signifiers and identify signifieds or signifiers throughout the performance.

C. "AUTOMATISM" OF A SEMIOLOGY OF COMMUNICATION

Barthes' metaphor about theatre as a "kind of cybernetic machine" has often been taken literally: "When it is not working, this machine is hidden behind a curtain. But as soon as it is revealed, it begins emitting a certain number of messages. These messages have this peculiarity, that they are simultaneous and yet of different rhythm; at a certain point in the performance, you receive at the same time six or seven items of information (proceeding from the set, the costumes, the lighting, the placing of the actors, their gestures, their speech)" (1964a, 258; Eng. 1972a, 261–262). On this basis, attempts have been made to apply the conceptual apparatus of a semiology of *communication** to theatre. This approach has tried to define the process of exchange in theatre as a reciprocal one, attempting to automatically translate a particular signifier into a particular signified – decidedly still very "philological" – making the staging the (almost superfluous) signifier of a textual signified, itself known and primordial, and wondering how to reconcile "the presence of multiple signifiers with one and only one signified" (GREIMAS/COURTÈS 1979, 392; Eng. 1982, 342).

D. UNIVERSALITY OF THE SEMIOLOGICAL MODEL

A semiological model based on a typology of signs does not explain the specific functioning of a dramatic text or a performance.

Similarly, the *actantial models** inspired by PROPP (1929), SOURIAU (1950) and GREIMAS (1966) have often been applied in an overly schematic and indiscriminate manner, so that the world of meaning of the plays was strangely alike. When used in a strictly Greimasian spirit, the actantial model retains its abstract and non-figurative nature. As soon as it is applied too specifically to the dramatic universe of the dramatic text and the actants are no longer "a kind of syntactic unit, of a strictly formal nature, prior to any semantic and/or ideological investment" (GREIMAS 1973, 3), it is easy to fall back on the notion of *character** and *plot**. Narratology, when applied erroneously to theatre, does not allow us to speak specifically of theatre performance.

Without entirely discrediting this kind of non-figurative semiotics, we prefer to follow the process of *reception** by a particular audience under particular conditions, thus effecting a semiology *in situ* to relate its explanatory schemes to the spectator's interpretative path (*parcours**): "Someone who watches the performance does not practice semiotics in the sense of semiotic theory, but the processes whereby he sees, hear and feels become processes of evaluation, which are always processes of a semiotic nature" (NADIN 1978, 25). See entry for *description**.

E. CODE* FETISHISM

The frequent confusion between *stage materials* (i.e. real objects) and *stage system** or *code** (i.e. objects of knowledge, a theoretical and abstract notion) has often led semiologists to draw up an exhaustive list of specifically theatrical codes or to decide *a priori* which codes are theatrical and which extratheatrical. The hierarchies they have proposed (code of codes) have often reified the performance peremptorily and made into a normative model what was only a particular case. It is preferable not to try to establish a taxonomy of codes in advance but rather to observe how each performance builds or conceals its codes, weaves its *performance text**; how the codes evolve throughout the performance, how we go from explicit codes or *conventions** to implicit codes. Instead of considering the code as a system buried in the performance that is to be updated by analysis, it would be more accurate to speak of a *process of establishing a code* by the interpreter, for it is the receiver who, as hermeneut, decides to read a particular aspect of the performance according to a particular, freely-selected code. The code, thus conceived, is a method of analysis rather than a fixed property of the object analyzed.

F. THE LIMITS OF A "CONNOTATIVE DELIRIUM"

Following BARTHES (1957, 1970), a major branch of semiology began to note the connotations and secondary meanings that a sign could evoke in the receiver. It is also necessary, however, to structure the series thus obtained intrinsically and in relation to the various stage systems, either according to a meaning that can be "constructed" based on connotations or according to a latent text comparable to symbolic dream-work as analyzed by FREUD (1900) or BENVENISTE (1966, 75–87). This allows us to produce more than a mere list of secondary meanings, no matter how subtle, and to gain a better grasp of how the connotations of the performance text are contained in the deep structure of the meaning of the staging and how they help build that meaning.

G. TEXT/PERFORMANCE RELATIONSHIP

This relationship has not yet been fully clarified, since parallel research has often been undertaken on text semiology and performance semiology without always comparing the results. Textual semiology has often been content with a philological approach to the text, considered as a fixed and central part of performance; or, inversely, the text has been trivialized and reduced to one system among others, without its privileged position in creating meaning being taken into account. It would seem useful to refer to a *performance text**, a kind of *score** in which all of the resources of performance are connected in time and space (cf. 3B below). In this way, the rhythms, redundancies and cross-references of the various signifying systems can be conveyed both diachronically and synchronically. This approach enables us to visualize the performance in the abstract space of the score while implying that the staging, as the overall rhythm of the rhythms specific to each signifying system, can be reconstructed in that diagram, a reduced-scale model of the performance.

Even among some semiologists, it is still believed that the staging of a text is only an intersemiotic *translation**, a transcoding from one system to another – the idea is a semiological monstrosity! Sometimes the text is even considered to be the deep structure of the performance, an invariable signified that can be expressed more or less "faithfully" in different signifieds of the staging. These conceptions are clearly erroneous; it is not because the textual signifiers remain the same when they are taken up by the actors of PLANCHON, VITEZ or BROOK, that the text keeps the same meaning. The staging is not the formalization of something that is obvious in the text. It is the enunciation of the dramatic text in a particular staging that confers a given meaning on the text (*text and performance**).

3. New Trends and New Directions

A. STAGING AND SEMIOLOGY

After the first theoretical debates of the semiologists who proposed a "well-oiled" method that was so general and abstract as to be out of touch with reality, the question came back to a much more *pragmatic** approach to the theatrical object, as it had in the early days of the Prague Circle (HONZL, VELTRUSKÝ, MUKAROVSKÝ, BOGATYREV). The semiological model selected is asked to justify itself in the specific context of a given theatrical performance; the staging is conceived as a "semiology in action" that may or may not erase the traces of its work but always reflects on the establishment and decoding of its signs. The director inclined to semiology (R. DEMARCY or C. REGY, for instance) "thinks" in parallel series of signs, is conscious of the dosage of the materials, sensitive to redundancies and the correspondences between systems: plastic, musical, spatial diction, gestures in accord with the rhythm underlying the text.

B. STRUCTURING SIGN SYSTEMS

Semiology pinpoints the oppositions between the various signifying systems and comes up with a hypothesis on the relationship between codes, the discrepancies between stage systems, foregrounding and focusing effects. Understanding the performance means being able to segment it according to various criteria: narrative, dramaturgical, gestural and prosodic (*rhythm**).

C. RAMIFICATIONS OF SEMIOLOGY

Semiology relays and is relayed by several more specific disciplines related to particular aspects of theatre. This is a narrowing down, or specialization, rather than a scattering. Among those new disciplines are:

- *Pragmatics**;
- Enunciation theory;
- *Sociocriticism**;
- *Reception** theory;
- Relational theories (which have borrowed from phenomenology the notion that the perceiving subject should be associated with the structure of the object perceived) (cf. HINKLE 1979; CHAMBERS 1980, HELBO 1983a; STATES 1987).

4. Other Trends

Alongside these discplines we find a series of trends, or rather temptations, in semiology:

A. THE PEDAGOGICAL TEMPTATION

Semiology is no more than a way of talking about the performance in a systematic and clear way (though that in itself is a considerable feat). It may try out various kinds of *questionnaires** and become a "school for spectators" (after the title of A. UBERSFELD's book, 1981). Is this semiology's suicide as an autonomous discipline, as Marco DE MARINIS (1983b) fears, or a detour toward a "normative pedagogy of enjoyment of the performance" (1983b, 128)? The risk is a real one. We would rather see this questioning of semiology as a desire on its part to be an epistemology of the performing arts.

B. THE ANTI-THEORY TEMPTATION

Given the complexity of the description and the number of neologisms in its metalanguage, critics often complain that semiology is unproductive, protesting the idea of a mise-en-scène as a "rendering into signs" (*mise-en-signes*). They advocate a return to an aesthetics of the "je-ne-sais-quoi," the indefinable and ungraspable (which may be called the "non-semiotizable" or "pure presence"). B. DORT sees this as a regression to a literary conception of theatre, as soon as the notions of reading or performance text are introduced: "We have gone from the notion of text to the notion of theatrical performance, only to rediscover, thanks to certain semiological methods, the notion of a stage text or a reading of theatre" (*Actes du colloque de Reims*, 1985, 63).

C. CRITIQUE OF THE SIGN

Criticism of the notion of sign is nothing new, since ARTAUD (1938), DERRIDA (1967), BARTHES (1982) AND LYOTARD (1973). ARTAUD dreamed of a notation of "theatrical language" with a system of hieroglyphs: "As for ordinary objects, or even the human body, raised to the dignity of signs, it is evident that one can draw one's inspiration from hieroglyphic characters, not only in order to record these signs in a readable fashion which permits them to be reproduced at will, but in order to compose on the stage precise and immediately readable symbols" (1964b, 143; Eng. 1958, 94). He was searching for signs that would be both iconic ("directly readable") and symbolic (arbitrary), and found such a synthesis in the hieroglyph. Thus he cast doubt on the very possibility of representing and repeating signs. DERRIDA, rereading ARTAUD, arrived at a critique of "the closure of representation" and thus of any closed semiology based on recurring units: "To think the closure of representation is to think the tragic: not as the representation of fate, but as the fate of representation." (1967, 368; Eng. 1978, 250) For his part,

BARTHES set up an opposition between the notion of *work* (*oeuvre*), which is based on readable signs, and *text* (*texte*), which can be entirely constructed and deconstructed by the reader. But he also notes that art could not "stop being metaphysical, that is significant, readable, representational, fetishistic?" (1982, 93). LYOTARD dreamed of a "generalized desemiotics" that would put an end to the "lieutenance" of the sign, of an "energetic theatre" that "need not suggest that this means that; nor need it say so, as Brecht wished. It is to produce the highest intensity (by excess or by default) of what is there, unintentionally. Here is my question: is it possible?" (1973, 104).

The semiologist's response could only be negative. But at least the question would have had the merit of denouncing the inertia that affects any semiological system of equivalence, particularly any semiotics based on the visual, massive and fixed nature of the sign and the signifying structure in which it resides. As for proposing a different model based on music, the text, energy or the body-hieroglyph, it seems that we are always at the stage of prophetic proclamations and never at the stage of actual achievements. This comes as no surprise considering that each of the four theoreticians has resigned himself to the inevitability or fatality of the closure, where "it is *fatal* that, in its closure, representation continues" (DERRIDA 1967, 368; Eng. 1978, 250) or to the fatality of the sign that, in any case, in spite of its crisis "which began in the last century with the metaphysics of truth (Nietzsche)" (BARTHES, "Text" in *Encyclopédia Universalis*), inevitably closes the text and turns it into an *oeuvre*?

Despite this failure of a return to a logocentric and representational perspective, semiology and its notation are undergoing a crisis, a crisis of the sign which Raimundo GUARINO diagnosed as this "substantialist semiology that is still governed by notions such as substitution and replacement and has difficulty thinking of matter and meaning at the same time" (1982a, 96). It is a real crisis, but we have learned to live with it; otherwise, to overcome it and escape the substitutional and visual trap of the semiological model, we would have to invent a theory concerned solely with the effects of the performance on the spectator.

A theory of passions and affects existed from Aristotle's notion of catharsis to the eighteenth century treatises on the actor. JAUSS's *Rezeptionstheorie* revived it with its analysis of the mechanisms of the comic and the tragic. A more precise model is conceivable, though it would run the risk of veering off course toward a theory of emotions that no longer has any influence on the way in which text and performance are produced. We can conceive of a notation system for the affects of the performance, a classification of their intensity, kind and duration: that would mean an in-depth study of the reception of art by human beings, but we must not forget to account for the manufacture of the performance.

5. Towards an Integrated Semiology

Repeated critiques of semiology have enabled it to survive and move beyond a static theory of signs. We would propose a description of the staging as a series of structural operations, starting once again from rhetoric and the metonymy/metaphor opposition, which in dreamwork is related to the difference between displacement and condensation. Representation is imagined as a rhetoric of four major types of vectors:

Metonym (Displacement)	Metaphor (Condensation)
Connecting vector	Accumulating vector
Cutting vector	Shifting vector

Integrated semiology identifies the major vector movements and the relationships between the major vector types. It looks at the major axes governing the production's workings, pinpoints the starting and ending points of the vectors without determining in advance the energy forces that link them to one another. The vectorization stays open: identifying the dominant vector at a given point in the play is a delicate business, and the relationship between connecting, accumulating, cutting and shifting remains to be established.

We can see what semiology has taken and learned from post-structuralist theories, and that borrowing becomes a theoretical oxymoron, a productive contradiction between the following items:

A. Sign and energy: Identifying the sign and its vectorization does not mean forgoing reference to energy and the flow of drives.

B. Semiology and energy: Semiology puts in place networks of energy within which meaning and sensation circulate.

C. Vector and desire: Vectors carry the actor/director's interest and aesthetic experience, but also of the spectator's receptiveness and desire.

D. Semiotization and desemiotization: The stage and matter produce signs, and inversely the sign lapses into a signifying materiality.

These oxymorons call into question the typical operations of classical semiology. They suggest that a rigid semiology is obsolete, or at least ought to be reexamined.

Further reading: Arnold 1951; Prieto 1966; Kowzan 1968, 1975; Pagnini 1970; Corvin 1978b; Ducrot and Todorov 1972; Lyotard 1973; Ruffini 1974, 1978; Bettetini 1975; Vodicka 1975; Diez Borque and Lorenzo 1975; Pavis 1975, 1987; Gossman 1976; Gulli-Pugliati 1976; Pfister 1977; Lyons 1977; Ubersfeld 1977a, 1991; Krysinski 1978; Angenot 1979; Fischer-Lichte 1979, 1984, 1985; Helbo 1979, 1983a, 1983b, 1986; Bassnet 1980; Durand 1980; Hess-Lüttich 1981; Caune 1981; Ferroni 1981; Alter 1981, 1982; Kirby 1982; Gourdon 1982; Barthes 1982; Steiner 1982; Sinko 1982; Strihan 1983; Rozik 1992; Prochazka 1984; Carlson 1984; Schmid and van Kesteren 1984; McAuley 1984; Toro 1984, 1986; Segre 1980, 1984; Piemme 1984; Slawinska 1985; Pradier 1985; Urrutia 1985; States 1985; Corvin 1985; Issacharaoff 1986; Issacharaoff and Whiteside 1987; Schoenmakers 1986; Naltiez 1987; Reinelt 1992; Watson 1993; Pavis 1996a.

Additional bibliography in: Helbo 1975, 1979; de Marinis 1975, 1977; Ruffini 1978; Serpieri 1978; Rey-Debove 1979; Carlson 1984, 1990; Schmid and van Kesteren 1984; Issacharoff 1985; Jung 1994.

Special issues: *Langages*, 1968, 1969, (no. 13), 1970 (no. 17); *Biblioteca teatrale*, 1978; *Versus*, 1975, 1978, 1979, 1985; *Degrés*, 1978, 1979, 1982; *Études littéraires*, 1980; *Drama Review*, 1979; *Organon*, 1980; *Poetics Today*, 1981; *Modern Drama*, 1982; *Dispositio*, 1988.

SEMIOTIZATION

Fr.: *sémiotisation*; Ger.: *Semiotisierung*; Sp.: *semiotización*.

The semiotization of an element of performance occurs when it appears clearly as the sign of something. Within the *framework** of the stage or the theatrical event, all that is presented to the audience becomes a sign that "wishes" to communicate a signified. The Prague Circle was the first to theorize about this basis of the semiological approach: "on the stage things that play the part of theatrical signs can in the course of the play acquire special features, qualities, and attributes that they do not have in real life" (BOGATYREV 1938; in MATEJKA and TITUNIK 1976, 35–36). "All that is on the stage is a sign" (VELTRUSKÝ 1940; 1964, 84).

The process of semiotization takes place as soon as we integrate a sign into a signifying system and establish its aesthetic function. The stage becomes the site of a symbolic action by differentiating itself from the real world.

But semiotization exists only in relation to a reality which itself does not turn into a sign, and can lead at any time to a *desemiotization*: "On stage, everything can also stop becoming a sign, can undergo a desemiotization" (ALTER 1982, 111). This occurs whenever the audience has the feeling of witnessing a real event: an incident in the unfolding of the performance, an error in timing, a break in the acting, an erotic perception on the part of the spectator, or an interest in the actor as a star or a person (rather than as a character).

The dialectics between semiotization and desemiotization is, in short, quite specific to theatre: we take real "objects," human beings, props, space and time to make them mean something other than themselves and construct a fiction. No wonder that finally we confuse the thing with the sign, stage reality with that of the *other stage* where the fiction is presumably taking place.

See also: semiology, sign, theatrical reality.

Further reading: Mukarovský 1934; Bogatyrev 1971; Deák 1976; Osolsobe 1980.

SENTENTIA

See MAXIM

SENTIMENTAL COMEDY

Fr.: *comédie sentimentale;* Ger.: Rührstück; Sp.: *comedia sentimental.*

See MELODRAMA

SEQUENCE

Fr.: *séquence;* Ger.: *Sequenz;* Sp.: *secuencia.*

This term from narratology refers to a narrative unit. The order of the sequences determines the plot. A sequence is a directed series of *functions**, a segment made of several assertions that "gives the reader the impression of a complete whole, a story, an anecdote" (TODOROV 1968, 133).

Classical dramaturgy proceeds by large sections of action divided into five *acts**. Within each act, scenes are defined by action performed by the same number of characters. Consequently, we can speak of sequences only at this level of the scene. Within a long scene we may distinguish several moments or sequences defined according to a focus of interest or a particular action.

Within the sequence, we can isolate a series of microsequences, a "fraction of theatrical time (text or performance) in the course of which something happens that can be isolated" (UBERSFELD 1977a, 255). Other notions, such as that of movement within the continuous line of action or the performative-deictic unit (SERPIERI, 1977), may serve the analyst in a similar way.

See also: unity, segmentation, tableau, narrative analysis.

SERVANT ROLE

Fr.: *valet;* Ger.: *Diener;* Sp.: *criado.*

See VALET

SET

Fr.: *décor;* Ger.: *Bühnenbild;* Sp.: *decorado.*

See SCENERY

SHORT-CUT

Fr.: *raccourci.*

This term is often used by mimes to describe how a sequence is telescoped into a gesture. DORCY spoke of "condensing idea, space and time" (1958, 66). According to DECROUX, COPEAU's body mime at Vieux-Colombier concentrated gestures: "the unfolding of the action was done so cleverly that several hours became a few seconds, and several places became a single one" (1963, 18). MEYERHOLD uses the word *rakurz* to denote a notion similar to CHEKHOV's *psychological gesture* (1980, 1995): the way one's body is placed so that "emotional expression issues from the right expression" (COPEAU 1974, 211), the search for the right tone: "An actor situated in the right physical short-cut will say his text in just the right way [...] Just as a writer looks for the right word, I look for the most accurate short-cut" (MEYERHOLD 1992, 329). A short-cut should give the actor a summary of his situation, his tone, and a whole sequence of gestures that are typical of his role.

SHOW

Fr.: *spectacle;* Ger.: *Vorstellung;* Sp.: *espectáculo.*

See SPECTACLE

SIGN, THEATRICAL

Fr.: *signe théâtral;* Ger.: *theatralisches Zeichen;* Sp.: *signo teatral.*

1. Definition of the Sign

In Saussurian-inspired *theatre semiology**, the theatrical sign is defined as the union of a signifier with a signified, or more restrictively as "the smallest meaning-bearing unit proceeding from a combination of elements of the signifier and elements of the signified" (JOHANSEN and LARSEN in HELBO *et al*, 1987), such combination being the meaning of the sign.

A. SAUSSURIAN SIGN

The linguistic sign (defined by SAUSSURE as that which "joins, not a thing with a name, but a concept with an acoustical image," 1915, 98) when transposed to the theatrical performance and the dramatic text does pose serious problems. In theatre, the signifier level (of expression) is made up of stage materials (an object, a colour, a form, a lighting effect, a facial expression, a movement), whereas the signified level is the concept, the meaning one attaches to the signifier, it being understood that the signifier varies in its dimensions, nature and composition.

For Saussurian semiology, signifier and signified (or, if preferred, the level of signifying systems and the level of signifieds or *semes*), when joined together, are sufficient to create meaning, precluding the need to resort to the *referent*, the actual or imaginary object to which the sign refers in reality.

The meaning of the linguistic sign, that is, the union of signifier and signified, is non-motivated, which means that the relationship between the two elements is not one of analogy.

When it comes to signs in theatre, on the other hand, there is always a certain motivation (or analogy or iconicity) between signifier and signified, simply because the sign's referent gives the illusion of being identical to the signifier, so that one naturally compares the sign with the outside world. In some aesthetics, in fact, theatre is deemed to be an art of *mimesis**. Some branches of semiotics (those of OGDEN and RICHARD 1923, or PEIRCE 1978, for example) are concerned with the sign's relationship with the referent and propose a typology of signs based on a typology of such relationships (motivated for the *icon**, arbitrary for the *symbol**, one of spatial contiguity for the *index**).

B. PEIRCE'S TYPOLOGY OF SIGNS

See entries under icon, index, symbol.

2. Refuting the Theory of the Actualized Referent

Stage reality is not the actualized referent of the dramatic text. The stage and the staging are not responsible for receiving and representing a textual referent. It is not possible "to show a referent" but at the most a signifier, which is given as an illusory, or imaginary referent. The referential illusion (also called *reality-effect**) is the illusion that we are seeing the *referent* of the sign, when we are in fact seeing its *signifier*, whose sense we apprehend only through its *signified*. It is incorrect, then, to speak of a "theatrical sign" whose referent is supposed to be actualized on stage. In fact, the spectators are only the (consenting) victims of a referential illusion: they think they are seeing Hamlet, his crown and his madness, when all they are seeing is the actor, his prop and simulated insanity.

Theatre, at least in its mimetic (representational) tradition, could be defined not only as a "rendering into signs" of reality, but as a stage reality that the spectators are constantly turning into signs of something (process of *semiotization**). Here we could invert A. UBERSFELD's formula defining theatre semiologically: "A referent (a reality) that 'makes signs'" (*Travail théâtral*, 1978, 121) and say that, on the contrary, theatre is also a *sign that makes reality* (process of desemiotization). Moreover, it would appear that A. UBERSFELD arrives at the same proposition when she states that "the concrete theatrical sign (is) at the same time sign and referent" (1978, 123).

3. Specificity of the Theatrical Sign

A. In an early phase of general semiological research (i.e. not only related to theatre), it was thought essential to identify a sign or *minimal unit** in order to elaborate a theory. But this search for a semiological model copied from language led to an excessive fragmentation of the continuum of the performance, by defining the minimal unit only in terms of time, as "a slice the duration of which is equal to the sign lasting least" (KOWZAN 1975, 215; Eng. 1968, 79). Despite KOWZAN's clear warning, this led researchers to effect "an excessive atomization of the units of performance and may make it necessary to introduce a distinction between small and large units (particularly as regards speech and kinesic signs)" (1975, 215).

B. On the other hand, the search for the minimal sign sometimes prevents us from observing the interaction between the various sign systems and studying their connections and dynamics. It might have been more productive, in analyzing performance, to observe the convergence or divergence of the sign networks, or *signifying systems**, and to stress the role played by the producer and the spectator in setting up those networks and in their dynamics (PAVIS 1985, 1996a).

4. Qualities of the Sign in Theatre

A. HIERARCHY

No performance sign can be understood in isolation, but must be seen within the network of signs, which is constantly evolving, particularly as to the hierarchy of the stage systems – now it is the dramatic text, now the visual sign that is at the centre of communication (*focalization**).

B. MOBILITY

The sign is mobile with respect to both signifier and signified. A single signified, such as "house," may be realized in several signifiers – scenery, music, gesture and so on. Inversely, a single signifier may have various signifieds in turn: In BROOK's *Ubu aux Bouffes*, for instance, the bricks signify in turn food, arms, steps, and so on. In this sense, HONZL states that action is an electric current that provides a way of getting from one signifying system to another by setting up a hierarchy and dynamics of signs on an imaginary score according to a *vectorization** that is as dependent on production as reception.

Further reading: Gossman 1976; Pladott 1981; Brach 1965; Brusak 1939.

SIGNIFIER

Fr.: *signifiant*; Ger.: *Bezeichnendes, Signifikant*; Sp.: *significante.*

See SIGN

SIGNIFIED

Fr.: *signifié*; Ger.: *Bezeichnetes, Signifikat*; Sp.: *significado.*

See SIGN

SIGNIFYING PRACTICE

Fr.: *pratique signifiante*; Ger.: *Signifikantenpraxis*; Sp.: *práctica significante.*

This term contrasts with the (itself problematic) conception of text or performance as a static, closed structure that is given at the beginning of the play without the active involvement of the reader/spectator.

The application of the theories of the productive work of ideology (MARX, ALTHUSSER) or dream (FREUD) ushers in a semiotics that, in addition to studying how meaning is communicated, examines how it is produced in the act of reading/writing (*reception**). With respect to the staging, the signifying practice of the interpreter (director or spectator) leads us to reconstruct the meaning on the basis of the stage signifiers: before "translating" those signifiers into univocal signifieds, we stop to look at what they are made of, and to extract all the meanings they are capable of producing, to understand the many enunciatory voices of which it consists.

Signifying practice comes close to the structural notion of mise-en-scène, in so far as it is defined, following Jean CAUNE, as "an aesthetic signifying practice that transforms particular materials (text, space, body, voice) in a particular way that is meant to create perceptible relationships and effects of meaning between the stage

space and the spectators gathered in a space and for a period of time" (1981, 230).
See also: theatre practice, theatre production, semiology.
Further reading: Greimas 1977; A. Simon 1979; Barthes 1984.

SIGNIFYING SYSTEM

Fr.: *système signifiant;* Ger.: *Signifikantensystem;* Sp.: *sistema significante.*
See STAGE SYSTEM

SILENCE

Fr.: *silence;* Ger.: *Schweigen;* Sp.: *silencio.*

Silence is difficult to define absolutely, as it is the absence of noise. Silence is all the more important because such absence is infrequent, if not impossible, and because the purpose of music, like the performing arts, has traditionally been to fill the void by producing a word that originates on stage. In theatre, however, silence is a crucial component of the actor's voice and gesture, whether it is called for in the stage directions ("a pause") or added by the staging or the actor. A dramaturgy of silence has appeared since the turn of the century, and there are various kinds of silence.

1. Silence in Acting: Pauses
Any recitation of the dramatic text includes a certain number of pauses. Often, and particularly in the case of alexandrine verse, pauses are established by the rhythmical scheme (at the end or the middle of the line of verse; at the end of a phrase, argument or speech). Pauses contribute to establishing the rhythm, thus structuring, invigorating, animating the actor's delivery and the performance. They may be motivated by the psychological situation or may be voluntary or involuntary *breaks** that heighten the tension, prepare for an effect or make a space in which reflection and disillusionment are quickly engulfed. In the realistic text (which may appear to be taken from an ordinary conversation), the interpretation of silences is left up to the actor, who uses them (in agreement with the director) according to a psychological character analysis, trying to discover by intuition when, owing to reflection, allusions or incoherence of thought, they are necessary. Gesture and facial expression fill the void, and silences are the reverse of and preparation for words: "There are silences and words make them and help to make them" (CAGE 1966, 109). This kind of silence is not problematic in itself, but may become so if the actor stresses the pause, inferring something unsaid that quickly contaminates, even contradicts, the lines.

The use of pauses, rhythms and accelerations in a psychological manner destabilizes the situation but communicates the verbal structure of the text, its rhetorical construction and gestuality. This is how MNOUCHKINE proceeds in her stagings of SHAKESPEARE with the Théâtre du Soleil (*Richard II, Henry IV*).

2. A Dramaturgy of Silence
Playwrights have always scattered silences and pauses throughout the text, but not until the concept of staging arose did they come to be a full-fledged element of the performance. In *De la poésie dramatique,* however, DIDEROT was already pointing up the need to write silences into the text: "Pantomime must be written in whenever it forms a tableau, gives energy or clarity to a speech, connects the dialogue, characterizes, consists in a difficult manoeuvre that cannot be guessed, gives time for reply, and almost always at the beginning of a scene" (1975, 103).

Silence seemed to take over the theatre toward the end of the nineteenth century, along with the need for mise-en-scène. It was no longer something used to "spice up" the text, but a central compositional element.

Naturalism had already shown a strong interest in displaying the oppressed speech of ordinary people. With CHEKHOV, particularly in STANISLAVSKY's productions, the dramatic text tended to be a kind of preliminary text of silences, with characters unwilling or unable to follow through with their thoughts, or communicating in inferences, or speaking empty words while making sure those words were understood by the listener to be pregnant with meaning. In the 1920s, J.-J. BERNARD, H. LENORMAND and C. VILDRAC were the representatives of a theatre of silence (or of the unexpressed) that put into practice, sometimes crudely, that dramaturgy of the unspoken (cf. J.-J. BERNARD in *le Feu qui prend mal*, 1921 or *Martine*, 1922). But silence used too systematically quickly becomes talkative. BECKETT knew this, and his protagonists switch without warning from absolute aphasia to verbal delirium.

3. The Thousand Voices of Silence
An overview of the various kinds of silence used in theatre reveals dramaturgies that are radically opposed to one another in their aesthetics and social scope.

A. DECIPHERABLE SILENCE
This is the psychological silence of the repressed word; as in STRINDBERG, CHEKHOV and, today, VINAVER's *chamber theatre**. It is fairly clear that the character is refusing to reveal something, and the play is based on the *unspoken/decipherable* dichotomy: the "meaning" of the text is knowing how to set up the opposition between *spoken* and *unspoken**.

B. THE SILENCE OF ALIENATION
This kind of silence, whose ideological origins are clear, is heavy with useless words poisoned by the media and the formulas of convention, always letting the sociological reasons for alienation show through. KROETZ and the ensuing *theatre of the everyday** (WENZEL, DEUTSCH, LASSALLE) are its current advocates.

C. METAPHYSICAL SILENCE
This is the only kind of silence that is not easily reduced to words spoken in a low voice. Its only cause appears to be a congenital inability to communicate (PINTER, BECKETT), being condemned to playing with words without being able to relate them to things in any way but through play (HANDKE, BECKETT, HILDESHEIMER, PINGET).

D. TALKATIVE SILENCE
Falsely mysterious, this kind of silence, which is not really silence at all, often shows up in melodrama, boulevard theatre and soap operas. It uses its phatic function as a cheap trick.

Silence is the most difficult ingredient to deal with in staging work, as it can easily escape the author's control to become an unfathomable (*ergo* difficult-to-communicate) mystery, or a too-visible (*ergo* soon tiresome) device.

SIMULTANEOUS SETTING

Fr.: *décors simultanés*; Ger.: *Simultanbühne*; Sp.: *decorados simultáneos.*

Scenery which is visible throughout the performance and arranged in the space in which actors play simultaneously or by turns, sometimes taking the audience with them from one place to another. In the Middle Ages, each scene had its own *mansion*, a stage device that provided the framework for a separate action. This kind of scenery is currently very fashionable, as it answers the need to fragment *space** and present a multiplicity of times and *perspectives**. (cf. the scenery in *1789*, *l'Age d'Or* at the Cartoucherie, *Faust I* and *II* staged by C. PEYMANN in Stuttgart in 1977.)

SITE-SPECIFIC PERFORMANCE

Fr.: *mise en scène liée à un lieu donné*; Ger.: *Ortsgebundene Inszenierung*; Sp.: *puesta en escena ligada a un lugar específico.*

This term refers to a staging and performance conceived on the basis of a place in the real world (ergo, outside of established theatre). A large part of the work has to do with researching a place, often an unusual one, that is imbued with history or permeated with atmosphere: an airplane hangar, unused factory, city neighborhood, house or apartment. The insertion of a classical or modern text in this "found place" throws new light on it, gives it an unsuspected power, and places the audience at an entirely different relationship to the text, the place, and the purpose for being there. This new context provides a new situation of enunciation and, like *land art*, leads us to a rediscovery of nature and land use and gives the performance an unusual setting of great charm and power.

This staging technique has been tried out many times in the twentieth century. Examples are EVREINOFF and his reconstruction of the taking of the Winter Palace, COPEAU and his mystery plays in Beaune and Florence, the Théâtre du Soleil and their renovations of the Cartoucherie for each new production; the Royal de Luxe, the Fura dels Baus et Brith (GOF), who specialize in rerouting places and the staging in their imagination.

SITUATION OF ENUNCIATION

Fr.: *situation d'énonciation;* Ger.: *Aussagesituation;* Sp.: *situación de enunciación.*

*Semiology** and the theory of enunciation use this term to describe the place and circumstances of production of an act of enunciation in the reading or staging of a dramatic text. "Enunciation is this implementation of language [*langue*] through an individual act of enunciation" (BENVENISTE 1974, 80).

Enunciation, continues BENVENISTE (1974, 79–88) is the "vocal realization of language [*langue*]," and "presupposes the individual conversion of language into discourse," is "a process of appropriation" of the formal apparatus of language, whereby "language is employed to express a certain relationship with the world." In the written enunciation of the writer – and this is even more true of the writer for theatre, one might add – "the writer utters (enunciates) himself in writing and, within his writing, makes individuals utter (enunciate) themselves" (88).

In theatre, the enunciation is that of the playwright or author, relayed by the utterances of the characters/actors and by everyone involved in the staging. But this opposition, this "dual enunciation" (UBERSFELD 1977a, 250) is not an absolute one, first because it is in fact the "author" who makes the characters talk, and second because the author cannot be reduced to a single voice or to a coherent and unified discourse that could be read clearly in the stage directions or in an apparent structure of the dialogues and the conflicts to which they refer.

1. Visualization of Enunciation

The situation of speech (*parole*) is actualized in the staging, as the characters are shown talking. In his reading of the text, the director seeks out a situation in which the characters' utterances, the stage directions and the director's own commentary on the text can be given concrete expression. The director's dramaturgical analysis exists only once it is given concrete expression in the play on stage, using space, time and the materials and actors. Such is stage enunciation: bringing into play all the scenic and dramaturgical elements deemed useful for the production of meaning and its reception by the audience, which is thus placed in a certain reception situation.

2. "Latitude" of Enunciation

Interpreting or performing a text involves taking a position on the situation of enunciation. Certain texts, particularly naturalistic ones, contain precise information on situations and characters. The staging, then, is often confined to merging text and situation in a single message. When the text or *stage directions** say little about the situation, however, the director/enunciator has much more room for manoeuvre and the choice of a situation of enunciation often produces a reading in a new light.

3. Conditions of Speech

Not only do we need to determine who is speaking and to whom, but we also need to grasp how the staging, as an overall stage enunciation, opens up and presents itself to the audience, how it is a rendering visible (and audible), in space and time, of the condition of enunciation so that the staging may be received by the audience.

The enunciation is also clarified by the *attitudes* of the speakers toward their utterances. These *attitudes* (in the Brechtian sense of *Haltung*, a way of holding oneself and behaving, as well as a position on an issue) are not confined to the actors' gestural enunciation; stage design, diction and lighting also reflect the relationship with the act of speaking and the utterance.

The various stage enunciators give a concrete image of the situation of enunciation by proposing a hierarchy or, at the very least, an interdependence of the sources of enunciation.

4. Hermeneutics of Enunciation

Just as, in the sentence, enunciation always has the "last word" over the utterance, diction is a hermeneutic act that gives the text a particular volume, vocal colouring, corporality, or modalization that is responsible for its meaning. By impressing on the text a certain *rhythm**, whether smooth and continuous or jerky, the actor presents the events, builds the *fabula*, conveys the dramatic text and the metatextual commentary. It is the alliance of this enunciation proper to the actor (and through him to the staging) and of the dramatic text that produces the staging.

There are, therefore, two linguistic texts and two ways of analyzing them and founding a semiology: the dramatic text studied "on paper" and subject to a text semiology that borrows some of its methods from other kinds of texts, and the text uttered on stage, onto which are grafted all possible signifying systems, based on the visual or acoustic image. As Jean CAUNE writes: "The text will be considered as a raw material, transformed by stage writing just like gesture, voice or space. The verbal expression of the actors is not of the same nature, on the level of expression, as the written text. And it is not so much the substance that has changed as its formal organization. The verbalized text is introduced into a way of breathing, a system of gestures, an activity, a space. It is one of the elements of the performance and, as such, its value lies only in its place within the overall form and the relationships it maintains with the other elements" (1981, 234).

It is precisely in terms of the relationships and interactions among the various signifying systems and therefore their enunciation that *stage enunciation* or mise-en-scène may best be defined.

See also: situation, dramatic situation, deixis, discourse, pragmatics.

Further reading: Veltruský 1977; Pavis 1978a; Kerbrat-Orecchioni 1980.

SITUATION COMEDY

Fr.: *comédie de situation;* Ger.: Situationskom*ödie;* Sp.: *comedia de situaciones.*

A play characterized by fast-paced action and a complicated plot rather than finely-drawn characters. Like *comedy of intrigue**, situations succeed each other constantly; surprise, *mistaken identity** and *coups de théâtre* are its favourite mechanisms (for example, SHAKESPEARE's *The Comedy of Errors*).

SKETCH

Fr.: *sketch;* Ger.: *Sketch;* Sp.: *sketch.*

A sketch is a short scene that presents a situation, generally a comic one, played by a small number of actors with no profound characterization or plot development, emphasizing funny and subversive moments. The term refers particularly to variety entertainment in which a character or a scene is played using a humourous and satirical text, in music hall, cabaret, on television or in café *theatre**. It is driven mainly by a satire of contemporary life, sometimes literary (as in a parody of a well-known text or famous person), sometimes grotesque and burlesque (as on television or in the movies) (R. DEVOS, G. BEDOS, formerly F. RAYNAUD, COLUCHE and P. DESPROGES).

See also: playlet.

SOCIAL CONDITION

Fr.: *condition;* Ger.: *gesellschaftlicher Stand;* Sp.: *condición social.*

See CONDITION

SOCIOCRITICISM

Fr.: *sociocritique*; Ger.: *Soziokritik*; Sp.: *sociocrítica*.

Method of textual analysis intended to examine the relationship between text and society, to study "the status of the social in the text rather than the social status of the text" (DUCHET 1973, 14). Sociocriticism looks at how the social dimension is reflected in the structure of the text: structure of the fiction, structure of the *fabula* and specificity of writing; it sees itself as "a poetics of society, inseparable from a reading of the ideological in its textual possibilities" (DUCHET and GAILLARD 1976, 4).

1. Sociocriticism in Theory and in Literary Criticism

This method was first applied to the (essentially realistic and naturalistic) novel, to works whose relationship with the society and ideology of their times was fairly clear (DUCHET 1979). It was developed in the early 1960s as a continuation of a sociology of literature and a formalist approach to the literary fact. Sociology seemed too general, too preoccupied with great themes and the explicit content of a work, to be used to analyze texts by identifying the social or mental structures they hypothesized. Formalism, on the other hand, claimed to exclude all social references in textual analysis, leading to descriptions of micromechanisms that failed to account for historical origins or connections with the world of ideas. Briefly, sociocriticism aims, if not to reconcile sociological and formalist perspectives, then at least to compare them. It attempts to describe the inner workings of specific works without excluding the relevance of the social context in which they are produced and received.

2. Problems in Sociocriticism

Sociocriticism applied to theatre is in its early stages, in the strict sense at least, for attempts to relate text and history are clearly not new. Before proposing a specific program for such an approach, we should first look at the problems in the theory of ideology, of the relationship between text and history, of determination by social context.

Clearly, a theory of ideology is badly needed, if we understand this to mean a theory that would go beyond the conception of ideology as *camera obscura* (MARX), as false consciousness, a manoeuvre to divert and exploit. It would be a little hasty to say (along with a certain Marxist line of thinking) that ideology is made only to mask reality, camouflage truth, to govern one group and serve another. For one thing, we would have to see how such ideology functions in and for the literary text!

Setting up an opposition between the individual and the social, as both sociology and common sense are prone to do, poses the problem of that opposition which is precisely what should be overcome, in order to "get beyond the mechanistic duality: individual *and* society, artistic work *and* external conditions of production" (JAFFRÉ 1974, 73), in order to link sociology and psychoanalysis.

3. Program of a Sociocriticism of the Theatre

The program is an ambitious one; still, Claude DUCHET is right in seeing theatre as a privileged field of (future) sociocriticism, for "theatre displays a socialized usage of words and its text can go back to such a usage, by reflecting the very value of the words and he who speaks them, by basing its problematics on the verbal exchange that constitutes it" (DUCHET 1979, 147).

A. THE EXCHANGE OF WORDS

Besides the obvious fact of a dialogue, of roles and characters, the questions one asks include who is ultimately speaking to whom, what roles and strategies are put into play, what social forces – ideological and discursive formations – establish a "dialogue" through the conflicts and actants (cf. FOUCAULT, ALTHUSSER).

B. THE DRAMATIC SYSTEM

If there is theatre, and therefore words in conflict and imbalance, it is also because the social microcosm of the characters finds its best expression in this conflictive form where no one ever has the last word.

C. TEXT AND STAGE PRACTICES

Theatre is more than the dramatic text. It only really exists once it is enunciated on stage, set off (rather than served) by the many sign systems (actors, lighting, rhythm, stage design, etc.). It is an ideal subject for sociocriticism, which must examine the actual stage work and the origins and functions of paraverbal systems, which sees performance as a social practice: Which troupe performs (or performed) Molière? What kind of actors were used? Who co-ordinated their work, and for what social and aesthetic purpose? What hierarchy was established in the performance? These questions are asked in order to acquire a grasp of the social dimension of stage practice, the meaning of the forms and materials used. They are often quite ambitious, attempting to determine the links between a society, a dance and a particular stage design, for example (FRANCASTEL 1970), or how to analyze "the situation of the audience within the theatre space" (HAYS 1981, 369).

D. MEDIATION OF THE MISE-EN-SCÈNE

The mise-en-scène effects a highly "socialized" and sometimes personalized link in the director's function between the text and the audience that is to be reached intellectually and emotionally. This makes it necessary to take into account the evolution of the audience, the social context and the changing function of theatre.

E. CONCRETIZATION OF TEXT AND PERFORMANCE

In order to adapt to those changing circumstances, sociocriticism observes how the text is realized in the director's reading, then the audience's viewing. It must reconstruct the social context (the "total context of social phenomena," according to MUKAROVSKÝ) for the production of the play and its current reception.

F. IDEOLOGICAL CONTRADICTIONS

Essentially, sociocriticism assumes that the dramatic text bears the marks of ideological contradictions that are visible to some degree in the conflict of ideologems or the configuration of the dramatic system. It refuses to decide whether the author is *x* (reactionary) or *y* (progressive), the better to perceive the contradictions, the incompatibilities between worldviews. BENICHOU, who practised sociocriticism before the term existed, stated in *Morales du Grand Siècle* (1948) that MOLIÈRE does not reflect a bourgeois ideology but bears witness to an aristocratic idealism. It is not in the characters' words but in the way conflicts are represented theatrically that BENICHOU detected the balance and deep meaning of MOLIÈRE's theatre: the main difficulty continues to be to support such major divisions using the text, and to articulate them as much in relation to discursive oppositions as actantial relations (without discourse and action necessarily coinciding).

4. Sociocriticism and Other Disciplines

Although it is still searching for its own identity and path, sociocriticism differs from other "social" approaches in its methods and ends.

- Sociology of audiences analyzes the composition of and changes in the audience, and explains reception according to socioeconomic and cultural classifications (GOURDON 1982).
- Sociology of culture looks at theatre in the context of overall cultural development.
- Sociology of institutions examines literary institutions, modes of production and consumption, criticism and publishing (SARKANY 1984).

Like semiology, its older sister, sociocriticism is in great danger of losing all specificity by including the results of neighbouring disciplines without making the connection between the text and performance and the social data. At least it will have learned from semiology that text and performance can be analyzed only by going beyond their narrow bounds and accepting the constant incursions of the social into the fortress of text or performance.

Further reading: Lukács 1914; Goldmann 1955; Adorno 1984; Jameson 1981; Pavis 1983a, 1986; Viala 1985; Féral, 1990.

SOCIOLOGY OF THEATRE

Fr.: *sociologie du théâtre;* Ger.: *Soziologie des Theaters;* Sp.: *sociología del teatro.*

Discipline that examines the way the performance is produced and received by a human audience by conducting an empirical survey (on the socio-demographic make-up of the audience, for instance) or by inquiring into the spectator's "incorporated cultural capital" (BOURDIEU).

Sociology does not establish the play's links to economic infrastructure but rather assesses the relationship of the play (text or performance) with the mentality or ideological conceptions of a group, a social class, or a historic period. The program designed by GURVITCH (1956) and carried further by DUVIGNAUD (1965) and SHEVTSOVA (1993) is still current today:

- Study of audiences to "understand their diversity, their different degrees of cohesion, the importance of their possible conversions into more formal groupings" (1956, 202).
- "Analysis of the theatrical performance itself as unfolding within a particular social framework."
- "Study of the group of actors as a troupe and, more generally, as a profession."
- Analysis of the relationship between the fiction (text and performance) and the society where it was produced and is received.
- Comparison of the possible functions of theatre according to the status of a society at a given point in time.

Sociology stands to gain from comparing its results to the aesthetics of reception (JAUSS 1982b) by determining the audience's horizon of expectations, the "theatrical system of pre-receptive preconditions" (DE MARINIS 1987, 88), and above all the spectator's aesthetic experience, without neglecting a hermeneutical reflection on the conditions of understanding and experiencing, thus undertaking an anthropology of spectator and performance.

See also: Sociocriticism, semiology.

SOLILOQUY

(From the Latin *solus*, alone, and *loqui*, to speak)
Fr.: *soliloque;* Ger.: *Monolog;* Sp.: *soliloquio.*

A soliloquy is a speech addressed by a person or character to himself. Even more than the monologue, the soliloquy refers to a situation in which a character reflects on his psychological and moral situation, using this theatrical convention to reveal what would have remained merely an interior monologue. This technique gives the spectator a glimpse of the character's soul or unconscious, hence its epic and lyric dimension and its ability to become a little gem that may be taken out of the play to stand on its own (cf. Hamlet's soliloquy "To be or not to be").

In dramaturgical terms, the soliloquy answers two requirements:

1. According to the dramatic rules, the use of the soliloquy is warranted in certain situations when it can be spoken realistically: a moment of self-examination by the hero, a dialogue betwen two moral or psychological necessities that the subject is required to state out loud (*dilemma**). The only condition for success is that it be sufficiently constructed and clear to be more than a monologue or an "inaudible" stream of consciousness.

2. By epic standards, the soliloquy is a way of objectifying thoughts that would otherwise not be voiced. Hence its believable nature within the purely dramatic form. The soliloquy breaks the illusion and institutes a theatre convention that enables direct communication to be established with the audience.

See also: dialogue, aside, address to the audience, stanza.

SONG

Fr.: *song;* Ger.: *Song;* Sp.: *song.*

BRECHT used the English word to describe the songs in his plays (beginning with *The Threepenny Opera* in 1928), to differentiate them from the "harmonious" singing that illustrates a situation or mood in opera or musical comedy. The Brechtian song is a means of *alienation**, a parodic and grotesque poem in a syncopated rhythm that is spoken or chanted rather than sung.

SOTIE

Fr.: *sotie;* Ger.: *satirische Posse, Sotie;* Sp.: *sotie, farsa.*

A medieval comic play (from the fourteenth and fifteenth centuries) in which fools attack conventions and the establishment under the cloak of madness (for example, *Jeu du prince des sots* by GRINGORE).

See also: play, farce, morality.

Further reading: Picot, 1902–1912; Aubailly 1976.

SOUBRETTE

(From the Provençal *soubreto,* meaning affected.)
Fr.: *soubrette;* Ger.: *Soubrette, Zofe;* Sp.: *criada.*

The soubrette is the maid to the main female character of the play. The servants often take the initiative to set their masters straight or to react strongly against their extravagant projects (as do Dorine and Toinette in MOLIÈRE). Often considered part of the bourgeois families they serve, these ladies' maids are more ladies' companions than domestics (e.g. Marton in *les Fausses Confidences,* Lisette in *le Jeu de l'amour et du hasard*). Although, unlike valets, they rarely initiate action, soubrettes do contribute to clarifying the psychology of their mistresses and influence the development of the plot.

SOUND EFFECTS

Fr.: *bruitage;* Ger.: Geräuschekulisse; Sp.: *efectos de sonido.*

Sound effects are artificial reproductions of natural and man-made sounds. Although it may not always be easy, they must be distinguished from words (as vocal material), music, *gibberish** and, particularly, stage-generated noise. They are the set of sound events included in musical composition (N. FRIZE).

1. Origins

Sound effects may be produced on stage as required by the *fabula,* or made in the wings or broadcast through the loudspeakers and "laminated" onto the show – i.e., they may be diegetic or extra-diegetic. Sometimes, however, the musicians and sound crew are located just between the stage and the wings, as, for example, in the Théâtre du Soleil's productions of SHAKESPEARE's plays or *Sihanouk.*

2. Techniques

Sound effects are rarely made on stage by the actor. They are most often produced in the wings by technicians using various kinds of machines. Sometimes they have been pre-recorded for the director's specific needs and retransmitted by loudspeakers distributed throughout the audience.

Sounds are taped using the most sophisticated techniques imaginable – mixing, synthesizing and modulation. Sound effects sometimes take over the performance altogether; a mechanical art penetrating the living tissue of the theatre event, leaving nothing to chance and threatening to take control. Using sound effects is always a little like letting a fox loose in a chicken coop.

3. Dramaturgical Functions

A. REALISTIC EFFECTS

Realistic sound effects made in the wings can imitate a sound (telephone, doorbell, tape recorder, etc.) and take part in the development of the action.

B. ATMOSPHERE

The sound track builds up a sound set by evoking noises characteristic of a given environment (PAVIS 1996a).

C. SOUND FRAME

In an empty set, a sound effect creates a space, a depth of field, an atmosphere for the duration of a sound frame, as in radio plays.

D. SOUND COUNTERPOINT
Sound effects act in parallel to the stage action, like off-screen sound in film, giving stage action a very full colouring and meaning. Placing loudspeakers in the wings or in the hall distributes the sound evenly and disorients the audience.
Further reading: Pavis 1996a.

SOUND MONTAGE

Fr.: *montage sonore*; Ger.: *Geraüschmontage*; Sp.: *montaje sonoro*.
See SOUND

SOUND SCENERY

Fr.: *décor sonore*; Ger.: *Geräuschkulisse*; Sp.: *decorado sonoro*.

Means of suggesting the framework of the play with sound. Sound effects draw on radio play techniques and are often substituted today for realistic and figurative scenery.

SOURCE

Fr.: *source*; Ger.: *Quelle*; Sp.: *fuente*.

All of the plays (both texts and performances) that may have influenced the playwright, either directly or indirectly.

In the narrow sense, a source is a text that inspired the playwright in doing preparatory work: other plays, archives, legends, myths, and so on. All dramatic writing implies a certain amount of *dramaturgical* adaptation**, and the playwright may use a great variety of materials according to need, sometimes bordering on plagiarism (BÜCHNER copied excerpts from history books for *Danton's Death*).

The notion of source is seldom used except by positivist critics in the style of LANSON ("the idea would have been" he wrote in the preface to his critical edition of VOLTAIRE's *Lettres philosophiques* (1909), "to discover for each sentence the event, text or words that had set in motion Voltaire's intelligence or imagination"). Today we voice no such vain or wild claim; sources are not seen as having an absolute explanatory value. We pay attention to stage and textual intertextuality by asking what other plays or styles are referred to by a text or staging and observing what acting and staging traditions are reactivated in contemporary theatre production.
See also: theme, reading, documentary theatre, adaptation, motif.
Further reading: Frenzel 1963; Demougin 1985.

SPACE

Fr.: *espace*; Ger.: *Raum*; Sp.: *espacio*.

The notion of space, a tremendously popular one in the theory of theatre as well as in the human sciences, is used for very different aspects of text and performance. Although to try to isolate and define all of the spaces involved is a vain and hopeless undertaking, we will make an attempt at classification for the sake of clarity.

1. *Dramatic space**, referred to by the text, is an abstract dramaturgical space that the reader or spectator must construct in the imagination (by "fictionalizing" it).

2. *Stage space** is the actual space on stage in which the actors move, whether they confine themselves to the stage area *per se* or mix with the audience.

3. *Theatre space** is the space occupied by the audience and actors in the course of a performance. It is characterized by the *theatrical relationship** between the two (R. DURAND 1980). The term "audience space" could be reserved for the place occupied by the audience during the performance and intermission (or just before the play begins). The *theatre space* is the total of spaces 1, 2, 4, 5 and 6 and is constructed, according to Anne UBERSFELD, "on the basis of an architecture, a (pictorial) view of the world, or a space sculpted essentially by the actors' bodies" (1981, 85).

4. *Gestural space** is created by the actors, their presence and movements, their interrelationships, and the stage arrangement.

5. *Textual space** is space from the point of view of its graphic, phonic or rhetorical materiality, the space of the "score" containing the actors' speeches and the stage directions. The textual space is realized when the text is used not as a dramatic space fictionalized by the reader or hearer but as raw material arranged for the audience's eyes and ears as a "pattern" (as in B. WILSON or MNOUCHKINE's recent productions with the Théâtre du Soleil) or as systematic repetition (HANDKE).

6. *Inner space** is stage space as an attempt to represent a fantasy, dream or vision of the playwright or a character, as for instance the space created by R. PLANCHON for *Arthur Adamov* or by P. ADRIEN for *Rêves de F. Kafka* (*fantasy**).

The way in which space functions in contemporary mise-en-scène is covered under each of these six kinds of space and in the entries for *stage design**, *stage arrangement**, *stage machinery**, *parcours**, *stage boards**, *street theatre**, *mass theatre** and *image**.

SPECIFICITY OF THEATRE

Fr.: *spécificité théâtrale;* Ger.: *Wesen des Theaters;* Sp.: *especificidad teatral.*

The search for the specificity of theatre is a somewhat metaphysical undertaking if the intention is to isolate a substance that would contain all properties of all theatres. This expression (as well as *theatrical language, stage writing** and *theatricality**) is used to differentiate theatre from literature and the other arts (architecture, painting, dance and so on). *Semiology** also asks whether there are theatrical *signs** and a set of *codes** proper to the theatre or whether the codes used on stage are borrowed from other artistic systems. It looks at the *essence** of theatre in terms of how signifying systems function.

1. A Theatrical Sign?

The existence of a *specificity of theatre* would imply that the iconic aspect of the stage (the visual) and the symbolic aspect of the text (the textual) could meld into a properly dramatic whole that could not be broken down. On the other hand, linguistic signs and visual signs always retain their autonomy, even when they are combined and allied in such a way as to produce a signified unattached to a single stage system. The sign in theatre is never a mixture of various codes, as a colour may be a mixture of two primary colours. The only possible "specificity" is the fact of using and regrouping different stage materials at the same time and in the same place. Still, this technique exists in other performing arts.

2. A Specific Combination of Signs?

The second question is whether theatre performance maintains the autonomy of its materials or creates a synthesis that can be called "specifically theatrical." In fact, each production has its own answer, based on aesthetic and ideological choices. The production may pursue harmony and "correspondences" among its materials (as in opera, particularly Wagnerian opera), or it may isolate systems, each of which retains its autonomy and may even be opposed to each of the other materials (as in BRECHT), to avoid creating the illusion of a seamless whole.

3. Other Specificities

A. VOICE

The iconic nature of the stage and the symbolic nature of the text, the figurative and the discursive (LYOTARD 1971), represent the two poles of performance: the actor's physical acting and his words. It is in the actor's *voice**, which simultaneously forms part of the body and of articulate language, that a tension is produced that is far from being resolved in an absolute synthesis (VELTRUSKÝ 1976, 94–117, BERNARD 1976).

B. ACTION AND "MOBILITY" OF THE THEATRICAL SIGN
Since ARISTOTLE's *Poetics*, action has often been considered an indispensable part of theatre. This may be attributed to the narrative's ability to move from one system to another without distinction, provided that all the systems come together in an overall project. The unifying function of action was also stressed by the Prague Circle: "Action – the very essence of dramatic art – fuses word, actor, costume, scenery and music in the sense that we recognize them as conductors of a single current that travels through them, passing from to the other or through several at a time." (HONZL 1971, 18). We can also speak of the *vectorization** of the staging, of the way in which it combines the motifs and materials of the performance.

C. DYNAMICS OF THE SIGN
Ultimately, the specificity of theatrical signs may lie in their ability to use the three possible functions of signs: as icon (mimetically), as index (in the situation of enunciation), or as symbol (as a semiological system in the fictional mode). In effect, theatre makes the sources of the words visual and concrete: it indicates *and* incarnates a fictional world by means of signs, such that by the end of the process of signification and symbolization the spectator has reconstructed a theoretical and aesthetic model that accounts for the dramatic universe.

D. THE DEMISE OF SPECIFICITY?
When faced with the *media**, like it or not, the theatre either sells its soul or finds a new specificity through new exchanges. This "mediatization" of theatre is reflected in the growing frequency of exchanges with the mechanical arts: theatre practice blithely trespasses on media property, using video, television and audio recordings within the theatre performance, and is constantly being recorded, taped and filed. There is so much borrowing and exchange going on between theatre and the media that there is not much sense in defining theatre as a "pure art," or even in drawing up a *theory of theatre** that does not take account of the media practices to be found on the fringes of, and sometimes within, contemporary staging practice (PAVIS 1985a).

Today we no longer assume that theatre exists as an autonomous, unified art. In view of the above process, the only legitimate search would seem to be for a minimal theatre, for what is left when everything is taken away, in the sense of the *poor theatre* of GROTOWSKI, "the proper spectator-actor relationship for each type of performance" (GROTOWSKI 1971, 19; Eng. 1968, 20).

See also: minimal unit, Gesamtkunstwerk, ethnoscenology.

Further reading: Appia 1895, 1963; Ellis-Fermor 1945; Fergusson 1949; Bentley 1957, 1964; Bazin 1959; Artaud 1958; Brach 1965; Kowzan 1968; Gouhier 1958, 1968, 1972; Havel 1977; *Versus*, 1978; Pavis 1983a.

SPECTACLE

Fr.: *spectacle*; Ger.: *Vorstellung*; Sp.: *espectáculo*.

A spectacle is anything that is the object of the gaze ("something presented to the view," Oxford English Dictionary), especially something intended for public display. "The spectacle is the universal category in whose species the world is seen" (BARTHES 1975, 179).

The French term applies generically to the visible part of a play (usually rendered as "performance" in English, as in the text/performance opposition), and to all kinds of performing arts (dance, opera, cinema, mime, circus) and other activities involving audience participation (sports, ritual, religious experiences, social interaction).

In current English usage, "spectacle" is generally construed as "a piece of stage-display or pageantry, as contrasted with real drama" (Oxford English Dictionary). Here, however, it is used in the technical sense of the visual aspect of the theatre phenomenon.

1. Spectacle as Superfluous

In classical dramaturgy, *spectacle* equalled *staging** (*mise en scène*), a term not yet in existence. In the nineteenth century there were *spectacle plays*, in which a great array of visual stage elements were deployed. *Spectacle* had a pejorative connotation, as opposed to the deep, lasting nature of the text. ARISTOTLE listed it in his *Poetics* as one of the six parts of tragedy, only to diminish its importance with respect to action and content: "Spectacle, though fascinating in itself, is of all the parts the least technical in the sense of being least germane to the art of poetry." (1450b) Theorists (e.g. MARMONTEL) long continued to reproach it for its external, material nature, apt for amusement rather than entertainment. The spectacle was distrusted, as in *Spectacle dans un fauteuil* (MUSSET 1832) or *Théâtre en liberté* (HUGO 1886), created in reaction to the staging, which did not wish to run the risk of imposing a too-visual and "unfaithful" staging on the written text.

The classical conception was not opposed to spectacle on principle, however. D'AUBIGNAC (1657) stressed its use in representation, but there was a categorical separation of text and spectacle, or performance, rather than a sensitivity to their interdependence.

2. Spectacle Reconquered
With the emergence of the mise-en-scène and the awareness of its decisive importance to an understanding of the play, the visible aspect of theatre recovered its status. ARTAUD saw it as being the heart of theatre: "We intend to base the theatre upon spectacle before everything else, and we shall introduce into the spectacle a new notion of space utilized on all possible levels and in all degrees of perspective in depth and height, and within this notion a specific idea of time will be added to that of movement" (1964b, 188; Eng. 1958, 124). He notes the contrast with the existing concept of the term: "... the kind of performance improperly called spectacle, with everything pejorative, accessory, ephemeral, and external that that term carries with it" (1964b, 160; Eng. 1958, 105–106).

3. Nature of Contemporary Spectacle
- Everything is meaningful: text, stage, location of theatre, auditorium space. The spectacle is not confined to the playing area but invades the auditorium and the city beyond, bursting the bounds of its *frame**.
- All possible methods are permissible: speech, acting, new technology. Theatre has abandoned its requirement of pure form to embrace any means of expression that may be useful to it.
- The aim is no longer to produce illusion by concealing its process of manufacture; that process is integrated with the performance in stressing the sensorial and sensual aspect of theatre without being concerned with meaning.

4. Which Theory of Spectacle?
A general theory of spectacle would seem to be premature at present, first of all because the borders between reality and spectacle are not easy to define. Can anything be transformed into spectacle? Yes, if the aim is to make it the object of *ostension** and observation; no, if that object must also be *spectacular*, astonishing and fascinating to the observer. At the very least, we can arrive at a minimal and purely theoretical definition: "The definition of show [*spectacle*], then, includes, from an internal point of view, characteristics such as the presence of a closed tridimensional space, proxemic distribution, etc., whereas, from an external point of view, it involves the presence of an observer actant (excluding from this definition ceremonies, mythical rituals, for example, in which the presence of spectators is not necessary)." (GREIMAS and COURTÈS 1979, 393; Eng. 1982, 343).

What practices might be categorized as "spectacular"? Theatre, cinema, television, but also strip tease, street performances, and even erotic play and domestic scenes when they are observed either deliberately or accidentally.

A typology of spectacle is risky as well, although it might be divided into *performing arts** and *stage arts**. Another criterion might be fictional status, giving us fictional arts (e.g. theatre, non-documentary film, mime) and non-fictional arts (e.g. circus, bull fights, sports). The latter do not seek to create a reality different from our own reference reality, but to generate a performance

based on their ability to appeal to the audience through strength or expertise.
See also: performance art, text and performance, (re)theatricalization, theatricality, play.
Further reading: *Spectacles à travers les âges (les)*, 1931; Dumur 1965; Debord 1967; Giteau 1970; Dupavillon 1970–1978; Rapp 1973; Zimmer 1977; Kowzan 1975; Dort 1979; *Cahiers de médiologie*, 1996.

SPECTACULAR

Fr.: *spectaculaire;* Ger.: spektakulär; Sp.: *espectacular.*

"Of the nature of a spectacle or show; striking or imposing as a display" (*Oxford English Dictionary*). This is a fluid notion since, like the uncanny, the strange and all other categories defined on the basis of *reception** by the spectator, it depends as much on the perceiving subject as on the object perceived.

The degree of spectacularity of a particular play depends on the staging and the aesthetics of the era, which may reject (classical stage) or encourage (contemporary stage) the emergence of the spectacular. Theatre is often accused of making sacrifices for the spectacular, i.e. seeking facile effects or masking the text and reading beneath a mass of visual signs.

The spectacular, then, is a historical category that depends on the ideology and aesthetics of the time, which decide what can and must be shown and how – by visualization, allusion in the narrative, use of sound effects, etc. Although it is associated in theatre history with visuality and visual *representation**, this may be only an accident of civilization; the spectacular could also be linked to hearing, touch or taste.
See also: performance.
Further reading: Alexandrescu 1984.

SPECTATOR

Fr.: *spectateur;* Ger.: *Zuschauer;* Sp.: *espectador.*

1. Long forgotten or considered of negligible importance, the spectator is at present the favourite object of study of *semiology** or *reception** aesthetics. However, there is no homogeneous perspective that could encompass all possible approaches from the spectator's point of view, such as sociology, *sociocriticism**, psychology, semiology, *anthropology**, etc. It is not an easy matter to grasp all the implication of the fact that the spectator cannot be separated as an individual from the audience as a collective agent. Each individual spectator contains within him the ideological and psychological codes of several groups, while, on the other hand, the audience sometimes forms a single entity, a body that reacts *en masse* (*participation*).

2. The sociological approach generally confines itself to the composition and sociocultural origin of audiences, their tastes and reactions (GOURDON, 1982). *Questionnaires** and tests administered during and after the performance help refine results and measure reactions to the performance, which is considered a set of stimuli. Experimental psychology, and even physiology, undertake the task of quantifying reception. This does not make the process of staging easier to understand. This sociological model would have to be related to a perception of theatrical forms, without setting up an opposition between statistical quantitative data and the qualitative perception of forms, since (and this could be the motto of sociocriticism) "what is truly social in literature is form" (LUKACS, 1961, 71).

3. Semiology is concerned with the way the spectator builds meaning on the basis of the series of performance signs, of the convergences and discrepancies among the various signifieds.

The spectator's work (and pleasure) consists in continuously effecting a series of micro-choices or mini-actions to focus, exclude, combine, compare, an activity that affects the performance as well: "The effect of an artistic performance on the spectator," remarks BRECHT, "is not independent of the effect of the spectator on the artist. In theatre, the audience regulates the performance" (*Arbeitsjournal*).

4. Reception aesthetics looks for an implicit or ideal spectator. It is based on the principle (albeit a very debatable one) that the staging must be received and understood in a single right way and that everything is arranged according to that all-powerful receiver. In fact, it is the spectator's gaze and desire that establish the stage production by giving sense to the performance, conceived as a changing set of enunciators. The spectator's pleasure at such instances of enunciation varies: being deceived by the illusion, believing and not believing (*denial**), regressing to an infantile state in which the motionless body experiences, without too much risk, dangerous, frightening and gratifying situations. Its vulnerability limited, the audience is not really threatened by the performance. While the cinema can easily activate fantasy and plumb the depths of the psyche, in theatre the spectator is conscious of the conventions (the fourth wall, the character, dramaturgy); he remains the chief manipulator, the stage-hand for his own emotions, the craftsman of the theatrical event. The theatregoer moves toward the stage of his own accord, while the filmgoer is relentlessly absorbed by the screen. In the theatre, the spectator can (theoretically) intervene on stage, be a troublemaker, applaud or whistle; in fact, he internalizes such intervention rites without disturbing the ceremony staged so painstakingly by the artists.
Further reading: Poerschke 1952; Rapp 1973; Ruprecht 1976; Fieguth 1979; Turk 1976; Hays 1981, 1983; Hanna 1983; Avigal and Weitz 1985; *Versus*, 1985; Pavis 1985d; Wirth 1985; Schoenmakers 1986; Deldime 1990; Dort 1995; Guy and Mironer 1988.

SPOKEN ACTION

Fr.: *action parlée*; Ger.: *Sprechhandlung*; Sp.: *acción hablada*.

1. In theatre, action is not simply a question of perceptible movement. It is situated *also*, and in classical tragedy *especially*, within a character in its progression, in decisions, and therefore in *speeches** (cf. *action parlée* in French, from *azione parlata* as defined by PIRANDELLO).

All speech on stage is active – here, more than anywhere else, "saying is doing." D'AUBIGNAC was well aware of this, CORNEILLE made his monologues into discursive mimes (PAVIS 1978a), CLAUDEL contrasted Kabuki (in which the actors speak) to Bunraku (in which words act). All theatre people know, like SARTRE, "that language is action, that there is a language proper to theatre and that this language must never be descriptive [...] that language is a point in action as in life and that it is used only to give orders, present a defence, state emotions in the form of pleadings (thus for an active end), to convince or to defend or to accuse, to embody decisions, for verbal duels, refusals, avowals, etc.; in other words, always as an act" (1973, 133–134).

2. In view of the foregoing, *pragmatics** sees dialogue and stage events as performative actions and as a play on the presuppositions and the implicit elements of any conversation; that is, as a way of acting on the world by using words.
Further reading: Searle 1975; *Poetica*, 1976; Pfister 1978; Ubersfeld 1977a, 1981; Pavis 1980a.

SPOKEN AND UNSPOKEN

Fr.: *dit et non-dit*; Ger.: *Gesprochenes und Unausgesprochenes*; Sp.: *dicho y no dicho*.

How to speak about the unspoken – and, to begin with, where to locate it? Both the *dramatic text** and the staging are necessarily incomplete and do not say everything there is to say about the meaning of a character, an action or a non-verbal element. It is up to the reader or spectator to fill in the blanks of the ellipsis, of the points of suspension, of the implicit and unspeakable.

1. The discourse of character is always incomplete. Certain thoughts and motivations remain unknown to us (and to him), either because that is the way he is charac-

terized or because the textual strategy chooses to leave us in ignorance in order to build suspense, force us to complete the text, or play on its incompleteness.

2. The unspoken also abounds in the *fabula*, whether it is referred to as blank spots, spots of indeterminacy (INGARDEN, ISER), gaps (UBERSFELD 1977a) or the unconscious of the text. Any text is incomplete by nature, inconsistent and filled with presupposition and implicit statements (*pragmatics**). The task of the *dramaturg** and director is to reconstruct a possible trajectory (*parcours**) through the dramatic text, to determine its *fabula** and to suggest a possible concretization. There are many ways to reduce these pockets of the unspoken, though not all of them are equally valid. It must first be decided what the text is to say, and above all what *modality** the spoken is assigned – is to be believed, suggested, presented as a possibility or a certainty. In the last analysis, this major *hermeneutical** issue is resolved by the staging and the performers.

3. The unspoken aspects of the mise-en-scène are found in the ways in which it decides to clarify or complicate the text, by giving information about the characters' motivations and the psychological and/or socioeconomic basis for their behaviour, in other words releasing what STANISLAVSKI called the subtext (see *text and performance**). These unspoken aspects "expressed" by the mise-en-scène and the actors in non-verbal communication are often considered a betrayal of the dramatic text. It would seem more proper to see them as the production of the text on stage, hence as a way of saying the unsaid, of producing meaning.

See also: silence, discourse, interpretation, staging.

Further reading: Ellis-Fermor 1945; Ducrot 1972; J. Miller 1972; Ubersfeld 1977a, Pavis 1986.

SPONTANEOUS THEATRE

Fr.: *théâtre spontané*; Ger.: *spontanes Theater*; Sp.: *teatro espontáneo*.

Spontaneous theatre (or *autonomous theatre*, in the words of N. EUREINOFF (1930) and later T. KANTOR) tries to eliminate the boundary between life and theatre, between audience and actor. Spontaneous activity takes place as soon as there is a creative exchange between spectator and actor, and the performance takes on the appearance of a *happening**, *dramatic play** and an improvisation that encroaches on external reality, or a *psychodrama**.

See also: psychodrama, improvisation, happening, invisible theatre.

Further reading: Pörtner 1972; Kantor 1977.

STAGE

Fr.: *scène*; Ger.: *Bühne*; Sp.: *escenario*.

1. The Greek *skênê* was, at the beginning, a cabin or tent behind the *orchestra*. *Skênê*, *orchestra* and *theatron* were the three elements of the Greek stage; the orchestra, or performing area, connected the stage with the audience.

The *skênê* developed above, containing the *theologeion* or playing area of gods and heros, and at surface level with the proscenium, the architectural facade that was the predecessor to the walled set and, later, the apron.

STAGE ARRANGEMENT

Fr.: *dispositif scénique*; Ger.: *Bühnengestaltung*; Sp.: *dispositivo escénico*.

The term implies that the stage is not fixed and that the scenery does not remain unchanged from beginning to end. The stage designer uses playing areas, objects and different planes according to the action needed, and does not hesitate to vary this structure in the course of the performance. The theatre is a *machine** with greater affinities to a child's building set than to a decorative fresco. The stage arrangement visualizes the *actantial** relations and facilitates the actors' movements.

See also: space, parcours, stage boards.

STAGE-AUDIENCE RELATIONSHIP

Fr.: *rapport scène-salle;* Ger.: *theatralisches Grundverhältnis;*
Sp.: *relación escena-sala.*

1. Stage Design

The relative placement of the audience and the playing area influences the transmission and reception of the performance. Things change depending on whether they are spoken on a picture-frame stage, a theatre-in-the-round or an Elizabethan stage. Each stage has its own way of relating to the audience: illusionism, participation, interrupted play, consumption, etc. Each kind of stage tends to reproduce the structures of a given society: the proscenium-arch theatre, a hierarchy; the popular theatre-in-the-round, community; the total environment theatre, a fragmented reality. We should not, however, establish an overly-narrow determinism between the type of stage and the type of society (for instance, BRECHT often used a picture-frame stage, and there is often a false democratization of round stages where the audience is encouraged to participate). Nevertheless, contemporary mise-en-scène very carefully establishes an appropriate relationship, when necessary building a new structure within the existing theatre building.

2. Exchange between Stage and Audience

In addition to this concrete spatial relationship, there are psychological and social relationships between stage and audience that reflect the aim of the performance.

A. IDENTIFICATION*

The picture-frame stage requires the *spectator** to identify with the fiction by projection. The stage then supposedly reproduces the structure of the audience, which is supposed to give in *en masse* to the actors-illusionists (*denial**).

B. CRITICAL DISTANCE*

The Brechtian stage, on the other hand, widens the gap between stage and audience, prevents the interest from being "displaced" from the audience to the stage, produces a critical distance and divides the audience through the play. The social contradictions of the audience (if there are any) refer back to those of the fiction, and vice versa. The stage-audience relationship is therefore a kind of barometer that indicates how theatre acts upon an audience.

C. ALTERNATION

Some directors (WILSON, DEMARCY, LASSALLE) attempt to establish a variable relationship between stage and audience; closeness and distance, uniqueness and reception. This new kind of relationship appears to be intended to transcend the identification/alienation opposition.

D. MODIFICATION OF THE FICTION-REALITY RELATIONSHIP

Theatre plays at modifying the relationship between the playing area (fiction) and the audience (reality). By breaking the *framework** of the traditional stage, it attempts to use the fiction to encroach upon the spectator's real space, to question the security of that place where one may watch without getting involved. In fact, some productions (dramatic play or *happenings**) would like to do away with that place altogether and integrate the spectator's gaze into the fiction, destroy the barrier between stage and audience. All such attempts, however, must contend with the spectator's gaze, which immediately establishes the division between his own real world and the fictional universe.

3. Permanence of Stage/Audience Duality

In fact, far from being eliminated, the *distance** between stage and audience has widened, is even the hallmark of theatrical performance. Only the playwright's aesthetic project has changed, shortening or lengthening that distance. In Wagnerian musical drama, for instance, the orchestra is buried so as not to interfere with the merging of stage and audience. Epic theatre, however, accentuates the difference; if it wishes to "bury the orchestra" (W. BENJAMIN) it is to install a podium in its place, the better to lay bare the devices of stage illusion. There have been many experiments on stage-audience distance in the Wagnerian direction of merging, to encourage participation. MEYERHOLD links stage and audience with a passageway of flowers borrowed from Japanese theatre. The theatre-in-the-round and the environmental theatre have the same integrational objective. But whether the relationship is frontal, lateral or all-encompassing, the rule of duality applies to any performance. What does change is the aesthetic distance between spectator and stage, the way in which *reception** determines the understanding of the performance. This confusion in the use of *distance** or *perspective**, sometimes concrete, sometimes cognitive, underlies all the paradoxes of illusion, as well as all reflection on the specificity of communication in theatre.

Further reading: Hays 1977; Pavis 1980c; R. Durand 1980; Chambers 1980; States 1985.

STAGE BOARDS

Fr.: *tréteau*; Ger.: *Gerüst, die Bretter*; Sp.: *tablado*.

Historically, the "boards" were the popular stage reduced to its simplest expression (boards resting on supports every one to one and a half meters). The term refers to the *popular theatre** performed in the open air, as for example on the Pont-Neuf at the beginning of the seventeenth century.

Following the excesses of *stage machinery** and the illusionism of the picture-frame stage, *stage design** rediscovered the bare *space** which enhances the actor's gestural virtuosity and the text's purity: "Good or bad, rudimentary or refined, artificial or realistic, we mean to deny the importance of machinery [...] For the new play, give us a bare stage" (COPEAU 1974, 31–32).

The return of the stage boards is connected to the (debatable) idea that the great dramatic text speaks on its own without the director having to fill it with visual commentary. One kind of machinery disappears, another comes along to replace it: that of the actor who provides spatial coordinates, show where the stage ends and the wings begin, invent new conventions constantly, enhance theatricality (as in the scenes of buffoonery or improvised boards and, today, the Théâtre du Soleil). The boards may be used as a podium for social demonstration (in BRECHT, the "street scene" forces the actor to reconstruct the scene he has witnessed), a trajectory traced out, a historical tribunal or a kind of perch for the actor, who recreates and "projects" space from himself. They are a magnificent trampoline for an actor left to his own devices and master of his text.

See also: *parcours*, space.

STAGE BUSINESS

Fr.: *jeu de scène*; Ger.: *äussere Handlung, Bühnengeschenen*;
Sp.: *juego escénico*.

Wordless action by the actor that uses exclusively the actor's presence or gestures to express a feeling or situation before or during a speech. Classical theorists spoke of *jeu de théâtre* in this sense, as when one "put pantomime in the place of eloquence" (VOLTAIRE).

STAGE DESIGN

Fr.: *scénographie*; Ger.: *Bühnenbild*; Sp.: *escenografía*.

Skênographia, for the Greeks, was the art of decorating theatre, and the resulting painted set. In the Renaissance, scenography referred to the technique of designing and painting a backdrop in perspective. In the modern sense, stage design is the science and art of organizing the stage and theatre space. By metonymy, it is also the scenery itself, the result of the stage designer's work.

The concept of stage design today goes beyond the notion of ornamentation and packaging, which is often still tied to the outmoded conception of theatre as decoration. Stage design aspires to be a kind of writing in three-dimensional space (to which we could even add the dimension of time) rather than a pictoral art of painted canvas, just as theatre is no longer content with naturalism. The stage should not be considered to be the concretization of problematic *stage directions**; it refuses to merely "figure" (represent) a pre-existing and prevailing text.

1. A Writing in Space

If the set conceived as decoration was a two-dimensional one executed in painted canvas, contemporary stage design is a "writing" in three-dimensional space, a transition analogous to moving from painting to sculpture or architecture. This mutation in the function of stage design is connected to the evolution of dramaturgy, and has more to do with an autonomous development of stage aesthetics than with a profound change in the understanding of the text and its representation on stage.

It was long believed that the scenery should materialize the believable and ideal spatial coordinates of the text as the author envisaged them when writing the play: stage design consisted in providing the spectator with the means of localizing and recognizing a universal neutral place (palace, square) that was adaptable to any situation and able to situate mankind as abstract, eternal, and bereft of ethnic or social roots.

Today, however, stage design no longer sees its task as an ideal and univocal illustration of the dramatic text but as an *arrangement** capable of clarifying (rather than illustrating) the text and human action, of representing a situation of *enunciation** (rather than a fixed place), and of placing the meaning of the mise-en-scène in the exchange between a space and a text. Stage design is therefore the result of a semiological conception of mise-en-scène: the concordance of the various stage materials, their interdependence, particularly image and text; the search for a situation of enunciation that is no longer "ideal" or "faithful" but as productive as possible for reading the dramatic text and relating it to other theatre practices. Its object is to set up a series of correspondences and proportions between textual and stage space; it is to structure each system "in itself" but reflecting the other in a series of agreements and discrepancies.

2. The Original Writing of the Stage Designer

Fortified with these newly-acquired powers, the stage designer is becoming aware of his autonomy and unique contribution to the production. Once a shadowy figure entrusted only with painting backdrops for the glory of actor or director, the stage designer's mission today is a complete exploration of the different *spaces** of theatre. He must take into account an ever-widening *framework**: the stage and its configuration, the stage-audience relationship, the location of the auditorium in the theatre building or social space, the immediate surroundings of the playing area and of the theatre building.

This process sometimes leads the stage designer to turn the mise-en-scène to his own advantage: that is the case when the stage space is only a pretext for an exhibition of paintings (*installation**) or a formal experiment with volumes and colours. Famous painters like PICASSO, MATISSE and the painters of the Russian ballets have felt tempted by this free expression and "theatrical" exhibition of their works, and the temptation of aestheticism in a set that is beautiful in itself continues to be a significant one, in spite of the warnings of directors who are careful to bring the scenery back to more reasonable proportions and to involve it in the production of the overall meaning of the performance.

In spite of the extreme diversity of contemporary experiments in stage design, a few trends can be identified:

- *Breaking the frontality* of the picture-frame stage in order to open the stage up to the auditorium and the spectator's gaze, to bring the spectator closer to the action. The proscenium-arch stage is felt to be an anachronism, based as it is on a remote, illusionist conception of theatre. This does not, however, rule out its revival in order to experiment with illusion, *fantasy** and stage machinery. Here the reversal is complete, for the picture-frame stage is then no longer the refuge of the believable but the reference point of deception and fantasy.

- *Opening up space* and presenting multiple points of view to relativize perceptions of the stage, by seating the audience all around and sometimes within the theatre event.
- *Arranging the stage design* according to the needs of the actor and a specific dramaturgical project.
- *Restructuring the scenery* by basing it in turn on space, objects, costumes, or anything else that goes beyond the fixed view of a surface to be dressed up.
- *Dematerializing the stage design* with the use of light and mobile materials. Here the scenery is employed as a prop or an extension of the actor. The light produced by the projectors can carve out any place or atmosphere from the darkness.

In all of these contemporary practices, stage design is no longer the mandatory painted canvas of yesteryear, but a dynamic and versatile element of theatre performance.

3. Points of Reference

Rather than provide an inevitably incomplete list of the major stage designers of the twentieth century, one should stress the founding role played by Adolphe APPIA (1862–1928) and Edward Gordon CRAIG (1872–1966). With them, stage design became for the first time the soul of the theatre performance. More than painters or decorators, APPIA and CRAIG were theatre reformers with an overall conception of mise-en-scène. They are more important for their sketches, projects and theoretical musings than for their actual designs for specific productions. Both reacted against the naturalistic style that presented the stage milieu as a passive and mimetic reflection of reality in opposition, for instance, to the conception of ANTOINE, who said "it is the milieu that determines the characters' movements, not the characters' movements that determine the milieu" (1903, 603). According to the aesthetics of APPIA and CRAIG, the breathing of a space and its rhythmical value form the core of the stage design, which is not a fixed two-dimensional object but a living body subject to time, musical tempo and variations of light. The scenery (no longer the décor, a term that is too tied to painting) is considered to be in itself a world of meaning that, far from illustrating and restating the text, presents it to the eye and ear as if from within (reflecting a Symbolist influence). APPIA "has taught us," writes COPEAU, "that the musical duration that envelops, directs and regulates the dramatic action engenders at the same time the space in which it develops. For him, the art of mise-en-scène in the pure sense of the term is nothing but the configurations of text or music, rendered perceptible by the living action of the human body and by its reaction to the resistance put up by the planes and volumes constructed on the stage. Hence the banishment from the stage of all inanimate decoration, of all painted canvases, and the primordial role of that active element, light." (*Comoedia*, 12 March 1928).

APPIA's work, besides his books – *la Mise en scène du drame wagnérien* (1895), *Die Musik und die Inszenierung* (1899), *l'Oeuvre d'art vivant* (1921) – consists of approximately one hundred sketches of scene designs for operas (WAGNER), plays (SHAKESPEARE, IBSEN, GOETHE) and "rhythmical spaces" for JAQUES-DALCROZE. "The art of staging," wrote APPIA, "is the art of projecting into space what the playwright has been able to project only in Time." The actor is no longer shut up in a constrictive milieu or shown against a fixed canvas; he is at the centre of a space animated by light. Stage design builds massive but fragile and manageable volumes: stairs, podiums, portals, pillars, shadows that do not overwhelm the actor but incorporate the human body in the musical and architectural order. Space becomes a mental landscape, a perfect architecture, dream or music become form, idea become matter; the text comes alive in the rhythmic universe of time and space.

CRAIG shares APPIA's rejection of historical accuracy, of the mise-en-scène led astray by superstar actors or pictoral illustrations, as well as his admiration for WAGNER's complete work of art, his belief in the autonomy of stage design and a dynamic synthesis of the elements of performance: "The Art of the Theatre is neither acting nor the play, it is not scene nor dance, but it consists of all the elements of which these things are composed... Action, words, line, colour, rhythm" (1905, 138; Fr. 1942, 115).

While APPIA assigned the actor a central role in the eurhythmics of space and time, CRAIG's tendency to neutralize the actor led to his theory of the Übermarionette, conceived not to replace the actor but to avoid the "involuntary confessions" of a human being overly subject to emotion, chance, the improvisation proper to living matter.

After this brilliant opening by APPIA and CRAIG, the twentieth century entered the space of stage design directly. Experiments and styles followed each other in quick succession. First came the Russian Constructivists who, like TAIROV (1885–1950) and his *Liberated Theatre* (1923), structured space according to planes, lines and curves that turned the stage into a performance machine.

In reaction against both the aestheticism of the advocates of eurhythmic space and the militant Constructivism of the Russian set designers, Jacques COPEAU (1879–1949) proposed a revival of the empty stage, a bare-boards theatre that "denies the importance of all machinery" and gives the last word to actors and gestures. The stage design must come second to the staging project, which is at the service of the text and "the outline of the dramatic action." At the opposite extreme of this bare aesthetic is that of DIAGHILEV's Russian Ballet, all the rage in Paris around 1909 with sets and costumes created by Leon BAKST, then the productions of GONTSCHAROVA and LARIONOV. A profusion of bright colours (red, orange, yellow and green) and motifs from Russian folktales enliven the painted set and the costumes of the singers, dancers or choristers. With what has been called "painters' theatre," stage design runs a risk (thought it is an exquisite one) of losing control of the painting and promoting a generalized exhibition of canvases that have only a loose connection with the action on stage. The result is no less surprising when the painters, often working for the Russian Ballet, were called PICASSO (SATIE's *Parade*, 1917), MATISSE (STRAVINSKY's *Le chant du rossignol*, 1920), Fernand LÉGER (MILHAUD's *La Création du monde*, 1923), BRAQUE (AURIC's *Les Fâcheux*, 1924; MOLIÈRE's *Le Tartuffe*, 1950), UTRILLO (CHARPENTIER's *Louise*, 1950), DUFY (MILHAUD's *Le Boeuf sur le toit*, 1920; SALACROU's *Les Fiancés du Havre*, 1944), DALI (*As You Like It* at Teatro Eliseo in Rome, 1948), MASSON (SARTRE's *Morts sans sépulture*, 1946).

Today it appears to be more difficult for painters to work successfully for theatre; they seem to fall back into the time of "illustrator" decorators, except for scene designers who work closely with a particular director (R. PEDUZZI and P. CHÉREAU, R. ALLIO and R. PLANCHON, Y. KOKOS and A. VITEZ, J. SVOBODA and O. KREJCA, W. MINKS and P. ZADEK, G. AILLAUD and K.M. GRÜBER).

In their best work, however, contemporary stage designers have succeeded in animating the space, duration and acting in a total creative process that is similar to the work of a director, lighting designer, actor or musician.

Further reading: Bablet 1965, 1975; Rischbieter and Storch 1968; Badenhausen and Zielske 1972; Bellmann 1977; Banu and Ubersfeld 1979; Pierron 1980; Banu 1989.

STAGE DIRECTIONS

Fr.: *indications scéniques*; Ger.: *Bühnenanweisungen*;
Sp.: *indicaciones escénicas.*

Stage directions include any text (usually written by the playwright but sometimes added by editors, as in the case of SHAKESPEARE) which is not spoken by the actors and is meant to clarify the understanding or mode of presentation of the play for the reader. Examples include names of characters, indications of entrances and exits, descriptions of space, notations on acting.

1. Evolution of Stage Directions

A. The use and importance of stage directions has varied considerably in the history of theatre, from the absence of external directions in Greek theatre and their infrequence in classical French theatre to their proliferation in melodrama and naturalism and their total invasion of the play in BECKETT and HANDKE. The dramatic text can do without stage directions when it already contains all the necessary information (self-introduction of the character as in Greek theatre or the mystery plays, word scenery as in the Elizabethans, clear expositions of feelings and projects in classical drama) (*indications of time and space**).

B. Classicism shuns such directions as being external to the dramatic text, and requires them to be expressly written into the speeches of the play, especially in the narratives. According to D'AUBIGNAC (1657), "all of the poet's thoughts, whether regarding the decoration of the theatre or the movements of his characters, dress and gestures required for an understanding of the subject, must be expressed by the verses he has them recite" (1927, 54). But dramatists like CORNEILLE wished to write them in the margins to remove unnecessary material from the dramatic text: "I would be of the opinion that the poet takes great care to mark in the margin the same actions which do not warrant his burdening his verses with them, and which would even take away from their dignity. The actor easily makes up for them on stage, but in reading the book one would often be reduced to guessing" (*Discours sur les trois unités*, 1657). Stage directions did not really appear until the beginning of the eighteenth century with authors such as HOUDAR DE LA MOTTE (in his *Inès de Castro*, 1723) and MARIVAUX; they became general practice with DIDEROT, BEAUMARCHAIS and naturalistic theatre. Dramatic writing is no longer self-sufficient; it needs a mise-en-scène that authors endeavor to provide for through their stage directions.

This sudden development is explained to some extent by the status of stage directions within the written text as a whole.

2. Textual Status of Stage Directions

A. As soon as the character becomes more than just a role, taking on individual and naturalistic traits, it becomes important to state these facts in an accompanying text. This is what happened in the eighteenth and nineteenth centuries: the search for the socially marked individual (bourgeois drama) and the awareness of the need for mise-en-scène brought with them an expansion of the *didascalia**. It is as if the text were notating its own future staging. The stage directions then have to do not only with coordinates of space and time, but mainly with the character's interiority and the mood of the stage. This information is so precise and subtle that it requires a narrative voice. Here theatre approaches the novel, and curiously enough it is just when it aims to be believable, objective, "dramatic" and naturalistic that it falls into psychological description and restorts to a descriptive or narrative approach.

B. Paradoxically, this text in which the author is supposedly speaking in his own name is aesthetically neutral, having a purely utilitarian function. Very little attention is paid to how stage directions are written; one is tempted to consider them "one of the rare kinds of 'literary writing' in which one may be fairly sure that the author's 'I' – which, however, never appears – is not another" (THOMASSEAU 1984c, 83). In fact, like any text, the didascalic (or *paratextual*) text misleads us as to its exact origin. In addition, it is by no means necessarily transformed into the performance signs, as those who advocate being faithful to the author would have it. We think it would be a mistake to try to infer the mise-en-scène from the "paratextual virtualities of the text in dialogue" (THOMASSEAU 1984c, 84). The mise-en-scène is "big enough" to bring in its discourse from outside the text, to assert itself as an autonomous artistic practice unrelated to the text. This does not mean, however, that the dramatic text is written without taking into account a past or future stage practice.

C. As we can see, the status of stage directions is always ambiguous and incomplete: stage directions are not an autonomous genre or a homogeneous kind of writing, but a supporting text for the dialogues which replaces the pragmatic act of enunciation of the text, an enunciation which is removed from the dramatic text (particularly the classical text). Stage directions can only be studied within the whole dramatic text, as a system of references and conventions, i.e. as closely connected to the dramaturgy. It is dramaturgy that calls for them (according to a particular theatre tradition and specific notions of verisimilitude and decorum), but, inversely, they impose a certain type of dramaturgy in relation to the situation and development of the text. In this way, they always serve as an intermediary between text and performance, between the dramaturgy and the social imagination of a given period (i.e. its code of human relationships and possible actions).

3. Function within the Staging

The question is to determine the respective status of the text of the play and the stage directions. There are two possible approaches:

A. Stage directions are considered an essential part of the text and directions as a whole, and are made into a metatext that informs the actors' text and takes prominence over it. One is therefore "faithful" to the author by following the stage directions in staging the play, which is interpreted according to them. This is a way of accepting as true the interpretation and mise-en-scène suggested by the playwright. Stage directions are considered *staging directions*, a kind of "pre-notation" for a future staging, a *pre-staging**.

B. Inversely, however, when the primordial, metatextual nature of the stage directions is questioned, they may be ignored or do the opposite of what is intended. The mise-en-scène often gains thereby in inventiveness, and the new light shed on the text easily compensates for the "betrayal" of a certain "faithfulness" (illusory in any case) to the author and a certain theatre tradition. The director may choose to have them spoken by a character or a *voice off**, or may even post them on a panel (BRECHT). In such cases, they lose their metalinguistic function to become material that can be used in different ways on the basis of a specific reading. The staging may appear unrelated to what the dramatist had in mind when composing the stage directions. The director then becomes a commentator of both text and stage directions, the only depositary of the work's critical metalanguage. This is not always to the liking of the playwright, and understandably so.

See also: main text and side text, text and performance.

Further reading: *Enciclopedia dello spettacolo*, 1954; J. Steiner 1968; Ingarden 1971; Thomasseau 1984c, 1996.

STAGE HAND

Fr.: *machiniste;* Ger.: *Bühnenarbeiter, Bühnentechniker;* Sp.: *técnico.*

Person who takes care of set changes, special effects and props during the performance. Until the advent of epic (particularly Brechtian) theatre, the stage hand worked "in the wings," i.e. in the dark or hidden by the curtain. He was not allowed to break the *illusion** of a natural, autonomous stage world. It should be remembered, however, that even before BRECHT and his "alienating" followers, the stage hand sometimes had the task of "dis-illusioning." In ancient comedy (ARISTOPHANES), for instance, the stage hand and the theatrical machinery were mentioned, thus breaking the illusion. In avant-garde theatre today, the stage hand's work is no longer concealed, and he has become the guarantor and the sign of theatrical *practice**, to the point where it may appear that he holds this position within the reported *fiction** (for instance, stage hands in WILSON's performances). Some of this work, such as the handling of light objects, is often done by the actors. Changes are made in full view of the audience and there is no longer a clear division between the stage action and pauses; the actors appear as what, in fact, they are: stage workers. The stage hands, meanwhile, are "theatricalized" and integrated into the performance as observers mediating between actors and audience.

STAGE LEFT, STAGE RIGHT

Fr.: *côté cour, côté jardin*; Ger.: *rechts vom Zuschauer, Links vom Zuschauer*; Sp.: *derecha e izquierda del escenario*.

Stage left is the audience's right; and stage right is the audience's left. In pre-revolutionary France, the terminology was "king's side" and "queen's side," according to the way their chairs were arranged in the Tuileries theatre, between the garden and the palace.

STAGE MACHINERY

Fr.: *machine théâtrale*; Ger.: *Theatermaschinerie*; Sp.: *maquinaria teatral*.

1. There is only a small step from the use of stage machinery in dramaturgy to the conception of stage as machine, but it is one that took theatre twenty-five centuries. ARISTOTLE attempted to restrict the use of machinery (particularly the *deus ex machina**) to episodes that could not be carried through unaided by men, and to exceptional circumstances, so as not to deprive the playwright of his faculty for giving realistic explanations for all actions. Machinery is always a materialization on stage (once frightening, now laughable) of the principle of the fantastical or supernatural element (embodied in acts of flying or disappearing), an element that delights the credulous but irritates the more rational or sophisticated spectator.

2. Machinery is both a metaphysical theme – man outmatched by mechanics, whether it be celestial, diabolical or automated – and a principle of theatricality. The current fascination with the opera, with spectacle plays and with Renaissance and seventeenth-century plays employing machinery, with the *Traité sur les machines de théâtre* by N. SABBATINI (1637), *Andromède* (1650) by P. CORNEILLE, *Amphitryon* (1668) and Psyché (1671) by MOLIÈRE, is attributable to the penchant for stage machinery cultivated and described by Constructivist directors (OKHLOPKOV, MEYERHOLD, MALEVITCH, STENBERG, TATLIN) and, today, by "baroque" directors such as J. LAVELLI, L. RONCONI, V. GARCIA and H. RONSE.

3. Stage machinery necessarily bears the stamp of theatre's *materiality*, of its constructive or deconstructive nature and of the *artificiality* of the illusion and fantasy it evokes. There is an ambiguity here that delights both large and small, for different reasons.

See also: space, object, properties, *deus ex machina*, stage arrangement.

Further reading: Allio 1977; Guarino 1982b; Bataille 1990; Freydefont in Corvin 1995.

STAGE MANAGEMENT

Fr.: *régie*; Ger.: *Bühnenregie*; Sp.: *regiduría*.

Material organization of the production by the stage manager before, during and after the performance. Before the advent of mise-en-scène in the nineteenth century, stage work was conceived as the only extraliterary activity, and the stage manager organized practical tasks. There are some exceptions; for example IFFLAND, a stage manager at the MANNHEIM theatre around 1780, had an important role in artistic direction. Moreover, any arrangement of the stage is a mise-en-scène, whether or not it is recognized as such. Once there was an awareness of the need for an overall control of artistic resources, the responsibilities of the stage manager were split up. Some of them were taken over by a director and some by a stage manager (*régisseur*) in the current sense of a person who is responsible for the stage, including sound, lighting and props, and coordinating these different areas. The German has retained the terms *Regisseur* and *Regie* for director and staging, and the French still sometimes uses the term *régisseur* at times to mean a director, considered (as in VILAR 1955) more as an executor than a creative interpretor. The aesthetic, theoretical and dramaturgical impact of stage management on the staging is, however, undeniable.

STAGE MANAGER

Fr.: *régisseur*; Ger.: *Spielleiter*; Sp.: *regidor de escena*.

The stage manager's job is distinct from that of the director's, being responsible for the material organization of the performance. The two complement each other, however: "for if the director creates the performance and gives it life, the stage manager conserves it and ensures its conduct and duration. As a play approaches opening night, it can be said that it passes from the director to the stage manager, somewhat as it has passed from the author to the director and actors" (COPEAU, "La mise en scène," *Encyclopédie Française*, 1935, XVII: 1764–3). The stage manager is in charge of technical adjustments to the machinery and the stage, while the director manages the use of the various materials and oversees their aesthetic production. "The discreet charm of good management" describes a good stage manager, while the director is often the only one to reap any recognition.

STAGE MATERIALS

Fr.: *matériaux scéniques*; Ger.: *Bühnenmaterial*; Sp.: *materiales escénicos*.

1. Signifying System

This term refers to the various stage arts and practices (painting, architecture, static and animated projections, music, sound effects, recitation) considered as systems of *signs**, *signifying systems** or a *stage system**. Stage materials are therefore the signs used in the performance in their signifying dimension, i.e. in their materiality.

Even if the stage is only an empty space, it is always a place where materials of various kinds are produced in tangible form to illustrate, suggest or frame the action of the play. Such materials include the objects and shapes conveyed by the stage, as well as the actors' bodies, lighting, sound and the spoken or declaimed text. The effects of materials and textures are particularly great when natural materials are used such as wood, marble or textiles. These appeal to sight but can also appeal to our sense of touch, hearing and smell.

2. Materiality of the Stage

The set of the raw materials of performance is a stock of signifiers that the spectator receives without being able, or wishing, to translate them into signifieds. The *signifiers** may "resist translation" or take on very different meanings or values. The materiality of the stage constrasts with the fiction that is established on the basis of the elements of *fabula* and character. Its materiality is related to the event, the way the staging mechanisms grip the audience directly.

The stage in theatre aesthetics varies from being a neutral, symbolic, aseptic and abstract space with no function other than allowing the text to be heard (as in classicism), to being a tangible, moving space that brings out the materiality of theatrical language and of the stage. Then, ARTAUD tells us, "it seems that on the stage, which is above all a space to fill and a place where something happens, the language of words may have to give way before a language of *signs* whose objective impact is the one that has the most immediate impact upon us" (1964a, 162; Eng. 1958, 107).

See also: code, represented reality, semiology, aesthetics.

Further reading: Althusser 1965; Macherey 1966; 1996; Voltz 1974.

STAGE PLASTIC

Fr.: *plastique animée*; Ger.: *belebte Plastik*; Sp.: *plástica escénica*.

The art which, "in opposition to the fixed arts of painting and sculpture, we could call *stage plastic* or *living plastic* (JAQUES-DALCROZE 1920, 133), is quite simply the art of theatre. In the classical period one spoke of "spoken painting" or "living tableau" when the actors were arranged in a motionless whole. BABLET (1975) uses the term *stage plastic* to describe what the plastic or visual arts contribute to the stage; the scene designer is charged by and iwth the director with the "plastic staging of the drama" (J. SVOBODA).

STAGE SPACE

Fr.: *espace scénique;* Ger.: *Bühnenraum;* Sp.: *espacio escénico.*

This is the space actually visible to the audience on the stage or stages, or part-stages, in any imaginable stage design. It corresponds more or less to what we call "the stage." Stage space is given to us here and now in the performance by the actors and their movements.

1. Boundaries and Forms

Theatre always takes *place* in a space that is marked off by the division between the gaze (audience) and its object (stage). The boundary between acting and non-acting is defined by each particular kind of performance and stage. As soon as the spectators cross that line, they cease to be observers and become participants in an event that is no longer theatre but rather *dramatic play** or a *happening**, and the stage and social spaces merge. Aside from such instances, the stage space remains inviolate, regardless of how it is set up or transformed.

The stage space is structured closely around the theatre space (location, building, house), and may take any form or establish any relationship imaginable with the place where the spectators sit. If we acknowledge the ritual origins of theatre, as participation by a group in a ceremony or rite, then in a ritualized action, the circle represents the primordial place and the stage can claim no specific viewpoint or distance peculiar to it alone. The circle that inspired Greek theatre – which was both built and buried on the banks of a hill – keeps reappearing wherever participation is not limited to an external gaze on an event. It is, then, the angle and the optical beam connecting an eye to a stage that becomes the link between audience and stage. In the Italian-style or picture-frame stage, action and actors are confined to a box that is open in front to the gaze of the audience and the prince, who has a privileged viewing and listening position. This type of stage structures space according to the principle of distance, symmetry and the reduction of the world to a cube that signifies the entire universe, through the interplay of direct presentation and illusion.

The combination of the two principles – circle and line, the *chorus* of the officiants and the master's *eye* – produces all kinds of stage and theatrical relationships. Theatre history has experienced them without any definitive formula being imposed, for the representation and depiction of reality is subject to an infinite number of variations that also affect the writing and structure of the text.

2. Dependence and Independence of Stage Space

On one hand, stage space is determined by the type of stage design and its visualization by the director in his reading of the *dramatic space**. On the other hand, however, the stage designer and director have quite a bit of room for manoeuvre to shape it as they wish. This dialectics between determinism and freedom gives rise to the particular stage space used in performance, which is why it has often been noted that space mediates between dramatic vision and stage realization. "It is at the level of space, precisely because it is largely an *unspoken aspect of the text*, an area that is particularly full of blind spots (what is *lacking* in the text) that the link between text and performance is forged" (UBERSFELD 1977a, 153). (See also JANSEN 1984.)

3. Functioning of Stage Space

Because it acts as a sign, space oscillates constantly between tangibly perceptible *signifying* space and the external *signified* space to which the spectator must refer in the abstract in order to enter the fiction *(dramatic space*)*. This essential ambiguity of the *theatre* space (i.e. *dramatic* space plus *stage* space) gives the spectator a dual view. One never knows whether the stage should be considered real and tangible or as *another stage*, that is, as a latent, unconscious representation. In the latter event, it is possible to read the stage as a set of rhetorical figures whose deep meaning is to be discovered (*rhetoric**). What is represented on stage is not the manifestation of another reality that is not represented, and therefore not figurative – it is as much the reality of the observer who projects himself into it as of the director who outlines it through the stage location and the presence of actors. To represent or *figure* the stage is to use a rhetorical figure to make the transition from one element – tangible space – to another, imagined space, what is beyond the stage, and dramatic space. Two figures are appropriate for this transition: metaphor and metonymy. The first transforms its object by similarity or dissimilarity; the second by spatial contiguity. These two combinatory principles, which have been shown by JAKOBSON (1963) to govern all production of meaning and semiosis, are the key to all stage figures, their nature, their ability to signal the real and to manipulate space (*text and stage**).

4. Typology and Quality of Stage Space
Every aesthetic approach has its own particular conception of space, so that an examination of space enables us to draw up a typology of dramaturgies (cf. KLOTZ 1960; HINTZE 1969):

A. Space in classical tragedy is conspicuous by its absence. It is a neutral place of transition that provides intellectual and moral support for the characters rather than characterizing the milieu. It is the abstract, symbolic place of the chessboard: everything there is made meaningful by difference, and any characterization of the squares is superfluous.

B. Romantic space often succumbs to the temptation of flashiness, local colour and "subjective" archeology intended to suggest extraordinary worlds to the imagination.

C. *Naturalistic** space imitates the world it represents to the greatest possible extent. Its material construction (based on economic infrastructure, heredity, historicity) is focused on a *milieu** that surrounds the characters.

D. Symbolist space, on the other hand, dematerializes the place and stylizes it in subjective, oneiric worlds ruled by a different logic (cf. STRINDBERG, CLAUDEL, the stage design projects of APPIA and CRAIG). Here specificity gives way to a synthesis of stage arts and an overall atmosphere of unreality (*Gesamtkunstwerk**).

E. Expressionist space is characterized by parabolic places (prison, street, madhouse, city). It bears witness to a profound crisis that racks the ideological and aesthetic consciousness.

Space in contemporary theatre has been the subject of too many experiments to be reduced to a few features. Any dramaturgy, in fact any performance, is subjected to a spatial analysis and an examination of its inner workings. Space is no longer conceived as a shell within which certain arrangements are allowed, but as a dynamic element of the entire dramaturgical conception. It ceases to be a problem of packaging and becomes the visible place where *meaning** is produced and made manifest.

Further reading: Brook 1968; Bablet 1972, 1975; Hays 1977, 1981; Banu and Ubersfeld 1980; Jansen 1984; Carlson 1989; Regy 1991; Boucris 1993; Pavis 1996a.

STAGE SYSTEM

Fr.: *système scénique*; Ger.: *Bühnensystem*; Sp.: *sistema escénico*.

A stage system (or signifying system) brings together a set of signs of the same kind (lighting, gesture, scene design), which establish a semiological system of oppositions, redundancies, complementarity, and so on.

This notion is preferable to the overly-narrow ones of *sign** or *minimal unit**. It encompasses both the inner structure of one of the systems and the relationships among several of them. It invites us to imagine the performance as an object crossed by vectors moving in all directions.
See also: code, semiology, questionnaire.

STAGE VERSION

Fr.: *version scénique;* Ger.: *Bühnenfassung;* Sp.: *versión escénica.*

Version of a non-dramatic work that has been adapted or rewritten for performance, or of a translation that was first intended to be read and has been modified or shortened for the stage.

STAGE WRITING

Fr.: *écriture scénique;* Ger.: *szenische Schreibweise;* Sp.: *escritura escénica.*

1. *Dramatic writing* (dramatic *art* or dramatic *text*) refers to the theatrical world as it is inscribed in the text by the dramatist and received by the reader. The *drama* is conceived as a literary structure supported by certain dramaturgical principles: separate roles, dialogues, dramatic tension and action by the characters. The features of this dramatic writing are such that it easily becomes (or confronts) the stage writing, as in casting, the gaps and ambiguities left in the text, an abundance of *indications of time and place**. The dramatic writing should not, however, be mistaken for stage writing, which takes into account all possible stage expression (acting, space, time).

The stage designer's task is to help the director find a stage writing (or language): "for each play, to invent a kind of language for the eye that upholds the play's meanings, stretches them out and echoes them, sometimes precisely and almost critically, sometimes vaguely and subtly, in the manner of a poetic image (in which chance meanings may be no less important than intentional ones), within the register and mode of expression selected" (René ALLIO, quoted in BABLET 1975, 308).

2. *Stage writing* (or stage *art*) is the way in which the stage apparatus is used to stage the characters, place and action developed on it. This "writing" or *écriture* (in the current sense of a style or personal mode of expression) is obviously not equivalent to the writing of the text – it is a metaphor for the staging practice, which uses specific tools, materials and techniques to communicate a meaning to the spectator. To warrant the comparison with writing, a lexicon of registers, units and modes of stage practice should first be established. Although *semiology** can help identify certain principles, we are far from an alphabet or a writing system in the traditional sense.

The notion of stage writing is equivalent to that of mise-en-scène when it is undertaken by a creator who controls the stage systems as a whole, including the text, and organizes their interactions, so that the performance is not a byproduct of the text but rather the foundation of meaning. When there is no text to stage (when a text is not being staged), we have stage writing in the strict sense, as in (early) WILSON, KANTOR, and LEPAGE.

The dramaturgical work has to do with the *dramatic text* from the point of view of its *stage writing*.

3. According to PLANCHON, stage writing and dramatic writing have always existed, but each period gives preference to one over the other. Medieval theatre writes in images to portray the characters of its mystery plays. Classicism starts from the dramatic text, adapts and reworks textual materials without concerning itself with how they were presented visually. Our own period distinguishes between the two kinds of writing, and chooses one of them in performance: "Sometimes it is the dramatic text that occupies all of the space, sometimes the stage writing, and sometimes a combination of the two" (*Pratiques*, no. 15–16, 1977, p. 55) Such a distinction, perpetuated by directors and scholars, is in itself debatable, since although historically a dis-

tinction has been maintained between *mimesis* (imitation of a thing) and *diegesis* (narrative describing a thing), it has been based on a criterion of imitation and realism, i.e. in relation to the referent, which is by no means the only possibility. Furthermore, any text forces the reader to make a fictional representation of it and, inversely, any stage image can also be read according to a set of codes and circuits that render it linear and break it down into units.

See also: rhetoric, text and performance.

Further reading: Barthes 1953; Artaud 1964a; Bartolucci 1968; Larthomas 1972; Martin 1977; Vaïs 1978; Alcandre 1986; Vinaver 1993.

STAGING

Fr.: *mise en scène*; Ger.: *Inszenierung, Regie*; Sp.: *puesta en escena.*

The notion of staging, or *mise-en-scène*, is a recent one, having been introduced in the second half of the nineteenth century (the French term dates from 1820, cf. VEINSTEIN 1955, 9), when the director became the "official" responsible for organizing the production. Previously, the stage manager or, sometimes, the leading actor (as actor-manager) were in charge of casting the production in a pre-existing mould. Staging was comparable to a rudimentary technique of *blocking** the movements of the actors. This conception sometimes prevails among the general public, who believe that the director does no more than sort out the actors' movements and the lighting.

B. DORT explains the advent of mise-en-scène not by the technical complexity of theatre and the need for a central "organizer," but by a change in the structure of the audience: "Since the second half of the nineteenth century theatres have no longer had a homogenous audience clearly differentiated according to the type of productions offered to them. Therefore, there is no longer any basic prior agreement between spectators and theatre people concerning the style and meaning of those performances" (1971, 61).

1. Functions of Staging

A. MINIMUM AND MAXIMUM DEFINITIONS

A. VEINSTEIN proposes two definitions of mise-en-scène, according to the general public and according to the specialist: "In a broad sense, the term *mise-en-scène* refers to all of the resources of stage performance: décor, lighting, music and acting [...]. In a narrower sense, the term *mise-en-scène* refers to the activity that consists in arranging, in a particular time and space, the various elements required for the stage performance of a dramatic work" (1955, 7).

We will leave aside the historical reasons for the emergence of mise-en-scène at the end of the nineteenth century, without however downplaying their importance. It would be a simple matter to trace the drastic changes that occurred on the stage between 1880 and 1900, particularly the automation of the stage and improvements in electric lighting. Other factors were the crisis in drama and the collapse of classical dramaturgy and dialogue (SZONDI 1956).

B. THE REQUIREMENT OF TOTALITY

Originally, mise-en-scène reflected a classical conception of the stage work as a total, harmonious work that was more than the sum of its parts or materials, which were once considered to be the fundamental units. Mise-en-scène asserts the subordination of each art, or simply of each sign, to a whole that is harmoniously coordinated by a unifying thought: "A work of art cannot be created unless it is directed by a single thought" (E.G.CRAIG). Since the emergence of the concept of mise-en-scène, this requirement has been accompanied by an awareness of the historicity of texts and performances, of the series of successive "concretizations" of a single work. This historicity is evident in the application to the text of a new body of knowledge, that of the human sciences: "Knowledge is a constituent part of the mise-en-scène" (PIEMME 1984, 67).

C. PROJECTION INTO SPACE

Mise-en-scène consists in transposing the dramatic writing of the text (written text and/or *stage directions**) into scenic writing. "The art of stage-directing is the art of projecting into space what the dramatist has been able to project only into time" (APPIA; Eng. 1982, 57). The staging is "in a play the truly and specifically theatrical part of the spectacle" (ARTAUD 1964b, 161–62; Eng. 1958, 107). In short, it is the transformation or, better, the "concretization" of the text, using actors and the stage space, into a duration that is experienced by the spectators.

Space is, so to speak, rendered into words; the text is memorized and inscribed in the gestural space of the actor, speech by speech. The actor seeks the most appropriate movements and attitudes for his spatial inscription. The words of the dialogue, contained in the text, are now scattered through and inscribed in the time and place of the stage, presented to be seen and heard: "The type of enunciation of the dramatic text contains the requirement that it be shown" (P. RICOEUR 1983, 63). Gestures, for instance, are worked out systematically in order to be readable (rather than visible); they are stylized, abstracted, broken down, associated mnemonically with the unfolding of the text, anchored to a few points of reference, a few supports (sub-*score**).

D. CO-ORDINATION

The various components of the performance, which are often attributable to various different individuals (dramaturg, musician, stage designer, etc.), are assembled and co-ordinated by the director. Whether the aim is to achieve an integrated whole (as in the opera) or a system in which each art remains autonomous (BRECHT), the director's mission is to decide on the links between the various scenic elements, which naturally has a decisive influence on the production of the overall meaning. This process of coordination and homogenization is done, in the case of a dramaturgy where an action is shown, through the explanation and commentary of the *fabula**, which is made intelligible by using the stage as the keyboard of the theatre production. The mise-en-scène must form a complete organic structure, in which each element is integrated into the whole, in which nothing is left to chance and everything has a function within the overall design. Any mise-en-scène establishes a *coherence**, which may at any moment turn into an incoherence. COPEAU, for example, defines it as follows: "By mise-en-scène we understand the design of a dramatic action. It is the whole set of movements, of gestures and attitudes, the concordance of facial expressions, voices and silences; it is the totality of the stage performance, flowing from a single thought that conceives, organizes and harmonizes it. The director invents and makes to prevail among the characters this secret and visible bond, this reciprocal sensitivity, this mysterious correspondence of relationships, all elements without which the drama, even when performed by excellent actors, would lose the best part of its expression" (COPEAU 1974, 29–30).

E. HIGHLIGHTING MEANING

The staging, then, is no longer considered to be a "necessary evil" that the dramatic text could very well do without, but the very place where the meaning of the theatrical work will emerge. STANISLAVSKY, for example, saw designing a mise-en-scène as finding a way to make the deep meaning of the dramatic text tangibly evident, for which purpose all resources are available, both scenic (stage machinery, lighting, costumes, etc.) and actor-related (acting, body expression and gestuality). The staging has to do with both the milieu in which the actors move and the psychological and gestural interpretation of those actors. Any staging is an interpretation of the text or script, an explanation of the text "in the making." We have access to the play only through this reading by the director.

F. THREE KEY QUESTIONS ON THE "TUNING" OF MISE-EN-SCÈNE

In order to understand the concretization which any new staging of a text implies, we must establish a link between the dramatic text and its context of enunciation by asking three theoretical questions:

1. What *concretization** is made of the dramatic text by any new reading or staging? What circuit of concretization is then established between the work as a signifier, *social context* and aesthetic object (going back to the terms of MUKAROVSKY 1934; cf. PAVIS 1983)?

2. What *fictionalization**, i.e. what production of a fiction, based on both text and stage, is established through the concerted efforts of text and reader, stage and spectator? In what way is the intermingling of the two fictions, textual and scenic, fundamental to theatrical fictionalization (cf. PAVIS 1985d)?

3. What *"ideologization"* do the dramatic text and the performance receive? Both the dramatic and the performance texts can be understood only in their *intertextuality**, particularly in relation to the discursive and ideological formations of a particular era or corpus of texts. One has to imagine the relationship of the dramatic and performance text with the *social context*, i.e. with other texts and discourses on reality produced by society. As this relationship is extremely fragile and variable, the same dramatic text easily produces an infinite number of readings, and therefore stagings that cannot be predicted solely from the text.

G. IMAGINARY SOLUTION

The confrontation between textual and scenic fictions is not confined to establishing a circularity between utterance and enunciation, absence and presence. It compares the spots of indeterminacy and the ambiguities of text and performance, as they do not necessarily coincide in the text as well as in the staging. The performance may render a passage of text ambiguous, i.e. polysemic, or, on the contrary, devoid of meaning. Or the performance may take a stand on a contradiction or indeterminacy in the text.

Obscuring on stage what was clear in the text, or clarifying what was obscure in the text, are operations central to the staging. Most of the time the staging is an interpretation of text that mediates between the original receiver and the contemporary receiver. Sometimes, however, it is a "complication of text," a deliberate attempt to prevent any communication between the *social contexts* of the two instances of reception.

In some stagings (for instance, those inspired by a Brechtian dramaturgical analysis), it is a question of showing how the dramatic text itself was the imaginary solution to real ideological contradictions, those of the time in which the fiction was established. The mise-en-scène then has to make the textual contradiction imaginable and representable. For productions that are concerned with the revelation of a subtext in the Stanislavskian manner, the unconscious of the text is supposed to accompany, in a parallel text, the text actually spoken by the characters.

H. PARODIC DISCOURSE

Whether or not there is a clear intention to show the contradiction of the *fabula* or the deeper truth of the text by presenting its subtext, the staging is always a discourse *adjacent* to a flat neutral reading of the text; it is, in an etymological sense, parodic. But neither the contradiction nor the unconscious subtext is truly adjacent to or above the text (as in the metatext). They are to be found in the collision between or interlacing of the two readings, within the concretization, the fiction, the relationship with ideology, like a parody that cannot be separated from the object parodied.

I. DIRECTING OF ACTORS

Concretely, mise-en-scène starts with the directing of actors. The director gives the actors guidance by returning to them and explaining the images they produce on the basis of his suggestions, and by adjusting their acting to that of the remaining actors. He ensures that the gestures, intonations and pace are consistent with the overall discourse of mise-en-scène and are integrated into sequences, scenes and the performance as a whole. During rehearsals, the actors try out different *situations of enunciation**. Little by little, they occupy the space, looking for a possible trajectory, adapting and following all the stage systems: "That is what the directing of actors is all about; to manage to motivate you and to ensure that the gestures you make on stage seem to you not only as something to be done, but as self-evident: feeling that the role is played through movements alone, for instance" (C. FERRAN, *Théâtre/Public*, 1985, 60). This kind of directing assumes that the signs produced by the actor are transmitted clearly, without "noise" or interference, in line with the effect sought by the staging discourse overall, that the actors play with each other, are audible and "readable." Particular care is often taken with intonation and rhythm, with what the Germans call *Sprachregie* (language staging).

Although it is fashionable to say so, the staging is not necessarily an exercise in authoritarianism by a director who plunders authors and sadistically tyrannizes the actor-puppets. As BRECHT used to say: "With us, the director does not come to the theatre with his own 'idea' or 'vision,' with a 'blocking scheme' and ready-made sets. His desire is not to 'realize' an idea. His task consists in awakening and organizing the productive activity of the actors (musicians, painters, etc.). For him, rehearsing does not mean being forcefed some conception established *a priori* in his head, but trying [things] out" (1972, 405).

J. NOTES

Directors give "notes" to actors. These are not easy to give or receive: "It's very difficult to know how to take notes well, just as it is difficult for the director to give them clearly. The idea is to grasp the spirit of them rather than the letter" (DULLIN 1946, 48). This is advice that nearly all directors follow. Notes should not lead to imitation. They do not dictate; rather, they suggest, inform, show a possible way.

2. Staging Problems

A. ROLE OF THE STAGING

The emergence of the director in the history of theatre is indicative of a new attitude toward the dramatic text. The text was long considered a closed-off place for a single possible interpretation that had to be tracked down – as, for instance, in LEDOUX's formula recommending that a director faced with a text should "serve it rather than serving himself" (*servir et non se servir*). Today, however, the text is an invitation to seek out its many meanings, even its contradictions; it lends itself to new interpretations. The advent of mise-en-scène proves that *theatre** is now established as an autonomous art. Its significance is to be found as much in its form and dramaturgical structure as in the meaning or meanings of the text. The director is not an element external to the dramatic work: "He does more than establish a framework for or illustration of a text. He becomes the fundamental element of the performance; the necessary mediation between text and performance [...] Text and performance are mutually dependent, and each expresses the other" (DORT 1971, 55–56).

B. THE DISCOURSE OF MISE-EN-SCÈNE

The mise-en-scène of a text always has something to say, and this is essential for it will be the "last word" of the performance. There is no universal, definitive discourse of the work that the performance should bring to light. The alternative conception, which is still current among major directors who speak of "playing the text" or "playing the performance," is therefore false from the outset. Neither of the two terms should be given priority over the other. Hardly anyone still believes that the text is a fixed point of reference for a single possible performance, and that there is only one "true" staging (*scenario**, *text and performance**).

C. LOCATION OF THE DISCOURSE OF MISE-EN-SCÈNE

1. The *stage directions** give very precise instructions for the stage performance, but the staging need not follow them to the letter.

2. The text itself often makes direct suggestions as to where and how the action takes place, the positioning of the characters, etc. (*indications of time and place**). No dramatic text can be written without a vague idea of

a possible performance, without a knowledge, however rudimentary, of the laws of the stage used, the conception of represented reality, and the sensitivity of a particular period to the problems of time and space (*pre-staging**).

3. The stage directions and suggestions made by the text are never really imperative, and the director's personal touch, external to some extent to the text, is decisive. Where and how this takes place, however, is very difficult to establish. Even if it takes shape in a staging book, it is difficult to isolate from the performance, being its *enunciation**, a metalanguage that is perfectly integrated into the way the action and characters are presented. It is not added to the verbal text and the stage, does not exist as a finished text; it is disseminated in the acting choices, the stage design, the rhythm, etc.

According to our productive-receptive conception of staging, it does not exist until it is recognized and shared in part by the audience. Rather than a performance text accompanying the dramatic text, the metatext organizes the concretization on stage from within, something that is not *beside* but *inside* the dramatic text, as the result of the circuit of concretization (circuit between signifier, *social context** and signified of the text) (PAVIS 1985e, 244–268).

4. In addition to the conscious work done by the director, we must take into account the visual or unconscious work of the creators. If, as FREUD suggests, visual thinking is closer to the unconscious than is verbal thinking, the director or stage designer could act as a "medium" between dramatic language and stage language. Thus the stage always refers to "the other stage" (*interior space**).

3. A Staging Typology

A. STAGING OF THE CLASSICS

Classifications are risky and categories volatile (PAVIS, 1996a). Some categories of staging apply, *mutatis mutandis*, to contemporary texts as well. Classics pose all the aesthetic questions even more acutely. The fact that they involve texts that are older and difficult to receive without some explanatory work practically forces the director to take a position as to his interpretation, or to situate himself within the tradition of the different interpretations. There are several possible solutions:

1. *Archeological reconstruction*

This is not a staging but a restaging of the play, inspired by the original one and done with archeological fervour when documents from the period are available.

2. *Flat rendering*

The choices offered by the stage are discarded in favour of a flat reading of the text, with no position being taken as to the production of meaning, giving the (false) illusion that the text is being followed and that visualization is redundant.

3. *Historicization*

It takes into account the distance between the time of the represented fiction, the time when it was composed, and our own time, laying stress on this distance and indicating the historical reasons on three reading levels; i.e., *historicizes**. This type of staging reconstructs the hidden ideological presuppositions more or less explicitly and does not hesitate to lay bare the devices of the text's aesthetic construction and of the performance. PLANCHON, VILAR, STREHLER, FORMIGONI and VINCENT are proponents of this kind of "sociological staging" (VITEZ 1994, 147).

4. *Use of text as raw material*

Old texts are used as raw material for a quite different aesthetic or ideological purpose (Brechtian *contemporization*, modernization, adaptation, rewriting). Quotes or excerpts from other works clarify the work intertextually (MESGUISCH, VITEZ).

5. *Staging of multiple possible meanings of the text*

This is done by establishing *signifying practices** (KRISTEVA) that present the performance text for manipulation by the spectator (A. SIMON 1979, 42–56). Such practices may range from abstraction to a proliferation of stage objects.

6. *"Mise en pièces" of the original text*
(The French term evokes both a destruction and a remaking of the play.) The play's superficial harmony is destroyed and ideological contradictions are revealed (cf. PLANCHON and his *Mise en pièce(s) du Cid, Arthur Adamov* and *Folies bourgeoises*, or, curiously, the productions of the Théâtre de l'Unité).

7. *Return to myth*
The production leaves aside the specific dramaturgy of the text and exposes its mythical core (ARTAUD, GROTOWSKI, BROOK and CARRIERE in their adaptation of *The Mahabharata*).

B. BACK TO WRITING
One way of getting one's bearings among different types of stagings is to observe how they treat the text: "No matter how you look at it, all the questions asked by theatre always come down to this: what happens to the text on stage?" (SALLENAVE, 1988:93). Every decade seems to invent its own relationship between text and stage:

- The 1950s called for a (respectful) *reading* of plays in the national heritage (VILAR).
- The 1960s introduced a critical, distanced *rereading* (PLANCHON).
- The 1970s preferred a *dereading*, or polyphonic, dialogic (BAKHTIN 1978) deconstruction of signifying practices (VITEZ).
- The 1980s examined the aesthetics of reception and the "reader's role" (ECO, 1980), taking an overview to propose *metareadings* that identify all observations as commentary, whether marginal or all-encompassing (MESGUICH).
- The 1990s are restoring the power of writing and ushering in a time of writings both autonomous and open to staging: an *overreading* that lends itself to all situations (COLAS or PY).
- What will the next millennium bring? Perhaps the text, or the hypertext, will pass from human memory to machine memory, from the body to virtual reality, without anyone realizing it, as hyperwriting and hyperreading combined.

See also: questionnaire, visual and textual.

Further reading: Becq de Fouquières 1884; Antoine 1903; Appia, 1954, 1963; Rouché 1910; Allevy 1938; Baty 1945; Moussinac 1948; Blanchart 1948; Veinstein 1955; Jacquot and Veinstein 1957; Dhomme 1959; Pandolfi 1961; Reinhardt 1963; Artaud 1964a; Bablet 1968; Touchard 1968; Dullin 1969; Dort 1971, 1975, 1977a, 1979; Girault 1973; Sanders 1974; Vitez 1974, 1981; Pignarre 1975; Bettetini 1975; Wills 1976; *Pratiques*, 1977; Benhamou 1977; Ubersfeld 1978b; Strehler 1980; Pavis 1980b, 1984a; Hays 1981; Jomaron 1981; Braun 1982; Brauneck 1982; de Marinis 1983; Melrose 1983; Piemme 1984; Banu 1984; Javier 1984; Fischer-Lichte 1985; Mesguisch 1991; States 1985; Thomsen 1985; Alcandre 1986; Bradby and Williams 1988; Lassalle 1991; Regy 1991; Abirached 1992; Sallenave 1988; Piemme 1989; Lehmann 1989; Jomaron 1989.

STANCES

Fr.: *stances*; Ger.: *Stanze*; Sp.: *estancias*.

Kind of verse used in French classical dramaturgy (essentially between 1630 and 1660). Stances are characterized by regular stanzas built around the same rhythmical model and rhyme scheme and spoken by the same character, who is often alone on stage. Each stanza ends with a cadence, marking a phase in the character's reflection: "In its most regular form... according to the ear as well as the mind, the most well-rounded *stance* is one that encloses a single thought, ending like it and with it in complete repose" (MARMONTEL 1787, entry on 'stance').

The accomplished formal structure of stances makes them a veritable exercise in style that requires great semantic, prosodic and consonantal precision. Their formal beauty is sometimes excused by theoreticians with the fiction that they were composed by the character in the wings (D'AUBIGNAC 1657). Their originality lies in their status as a poem within a poem, and in the emphasis on their poetic nature. Finally, their dramaturgical function should not be underestimated, as a poetic reflection by the hero whose actions and decisions are determined by the rhetorical machinery of the poetic text.

Further reading: Scherer 1950; Hilgar 1973; Pavis 1980a.

STEREOTYPE

Fr.: *stéréotype*; Ger.: *Stereotyp*; Sp.: *estereotipo*.

A fixed, trite conception of a character, situation or improvisation.

Several stereotyped elements can be identified in theatre: stock characters, trivial and repetitive situations, the use of verbal clichés, uninspired gestures, dramatic structure and development of the action according to a fixed model.

1. Characters

Stereotypes (or *types**) talk or act according to an extremely repetitive formula that is known in advance. They have no individual freedom of action and are only the rudimentary instruments of the playwright (for example, the braggart). Their actions are mechanical, and they look like a composite picture. Often they represent the result of a long literary evolution and reappear in slightly different variations (*caricature**, *typecasting**, *type**, *role**).

2. Situations

Examples of situations that are historical and thematic stereotypes are, for instance, rivalry in love or war, the love triangle of boulevard theatre, the hero's indecision before acting, beauty and the beast, man as prey to the elements. All of these examples are combinations of predictable performance situations. By reconstructing the possible relationships among the characters, we can identify, among all the variants, a small number of situations and *actantial** models that can be found in abundance in the history of theatre (SOURIAU 1950; POLTI 1895). Mise-en-scène sometimes enjoys translating the verbal cliché into a stage rhetoric that illustrates and deconstructs it (AMOSSY 1982).

3. Dramaturgical Structure

The *well-made play** (or neoclassical drama, e.g. by VOLTAIRE) tries for a dramatic structure that is as close as possible to an ideal model, and falls into all the clichés of dramatic construction: balancing the five acts, precise phases of action, artifical conclusion, monologues and obligatory scenes.

4. Ideology

Stereotypes take no artistic or ideological risks; they use preconceived ideas and unverified truisms. Boulevard comedy, a great consumer of ideological stereotypes, returns again and again to its favourite themes (cuckoldry, social mobility, witty repartee), thus surreptitiously reassuring the audience in its beliefs and presenting stereotypes as immutable, inevitable laws.

5. Possible Use of Stereotypes

Most of the time, plays with stereotyped characters or actions hold little interest from the point of view of dramaturgical originality or psychological analysis. Still, the playwright may turn the congenital poverty of stereotypes to good account. By referring the spectators to a type of character already known to them, the playwright saves time that can be used to better develop the plot or enhance the theatricality of the acting. This probably explains the current revived interest in *commedia dell'arte**, *melodrama** and the circus. Dramaturgical stereotypes immediately resolve the question of characterization and psychological acting; they invite the director to use a very theatrical, imaginative and often parodic acting style. The spectators, frustrated at first in their catharctic need for psychology and identification, can then derive much theatrical pleasure from this kind of dramaturgy and acting.

Finally, and above all, any use of stereotypes is accompanied by an ironic distancing of the device and exposure of the play's strings. The playwright and the director take up the fixed scheme, varying it and criticizing it from within. BRECHT used this method to help the spectators acquire an awareness of the ideological common-

places imprisoning them (cf. *The Threepenny Opera*, parodying the bourgeois comedy with a happy ending; *Arturo Ui*, playing on the popular imagination by caricaturing American gangsters, etc.). Dramatic play uses it to sensitize players to the language and ideological forces that confine them (RYNGAERT 1985).
Further reading: *Dictionnaire des personnages*, 1960; Aziza et al. 1978.

STICHOMYTHIA

Fr.: *stichomythie;* Ger.: *Stichomythie;* Sp.: *stichomithia.*

Rapid verbal exchanges between two characters (a few lines or sentences, one line, even two or three words), most often at a particularly dramatic point in the action.

Already present in Greek and Latin theatre, stichomythia enjoyed a certain amount of success in the classical period (sixteenth and seventeenth centuries) at emotional points in the play. It was denounced, however, when it degenerated into an overly obvious *device** that hindered the rhetorical organization of the *tirades*: it was frequently used in naturalistic drama and so-called psychological theatre, always at the key point of the *well-made play**.

1. "Psychologization" of Discourse
Stichomythia gives the effect of a verbal duel between protagonists as their conflict comes to a climax. It provides a talking picture of the contradiction between their speeches and points of view and marks the appearance of the emotional, the uncontrolled or the subconscious within the very strict discursive structure of the tirades.

2. Semantic Inversions
All *dialogue** alternates an *I* and a *you*, the rule being that one must wait to speak until the other has finished. The participants are connected by a common *theme** and a *situation of enunciation** that encompasses both and threatens at every moment to influence the theme. Each, however, has his own semantic context: we can never predict exactly what will be said, and the dialogue is a series of contextual breaks. The shorter the lines of each, the more probability there is of a brutal change of context. This makes the stichomythia the truly dramatic moment of the play, because suddenly it seems that anything can be said, and the spectator's suspense (and that of the participants) grows with the liveliness of the exchange. The stichomythia is the verbal image of the collision between *contexts**, characters and points of view. A *discourse** that is at once full (intense, hyperdramatic) and empty (foregrounding of the semantic gaps in context), stichomythia is the exaggerated form of theatre discourse.
Further reading: Mukarovsky 1941; Scherer 1950.

STORY-TELLER

Fr.: *conteur;* Ger.: *Erzähler;* Sp.: *cuentista.*

A story-teller is not to be confused with a *narrator**, who may be a person recounting an event as in classical *narrative**.

A story-teller is an artist at the crossroads of the other arts; (most often) alone on stage, he tells his (or a) story directly to the audience, evoking events by word and gesture, playing one or more characters, but always coming back to his story. In reviving oral story-telling, he is part of a long secular tradition and influences Western theatre practice by setting it against long-lost popular traditions such as Arab story-telling and African "griot." The story-teller (who most often composes his texts himself) seeks to reestablish direct contact with the audience, assembled together in one place as at a festival or in a theatre. He is a *performer** who carries out an action and delivers a poetic message that is directly transmitted and received by the listener-spectators. As in the various oral traditions, text and gesture are memorized together: "every oral formula, like every gestural formula, is always imbued with the entire tradition" (M. JOUSSE).

The story-teller's art has renewed theatre practice today. It falls within the movement of narrative theatre, which dramatizes non-dramatic materials and generally marries acting to narrative, a practice begun by

VITEZ with *Vendredi ou la vie sauvage*: "What we cannot act, we tell; what cannot be fully told, we act." The story-teller's art has become a very popular genre that is addressed to a different audience than that of staged theatre. With the minimal resources of voice and bare hands, the story-teller breaks the fourth wall, speaks directly to the audience, confines himself to a confrontation that is not a sophisticated staging and uses all available resources, chiefly dramatic techniques, though tie mikes, lighting and musical accompaniment may be used as well (P. MATEO).

When telling *autobiographical** stories (J.-P. CHABROL), a story-teller may recall *performance art** (L. ANDERSON, S. GRAY). Any imaginable relationship may obtain between the word and the speaker's stage situation; any means may be used to theatricalize the narrative by introducing characters who speak for themselves (e.g., P. CAUBÈRE plays all the characters in *Le Roman d'un Acteur*, and not only his "double," Ferdinand, the hero). The story-teller enriches theatre practice and himself benefits greatly from the miracles of the stage.

See the periodical *Dire* on story-telling and the oral tradition. France's 150 professional story-tellers include H. GOUGAUD, M. HINDENOCH, B. DE LA SALLE (*Le Conteur amoureux*, 1996).

Further reading: Haddad 1982; Gründ 1984.

STRATEGY

Fr.: *stratégie*; Ger.: *Strategie*; Sp.: *estrategia*.

The playwright's or director's attitude and approach to the subject to be dealt with or the staging to be produced and, in the last analysis, to the symbolic action to be exercised over the spectators.

1. Authorial Strategy

In order to be systematic and effective, the *dramaturgical** work, whether it is done by the playwright or the *dramaturg**, must involve a reflection on the meaning of the text staged and the purpose of the performance in the actual circumstances in which it will be shown to the audience. So the dramaturgical work and the strategy required for proper reception depend on both the internal interpretation of the text and its mode of reception. The determination of these parameters constitutes the overall performance strategy.

2. Textual Strategy

The authorial strategy exists only virtually, and must be reflected in the text (and be read there by its interpreters). The textual strategy imposes certain reading methods, presents "clues" that throw light on the play as a whole, put forward choices in understanding characters. The strategy is often far from being univocal; the play's internal contradictions remain unexplained and, in the modern text, there are several reading *isotopies** (methods and clues). Any reading of the script has to overcome these obstacles to interpretation, with varying degrees of success. The ensuing choice is made with guidance from the overall theatre project and the director's aesthetic and social discourse.

3. Staging Strategy

The staging strategy goes beyond the reading strategy and represents the final step, in which the reading choices are materialized on stage. This may be done by exemplifying and directly applying the reading choices, or through a more discreet application that does not spell out the message.

This strategy is often used for the sole purpose of manipulating the spectators' sympathy toward certain characters, to have them choose the right point of view or hesitate over different solutions. In any case, the basic strategy is to trap the audience. The staging strategy is, in fact, sometimes more deceptive than constructive, and many productions are constructed in such a way as to make a definitive reading of the performance impossible.

4. Reception Strategy

Reception ultimately conditions any theatrical undertaking, by bursting its confines. For the final aim of all theatre is to act on the spectator's consciousness and to remain there vibrating even after the play is over. Here we see the illocutory, even perlocutory nature of a performance that demands that the spectators come away with a new awareness and take up a position (*speech act**).

In short, the art of theatre consists in having the spectators perform a series of symbolic acts and engaging in a dialogue with them through the interaction of tactics and the gradual discovery of the rules of the game.

Further reading: Bataillon 1972; Genot 1973; Marcus 1975.

STREET THEATRE

Fr.: *théâtre de rue*; Ger.: *Strassentheater*; Sp.: *teatro de calle*.

Theatre produced outside the traditional buildings, in the street, in a square or marketplace, in the subway, at the university, etc. It is usually done in a desire to reach a non-theatregoing audience, to create a direct sociopolitical action, to join cultural *animation** and social demonstration, to find a place between provocation and convivialty in the urban environment. Street theatre has long been confused with *agit-prop** and political theatre (1920s and 1930s in Germany and the Soviet Union). Since the 1970s, it has taken on a less political and more aesthetic cast.

Street theatre was particularly prevalent in the 1960s (Bread and Puppet, Magic Circus, *happenings** and union activities). It is actually a return to theatre's roots; THEPSIS played to the Athens marketplace from a chariot in the sixth century B.C., and the medieval *mystery plays** took place in church courtyards and town squares. Paradoxically, street theatre has a tendency to become institutionalized, organized into festivals (*Éclats*, held since the 1980s in Aurillac), to become established within an urban context, land art or urban development policy, while attempting to remain faithful to its quest of diverting daily existence.

See also: agit-prop, theatre of participation.

Further reading: Kirby 1965; Beck 1972; Boal 1977; Barba 1982; Obregon 1983.

STYLIZATION

Fr.: *stylisation*; Ger.: *Stilisierung*; Sp.: *estilización*.

A device that consists in representing reality in a simplified way, stripped to its essential features, eliminating excess detail.

Stylization, like *abstraction**, refers to a series of general structural features that point up a master scheme, an in-depth grasp of phenomena. According to GOMBRICH's formula (1977), the artist "tends to see what he paints rather than paint what he sees."

Dramatic and stage writing employ stylization when they eschew the mimetic reproduction of a complex reality or whole. Any kind of representation, even if it is *naturalistic** or *verist**, is based on a simplification of the object represented and a series of *conventions** that signify the object represented.

1. Human action never unfolds in its entirety on stage. Its strong, significant moments may be chosen (*parable**), or it may be explained in an implicit commentary that discloses its principles. A statement of human *motivations** would quickly become annoying in theatre. Even when the intention is to show a particular behaviour or repetitive activity from the outside (cf. the neonaturalism of the *theatre of everyday life**), the actor plays what is characteristic and therefore identifiable by an audience. In his requirement that theatre be an account of a totality, HEGEL (1832) and, later, LUKACS (1963), marked out the extreme position of classical aesthetics: it could legitimately formulate that rule to the extent that action, speech and character coincide perfectly. But that requirement is necessarily accompanied by a generalization and universalization of the human action represented. The typical and the characteristic serve the purpose of an exemplary portrayal of existence. After HEGEL and the decline of classical form, dramatic

action encompasses only a particular, even fortuitous fragment of reality. But here too, even in the case of the naturalistic aesthetic of showing all, that fragment must be simplified and adapted to the spectator's view. As a result, it does not actually gain in accuracy what it loses in universality.

2. The stage act (eating or dying, for instance) never fulfills all of its conditions of production and therefore its primary efficiency. The actor replaces the real act with a signifying act that is not given as real but is indicated as such by virtue of a *convention**. Paradoxically, the act often becomes theatrically valid and believable to the extent that it is stylized. It does not bother us to watch the actors eat a meal from empty plates. Stylization even enhances our fascination with theatrical play, in that we must superimpose a real act on the stage act, within the *fiction**.

3. Dramatic language is also subject to the refinement of stylization. Differences in language level according to character or social class are smoothed out by the playwright's personal stamp. Naturalistic dialogue, for instance, uses language conventions and stylistic cross-references within the various speeches. Even when the playwright's intention is to convey a crude characterization of a kind of speech, stage custom always imposes a certain rhetoric: the repetition of turns of phrase to be stressed, a vocabulary comprehensible to most of the audience, the exaggeration of individual features – all stylizations of "raw" reality.

4. It is stage reality (stage design, objects, costumes) that is least tolerant of unstylized representation. The spectators are lost in a mass of "true facts"; they recognize elements of their own environment but, at the same time, do not know what to do with this archeological reconstruction. On the contrary, the director's task is to simplify the real, to "pin it down" in a few object-signs that identify and place it. Stylization comes somewhere between servile *imitation** and abstract *symbolization*.

See also: represented reality, realism, mimesis, imitation, semiology.

SUBPLOT

Fr.: *intrigue secondaire;* Ger.: *Nebenhandlung;* Sp.: *intriga secundaria.*

A subplot (or by-play) completes the main plot and is structured in parallel to it, commenting on it, repeating it, varying it or distancing it. It generally has fewer and less important characters. Its connection with the main action may be fairly loose; it may even present a separate *fabula*. This device, used particularly in Elizabethan theatre, is fairly frequent in classical dramaturgy; it often contrasts a collective *action** with a private one, a noble acting style with a comic or grotesque one (SHAKESPEARE, MOLIÈRE), a parodied with a parodying level, a story of masters with one of servants (MARIVAUX). Often, but not necessarily, the two plots finally converge in a single stream.
See also: isotopy, narrative analysis, fabula.
Further reading: Scherer 1950; Klotz 1960; Pfister 1977.

SUBTEXT

Fr.: *sous-texte;* Ger.: *Subtext;* Sp.: *sub-texto.*

The term refers to something that is not explicitly said in the dramatic text but emerges from the way it is interpreted by the actor. The subtext is a kind of commentary made by the *staging** and the acting style, providing the spectator with clarification needed for a proper *reception** of the performance.

This notion was introduced by STANISLAVSKY (1977, 1989), who saw it as a psychological tool to tell about the character's inner state, creating a significant discrepancy between what is said in the text and what is shown on stage. The subtext is the psychological or psychoanalytical mark left by the actor or character through his acting.

Although it is in the nature of the subtext not to be entirely graspable, it can be compared to the notion of the discourse of mise-en-scène: the subtext comments on and controls the entire stage production, is imposed on the audience more or less clearly and affords a glimpse of a whole unexpressed dimension of the discourse, "a pressure behind the words" (PINTER). It is useful to distinguish between subtext and subscore (*score**).

See also: situation, discourse, silence, dramatic text.

Further reading: Strasberg 1969.

SUSPENSE

Fr.: *suspense;* Ger.: *Spannung;* Sp.: *suspenso.*

Anxious *expectation** of the spectator when faced with a situation in which the hero is threatened and the worst is feared. A point in the action at which the spectator or reader is kept on tenterhooks.

Suspense is a psychological attitude produced by a very tense dramatic structure: *fabula* and action are managed such that the character who is the object of our concern seems no longer to be able to escape his or her fate.

See also: reading, tension, deus ex machina, dramatic and epic.

SYMBOL

(From the Greek *symbolon,* sign of recognition.)
Fr.: *symbole;* Ger.: *Symbol;* Sp.: *símbolo.*

1. In PEIRCE's semiotics, the symbol is "a sign which refers to the Object that it denotes by virtue of a Law, usually an association of general ideas" (in SEBEOK 1986, 2:1030). The symbol is a sign that is chosen *arbitrarily* to denote its referent, as, for example, in the use of red, amber and green, established by *convention**, in traffic lights.

2. The term *symbol* is often used in the opposite sense. In Saussurian linguistics, the symbol shows "at least a vestige of natural connexion between the signal and its signification" [between the signifier and the signified] (SAUSSURE 1971, 101; Eng. 1986:68). The scales is the symbol of justice, evoking by analogy through its balanced pans the weight of pro and con. What PEIRCE called *symbol,* SAUSSURE termed *sign* or *arbitrary sign.*

3. The use of the term *symbol* has become widespread in dramatic criticism, with all the imaginable imprecisions and with little advantage for theory. Clearly, everything on stage symbolizes something; the stage is *semiotizable**, it gives the spectator a sign.

We could study the stage processes of symbolization by considering the stage as rhetoric:

- metaphor: iconic use of the symbol; a certain colour or piece of music refers to a certain atmosphere; related to condensation and to accumulating and shifting vectors;
- metonymy: indexical use (*index**) of the sign; a tree stands for a forest; corresponds to displacement and the connecting and cutting vectors;
- allegory: the seagull, in the eponymous play, not only refers to Nina but "symbolizes" innocence stained by idleness.

4. A literary movement at the end of the nineteenth century, Symbolism generalized the notion of symbol, making it the code of reality. Symbolism sought to "dress the idea in a perceptible form" (Jean MOREAS). Authors such as MAETERLINCK, WAGNER, IBSEN, HOFMANNSTHAL, ELIOT, YEATS, MALLARMÉ, HAUPTMANN, SYNGE, D'ANNUNZIO, STRINDBERG, PESSOA and CLAUDEL make use of symbols to invent a self-sufficient language.

This aesthetics can still be seen today in what B. DORT terms symbolist representation: "the attempt to organize, on stage, a (closed or open) universe that borrows some elements from apparent reality but which, through the actor, refers the spectator to another reality that he must discover" (DORT, 1984:11).

See also: icon, represented reality, semiology.

Further reading: Appia 1895, 1963, 1921; Craig 1905; Robichez 1957; Frenzel 1963; Styan 1981 Marty 1982.

SYMBOLISM

Fr.: *symbolisme;* Ger.: *Symbolismus;* Sp.: *simbolismo.*
See STYLIZATION, SYMBOL

SYMBOLIZATION

Fr.: *symbolisation;* Ger.: *Symbolisierung;* Sp.: simbolizació*n.*
See SIGN

SYNOPSIS

Fr.: *résumé de la pièce;* Ger.: *Zusammenfassung;* Sp.: *resumen de la obra.*
See PLOT

SYNTHETICAL THEATRE

Fr.: *théâtre synthétique;* Ger.: *synthetisches Theater;* Sp.: *teatro sintético.*
See TOTAL THEATRE

T

TABLEAU

Fr.: *tableau*; Ger.: *Tableau*; Sp.: *cuadro*.

Unit of the play from the point of view of major changes in location, atmosphere or period. There is usually specific scenery for each tableau.

1. Act vs. Tableau

Structuring a play in tableaux is quite different from using the *act**/*scene** system, which functions more on the level of *action** and *entrances** and *exits** of the characters.

The reference to painting implied by the term *tableau* is indicative of the difference between this notion and that of the act. The tableau is a spatial unit of atmosphere, milieu or period; it is a thematic unit, not an actantial one. The act is the result of a strict narratological *segmentation** and is only one link in the actantial chain, while the tableau covers much more ground, and is a much looser term. It covers an epic world of characters, and the relatively stable relationships among them give the illusion of forming a fresco, a corps de ballet or a *tableau vivant**.

2. Emergence of Tableau Structure

The tableau aesthetic arose in the eighteenth century, along with a pictorial view of the dramatic stage. The tableau is "an arrangement of the characters on stage that is so natural and so true that, were it rendered faithfully by a painter, it would please me on the painting [...] The spectator in theatre sits as before a canvas on which different paintings appear by magic [...] The pantomime is a painting that existed in the poet's imagination as he wrote, a painting he wished the stage to show at each moment of the play" (DIDEROT 1975, 110). Similarly, some playwrights divide their texts into autonomous scenes focused around a theme or situation (LENZ, GOETHE in *Faust*; in the nineteenth century, BÜCHNER, MUSSET or HUGO; in the twentieth, WEDEKIND, BRECHT and others).

3. Tableau Dramaturgy

The tableau appeared in the company of epic elements of drama. According to the epic approach, the playwright, rather than focusing on a crisis, breaks down a duration, puts forth fragments of discontinuous time. He is interested not in gradual development but in breaks in the action. The tableau provides the necessary framework for a sociological survey or a genre painting. Rather than dramatic movement, it is like a still photograph of a scene. The tableau structure is a way of arranging the *stage** visually overall, and arose with the emergence of the mise-en-scène.

Still, the ideology underlying its use can vary widely. For DIDEROT, the tableau effected a harmonious synthesis of mobility, dramatic concentration and action: "A well-composed tableau is a whole enclosed according to a point of view, in which the different parts work towards a single goal and form, through their mutual correspondence, a whole as real as that of the parts of an organic body" (entry on "Composition," *l'Encyclopédie*). For BRECHT, on the other hand, the tableau is a typical but incomplete fragment without the spectator's critical and reconstructive perspective: each tableau forms a whole and is not projected into the following one; each tableau ends brusquely as soon as it threatens to "set" into a substance that is valid in itself and does not require comparison with the following one.

Further reading: Szondi 1972b; Valdin 1973; Barthes 1973b.

TABLEAU VIVANT

Fr.: *tableau vivant;* Ger.: *lebendes Bild;* Sp.: *cuadro viviente.*

Staging of one or more actors who are immobile and fixed in an expressive pose suggestive of a statue or painting.

1. The technique existed as early as the Middle Ages and the Renaissance, but the fashion and theory date back mainly to the eighteenth century. (C. BERTINAZZI is considered to be one of the inventors of this stage practice; he composed a tableau reconstructing GREUZE's painting *l'Accordée du village*.) The technique became a genre advocated by DIDEROT in *De la poésie dramatique*: "The figures must be placed together, brought closer or dispersed, isolated or grouped together, to form a series of tableaux, all composed in a great and true fashion" (1975, 110).

2. The tableau vivant inaugurated a dramaturgy that described a milieu, captured life in its everyday guise and showed a series of pathetic images of man with the help of genre painting. As in GREUZE, immobility is considered to hold the germ of movement and the expression of inner self. The tableau vivant lends itself to an evocation of *situations** and *conditions** rather than of actions and characters. Some plays used it systematically (DIDEROT, but also GOGOL in *The Inspector General*, 1836, which ends with the catastrophic fixed image of the characters waiting for the finance inspector). But at present the technique is used mainly in staging work. Some productions of the *theatre of everyday life** or *theatre of images** (LASSALLE, WENZEL, DEUTSCH, KROETZ) end each sequence with a freeze that is suggestive of the grip of environment and the way this dramaturgy proceeds, with small strokes creating scenes that are barely glimpsed in a flash of awareness.

TASTE

Fr.: *goût;* Ger.: *Geschmack;* Sp.: *gusto.*

1. In the Western theatre tradition, taste in the literal sense does not play a significant role in the spectators' *aesthetic experience**, whereas certain poetics, such as the Sanskrit, allude to the taste and flavour of the spectacle, to what BARTHES calls the *Sapientia* of the text: "No power, a bit of knowledge, a bit of wisdom, and as much flavour as possible" (1978a, 46).

2. Taste in the larger sense of *expectations** and definite subjective judgment, however, is an essential concept to appreciate the way in which the audience receives the performance and reads the text or mise-en-scène on the basis of *codes**, as well as the way tastes change with times and ideologies, how good and bad taste undergo constant change, much to the displeasure of normative theorists such as LA BRUYÈRE, who claim that "there is, therefore, a good and a bad taste" (*Les Caractères*, 1688). Studies on taste would require empirical surveys on theatre audiences and their makeup, culture and habits.

See also: sociosemiotics, semiology.

Further reading: Bourdieu 1979.

TEACHING OF THEATRE

Fr.: *enseignement de théâtre;* Ger.: ; Sp.: *enseñanza de teatro.*

1. An Immoderate Program

Although programs of *theatre studies**, in theory at least, are highly ambitious, being borrowed from disciplines of prestige, the teaching of theatre is much more limited and modest in its everyday reality. Difficulties seem to accumulate, confounding apprentice actors as well as school and university authorities. These difficulties are all the more insurmountable since Western tradition does not confine such teaching to physical training and apprenticeship within a tradition but proposes to mould the entire personality of the actor, including physical, intellectual, emotional, even metaphysical and moral qualities. From more or less academic *teaching* to *training*, even self-training or the "training of trainers," there is a significant shift in vocabulary.

The program of such an ideal school is unlimited: all authors, all techniques, all branches of stagecraft and avenues of research come under study. Seen in the light of its two aspects, text and performance, theatre has numerous areas in which actors may exercise their talent. The epistemological chaos of theatre studies is matched only by the anarchy of art studies (both in France and abroad) and the lack of cooperation and coordination among government departments and organizations. It is much more important to the young actor, however, to discover his own personal style – to find his way around the maze of theories, methods and traditions – than to be crammed with impressive technical knowledge but incapable of adapting to new situations or reflecting on himself and his art. And rather than trying to cover the whole field of theatrical knowledge, it might perhaps be more reasonable to restrict teaching and learning to certain priority areas. For instance, the theatre department at the Université de Paris VIII focuses on the following seven main branches of research: theatre writing, acting, space, staging, institutions, relationships with other arts, and reception. This should make it possible to adopt an approach that is both theoretical (academic in the sense of a description) and practical (an actualization of theory that produces an artistic object and then attempts to analyze it).

2. The Place of Learning

The same uncertainty reigns in regard to the place where such complex knowledge should be transmitted. In Western Europe, dramatic art is taught at both universities and professional schools (conservatories or private institutions). This separation, supposedly legitimated by the distinction between theory and practice, is particularly unfortunate because it prevents both aspects from being explored in depth and perpetuates an artificial dichotomy that would be in the interests of both the university and the schools to overcome.

A. UNIVERSITY TEACHING

Universities discovered theatre only recently, when they acknowledged, not without much vacillation, that it was in fact neither a branch of literature nor a refuge for hotheads, but an artistic practice (without however according it the means for decent survival or multidisciplinary teaching). The universities have not managed to redraw the boundaries of disciplines of knowledge on the basis of this artistic practice, or to decide what is in fact their object of study: professional or amateur theatre, dramatic play or the hybrid forms of the "inter-artistic." Nor is it clear whether the student is supposed to learn by doing or should be placed in *"l'école du spectateur"* [school for spectators] to better *"lire le théâtre"* [read theatre] – according to the titles of Anne Ubersfeld's famous books – or whether (as one might hope) the two are not mutually exclusive. For the teaching of theatre should make as much use of the academic study of texts and performances and the learning of techniques and performance skills as of artistic practice itself. Universities would be wrong to confine such teaching to academic studies, if only because in order to be fully comprehensible it requires a knowledge of the techniques and the craft of performance.

In continental Europe, teaching covers essentially texts, sometimes dramaturgical analysis and, in the best cases, performance analysis. In the English-speaking countries theatre is taught at school or at university, more as an activity of personal development ("drama in education") than as an art. Universities encourage the presentation of plays that give students experience in putting on actual performances. Often these public presentations (which serve to legitimate the university within the community) are so time-consuming that they afford participants no opportunity for critical reflection during or after the event, while giving them the illusion of professionalism and providing the authorities with the facile satisfaction of a show at low cost.

It is very difficult for universities to reconcile their traditional view of universal humanist culture with the short-term professional needs that call for the careful management of profitability. Research and experimentation, anarchy and incompetence do not mix well with the requirement of professionalism and immediate financial return. It hardly needs repeating that universities in Western Europe rarely have the resources to function properly. In France, faculties of arts have to contend with conditions that are worse than those in many third-world countries: nonexistent or insufficient rehearsal and theatre space, materials and funds; uncomfortable, dirty premises, inadequate libraries, a lack of skilled technicians, etc. It is quite amazing, in fact, that people from all over the world persist in coming to study in Paris. In Eastern Europe the situation is (or was) one of comparative luxury: access to advanced schools of dramatic art is controlled much more strictly and training is much more technical and comprehensive, although the admission criteria are (were) not always based on merit.

B. ACTING SCHOOLS

The level of such institutions varies considerably, from national schools and advanced conservatories of dramatic art to private courses that are sometimes administered by unscrupulous and unqualified people but often by "course leaders" [*animateurs*] and professionals, generous with their time, who are anxious to pass on their art. Entrance to conservatories and schools of theatre is very selective, and the selection criteria are poorly defined, contradictory or obsolete – for example, admission may depend on prior knowledge that the student could have acquired only with great difficulty. The program is addressed to young people who, in three years, are supposed to acquire all the performance and acting skills and feel at ease in all different roles and types of dramaturgy ("conserve tradition while opening windows wide" National Centre of Dramatic Arts, Paris). In all such advanced schools, learning basic techniques (voice, body expression, improvisation, dance, relaxation, declamation, singing, fencing, archery, Tai Chi, riding, etc.) lays an indispensable foundation for subsequent learning and creation.

Nevertheless, the way in which this learning takes place – in what spirit and for what purpose – is of prime importance. By separating technical training in basic courses in the morning from blocking and staging work in the afternoon, one runs the risk of giving credit to the notion that the body must first be warmed up mechanically before beginning any exercise involving the mind.

Between the basic training (which is undisputably necessary) and its actualization in dramatic work (which is, of course, the final aim), there is a disturbing no-man's land. When will these basic techniques be put to the test in dramaturgical analysis or the reading of performances or, above all, in signs conveyed by actor and performance? Only rarely is dramaturgical analysis taught in connection with the actor's work, or stagecraft as a theory of the production of meaning on stage. It is true that, tied as it is to each individual's development, it is not easy to teach or induce creativity – the intransmissible creative spark that is an essential ingredient of art.

Private courses differ more in the cost of tuition (often unduly high) than in the diversity of the teaching they offer. Their main purpose is to give aspiring actors a veneer of credibility and assurance by having them work unremittingly on selected pieces, by instilling in them the mythology of their characters, and by giving them the false notion that learning their craft means knowing how to create illusion on the basis of a carefully rehearsed scene (cf. *Acteurs*, no. 68, 1969).

Despite the differences in status and resources, all of these establishments, whether public and private, are torn between the desire to be comprehensive and the awareness that they must necessarily fail at their mission.

3. A Thorny Problem, and a Few Dreams
It can safely be said that, at least in France, ideas circulate poorly between the university and the theatre profession, and between the university and the professional schools (National Conservatory, École Nationale Supérieure des Arts et Techniques du théâtre, Théâtre National de Strasbourg), whether this be attributable to mutual disregard, differing interests or narrow-mindedness.

Added to this is a basic distrust of schooling on the part of theatre people, and a refusal to participate in shared teaching activities. Perhaps, after all, universal humanism and immediate professional needs are naturally incompatible. This is all the more true since it is not easy, in order to please the technocrats, to reverse the roles and have a university open to professional techniques alongside theatre creation that could be used by teaching institutions. Universities and the state refuse to bear the brunt of a costly training, refuse to carry out their mission properly, and encourage rampant privatization, the sponsoring of spectacular but "corrupting" operations; they will not associate themselves with projects situated an equal distance from teaching and culture.

The status of the teaching staff at schools and universities ought to be redefined, distinguishing clearly between:

1. a teaching and academic function in which exercises and practical work proposed by professionals giving courses on a part-time basis are integrated as teaching aids within the teaching of theory;
2. a professional and artistic function assumed by professional schools and conservatories by employing real professionals and frequently bringing in intellectuals, theoreticians and outside personalities.

Not only are these functions poorly defined or muddled at present, but interaction among university professors and professionals who teach on a part-time basis is impeded by the difference in status, by symbolic rivalry, and by the distorted image each has of the other. It sometimes happens that course leaders recruited normally within the profession have no time to do anything but teach (given the poor pay they receive), while university professors, too caught up in their artistic or administrative work, no longer have the desire or the leisure time to do basic research.

In spite of these endemic structural differences, however, such a reconciliation between the university and the profession needs to be well thought out if the teaching of theatre is to remain within the university and if a decompartmentalization of skills and approaches is truly desired.

1. A first dream of reconciliation has already been realized in the "From Page to Stage" projects coordinated by Gay McAuley at the University of Sydney. She brings together a professional team at the university theatre and they rehearse for two or three weeks in the presence of the students, lending themselves to their research. The entire creative process is analyzed and assessed by teachers and students.

2. Conversely, the university can go to the theatre; for instance, the theatre department of the Université de Paris VIII once assigned a number of European students and professors to Avignon before and during the festival. The aim was to comment on and analyze performances immediately after the fact, to confront reflection with the need for immediate action, to facilitate placing apprentices in the professional milieu, to attend rehearsals and to draw conclusions about the production and reception of the performance.

3. On a more modest scale, one might plan acting exercises designed to reconsider the mind/body dichotomy, to lead to theoretical reflection through experimentation with play, to ensure a constant dialogue between theoretical questioning and stage testing, to move between the seminar and the workshop. Studying texts and performances is no longer an emotional and play activity for its own sake. Study and play may be reconciled with each other if a teaching and training framework is created for them, a seminar/workshop where ideas and actions can be tried out. This framework could be created at the university but also in workshops or "thematic studios" at conservatories, national theatres or drama centers (following the technique launched by STANISLAVSKY and MEYERHOLD, and revived by Vitez at the conservatory and at Chaillot, or by the Théâtre National de Strasbourg).

4. The year-end performance should also be revamped to make it not merely a student performance directed by a teacher or professional, but an individual or collective project, a "self-course" (*autocours* in the sense of Jacques Lecoq) – a "thematic studio," a project of artistic research accompanied and followed by reflection, for example in the form of a master's program (as at the Université du Québec à Montreal or the Higher Institute of the Arts in Havana.

Many failings can be found within the teaching of theatre, as well as a striking waste of human and institutional energy. In spite of everything, however, it is also a bearer of hope, presenting as it does a summary of human knowledge that is to be assessed, transmitted and replayed. The process of reflection now under way on such possibilities holds out the expectation that, given decent means of survival, it could contribute to improving the quality of a teaching activity that is still too approximate.

Further reading: *Théâtre/Public*, no. 34–35 (1980), no. 82–83 (1988); *Acteurs*, no. 68 (April 1989) (theatre schools); *Voies de la création théâtrale*, "La formation de l'acteur," Paris, CNRS; McAuley, 1985; Vernois and Henry 1988.

TEICHOSCOPY

(From the Greek *teichoskopia*, seeing through the wall.)

Fr.: *teichoscopie*; Ger.: *Teichoskopie, Mauerschau*; Sp.: *teichoscopia*.

The term is used to describe a scene from HOMER (The *Iliad*, 3: 121–244) in which Helen describes for Priam the Greek hero she alone can see.

A dramaturgical means of having a character describe something that takes place in the wings just as the observer is telling about it (*off stage**). This avoids having to show violent or unseemly actions on stage, while giving the spectators the *illusion** that they are actually happening and allowing them to experience them at second hand. Similar to radio reports (for example, sports broadcasts), teichoscopy is an epic technique; it does without visual aids while focusing on the enunciator and producing tension perhaps more acutely than if the event were visible. It enlarges the stage space and connects several scenes, reinforcing the authenticity of the visible place from which the reporting takes place.

Examples of teichoscopy can be found in SHAKESPEARE (*Julius Caesar*), KLEIST (*Penthésilée*), GOETHE (*Götz von Berlichingen*), SCHILLER (*Maria Stuart, Die Jungfrau von Orléans*), BEAUMARCHAIS, GRABBE (*Napoléon*), BRECHT (*Galileo*), GIRAUDOUX (*Electre, la Guerre de Troie n'aura pas lieu*).

See also: messenger, narration, dramatic and epic.

TELEVISION AND THEATRE

Fr.: *television et theatre*; Ger.: *Fernsehen und Theater*; Sp.: *television y teatro*.

Theatre plays a fairly important role on television. The only theatre many people will ever see is a television broadcast or television drama. Many theatre productions are now videotaped. It is crucial, then, to examine the relationship between television and theatre, and to study the way the theatre event changes when broadcast on television.

1. Television as a New Medium

Television can easily multiply a play's average audience by 10,000 in a single evening. In this way, over the space of a few years, a whole repertory (mainly classical) is built up for a huge audience. Theatre is also covered in educational programs and reports on productions under way. The scenes filmed are considered to be a representative sample of the theatrical performance.

The selection and presentation of particular shows hinges, naturally, on their conditions of production. Until the late fifties, only live broadcasts were possible, mainly from a studio, with all the uncertainties involved in live theatre in addition to technical hazards. Televised theatre retained its essential aspect as an ephemeral and elusive, difficult-to-codify live event. Thus the classics, which were often shown at the time, naturally retained their unities. However, television did not take advantage of this immediacy: what prevailed was a concern with perfection, with reliability and an accomplished performance. A technical incident, which is always of interest on the stage, means only a blackout on television and the end of communication. Nowadays, plays are no longer filmed live but in a studio and on location, as in the movies. Television has moved further and further away from the theatrical mode of production and closer to the work of the cinema. Whether or not the broadcast is done in front of an audience (be it live or recorded), the public recording aims to give the television audience the illusion that they are really in a theatre, with all the ingredients of fantasy (the red curtain, the whistling to indicate that the performance is to begin immediately, the applause, the well-known stars of boulevard theatre, the sight of spectators leaving the auditorium). Like early live studio filming, the technique is rather basic, consisting of a few cameras arranged frontally from the audience's perspective, generally two heavy cameras for close-ups and a light camera on a crane for group shots and movement. The repertory of these broadcasts is that of the worst boulevard theatre; sometimes "worn-out" classics are chosen, very rarely contemporary plays. The staging is very conservative. In France, unlike Great Britain, playwrights are rarely asked to write original screenplays for television.

2. Theatre and Television: A Collision of Specificities

A. SITUATION OF RECEPTION

The small screen at home is the point of attraction and umbilical cord of an elsewhere that is hard to place. Both voluntary and involuntary interruptions of the broadcast are possible, and the television viewer, who is in demand for many other programs, is a fundamentally unstable being. The result of the need to keep the spectator's interest is a much faster-paced show that the stage version, which often lasts three hours or more. The television production should therefore never be boring or lose its narrative force.

B. MEDIATIONS BETWEEN PRODUCERS AND RECEIVERS

There are many of these – technological mediations, but also interferences and semiotic transformations of meaning through the various stages of acting on the theatre stage, then in the studio, then in the framing and editing of the film or video, and finally in adaptation and miniaturization for the small screen.

C. EFFACING THEATRICALITY

The television director of a pre-existing theatre performance or television drama may choose either to eliminate the most visible and stagy aspects of theatricality by choosing filmic effects and giving the acting and setting a more natural look, or to underscore the theatricality, underlying it with an abstract setting and theatrical diction, as if the camera were doing a report in the theatre premises.

D. PRINCIPLES OF TRANSPOSITION FROM THEATRE TO TELEVISION

Whereas in theatre it is the spectator who sifts through the performance signs, in television (as in film) an orientation of meaning is given in the framing, editing and camera movements. In a broadcast based on a theatre staging, this implies that the film staging has the "last word" in giving meaning to the performance. Even the most compact and finished theatre object is always deconstructed and reconstructed in the filmic discourse in the process of filming and editing and in the television discourse (miniaturization, delayed private reception, etc.), all of which pleads for a specific television dramaturgy.

3. A Television Dramaturgy

We will leave aside the case of a live or delayed broadcast of a pre-existing theatre performance, for such a process retains the look of live reportage, an excerpt and a loss of meaning (along with, in a live broadcast, a remnant of authenticity). The dramaturgy of television drama is based on a few general principles:

A. The *image* must be framed with precision and composed with care in order to be easily readable within the smaller dimensions of the television screen, hence a certain stylization, abstraction of the elements of set and costume, and a systematic treatment of space. The miniaturization of the image makes the sound track more important.

B. The quality and proximity of the *sound* is most capable of ensuring an effect of reality. Words come out very well on television, often better than in theatre. They can be modulated, transmitted by voice-over, connected to the situation and the image. The impression of disembodied sound in the image is much less noticeable than on the big screen. Television is often nothing more than visual radio; we listen to it in a way that is both private and absent-minded, like a nearby, convincing voice, and the image only confirms the authenticity of that voice.

C. As to the setting, we often see only bits of it behind the actors, except when a close-up or a panoramic shot is used to stress a particular detail or characterize an atmosphere. As long as performances were filmed mainly in a studio (in France this was true until about 1965), the reconstructed studio sets remained close to theatrical stylization; later on, exteriors provided a more cinematic framework and the effect of reality began to prevail, with a resulting loss of clarity and stylization.

D. *Lighting* is rarely as varied or as subtle as in theatre or cinema; when television sets were in black and white, the lighting had to accentuate contrast and carefully manage light and shadow.

E. The *editing* uses strong punctuation, dramatized breaks and pauses. The narrative must be readable and clearly organized, managing a rapid and coherent suspense.

F. *Acting*: The camera is focused on the actor-speakers, most often in medium shot, to show their psychological and physiological reactions. Using too many close-ups in colour risks revealing skin imperfections. Like the other elements of film and screen, the actor is only one element, integrated and subordinated to the industrial and artistic plans of the directors. Hence a certain disembodiment; the actor exists only in his fragmentation, by metonymy, by his position in the filmic discourse.

G. *Story and theme* are variable, of course, but refer often to social reality, journalism, everyday life. This kind of narrative material lends itself to soap operas and serials; heir to the trivial literature of penny dreadfuls and melodrama, the television drama is fond of proven formulas, unfortunate heros, switchback destinies. On television, theatre is consumed in the same way as news, weather reports or commercials. The news look like a spectacular show, with blood and death and operetta weddings; inversely, television fiction never relinquishes its core of realism and its everyday quality that suits a naturalistic repertory and an aesthetic of reality-effects.

H. *Mise-en-scène* in television is the outcome of the preceding elements. It is the vast assembly line on which the framing and editing has finally to rank and correlate the different components of the television film. The more perceptible its coherence, the more indistinct is form from content, the more television dramaturgy proves its specificity, thus successfully moving from theatron to electron.
Further reading: Erenstein 1988.

TEMPO
(Italian word for time)

A musical term sometimes used in theatre that indicates a movement not marked by the number of beats on a metronome. In music, as in theatre, the interpretation of tempo is for the most part left to the discretion of the director, or even the actor. Stage directions about the quality of delivery and acting abound only in naturalistic, psychological or conversational plays.

TENSION
Fr.: *tension;* Ger.: *Spannung;* Sp.: *tensión.*

Dramatic tension is a structural phenomenon that connects the episodes of the *fabula* to one other, particularly toward the end of the play.

Tension is produced by anxious anticipation of the ending. By anticipating the events to follow, the spectator creates *suspense**, imagining the worst and feeling very "tense."

A episode or motif in the dramatic text acquires meaning only through projection into the next one. STAIGER (1946) even makes tension a specific principle of dramatic art. Dramatic structure resembles a bow, with each action stretching it further until it releases the fatal arrow.

Epic (notably Brechtian) dramaturgy calls for tension on the development (*Gang*) rather than the ending (*Ausgang*) of the play.

When the outcome of the conflict is known in advance, as in *analytical** drama, the tension is defused and the spectator concentrates on the development of the *fabula*.
See also: dramatic and epic, reading, dramatic structure.
Further reading: Freytag 1965; Beckerman 1970; Pütz 1970; Genette 1972; Demarcy 1973.

TEXT AND COUNTERTEXT
Fr.: *texte et contre-texte;* Ger.: *Text und Gegentext;* Sp.: *texto y contratexto.*
See INTERTEXTUALITY

TEXT AND PERFORMANCE
Fr.: *texte et contre-texte;* Ger.: *Text und Gegentext;* Sp.: *texto y contratexto.*

Any reflection on the relationship between text and performance involves an in-depth debate on mise-en-scène, the status of the word in theatre, and the *interpretation** of the *dramatic text**.

1. Historical Background

A. THE LOGOCENTRIC POSITION
For many years theatre was imprisoned within a logocentric conception, from the time of ARISTOTLE until the staging became a systematic practice near the end of the last century, with the exception of certain popular shows and spectacular productions. Whether that attitude was characteristic of *classical dramaturgy**, Aristotelianism or the Western tradition, the result was to make the text the primary element, the deep structure and the essential content of dramatic art. The performance (the "spectacle," or *opsis** as ARISTOTLE termed it) comes only afterwards, as a superficial and superfluous expression that addresses itself solely to the senses and the imagination and distracts the audience from the literary beauty of the

story and from reflecting on the tragic conflict. There is a theological assimilation that takes place between *text*, as sheltering the immutable meaning and the soul of the play, and *performance*, as the peripheral place of the flashy and the sensual, of the body, of instability – in short, of *theatricality**.

B. THE COPERNICAN REVERSAL

The late nineteenth century saw the beginnings of a reversal in the logocentric attitude. Suspicions about words as the bearers of truth and the liberation of the unconscious forces of image and dream brought about the exclusion of theatre from the verbal domain, considered as the only relevant one. The stage and all one might do on it were promoted to the rank of supreme organizer of the meaning of theatre *performance**. A. ARTAUD marked the outcome of the trend in the clarity of his aesthetic and this forcible formulation: "In any case, and I hasten to say it at once, a theatre which subordinates the *mise en scène* and production, i.e., everything in itself that is specifically theatrical, to the text, is a theater of idiots, madmen, inverts, grammarians, grocers, antipoets and positivists, i.e., Occidentals." (1964, IV:49–50; Eng. 1958, 41).

2. Dialectics of Text and Performance

The historical background of the text-performance relationship only illustrates the dialectics between them. There are two possibilities: either the performance seeks to render and "respeak" the text, or it creates a gap between them, criticizing or relativizing the text by not reduplicating it.

A. PERFORMANCE POTENTIAL OF THE TEXT

In the first instance, that of the *redundancy** of performance, the production seeks out stage signs that illustrate or give the spectator the illusion of illustrating the text's referent. Strangely enough, for the audience, and even for many "realistic" directors and "philological" critics, as well as actors, this is considered an exemplary solution, as a goal to be achieved: "A good production is script-into-performance, an intimate, point-to-point transformation that moves us only in its wholeness. Script has *become* performance, by pursuing a line of potentiality that had previously been only implicit, and therefore hidden, but which is now actualized in such a way as to seem inevitable" (HORNBY 1977, 109). According to this view of the text as hidden potentiality (HORNBY 1977) or as "stage virtuality" (SERPIERI 1978), the text contains one right staging that needs only to be discovered, and the stage performance and stage work do not come into conflict with, but serve, the meaning of the text. This reflects a philological attitude toward theatre (without meaning anything offensive thereby). It is to its credit that such a theory refrains from throwing out the (textual) baby with the (performance) bathwater, something that is certainly salutary today given the sometimes out-of-control experiments of our textual obsessives and manipulators. It risks, however, blocking experimental theatre by perpetuating a certain logocentrism.

B. THE IRREDUCIBLE HERMENEUTICAL* DIFFERENCE

Inversely, it would appear much more accurate to note a divergence between text and performance. As soon as the performance is freed from its ancillary role toward the text, a significant distance opens between the two and an imbalance is created between the visual and the textual. That imbalance generates a new look at the text and a new way of showing the reality suggested by it.

The difference is an impassable gulf between the text and when and where it is uttered. "It may be," writes B. DORT, "that our pleasure in theatre is supported precisely by seeing in it a text, by definition foreign to time and space in the transitory moment and the particular time of the performance. The performance of theatre, then, does not represent a rediscovered unity but a never-to-be-resolved tension between the eternal and the transitory, between the universal and the particular, between the abstract and the concrete, between text and stage. It does not realize a text to a greater or lesser degree; it criticizes it, forces it, questions it; sets up a confrontation. It is not an agreement, but a struggle" (*Le Monde du dimanche*, 12 October 1980).

3. Fictionalization in Text and Performance

The theory of *fiction** has us see the text-performance relationship in connection with the process of fictionalization effected by the staging. The fiction may seem to be the middle term, the mediation between what the dramatic text relates and the performance represents, as if the mediation were effected by the textual and visible figuration of a possible fictional world, first constructed through dramaturgical analysis and reading, then figured by the blocking. The hypothesis is not false, provided we are careful not to let in, by the back door so to speak, the theory of the actualized referent figured by that mediation. Naturally there is an obvious relationship between text and performance, though not in the form of a translation or reduplication of the first in the second; rather, it is a confrontation between a fictional world structured on the basis of the text and a fictional world produced by the performance.

A. TWO KINDS OF FICTIONAL STATUS

The two kinds of fictional status, of text and performance, have very specific characteristics, although the fictional world of the performance does, simultaneously, two things:

1. Encompasses and integrates the fictional world of the text spoken on stage, supplies the situation of enunciation;
2. May be at any time *contradicted* and deconstructed from within through the intervention of the text spoken within the performance. For this dramatic *text* is a semiological system whose semantic precision and immediately perceptible verbal nature throw a certain light on the other signifying systems and provide them with the possibility of anchoring themselves to the signifieds uttered by the linguistic text.

The encounter between the two comes about by means of a dual fiction in the case of a theatre production.

1. Fictionalization in performance: through stage enunciation, the visible and audible situation in which the dramatic text is uttered.
2. Textual fictionalization: through fictionalization by the text's listeners, for although it is true that the text is meaningless except in stage enunciation, the spectator is free to build a different fiction than that chosen for the production, and to treat the text as a continent accessible only through reading and imagination ("in the mind's eye," as Hamlet would say).

This very real distinction is no less purely theoretical, for both fictional modes interfere and cover up their traces for the spectator's pleasure and illusion. The stage and the representation of time and place establish at the outset a *framework** that is given as the place of the fiction, an imitation of the fictional world. This first fictionalization of performance becomes all the stronger as the actors, atmosphere, pace and other elements do their best to persuade us that they are fiction incarnate.

Fictionalization in performance cements the textual fiction (even in the incarnation of the verb, the only staging possible, etc.). The two fictions finally interpenetrate each other to the point that we can no longer say whether it is the dramatic text that has created the situation of enunciation, or the enunciation that is not capable of leading to another text than the one understood. The mingling of the two fictional modes occurs as if to better anchor and stress the spectator's illusion of being in a foreign fictional world, to the point that what he sees before him (an actor, a lighting or sound effect) seems to him to exist elsewhere, on "another stage," as MANNONI (1969) puts it.

B. PRESENCE/ABSENCE

This general confusion of the two kinds of fictionalization, which we might call one of the specific traits of theatrical perception, proceeds – at least in the production of a pre-existing dramatic text – from the exchange of two semiotic principles for the linguistic text and the stage figuration:

1. The linguistic text signifies through its signs alone, as an *absence* for a *presence*, i.e. as the fictional reality experienced as present and real.
2. The performance is given as the immediate *presence* of something that is only *absence* and confusion of signifier with referent.

Once these precautions have been taken into account as to the relationship between textual and stage fiction and how difficult they are to dissociate, the theory of fiction is in a position to specify some of the operations that take place between text and performance.

See also: scenario, visual and textual, pre-staging.

Further reading: Tonelli 1978; Aston et al. 1983; Pavis 1983b, 1986; Fischer-Lichte, Riley and Gissenweirer 1990; Carlson 1985; Swiontek 1986.

TEXTUAL LINGUISTICS

Fr.: *grammaire du texte*; Ger.: *Textlinguistik*; Sp.: *gramática del texto*.

See NARRATIVE ANALYSIS

TEXTUAL SPACE

Fr.: *espace textuel*; Ger.: *Textraum*; Sp.: *espacio textual*.

1. Textual space should not be confused with the *indications of time and place** contained in the dramatic text. Like any text that talks about the world (represents a given reality), the dramatic text contains certain expressions of space (adverbial phrases of place, shifters, personal pronouns) that link any enunciation to its time and place. Indications of time and place, which are by no means specific to theatre, arise at the level of the content, of utterances.

2. When we speak of textual space, however, we are referring to the enunciation of the text, the way in which the sentences, speeches and lines unfold in a given place. This visual dimension of discourse is, or can be made, perceptible in theatre. The enunciators are present; we can see where their speeches and exchanges come from. Theatre offers up to the eyes of the audience texts that reply to each other and are comprehensible only in quasi-physical interaction (*stichomythia**). In this sense, textual space and rhythmic architecture are always perceptible on stage.

But space is also inserted in certain forms of textuality, as soon as attention is drawn not to what the discourse seeks to represent (what it is representing dramatically), but its signifying presentation and formalization. When a text is too poetic (opaque) to represent a referent, it tends to become crystallized and fixed (for example, *les Burgraves* by HUGO is one of the first attempts to draw the spectator's attention to the tangible and "spatial" nature of the verses spoken). A repetitive structure of terms or paragraphs produces the same effect; though he may not be able to understand the text or the reason for the repetition, the hearer is sensitive to the enunciation of masses of words or phrases (cf. G. STEIN, R. FOREMAN, or R. WILSON in *A Letter to Queen Victoria* or in *I Was Sitting on my Patio*, where the text was spoken twice by two actors without any new information being added, reinforcing the image of a text projected into space).

See also: discourse, text and performance, rhythm.

Further reading: Ryngaert 1984; Pavis 1984b.

THEATRE ART

Fr.: *art théâtral*; Ger.: *Theaterkunst*; Sp.: *arte teatral*.

The term *theatre art* brings together two words that sum up all of the contradictions of theatre. Is it an autonomous art with its own laws that possesses an aesthetic *specificity**? Or is it the result (synthesis, conglomeration or juxtaposition) of several arts such as painting, poetry, architecture, music, dance and gesture? Both points of view are represented in the history of aesthetics. Below is an overview of the origins and tradition of theatre art in the West.

1. Origins of Theatre

The infinite wealth of theatre traditions and forms throughout history makes any definition of theatre art impossible, however general. The etymology of the Greek word *theatron*, which referred to the place where spectators sat during the performance, gives only a partial account of one component of that art. A visual art *par excellence* and an institutionalized space for voyeurism, theatre has nevertheless often been "reduced" to a literary genre, to dramatic literature, the performative aspect being considered since ARISTOTLE as accessory and necessarily subordinate to the text.

Accompanying these scattered forms of theatre and dramatic genres is a similar diversity of material, social and aesthetic conditions in theatre. What similarities are there, for instance, between a primitive ritual, a light comedy, a mèdieval mystery or a performance in the Indian or Chinese tradition? Sociologists and anthropologists have great difficulty identifying the reasons underlying man's need for theatre. They have cited the desire to imitate, the love of play in children and adults, initiation to ceremony, the need to tell stories or mock a particular condition of society with impunity, the actor's pleasure in metamorphosis. The origins of theatre are supposedly *ritual** and religious, and the individual within the group originally participated in a ceremony, before gradually delegating this task to an actor or a priest. Theatre is conceived as having only gradually lost touch with its magic and religious essence as it became sufficiently strong and autonomous to defy society; hence the historical problems that have plagued its relationship with authority and law, or even its difficulty in being accepted. Whatever the value of these theories, the theatre of today no longer has anything to do with its cultic origins (except in experiments that revive myth or ceremony to capture the original purity of the theatre act, as in ARTAUD). It has been diversified to the point where it now fulfills many new aesthetic and social functions. Its development is closely linked to that of social and technological consciousness, a fact demonstrated by the periodic predictions of its imminent demise as a result of the development of the *media** and mass art.

2. The Western Tradition

Although the question of the *essence** and specificity of theatre art has always been rather idealistic and metaphysical, far removed from the reality of theatre practice, we can at least indicate several features that have characterized it in the Western tradition from the Greeks to the present day. The notion of *art* differs from that of craft, technique or ritual. Although it has various different techniques available to it (acting and set design, for instance), and although it still contains an element of unchanging, prescribed actions, theatre is more than either of these aspects. It always presents an action (or the mimetic representation of an action) through actors who incarnate or show characters for an audience gathered together to receive it at a time and place that may or may not be specified in advance. A text (or an action), an actor's body, a stage, a spectator – this would seem to be the necessary sequence of all theatre communication. Each link in the chain, however, can take very different forms. The text is sometimes replaced by a non-literary style of acting, although this social text too is fixed and readable. The actor's body may lose its value as a human presence if the director makes an "Übermarionette" of it or if it is replaced by a stage arrangement or object. The stage does not have to be in a theatre building designed specifically for putting on plays; a public place, a shed or any other such place is perfectly suitable for theatre activity. It is impossible to eliminate the spectator entirely, however, without changing theatre art into a dramatic game in which everyone participates, a rite that does not require an external gaze to be fulfilled or an elitist activity sufficient unto itself that lacks critical openness to society, a self-theatre.

The concept of dramatic art was originally (in PLATO's *Republic* and ARISTOTLE's *Poetics*) founded on a distinction between *mimesis* (representation through direct imitation of action) and *diegesis* (narration by a narrator of the same actions). Mimesis then became the mark of the "objectivity" of theatre (in the sense of SZONDI 1956). The *he* or *she* of the (speaking and acting) characters is turned into dialogue by the *I* of the playwright; the re-presentation appears as an image of an already existing world. In fact, we know today that mimetic representation is neither direct nor immediate, but that it means placing text and actors in a situation of discourse. Theatre performance consists of a set of instructions, advice and guidelines contained in the *score**, text and stage directions.

There can be no definitive hierarchy of genre, as classical poetics claimed on the basis of a normative view of genres and their social functions. All contemporary theatre art escapes this theatre/poetry/novel trio. Similarly, the tragedy-comedy polarity, which is also found in the double tradition of the "noble" (tragedy, high comedy) and the "vulgar" (farce, lavish productions) genres, becomes meaningless as the social relationships underlying such class distinctions are altered.

3. Theatre within a System of the Arts

A. Most theoreticians are willing to concede that theatre art has access to all of the artistic and technological resources known to a given era. CRAIG, for example, defines it (somewhat tautologically) as follows: "The Art of the Theatre is neither acting nor the play, it is not scene nor dance, but it consists of all the elements of which these things are composed: action, which is the very spirit of acting; words, which are the body of the play; line and colour, which are the very heart of the scene; rhythm, which is the very essence of dance" (CRAIG 1905, 101).

B. There is no such consensus, however, as to how the various arts relate to each other. Adherents of the Wagnerian *Gesamtkunstwerk** or total theatre concept believe the performing arts should converge in a synthesis and become unified because their systems overlap.

C. According to another point of view, however, different arts should never be unified, as the result would be at best an unstructured amalgam. The important thing is to establish a hierarchy of resources and articulate them on the basis of the desired result according to the director's taste. The hierarchy proposed by APPIA (1954) – actor, space, light, painting – is only one of the innumerable possibilities of *aesthetics**.

D. Other theoreticians criticize the notion of theatre art conceived as *Gesamtkunstwerk* or total theatre in favour of *theatrical work** (*Theaterarbeit* for BRECHT). Performing arts exist and produce meaning only through their differences or contradictions (cf. BRECHT, *A Short Organum for the Theatre*, sect. 74). The staging makes the stage work against the text, the music against the meaning of the language, the gesture against the music or the text, etc.

4. The Specificity and Boundaries of Theatre Art

An overview of different writings on theatre shows that no one theory can reduce theatre art to a series of necessary and sufficient elements. It cannot be restricted to a set of techniques, and the boundaries of the stage are constantly being redrawn through various practices: the *projection** of slides or films (PISCATOR, SVOBODA), expansion into sculpture (Bread and Puppet), dance and mime, political action (*agit-prop**) or *happening**.

As a result, the study of theatre art branches out into numerous areas of study. In this vast context, SOURIAU's program appears almost too timid: "A treatise on theatre ought to examine successively at least the following factors: playwright, dramatic world, characters, place, stage space, set, exposition of subject, action, situations, dénouement, acting, spectator, categories of theatre (tragic, dramatic, comic); then the syntheses: poetry/theatre, music/theatre and dance/theatre; and finally the phenomena on the fringes of theatre: various kinds of shows, circus, puppets, and so on. Not to mention areas where theatre overlaps with other arts, particularly with the new art of cinematography" (SOURIAU, quoted in ASLAN 1963, 17).

See also: essence of theatre, staging, theatre anthropology, ethnoscenology.

Further reading: Rouché 1910; Craig 1964; Touchard 1968, Kowzan 1970; Schechner 1977; Jomaron 1989; Corvin 1995.

THEATRE CRITICISM

Fr.: *critique dramatique;* Ger.: *Theaterkritik;* Sp.: *crítica teatral.*

1. A type of criticism done mainly by journalists in immediate response to a particular production and published in the press or broadcast over radio or television. The informational aspect is just as important as the critical aspect of the message, the purpose being to indicate what plays may/should be seen, while giving the opinion of a critic who represents his readership more than his own aesthetic or ideological opinions. Much has changed since the impressionistic criticism of the late nineteenth century by critics such as FAGUET, SARCEY or LEMAITRE, who had the space to write long articles to express their enthusiasm or rage, peppering their arguments with theatre scandals and gossip. Today, criticism is of limited importance and has little impact on the show's success.

2. This type of writing is very dependent on working conditions and the situation of the media. Since the turn of the century theatre writing has lost most of the space in the newspaper, which complicates analysis and evaluation. Despite the difficult conditions involved, we should not make a strict distinction between what a theatre critic does and what the author of an article in a theatre review or academic essay does. It does not seem possible to define a standard discourse of dramatic criticism, as the evaluation criteria vary widely depending on the aesthetic and ideological position of the author and his or her implicit conception of theatre and mise-en-scène. Today many critics are aware of the importance of the director and his options, are open to experimentation in general, but have the feeling they are not equipped to describe a show and a certain distrust of theory and of human sciences, which offer their services to performance analysis.

Further reading: Lessing 1767; Brenner 1970; Dort 1971, 31–48; *Travail théâtral*, no. 9 (1972); *Yale Theater*, vol. 4, no. 2 (1973); Pavis 1979a, 1985e, 135–144, "Le discours de la critique"; *Pratiques*, no. 24 (1979); Descottes 1980; Ertel 1985. See also the critical collections of R.Kemp, G.Leclerc, J.-J.Gautier, B.Poirot-Delpech, G.Sandier, R.Temkine, B.Dort.

THEATRE INSTITUTION

Fr.: *institution théâtrale;* Ger.: *Theaterinstitution;* Sp.: *institución teatral.*

See SOCIOCRITICISM

THEATRE MANAGER

Fr.: *directeur de théâtre;* Ger.: *Theaterleiter, Intendant;* Sp.: *director de teatro.*

The theatre manager, administrator, *Intendant* (in German), or ministerially appointed artistic director contributes greatly, not only to the management but also to the aesthetics of plays. He thinks along the lines of the director in the *Prologue on Theatre* in GOETHE's *Faust* who aspires to please the crowd. "The infernal cast of manager-directors" complains J. LASSALLE, former administrator of the Comédie-Française.

The manager is there to remind us that management is an integral part of creation: in the operating budget, but even before that in programming. He will tend to favour subscriptions, for a season without surprises; will request time-tested plays or styles; will only become involved in profitable coproductions: will heed all the economic imperatives that apply to young companies and directors. Cultural policy can no longer guarantee the survival of art, even average fare.

THEATRE OF EVERYDAY LIFE

Fr.: *théâtre du quotidien*; Ger.: *Theater des Alltags*; Sp.: *teatro cotidiano.*

A neonaturalistic trend in theatre in the 1970s, given the generic name of "theatre of everyday life," aimed to discover and display everyday life, which had always been considered too insignificant and specific to be shown on stage. This label has been given to very diverse experiments, including "Kitchen Sink Drama" from the 1950s in England (WESKER), the neonaturalism of KROETZ, the creations and productions of WENZEL, DEUTSCH, LASSALLE and TREMBLAY (*Les Belles-Soeurs*). This movement has restored the historical fresco of critical realism (BRECHT) and provided a counter-balance to the theatre of the *absurd**, locked into its metaphysics of "nothingness." The everyday was always relegated to a decorative, anecdotal second place, like "the people" in the classical tragedies and historical dramas of the nineteenth century. It was part of a higher dramaturgical plan (as the backdrop to the sphere in which the hero moved, for instance). By definition, what was atypical or irrelevant to historical development was considered uninteresting. Not even BRECHT described the daily life of the people except from the point of view of an overall sociological scheme, as a counterpoint to the life of "great men" (cf. *Mother Courage*). The theatre of everyday life is content to present an assemblage of fragments of reality, tatters of language.

1. Themes

Showing the banal everyday life of the disadvantaged classes closes the gap between the history of great men and the "petty" but insistent and obsessive history of little people who have no voice (a story that the history of mentalities, objects and daily life has rehabilitated). This "minimal" theatre attempts to use a few episodes or phrases from daily experience to reconstruct a milieu, a period and an ideology. A hyper-realistic theatre that piles up details, the theatre of everyday life brings naturalism back to stage and acting styles, though with a critical perspective – it shows us often repetitive, always down-to-earth events, an accumulation of things and stereotypes. It is a mix of notations on reality, autobiography, and intimacy.

2. Vanishing Language

The dialogues are often flat and minimal, going beyond the thoughts of the speakers, who merely repeat the hackneyed phrases inculcated in them by the prevailing ideology (commonplaces, proverbs, "elegant" phrases from the mass media, speeches about the individual's freedom of expression). All that matters to the spectator are the silences and what is left unsaid. The speaking "subjects" are deprived of all verbal initiative; they are only cogs in the ideological machine of reproduction of social relationships.

This conception of man imprisoned in a milieu that has robbed him of everything, even his own language, would be nothing more than a revival of the naturalistic aesthetic were it not for the new status of theatricality.

3. Ever-changing Theatricality

Far from being overwhelmed by a meticulous representation of reality, theatricality is constantly in evidence, like a kind of persistent bass that no reality-effect can drown out. We are meant to sense the manipulation of reality behind the accumulation of facts and spicy details, the derision behind the "natural" appearance, the imaginary behind the commonplace. Such a subjective attitude toward reality is often conveyed by the directing of actors (LASSALLE) by an unrealistic stage design (CHÉREAU's staging of *Loin d'Hagondange*). A constant play of breaks between reality produced and theatrical production of reality is the ideological underwriter of this form of theatre: the spectators should not receive raw images of their everyday reality. The very accumulation of representations of their reality and the fact that they are presented after a time lag should grant them an awareness of their incongruity and show reality to be "curable."

4. Transformation of the Everyday?

Still, unlike Brechtian critical realism, which was based essentially on an optimistic attitude that the world could be changed, everyday theatre always maintains a certain ambiguity and pessimism about the possibility of changing ideology and society. There is a kind of disillusionment at the representations of reality and ideology in human consciousness that lead to resignation and immobilism, and the characters' entanglement in the prevailing discourse only illustrates this fatalistic view of verbal alienation. With this mythical drift toward a reification of ideology and social relations, the text sometimes has the author's lyrical voice intervene directly to openly criticize the alienation of the characters and to provide a subjective view of their problems (as in WENZEL's *Dorénavant I* (1977), *Les Incertains* (1978); *La Fin des monstres* (1994), KROETZ and some scenes in DEUTSCH's *l'Entraînement du champion avant la course*). Like naturalism, the theatre of everyday life cannot escape the subtle dialectics between scientific reporting and a subjective rendering of reality.

See also: naturalistic staging, reality-effect, realistic, represented reality, history.

Further reading: Lefèbvre 1972; Vinaver 1982; Sarrazac 1989, 1995; *Travail théâtral*, no. 24–25, 37, 38–39.

THEATRE PRACTICE

Fr.: *pratique théâtrale*; Ger.: *Theaterpraxis*; Sp: *práctica teatral*.

This is the collective and productive work done by the various practitioners (actors, stage designer, director, light designer, and so on). The neutrality of the term is supposed to guard against idealizing the process of "creation" by stressing the *collective doing* of the stage enunciators. This is far from the normative approach that, as in *Pratique du théâtre* by d'AUBIGNAC (1657), dictated theoretical rules for the proper functioning of theatre practice.

See also: dialectics, historicization, represented reality, theatre production, materialist theatre.

THEATRE RESEARCH

Fr.: *recherche théâtrale*; Ger.: *Theaterforschung*; Sp.: *investigación teatral*.

A distinction should be drawn between basic research in professional training and the teaching of theatre in conservatories and universities. Basic research imposes a certain distance on the object of study, an intellectual and institutional availability to conduct an in-depth inquiry into a particular aspect of theatre activity.

1. Researchers

Research, however, concerns only specialists and the erudite. Every artist must solve a series of practical questions having to do with his situation in theatre. The director, the dramaturg-literary advisor, professor in charge of redistributing and organizing knowledge in *Theaterwissenschaft* (theatre science) have all the more need to study such and such a historical or theoretical detail in depth, and visits to the archives are inevitable.

2. Location

Independent scholars no longer exist, as erudite individuals devoting their lives to theatre. Research takes place in *universities** as students pursue master's and doctoral degrees, in academies of sciences (in former Eastern Europe), or at the national centre for scientific research (despite the cruel distance between researchers and the study body), and only rarely in theatres "documenting" their performances or issuing publications (*Théâtre/Public*, *Comédie Française*). Without the official sanction of a university diploma (M.A., PhD, accreditation to supervise research), research does not appear to carry sufficient weight, and publication is only viable when subsidized by the university or the CNRS. Documentation centres and libraries (department of performing arts at Arsenal, national theatre centre, Maison Jean Vilar, theatre museums in Western Europe) lack the resources to publish the results of research or even indicate its scope. The "loneliness of the long-distance researcher" will last only a short moment, interrupted by the jury distractedly giving an opinion on his thesis but not really influencing the circulation and dissemination of results.

3. Forms

Most frequently seen is an individual study that leads to a doctoral thesis in the form of a monograph, nearly always too long or unreadable, which should be condensed and rewritten for publication: a huge effort for a result that is unsuited to "modern communication."

Fortunately, other kinds of research have appeared recently and are renewing research:

- Master's degrees, and even doctorates, are being opened up to practical experience, so that a dissertation accompanies an experience (though limited) with directing, acting or writing. However, few universities can provide the necessary facilities for practical experiments.
- Observation of preparations for a production throughout rehearsals, "participatory observation" by apprentices or assistants in directing, scene design, and technicians.
- More and more frequent observation of seminars on aspects of theatre creation or current events.
- Meetings of practitioners and historians/theoreticians to which artists are invited to demonstrate their work methods for actors or dancers under the critical gaze and commentary of academia. Examples are the International School of Theatre Anthropology organized by E. BARBA, the *Transversales* or (*Matières à conversations* of the Théâtre du Mouvement, meetings organized by the Académie Expérimentale des Spectacles directed by M. KOKOSOWSKI. The aim is to recreate a laboratory situation in which a small, specialized audience can witness the genesis and approach to work of artists, though this always distorts acting conditions to some extent.

4. Reevaluation: History and Theory

In tackling the creative process head-on, a researcher comes out of isolation but remains — and this is a requirement of "theatre science" — an independent subject, a deliberate anarchist and freelancer who strives for objectivity while recognizing the limits of his search. In particular, he must adapt his methods and questions to the object of study.

Research is both diversifying and focusing more closely on issues and methodologies, travelling to the field (as in *ethnoscenology**) and conducting research on forms of paratheatre (in *ethnodrama**), on formerly alien cultural traditions.

History is no longer the only or even the prevailing approach. Changes in the canon, the acceptance of new genres and the questioning of hierarchies all contribute to modifying the object of research and giving rise to an ongoing reevaluation of historical methods. Research on historical documents is not exempt from theory, and is no longer a self-confident positivist discipline. It no longer sets itself up as an objective science as opposed to the subjective reading of texts and interpretation of stagings. It reflects on the way in which the history of theatre is written, borrows its narrative and rhetorical models from literature and hermeneutics (RICOEUR), gains awareness of its writing and the influence of the surrounding culture that suggests such a mode of expression. Research, particularly historical research, thus comes back to the theoretical debate where everything must be reconstructed at every moment; it opens up prospects unsuspected by the orderly stacks of archives.

THEATRE SPACE

Fr.: *lieu théâtral*; Ger.: *theatralischer Raum*; Sp.: *lugar teatral*.

A term that, today, often replaces *theatre*. With the transformation of theatre architec-

ture – particularly the decline of the frontal proscenium-arch stage – and the growing use of new places such as schools, factories, city squares, marketplaces and so on, a theatre can be set up anywhere, seeking above all closer contacts with a social group and avoiding the traditional circuits of theatrical activity. The place is sometimes surrounded by a sense of mystery and poetry that imbues the performance. The dilapidated Bouffes du Nord theatre, for instance, religiously conserved in its original state when it was "found," lends itself marvellously well to the "raw," "immediate" style of Peter BROOK's productions. The old Cartoucherie factory that houses the Théâtre du Soleil retains a look that is half-industrial, half-craftsmanlike, favouring the creation for each new production of a *stage design** appropriate to the specific dramaturgy and atmosphere in question.
See also: frame, playing area, space.
Further reading: Jacquot and Bablet 1963; Bablet 1965, 1972, 1975; Rischbieter and Storch 1968; Banham 1988; Banu 1989; Carlson 1989.

THEATRICAL

Fr.: *théâtral*; Ger.: *theatralisch*; Sp.: *teatral*.

We can define this category as having the following characteristics:

1. Concerns the theatre;
2. Is easily adaptable to the demands of the stage (for example,, a very visual scene in a novel);
3. (pejoratively) Aims for an easy, i.e. artifical and affected, effect on the spectator, which is seen as not very *natural** (overly theatrical acting).

See also: theatricality, dramatic and epic, (re)theatricalization, specificity, declamation, theatrical effect.

THEATRICAL CATEGORY

Fr.: *catégorie dramatique, théâtrale*; Ger.: *Kategorien des Theaters*; Sp.: *categoría teatral*.

A general anthropological principle that goes beyond actual historical forms; for instance, the *dramatic**, the *comic**, the *tragic**, the *melodramatic**, the *absurd**. These categories go beyond the narrow bounds of literary works and reflect man's basic attitudes toward existence. They do apply to other contexts than Western theatre, though always with very specific values.
See also: essence of theatre, specificity, theatricality.
Further reading: Gouhier 1952, 1958, 1968, 1972.

THEATRICAL EFFECT

Fr.: *effet théâtral*; Ger.: *theatralischer Effekt*; Sp.: *efecto teatral*.

This term, as opposed to the *reality-effect**, refers to stage action that immediately reveals its playful, artificial and theatrical origins. Staging and acting styles renounce illusion and are no longer presented as an eternal reality, but rather stress the artistic techniques and devices used, accentuating the artificial nature of the performance. The theatrical effect is banned from the illusionist stage, as it reminds the audience of its spectator status by bringing out the *theatricality** or *theatricalization** of the stage.
Further reading: Meyerhold 1969; Brecht 1967, 15:339–388.

THEATRICALIZATION

Fr.: *théâtralisation*; Ger.: *Theatralisierung*; Sp.: *teatralización*.

To theatricalize an event or a text is to interpret it on stage using stage and actors. The visual aspect of the stage and the contextualization of the characters' speeches in an actual situation are the marks of theatricalization.

*Dramatization**, on the other hand, has to do with the textual and narrative structures only: writing dialogue, creating dramatic tension and conflicts among the characters, building up a dynamics of action (*dramatic and epic**).
See also: adaptation, translation, theatricality.

(RE)THEATRICALIZATION OF THEATRE

Fr.: *(re)théâtralisation du théâtre;* Ger.: *Theatralisierung;* Sp.: *(re)teatralización del teatro.*

1. Movement against the current of naturalism. While naturalism obliterates the traces of theatre production to give the illusion of a believable and natural stage reality, theatricalization or, more accurately, *re*theatricalization highlights the rules and *conventions** of the stage, presenting the performance as playful fiction only. The acting points up the difference between the character and the actor. The production makes use of traditionally "theatrical" "gadgets" such as exaggerated make-up, stage effects, melodramatic acting, stagy costumes, music hall and circus techniques, exaggerated body language, and etc.

2. According to the typology proposed by DORT (1984), theatricalized performance is "the attempt to create, on a stage that appears as such, a multiple interplay in which the actor, consciously using certain traditional devices or reinventing them spontaneously, appeals to the spectator's pleasure and instinct for play" (1984:11).

3. Artists as diverse as MEYERHOLD (1963), BRECHT and COPEAU have called for the retheatricalization of theatre as a place of play and artifice, and the "re-establishment of theatrical reality (as) a necessary condition for realistic representations of human social life" (BRECHT 1967, 15:251).

THEATRICALITY

Fr.: *théâtralité;* Ger.: *Theatralik, Theatralität;* Sp.: *teatralidad.*

The term was probably formed according to the model of the literature/literariness pair. Theatricality is that which is specifically theatrical, in performance or in the dramatic text, in the sense it is understood by A. ARTAUD, for example, when he notes the suppression of theatricality on the traditional European stage: "How does it happen that in the theater, at least in the theater as we know it in Europe, or better in the Occident, everything specifically theatrical, i.e., everything that cannot be expressed in speech, in words, or, if you prefer, everything that is not contained in the dialogue (and the dialogue itself considered as a function of its possibilities for 'sound' on the stage, as a function of the *exigencies* of this sonorisation) is left in the background?" (1964b, 38; Eng. 1958, 37). Our times are characterized by a search for that long-lost theatricality. But there is something mythical, overly general, even idealistic and ethnocentrist about the concept. It covers too much ground, and all we can do is note certain associations with the term.

1. A Density of Signs

Theatricality can be opposed to the *dramatic text** read or conceived without the mental representation of a production. Rather than flattening the dramatic text with a reading, i.e. a visualization of the enunciators, it helps point up its visual and auditory potential, grasp its theatricality: "What is theatricality? It is theater-minus-text, it is a density of signs and sensations built up on stage starting from the written argument; it is that ecumenical perception of sensuous artifice – gesture, tone, distance, substance, light – which submerges the text beneath the profusion of its external language" (BARTHES 1964a, 41–42; Eng. 1972a, 26). Just so, in the Artaudian sense, theatricality is opposed to literature, to the theatre of text, to written means, to dialogues and even at times to the narrativity and "dramaticity" of a logically constructed story.

2. The Location of Theatricality

The next problem is the origin and nature of this theatricality:

- should we look for it in the themes and content of the text (outside spaces, visualization of characters);
- the way the text talks about the outside world and shows (iconicizes) what it evokes in text and performance?

A. In the first case, *theatrical* simply means spatial, visual, expressive, as one might speak of a spectacular and impressive scene. This is a widespread use of the concept, but a trivial and irrelevant one.

B. In the second case, *theatrical* means the specific form of theatre enunciation, the movement of words, the dual nature of the enunciator (character/actor) and his utterances, the artificiality of performance (representation). This notion is similar to ADAMOV's concept of performance (representation): "the projection into the sensible world of states and images that constitute its hidden forces [...] the manifestation of the hidden, latent content, which holds the germs of drama" (ADAMOV 1964, 13).

3. The Origins of Theatricality and Theatre

The Greek origin of the word *theatron* reveals a forgotten, though fundamental property of this art; it is the place from which the audience watches an action that is presented in another place. Theatre is indeed a point of view on an event, made up of a gaze, an angle of vision and optical beams. The word came to mean the building where a performance is held only through a shift in the relationship between the gaze and the object contemplated. In the classical language of the seventeenth and eighteenth centuries, theatre meant the stage itself. Through a second metonymic translation, theatre came to mean the art, the dramatic genre (hence its interference with literature, so often fatal to theatre), but also the institution ("Théâtre-Français" for Comédie-Française) and, finally, the repertory and works of a particular author (SHAKESPEARE's theatre). The consequences of theatre's exile from the place of the gaze are crystallized in the metaphors of the world as a stage (*Theatrum Mundi**) or the sense of a place of action (theatre of operations), or hamming it up in everyday life (theatricals).

The French word *théâtre* has maintained the idea of a visual art, though there is no word that has taken on the concept of text. The word *drame* (unlike its English and German counterparts) refers not to the written text but to a historical form (bourgeois or lyrical drama, melodrama) or, by extension, to a catastrophe ("drôle de drame").

4. Pure Theatre or Literary Theatre?

Is theatricality a property of the *dramatic text**? Such claims are often made, as when a text is called very "theatrical" or "dramatic," suggesting that it lends itself to a stage presentation (visuality, open conflict, rapid exchange of dialogue). This is not a purely stage property, however, and the opposition between "pure theatre" and "literary theatre" is based not on textual criteria but on the ability of "theatrical" theatre, to use MEYERHOLD's (1963) expression, to maximize the use of stage techniques that replace characters' speeches and tend to be self-sufficient. Paradoxically, then, a text is theatrical when it cannot stand on its own, when it lacks sufficient indications of time and place or acting directions. The same ambiguity can be seen in the adjective *theatrical*; sometimes it means total illusion, other times that the acting is too artificial and reminds us constantly that we are in the theatre, while we would like to be transported into another world even more real than our own. It is because of this confusion about the status of theatricality that we have often sterile polemics about whether acting should be *natural** or not.

The eternal polemics between partisans of text and partisans of *performance** has recurred throughout the history of theatre. Almost always, it is the text and literature that are deemed to belong to the more noble genre, as they offer the advantage of being conserved intact (or at least supposedly intact) for future generations, while the most beautiful stage expression is as ephemeral as the smile of a beautiful woman. The opposition is an ideological one: in Western culture we tend to give preference to text, writing and discourse. Added to this is the rise of the director (who in the late nineteenth century took charge of the visualization of the text on stage) and of theatre as an autonomous art. Consequently, theatricality became the essential and specific nature of theatre and, in the era of the director, the object of contemporary artistic study. A textual study of the great playwrights (from SHAKESPEARE to MOLIÈRE and MARIVAUX), however, is unsatisfactory unless we attempt to situate the text in a stage practice, a style of acting and an image of the performance. Although there is no irrevocable, absolute opposition between pure theatre and literature, there is a dialectical tension between the actor and his lines, between the significance the text may take on when read and its modalization by the staging once it is uttered using extraverbal means. Theatricality no longer seems a quality or *essence** inherent in a text or situation, but a pragmatic use of stage tools such that the components of performance enhance one another and break the linearity of text and word.

5. Theatricality and Specificity

There is no such thing as absolute essence. Although there is no such thing as an *essence** of theatre, we can at least specify what elements are indispensable to any theatrical phenomenon. Two parallel definitions provide an excellent summary of how theatre functions:

Alain GIRAULT: "The common denominator of everything we habitually call 'theatre' in our civilization is this: from a static point of view, a playing area (stage) and a watching area (auditorium), an actor (gesture, voice) on stage and spectators in the auditorium. From a dynamic point of view, the creation of a 'fictional' world on stage in opposition to the 'real' world of the auditorium, and, simultaneously, the establishment of a current of 'communication' between actor and spectator" (*Théâtre/public*, Nos. 5–6, June 1975, p. 14).

Alain REY: "It is precisely in the relationship between the tangible reality of speaking and acting human bodies, such reality produced by a performance construction, and a fiction thus *represented*, that what is specific to the theatrical phenomenon lies" (COUTY and REY 1980).

See also: staging, semiology.

Further reading: Jarry 1962; Burns 1972; Jachymiak 1972; Jaffré 1974; Bernard 1976, 1986; Krysinski 1982; Féral 1985.

THEATRICAL PERFORMANCE

Fr.: *représentation théâtrale*; Ger.: *Theatervorstellung*; Sp.: *representación teatral*.

1. Terminology

To define this key term, and to highlight each of its many facets, it is useful to see how various languages convey a particular image of the stage presentation of a play:

A. The French *représentation* stresses the idea of representing or portraying something that already exists (in the form of a text to be used in rehearsals) before being shown on stage. But to re-present is also to make present, at the moment of stage presentation, that which existed at another time in a text or a theatre tradition. These two criteria, the repetition of a pre-existing datum and temporary creation of a stage *event*, in fact form the basis of any staging.

B. In German, *Vorstellung*, *Darstellung* and *Aufführung* all use the spatial image "to place before" or "to place there." They accentuate the frontality and display to public view of the theatre product and the fact that the *spectacular** aspect is highlighted.

C. The English *performance* gives the impression of an action carried out, or performed, in the act of presentation. The theatre performance involves both the stage (and all that has gone before to prepare the performance) and the audience (with all the receptiveness of which it is capable). The linguistic concept of performatives gives further support to the idea of an act performed by the speaker, in the case of theatre, by the whole team, an act that is "realized" on stage (both artistically and socially). We could also use the performance/competence opposition established by generative grammar to illustrate one of the aims of performance; to go from systematic and theoretical know-how (competence) to the specific practical materialization (performance) (SCHECHNER 1977).

2. Functions of Performance

A. THE PRESENT OF THE PERFORMANCE

Theatre does not represent something having a previous autonomous existence (the text) which it presents "a second time" on the boards. The stage performance must be taken as a unique event, as a construction that refers to itself (like the poetic sign) and does not imitate a world of ideas. "the Drama is primary. It is not a (secondary) representation of something else (primary); it presents itself, is itself" (SZONDI 1956, 16; Eng. 1987, 9). The performance exists only in the present common to the actor, the stage space and the spectator. This is what differentiates theatre from the other representational arts and literature.

B. THE TEXT IN ABEYANCE

The *dramatic text** is a "script," incomplete and awaiting staging. It acquires meaning only in performance, as it is by definition "cast" in several speeches and roles and can be understood only when uttered by actors in the context of enunciation chosen by the director. This does not mean, however, that there is only one form of performance possible for a particular text. Rather, the reverse is true: the many different performances that are possible multiply the meanings of the text, which is no longer the fixed centre of the theatrical performance, as it was long thought to be.

C. EXTERNALIZATION OR STARTING POINT?

Performance today is considered the starting point for an analysis of *mise-en-scène*. This conception, which is definitely *theatrical** (rather than *literary* or even *dramatic*), has only been in current use since the practice of *staging** (mise-en-scène) became systematic. Before that, the classical performance appeared to be the external and therefore secondary part of the text. It did not involve the meaning of the play but gave the word an artistic boost. HEGEL's definition of theatre reflects that conception: "the properly theatrical art of the actor in so far as it is so limited in action, recitation, and play of features that poetic language may always remain the determining and dominant feature [...] that kind of execution which uses every means of scenery, music, and dance and makes them independent of the poet's words" (HEGEL 1832, 357; Eng. 1975, 1182). Text and performance here are quite independent of each other, the performance being despised (since ARISTOTLE'S *Poetics*) as the material husk of the soul of the drama (i.e. the linguistic text). This latent Platonism, tied to the ideological hegemony of Text and Word, marked the entire development of Western theatre until the discoveries of the twentieth century, one of whose most passionate prophets was A. ARTAUD: "So long as the *mise-en-scène* remains, even in the minds of the boldest directors, a simple means of presentation, an accessory mode of expressing the work, a sort of spectacular intermediary with no significance of its own, it will be valuable only to the degree it succeeds in hiding itself behind the works it is pretending to serve. And this will continue as long as the major interest in a performed work is in its text, as long as literature takes precedence over the kind of performance improperly called spectacle, with everything pejorative, accessory, ephemeral, and external that that term carries with it." (1964b:160; Eng.: 1958:106)

D. REPRESENTATION OF ABSENCE

Nevertheless, we should not follow current practice and draw an equivalence between performance and visuality, the Aristotelian *opsis**. To represent is also to render temporarily and auditorially *present* something that was not; it is to appeal to the time of enunciation to show something, thus to stress the temporal dimension of theatre. The representation, or performance, is not, or at least not only, spectacle; it is rendering absence present, presenting it again to our memories and our ears, to our temporality (not only to our eyes).

E. RELATIONSHIP BETWEEN TEXT AND PERFORMANCE

The status of the performance is an ambiguous one: does it belong solely to the visualization created by the mise-en-scène, or is it already perceptible, performed in the dramatic text? *Semiology** must deal with this question, as it must decide whether to base its analyses on the mise-en-scène alone or on the text as it is apparent in its indications of time and place. The problem, then, is knowing whether the text contains a vision of the performance, a kind of *pre-performance**. We would reject such a thesis, since it is overly logocentric and considers theatricality as a textual property. It must be recognized, however, that the hypothesis of a specifically theatrical writing, something that imposes its vision of the performance straight away, is often defended by playwrights and directors who "sense" intuitively whether or not the text lends itself to the stage. For DIDEROT, theatrical writing "does not mislead": "Whether or not a poet has written the pantomime, I will know at once if he has composed according to this pantomime. The play will behave differently; the scenes will take quite a different turn; his dialogue will show the effects [...] The pantomime is the tableau that existed in the poet's imagination as he wrote, what he wished the stage to show at every moment" (1758, 110–111). Some dramaturgical research has attempted to define the predeterminations of the mise-en-scène in the text that the author necessarily has in mind: stage conventions of the time, conceptions of time and place, dramaturgical *segmentation**, etc. (SERPIERI 1977; GULLI-PUGLIATI 1976). Such research is legitimate provided that it does not try to dogmatically impose *one* mise-en-scène, i.e. *the* mise-en-scène, based solely on a reading of the text. We prefer, however, to start with the actual situation of enunciation that constitutes every performance, in order to examine how it influences the text and its reading. We are thus very far from the Hegelian conception of theatre as an externalization of the text, for it is, on the contrary, the mise-en-scène and the performance that give the text its meaning (PAVIS 1986).

See also: visual and textual, performing arts, text and performance, ethnoscenology.

Further reading: Pavis 1983b; *Littérature*, no. 57 (1985); Williams 1968.

THEATRICAL PROCESS

Fr.: *processus théâtral*; Ger.: *Theatervorgang*; Sp.: *proceso teatral*.

The actions or events staged are processes when their dialectical nature, perpetual motion and dependence on earlier or outside events are all clear. *Process*, as opposed to a *state* or fixed *situation*, is the corollary of a transforming view of man as a "work in progress," and presupposes an overall scheme of psychological and social movements, a set of rules for change and interaction. This is why the concept is used mainly within an open, dialectical, even "Marxist" dramaturgy (P. WEISS, B. BRECHT).

See also: reproduction, dramaturgy, action, represented reality, signifying practice.

Further reading: Dort 1960; Wekwerth 1974; Knopf 1980.

THEATRICAL REALITY

Fr.: *réalité théâtrale*; Ger.: *theatralische Wirklichkeit*; Sp.: *realidad teatral*.

The status of stage or theatrical reality has been a subject of debate since the days of ARISTOTLE, but no final or definite answer has been found. This is because here we are victims of the theatrical *fiction** and *illusion** on which our view of the performance rests, and because we combine several realities.

What is it that we see on stage? Objects, actors, sometimes a text. Several elements are to be found there, distinguishable as follows:

1. The "Social" Reality of Stage Machinery

The concept of stage *machinery** extends to everything that is used to manufacture the performance and is identifiable as such within it (panels, walls, floors, etc.). This machinery may be modestly concealed in "illusionist" theatre, but it can always be detected when we zero in on the "secret recipe." By definition, this mechanical reality is foreign to the fictional world suggested by the stage. It is the only object with no sign value (except, of course, when the staging uses it in its theatre practice, as in PIRANDELLO's *Six Characters in Search of an Author*). In BRECHT or a Brechtian staging even the podium and the curtain become *signs** of "showing how it works" and, today, of "this is Brechtian critical epic theatre." P. BROOK describes this process of semiotization as follows: "I can take any empty space and call it a bare stage. A man walks across this empty space whilst someone else is watching him, and this is all that is needed for an act of theatre to be engaged" (1968, 11).

2. The Reality of Stage Objects

We can identify stage objects by their usual social function (a table, a glass) and decode them as non-functional materials or objects, "unidentified stage objects." The problem is knowing whether the objects are to be taken literally as things or whether they should be assigned a value as *signs**, which means looking beyond their materiality at what they represent (such and such a symbol, emotion or social connotation). In other words, are we dealing with real or aesthetic objects, and have they already been semiotized or not?

In theatre, we spend our time chasing referents that always elude us (*reality-effect**). The referent, or object to which the sign refers (the real table is the referent of the sign /table/), is always apparently present on stage, but as soon as we think we have identified it, we realize it is a signifer that we define by its signified. The only possible referent can be theatrical machinery again. All other objects, as soon as they are used in the context of a fiction, are elements that refer to something besides themselves. Consequently, they have a *sign* value: they are put in the place of something else that they *suggest* but do not encarnate. So, the table under which Orgon is hidden is not a prop, or even a real seventeenth century table; it is a convention, a sign agreed to by the spectators, which *means* a piece of Orgon's furniture in the style of the period that makes a good hiding-place. Orgon's table is a sign that has value not because of its referent (which is fictitious in any case), hardly at all because of its signifier (it is unimportant whether it is made of oak or plywood), and entirely because of the signified we attribute to it: a table that acts as a trap into which Tartuffe may fall. The signifier – that is, the form and matter of the table – has a transitional function; it leads the spectator to identify a certain signified. This does not mean, however, that the spectator need not pay attention to the materiality of the performance, and therefore of the signifier.

But what happens to the other objects on stage (the floor, chairs, set) that are not being used in stage business or dialogue at a given moment? They remain "raw" objects, signifying material that has yet to find its signified, that does not yet have sign value. As soon as they are foregrounded by the dialogue or acting, however, these objects become signs, and the spectator, by analyzing their significant properties, assembles their signifieds and integrates them into the scene. *Staging** is the art of breathing in the outside world and making it play a role in the fiction.

3. The Reality of Actors

The same reasoning can be applied to actors on stage as to objects. They have value through their signified, not their referent (/body of actor X/ or /Orgon's real body/). Their interest lies only within a signifying whole in relation to other signs, other characters, situations, scenes, etc.

As soon as an actor comes on stage, he is placed in a semiological and aesthetic *frame** that employs him in the fictional dramatic world. All the actor's physical properties (beauty, sexuality, "mysterious aura") are *semiotized**, transferred to the character represented: a beautiful, sexy and mysterious heroine, for example. The actor is only a physical medium that stands for something else. This does not mean that we cannot perceive the actor directly as a human being who exists just as we do, and whom we may desire. Then we are seeing the actor as a person, not as a character or as a sign of a character or a fiction.

True, attempts are made to deny the sign-aspect of the actor: the *happening** in which the "actor"-person plays himself; forms of circus in which physical feats refer not to the foreign body of a character but to the artists themselves, and performance art in which the actor does not refer to a character or a fiction but to himself as a person communicating with an audience.

4. The Reality of the Dramatic Text
Like the stage object or actor, the dramatic text has value first of all as a reality that can be grasped in its material nature, its musicality, and not as a sign of something. But this "text-thing" is itself immediately reframed, semiotized, considered as the signifier of a global signified that can only be identified once it is relocated in the overall system of stage signs, compared in particular to non-linguistic stage signs.

The principle of the semiotization of theatrical reality therefore applies equally to objects, actors, text; in short, to everything that is presented to the spectator's view in the stage space.

See also: main text and side text, discourse, realism.

Further reading: Honzl 1940; Krejca 1971; Ertel 1977; Pavis 1978c, 1978d.

THEATRICAL (STAGE-AUDIENCE) RELATIONSHIP

Fr.: *relation théâtrale*; Ger.: *theatralisches Grundverhältnis*; Sp.: *relación teatral*.

The visualization and concretization of many relationships within the creative process: between author, director, actor and all other members of the production team; between characters and, overall, between performance and audience.

1. Relationships among the Various creators
Between the playwright, who is already subject to the influence of a period, a class, a horizon of *expectation**, and the actor playing a character, there is a long chain of *interpretations** and transformations of theatrical meaning. Although it is almost impossible to clarify the various stages of the process, any staging is an attempted response to that dialectics among the various subjects of the final stage enunciation.

2. Relationships among Characters
Theatre is the art of social relationships among men, and its history can be traced back through the nature of the ties between human beings. It was determined in pre-Renaissance times by the relationship between man and God; then the human relationship became the pivot of human action, oscillating between freedom and necessity. Toward the end of the nineteenth century, the crisis in drama announced a break in that relationship and there were various dramaturgical attempts to rescue or transcend dialogue among humans (SZONDI 1956).

3. Relationship between Spectator, Actor and Character
The identification of the actor with the character and the spectator with the actor-character is necessary to establish the *illusion** and the *fiction**, but it is also very fragile and subject to fracture and *denial**. When this happens, a critical distance is created through aesthetic breaks (alienation-effects) or by an ideological device (BRECHT). The audience's relationship with the performance is symptomatic of what the staging expects of the theatrical act: submission, criticism, entertainment, etc. The stage-audience relationship is always one of confrontation, whether it reconciles (in an identification with the stage) or deeply divides the audience (as BRECHT wished to do). The minimum definition of theatre is contained in "what takes place between spectator and actor. All the other things are supplementary" (GROTOWSKI 1971, 31; Eng. 1968, 32).

4. Critical Relationship
The visualization of the *stage-audience relationship** should not let us forget a final rela-

tionship, by far the most important: the work of reception and the work of critical *interpretation**. The spectators are involved in the performance by having to look beyond a mere description of the play's internal structure.

Such a critical relationship is not confined to "a scrupulous inventory or the parts of the play or an analysis of their aesthetic correspondences"; it must also include a variant of the relationship established between critics and the play. It is thanks to that variant that the play may deploy its various aspects, and that critical consciousness captures itself, goes from heteronomy to autonomy" (STAROBINSKI 1970, 14).

THESIS PLAY

Fr.: *théâtre à thèse*; Ger.: *Thesenstück*; Sp: *teatro de tésis*.

A thesis play is a systematic form of *didactic theatre**. It develops a philosophical, political or moral thesis and seeks to convince the audience that it is valid, using reason rather than emotion. Every play necessarily presents a thesis within its packaging, which may be discreet or unsubtle: man's freedom or servitude, the dangers of a particular attitude, the force of destiny or passion. Thesis drama, however, formulates its problems in a very didactic commentary. Playwrights such as IBSEN, SHAW, GORKY and SARTRE all wrote plays with the intention of making the audience think, or even of obliging them to change society.

This genre has a bad reputation today, as it is (often too hastily) identified with a lesson in catechism or Marxism and seen as talking down to the audience instead of letting the audience "look for the solution" (BRECHT). Quite often the importance of the issues leads the playwright to neglect the dramatic form and use a ready-made dramatic structure and overly direct discourse, which quickly becomes tedious. Hence the aesthetic weakness of many thesis plays, and the audience's frustration. (Examples are IBSEN's *A Doll's House*, most of SHAW's plays and, for philosophically advanced pupils, SARTRE's *Huis-Clos*).
See also: agit-prop, message.

THEATRE OF THE ABSURD

Fr.: *théâtre de l'absurde*; Ger.: *absurdes Theater*; Sp.: *teatro del absurdo*.
See ABSURD

THEATRE OF CRUELTY

Fr.: *théâtre de la cruauté*; Ger.: *Theater der Grausamkeit*; Sp.: *teatro de la crueldad*.

An expression forged by Antonin ARTAUD (1938) to describe a kind of theatre that would subject the spectators to an emotional shock treatment, in order to free them from the grip of discursive and logical thought processes to rediscover a more immediate avenue of experience in a new *catharsis** and an original ethical and aesthetic experience.

The theatre of cruelty has nothing to do, at least in ARTAUD, with physical violence directly imposed on actors or spectators. The text is offered in a kind of ritual incantation (rather than being spoken in the mode of psychological interpretation). The whole stage is used as in a ritual, as a producer of images (hieroglyphs) addressed to the spectator's unconscious, using the most diverse means of artistic expression.

There are many groups today claiming such an ethics of cruelty for themselves. The aesthetics of J.-L. BARRAULT and R. BLIN, P. BROOK's staging of P. WEISS's *Marat/Sade*, ARRABAL's *teatro pánico*, the Living Theater and Fura dels Baus represent some of the more successful attempts.
Further reading: Girard 1974; Blüher 1971; Borie 1981, 1989; Grimm 1982.

THEATRE OF PARTICIPATION

Fr.: *théâtre de participation*; Ger.: *Mitspieltheater*; Sp.: *teatro de participación*.

The term would appear to be pleonastic, as there is clearly no such thing as theatre without audience particiation, whether emotional, intellectual or physical. In spite of its ritual or mythical origins, however, theatre has sometimes lost its aspect as an immediate event, and there has been a drive to return to participation since the turn of the century for various reasons: critical activity, psychic shock as in ARTAUD and the ritual and mystical tendencies that followed him (BROOK, GROTOWSKI), but also the practice of collective affectivity in Fascist ceremony or illusionist drama as described by BRECHT in barely exaggerated terms: "Looking about us, we see somewhat motionless figures in a peculiar condition: they seem strenuously to be tensing all their muscles, except where these are flabby and exhausted. They scarcely communicate with each other; their relations are those of a lot of sleepers, though of such as dream restlessly because, as is popularly said of those who have nightmares, they are lying on their backs. True, their eyes are open, but they stare rather than see, just as they listen rather than hear. They look at the stage as if in a trance: an expression which comes from the Middle Ages, the days of witches and priests. Seeing and hearing are activities, and can be pleasant ones, but these people seem relieved of activity and like men to whom something is being done" (*A Short Organum for the Theatre*, sect. 26).

Such intense emotional participation was, for BRECHT, the antithesis of intellectual and critical participation: such is the ambiguity of a notion that can describe very different modes of action. It can be social, as when the spectator associates with others in a festival or popular play, joining in collective laughter or action; it can be physical, if the audience is invited to move between stages and interact with the actors or receive charges of electric current; it can be playful, when in dramatic play or *invisible theatre** (BOAL) the actors do not realize they are acting. There is no one form or genre of theatre of participation, but a style of acting and staging that activates the spectators by inviting them to a dramaturgical reading, a decoding of signs, a reconstruction of the story and a comparison of the reality represented with their own world.

Further reading: Pörtner 1972.

THEATRE IN THE ROUND

Fr.: *théâtre en rond*; Ger.: *Rundtheater, Arenabühne*; Sp.: *teatro circular.*

Theatre in which the audience is seated around the playing area, as in the circus or stadium. In use in the Middle Ages for the performance of mystery plays, this kind of stage design has been favoured in this century (M. REINHARDT, A. VILLIERS 1958), not only to unify the audience's vision but, above all, to enable the spectators to participate in a ritual that involves them emotionally.

THEATRE OF IMAGES

Fr.: *théâtre d'images*; Ger.: *Bildertheater*; Sp.: *teatro de imágenes.*

This term refers to a kind of staging that tends to produce stage images, generaly of great formal beauty, rather than offering a text or presenting physical actions "in relief." Images are seen from afar in two dimensions, flattened by distance and by the technique used in their composition. According to FREUD, images are in a better position than conscious thought and language to render subconscious processes: 'Images provide ... a very imperfect means of conveying conscious thought; it could be said that visual thought comes closer to unconscious processes than verbal thought and predates it both phylogenically and ontogenically.' ('Essay on psychoanalysis').

This is probably why directors from WILSON to KANTOR, from CHÉREAU to BRAUNSCHWEIG naturally employ a visual train of thought to suggest the deep subconscious dimension of the play.

Further reading: Marranca 1977; Simhandl 1993.

THEATRE OF OBJECTS

Fr.: *théâtre d'objets*; Ger.: *Theater der Gegenstände*; Sp.: *teatro de los objetos.*

This relatively recent term is sometimes used in place of "puppet theatre," a name which is considered outmoded and pejorative. In addition to puppets, it refers to moving scenery, *installations**, and alliances between actors and figures (Philippe GENTY). (See the periodical *Puck* published by the Institut International de la Marionnette de Charleville.)

THEATRE STUDIES

Fr.: *études théâtrales*; Ger.: *Theaterwissenschaft*; Sp.: *estudios teatrales*.

Theatre studies (the term is perhaps the least objectionable of all) stakes out a position that excludes literature (and therefore written drama) on the basis of this radical difference: theatre studies belong to the world of stage, performance, and performing arts. They are not concerned with the dramatic text, or at least not exclusively, but rather with all possible artistic practices that employ a stage and actors; i.e. all of the arts and techniques available to a given era. To this we must add what *ethnoscenology** defines as performance practice in every possible cultural context.

1. The Object of Study

The object of study may be to inform readers about one of the many aspects of theatre creation. The critical discourse may vary from journalistic-type information about the place and date of a performance, to a learned study of one aspect of theatre activity in a scholarly journal. Studies are often undertaken to pass on a certain know-how and train actors, stage designers or lighting technicians; i.e. to provide vocational training. They then focus on technical knowledge that the future practitioner will be putting into practice in his or her professional activities. Each field branches off into specialized areas having their own unique analytical procedures and learning techniques. In this case, the aim of the study is to train people in one of the theatre professions. It is judged by the effectiveness of the know-how and training provided for a future technical or artistic activity. We can imagine as many bodies of knowledge and fields of study as there are techniques required to produce a performance. The difficulty is not to specify and to specialize knowledge but to ensure it homogeneity from one branch to another and to be able to confront the different fields in a fruitful manner. There is no place or institution where theatre can be studied as a whole. Professional schools give some training in the difference stage crafts (stage design, lighting, costumes); acting schools teach acting techniques; university literature departments teach the great texts of theatre; some theatre departments at university study the production of meaning through acting and staging, usually meditating at length on the relationship between theory and practice. We should no longer expect a university to teach everything there is to know about a subject, but at least a process of epistemological reflection on the prerequisites for knowledge about a particular component of the dramatic or theatrical work, and on theatre activity in all its forms. Instead of an illusory unified theory of theatre, we will be satisfied with an epistemology of theatre studies that outlines the framework of the different fields of knowledge and the limits of this knowledge.

2. Epistemology

Theatre people sometimes feel strongly that theatre art cannot be studied, that one can only guess at some of its laws, and that actors' or directors' intuition is more valuable than any theory. There are more myths about theatre than about any other art, and a theoretical or scientific approach is often considered to be sacrilegious. However, a scientific approach (in the strict sense of the term) is trying to find its way through, though indirectly. Based on scientific disciplines such as biology, psychology or medicine, such theories effect a transfer of knowledge into the field of the actor's or spectator's performance behaviour and through their hypotheses they try to apply their results to performance. If we think of the scientific not in terms of verifiable and quantifiable results but in terms of coherence and non-contradiction, we may arrive at a *dramaturgy** or *semiology** which starts out with no other ambition than to elucidate the production of meaning and manipulation of signs, whether at the level of a specific work or of a whole (period, genre, the work of a particular playwright or director). The analysis would deal at times with the production of the text and the staging by the creative team, at times with the reception by the reader or spectator or better still, with the dialectics of these elements within a semiotics that describes both the communication between stage and audience, the inscription of theatre within a semiotics of culture.

3. Perspectives and Fields

To learn about this strange object called theatre, however, we must first determine how we are to approach it, and from what angle we are to perceive it. For it is our gaze that creates, not the theatre object itself, but the discourse formulated about it. This gaze is coloured with methodologies from the various human sciences: anthropology (BARBA 1985), sociology and phenomenology (STATES 1985) semiology (UBERSFELD 1977, 1981), pragmatics. It is predetermined by the kinds of questions asked by each of these methodologies and it only finds what it would like to find, but at least it is aware of its limitations and shortcomings. Then we can identify a series of fields of study based on internal divisions within the object and methodology. These fields of study may either be components of the theatre object or modes of approach which touch upon various components at once. It quickly becomes evident that no fields can survive in isolation and that each field draws upon all other approaches. Therefore there is no ideal program of study, but at best a series of approaches that give more or less an account of their object of research.

4. Knowledge in Process

The knowledge thus staked out should be reconstructed constantly in an overall theory, by effecting passages between study of text and study of performance, and by associating different fields of study and methodologies. The larger perspectives are essential to relate the scattered fragments – thus, a semiological approach will enable the production of signs to be tested on the basis of a dramaturgical project.

Rather than covering all theatrical activity, it would be preferable to study areas as yet unanalyzed. Among them are gestural theatre, radio plays, dance and dance theatre, interartistic aspects of staging, intercultural relationships in contemporary staging.

As well as the danger of overspecializing there is a very real danger that theatre studies will be lost in much larger disciplines or methodologies that no longer belong to aesthetics, such as anthropology, media theory, narratology and even semiology, when it is limited to JAKOBSON's model of communication functions, or to a typology of signs, or to the search for minimal units, or to an inventory of codes or the connotative proliferation of signifieds.

Can theatre be studied, after all? As a modelling system and distorting mirror of the world, it lends itself to all questions, approaches, desires for knowledge and fields of study and *research**.

TOTAL THEATRE

Fr.: *théâtre total;* Ger.: *Totaltheater;* Sp.: *teatro total.*

A production that endeavours to use all available artistic resources to come up with a spectacle that appeals to all the senses, thereby creating the impression of a totality and a wealth of meaning that overwhelms the audience. All possible technical means (from existing and future genres) are available to this kind of theatre, particularly modern machinery, movable sets and audiovisual technology. The architects of the Bauhaus sketched it out quite completely: "Total theatre must be an artistic creation, an organic set of bundles of relationships between light, space, surface, movement, sound and human being with all possible variations and combinations of those diverse elements" (SCHLEMMER, quoted in MOHOLY-NAGY and SCHLEMMER 1925).

1. Achievements and Aims

Total theatre is more an aesthetic ideal and a futuristic project than an actual achievement in the history of theatre. Certain dramatic forms, such as Greek theatre, medieval mystery plays and spectactular baroque productions made some progress toward it. But it was mainly after WAGNER and his *Gesamtkunstwerk** that this aesthetic materialized in theatrical reality and imagination (GROPIUS, SCHLEMMER). It shows a desire to deal with theatre in *itself* rather than as a literary by-product: "What we wish to do is to break with the theatre considered as a distinct genre, and bring up to date that old idea, never truly realized, of the integrated spectacle. Without, of course, theatre being confused at any time with music, pantomime or dance, and above all with literature" (ARTAUD 1964a, 149).

2. Fundamental Principles

A. CONSTRUCTING "LITERALLY AND IN EVERY SENSE OF THE WORD" (RIMBAUD)

Freed from the constraint of linear action, total theatre explores all dimensions of the stage arts, not confining the text to one meaning that is staged explicitly, but offering several possible interpretations, and allowing each system to enrich the immediate meaning of the story.

B. REGISTERING THE ORIGINAL, DEFINITIVE GESTUS

As the actor is generally thought of as the basic material, total theatre attaches great importance to gestuality. Besides its hieroglyphic nature, it registers a man's relationship with others, with his partner and his milieu (Brechtian *gestus**). The *attitudes** that flow from these gestural exchanges provide the key to any dramatic universe: "Words alone cannot say everything. Hence there must be a pattern of movement on the stage to transform the spectator into a vigilant observer, to furnish him with that material which the two people in conversation yielded to the third, the material which helps him grasp the true feelings of the characters. Words catch the ear, plasticity the eye. Thus the spectator's imagination is exposed to two stimuli: the oral and the visual. The difference between the old theatre and the new is that in the new theatre speech and plasticity are each subordinated to their own separate rhythms and the two ado not necessarily coincide" (MEYERHOLD 1973, I:217; Eng. 1969, 56).

C. ORCHESTRATING THE PERFORMANCE FOR THE MISE-EN-SCÈNE

Any total theatre implies a unifying or at least organizing consciousness. The impression of globality or fragmentation depends on the staging. So, when J.-L. BARRAULT staged CLAUDEL's *Christophe Colomb* (1953), "The most valuable point in the production of a play consists, then, in finding a way to elevate the level of the performance sufficiently ([through] scenery, properties, lighting, sound effects, music) so that it can no longer content itself with its secondary role as the 'framework' or combination of the arts, but manages to humanize itself to such an extent that it somehow becomes part of the action and can make its own contribution in the same way as a human being, in other words, so that it serves the theatre in its totality – and at that moment, theatre discovers its unity" (*World Theatre*, 1965, 543).

D. OVERCOMING THE STAGE/AUDIENCE DIVISION AND PARTICIPATING IN RITUAL

One of the aims of total theatre is to rediscover a unity thought to have been lost; that of the festival, of ritual and ceremony. The requirement of totality goes beyond the aesthetic plane and applies to reception and the action exerted on the audience. It is meant to enable all individuals to participate.

E. REDISCOVERING A SOCIAL TOTALITY

It must be noted, however, that even the epic theatre of PISCATOR and BRECHT call for audience participation in the event. PISCATOR, in fact, was one of the first to employ (along with GROPIUS) the expression *Totaltheater*, which he translated as *theatre of totality* (not as *total theatre*, a term reserved for a "dramatic-aesthetic concept, a rather vague notion of liberating the figurative arts as a whole," *World Theatre*, 1965, 5). Theatre of totality, for him, is synonymous with epic theatre, "that is, a theatre of quasi-scientific analysis, of critical objectivity. One no longer displayed personal conflicts on stage, one no longer dissected feelings, but rather presented, crudely and straightforwardly, social processes. One asked the audience to take a position and not to enjoy the performance. Theatre was no longer content to apprehend fragments of reality, but wanted it all. [...] 'Theatre of totality' is a construction, 'totally' conceived by the acting, in which the spectator, the spatial centre, is surrounded with a total stage, is 'totally' confronted with it. The simultaneity of the historical events, the synchronization of social and political 'action' and 'reaction' may, on this stage, on this set of stages, be represented at the same time. 'Total theatre,' on the other hand, refers only to the constant tradition from one kind of acting, one form of expression, to another, assuming that the performer's talents and training enable this transition to be realized happily. In this sense, total theatre is the perfectly homogeneous fusion of all the figurative arts (which necessarily recalls the 'total art-work' of Richard Wagner) [...] the so-called total theatre, as eclectic theatre, produces no more than a totality of appearances. It is staged for itself. It is a formalist theatre" (*World Theatre*, 1966, 5–7).

In all of the foregoing, we should keep in mind both aims and actual achievements. The often prophetic and dogmatic tone of the various definitions reminds us that there are many theatre aesthetics, and even more conceptions of the totality of the reality to be represented. Finally, total theatre is none other than theatre *par excellence*.

Further reading: Nietzsche 1967; Appia 1895; Craig 1905; Mohol-Nagy and Schlemmer 1925; Piscator 1980; Barrault 1959; Kesting 1965; *World Theatre*, 1965, 1966; Boll 1971.

THEATRON

Fr.: *théâtron*; Ger.: *Theatron*; Sp.: *theatron*.

Greek word that refers to the place where one watches the performance, the spectators' area. Not until much later was the theatre thought of as an entire building, then the dramatic art or the work of a playwright.

THEATRUM MUNDI

(Latin for "theatre of the world.")
Fr.: *theatrum mundi*; Ger.: *Theatrum Mundi*; Sp.: *theatrum mundi*.

A metaphor invented in antiquity and in the Middle Ages that became widespread in baroque theatre, which sees the world as a show staged by God and performed by mediocre human beings (cf. CALDERON's *El Gran Teatro del Mundo* of 1645) and, in the twentieth century, HOFMANNSTHAL's *Das Salzburger Grosse Welttheater* of 1922). This is the term used for the *cross-cultural** shows mounted by BARBA as the culmination of ISTA training courses that bring together Eastern teachers and Western students.

THEME

Fr.: *thème*; Ger.: *Thema*; Sp.: *tema*.

1. Central Idea or Structure

The general theme is the summary of the dramatic action or universe, its central idea or organizational principle. This notion, much used in critical language, lacks precision.

Themes are the elements of content: main ideas, images, *leitmotifs**, what is being discussed. But how are they discussed? *Motifs** are abstract, universal concepts (the motif of betrayal), while themes are the concrete, individualized forms of motifs (the theme of Phèdre's betrayal of her husband). Themes are pertinent as soon as they are organized in a structure, whether as an "organized network of obsessions" (BARTHES), a "concrete organizational principle" and a "constellation of words, ideas and concepts" (RICHARD), an "involuntary archetype" (DELEUZE), a "personal obsessive myth" (MAURON 1963) or a "traumatic obsessional image" (WEBER). This notion of theme, in spite of its obvious usefulness as a teaching aid, is difficult to manage in dramatic analysis, for it assumes that there is prior agreement on the nature and number of themes in a work, which is rarely the case. Otherwise, talking of general themes is a superficial and gratuitous exercise. Every person who interprets tracks down an infinite number of themes in the text and the performance, but the important thing is to establish a hierarchy of them.

2. Dimensions of Theme

It would be practically impossible to describe all the forms in which a theme may be detected, for the notion is scattered throughout the dramatic text (and even the production, which also creates recurrent images or themes). Isolating a theme, that is a content exclusive of its form, is equally difficult. In the poetic and dramatic text, form and *meaning** are not dissociated, but overlap, and it is the unique and fluid manner of overlapping that reflects the poetic nature of the text.

In identifying certain themes in the play, we engage in an extraliterary operation of commentary or interpretation rather than a scientific analysis. Any thematic crticism should therefore be structural as well, and describe a *parcours* or an arrangement. As the theme is a more or less conscious and obsessive pattern of the text, it is incumbent on the critic to unearth these thematic structures, but also to decide which themes render the play most easily explained or produced.

See also: thesis, represented reality, realism, myth.

Further reading: Fergusson 1949; Frenzel 1963; Mauron 1963; Tomachevsky 1965; G. Durand 1969; Bradbrook 1969; Starobinski 1970; Monod 1977; Aziza et al. 1978a; Trousson 1981; Demougin 1985.

THEORY OF ACTING

Fr.: *théorie de l'acteur*; Ger.: *Theorie der Schauspielkunst*; Sp.: *teoría del actor.*

See ACTOR

THEORY OF TEXT

Fr.: *théorie du texte*; Ger.: *Texttheorie*; Sp.: *teoría del texto.*

See DRAMATIC TEXT

THEORY OF THEATRE

Fr.: *théorie du théâtre*; Ger.: *Theatertheorie*; Sp.: *teoría del teatro.*

A discipline that concerns itself with theatrical phenomena (text and performance). Only after the advent of mise-en-scène, around the end of the nineteenth century, did theory reach beyond *dramaturgy** and poetics to encompass stage art in all respects.

1. Theatricality and Literariness

Following the example of literary theory, whose object of study is literariness, the theory of theatre studies *theatricality**, i.e. the specific properties of the stage and forms of theatre actually occurring in history. The general system it seeks to construct must take into account historical examples as well as theoretically imaginable forms: theory is a hypothesis of how a particular performance functions. Armed with this hypothesis, the researcher will then be induced to clarify the model and restrict or expand the theory.

2. Theory and Performance Studies

We are still very far from a unified theory of theatre, given the scope and diversity of the aspects involved: *reception** of the performance, discourse analysis, *description** of the stage, and so on. This diversity of perspective makes it very difficult to choose a unifying point of view and a scientific theory capable of encompassing dramaturgy, aesthetics and semiology. Up to now, prior to the structuralist search for a system that would be vast enough to account for the actual manifestations of theatre, theory was generated by various different disciplines: *dramaturgy** (composition of the play, relationships of time and place in the fiction and the staging); *aesthetics** (production of beauty and the performing arts); *semiology** (description of stage systems and the construction of meaning).

These three disciplines, which are as "scientific" as possible, are useful tools for a theory of theatre; they do not compete but permit a back-and-forth methodology between the particular play and the theoretical model of which they comprise a possible variant. In this sense, it is useless to wonder which discipline encompasses the others: sometimes it is aesthetics as the theory of production and reception of the work of art; sometimes it is dramaturgy as the scheme of all possible interactions between the time and place of the fiction and of the performance; sometimes it is semiology that furnishes an analysis of all the signifying systems and how they are organized within the theatre event; sometimes, finally, *ethnoscenology**, extending beyond a European perspective and theory, takes an interest in all the performance practices in the world in the various geographical and cultural areas, at the (not insignificant) risk of relinquishing all epistemological rigour.

Further reading: Mukarovský (1941) in Schmid and van Kesteren 1975; Bentley 1957; Else 1957; Nicoll 1962; Clark 1965; Calderwood 1968; Goodman 1968; Steinbeck 1970; Adorno 1984; Chambers 1971; Klünder 1971; Artioli 1972; Lioure 1973; Dukore 1974; Fiebach 1975; Schmid and van Kesteren 1975; Autrand 1977; Angenot 1979; Klier 1981; Paul 1981; Styan 1981; Mrlian 1981; Pavis 1983a; Slawinska 1985; Carlson 1984; Schneilin and Brauneck 1986; Heistein 1986; Fitzpatrick 1986; Hubert 1988; Roubine 1990; Ryngaert 1993.

TIME

Fr.: *temps*; Ger.: *Zeit*; Sp.: *tiempo*.

Time is one of the fundamental elements of the dramatic text and of the stage presentation of a play. It is a notion that, though rather obvious, is not easy to describe, as description implies being outside time, not an easy thing to achieve. Like Saint Augustine, we could say, "I know what time is, as long as no one asks me."

A fundamental point is the dual nature of time: there is the time that refers to itself, or *stage time*, and the time that must reconstructed using a symbolic system, or *off-stage time*.

1. Dual Nature of Time in Theatre

For the spectator, whose perspective we will adopt here, if only as a point of reference, there are two kinds of time:

Stage time: time experienced by the spectator when faced with the theatre event, factual time related to enunciation, to the here and now, to the unfolding of the performance. This time unfolds in a continuous present, for the performance takes place in the present: what happens in front of us happens in our spectator's time scheme, from the beginning to the end of the performance.

Off-stage or *dramatic time* is the time of the fiction. It is not tied to enunciation *hic et nunc* but to the illusion that something is happening, or has happened or will happen in a possible world, the world of the fiction. To return to our distinction between *stage space** and *dramatic space**, we could call this *dramatic time*, and define theatrical time as the relationship between stage and off-stage time. Some have termed what we call *theatrical time, dramatic time*, or time "created by the co-existence of two times of different natures: stage time and off-stage time" (MANCEVA 1983, 79). We prefer to speak of *theatrical time* (like A. UBERSFELD 1977, 203; 1981, 239), defined as the relationship between the temporality of the performance and the temporality of the action represented.

A. *Stage time* is both the time of the performance under way and of the spectator watching it. It consists of a continual present that is constantly vanishing and being renewed. It is measurable chronometrically – from 8:31 to 11:15, for instance – and is psychologically tied to the spectator's subjective sense of duration. Within an objective, measurable framework, the spectators organize their perception of the performance according to an impression of duration (in the form of boredom or enthusiasm) unique to each. The same length of time can vary depending on the play, its location on the dramatic curve, and its reception by the spectators.

It is very easy, albeit uninteresting, to segment the continuum of stage time numerically, but it is very more difficult – and fascinating – to organize it in pertinent units based on its perception. The performance is like a series of events, the present being composed of a series of presents: "The present as perceived has a temporal density whose duration has the very same limits as the organization of continuity in one unit" (FRAISSE 1957, 71).

Stage time is incarnated in the performance signs, both temporal and spatial: changes in objects and scenery, lighting effects, entrances and exits, blocking, and so on. Every signifying system has its own *rhythm**, according to which time is structured in a particular way depending on the materiality of the signifier.

B. *Dramatic time* also is analyzed in a dual fashion, by the opposition between action and plot (GOUHIER), *fabula* and *szujet* (Russian formalists), *story* and *narrative* (BENVENISTE, GENETTE); i.e. the relationship between "the temporal order of succession of the elements in the diegesis and the pseudo-temporal order of their description in the narrative" (GENETTE 1972, 78). The object is to grasp the way in which the plot organizes (selects and arranges) the story materials, how it proposes a temporal assembly of certain elements. This time of the fiction is not specific to theatre, but can be identified in any narrative discourse that announces and establishes a time scheme, refers to an *other-scene**, gives the referential illusion of another world, seems to us to be structured as logically as calendar time.

An examination together of these two temporalities, stage time and dramatic time, quickly leads to a confusion between the two. Just as the spectators' pleasure lies in confusing stage fiction and dramatic fiction (from the text), it also consists in not knowing where they are. They live in a present but forget its immediacy to penetrate a different world of discourse, a different temporality: that of the story told to me, to whose construction I contribute by looking forward to what comes next (*dramatic text**).

2. Ways of Relating the Two Temporalities
All possible combinations are imaginable.

A. dT (dramatic time) > sT (stage time): Dramatic time is very long (years in SHAKESPEARE's historical plays) but is evoked in a performance lasting two or three hours. According to the classical aesthetic, dT should not exceed 24 hours for a two-hour performance.

B. dT = sT: The classical aesthetic sometimes went so far as to require that dT action coincide with sT action on the stage. The result is a naturalistic approach in which stage reality reproduces dramatic reality as is. The time of performance art, rather than imitating a time outside it, may be itself and not seek a fiction or time beyond the stage.

C. dT < sT: It is infrequent, but does occur (MAETERLINCK, B. WILSON) that the stage time is dilated, reconstructing a reference time that is much shorter.

In any case, stage time, i.e. present time, organizes the world on the basis of itself and dips into the reservoir of dramatic time, which flows into the stage enunciation. Like BENVENISTE, we would stress the definition of time according to its enunciation, in this case the stage enunciation of all the materials. "One might think," writes BENVENISTE, "that temporality is an innate framework of thought. Actually, it is produced in and by enunciation [...] The present is properly the source of time. It is this presence in the world that only the act of enuncation makes possible, for man has no other way of living the 'now' and making it real than by realizing it through the insertion of discourse into the world" (1974, 83).

Also like BENVENISTE, we would note the ever-present performance aspect of theatre and the need to reduce the entire fiction to the present enunciation of the performance.

Stage time carries a number of indexical marks or deictic signs that bear witness to its place in space and in the characters (*deixis**).

The stage present is established through other temporalities that must also be taken into account:

A. SOCIAL TIME
I need to know on what day and at what time the performance begins, whether I can go to the theatre that evening, whether the subway will be running after the performance, and so on. It is useful to know whether the audience has an attention span of half an hour, three hours or two days and what units of time they relate to, what their "sense of time" is.

B. INITIATORY TIME
This is the time that enables me to attend the big evening, before arriving at the theatre (purchasing tickets, making reservations) and before the curtain rises (small talk in the lobby, PA announcement, darkness, silence). "In every case," remarks A. UBERSFELD, "there is a kind of initiatory time that precedes the theatre time [...] a threshold and a preparation, the psychological preparation for another time, the threshold of the performance" (1981:240). This initiatory time effects the transition from a social time to a time proper to the play and its reception, combining the real time of the spectator with the fictional time of the theatre. But without this ceremony, this "space of privileged, solemn time opened and closed by the curtain being raised and lowered, the three knocks sounded before the curtain rises or the blackout ..." (DORT 1982, 5), there is no true theatre!

C. MYTHICAL TIME
The time of "events that took place *in principio*, i.e. 'in the beginning,' at a primordial, atemporal moment, in a lapse of *sacred time*" (ELIADE 1963, 73) or in the time of the "ceremonial return" (UBERSFELD 1977a, 205), we do not consider to be a component of theatre performance, except for seeing it as an unrepeatable ritual or, of course, as a theme taken up in the story. The studies that mention it do not explain its precise function within performance but go back to the metaphor of theatre as a return to an external mythical present or a ritual that takes place outside historical time. Such may be the origins of theatre, in fact, but its present functioning make little reference to them.

D. HISTORICAL TIME
Historical time, on the other hand, is a reality that must necessarily be reflected in both text and performance. Because of its multiple time schemes and its mode of production, theatre is always situated in history. The difficulty in reading there the fictional history of the story and our own history is largely attributable to the confusion between the time represented (dramatic time) and that of the representation or performance (stage time) (see 3.B below).

3. Modulations of Time

A. DRAMATURGICAL CONCENTRATION
In *classical dramaturgy**, there is a tendency to concentrate and dematerialize dramatic (off-stage) time: it is filtered through the character's words and is evoked only in relation to the stage presence of that character in a given situation or conflict. Off-stage time is always related to stage time and tends to efface itself, to exist only in the form of words and an unrealized fictional world that is shown on stage but evoked through the combined imagination of the poet and the spectator who listens and imagines a referential reality beyond the stage. This explains the logical necessity for the classical unity of time: off-stage temporal reality must be reduced as much as possible (to 24 or 12 hours, for instance), for in order to be evoked on stage it must be filtered through the consciousness of the hero visible on stage, who has only two or three hours to effect this flattening of the world and its off-stage temporality. Classical theatre dematerializes off-stage time by creating the illusion of pure words, of a discourse in which the world and the character coincide, in which its present discourse and external fictional existence become one.

B. DIALECTICS OF HISTORICITY

In the staging of a classical text, the question of the play's historicity must be dealt with as well as the relationship between stage and off-stage time.

At least three kinds of historicity have to be considered:

1. The time of the stage enunciation (the historical time when the play is staged);
2. The time of the *fabula* and of its actantial logic (dramatic time);
3. The time when the play was created and the artistic practices then prevailing.

Our knowledge of these three variables is constantly changing; that is obvious in the first case, but it applies equally to our retrospective recognition of the era when the play appeared. As to the temporal logic of the story, it is not fixed forever but is constructed on the basis of the point of view selected to reconstruct the *fabula* and evalute the events reported. Whoever wishes to interpret a classical play today must first relate these three historical times. They are never situated on the same level; any transition from one period to another seems to be the result of a shift bringing them closer together. To take the example of MARIVAUX's *Triomphe de l'amour*, the eighteenth-century temporality drew toward itself that of the fictional Greek antiquity when the story was situated, the twentieth-century temporality draws toward itself that of the eighteenth century that produced the text and its relation to antiquity. The important thing in establishing these temporal levels is the process on arrival (in our time), the way in which the last temporality (that which reaches the current spectator) functionalizes and semiotizes the preceding one. It is impossible to treat the three kinds of historicity on the same level as different reference worlds. We have access only to the system of their successive functionalizations, the compression of each set within the one that succeeds it in time.

C. MANIPULATING STAGE TIME AND OFF-STAGE TIME

All the operations of concentration/expansion, acceleration/slowing, stopping/starting, flashback/flash-forward are possible in both stage and off-stage time. Any manipulation of either level, however, necessarily affects the other. For instance, if I wish to concentrate the dramatic time of the *fabula*, I will have to show a stage time – a way of doing – that suggests that concentration, as well as a certain speed of execution or evocation of stage actions. If, however, I slow down and stretch out the stage time as much as possible, as R. WILSON does, for instance, I thereby indicate the slowness of the corresponding process in a possible fictional world that necessarily bears some relation to our own. Ironically, WILSON's slowness may allude to the vivacity and brutality of human relationships. So the stage time "escapes" at every moment towards another place that is the fictionalization of an off-stage time and world and, conversely, that exteriority threatens at every moment to burst onto the stage and the stage time of the theatrical event.

See also: intermission, history, dramatic text, unities.

Further reading: Langer 1953; Pütz 1970; Weinrich 1974; Lagrave 1975; Ricoeur 1983, 1984, 1985; Slawinska 1985; Mesguich 1991; García-Martínez 1995.

TIRADE

Fr.: *tirade;* Ger.: *Tirade;* Sp.: *parlamento.*

The speech of a character who has time to outline his ideas. The tirade is often long and vehement. It is structured rhetorically in a series of propositions, questions, arguments, assertions, bravura pieces, or witticisms (the "nose tirade" in *Cyrano de Bergerac*). Tirades are frequently seen in classical dramaturgy, where the text is divided up into fairly long, autonomous dialogues that form almost a series of *monologues**. Tirades tend to become poems, each with its own inner structure that replies to the preceding one.

See also: Stichomythia, narrative, stanza, soliloquy.

TITLES OF PLAYS

Fr.: *titre de la pièce*; Ger.: *Titel des Stückes*; Sp.: *título de la obra*.

There are no rules and no recipes for finding a good title for a play, nor are there comprehensive studies on the choice of titles. The title is a text external to the dramatic text *per se*; in this sense it is a *didascalic* (extra-textual or *paratextual**) element, but the fact that it must be known – we still go to the theatre on the basis of the title of a play, even though we are mainly interested in the staging – influences our reading of the play. The title sets up expectations that will either be disappointed or satisfied; the spectators will judge whether the story fits the label. Some dramaturgies, such as those of Romantic or mock-heroic drama, give a title to each act (or *tableau**), so that the story is summarized perfectly in the sequence of titles (as in *Cyrano de Bergerac*).

1. Conciseness

The title is often concise, as it should be easily remembered and not give everything away (like those eighteenth-century novels that have mini-narrations for titles). If it is too long and complicated people will simplify it, as in *Hamlet* for *Hamlet, Prince of Denmark*, or the (parodic) title of Peter WEISS's play, *The Persecution and Assassination of Marat as Performed by the Inmates of the Asylum of Charenton under the Direction of the Marquis de Sade*, shortened to *Marat/Sade*.

2. Proper Names

The title usually bears the name of the main hero (*Tartuffe*, *Andromaque*), with the danger that our time no longer sees the hero as being most important: *Britannicus* is the name of the main victim, but it is Nero who holds our fascination now. For kings, particularly in SHAKESPEARE, the name is preceded by the title and the part in question: *The First Part of King Henry the Fourth*.

3. Quick Characterization

The title often seeks to characterize the hero, either by making a general statement about character (for example, *le Misanthrope*, *l'Avare*, *le Menteur*) or by making a play on assonance, as in *Tartuffe*, le *Ping-Pong* (ADAMOV), *Man is Man* (BRECHT). Sometimes a subtitle sharpens the focus and insinuates the plot, as in SHAKESPEARE in Elizabethan theatre (*All for love* for *Antony and Cleopatra*).

4. Metatextual Commentary

The title can easily slide into a metatextual commentary on the story: *le Jeu de l'amour et du hasard* invites us to elucidate the relationships between those two motifs in the plot. *Grand-peur et misère du IIIe Reich* reflects the feelings experienced by a spectator watching all the sketches of the play.

5. A Taste for Provocation and Publicity

Who's Afraid of Virginia Woolf? (ALBEE), *An Italian Straw Hat* (LABICHE), *T'is Pity She's a Whore* (FORD) are eye-catching titles that excite curiosity and attract attention, the dream of contemporary filmmakers.

6. Proverbs

MUSSET's *Comedies and Proverbs* provide the theme illustrated by the play, as if had been commissioned or were based on the guessing game played in seventeenth and eighteenth-century France. A somewhat enigmatic witticism may be used, as in *The Importance of Being Ernest*.

7. Choice of Title

The avant-garde is much more conservative today in choosing titles, considering them merely a convention or nomenclature for a text that is seen as the only important part. They seem to be all a little alike. And still, the title is important to the play's career, especially in boulevard theatre where the audience must be tantalized and promised a good bang for their buck (*On dînera au lit*, *les Baba-cadres*, *le Dindon*, *Reviens dormir à l'Élysée*). Authors of melodrama were well aware of this; they knew that "To make a good melodrama one must first choose a title. Then any subject can be adapted to the title" (*Traité du mélodrame*, 1817).

See also: names of characters.

TONE

Fr.: *ton*; Ger.: *Tonfall*; Sp.: *tono*.
See DECLAMATION

TRAGEDY

(From the Greek *tragoedia*, song of the goat sacrificed to the gods by the Greeks.)
Fr.: *tragédie*; Ger.: *Tragödie*; Sp.: *tragedia*.

Play portraying a disastrous human action, often ending in death. ARISTOTLE's definition was to have a profound influence on playwrights up to the present day: "Tragedy is an imitation of an action that is serious, complete, and possessing magnitude; in embellished language, each kind of which is used separately in the different parts; in the mode of action and not narrated; and effecting through pity and fear [what we call] the *catharsis* of such emotions" (1449b).

There are several fundamental elements that characterize the tragic play: *catharsis**, or the purging of passion through pity and terror; *hamartia**, or the hero's act that initiates the process leading to his loss; *hubris**, the stubborn pride of the hero in persevering and refusing to give up despite the warnings. The typically tragic sequence, in its "minimal formula," would be as follows: *mythos** is the *mimesis** of *praxis** through *pathos** to *anagnorisis**. In other words, the tragic story imitates human actions in which the prevailing note is suffering and *pity**, until the moment of *recognition** by the characters of one another, or of realization of the source of the affliction.

Tragedy flourished mainly in three periods: the classical Greece of the fifth century, Elizabethan England, and France in the seventeenth century (1640–1660).

See also: tragic, poetics.
Further reading: Güthke 1966; Williams 1968; Lehmann 1991.

TRAGIC

Fr.: *tragique*; Ger.: *tragisch*; Sp.: *trágico*.

We must be careful to distinguish between *tragedy**, a literary genre having its own rules, and the *tragic**, an anthropological and philosophical principle that is found in several other forms of art and in human existence. However, the tragic is clearly best studied in tragedies (from the Greek tragedies to modern ones by GIRAUDOUX or SARTRE), since, as P. RICOEUR remarks, "the essence of tragedy (if there is such a thing) can be discovered only through a poem, a performance, a creation of characters, that is, the tragic is first shown *on* tragic works, effected *by* heroes who exist wholly in the imagination. Here, tragedy instructs philosophy" (1953, 449). The same dichotomy is found in every philosophy of the tragic:

- A literary and artistic conception of the tragic related essentially to tragedy (ARISTOTLE);
- An anthropological, metaphysical and existential conception of the tragic that sees tragic art as proceeding from the tragic situation of human existence, a conception that began to prevail in the nineteenth century (HEGEL, SCHOPENHAUER, NIETZSCHE, SCHELER, LUKÁCS, UNAMUNO).

There is no point proposing an overall, complete definition of the tragic, for the phenomena and kinds of plays involved are too diverse and too tied to history to be reducible to a corpus having tragic properties. Still, it may be useful to outline the classical system of tragedy and its extensions into the modern day.

1. The Classical Conception of the Tragic

A. CONFLICT AND MOVEMENT

The hero carries out a tragic action when he voluntarily sacrifices a legitimate part of himself to higher interests; such a sacrifice may extend to death. HEGEL gives a definition that points up the hero's agonizing struggle between conflicting necessities: "The original essence of tragedy consists then in the fact that within such a conflict each of the opposed sides, if taken by itself, has *justification*; while each can establish the true and positive content of its own aim and character only by denying and infringing the equally justified power of the other. The consequence is that in its moral life, and because of it, each is nevertheless involved in *guilt*" (1832, 377; Eng. 1975, 1196). The tragic is generated by an inevitable and insoluble problem, not by a series of horrible natural disasters or catastrophes, but because of fate, which exerts its power over human existence. There is no escape. In the words of LUKÁCS, "when the curtain rises, the future is already present, since eternity."

B. PROTAGONISTS

Whatever the exact nature of the forces present, the classical tragic conflict always sets up an opposition between man and a higher moral or religious principle. With the appearance of Greek tragedy, "in order for tragic action to exist, we must be rid of the notion that human nature has its own characteristics, and consequently the human and the divine must be different enough to be opposed; but they must not cease to appear inseparable" (VERNANT 1974, 39). For HEGEL, "the proper theme of the original type of tragedy is the Divine; not, however, the Divine as the object of the religious consciousness as such, but as if enters the world and its individual action" (Eng. 1975, 1195).

C. RECONCILIATION

The ethical order always has the last word, regardless of the hero's motivations. According to HEGEL, the ethical order of the world, threatened by the partial intervention of the tragic hero in the conflict of equal values, is re-established by eternal justice when the hero succumbs (HEGEL 1832, 377). Despite punishment or death, the tragic hero is reconciled with moral law and eternal justice, for he comes to realize that his desire was unilateral and offended the absolute justice on which rests the moral universe of common mortals. This makes him a character to be admired, even if he is guilty of the worst crimes.

D. DESTINY

The divine may take the form of a fate or destiny that crushes man and reduces his actions to nothing. The hero is aware of this higher authority and faces it knowing that he cannot win. Tragic action comprises a series of episodes that follow one another in a way that can only lead to catastrophe. Motivation is both interior, within the hero, and dependent on the outside world, on the will of the other characters. Transcendency has appeared in many guises in the course of literary history: fortune and moral law (CORNEILLE), a hidden god (RACINE according to GOLDMANN 1955), passion (RACINE, SHAKESPEARE), social determinism or heredity (ZOLA, HAUPTMANN).

E. FREEDOM AND SACRIFICE

Man thus recovers his freedom: "It was a great idea to admit that man consents to a punishment even for an *inevitable* crime, in order to make manifest his freedom in the loss of his freedom and to sink because of a declaration of the right to free will" (SCHELLING, quoted in SZONDI 1975b, 10). The tragic, therefore, is as much the hallmark of fate as the hero's freely accepted fate: the hero takes up the tragic challenge, agrees to fight, takes upon himself the flaw (that is sometimes attributed to him in error) and does not seek any compromise with the gods; he is ready to die to reaffirm his freedom by basing it on the recognition of necessity. By his sacrifice, the hero shows himself to be worthy of tragic greatness.

F. THE TRAGIC FLAW

It is both the origin of and the reason for the tragic (*hamartia**). For ARISTOTLE, the hero commits an error and "does not fall into misfortune through vice or depravity, but falls because of some mistake" (*Poetics*, 1453a). This tragic paradox (a combination of moral *flaw* and *error* in judgment) is a component of the action, and the various forms of the tragic are explained by a constant re-evaluation of that flaw. The playwright's golden rule, in any case, is to present heros who are neither too guilty nor completely innocent. Sometimes the tragedian minimizes the scope of the flaw and makes it a moral dilemma that transcends the hero's individuality and freedom

(CORNEILLE). Sometimes he makes the hero a being who is delivered up mercilessly to a hidden god; according to GOLDMANN, the tragic aspect of the Racinian hero lies in "the radical opposition between a world without a genuine conscience and without human greatness and the tragic character whose greatness consists precisely in the *rejection* of that world and of life" (1955, 352).

The flaw varies with the tragic conflict, but BARTHES says rightfully that "every tragic hero is born innocent: he becomes guilty in order to save God" (1963, 54; Eng. 1964b, 46). So, in RACINE's case, "the child discovers that his father is wicked, yet wants to remain his child. This contradiction admits on only one solution (and this is the tragedy itself): that the son assume the Father's transgression, that the creature's guilt exempt the Creator" (1963, 54; Eng. 1964b, 45). But the term *hamartia** is very ambiguous, and can also be translated as an *error* in judgment or a *sin* (in the Christian tradition).

G. THE EFFECT PRODUCED: CATHARSIS

Tragedy and the tragic are defined essentially according to the effect produced in the spectator. Beyond the famous purging of the passions (and we are never sure whether that means the *elimination* of passion or *purification* by passion), the tragic effect must leave the spectator with the impression of edification, of psychological and moral enrichment. That is why action is truly tragic only when the hero offers the audience, by way of a sacrifice, this feeling of having been transfigured (*pity and fear**).

H. OTHER CRITERIA OF THE TRAGIC

The various aesthetic approaches do not confine themselves to viewing the tragic from an ontological or anthropological point of view. Often confusing the tragic with tragedy, they redefine the tragic on the basis of dramaturgical and aesthetic criteria rather than philosophical ones, since ARISTOTLE's famous definition of tragic action as the imitation of the *incidents** of the plot.

French classicism stressed the three unities. Some playwrights, such as RACINE, made an internal necessity of those rules, particularly the unity of time. GOETHE, commenting on ARISTOTLE, said that tragedy was characterized by a finished construction, *catharsis**, as a "conclusion that reconciles and ends, which is required in fact of any drama, and even of poetic works" (1970, 6:235). It is the hero, even more than the audience, who experiences tragic expiation and reconciliation; it is only later, as a indirect consequence, that "the same thing happens in the mind of the spectator, who returns home without having been better at all" (1970, 6:236).

Other dramatists have different interpretations of the tragic conflict, depending on their conception of the object of the hero's actions. For SCHILLER, the tragic is born of the character's resistence against an all-powerful destiny, with moral resistence to suffering, which leads the hero to the sublime.

A psychological view of the tragic sees the moral conflict as a subjectivity torn between two contradictory passions or aspirations. Hamlet is divided between his desire for vengeance and the impossibility of acting in accordance with his humanism.

As demonstrated admirably by GOETHE, SHAKESPEARE appears at a turning point in tragic conscience, at a time when the tragic was weakening, a time of transition between old and new, between duty (*sollen*) and desire (*wollen*): "Through duty tragedy becomes great and strong, through desire small and weak. It was through the latter that the *drame* was born, when monstrous duty was replaced with desire, and because that desire panders to our weakness we feel moved, as after a painful wait we are finally consoled in a mediocre way" (GOETHE 1970, 6:224). SHAKESPEARE "links the old with the new in an overwhelming way. Desire and duty try to remain in balance in his plays; both fight valiantly but always in such a way that power loses. No one else has portrayed so magnificently the primary connection between desire and duty in the individual character. The character, considered from the point of view of his traits, 'must': he is limited, destined to be particular. As a human being, however, he 'wants': he is unlimited and appeals to the general" (GOETHE 1970, 6:224).

2. Beyond the Classical Conception

A. FAILURE OF THE TRAGIC

The very possibility of the tragic is linked to the social order, as it presupposes an all-powerful transcendent force and fixed values to which the hero willingly submits. Order is always restored at the end, whether divine, metaphysical or human.

History and tragedy are contradictory elements. When a historical backdrop is glimpsed behind the destiny of the tragic hero, the play ceases to be a tragedy of the individual and takes on the objectivity of historical analysis.

A historical worldview, then, displaces the conception of the tragic. If, like MARX, we think of the character not as an atemporal substance but as a representative of certain classes and trends, the character's motivations are no longer petty individual desires but aspirations common to a class. Only a collision between a "necessary historical postulation and its realization which is practically impossible" (MARX 1967, 187) can thus be tragic. The tragic then becomes the fact that individual postulation is out of step with social reality, the loss of the individual against a new social order. From the point of view of Marxism, or simply one of social change, the tragic lies in a contradiction (between individual and society) that has not been or cannot be eliminated except by struggle and sacrifice: "The tragic thing about Mother Courage and her life, which the audience felt deeply, lay in a terrible contradiction that was destroying a human being, a contradiction that could be resolved, but only by society itself and at the cost of long and terrible struggles" (BRECHT).

GOLDMANN rightly makes the following distinction between tragedy, in which the conflict is irreparable, and drama, in which it is accidental: "I shall call 'tragedy' any play in which the conflicts are necessarily insoluble, and a 'drama' any play in which the conflicts either are solved (at least on a moral level) or fail to be solved because of the fortuitous intervention of a factor which, according to the laws governing the universe of the play, might not have operated" (1970, 75; Eng. 1972, 4).

B. TRAGIC VISION, IRONIC VISION

N. FRYE (1957) has shown how tragedy has developed toward *irony**, i.e. the realization of *avoidability* (the "resistible rise," as BRECHT would say) of the tragic event and its consequences. The tragic fact begins to take a human or social form, "Tragedy's 'this must be so' becomes irony's 'this at least is so'" (1957, 285). Out of this process emerged, in the nineteenth century, the *Schicksalsdrama* (tragedy of destiny) (BÜCHNER, GRABBE, HEBBEL, IBSEN and even HAUPTMANN), in which the supreme authority lies in societal constraints and the lack of prospects for the future.

C. TRAGIC VISION, ABSURD VISION

The road from the tragic to the *absurd** can be very short, especially when man does not manage to identify the nature of the force crushing him, or when the individual doubts the fairness or justification of the tragic authority. All the metaphors of history as a blind force reveal the seeds of the absurd in tragic action. BÜCHNER, seeking to explain history, can find no meaning or means of action in it: "I felt overwhelmed by the dreadful fatalism of history. I find in human nature an atrocious uniformity, in human relations an unstoppable force that belongs to all and to none. The individual is nothing but the foam on the wave, greatness mere chance, the domination of genius a game of puppets, a ridiculous struggle against an implacable law which it would be sublime to recognize but which is impossible to master" (1965, 162). Today, the confusion between the tragic and the absurd is even greater, as the absurd playwrights (CAMUS, IONESCO, BECKETT, etc.) appear to have taken over the former territory of tragedy and renewed the approach to genre by combining comic and tragic as basic ingredients of man's absurd condition. Tragedy according to the rules no longer exists, rather we have a persistent feeling of the tragic nature of existence.

Further reading: Benjamin 1928; Scherer 1950; Goldmann 1955; Frye 1957; Steiner 1961; Szondi 1961, 1975b; Jacquot 1965a; Barthes 1963; Morel 1964; Vernant 1965, 1972; Dürrenmatt 1966; Green 1969, 1982; Romilly 1970; Vickers 1973; Hilgar 1973; Girard 1974; Truchet 1975; Saïd 1978; Bollack and Bollack 1986; files in *Théâtre/Public*, nos. 70–71, 82–83, 88–89, 100.

TRAGICOMEDY

Fr.: *tragi-comédie;* Ger.: *Tragikomödie;* Sp.: *tragicomedia.*

Play with both tragic and comic elements. The term *tragico-comoedia* was first used by PLAUTUS in his prologue to *Amphytruo*. Tragicomedy is defined in theatre history by the three criteria of the *tragicomic** (character, action, style).

Tragicomedy was developed mainly after the Renaissance: in Italy by GUARINI with *Pastor Fido* (1590), in England by FLETCHER, and in France, where it flourished between 1580 and 1670 as a precursor and then a rival to classical tragedy. In the classical period, the term was used for any tragedy that ended well (CORNEILLE used the name for *le Cid*). Tragicomedy may be seen as an adventure story or a tale of chivalry in which many things occur: encounters, recognition, cases of mistaken identity, gallant adventures. While classical tragedy is respectful of the rules, the tragicomedy of ROTROU or MAIRET, for example, is concerned with the spectacular, the heroic, the surprising, the pathetic, the baroque.

Sturm und Drang (GOETHE, LENZ), and then bourgeois drama and Romantic drama, were interested in this mixed genre capable of allying the sublime with the grotesque and clarifying human existence through vivid contrasts. The realistic or pre-absurd period saw it as the expression of man's desperate situation (HEBBEL, BÜCHNER), while our own time identifies with it fully (IONESCO, DÜRRENMATT).

TRAGICOMIC

Fr.: *tragi-comique;* Ger.: *tragikomisch;* Sp.: *tragicómico.*

1. The tragicomic genre is a mixed genre based on three essential criteria: the characters belong to both the popular and the aristocratic classes, eliminating the boundary between comedy and tragedy; the action, though serious and even *dramatic**, does not lead up to a *catastrophe**, and the *hero** does not perish; and the style has "ups and downs," combining the elevated and emphatic language of tragedy with the everyday or vulgar language of comedy.

2. According to HEGEL, *comedy** and *tragedy** are reconciled in tragicomedy and cancel each other out: subjectivity, which is usually comic, is treated seriously; the tragic is attenuated in reconciliation (bourgeois in the *drama**, worldly, as termed by GOLDMANN, in classical tragedy with a happy ending). On the other hand, each genre appears to carry its own antidote secretly within it. Tragedy always reveals a moment of tragic irony or a *comic interlude**; comedy frequently opens up disquieting prospects (cf. *le Misanthrope, l'Avare*). Some critics have gone so far as to see the two genres as overlapping structurally. According to N. FRYE (1957), comedy implicitly contains tragedy, which is only an unfinished comedy.

3. As a constitutionally ambiguous and dual structure, the tragicomic reveals man's inability to stand up to an adversary worthy of him: "It appears wherever a tragic fate manifests itself in a non-tragic form, where on the one hand we have struggling man being eliminated, but on the other hand we find not moral force but a bog of circumstances that swallows up thousands of men without any one of them deserving it" (HEBBEL, Preface to *Ein Trauerspiel in Sizilien*, 1851; cf. also LENZ, *Anmerkungen über das Theater*, 1774).

This explains the current predilection for the derisory, the *absurd** and the *grotesque** aspects of the tragicomic. DÜRRENMATT saw tragic elements in our time that could not always be embodied in a tragedy. For IONESCO, comic and tragic are interchangeable and cosubstantial: "A bit of the mechanical tacked onto the living, that's comical. But if there is more and more of the mechanical, and less and less of the living, it becomes stifling, tragic, for one has the impression that the world eludes us."

Further reading: Frye 1957; Güthke 1961, 1966; Styan 1962; Kott 1965; Dürrenmatt 1966, 1970; Girard 1968; Guichemerre 1981.

TRANSLATION

Fr.: *traduction théâtrale;* Ger.: *Übersetzung;* Sp.: *traducción.*

1. Specificity of Translation for the Stage

To do justice to theory of theatre translation, especially the translation of plays for staging, it must be acknowledged that there is a *situation of enunciation** specific to theatre; that of a text proferred by an actor, at a given time and place, to an audience who thereby receive a text and a production. To reflect on the process of theatre translation, we would have to talk to both the theoretician of translation and the director or actor, make sure of their co-operation and see the art of translation as part of that much larger translation that is the staging of a dramatic text. In theatre, in fact, the phenomenon of translation for the stage goes far beyond the limited problem of translating a dramatic text from one language to another. In attempting to address certain problems of translation specific to the stage and the staging, it is essential that we take into account two obvious facts – first, in theatre, translation is determined also by the actors' bodies and the spectators' ears; second, one linguistic text is not merely translated into another – situations of enunciation and cultures which are heterogeneous and separated by space and time are made to communicate. A clear distinction should be made between translation and *adaptation**, especially as in BRECHT (*Bearbeitung*, literally "reworking"). By definition, adaptation escapes any control. "Adapting means writing another play, replacing the author. Translating means transcribing an entire play in the same order, with no additions or omissions, no cuts, development, reversal of scenes, recasting of characters, changes in lines" (DEPRATS, in CORVIN 1995, 900).

2. Interference from Situations of Enunciation

The translator and the translation text are at the intersection of two sets to which they belong to different degrees. The translated text is part of both the source text and culture and the target text and culture, since the transfer involves both the source text, in its semantic, rhythmic, acoustic and connotative aspects, and the target text, in those same aspects, as adapted to the target language and culture. In addition to this phenomenon, which is standard for any translation, in the theatrical relationship there are the situations of enunciation. They are, for the most part, virtual ones, as the translator generally works from a written text; in rare cases, he may have encountered the text to be translated in an actual staging, i.e. already "surrounded" by a situation of enunciation that has been realized.

Contrary to the situation in film dubbing, however, even in the latter case the translator is well aware that the translation will not be able to keep its original situation of enunciation but will be subject to a future situation of enunciation that is not yet known, or at least not well known. In the case of an actual staging of the translated text, the situation of enunciation can be seen perfectly well in the target language and culture. But, for the translator, before the actual staging, the problem is much thornier, for in translating he must adopt a virtual but past situation of enunciation that is not (or no longer) known, or a situation of enunciation that is current but not (yet) known. Even before looking at the question of the dramatic text and its translation, we can observe that the real situation of enunciation (that of the text translated and placed in a reception situation) is a compromise between the source and target situations of enunciation; the translator has to focus a little on the source and a lot on the target.

Theatre translation is a hermeneutic art. In order to determine what the source text says, I must bombard it with practical questions on the basis of a target language. I need to ask this: placed here where I am, in this ultimate situation of reception, and transmitted in the terms of this other language which is the target language, what do you want me to say for me and for us? This is a hermeneutic act that, in order to *interpret* the source text, consists in identifying a few basic brushstrokes, translated into another language, in pulling this foreign text toward oneself, toward the target language and culture, to make all the difference between its origins and its source. Translation is not an attempt to establish the semantic equivalence of two texts but an appropriation of a source text by a target text. To describe this process of *appropriation* we must follow it along through all the stages from source text and culture to actual reception by the audience (PAVIS 1990).

3. Series of Concretizations

To be in a position to understand the transformations of the dramatic text, which is successively written, translated, analyzed dramaturgically, uttered on stage and received by the audience, we need to reconstruct that process and the changes it undergoes throughout.

The starting text (T^0) is determined by the author's choices and formulation. It cannot be read itself except in the context of its situation of enunciation, its intertextual and ideotextual dimension; that is, its relationship with the surrounding culture.

A. The text of the written translation (T^1) depends on the virtual and past situation of enunciation of T^0 and that of its future audience, who will receive the text in T^3 and T^4. T^1 is a first concretization. The translator is in the position of a reader and dramaturg, making choices among the possible virtualities and paths of the text to be translated. The translator is a dramaturg who must first carry out a *macrotextual* translation, i.e. a dramaturgical analysis of the fiction conveyed by the text. He must reconstruct the story according to the actantial logic deemed appropriate; he reconstructs the dramaturgy, the system of characters, the space and time in which the actants move, the ideological point of view of the author or period, the specific individual traits of each character and the suprasegmental traits of the author, who tends to homogenize the speeches, and the system of echos, repetitions, recurrences and correspondences that ensure the coherence of the source text. But the macrotextual translation, although it is only possible upon a reading of the text's textual and linguistic microstructures, in turn involves the translation of those same microstructures. In this sense, theatre translation (like all literary translation or translation of fiction) is not a simple linguistic operation; it involves too much stylistics, culture and fiction to be able to do without those macrostructures.

B. The text of the dramaturgy (T^2), then, can always be read in the translation of T^0. It may even happen that a dramaturg comes between translator and director (in T^2) to lay the groundwork for the future staging through systematic dramaturgical choices, both in reading translation T^1 (which is, as we have seen, imbued with dramaturgical analysis) and, when appropriate, in making reference to the original T^0.

C. The following stage, T^3, is the test of the text translated in T^1 and T^2 in contact with the stage – it is the concretization of the stage enunciation. This time the situation of enunciation is finally realized; it is plunged into the audience, the target culture, to sink or swim. The staging, as a comparison of the virtual situation of enunciation of T^0 and the actual situation of enunciation of T^3, proposes a *performance text*, suggesting an examination of all possible relationships between textual signs and stage signs.

D. The chain is not yet complete, though, for the spectator needs to receive T^3, the stage concretization, and appropriate it in turn. We could call this last phase receptive concretization or receptive enunciation. At this point the source text has finally succeeded in its aim – to reach a spectator in the course of an actual staging. That spectator appropriates the text only after a series of concretizations, of intermediary translations which themselves reduce or enlarge the source text at each stage, making it a text that is always yet to be found or constructed. It is no exaggeration to say that translation is simultaneously a dramaturgical analysis (T^1–T^2), a staging (T^3) and an address to the audience (T^3), all unaware of this fact.

4. Conditions of Reception of Theatre Translation

A. THE HERMENEUTIC COMPETENCE OF THE FUTURE AUDIENCE

We have seen that the translation leads, by the end of the process, to a receptive concretization that ultimately decides on the use and meaning of the source text, T^0. That is a measure of the importance of the target conditions of the utterance translated, conditions that are very specific in the case of the theatre audience who must hear the text and, specifically, understand why the translator made the choices he did, assuming a particular "horizon of expectation" (JAUSS) in the audience. It is in the evaluation of himself and the other that the translator will form an idea of the character that is more or less appropriate to the translation. But the latter depends on many other factors, specifically on a different kind of competence.

B. THE RHYTHMIC, PSYCHOLOGICAL AND AUDITORY COMPETENCE OF THE FUTURE AUDIENCE

Equivalence, or at least the rhythmic and prosodic transposition of the source text (T^0) and the staging text (T^3), is often noted as being essential to a "proper" translation. It is true that consideration must be given to the form of the text translated, particularly its duration and rhythm, which form part of the message. But the criterion of whether a text can be acted or spoken is both valid, for establishing the mode of reception of the text, and problematic, when it degenerates into a standard of proper acting or verisimilitude. True, the actor must be physically capable of acting and speaking his lines. This implies avoiding euphony, gratuitous plays on the signifier and multitudinous detail at the expense of a quick overview of the whole. The requirement that a text be capable of being *acted* or *spoken* may, however, lead to a standard of proper speaking, to a facile simplification of the rhetoric of the actor's respiratory and articulatory performance and phrasing (cf. translations of SHAKESPEARE). The staging work carries a risk of trivialization for the sake of a text that "sounds right."

As to the corresponding notion of the text that is capable of being *heard* or *received*, it too depends on the audience and on its ability to assess the emotional impact of a text or fiction on the spectators. It is clear that contemporary staging no longer recognizes such rules as phonic correctness, clarity of speech or pleasing rhythms. Other criteria have replaced those normative bench-marks of a text that rolls off the tongue and is pleasing to the ear.

5. Staging Translations

A. IMPORTANCE OF THE SITUATION OF ENUNCIATION

The translation at T^3, which is already part of an actual staging, is "plugged into" the stage situation of enunciation through a system of deictics. Once this has occurred, the translated text can get rid of terms that are understandable only in the context of their enunciation. The dramatic text makes much use of deictics, personal pronouns and silences, or places the description of beings and things in the stage directions, expecting the staging to convey the text.

This property of the dramatic text, and thus of its translation for the stage, enables the actor to flesh out his lines with all sorts of acoustical, gestural, expressive and postural means. Then the actor's entire range of rhythmical possibilities comes into play: intonation, which can speak louder than a long speech; pace, which can lengthen or shorten his speeches, structure or destructure the text; and many gestural devices that ensure the interaction between words and body.

B. TRANSLATION AS STAGING

There are two schools of thought among translators and directors as to the status of the translation in relation to the staging. This is the same debate as between the dramatic text and the staging.

1. For translators who would like to protect their autonomy and who often feel their work is publishable as is, and not tied to a particular staging, the translation does not necessarily or fully determine the staging, but leaves it to the discretion of future directors. This is position taken by DÉPRATS (in CORVIN, 1995).

2. The opposite view treats the translation as practically a staging, since the text of the translation already contains and directs its staging. This would imply that the text, whether original or translated, contains a *pre-performance**, an assumption that is difficult to defend since it suggests that the pre-performance must be borne in mind to carry out the staging and prepare the translation (DÉPRATS).

6. Theory of Language-body

The alliance of gesture and word is called the language-body. It is an arrangement, specific to a language or a culture, of the (gestural and vocal) rhythm and the text. It is a question of grasping the way the source text, then its source performance, associate a kind of gestural and rhythmic enunciation with a text; then one looks for an equivalent language-body that is appropriate to the target language. To translate the dramatic text, then, it is necessary to create a visual and gestural image of this language-body of the source language and culture, to try to appropriate it based on the language-body of the target language and culture. It has often been stressed that the acting and staging must convey gesture and body in the source language to restore its physicality. The point is always to bring about a meeting between the language-body of the source language and culture and the language-body of the target language and culture.

Further reading: *Théâtre/public*, no. 44 (1982); Pavis 1987; *Sixèmes Assises*, 1990.

TRESTLE STAGE

Fr.: *tréteau*; Ger.: *Gerüst, die Bretter*; Sp.: *tablado*.
See STAGE BOARDS

TRITAGONIST

Fr: *tritagoniste*; Ger.: *Tritagonist*; Sp.: *tritagonista*.
See PROTAGONIST

TURNING POINT

Fr.: *point de retournement*; Ger.: *Wendepunkt, Umschlag*; Sp.: *punto decisivo, viraje*.

Point at which the play or the action takes a new turn, often in a direction opposite to the expected. Point at which the action changes direction, when a *coup de théâtre** changes the face of things and "takes the characters from misfortune to prosperity or from prosperity to misfortune" (MARMONTEL). This notion is very similar to that of *peripeteia**.

TYPE

Fr.: *type, personnage typique*; *Typus*; Sp.: *tipo*.

Conventional *character** possessing physical, psychological or moral attributes that are known to the audience in advance and remain constant throughout the play. The attributes are established by literary tradition (the generous bandit, the prostitute with a heart of gold, the braggart and all the stock characters of the *commedia dell'arte**). This notion differs somewhat from that of the *stereotype**, which is more superficial, repetitive and dull. The type represents, if not an individual, at least a *role** characteristic of a state or failing (the miser, the traitor). Although it is not individualized, it at least has some human and historical traits.

1. A type is created whenever individual and original characteristics are sacrificed to generalization and magnification. The spectator has no difficulty identifying the type

in question by a psychological trait, a social milieu or an occupation.

2. The type has had bad press; it is reproached for its superficiality and dissimilarity to real people. It is equated with the well-defined comic figure in Bergsonian terms, as "the mechanical grafted onto the living" (BERGSON, 1899). It is observed that tragic characters possess a much more human and individual dimension. Even the most polished character, however, can be reduced to a set of traits, or even distinctive signs, and has nothing to do with an actual person. And, inversely, the type is none other than a character who states frankly its limits and simplification. Finally, types are easier to fit into the plot and better serve as the object of acting by showing, in that they are characterized by an obsession that places them in conflict with the other characters (whether individualized or types themselves).

3. Types are found mainly in theatrical forms having a strong historical tradition in which the recurring stock characters represent the major human types or failings being attacked by the dramatist. Historically, the appearance of the stock character is often explained by the fact that each character was played by the same actor, who evolved an original gestuality and psychology over the years. There are some dramaturgies that cannot do without types, such as the farce. Sometimes the representation of the typical, i.e. the general or "philosophical," can be the playwright's revenge.

See also: actantial model, actor, role, typecasting, casting.

Further reading: Bentley 1964; Aziza et al. 1978b; Herzel 1981; Amossy 1982.

TYPECASTING

Fr.: *emploi*; Ger.: *Rollenbesetzung, Rollenfach*; Sp.: *parte*.

This is a type of casting in which actors are given parts that correspond to their age, appearance and acting style; for instance, the role of leading man, ingenue, and so on.

Typecasting is based on the actor's age, physique, voice and personality. We can distinguish between comic and tragic types, but the classifications are endless. The tendency to codify or legislate in the arts is reflected, for instance, in the list of character types published by Napoleon in his Moscow decree. A hybrid notion somewhere between the *character** and the actor playing it, the type character is a synthesis of physical, moral, intellectual and social attributes. A classification may be based on various different criteria:

- social status: king, valet, dandy;
- costume: cloak (leading roles and fathers in comedy), bodice (countrywomen in comic opera wearing bodice and petticoat);
- character: ingenue, lovers, traitor, noble father, duenna.

Such a "physiological" conception of the actor's work is already part of the past, though it lives on in genres such as bourgeois comedy, classical comedy and *commedia dell'arte**. It is based on the idea that the actor should correspond to the great character types of repertory and incarnate the character, a notion that is falling into disuse, at least in experimental theatre. In another context entirely, it has been revived by directors such as MEYERHOLD (1975, 81–91).

See also: type, characterization, stereotype, casting.

Further reading: Pougin 1885; Abraham 1933; Herzel 1981; *Annuel du spectacle*, 1982–1983.

U

UBERMARIONETTE

Fr.: *sur-marionnette;* Ger.: *Über-marionette;* Sp.: *Uber-Marionette.*

Name given by E.G. CRAIG to his notion of an actor placed entirely at the director's disposal: "The actor must go, and in his place comes the inanimate figure – the uebermarionette we may call him, until he has won for himself a better one." (CRAIG 1905, 72; COLE and CHINOY 1973, 383). This notion came as the culminating point of a theatre tradition that sought to control the staging completely and to subject the living material to the intellectual grip of the director. It dates back, at least, to DIDEROT's *Paradoxe sur le comédien,* where the actor "is enclosed within a great wicker mannequin of which he is the master" (1994:406).

Further reading: Kleist 1978; Stanislavski 1977, 1989; Bensky 1971.

UNITIES

Fr.: *unités;* Ger.: *Einheiten;* Sp.: *unidades.*

The system of the three unities is the touchstone of and the key to *classical dramaturgy*.* It is meaningful only within the aesthetic and ideological context of its time.

1. Origins

The rule of the three unities appeared in aesthetic doctrine in the sixteenth and seventeenth centuries (CHAPELAIN from 1630 to 1637, D'AUBIGNAC in 1657, LA MESNARDIÈRE), based on ARISTOTLE's *Poetics,* which was considered – wrongly – to have decreed those three unities as necessary. In addition to the *unity of action*,* which was in fact recommended by ARISTOTLE (*Poetics,* Chap. 5), the *unity of time** and the *unity of place** were introduced under the influence of CASTELVETRO's translation and commentary on ARISTOTLE (1570). The latter two unities have rarely been honoured completely, however, as they impose very severe restrictions on the playwright. Instead, they functioned as a kind of restraint on experimentation and the epic temptations of drama.

2. Dramaturgical Consequences

The rules are based on a supposed convergence of stage time and place (of the performance) and external time and place (of the material performed). The unity dogma called for these two systems of time and place to converge so that the action might unfold in a continuous and homogeneous fashion, one of the essential concerns of classical dramaturgy (for reasons of verisimilitude and good taste: to be capable of encompassing a limited whole with the mind).

That criterion puts a great strain on the dramatic material, concentrating it, distorting facts, isolating favoured moments (*crisis**), narrating external events and internalizing action.

3. Other Kinds of Unity

A. UNITY OF TONE

Classicism calls for unity in the presentation of actions. The play should not jump from one level of language to another, or from one genre to another. The atmosphere should be consistent (*coherence**). There should be unity of interest, "which is the true source of continuous emotion" (HOUDAR DE LA MOTTE, *Premier Discours sur la tragédie*, 1721).

B. UNITY OF THE HERO'S CONSCIOUSNESS: THE UNITIES SYSTEM

This kind of unity is similar to unity of action, but goes beyond it to constitute the basic unity of classical dramaturgy, on which all the others depend. As demonstrated by HEGEL, the hero is defined by his self-consciousness, which is at one with his actions. He cannot contradict himself and be completely in control of the situation. There is no social contradiction within him that he has not assumed, that is not reflected in his consciousness. His unity of consciousness imposes his unity of action, which cannot be broken down into contradictory processes (as, for example, in BRECHT), but forms a whole. The unity of time proceeds from the unity of action, as time can only be full and continuous; it issues from the unities of consciousness and of action. The last unity is that of place, which proceeds in turn from the unity of time: in a short, homogeneous period of time one cannot go very far or jump from one temporality to another. (That is how MAGGI introduced the unity of time in 1550, although it is not mentioned in ARISTOTLE.)

4. Functions

Although the classical treatises expended an inordinate amount of energy on justifying the need for such unifying rules, taking the Ancients as their authority and dictating to the quite conformist production of their time, they do not specify the philosophical and aesthetic foundations of those rules. The function of the unities is never clear, or at least varies from one text to another. The main justification is *verisimilitude**. A unified and concentrated performance is supposed to create a seamless illusion for spectators who, it is assumed, would not consent, in a two-hour performance, to visiting many times and places. That would point up the gaps and holes in dramatic construction, which would in turn have an annoying distancing effect. The opposite could be said, however: that concentrating the event forces it to be cut and manipulated in ways that are not believable. As HUGO remarked in his critique of classical tragedy, "the strange thing is that humdrum people claim to have based their rule of the two unities (of time and place) on verisimilitude, whereas it is precisely the real that kills it. What could be less believable than this vestibule, this peristyle, this antechamber, this trite place where our comedies deign to unfold, this place where (no one knows how) conspirators come to inveigh against the tyrant, where the tyrant comes to rant against the conspirators" (Preface to *Cromwell*, 1827).

The justification for the rule of the unities, then, must be sought elsewhere than in a notion of absolute verisimilitude. First of all, it can be attributed to the material stage conditions in the seventeenth century. In spite of all the machinery, changes of time and place were immmediately visible and forced the audience to accept a symbolic convention, for the stage was not yet transformed into a different place or time, as in the late nineteenth century.

Above all, however, we must remember that the notion of verisimilitude so often invoked for or against the unities is a historically flexible one that does not warrant the use or rejection of the unities in theory. The convention that sanctions those unities, however, is a decisive factor: it is simply a matter of knowing whether the intent is to mask it to give the illusion of a realistic rendering of human action, or whether it is accepted and emphasized to accentuate the artistic and theatrical nature of performance. When it comes to classical dramaturgy and its rules, the ambiguity is complete. On the one hand, it accepts abstraction, concentration and convention, and the unity is an asset rather than an obstacle. On the other hand, it has pretensions of naturalistic illusion, and it announces realism and naturalism in its desire for the representation of reality to coincide with the reality itself. In both cases, however, the unities are more theatrical conventions and codes than timeless principles drawn from an analysis of reality.

The justification for the unities lies elsewhere, and if classicism fails to breathe a word of it, it is not out of perverseness but because of a lack of historical perspective and a fixed, universalist belief in man that claims to be able to decide, once and for all, what is human nature and how it can be conveyed artistically. The unities, particularly that of action, on which scholars and playwrights are practically unanimous, are in fact the expression of a unitary and homogeneous view of man. Classical man is, before all else, an inalienable and undivided consciousness that can be reduced to an emotion, a property, a unity (regardless of the conflicts that are the play's theme, but which are made to be resolved). The theoretician, sure of that unity of motivation, never suspects for a moment that consciousness too can be shattered, as soon as it no longer reflects a unified, universalized world and appears as false consciousness, a rent in social or psychological fabric. As soon as cuts and dialogism appear (as in HUGO, BÜCHNER and MUSSET), the reassuring unity vanishes and is replaced by dialogue and diversity. The character and the theatre performance cease to be an indivisible whole. Dramatic writing cannot sustain such division, and the performance ceases to be a mimetic, autonomous world patterned after a unified reality; it needs to be constructed by a narrator. The dramatic form was gradually transformed by various epic efforts by BÜCHNER and GRABBE, but also by HUGO and MAETERLINCK. Since then, no unity – of time, place, action, tone or "interest" – has been able to mask that multiplicity. If our modern age (PIRANDELLO, BRECHT or BECKETT) has demolished all the unities, it is because the end of man and his unifying consciousness is no longer a secret to anyone. The demolition has been a relative one in any case, as it is not easy to admit that human action, the last bastion of the unity dispute, can be dismantled and still attract the attention of today's audience. This is an audience that, in spite of all evidence to the contrary, is not prepared to give up the principle formulated most clearly by D'AUBIGNAC in the seventeenth century: the inherent need for order in the human mind.

Further reading: Plato, *Phaedra, Symposium* (on the unity of discourse), Aristotle, *Poetics*, Chap. 5; Horace, *Ars poetica*, 100 B.C.; Maggi, *in Aristotelis librum de Poetica communes explicationes*, 1550; Scaliger, *Poetices libri Septem*, 1561; Castelvestro, *Commentaire d'Aristote*, 1570; Laudun, *Art poétique françois*, 1593; Mairet, *Préface de Silvanire*, 1630, *Sophonisbe*, 1634; La Mesnardière, *Poétique*, 1639; d'Aubignac, *Pratique du théâtre*, 1657; Corneille, *Discours sur les trois unités*, 1657; Dryden, *Of Dramatick Poesie*, 1668; Boileau, *l'Art poétique*, 1674; Gottsched, *Versuch einer critischen Dichtung für die Deutschen*, 1750; Johnson, *Preface to the edition of Shakespeare*, 1765; Lessing, *Dramaturgie de Hamburg*, 1767–1769; Herder, *Shakespeare*, 1773. For a more complete list, not centred entirely around the unities, see the bibliography provided in the entry for *poetics**.

UNITY OF ACTION

Fr.: *unité d'action*; Ger.: *Einheit der Handlung*; Sp.: *unidad de acción*.

Action is unified when all the narrative material is organized around a main story and the subplots are all connected logically with the common trunk of the story. Of the three unities, it is the most important, because it involves the entire dramatic structure. ARISTOTLE calls for the poet to show a unified action: "the plot [...] must be the imitation of a unified action comprising a whole; and the events which are the parts of the plot must be so organized that if any one of them is displaced or taken away, the whole will be shaken and put out of joint; for if the presence or absence of a thing makes no discernible difference, that thing is not part of the whole" (*Poetics*, section

1451a). Unity of action is the only unity that playwrights are required to respect, at least in part, not out of concern for the norm but in response to the internal necessity of their work. There is no way, in a three-hour performance, to present multiple actions or subdivide and ramify them infinitely. The spectators would be lost without the explanations, summaries and commentaries of a narrator placed outside the action. As this kind of authorial intervention is unthinkable in classical (non-epic) dramaturgy, the playwright must comply with the unity of action rule. Unity of action may perhaps be explained by the relative simplicity of the minimal narrative and by the need for the security felt by every reader when faced with a concise, finished narrative model. The action and its unity are as much categories of dramaturgical production as of spectator *reception**, as it is the audience who decides whether the action of a play forms a whole and can be summed up in a coherent narrative scheme.

UNITY OF PLACE

Fr.: *unité de lieu;* Ger.: *Einheit des Ortes;* Sp.: *unidad de lugar.*

This rule dictates use of a single place, one that the spectator can take in with his gaze. That one place may be divided up, however, as in the rooms of a palace, the streets of a town, "places where one could go in twenty-four hours" (CORNEILLE), with changing or simultaneous scenery.

UNITY OF TIME

Fr.: *unité de temps;* Ger.: *Einheit der Zeit;* Sp.: *unidad de tiempo.*

This rule, often challenged, limits the duration of the play's action to twenty-four hours. ARISTOTLE recommended that the action not exceed the time it takes for the sun to complete one revolution (12 or 24 hours). Some theoreticians (in France in the seventeenth century) went so far as to demand that the *time** represented not exceed the time of the performance.

The unities of time and place are closely connected. Since classicism, like any idealistic approach to human action, denies the progression of time and man's actions over the course of his destiny, time is compressed and reduced to the visible action of the character on stage, i.e. it is related to the hero's consciousness. In order to be shown to the audience, it is necessarily filtered through the character's consciousness. Moreover, since *analytical drama** (in which the catastrophe is inevitable and known in advance) is the model of tragedy, time is necessarily reduced to the minimum necessary to express the catastrophe: "The unity of time makes the story out to be, not a *process*, but an irreversible, unchangeable fatality" (UBERSFELD, 1977a:207).

UNIVERSITY AND THEATRE

Although the field of theatre studies has set a very ambitious theoretical program for itself, the teaching of theatre is much more limited. Difficulties seem to abound at acting schools, perplexing would-be actors and university authorities alike. These difficulties are all the more insurmountable because the Western tradition does not confine teaching to physical training and learning tradition and technique but aspires to form the actor's entire personality in every respect. From teaching — which may or may not be brilliant — to training, including self-training or the training of trainers, there is a significant shift in vocabulary.

1. An Insane Program

An ideal school would have an unlimited program, with all actors, all techniques, all stage arts, all research methods a legitimate object of study. The epistemological chaos of theatre studies is equalled only by the anarchy of artistic teaching (in France and abroad) and the lack of harmonization or concerted efforts among ministries and teaching establishments. Rather than attempting to cover the entire field of knowledge about the theatre, perhaps it would be more reasonable to limit teaching and learning to major subject groups such as theatre writing, acting, space, staging, institutions, intermedia, and reception. This should make it possible to take an approach that would be both theoretical (academic, in a descriptive sense) and practical (producing an artistic object and then endeavoring to analyze it).

2. The University as a Place of Learning
The same uncertainty reigns in terms of the place where such complex knowledge should be transmitted. In Western Europe, dramatic art is taught both at the university and at professional schools (conservatories or private programs). This split, rationalized by the distinction between theory and practice, is particularly unfortunate because it stands in the way of in-depth study of either one or the other, and perpetuates an artificial distinction whose elimination is in the interest of both universities and schools.

Universities have discovered theatre only recently, having acknowledged after much temporizing and only begrudgingly that it is not a branch of literature but an artistic practice in its own right (without however granting it resources to allow it decent subsistence or an interdisciplinary approach to teaching). They have not managed to carve out the domain of knowledge and disciplines of that artistic practice, or to decide what is in fact their object of study – professional or amateur theatre, drama or intermedia hybrids. Nor are they certain whether students should be expected to learn how to create theatre or placed in a "school for spectators" to "read theatre" (cf. the titles of two books by Anne UBERSFELD, 1977 and 1981); or whether the two are in fact contradictory and mutually exclusive. For the teaching of theatre should look equally to the academic study of texts and performances, the transmission of techniques and stage arts, and artistic practice itself.

In continental Europe, teaching focuses essentially on texts, sometimes on dramaturgical analysis, and includes performance analysis in the best cases. In the English-speaking countries, theatre is taught in schools and universities either as an enrichment activity (drama in education) or as an art. Universities encourage students to gain practical experience by putting on plays.

Universities are hard pressed to reconcile their traditional approach of universal humanistic culture with the short-term professional requirements dictated by their cautious management of profit, the needs of their impoverished students and the lack of a national conservatory.

3. Unresolved Problems
At least in France, ideas do not circulate freely between the university and the theatre profession or between the university and professional schools such as conservatories, the National Institute of Theatre Arts and Techniques (ENSATT) and the Strasbourg National Theatre School (TNS). This may be attributed to mutual disregard, divergent interests, even narrow-mindedness. Added to this is a distrust of schools and universities on the part of theatre people and a reluctance to take part in joint teaching activities. Perhaps after all a universal humanisitic approach is simply not compatible with immediate professional needs, so that it is not easy to reverse the roles and have universities that are open to professional techniques and theatrical creations that are exploited by teaching establishments. The university and the State balk at defraying costly training; they fulfill their mandate by encouraging a kind of hidden privatization and decline to associate themselves with projects situated halfway between teaching and culture.

The status of teaching staff at schools and universities should be redefined on the basis of the following distinction:

- a teaching and university objective whereby the exercises and practical exercises proposed by professional instructors are complementary activities which are fully integrated with theoretical teaching;
- a professional and artistic objective set at professional schools and conservatories by real professionals who constantly consult historians, theoreticians and authorities from outside.

Despite these endemic structural difficulties, however, a beginning needs to be made on bringing professional theatre closer to the university if the teaching of theatre is to remain in universities and truly aspires to decompartmentalizing skills and approaches.

Inversely, the university can go to the theatre, as by participating in festivals, analyzing performances afterwards, subjecting reflection to the discipline of immediate action, promoting practical study in the professional milieu, attending rehearsals, and drawing conclusions about the production and reception of performances.

On a more modest scale, exercises could be made up for actors that lead to a reconsideration of the body/mind dichotomy, to theoretical reflection through playful experimentation, to ensuring a mutual enrichment of theoretical questioning and experiments on stage, for performance between the seminar room and the workshop. The study of text and performance is simply an activity of play and emotion that is an end in itself. Study and practice may be reconcilable if they have a space for teaching and training, a seminar room/workshop where ideas and actions can be tried out immediately. Such a space could be part of both the university and the workshops or studios of conservatories or national theatre or dramatic centres (according to the technique inaugurated by STANISLAVSKY and MEYERHOLD, taken up by VITEZ at the Conservatory and at Chaillot, or by the TNS at Strasbourg).

Year-end productions also need revamping so that they go beyond merely a student performance under the direction of a teacher or professional to become an individual or collective project, a "self-course" in the words of Jacques LECOQ, a "thematic studio"; in short, an artistic research project accompanied and followed by a process of reflection, in the form of practical expertise.

The teaching of theatre is beset by many problems and shows a striking waste of human and institutional energy. But it is also promising as a bearer of human knowledge for evaluation, passing on and replaying.

Further reading: *Théâtre/Public*, (1980, 1982–83, 1988); "La formation du comédien," *Les Voies de la création théâtrale*, vol.IX, CNRS, 1981; Vernois and Herry 1988; Knapp 1993.
Source: Patrice PAVIS in Michel CORVIN (ed.), 1995.

UNRAVELLING

Fr.: *dénouement*; Ger.: *Lösung, Enthüllung*; Sp.: *desenlace*.
See DÉNOUEMENT

UPDATING

Fr.: *actualisation*; Ger.: *Aktualisierung*; Sp.: *actualización*.

Operation consisting of adapting an older text to the present time, taking into account contemporary circumstances and the new audience's tastes, and making changes in the plot as necessitated by the evolution of society.

Updating does not alter the main story, and preserves the nature of relationships among the characters. Only the dating and, perhaps, the frame of action are changed.

A play may be updated on several levels, from simply modernizing costumes to an *adaptation** for a different audience and sociohistoric situation. It was once thought, naively, that the classics had only to be played in street clothes to enable the spectators to feel involved in the issues. Stagings today are careful to give the audience the right instruments for a proper *reading** of the play; they seek not to eliminate but to accentuate differences between yesterday and today. Updating therefore tends to become a *historicization** (as in Brecht).
See also: Translation, dramaturgical analysis.
Further reading: Brecht 1963–1970; Knopf 1980.

UTTERANCE

Fr.: *énoncé*; Ger.: *das Aussagen*; Sp.: *enunciado*.
See DISCOURSE, SITUATION OF ENUNCIATION

V

VALET

Fr.: *valet*; Ger.: *Diener*; Sp.: *criado.*

The character of the valet or manservant appeared in theatre very frequently from Antiquity to the nineteenth century. Defined in advance by his social status and dependence on a master, the valet embodies the social relationships of a specific period, and becomes the barometer and the figurehead of that period. Although he is socially inferior to the master, his dramaturgical role is usually significant. He has two functions in the play; one as the master's helper or adviser and, sometimes, another as the master of the plot (Scapin, Figaro).

Through his association with the master or masters, the valet enables the playwright to reconstruct a social microcosm characteristic of the fictional universe represented in the play. The valet is rarely content to be a servile executor of his master's projects; he is an adviser (Dubois in *Les Fausses Confidences*), observer of the plot (*Figaro*), accomplice (Sganarelle in MOLIERE's *Dom Juan*), sometimes even a parodic form of slave (Vladimir and Estragon in *Waiting for Godot*). The valet stands up to the main character, who forces him to act, to express himself, to reveal his feelings (in MARIVAUX), to do the dirty work of aristocrats or bourgeois. Rather than an alter ego, he is the master's body and id, his consciousness and unconscious, his "unspoken" and "undone." Sometimes, depending on the play's ideology, his differences are stressed (his gluttony, his banal and coarse way of expressing himself, his bald desires, like the Harlequin of *commedia dell'arte** and MARIVAUX). Sometimes, however, the valet comes very close to the master, to the point of contesting his supremacy (as in *Le Mariage de Figaro*).

The valet of French theatre proceeds from two traditions: Italian, for the "buffoon" valet, having its roots in *commedia dell'arte** and specializing in farcical effects (Harlequin, Trivelin); and French, for the brilliant, ingenious valet who pulls strings to manipulate the action at will (Scapin, Crispin, Lubin, Dubois). The epitome of the popular character, the valet embodies all the contradictions of society and the theatrical genres; alienation and liberation are the stages in his journey.

The maid has not had the same brilliant career as her male counterpart; she is distinguished from the nurse only beginning with CORNEILLE's comedies and has no direct influence on the action.

Further reading: Emélina 1975; Aziza, Olivieri and Sctrick 1978b; Moraud 1981; Forestier 1988.

VALUE

Fr.: *valeur*; Ger.: *Wert*; Sp.: *valor.*

See AESTHETIC

VAUDEVILLE

Fr.: *vaudeville*; Ger.: *Vaudeville*; Sp.: *vodevil.*

Originally, in the fifteenth century, and until the early eighteenth century, vaudeville (*Vaux de Vire*) was a show composed of songs, acrobatics and monologues. FUZELIER, LESAGE and DORNEVAL composed shows for the Théâtre de la Foire that employed both music and dance. Light opera (*opéra comique*) appeared as the musical part developed. In the nineteenth century, vaudeville became, with SCRIBE (between 1815 and 1850) and then LABICHE and FEYDEAU, light comedy of intrigue with no intellectual pretensions: "Vaudeville [...] is to real life what the jointed puppet is to the walking man: a very artificial exaggeration of a certain natural rigidity of things" (BERGSON 1940, 78). Often as a *well-made play**, vaudeville lives on today in *boulevard theatre**, which has inherited its liveliness, its popular comic wit and its *authorial interventions**.
See also: comédie, théâtre bourgeois, farce.
Further reading: Sigaux 1970; Ruprecht 1976; Gidel in Beaumarchais et al. 1984; Thomasseau 1994; Lemahieu in Corvin 1995.

VERBAL SCENERY

Fr.: *décor verbal*; Ger.: *Wortkulisse*; Sp.: *decorado verbal*.

Scenery which is shown not through visual means but through a character's commentary (cf. Rosalind in *As You Like It*). This technique of verbal scenery is only possible by virtue of a *convention** that is accepted by the spectator, who must imagine the place and the immediate transformation of the place as announced. In SHAKESPEARE, transitions are easily made in this way from outside to inside, from forest to palace. Scenes are linked without having to provide more than a simple spatial indication or an exchange of words that evoke a different place (*indications of time and place**).
Further reading: Honzl 1940; Styan 1967.

VERISIMILITUDE

Fr.: *vraisemblance*; Ger.: *Wahrscheinlichkeit*, Sp.: *verosimilitud*.

1. Origins of the Notion

For classical dramaturgy, verisimilitude is that which, in actions, characters and performance, *seems real* to the audience, both in terms of action and the way they are represented on the stage. Verisimilitude is, therefore, a concept tied to spectator reception, but one which forces the playwright to invent stories and motivations that will produce the effect and illusion of truth. This requirement of believability dates back to ARISTOTLE, and was maintained and refined up to the classical period in Europe. It defines several other notions that describe the mode of existence of actions: the true, the possible, the necessary, the reasonable, the real. In ARISTOTLE's words, "the poet's function is not to report things that have happened, but rather to tell of such things as might happen, things that are possibilities by virtue of being in themselves inevitable or probable" (1451b). The important thing for the poet, then, is not historical truth, but the probable or creditable nature of what he is reporting, the ability to generalize his statements. Hence a fundamental opposition between poet and historian: "Thus the difference between the historian and the poet is not that the historian employs prose and the poet verse – the work of Herodotus could be put into verse, and it would be no less a history with verses than without them; rather the difference is that the one tells of things that have been and the other of such things as might be. Poetry, therefore, is a more philosophical and a higher thing than history, in that poetry tends rather to express the universal, history rather the particular fact." (1451b)

In choosing the general and the typical, the dramatist prefers persuasion to historical truth, banks on an "average" action that is credible but interesting, possible but out of the ordinary. There is therefore a tension to be observed between the action that captivates (because it is fantastic and exceptional) and the action that is acceptable to public opinion and belief. Hence the opposition, itself classical, between the believable and the marvellous, terms that should never be seen alone: "The marvellous is all that which goes against the ordinary course of Nature. The believable is all that which conforms to public opinion" (RAPIN, *Réflexions sur la poétique*, 1674).

The believable characterizes an action that is logically *possible*, given the interlocking logical series of motifs, thus *necessary* as the internal logic of the story: "In the characters and the plot construction alike, one must strive for that which is either necessary or probable, so that whatever a character of any kind says or does may be the sort of thing such a character will inevitably or probably say or do and the events of the plot may follow one after another either inevitably or with probability" (1454b).

There is a delicate balance between these components of the believable, which achieves perfection when there are grounds for agreement between author and spectator, when there is "perfect agreement between the poet's genius and the spectator's soul" (MARMONTEL 1763, III:478), when the theatrical illusion is perfect and achieves "the unity of the story, its precise length, in short, the verisimilitude so recommended and so necessary to any poem, with the sole intention of providing the onlookers with every possible opportunity to reflect on what they see and to doubt reality" (CHAPELAIN, *Lettre sur la règle des vingt-quatre heures*, 1630). Verisimilitude is therefore backed by a scrupulous respect for the three *unities**.

2. The Relative Nature of Verisimilitude

The rule of verisimilitude is valid for a normative dramaturgy based on illusion, reason and the universality of conflicts and behaviours. Contrary to classical belief, however, there is no such thing as an immutable verisimilitude that can be defined once and for all. There is only a set of codifications and norms that are ideological and tied to a historical moment, in spite of their apparent universal nature. It is only "an ideological and rhetorical code common to transmitter and receiver, which ensures the message's readability through implicit or explicit references to an (extratextual) system of institutionalized values that takes the place of the real" (HAMON 1973).

The believable is an intermediary link between the two extremes, the theatricality of theatrical illusion and the reality of the thing imitated in theatre. The author seeks a way of reconciling these two requirements: how to reflect reality by seeming to be true, how to signify the theatrical by creating a self-enclosed artistic system. This shifter between reality and stage is at once mimetic (it must create a reality effect by representing reality) and semiological (it must signify the real using a coherent system of signs, thus producing an effect of theatre). The very word "verisimilitude" implies both the illusion of truth (absolute realism) and the truth of illusion (consummate theatricality). Everything would seem to indicate, then, that the believable is constructed as a process of abstraction of the reality imitated and as a code of semantic oppositions.

The foregoing explains its relative nature in history. What is true changes, and appearances evolve. The primary reason for such changes is a particular period's belief in its ability to reproduce reality and its methods for doing so. Every school tries to describe reality: for classicism, the *truth* of human relationships and the use of the proper rules were essential; for naturalism, it was *reality* itself that must be described. Moreover, every literary genre has a specific "fictional status" with conventions that absolutely must be respected (in parables and folktales, for example, the *true* and the *real* are diametrically opposed). For the playwright, as well as the spectator, it is essential to know the key to the fiction, which is used to encode and then to read the action.

These reflections bring us to a turning point in the perspective and assumptions of the dogma of verisimilitude. In spite of the classical theorists, the point is not to know which reality is to be described and textualized in the text and on the stage, but rather to grasp which kind of discourse is the most appropriate to the reality one wishes to describe. The believable, like realism, is not

a question of imitating reality but an artistic technique for expressing that reality in signs.
Further reading: D'Aubignac 1927; Corneille 1660; Bray 1927; *Poétique*, 1973, no. 16.

VERISM

Fr.: *représentation vériste;* Ger.: *Verismus;* Sp.: *representación verista.*

An aesthetic attitude and movement that aims for a perfect imitation of reality.

1. Verism was an Italian literary and pictoral movement that followed on and was inspired by French *naturalism**, developing between circa 1870 and 1920. The movement's leading proponent was G. VERGA (1840–1922), and it drew inspiration from ZOLA, TOLSTOY and IBSEN.

2. Verism is similar to naturalism in its photographic subjection to reality and its belief in science and absolute determinism (regionalism, heredity). In theatre, verism presents a faithful reconstruction of place, has characters speak according to their regional origins (not only their social origins, as in naturalism), eschews all unrealistic *conventions** (confidants, monologues, long tirades, raisonneurs and choruses), and returns again and again to the theme of the environment that produces and stifles human beings. Beyond the movement as such, the verist (or naturalist) staging style is frequently seen in contemporary theatre. The spectators are meant to feel that they are no longer in the theatre but are watching a real event lifted from surrounding reality.
See also: realism, represented reality, theatrical reality, sign, history.
Further reading: "Verismo," *Enciclopedia dello spettacolo*, 1962; "Vérisme," *Encyclopedia universalis*, 1968; Ulivi 1972; Chevrel 1982.

VERSIFICATION

Fr.: *versification;* Ger.: *Versifizierung;* Sp.: *versificación.*

1. The dramatic text, particularly in classical tragedy, is often written in verse, which forces the actor to obey a rather strict prosodic scheme: pronouncing all 12 feet of the alexandrine, observing caesuras, breaking down hemistiches into six possible figures (one/five, two/four, three/three, four/two, five/one, two/two/two) and, particularly, noting deviations from the rule and connections with the prosodic structure and the meaning of the text. Theatre in verse is not necessarily poetic theatre, obeying a norm or poetics that imposes its own formal law and verse, from the Greeks to Romantic drama. The alexandrine cannot be avoided, whether classical (RACINE), free (HUGO), or neoclassical (ROSTAND).

Rather than making the alexandrine commonplace by drowning it in psychology or extracting from it those parts considered essential, today's staging often endeavours to use it to bring the text to life musically before taking on a meaning and merging with the situation and characterization. VITEZ is implacable: "We will train ourselves to reject and invert it without ever transgressing the laws of prosodic architecture. There is no way Racine's theatre can be played without dealing with the problem of the alexandrine. Racine without verse loses its form and its sense. A disastrous loss! Only the plot would be left, grievously changed." (*Le Monde-Dimanche*, 11–12 October 1981). Less confining forms than the alexandrine are found in the verse of CLAUDEL, free verse (DUJARDIN, YEATS, T.S. ELIOT, C. FRY, HOFMANNSTHAL), and today Heiner MÜLLER or T. BERNHARD).

Verse is no longer considered a necessary evil or a shameful form enveloping the textual substrata; in it we can see how the text is made, in it language appears as both the prisonhouse of the listener and that which structures and identifies the human being. By making "the alexandrine shine," by "stretching it to the utmost," like VITEZ, the actor also *tells* of his relationship with the world, and the story told by the play. At the same time, however, it becomes impossible to rely on psychology, characters, a story, a dramatic situation: the signifier dis-

plays its distrust toward a signified defined in terms of fiction and story.
See also: declamation, diction.
Further reading: Golomb 1979; Vitez and Meschonnic 1982; Bernard 1986.

VISUAL AND TEXTUAL

Fr.: *visuel et textuel*; Ger.: *visuell und textuell*; Sp.: *visual y textual.*

These two elements of the theatre of text are two fundamental components of theatrical performance. They are given various names:

1. *Visual*: acting, iconicity of the stage, stage design, stage images;
2. *Textual*: dramatic and textual language, symbolization, system of arbitrary signs.

Although it is clear that the mise-en-scène is an encounter between text and stage, that it is the text placed in a situation of enunciation, the reciprocal properties of the two systems are less well known. From LESSING's analyses of painting and poetry (cf. *Laokoon*, 1766) to JAKOBSON's systematization of visual and auditory signs (1971), comparison brings out the oppositions outlined below. They are major trends rather than absolute oppositions, for in the heat of the moment we are naturally incapable of determining the semiotic mode of each sign; hence the impression of the *spectacle* as a totality and synthesis of the arts (*Gesamtkunstwerk**).

1. Table of Oppositions

Visual	Textual
Principle of simultaneity	Principle of successivity
Figures and colours in space	Sounds articulated in time
Spatial contiguity	Temporal continuity
Possible permanence of the image	Fleeting nature of the text
Direction communication by ostension	Communication mediated by a narrator (actor), by a system of arbitrary signs
Ease in distinguishing visual indexes	Difficulty of distinguishing auditory indexes
Possibility of a description of objects	Possibility of a narration of episodes
Referent simulated by the stage (confused with the signifier)	Referent symbolized and imaginary
Possibility of anchoring in the visual signifieds from the text	Possibility of explanations of the text using visual elements
Immediate indications concerning situation of enunciation	Situation of enunciation to be reconstructed
Difficulty of verbalizing the visual sign	Difficulty of differentializing (concretizing) the text

2. Mediation of Voice

The actor is a "speaking image." Sometimes the text is "illustrated" by an image, sometimes it cannot be understood without the "legend" of a text. The synchronization is so perfect that we even forget we are in the presence of two modes of meaning production and can easily go from one to the other (VELTRUSKÝ 1941, 1977; PAVIS 1976a). The staging is a fine-tuning of textual and visual elements, the realization that this synchronization, trite and obvious in reality, is in theatre the effect of an art. The actor's physical presence monopolizes the audience's attention and prevails over the intangible meaning of the text: "In theatre, the sign created by the actor, owing to its subjugating reality, tends to monopolize the audience's attention at the expense of the intangible meanings conveyed by the linguistic sign. It tends to deflect attention from the text to its vocal realization, from speeches to physical actions and even to the physical appearance of the stage character

[...] Since the semiotics of language and the semiotics of acting are diametrically opposed as to their fundamental characteristics, there is a dialectical tension between the dramatic text and the actor, based primarily on the fact that the acoustical components of the linguistic sign constitute an integral part of the vocal resources available to the actor" (VELTRUSKÝ 1977, 15).

3. Reading Action

The staging is a *reading in action*: the dramatic text has no individual reader but a *possible reading*, the result of a "concretization" of text and performance. The reading of the staging and the dramatic text is therefore taken over by the various enunciators (actor, stage designer, light designer). The staging is always a parable about the impossible exchange between the verbal and the non-verbal. The non-verbal (i.e. the performance's representation and choice of a situation of enunciation) makes the verbal speak, duplicates its enunciation, as if the dramatic text, once *uttered* on stage, could succeed in speaking in itself without rewriting another text, through the obvious quality of what is said and what is shown. For the staging *speaks* by showing, says without saying, so that denial (FREUD's *Verneinung*) is its customary mode of existence. The staging, no matter how simple and explicit, "displaces" the text; it makes the text say what a critical text could not: it is, literally, *unspeakable*.

The relationship between the visual and textual is always "tense," particularly in the "new theatre," for the eye and the ear react differently to stimuli: "Words are addressed to the ear, plastics to the eye. In this way, the imagination works under the impact of two impressions, one visual and the other auditory. And what distinguishes the old theatre from the new is that in the latter plastics and words are each subject to their own rhythm and divorced even from the occasion." (MEYERHOLD 1973, 117).

See also: text and performance, theatrical sign, staging, situation of enunciation, inner space, semiology.

Further reading: Francastel 1970; Lyotard 1971; Freud 1976; Leroi-Gourhan 1974; Lindekens 1976; Barthes 1982; Gauthier 1982; Pavis 1996a.

VOICE

Fr.: *voix*; Ger.: *Stimme*; Sp.: *voz*.

The actor's voice is the last step before reception of text and performance by the spectator. That fact determines both its importance in establishing sense and affect and the difficulties we experience in trying to describe and evaluate it and grasp its effects.

1. The "Grain of the Voice": Phonic Criteria

The voice, that "intimate signature of the actor" (BARTHES), is first of all, a physical quality that is difficult to analyze except as the actor's *presence**, as an effect produced on the hearer.

Pitch, intensity, timbre and coloration are purely material factors, and therefore hardly subject to the actor's control. They enable us to identify the character immediately and at the same time have a direct sensorial influence on our sensibilities. ARTAUD, in describing his "theatre of cruelty," was in fact describing any enunciation of a text in theatre: "In this spectacle the sonorisation is constant: sounds, noises, cries are chosen first for their vibratory quality, then for what they represent" (1964b, 124; Eng. 1958, 81); "words will be construed in an incantational, truly magical sense – for their shape and their sensuous emanations, not only for their meaning" (1964b, 189; Eng. 1958, 125). Voice is an extension of body in space.

In theatre, perhaps more than in the everyday message, the voice's materiality is never effaced entirely for the sake of the text's meaning. The "grain of the voice" (BARTHES 1973a) is a message that is anterior to expression/communication (an accent, an intonation, a psychological coloration). There is nothing intentional or expressive in it, but rather an "erotic mix of timbre and language, [which] may therefore be, like diction, the raw material of an art: the art of handling one's body (hence its importance in Far Eastern theatres)" (1973a, 104).

The voice is the junction of the body and articulate language. It is a mediation between pure uncodable corporality and the textuality inherent in discourse, "the area in between body and discourse" (BERNARD 1976, 353), "constant oscillation, a dual movement in tension and a search for corporal resonance that jointly aims to surpass it in a meaning to be communicated to others" (358). The voice is therefore located at a point of junction or dialectical tension between body and text, acting and linguistic signs. Through his voice, the actor is simultaneously pure physical presence and the bearer of a system of linguistic signs. In him the language becomes body and *body** becomes system.

2. Prosodic Evaluation

A. INTONATION

Intonation governs pitch and stress. The actor's voice also carries the message of *intonation**, stress and rhythm. The intonation indicates right away (even before the meaning arises) the speaker's *attitude**, his position within the group, his social *gestus**. It modalizes the utterances by casting them in a very subtle light, hence the well-known test that consists in having actors perform in various situation, saying the same words in a different tone (see JAKOBSON 1963, 215). The intonation indicates the speaker's position in respect of his utterances, and expresses their modality, particularly emotion, volition, belief in utterance, etc. As shown by BAKHTIN, it also expresses contact with the listener, relationships with others, an assessment of the situation; hence its strategic value: "Intonation is always found at the border between the verbal and the non-verbal, what is said and what is left unsaid. In intonation, discourse enters into immediate contact with life." (quoted in TODOROV, 1981:74).

Intonation concerns the utterance as much as the enunciation, the meaning of the text as much as that of the actor's work, semantics as much as pragmatics.

B. THEATRICALIZATION

Directors like LEMAHIEU, VILLÉGIER, VITEZ (cf. his four productions of MOLIERE plays) or MNOUCHKINE (the SHAKESPEARE cycle) endeavour to theatricalize the actor's voice by avoiding effects of natural speech, psychology or expressiveness and by stressing or pacing the text according to an autonomous rhetoric having its own laws, which treat the text as phonic material, showing clearly the localization of the word in the body and its enunciation as a *gestus** that affects the whole body. It is up to the listener to let his thoughts float, like a psychoanalyst listening to an analysand, to better understand what this new *declamation** can say about the desires of the actor and of the character performed before us.

C. MATERIALITY

Voice possesses a certain "thickness" and conveys the actor's corporality. A sense of rhythm, spatialization of discourse, polyphony of words: all of this lends the voice its grain and theatricality.

D. ANALYSIS

Without using the scientific methods of phonetics, analysis at least endeavours to identify the effects of a fast or slow pace, frequency, duration and function of pauses, the physical aspects of language, pointing up breathing groups and melodic line, the existence of "rhythmic frameworks" (GARCÍA MARTÍNEZ, 1995), the way the actor invests his body in the text.

Further reading: Trager 1958; Veltrusky 1941, 1977; *Traverses*, 1980; R. Durand 1980b; Finter 1981, 1990; Meschonnic 1982; Barthes 1981, 1982, 217–277; Cornut 1983; Zumthor 1983; Fonagy 1983; Bernard 1986; Castarède 1987; J. Martin 1991; García-Martínez 1995.

VOICE OFF

This is a term borrowed from cinema, where it refers to a voice from out of shot, as distinguished from *voice over*, where a voice is heard that does not belong to any of the (visible or invisible) characters of the fiction, but rather a narrator who may be outside or inside the fiction.

In theatre, voice (as well as music, sound effects and the sound track) may be carried over loudspeakers rather than coming from actors on stage. *Voice off* in these circumstances is not the voice of a character in the fiction or an actor in the play who is invisible to the spectator, but from outside the fiction, embodied by the director, the author in his stage directions, a narrator commenting on the action on stage, a character who is heard and whose thoughts or interior monologue are imagined by another character.

By dissociating voice from an identifiable body and making it heard through non-body means, a staging may introduce uncertainty about its origin and about the speaker.

VOICE STAGING

Fr.: *mise en voix*; Ger.: *Sprachregie.*
See READING, PERFORMANCE

VULGAR

Fr.: *poissard;* Ger.: *vulgär*; Sp.: *vulgar.*
See PARADE

WALK-ONS

Fr.: *figurant*; Ger.: *Statist, stumme Nebenrolle*; Sp.: *figurante.*

Actors with secondary roles, usually with no lines, who come on stage as an anonymous crowd, a social group, servants or technicians disguised as characters in the play.

WELL-MADE PLAY

Fr.: *pièce bien faite*; Ger.: *well-made play*; Sp.: *obra bien hecha.*

1. Origins

Name given in the nineteenth century to a play characterized by the perfectly logical arrangement of its action. Both the expression and the play itself are attributed to E. SCRIBE (1791–1861). Other authors (SARDOU, LABICHE, FEYDEAU, even IBSEN) have constructed their plays by the same recipe. But beyond this historically placed "school of composition," the well-wrought play describes a prototype of post-Aristotelian dramaturgy that recalls the closed-structure drama; it has become synonymous with a play whose "strings" are sufficiently coarse and numerous to be identified.

2. Techniques of Composition

The first commandment is the continuous, tight and gradual unfolding of the motifs of the action. Even if the plot is very complicated (cf. SCRIBE's *Adrienne Lecouvreur*), the *suspense** must be maintained without fail. The curve of the action shows ups and downs and a series of cases of mistaken identity and *coups de théâtre**. The objective is clear; to keep the spectator alert and play on naturalistic illusion.

The dramatic material is arranged according to very precise rules. The exposition discreetly prepares the way for the play and its conclusion; each act comprises a rise in the action punctuated by a period. The story culminates in a central scene in which the various threads of the action are brought together, revealing and resolving the central conflict. This is the opportunity for the playwright (or his delegate, the *raisonneur**) to come up with some brilliant formulas or profound thoughts. It is the indicator of ideology *par excellence*, which takes the form of inoffensive general truths.

No matter how original and shocking the theme, it should not be problematic or propose a philosophy to the audience that would be foreign to it. *Identification** and *verisimilitude** are the golden rules.

The well-wrought play is a mould into which the events are poured systematically through the mechanical application of a scheme borrowed from the outdated neoclassical mould. The well-wrought play is the result and probably the (unknowingly parodic) "achievement" of classical tragedy. A genre attacked by the naturalists (ZOLA and others), it influenced playwrights like SHAW and IBSEN.

It is not surprising, then, that the well-made play, in spite of the apparent compliment in its name, has become the prototype of trivial dramaturgy and unimaginative technique, the symbol of an abstract formalism. It still used to good advantage, however, by the writers of *boulevard** theatre and television soap operas.
Further reading: Zola 1881 ("*Polémique*"); Shaw 1937; Taylor 1967; Ruprecht 1976; Szondi 1956.

WOMEN'S THEATRE

Fr.: *théâtre des femmes;* Ger.: *Frauentheater;* Sp.: *teatro de las mujeres.*

This term, implying a theatre made by women with specifically feminine themes, is appropriate to our times, with the past thirty years of an active feminist movement ("*feminisme diffus*," *Études théâtrales*, 1995:138). The question remains, however, whether it is possible to infer the principles governing specifically feminine dramatic writing or stage practice. Any generalization tends to be overly simplistic and easily refuted.

1. Feminine Dramatic Writing
Does the difference between the sexes result in a difference in thinking or feeling, in reading or choosing certain themes, in structuring plays, in attributing a particular purpose to the act of writing? The answer is an ambiguous one: yes, there is a difference, but it is difficult to perceive and generalize. Sieghild BOGUMIL believes there is "a different way of perceiving things that is reflected in a certain discrepancy in the actual writing. The differences are subtle ones and not sufficient to make a clear distinction between feminine writing and masculine writing" (*Études théâtrales*, op. cit., 149). This honest and humble statement about the difficult of pinpointing the feminine voice allows us to put forward only a few uncertain hypotheses:

- Themes in women's theatre tend to be more concrete and local, rather than abstract, general and universal as in men "thinkers."
- Dramatic structure is closer to the anecdotic, the fragmentary, life lived, feeling (N. SARRAUTE).
- The purpose attributed to writing is more conrete and more modest than among writers who aspire to major summations and universality.

These are extremely weak hypotheses, and are rejected by many women writers, who believe that "historical, political and social context is a more 'relevant' feature, in the words of linguists, than sex" (M. FABIEN Ibid, 27). Writing, for many, is much more decisive than masculine or feminine gender: "When I write, I am neither man nor woman, neither dog nor cat" (N. SARRAUTE).

Dramatic writing places a dilemma before women: to do like everyone else, i.e. like men, or to find their own voice. But is not every artist's voice mute, displaced, uncomfortable, persecuted or tolerated, just like the feminine condition? Hence the urgency of rethinking at least how women are represented in theatre, by authors as different and talented as Simone BENMUSSA, Hélène CIXOUS, Marguerite DURAS, Friederike ROTH.

2. Feminine Staging
It may be that a feminine way of making theatre is more easily observable in the concrete work of preparing for a performance, directing actors, and staging a play. Ways of relating to authority, the law, and metaphysical notions such as genius or inspiration differ quite clearly between the sexes as a result of conventional division of tasks. Directing actors – as long as male actors agree to be judged or directed by one or more women – allows a woman director to rethink all the traditional roles between the male director-Pygmalion and his actress-statue creation. Only a woman like Brigitte JACQUES, perhaps, in her *Elvire-Jouvet 40*, could understand the strange sadomasochistic but also perfectionist and generous relationship that ties a director to his actresses. Only a feminine sensibility like that of Ea SOLA or Gilberte TSAÏ can uncover the daily poetic gestures

of Vietnamese and Chinese women. Only H. CIXOUS and A. MNOUCHKINE have been able to render the feminine atmosphere, sweet and selfless, that held sway at the Khmer court of Sihanouk and the Indian administrations of Gandhi and Nehru.

To what extent can we formalize that working relationship and relate it to role sharing between the sexes? Drawing a distinction between paternal and maternal relationships is not quite convincing (Ibid., 121), nor is reapportioning roles based on the stereotypes associated with each sex. It would seem much more instructive to look at the image and representation of women (and men) conveyed by texts, productions, and the working methods of artists, both male and female.

Further reading: Bassnett in Schmid 1984; Féral 1984; Savona 1984; Miller 1994.

Special issues: *TheaterZeitSchrift*, no. 9–10 (1984); *Women in Performance: a Journal of Feminist Theory*, New York University; *Western European Stages*, vol. 7, no. 3 (1996) ("Contemporary Women Directors"); *Études théâtrales*, no. 8 (1995).

WORD SCENERY

Fr.: *décor verbal;* Ger.: *Wortkulisse;* Sp.: *decorado verbal.*

Scenery which is described or suggested not by visual means but through a character's commentary (cf. Rosalind in *As You Like It*, "Well, this is the Forest of Arden," act II, scene 4). The word scenery technique is only possible by virtue of a *convention** accepted by the spectator that allows him to imagine the scenery and the immediate change from one place to another as announced. In SHAKESPEARE, we can easily go from an exterior to an interior, from forest to castle. The scenes succeed each other without anything being supplied other than a simple spatial indication or an exchange of words evoking a different place. Modern theatre, having largely renounced realistic scenery, often uses verbal scenery, but in an epic fashion, i.e. without taking the trouble to provide a motivation for the description in a character's situation.

Further reading: Honzl 1940; Styan 1967; Elam 1977.

Bibliography

ABEL, L. 1963. *Metatheatre: A New View of Dramatic Form*. New York: Hill and Wang.

ABIRACHED, R. (1978) 1994. *La crise du personnage dans le théâtre moderne*. Paris: Grasset. Revised 1994.

– 1992. *Le théâtre et le prince*. Paris: Plon.

ABRAHAM, F. 1933. *Le physique au théâtre*. Paris: Coutan-Lambert.

Acteurs. 1989. No. 68 ('Les écoles de théâtre').

ADAM, J.-M. 1976. *Linguistique et discours littéraire*. Paris : Larousse.

– 1984. *Le récit*. Paris: PUF.

ADAMOV, A. 1964. *Ici et maintenant*. Paris: Gallimard.

ADORNO, T.W. 1970 *Ästhetiche Theorie*. Frankfurt: Suhrkamp.

– 1984. *Aesthetic Theory*. Trans. of 1970 by C. Lenhardt. London: Routledge & K. Paul.

ALCANDRE, J.-J. 1986. *Écriture dramatique et pratique scénique: Les brigands sur la scène allemande des XVIIIe et XIXe siècles*. 2 vols. Bern: Lang.

ALEXANDRESCU, S. 1984. 'Spectacle et spectaculaire.' *Kodikas/code* 7, no. 1–2.

ALIVERTI, I, ed. 1985. *Quaderni di Teatro*, no. 28 ('Rittratto d'amore').

ALLEVY, M.-A. 1938. *La mise en scène en France dans la première moitié de XIXe siècle*. Paris: Droz.

ALLIO, R. 1977. 'De la machine à jouer au paysage mental.' Interview with J.-P. Sarrazac. *Travail théâtral*, no. 28–29.

ALTER, J. 1975. 'Vers le mathématexte au théâtre: En codant Godot.' In HELBO 1975.

– 1981. 'From Text to Performance.' *Poetics Today* 2, no. 3.

– 1982. 'Performance and Performance: On the Margin of Theatre Semiotics.' *Degrés*, no. 30.

Alternatives théâtrales. 1994. No. 45.

ALTHUSSER, L. 1965. 'Notes sur un théâtre matérialiste.' In *Pour Marx*. Paris: Maspéro.

– 1970. *For Marx*. Trans. B. Brewster. London: Verso.

AMIARD-CHEVREL, C. 1979. *Le théâtre artistique de Moscou*. Paris: CNRS.

– 1983, ed. *Du cirque au théâtre*. Lausanne: L'Âge d'homme.

AMOSSY, R. 1981. 'Towards a Rhetoric of the Stage: Scenic Realization of Verbal Cliché.' *Poetics Today* 2, no. 3.

– 1981, ed. *Poetics Today* 2, no. 3 ('Drama, Theater, Performance: A Semiotic Perspective').

– 1982. *Les discours du cliché*. Paris: SEDES.

ANCELIN-SCHUTZENBERGER, A. 1970. *Précis du psychodrame*. Paris: Éditions universitaires.

ANDERSON, M., ed. 1965. *Classical Drama and Its Influence*. London: Methuen.

ANGENOT, M. 1979. *Glossaire pratique de la critique contemporaine*. Montréal: Hurtubise.

ANGIOLILLO, M.L. 1989. *Storia del costume teatrale in Europa*. Rome: Lucarini.

Annuel du théâtre, L. (ed. J.-P. SARRAZAC). 1981–1982 season, 1982–1983 season, Meudon.

ANTOINE, A. 1903. 'Causerie sur la mise en scène.' *Revue de Paris*, 1 avril.

– 1979. *Le théâtre libre*. Paris: Slatkine Reprints.

APPIA, A. 1895. *La mise en scène du drame wagnérien*. Paris: Léon Chailley.

– (1899) 1963. *La musique et la mise en scène*. Berne: Société Suisse du théâtre.

– 1921. *L'œuvre d'art vivant*. Paris: Atar-Billaudot.

– 1954. 'Acteur, espace, lumière, peinture.' *Théâtre populaire*, no. 5 (janvier-février).

– 1982. *Actor, Space, Light*. Eds. D. Bablet and M.L. Bablet. London: John Calder; New York: Riverrun Press.

– 1983–1992. *Œuvres complètes*. 4 vols. Lausanne: L'Âge d'homme.

ARISTOTLE. (330 B.C.) 1982. *Poetics*. Trans. James Hutton. New York: W.W. Norton.

ARMEGAUD, F. 1985. *La pragmatique*. Paris: PUF.

ARNOLD, P. 1946. *Frontières du théâtre*. Paris: Éditions du Pavois.

– 1947. *L'avenir du théâtre*. Paris: Éditions Savel.

– 1951. 'Éléments de l'art dramatique.' *Journal de psychologie normale et pathologique* (janvier–juin).

– 1957. Le *théâtre japonais – Nô-Kabuaki – Shimpa-Shingeki*. Paris: L'Arche.

– 1974. *Le théatre japonais aujourd'hui*. Bruxelles: La Renaissance du livre.

ARRIVÉ, M. 1973. 'Pour une théorie des textes polyisotopiques.' *Langages*, no. 31.

Art Press. 1989.

ARTAUD, A. (1938) 1964b. *Le théâtre et son double*. Paris: Gallimard.

– 1958. *The Theater and its Double*. Trans. of 1964b. by Mary Caroline Richards. New York: Grove Press.

– 1964a. *Œuvres complètes*. Paris: Gallimard.

ARTIOLO, U. 1972. *Teorie della scena – dal naturalismo al surrealismo. I: De Meininger a Craig*. Firenze: Sansoni.

ASLAN, O. 1963. *L'art du théâtre: anthologie de textes*. Paris: Seghers.

– 1974. *L'acteur au XXe siècle*. Paris: Seghers.

– 1977. ' L'improvisation, approche d'un jeu créateur.' *Revue d'ésthétique*, no. 1–2.

– 1993. *Le corps en jeu*. Paris: CNRS.

ASLAN, O., and D. BABLET, eds. 1985. *Le masque: du rite au théâtre*. Paris: CNRS.

ASTON, G., et al. 1983. *Interazione, dialogo, convenzioni: Il caso dil testo drammatico*. Bologna: Clueb.

ATTINGER, G. 1950. *L'esprit de la commedia dell'arte dans le théâtre français*. Paris: Librairie théâtrale.

ATTOUN, L. 1988. *Le théâtre ouvert à livre ouvert 1971-1988*. n.p.: Rato diffusion.

AUBERT, C. 1901. *L'art mimique*. Paris: E. Meuriot.

AUBIGNAC, F.-H., abbé D' (1657) 1927. *La pratique du théâtre*. Paris: Champion.

AUBRUN, C. 1966. *La comédie espagnole*. Paris: PUF.

AUERBACH, E. 1953. *Mimesis: The Representation of Reality in Western Literature*. Trans. Willard R. Trask. Princeton, NJ: Princeton University Press. Originally published in German, 1946.

AUSTIN, J. L. 1962. *How To Do Things with Words*. Oxford: Oxford University Press.

AUTRAND, M. 1977. Le Cid *et la classe de français*. Paris: CEDIC.

AVIGAL, S. 1980. *Les modalités du dialogue dans la discours théâtral*. Thesis, 3^d^ cycle, Université de Paris 3.

– 1981. 'What Do Brook's Bricks Mean? Towards a Theory of "Mobility" of Objects in Theatrical Discourse.' *Poetics Today* 2, no. 3.

AVIGAL, S., and S. WEITZ. 1985. 'The Gamble of Theatre: From an Implied Spectator to the Actual Audience.' *Poetics Today*, vol. 6

AZIZA, C., C. OLIVIERI, and R. SCTRICK. 1978a. *Dictionnaire des symboles et des thèmes littéraires*. Paris: Nathan.

– 1978b. *Dictionnaire des types et des caractères littéraires*. Paris: Nathan.

BABLET, D. 1960. 'Le mot décor est périmé.' *Revue d'esthétique* XIII: 1.

– 1962. *Edward Gordon Craig*. Paris: L'Arche.

– 1965. *Le décor de théâtre de 1870 à 1914*. Paris: CNRS.

– 1968. *La mise en scène contemporaine*. Bruxelles: La Renaissance du livre.

– 1972. 'Pour une méthode d'analyse du lieu théâtral.' *Travail théâtral*, no. 6.

– 1973. 'L'éclairage et le son dans l'espace théâtral.' *Travail théâtral*, no. 13, (octobre–décembre).

– 1975. *Les révolutions scéniques au XXe siècle*. Paris: Société internationale d'art XXe siècle.

– 1978. *Collage et montage au théâtre et dans les autres arts durant les années vingt*. Lausanne: La Cité.

BABLET, D., and C. JACQUOT. 1971. *L'expressionisme dans le théâtre européen*. Paris: CNRS.

BACHELARD, G. 1957. *La poétique de l'espace*. Paris: PUF.

BADENHAUSEN, R., and H. ZIELSKE, eds. 1972. *Bühnenformen, Bühnenräume, Bühnendekorationen*. Berlin: E. Schmidt.

BADIOU, A. 1969. *Le concept de modèle*. Paris: Maspéro.

BAKHTIN, M. (1929) 1970. *La poétique de Dostoievski*. Trans. Isabelle Kolitcheff. Paris: Le Seuil. Originally published in Russian.

– 1973. *Problems of Dostoevsky's poetics*. Trans. R.W. Rotsel. Ann Arbor, MI: Ardis.

– (1965) 1971. *L'œuvre de François Rabelais et la culture populaire au Moyen Âge et sous la Renaissance*. Trans. Andrée Robel. Paris: Gallimard. Originally published in Russian.

– 1984. *Rabelais and His World*. Trans. Hélène Iswolsky. Bloomington: Indiana University Press.

– (1979) 1984. *Ésthétique de la création verbale*. Trans. Alfreda Aucouturier. Paris: Gallimard. Originally published in Russian.

BALCERZAN, E., and Z. OSINSKI. 1966. 'Die teatralische Schaustelung im Lichte der Informationstheorie.' *Zagadnienia Rodzajow Literarckich*, vol. 8, Zeszyt, 2, 15.

BALME, C. 1995. *Theater im postkolonialen Zeitalter*. Tübingen: Niemeyer.

BANHAM, M., ed. 1988. *The Cambridge Guide to World Theatre*. Cambridge: Cambridge University Press.

BANU, G. 1981a. *Bertolt Brecht ou le Petit contre le Grand*. Paris: Aubier-Montaigne.

– 1981b. *Le costume de théâtre dans la mise en scène contemporaine*. Paris: CNDP.

– 1984. *Le théâtre, sorties de secours*. Paris: Aubier.

– 1989. 'Le théâtre art du passé, art du présent.' in *Art Press*.

BANU, G., and A. UBERSFELD. 1979. *L'espace théâtral*. Paris: CNDP.

BAR, F. 1960. *Le genre burlesque en France au XVIIe siècle: Étude de style*. Paris: d'Artrey.

BARBA, E. 1979. *The Floating Islands: Reflections with Odin Teatret*. Trans. Judy Barba, et al. Grasten: Drama.

– 1982a. 'Anthropologie théâtrale.' *Bouffonneries*, no. 4, Jan.

– 1982b. *L'archipel du théâtre*. Paris: Contrastes Bouffoneries.

– 1993. *Le canoë de papier*. Paris: Bouffonneries.

– 1995. *The Paper Canoe: A Guide to Theatre Anthropology*. Trans. of 1993 by Richard Fowler. London: Routledge

BARBA, E., and N. SAVARESE. 1985. *L'anatomie de l'acteur*. Paris: Bouffonneries.

– 1995. *L'énergie qui danse: L'art secret de l'acteur*. Boufonneries, no. 32–33.

BARKER, C. 1977. *Theatre Games: A New Approach to Drama Training*. London: Eyre Methuen.

BARRAULT, J.-L. 1959. *Nouvelles réflexions sur le théâtre*. Paris: Flammarion.

– 1961. *Le phénomène théâtral*. Oxford: Clarendon Press.

BARRET, G. 1973. *Pédagogie de l'expression dramatique*. Montréal: Presses de l'Université de Montréal.

BARRUCAND, D. 1970. *La catharsis dans le théâtre: la psychanalyse et la psychothérapie de groupe*. Paris: Épi.

BARRY, J. 1970. *Dramatic Structure: The Shaping of Experience*. BERKELEY: University of California Press.

BARTHES, R. 1953. *Le degré zéro de l'écriture*. Paris: Le Seuil.

– 1957. *Mythologies*. Paris: Le Seuil.

– 1963. *Sur Racine*. Paris: Le Seuil.

– 1964a. *Essais critiques*. Paris: Le Seuil.

– 1964b. *On Racine*. Trans. of 1963 by Richard Howard. New York: Hill and Wang.

– 1966a. 'Introduction à l'analyse structurale des récits.' *Communications*, no. 8. Also in TODOROV and GENETTE. 1977, 7–57.

– 1966b. *Critique et vérité*. Paris: Le Seuil.

– 1967. *Writing Degree Zero*. Trans. of 1953 by Annette Lavers and Colin Smith. London: J. Cape.

– 1970. S/Z. Paris: Le Seuil.

– 1971. 'De l'œuvre au texte.' *Revue d'esthétique*, no. 3.

– 1972a. *Critical essays*. Trans. of 1964a by Richard Howard. Evanston, IL: Northwestern University Press

– 1972b. *Mythologies*. Trans. of 1957 by Annette Lavers. New York: Hill and Wang.

– 1973a. *Le plaisir du texte*. Paris: Le Seuil

– 1973b. 'Diderot, Brecht, Eisenstein.' *Revue d'Ésthétique* 26, nos. 2–4. Also in BARTHES 1982.

– 1975. *Roland Barthes par Roland Barthes*. Paris: Le Seuil.

– 1976. *The Pleasure of the Text*. Trans. of 1973a by Richard Miller. London: J. Cape.

– 1978a. *La leçon*. Paris: Le Seuil.

– 1978b. *Prétexte: Roland Barthes*. Colloque de Cerisy. Paris: UGE.

– 1981. *Le grain de la voix*. Paris: Le Seuil.

– 1982. *L'obvie et l'obtus: Essais critiques III*. Paris: Le Seuil.

– 1984. *Le bruissement de la langue*. Paris: Le Seuil.

– 1986. *The Rustle of Language*. Trans. of 1984 by Richard Howard. New York: Hill and Wang.

– 1987. *Criticism and truth*. Trans. of 1966b by Katrine Pilcher Keuneman. Minneapolis: University of Minnesota Press

– 1991. *The Grain of the Voice: Interviews, 1962–1980*. Trans. of 1981 by Linda Coverdale. Berkeley: University of California Press.

– 1994. *Roland Barthes by Roland Barthes*. Trans. of 1975 by Richard Howard. Berkeley: University of California Press.

BARTHES, R., L. BERSANI, PH. HAMON, M. RIFFATERRE, and I. WATT. 1982. *Littérature et réalité*. Paris: Le Seuil.

BARTOLUCCI, G. 1968. *La scrittura scenica*. Roma: Lerici.

BARTOLUCCI, G., and G. URSIC. 1977. *Teatro-Provocazione*. Venezia: Marsilio Editori.

BASSNETT, S. 1980. 'An Introduction to Theater Semiotics.' *Theater Quarterly*, no. 38.

BATAILLE, A. 1990. *Lexique de la machinerie théâtrale à l'intention des praticiens et des amateurs*. Paris: Librairie théâtrale.

BATAILLON, M. 1972. 'Les finances de la dramaturgie.' *Travail théâtral*, no.7.

BATTCOCK, G., and R. NICKAS. 1984. *The Art of Performance: A Critical Anthology*. New York: Dutton.

BAUDELAIRE, C. 1951. *Œuvres complètes*. Paris: Gallimard. Particularly 'De l'essence du rire' (1855) and 'R. Wagner et Tannhäuser' (1861).

BAUDRILLARD, J. 1968. *Le système des objets*. Paris: Gonthier.

BAZIN, A. 1959. *Qu'est-ce que le cinéma*. Paris: Éditions du Cerf.

BEAUCHAMP, H. 1984. *Les enfants et le jeu dramatique: Apprivoiser le théâtre*. Bruxelles: A. de Boeck.

BEAUMARCHAIS, J.-P. DE, D. COUTY, and A. REY. (1984) 1994. *Dictionnaire des littératures de langue française*. 4 vols. Paris: Bordas.

BECK, J. 1972. *The Life of the Theatre*. San Francisco: City Lights.

BECKERMAN, B. 1970. *Dynamics of Drama*. New York: Alfred A. Knopf.

– 1979. 'Theatrical perception.' *Theatre Research International* 4, no. 3.

BECQ DE FOUQUIÈRES, L. 1881. *Traité de diction et de lecture à haute voix*: Paris: Charpentier.

– 1884. *L'art de la mise en scène: Essai d'esthétique théâtrale*. Paris: Charpentier.

BÉHAR, H. 'Le théâtre expérimental.' *Littérature*, no. 30.

BEHLER, E. 1970. 'Der Ursprung des Begriffs der tragischen Ironie.' *Arcadia* 5, Heft 2.

BELLMAN, W.F. 1977. *Scenography and Stage Technology*. New York: Crowell.

BELLOUR, R., and C. CLÉMENT, eds. 1979. *Claude Lévi-Strauss: Textes de et sur Claude Lévi-Strauss*. Paris: Gallimard.

BENHAMOU, A.-F. 1981. Britannicus *par le Théâtre de la Salamandre*. Paris: Solin.

BENHAMOU, M. 1988. 'Méandres d'un enseignement atypique.' *Théâtre/public*, no. 82–83.

BENHAMOU, M., and C. CARAMELLO, eds. 1977. *Performance in Postmodern Culture*. Madison, WI: Coda Press.

BÉNICHOU, P. 1948. *Morales du Grand Siècle*. Paris: Gallimard.

BENJAMIN, W. 1928. *Ursprung des deutschen Trauerspiel*. Berlin: E. Rowohlt.

– 1968. *Illuminations*. Trans. Harry Zohn. New York: Schocken Books.

– 1969. *Écrits sur Bertolt Brecht*. Paris: Maspéro.

– 1977. *The Origins of German Tragic Drama*. Trans. of 1928 by John Osborne. London: Verso.

– 1983. *Understanding Brecht*. Trans. of 1969 by Anna Bostock. London: Verso.

– 1985. *Origine du drame baroque allemand*. Trans. of 1928. Paris: Flammarion.

BENMUSSA, S. 1971. 'Le théâtre des metteurs en scène.' *Cahiers Renaud-Barrault*, no. 74.

– 1974. 'La déréalisation par la mise en scène.' In VERNOIS, 1974.

– 1977. 'Travail de scène; travail de rêve.' *Revue d'esthétique*, no. 1–2.

BENNET, T. 1979. *Formalism and Marxism*. London: Methuen.

BENSKY, R.-D. 1971. *Recherches sur les structures et la symbolique de la marionnette*. Paris: Nizet.

BENTLEY; E. 1957. *In Search of Theatre*. New York: Vintage Books.

– 1964. *The Life of the Drama*. New York: Atheneum.

BENVENISTE, E. 1966, 1974. *Problèmes de linguistique générale*. 2 vols. Paris: Gallimard.

BERG, J., and H. RISCHBIETER. 1985. *Welttheater*. Westermann: Braunschweig.

BERGALA, A. [1977?] *Initiation a la sémiologie du récit en images*. Paris: Les Cahiers de l'audio-visuel.

BERGEZ, D., V. GÉRAUD, and J.-J. ROBRIEUX. 1994. *Vocabulaire de l'analyse littéraire*. Paris: Dunod.

BERGMAN, G. 1964. 'Der Eintritt des Berufsregisseurs in das französische Theater.' *Maske und Kothurn*, no. 3–4.

– 1966. 'Der Eintritt des Berufsregisseurs in die deutschsprachige Bühne.' *Maske und Kothurn*, no. 12.

– 1977. *Lighting in the Theatre*. Stockholm: Almqvist et Wiksell International.

BERGSON, H. (1899) 1940. *Le rire: Essai sur la signification du comique*. Paris: PUF.

– 1911. *Laughter: An Essay on the Meaning of the Comic*. Trans. C. Brereton and F. Rothwell. London: n.p.

BERNARD, J.-J. 1922. 'Le silence au théâtre.' *La chimère*, no. 5.

BERNARD, M. 1976. *L'expressivité du corps*. Paris: J.-P. Delarge.

– 1977. 'Les mythes de l'improvisation théâtrale ou les travestissements d'une théâtralité normalisée.' *Revue d'esthétique*, no. 1–2.

– 1980. 'La voix dans le masque et le masque dans la voix.' *Traverses*, no. 20.

– 1986. 'Esquisse d'une théorie de la théâtralité d'un texte en vers à partir de l'exemple racinien.' In J. SCHERER 1986.

BERNARDY, M. 1988. *Le jeu verbal ou traité de diction française àl'usage de l'honnête homme*. Paris: Éditions de l'Aube.

BERRY, C. 1973. *Voice and the Actor*. London: Harrap.

BETTETINI, G. 1975. *Produzione del senso e messa in scena*. Milano: Bompiani.

Biblioteca teatrale. 1978. No. 20 ('Drama/Spettacolo').

BICKERT, H. 1969. *Studien zum Problem der Exposition im Drama der tektonischen Bauform*. Marburger Beitrage zur Germanistik, vol. 23.

BIRDWHISTELL, R. 1973. *Kinesics and Context Essays on Body-Motion Communication*. London: Penguin University Press.

BLANCHART, P. 1948. *Histoire de la mise en scène*. Paris: PUF.

BLOCH, E. 1973. '*Entfremdung et Verfremdiung*, aliénation et distanciation.' *Travail théâtral*, no. 11 (printemps).

BLÜHER, K. 1971. 'Die französischen Theorien des Dramas im 20. Jahrhundert.' In *Das moderne französische Drama*, ed. W. Pabst. Berlin: E. Schmidt Verlag.

BOAL, A. 1974. *Teatro del oprimado y otras poéticas políticas*. Buenos Aires: Edicionas de la Flor.

– 1977. *Théâtre de l'opprimé*. Trans. of 1974 by Dominique Lemann. Paris: Maspéro.

– 1979. *Theatre of the Oppressed*. Trans. of 1974 by Charles A. and Maria-Odilia Leal McBride. New York: Urizen Books.

– 1990. *Méthode Boal de théâtre et de thérapie*. Paris: Ramsay.

– 1995. *The Rainbow of Desire: The Boal Method of Theatre and Therapy*. Trans. of 1990 by Adrian Jackson. London: Routledge.

BODKIN, M. 1934. *Archetypal Patterns in Poetry*. Oxford: Oxford University Press.

BOGATYREV, P. 1938. 'Semiotics in the Folk Theatre' and 'Forms and Fonctions of Folk Theatre.' In MATEJKA 1976.

– 1971. 'Les signes au théâtre.' *Poétique*, no. 8.

BOILEAU-DESPREAUX, N. 1966. *L'art poétique*. Paris: Union générale d'éditions

BOLL, A. 1971. *Le théâtre total: Étude polémique*. Paris: O. Perrin.

BOLLACK, J., and M. BOLLACK. 1986. *Commentaire et traduction de Œdipe Roi*. 3 vols. Lille: Presses universitaires de Lille.

BONNAT, Y. 1982. *L'éclairage des spectacles*. Paris: Librairie théâtrale.

BOOTH, W. 1961. *The Rhetoric of Fiction*. Chicago: University of Chicago Press.

– 1974. *The Rhetoric of Irony*. Chicago: University of Chicago Press.

– 1977. 'Distance et point de vue.' *Poétique du récit*. Paris: Le Seuil. English original in *Essays in Criticism* 11, 1964.

BORGAL, C. 1963. *Metteurs en scène*. Paris: F. Lanore.

BORIE, M. 1980. 'Anthropologia.' In *Enciclopedia del teatro del 1900*. Ed. A. Attisani. Milano: Feltrinelli.

– 1981. *Mythe et théâtre aujourd'hui: Une quête impossible?* Paris: Nizet.

– 1982. 'Théâtre et anthropologie: L'usage de l'autre culture.' *Degrés*, no. 32.

– 1989. *Antonin Artaud: Le théâtre et le retour aux sources*. Paris: Gallimard.

BORIE, M., M. DE ROUGEMONT, and J. SCHERER. 1982. *Esthétique théâtrale: Textes de Platon à Brecht*. Paris: SEDES-CDU.

BOUCHARD, A. (1878) 1982. *La langue théâtrale*. Paris: Slatkine.

BOUCRIS, L. 1993. *L'espace en scène*. Paris: Librairie théâtrale.

Bouffonneries. 1982. No. 4 ('Improvisation. Anthropologie théâtrale').

BOUGNOUX, D. 1982. 'Questions de cadre.' *Journal du Théâtre national de Chaillot*, no. 9 (decembre).

BOUISSAC, P. 1973. *La mesure des gestes: Prolégomènes à la sémiotique gestuelle*. Paris et La Haye: Mouton.

– 1976. *Circus and Culture: A Semiotic Approach*. Paris and The Hague: Mouton.

BOURDIEU, P. 1979. *La distinction: Critique sociale du jugement*. Paris: Minuit.

BOWMAN, W.P., and R.H. BALL. 1961. *Theatre Language: A Dictionary of Terms in English of the Drama and Stage from Medieval to Modern Times*. New York: Theatre Arts Books.

BRACH, J. 1965. 'O znakach literackich i znakach teatralnych.' *Studia Estetyczne*, 2: 241–259.

BRADBROOK, M.C. (1935) 1969. *Themes and Conventions of Elizabethan Tragedy*. London: Cambridge University Press.

BRADBY, D., and D. WILLIAMS. 1988. *Directors' Theatre*. London: Macmillan.

BRAINERD, B., and V. NEUFELDT. 1974. 'On Marcus' Method for the Analysis of the Strategy of a Play.' *Poetics*, no. 10.

BRAUN, E. 1982. *The Direction and the Stage: From Naturalism to Grotowski*. London: Methuen.

– 1995. *Meyerhold: A Revolution in Theatre*. London: Methuen.

BRAUNECK, M. 1982. *Theater im 20. Jahrhundert*. Hamburg: Rowohlt.

– 1992. *Theaterlexikon*. Hamburg: Rowohlt.

BRAY, R. 1927. *La formation de la doctrine classique*. Paris: Nizet.

BRECHT, B. 1951. *Versuche* (25, 26, 35), Heft 11. Frankfurt: Suhrkamp.

– 1963–1970. *Petit organon pour le théâtre* (1948–1954). Paris: L'Arche.

– 1964. *Brecht on Theatre: The Development of an Aesthetic*. Trans. John Willett. London: Methuen.

– 1967. *Gesammelte Werke*. 20 vols. Frankfurt: Suhrkamp Verlag.

– 1972–1979. *Écrits sur le theâtre*. 2 vols. Paris: L'Arche.

– 1976. *Journal de travail*. Paris: L'Arche.

BRECHT, B. et al., eds. 1961. *Teaterarbeit*. Berlin: Henschelverlag.

BRÉMOND, C. 1973. *Logique du récit*. Paris: Le Seuil.

BRENNER, J. 1970. *Les critiques dramatiques*. Paris: Flammarion.

BROOK, P. 1968. *The Empty Space*. London: Mc Gibbon and Kee.

– 1991. *Le diable, c'est l'ennui*. Paris: Actes Sud Papiers.

– 1992. *Points de suspension*. Paris: Le Seuil.

BROOKS, P. 1974. 'Une esthétique de l'étonnement: le mélodrame.' *Poétique*, no. 19.

BRUSAK, K. 1939. 'Signs in the Chinese Theatre.' In MATEKJA and TITUNIK 1976.

BRUYER, R. 1983. *Le visage et l'expression faciale: Approche neuropsychologique*. Bruxelles: P. Mardaga.

BÜCHNER, G. 1965. *Werke und Briefe*. Frankfurt: DTV.

BÜHLER, K. 1934. *Sprachtheorie*. Jena: Fischer.

BURNS, E. 1972. *Theatricality: A Study of Convention in the Theatre and in Social Life*. New York: Harper and Row.

CAGE, J. 1966. *Silence*. Cambridge, MA: MIT Press.

Cahiers de médiologie. 1996. No. 1.

Cahiers du XXe siècle. 1976. No. 6 ('La Parodie').

Cahiers Renaud-Barrault. 1977. No. 96 ('Scène, film, son...': articles by M. Kirby, G. Fink, E. Rohmer, S. Benmussa).

CAILLOIS, R. 1958. *Les jeux et les hommes*. Paris: Gallimard.

CALDERWOOD, J. 1971. *Shakespearean Metadrama*. Minneapolis: University of Minnesota Press.

CALDERWOOD, J., and H. TOLIVER, eds. 1968. *Perspectives on Drama*. Oxford: Oxford University Press.

CAMPBELL, T. 1922. *Hebbel, Ibsen and the Analytic Exposition*. Heidelberg: n.p.

CARLSON, M. 1983. 'The Semiotics of Character in the Drama.' *Semiotica*, no. 44, 3/4.

– 1984. *Theories of the Theatre*. Ithaca, NY: Cornell University Press.

– 1985. 'Semiotic and Nonsemiotic Performance.' *Modern Drama*, Fall.

– 1990. *Theatre Semiotics: Signs of Life*. Bloomington: Indiana University Press.

– 1996. *Performance: A Critical Introduction*. London: Routledge and K. Paul.

CASTARÈDE, M.-F. 1987. *La voix et ses sortilèges*. Paris: Les Belles Lettres.

CAUBÈRE, PH. 1994. *Le roman d'un acteur*. Paris: Losfeld.

CAUNE, J. 1978. 'L'analyse de la représentation théâtrale après Brecht.' *Silex*, no. 7.

– 1981. *La dramatisation*. Louvain: Édition des Cahiers Théâtre Louvain.

CHABERT, P. 1976. 'Le corps comme matériau dans la représentation théâtrale.' Vol. 2 of *Recherches poétiques*. Paris: Klincksieck.

– 1981. 'La création collective dans le théâtre contemporain.' In *La création collective*, ed. R. Passeron. Paris: Clancier-Guénaud.

– 1982. 'Problématique de la répétition dans le théâtre contemporain.' In *Création et répétition*. Paris: Clancier-Guénaud.

CHABROL, C. 1973. *Sémiotique narrative et textuelle*. Paris: Larousse.

CHAIKIN, J. 1972. *The Presence of the Actor*. New York: Atheneum.

CHAILLET, J. 1971. 'Rythme verbal et rythme gestuel: Essai sur l'organisation musicale du temps.' *Journal de psychologie normale et pathologique*, no. 1 (janvier–mars).

CHAMBERS, R. 1971. *La comédie au château*. Paris: Corti.

– 1980. 'Le masque et le miroir: Vers une théorie relationnelle du théâtre.' *Études littéraires* 13, no. 3.

CHANCEREL, L. 1954. *L'art de lire, réciter, parler en public*. Paris: Bourrelier.

Change. 1968. No. 1 ('Le montage').

CHARLES, M. 1977. *Rhétorique de la lecture*. Paris: Le Seuil.

CHEKHOV, M. 1980. *Être acteur*. Paris: Pygmalion.

– 1995. *L'imagination créatrice de l'acteur*. Paris: Pygmalion.

CHEVREL, Y. 1982. *Le naturalisme*. Paris: PUF.

CHIARINI, P. 1970. *Brecht, Lukacs e il realismo*. Bari: Laterza.

– 1971. 'L'écriture scénique brechtienne: Style ou méthode.' *Travail théâtral*, no. 4.

CHION, M. 1990. *L'audio-vision*. Paris: Nathan.

CHRISTOUT, M.-F. 1965. *Le merveilleux et le théâtre du silence en France à partir du XVIIe siècle*. Paris et La Haye: Mouton.

CLARK, B.-H. 1965. *European Theories of the Drama*. New York: Crown Publishers.

CLAUDEL, P. 1983. *Réflexions sur la poésie*. Paris: Gallimard.

Clichés. 1985. No. 11.

COLE, D. 1975. *The Theatrical Event*. Middletown: Wesleyan University Press.

COLE, S. 1992. *Directors in Rehearsal*. London: Routledge and K. Paul.

COLE, T., and H.K. CHINOY, eds. 1970. *Actors on Acting*. New York: Crown Publishers.

COLLET, J., M. MARIE, D. PERCHERON, J.-P. SIMON, and M. VERNET. 1977. *Lecture du film*. Paris: Albatros.

Communications. 1964. No. 11 ('Le vraisemblable').

– 1966. No. 8 ('L'analyse structurale du récit').

– 1983. No. 38 ('Énonciation et cinéma').

COMPAGNON, A. 1979. *La seconde main ou le Travail de la citation*. Paris: Le Seuil.

COPEAU, J. 1955. *Notes sur le métier de comédien*. Paris: Michel Brient.

– 1959. 'Le théâtre populaire.' *Théâtre populaire*, no. 36, 4e trimestre.

– 1974. *Appels I*. Paris: Gallimard.

– 1974–84. *Registres*, I, II, III, IV. Paris: Gallimard.

COPFERMAN, E. 1969. *Roger Planchon*. Lausanne: La Cité.

COPPIETERS, F. 1981. 'Performance and Perception.' *Poetics Today* 2, no. 3.

COPPIETERS, F., and C. TINDEMANS. 1977. 'The Theatre Public: A Semiotic Approach.' In *Das Theater und sein Publikum*. Wien: Institut fur Publikumsforschung, Akademie der Wissenschaft.

CORNEILLE, P. (1660) 1982. 'Discours sur le poème dramatique.' In *Pierre Corneille: trois discours sur le poème dramatique: texte de 1660*. Ed. Louis Forestier. Paris: Société d'Édition d'enseignement supérieur.

CORNUT, G. 1983. *La voix*. Paris: PUF.

CORTI, M. 1976. *Principi della communicazione letteraria*. Milano: Bompiani.

CORVIN, M. 1969. *Le théâtre nouveau en France*. Paris: PUF.

– 1973. *Le théâtre de recherche entre les deux guerres: Le laboratoire art et action*. Lausanne: La Cité.

– 1976. 'Contribution à l'analyse de l'espace scénique dans le théâtre contemporain.' *Travail théâtral*, no. 22 (janvier–mars).

– 1978a. 'Analyse dramaturgique de trois expositions.' *Revue de la Société d'histoire du théâtre*, no. 30.

– 1978b. 'La redondance du signe dans le fonctionnement théâtral.' *Degrés*, no. 13 ('Théâtre et sémiologie').

– 1980. *Sémiologie et théâtre*. Organon. Lyon: Presses universitaires de Lyon.

– 1985. *Molière et ses metteurs en scène d'aujourd'hui: Pour une analyse de la représentation*. Lyon: Presses universitaires de Lyon.

– 1989. *Le théâtre de boulevard*. Paris: PUF.

– 1992. 'Une écriture plurielle.' In *Le Théâtre en France*, ed. J. Jomaron. Paris: Armand Colin.

– 1994. *Lire la comédie*. Paris: Dunod.

– (1991) 1995. *Dictionnaire encyclopédique du théâtre*. 2nd ed. Paris: Bordas.

Cosnier, J. 1977. 'Gestes et conversationnelle.' *Stratégies discursives*. Lyon: Presses universitaires de Lyon.

Couchot, E., and M.-H. Tramus. 1993. 'Le geste et le calcul.' *Protée* 21, no. 3.

Couprie, A. 1994. *Lire la tragédie*. Paris: Dunod.

Couty, D., and A. Rey, ed. 1980. *Le théâtre*. Paris: Bordas.

Craig, G. 1905. *On the Art of the Theatre*. Chicago: Browne's Bookstore.

– (1911) 1942. *De l'art du théâtre*. Paris: Lieutier.

– 1964. *Le théâtre en marche*. Paris: Gallimard.

Création collective, La. 1981. Ed., Groupe de recherche d'esthétique du CNRS. Paris: Clancier-Guénaud.

Critique et création littéraire en France au XVIIe siècle. 1977. (Collective work within the framework of the international colloquia of the CNRS, no. 557). Paris: CNRS.

Cube (von), F. 1965. 'Drama als Forschungsobjekt der Kybernetik.' In *Mathematik und Dichtung*, ed. H. Kreuzer. München: Nymphenburger Verlag.

Culler, J. 1975. *Structuralist Poetics*. Ithaca, NY: Cornell University Press.

Dallenbach, L. 1977. *Le recit spéculaire*. Paris: Le Seuil.

Danan, J. 1995. *Le théâtre de la pensée*. Paris: Éditions Médianes.

Dars, E., and J.-C. Benoît. 1964. *L'expression scénique*. Paris: Éditions sociales.

Daugherty, J. 1984. 'Structures chorégraphiques dans *Le bourgeois gentilhomme* de Molière.' *French Studies in Southern Africa*, no. 13.

Davis, J.M. 1966. 'Guerilla Theatre.' *Tulane Drama Review* 10, no. 4

Deak, F. 1976. 'Structuralism in Theatre: The Prague School Contribution.' *Drama Review* 20, no. 4, t. LXXII (December).

Debord, G. 1967. *La société du spectacle*. Paris: Buchet-Chastel.

Decroux, E. 1963. *Paroles sur le mime*. Paris: Gallimard.

Degrés. 1978. No. 13 ('Téâtre et sémiologie').

– 1981. No. 24 ('Texte et société').

– 1982. No. 29 ('Modèles théoriques').

– 1982. No. 30 ('Performance/représentation').

– 1982. No. 31 ('Réception').

– 1982. No. 32 ('Sens et culture').

Deldime, R. 1990. *Le quatrième mur: regards sociologiques sur la relation théâtrale*. Carnières: Éditions Promotion théâtre.

Delmas, C. 1985. *Mythologie et mythe dans le théâtre français*. Genève: Droz.

Deloche, J. 1977. *Des ambiguïtés du collage: Recherches à partir de deux spectacles de Roger Planchon*. Thesis, 3[d] cycle, Université de Paris 3.

Delsarte, F. 1992. *Une anthologie par Alain Porte*. n.p.: Institut de pédagogie musicale et chorégraphique.

Demarcy, R. 1973. *Élements d'une sociologie du spectacle*. Paris: UGE.

De Marinis, M. 1975. 'Materiali bibliografici per una semiotica del teatro.' *Versus*, no. 11.

– 1978–79. 'Lo spettacolo come testo.' *Versus*, no. 21–22.

– 1980. *Mimo e Mimi*. Firenze: Casa Usher.

– 1982. *Semiotica del teatro: L'analisi testuale dello spettacolo*. Milano: Bompiani.

– 1983a. *Al limite del teatro*. Firenze: Casa Usher.

– 1983b. 'Semiotica del teatro: una disciplina al bivio?.' *Versus*, no. 34 (gennaio–aprile).

– 1985. 'A Faithful Betrayal of Performance: Notes on the Use of Video in Theatre.' *New Theatre Quarterly*, 1: 4.

– 1987a. 'Dramaturgy of the Spectator.' *Drama Review* 31, no. 2: 100–114.

– 1987b. *Il nuovo teatro, 1947–1970*. Milano: Bompiani.

– 1993. *Mimo e teatro nel novecento*. Firenze: Casa Usher.

De Marinis, M., and G. Bettetini. 1977. *Teatro e communicazione*. Firenze, Guaraldi.

Demougin, J., ed. 1985. *Dictionnaire historique, thématique et technique des littératures*. 2 vols. Paris: Larousse.

Derrida, J. 1967. *L'écriture et la différence*. Paris: Le Seuil.

– 1972. *La dissémination*. Paris: Le Seuil.

– 1978. *Writing and Difference*. Trans. of 1967 by Alan Bass. Chicago: University of Chicago Press.

– 1981. *Dissemination*. Trans. of 1972 by Barbara Johnson. Chicago: University of Chicago Press.

Descotes, M. 1964. *Le public de théâtre et son histoire*. Paris: PUF.

– 1980. *Histoire de la critique dramatique en France*. Tübingen: Narr.

DESPROGES, P. 1986. *Pierre Desproges se donne en spectacle.* Paris: Le Seuil.

DHOMME, S. 1959. *La mise en scène d'André Antoine à Bertolt Brecht.* Paris: Nathan.

Dictionnaire des personnages littéraires et dramatiques de tous les pays. 1960. Paris: SEDE.

DIDEROT, D. (1758) 1975. *De la poésie dramatique.* Paris: Larousse.

– (1773) 1951, 1994. *Le paradoxe sur le comédien.* In *Œuvres.* Paris: Gallimard

– 1962. *Œuvres romanesques.* Paris: Garnier.

DIETRICH, M., ed. 1966. 'Bühnenform und Dramenform.' In *Das Atlantisbuch des Theaters.* Zürich: Atlantis Verlag.

– 1975. *Regie in Dokumentation, Forschung und Lehre: Mise en scène en documentation, recherche et enseignement.* Salzburg: Otto Müller Verlag.

DIEZ BORQUE, J.M., and L. LORENZO. *Semiología del teatro.* Barcelona: Planeta.

DINU, M. 1977. 'How to Estimate the Weight of Stage Relations.' *Poetics* 6, no. 3–4.

DODD, W. 1979. 'Metalanguage and Character in Drama.' *Lingua e Stile* 14, no. 1 (marzo).

– 1981. 'Conversation, dialogue and exposition.' *Strumenti critici,* no. 44, Feb.

DOMENACH, J.-M. 1967. *Le retour du tragique.* Paris: Gallimard.

DORAT, C.-J. (1766) 1767. La déclamation théâtrale. Paris: S. Jorry.

DORCY, J. 1958. *À la recherche de la mime et des mimes Decroux, Barrault, Marceau.* Neuilly-sur-Marne: Cahiers de danse et de culture.

– 1962. *J'aime la mime.* Paris: Denoël.

DORFLES, G. 1974. '*Innen* et *aussen* en architecture et en psychanalyse.' *Nouvelle Revue de psychanalyse,* no. 9 (printemps).

DORT, B. 1960. *Lecture de Brecht.* Paris: Le Seuil.

– 1967. *Théâtre public.* Paris: Le Seuil.

– 1971. *Théâtre réel.* Paris: Le Seuil.

– 1975. 'Les classiques ou la métamorphose sans fin.' In *Histoire littéraire de la France.* Paris: Éditions sociales.

– 1977a. 'Un âge d'or: Sur la mise en scène des classiques en France entre 1945 et 1960.' *Revue de l'histoire littéraire de la France,* vol. 4.

– 1977b. 'Paradoxe et tentations de l'acteur contemporain.' *Revue d'esthétique,* 1977, no. 1–2.

– 1979. *Théâtre en jeu.* Paris: Le Seuil.

– 1982. 'Un jeu du temps: Notes prematurées.' *Journal du Théâtre national de Chaillot,* no. 8.

– 1988. *La représentation emancipée.* Arles: Actes Sud.

– 1995. *Le spéctateur en dialogue.* Paris: POL.

DORT, B., and C. NAUGRETTE-CHRISTOPHE. 1984. 'La représentation théâtrale moderne (1880–1980): Essai de bibliographie.' In *Cahiers de la bibliothèque Gaston Baty,* I. Paris: Université de la Sorbonne nouvelle.

Drama Review. 1969. Vol. 42 ('Naturalism revisited').

– 1973. Vol. 57 ('Russian Issue').

– 1982. Vol. 94.

DUBOIS, J., et al. 1973. *Dictionnaire de linguistique.* Paris: Larousse.

DUBOIS, PH. 1983. *L'acte photographique.* Paris et Bruxelles: Nathan et Labor.

DUCHARTRE, P.-L. 1925. *La comédie italienne.* Paris: Librairie de France.

– 1955. *La commedia dell'arte et ses enfants.* Paris: Éditions d'art et d'industrie.

DUCHEMIN, J. 1968. *L'Agon dans la tragédie grecque.* Paris: Les Belles lettres.

DUCHET, C. 1973. 'Une écriture de la sociabilité.' *Poétique,* no. 16.

– 1979, ed. *Sociocritique.* Paris: Nathan.

DUCHET, C., and F. GAILLARD. 1976. 'Introduction to Sociocriticism.' *Substance,* no. 15.

DUCROT, O. 1972. *Dire et ne pas dire.* Paris: Hermann.

– 1984. *Le dire et le dit.* Paris: Minuit.

DUCROT, O., and J.M. SCHAEFFER. 1995. *Nouveau dictionnaire encyclopédique des sciences du langage.* Paris: Le Seuil.

DUCROT, O., and T. TODOROV. 1972. *Dictionnaire encyclopédique des sciences du langage.* Paris: Le Seuil.

DUKORE, B. 1974. *Dramatic Theory and Criticism: Greeks to Grotowski.* New York: Holt, Rinehart and Winston.

DULLIN, C. 1946. *Souvenirs et notes de travail d'un acteur.* Paris: Lieutier.

– 1969. *Ce sont les dieux qu'il nous faut.* Paris: Gallimard.

DUMUR, G., ed. 1965. *Histoire des spectacles.* Paris: Gallimard.

DUPAVILLON, C. 1970–78. 'Les lieux du spectacle.' *Architecture d'aujourd'hui,* no. 10–11, 1970 and octobre 1978.

DUPONT, F. 1989. *L'acteur-roi ou le théâtre dans la Rome antique.* Paris: Les Belles Lettres.

DURAND, G. 1969. *Les structures anthropologiques de l'imaginaire*. Paris: Bordas. (2nd edition Paris: Dunod, 1995).

DURAND, R. 1975. 'Problèmes de l'analyse structurale et sémiotique de la forme théâtrale.' In HELBO 1975.

– 1980a, ed. *La relation théâtrale*. Lille: Presses universitaires de Lille.

– 1980b. 'La voix et le dispositif théâtral.' *Études littéraires* 13, no. 3.

DÜRRENMATT, F. 1955–1966–1972. *Theaterschriften und Reden*. Zürich: Arche.

– 1970. *Écrits sur le théâtre*. Paris: Gallimard.

– 1976. *Writings on Theatre and Drama*. Trans. of 1955–1966–1972 by H. M. Waidson. London: J. Cape.

– 1991. *The Physicists*. Trans. James Kirkup. New York: Grove Weidenfeld.

DUVIGNAUD, J. 1965. *L'acteur: Esquisse d'une sociologie du comédien*. Paris: Gallimard.

– 1970. *Spectacle et société*. Paris: Denoël.

– 1976. *Le théâtre*. Paris: Larousse.

ECO, U. 1965. *L'œuvre ouverte*. Paris: Denoël.

– 1973. 'Tutto il mundo e attore.' *Terzoprogramma*, no. 2–3.

– 1975. *Trattato di semiotica generale*. Milano: Bompiani.

– 1976a. 'Codice.' *Versus*, no. 14.

– 1976b. *Theory of Semiotics*. Trans. of 1975. Bloomington: Indiana University Press.

– 1977. 'Semiotics of Theatrical Performance.' *Drama Review* 21, 1.

– 1978. 'Pour une reformulation du concept de signe iconique.' *Communications*, 29.

– 1980. *The Role of the Reader*. Bloomington: Indiana University Press.

– 1985. *Lector in fabula*. Paris: Grasset.

– 1989. *The Open Work*. Trans. of 1965 by Anna Cancogni. Cambridge, Mass.: Harvard University Press.

– 1990. *Les limites de l'interprétation*. Paris: Grasset.

– 1990. *The Limits of Interpretation*. Bloomington: Indiana University Press

EISENSTEIN, S. 1976. *Le film: Sa forme, son sens*. Paris: C. Bourgois.

– 1926–78. *La non-indifférente nature*. 2 vols. Paris: UGE.

ELAM, K. 1980. *The Semiotics of Theatre and Drama*. London: Methuen.

– 1984. *Shakespeare's Universe of Discourse: Language-Games in the Comedies*. Cambridge: Cambridge University Press.

ELIADE, M. 1963. *Aspects du mythe*. Paris: Gallimard.

– 1965. *Le sacré et le profane*. Paris: Gallimard.

ELLIS-FERMOR, U. 1945. *The Frontiers of Drama*. London: Methuen.

ELSE, G. 1957. *Aristotle's Poetics: The Argument*. Cambridge, MA: Harvard University Press.

EMÉLINA, J. 1975. *Les valets et les servantes dans le théâtre comique en France de 1610 à 1700*. Grenoble: PUG.

Enciclopedia dello spettacolo 1954–1968. Ed. S. d'Amico. Roma: Le Maschere.

Enciclopedia garzanti dello spettacolo. 1976–1977. Milano: Garzanti Editore.

Encyclopédie des spectacles. 1965. Paris: Gallimard.

ENGEL, J.-J. (1785–86) 1979. *Idées pour le geste et l'action théâtrale*. Paris: Slatkine Reprints. (Original title: *Ideen zu einer Mimik*).

ERENSTEIN, R., ed. 1986. *Conference on Theatre and Television*. Amsterdam: International Theatre Bookshop.

ERLICH, V. 1969. *Russian Formalism*. Paris and The Hague: Mouton.

ERTEL, E. 1977. 'Éléments pour une sémiologie du théâtre.' *Travail théâtral*, no. 28–29.

– 1983. 'L'éléctronique à l'assaut du théâtre.' *Journal du Théâtre national de Chaillot*, no. 12.

– 1985. 'Le métier de critique en question.' *Théâtre public*, 68.

ESCARPIT, R. 1967. *L'humour*. Paris: PUF.

ESCHBACH, A. 1979. *Pragmasemiotik und Theater*. Tübingen: Narr Verlag.

ESSLIN, M. 1962. *The theatre of the absurd*. New York: Doubleday.

Esprit. 1963. Novembre

Europe. 1983. No. 648 (avril: 'Le théâtre par ceux qui le font').

EVREINOFF, N. 1930. *Le théâtre dans la vie*. Paris: Stock.

FEBVRE, M. 1995. *Danse contemporaine et théâtralité*. Paris: Chiron.

FELDENKRAIS, M. 1964. *L'expression corporelle*. Paris: Chiron.

– 1972. *Awareness through Movement: Health Exercises for Personal Growth*. New York: Harper & Row.

FÉRAL, J., ed. 1977. *Substance*, no. 18–19.

– 1984. 'Writing and Displacement: Women in Theatre.' *Modern Drama* 27, no. 4.

– 1985. 'Performance et théâtralité: Le sujet démystifié.' In *Théâtralite: Écriture et mise en scène*, eds. J. Féral, J. Savona, and E. Walker. Montréal: Hurtubise.

FERGUSSON, F. 1949. *The Idea of a Theatre*. New York: Doubleday.

FERRONI, G., ed. 1981. *La semiotica e il doppio teatrale*. Naples: Liguori.

FIEBACH, J. 1975. *Von Craig bis Brecht*. Berlin: Henschelverlag.

FIEGUTH, R. 1979. 'Zum Problem des virtuellen Empfängers beim Drama.' In *Approaches to Ostrowski*, ed. A.J. Van Holk. Bremen: Kafka-Presse.

FINTER, H. 1981. 'Autour de la voix au théâtre: Voix de texte ou texte de voix.' In *Performance: Textes et documents*, ed. C. Pontbriand. Montréal: Parachute.

– 1990. *Der subjektive Raum*. Tübingen: Narr Verlag.

FISCHER-LICHTE, E. 1979. *Bedeutung: Probleme einer semiotischen Hermeneutik und Ästhetik*. München: Narr Verlag.

– 1983. *Semiotik des Theaters*. 3 vols. Tübingen: Narr Verlag.

– 1985, ed. *Das Drama und seine Inszenierung*. Tübingen: Niemeyer.

FISCHER-LICHTE, E., J. RILEY, and M. GISSENWEIRER, M. 1990. *The Dramatic Touch of Difference: Theatre, Own and Foreign*. Tübingen: Narr Verlag.

FITZPATRICK, T. 1986. 'Playscript Analysis: Performance Analysis toward a Theorical Model.' *Gestos*, no. 2.

– 1989. *Altro Polo-Performance: From Product to Process*. Sydney: Theatre Studies Service Unit, University of Sydney.

FLASHAR, H. 1974. 'Aristoteles und Brecht.' *Poetica* 6, Heft 1.

FLECNIAKOSKA, J.-L. 1961. *La formation de l'autoreligieux en Espagne avant Calderón (1550–1635)*. Montpellier: Éditions P. Déhan.

FLESHMAN, B. 1986. *Theatrical Movement: A Bibliographical Anthology*. Metuchen, N. J.: Scarecrow Press.

FLOECK, W. 1989. *Théâtre contemporain en Allemagne et en France*. Tübingen: Francke Verlag.

FO, D. 1991. *Minimum Manual of the Actor*. London: Methuen.

FONAGY, I. 1983. *La vive voix*. Paris: Payot.

FONTANIER, P. (1827) 1977. *Les figures du discours*. Paris: Flammarion.

FOREMAN, R. 1992. *Unbalancing Acts: Foundations for a Theater*. New York: Pantheon.

FORESTIER, G. 1981. *Le théâtre dans le théâtre sur la scène française du XVIIe siècle*. Genève: Droz.

– 1988. *Esthétique de l'identité dans le théâtre français*. Genève: Droz.

FOSTER, S. L. 1988. *Reading Dancing: Bodies and Subjects in Contemporary American Dance*. Berkeley: University of California Press.

FOUCAULT, M. 1966. *Les mots et les choses*. Paris: Gallimard.

– 1969. *L'archéologie du savoir*. Paris: Gallimard.

– 1971. *L'ordre du discours*. Paris: Gallimard.

– 1972. *The Archaeology of Knowledge*. Trans. of 1969 by A. M. Sheridan Smith. New York: Pantheon Books.

– 1973. *The Order of Things: An Archaeology of the Human Sciences*. New York: Random House.

FOURNEL, P., ed. 1982. *Les marionnettes*. Paris: Bordas.

FOWLER, A. 1982. *Kind of Literature: An Introduction to the Theory of Genres and Modes*. Cambridge, MA: Harvard University Press.

FRAISSE, P. 1957. *Psychologie du temps*. Paris: PUF.

FRANCASTEL, P. 1965. *La réalité figurative*. Paris: Gonthier.

– 1967. *La figure et le lieu*. Paris: Gallimard.

– 1970. *Études de sociologie de l'art*. Paris: Denoël-Gonthier.

FRENZEL, E. 1963. *Stoff, Motiv und Symbolforschung*. Stuttgart: J.-B. Metzlersche Verlagsbuchhandlung.

FREUD, S. (1905) 1930. *Le mot d'esprit et ses rapports avec l'inconscient*. Paris: Gallimard.

– 1969. *Studienausgabe*. 10 vols. Frankfurt: Fischer Verlag.

– 1976. *The Pelican Freud Library*. Trans. James Strachey. 15 vols. London: Penguin.

FREYTAG, G. (1857) 1965. *Die Technik des Dramas*. Darmstadt: Wissenschaftliche Buchgesellschaft.

FRIEDLANDER, L. 1989. 'Moving Images into the Classroom: Multimedia in Higher Education.' *Laserdisk Professional* (July).

FROW, J. 1986. *Marxism and Literary History*. Cambridge, MA: Harvard University Press.

FRYE, N. 1957. *Anatomy of Criticism: Four Essays*. Princeton, NJ: Princeton University Press.

FUMAROLI, M. 1972. 'Rhétorique et dramaturgie: Le statut du personnage dans la tragédie dassique.' *Revue d'histoire du théâtre*, no. 3.

GALIFRET-GRANJON, N. 1971. 'Le figural gestuel.' *Études philosophiques*, no. 3.

García-Martínez, M. 1995. *Réflexions sur la perception du rythme au théâtre*. Thesis, Université Paris 8, Paris.

Gaudibert, P. 1977. *Action culturelle: Intégration et subversion*. Paris: Casterman.

Gauthier, G. 1982. *Vingt leçons sur l'image et le sens*. Paris: Édilig.

Gauvreau, A. 1981. *Masques et théâtres masqués*. Paris: CNDP.

Genette, G. 1966. *Figures I*. Paris: Le Seuil.

– 1969. *Figures II*. Paris: Le Seuil.

– 1972. *Figures III*. Paris: Le Seuil.

– 1976. *Mimologiques*. Paris: Le Seuil.

– 1977. 'Genres,' 'Types,' 'Modes.' *Poétique*, no. 32.

– 1982. *Palimpsestes*. Paris: Le Seuil.

Genot, G. 1973. 'Tactique du sens.' *Semiotica* 8, no. 13.

George, K. 1980. *Rhythm in Drama*. Pittsburgh: University of Pittsburgh Press.

Ghiron-Bistagne, P. 1976. *Recherches sur les acteurs dans la Grèce antique*. Paris: Les Belles lettres.

– 1994. *Gigaku: Dionysies nippones*. Montpellier: Université Paul-Valéry.

Ginestier, P. 1961. *Le théâtre contemporain*. Paris: PUF.

Ginot, I., and M. Michel. 1995. *La danse au XXe siècle*. Paris: Bordas.

Girard, R. 1968. *R.M. Lenz: genèse d'une dramaturgie du tragicomique*. Paris: Klincksieck.

Girard, R. 1974. *La violence et le sacré*. Paris: Grasset.

Girault, A. 1973. 'Pourquoi monter un classique.' *La nouvelle critique*, no. 69 (décembre).

– 1982. 'Photographier le théâtre.' *Théâtre/public*, numéro special.

Gisselbrecht, A. 1971. 'Marxisme et théorie de la littérature.' *La nouvelle critique*, no. 39 bis.

Giteau, C. 1970. *Dictionnaire des arts du spectacle (français, anglais, allemand)*. Paris: Dunod.

Gobin, P. 1978. *Le fou et ses doubles*. Québec: Presses de l'Université de Laval.

Godard, C. 1980. *Le théâtre depuis 1968*. Paris: Lattès.

Goethe, F.W. 1970. *Werkausgabe*. 6 vols. Frankfurt: Insel.

Goffman, E. 1959. *The Presentation of Self in Everyday Life*. New York: Doubleday.

– 1967. *Interaction Ritual: Essays on Face-to-Face Behavior*. New York: Doubleday.

– 1974. *Frame Analysis*. Harmondsworth: Penguin Books.

Goldberg, R.L. 1979. *Performance: Live Art 1909 to the Present*. New York: H. Abrams.

Goldmann, L. 1955. *Le dieu caché: Étude sur la vision tragique dans les Pensées de Pascal et dans le théâtre de Racine*. Paris: Gallimard.

– 1964. *The Hidden God: A Study of Tragic vision in the Pensées of Pascal and the Tragedies of Racine*. Trans. of 1955 by Philip Thody. New York: Humanities Press.

– 1970. *Racine*. Paris: L'Arche.

– 1972. *Racine*. Trans. of 1970 by Alastair Hamilton. Cambridge, England: Rivers Press.

Golomb, H. 1979. *Enjambement in Poetry*. Tel Aviv: Tel Aviv Porter Institute for Poetics and Semiotics.

Gombrich, E. (1969) 1977. *Art and Illusion: A Study in the Psychology of Pictorial Representation*. London: Phaidon.

– 1972. *L'art et l'illusion: Psychologie de la représentation picturale*. Paris: Gallimard.

Gomez, J.A. 1968–86. *Scènogrammes: Textes dramatiques de la deuxième génération*. Barcelona: Investigación teatrológica.

Goodman, N. 1968. *Languages of Art*. New York: Bobb Merrills.

Gossman, L. 1976. 'The Signs of the Theatre.' *Theatre Research International* 2, no. 1 (October).

Gouhier, H. (1943) 1968. *L'essence du théâtre*. Paris: Flammarion.

– 1952. *Le théâtre et l'existence*. Paris: Flammarion.

– 1958. *L'œuvre théâtrale*. Paris: Flammarion.

– 1972. 'Théâtralité.' In *Encyclopaedia Universalis*. Paris.

Gourdon, A.-M. 1982. *Théâtre, public, réception*. Paris: CNRS.

Green, A. 1969. *Un oeil en trop: Le complexe d'Œdipe dans la tragédie*. Paris: Minuit.

– 1982. *Hamlet et Hamlet*. Paris: Balland.

– 1979. *The Tragic Effect: The Oedipus Complex in Tragedy*. Trans. of 1969 by Alan Sheridan. Cambridge and New York: Cambridge University Press.

– 1982. *Hamlet et Hamlet*. Paris: Balland

Greimas, A. 1966. *Sémantique structurale*. Paris: Larousse.

– 1970. *Du sens*. Paris: Le Seuil.

– 1972, ed. *Essai de sémiotique poétique*. Paris: Larousse.

– 1973. 'Les actants, les acteurs et les figures.' In C. CHABROL 1973.

– 1976. *Sémiotique et sciences sociales*. Paris: Le Seuil.

– 1977. 'La sémiotique.' In *La linguistique*. Paris: Larousse.

GREIMAS, A., AND J. COURTÈS 1979. *Sémiotique: Dictionnaire raisonné de la théorie du langage*. Paris: Hachette.

– 1982. *Semiotics and Language: An Analytical Dictionnary*. Trans. of 1979 by Larry Crist, Daniel Patte, James Lee, Edward McMahon II, Gary Phillips, and Michael Rengstorf. Bloomington: Indiana University Press.

GRIMES, R.L. 1982. *Beginnings in Ritual Studies*. Washington, DC: University Press of America.

GRIMM, J. 1982. *Das avantgardistische Theater Frankreichs (1895–1930)*. München: Beck.

GRIMM, R. 1971. Deutsche Dramentheorien. 2 vols. Frankfurt: Athenäum Verlag.

GROTOWSKI, J. 1968. *Towards a Poor Theatre*. New York: Simon and Schuster.

– 1971. *Vers un théâtre pauvre*. Lausanne: La Cité.

GRÜND, F. 1984. *Conteurs du monde*. Paris: Éditions de la maison des cultures du monde.

GUARINO, R. 1982a. 'Le théâtre du sens: Quelques remarques sur fiction et perception.' *Degrés*, no. 31 (été).

– 1982b. *La tragedia e le macchine: Andromède di Corneille e Torelli*. Roma: Bulzoni.

GUESPIN, L. 1971. 'Problématique des travaux sur le discours politique.' *Langages*, no. 23.

GUICHEMERRE, R. 1981. *La tragi-comédie*. Paris: PUF.

GULLI-PUGLIATI, P. 1976. *I segni latenti: Scrittura come virtualità scenica in* King Lear. Messina-Firenze: D'Anna.

GÜTHKE, K.S. 1961. *Geschichte und Poetik der deutschen Tragikomödie*. Göttingen: Vandenhœck.

– 1966. *Modern Tragicomedy: An Investigation into the Nature of the Genre*. New York: Random House.

– 1968. *Die moderne Tragikomödie*. Göttingen: Vandenhœck

GUY, J.-M., and L. MIRONER. 1988. *Les publics de théâtre*. Paris: La documentation française.

HADDAD, Y. 1982. *Art du conteur, art de l'acteur*. Louvain: Cahiers Théâtre.

HALL, T.E. 1959. *The Silent Language*. New York: Doubleday.

– 1966. *The Hidden Dimension*. New York: Doubleday.

HAMON-SIRÉJOLS, C. 1992. *Le constructivisme au théâtre*. Paris: CNRS.

HAMON, PH. 1973. 'Un discours contraint.' *Poétique*, no. 16.

– 1974. 'Analyse du récit.' *Le Français moderne*, no. 2, Apr.

– 1977. 'Pour un statut sémiologique du personnage.' In TODOROV and GENETTE 1977.

HANNA, J.-L. 1979. *To Dance is Human*. Austin: University of Texas Press.

– 1983. *The Performer-Audience Connection: Emotion to Metaphor in Dance and Society*. Austin: University of Texas Press.

HARNS, M., and E. MONTGOMERY. 1975. *Theatre Props*. London: Motley-Studio Vista.

HAVEL, V. 1977. 'Specificita del teatro.' In BARTOLUCCI 1977.

HARTNOLL, P., ed. 1983. *The Oxford Companion to the Theatre*. 4th ed. Oxford: Oxford University Press.

HAYS, M. 1977. 'Theater History and Practice: An Alternative View of Drama.' *New German Critique*, no. 12.

– 1981. *The Public and Performance*. Ann Arbor, MI: UMI Research Press.

– 1983, ed. *Theater* 25, no. 1 ('The Sociology of Theater').

HEFFNER, H. 1965. 'Towards a Definition of Form in Drama.' In ANDERSON 1965.

HEGEL, F.W. (1832) 1965. *Esthétique*. Trans. S. Jankélevitch. Paris: Aubier-Montaigne.

– (1962) 1975. *Hegel on Tragedy*. Eds. Anne and Henry Paolucci. New York: Harper and Row.

– 1964. *Sämtliche Werke*. Stuttgart: Frommann.

HEIDSECK, A. 1969. *Das Groteske und das Absurde im modernen Drama*. Stuttgart: Kohlhammer.

HEISTEIN, J. 1983. *La Réception de l'œuvre littéraire*. Wroclaw: Presses de l'Université de Wroclaw.

– 1986. *Le texte dramatique: la lecture et la scène*. Wroclaw: Presses de l'Université de Wroclaw.

HELBO, A., ed. 1975. *Sémiologie de la représentation*. Bruxelles: Complexe.

– 1979, ed. *Le champ sémiologique: Perspectives internationales*. Bruxelles: Complexe.

– 1983a. *Les mots et les gestes: Essai sur le théâtre*. Lille: Presses universitaires de Lille.

– 1983b. *Sémiologie des messages sociaux*. Paris: Edilig.

– 1986, ed. *Approches de l'opéra*. Paris: Didier.

HELBO, A., D. JOHANSEN, P. PAVIS, and A. UBERSFELD, eds. 1987. *Le théâtre: Modes d'approches*.

Bruxelles: Éditions Labor; Paris: Méridiens Klincksieck.

HELMICH, W. 1980. *Moralités françaises*. Genève: Slatkine.

HERZEL, R. 1981. *The Original Casting of Molière's Plays*. Ann Arbor, MI: UMI Research Press.

HESS-LÜTTICH, E., ed. 1981. *Multimedial Communication*. 2 vols. Tübingen: Narr Verlag.

– 1984. *Kommunikation als ästhetisches Problem*. Tübingen: Narr Verlag.

– 1985. *Zeichen und Schichten des Dramas und Theaters*. Berlin: E. Schmidt Verlag.

HILDESHEIMER, W. 1960. 'Erlangener Rede über das absurde Theater.' *Akzente*, 7.

HILGAR, M.-F. 1973. *La mode des stances dans le théâtre tragique français, 1610–1687*. Paris: Nizet.

HILZINGER, K.H. 1976. *Die Dramaturgie des dokumentarischen Theaters*. Tübingen: n. p.

HINKLE, G. 1979. *Art as Event*. Washington, DC: Georgetown University Press.

HINTZE, J. 1969. *Das Raumproblem im modernen deutschen Drama und Theater*. Marburg: Elwert Verlag.

Hiss, G. *Der theatralische Blick*. Berlin: Reimer

HODGSON, J., and E. RICHARDS. 1974. *Improvisation*. London: Methuen.

HOFFMANN, L., and D. HOFFMAN-OSTWALD, eds. 1973. *Deutsches Arbeitertheater 1918–1933*. München: Rogner & Bernhard.

HOGENDOORN, W. 1973. 'Reading on a Booke: Closet Drama and the Study of Theatre Arts.' In *Essays on Drama and Theatre (Mélanges Benjamin Hunningher)*. Amsterdam: Moussault.

– 1976. *Lezen en zien spelen*. Leiden: Karstens.

HONZL, J. 1940. 'Pohyb divadelníhoznaku.' *Slovo a slovesnost*, 6.

– 1971. 'La mobilité de signe théâtral.' (French translation of 1940) *Travail théâtral*, no. 4 (juillet). English translation in MATEJKA 1976.

HOOVER, M. 1974. *Meyerhold: The Art of Conscious Theater*. Amherst: University of Massachussetts Press.

HOPPE, H. 1971. *Das Theater der Gegenstände*. Bensberg: Schauble Verlag.

HORNBY, R. 1977. *Script into Performance: A Structuralist View of Play Production*. Austin: University of Texas Press.

HRUSHOVKI, B. 1985. 'Présentation et représentation dans la fiction littéraire.' *Littérature*, no. 57.

HUBERT, M.-C. 1988. *Le théâtre*. Paris: Armand Colin.

HÜBLER, A. 1973. *Drama in der Vermittlung von Handlung, Sprache und Szene*. Bonn: Bouvier-Verlag Grundmann.

HUGHES, G.E., and M.-J. CRESSWELL. 1968. *An Introduction to Modal Logic*. London: Methuen.

HUGO, V. (1827) 1968. Preface to *Cromwell*. Paris: Garnier-Flammarion

HUIZINGA, J. (1938) 1950. *Homo Ludens: A Study of the Play-Element in Culture*. Boston: Beacon Press.

HUTCHEON, L. 1985. *A Theory of Parody: The Teachings of Twentieth-Century Art Forms*. New York: Methuen.

INGARDEN, R. 1931. *Das literarische Kunstwerk*. Tübingen: Niemeyer.

– 1949. 'Les différentes conceptions de la vérité dans l'œuvre d'art.' *Revue d'esthétique*, no. 2.

– 1971. 'Les fonctions du langage au théâtre.' *Poétique*, no. 8.

– 1973. *The Literary Work of Art*. Trans. of 1931 by George G. Grabowicz. Evanston, IL: Northwestern University Press.

– 1983. *L'œuvre d'art littéraire*. Lausanne: L'Âge d'homme.

INNES, C. 1981. *Holy Theatre: Ritual and the Avant-Garde*. Cambridge: Cambridge University Press.

IONESCO, E. 1955. 'Théâtre et Antithéâtre.' *Cahier des saisons*, no. 2 (octobre).

– 1962. *Notes et contre-notes*. Paris: Gallimard.

– 1966. *Entretien avec Claude Bonnefoy*. Paris: Belfond.

ISER, W. 1972. 'The Reading Process: a Phenomenological Approach.' *New Literary History*, no. 3.

– 1975. 'The Reality of Fiction: a Functionalist Approach to Literature.' *New Literary History*, no. 1.

ISSACHARAOFF, M. 1981. 'Space and Reference in Drama.' *Poetics Today* 2, no. 3.

– 1985. *Le spectacle du discours*. Paris: Corti.

– 1986. 'Inscribed Performance.' *Rivista di letterature moderne et comparate* 39, no. 2.

– 1986, ed. *Performing Texts*. Philadelphia: University of Pennsylvania Press.

– 1988. *Le discours comique*. Paris: Corti.

– 1989. *Discourse as Performance*. Stanford, CA: Stanford University Press.

– 1990. *Lieux comiques*. Paris: Corti.

ISSACHARAOFF, M. and A. WHITESIDE, eds. 1987. *On Referring in Literature*. Bloomington: Indiana University Press.

IVERNEL, P., and J. EBSTEIN. 1983. *Le théâtre d'intervention depuis 1968*. Lausanne: L'Âge d'homme.

JACHYMIAK, J. 1972. 'Sur la théâtralité.' *Littérature, sciences, idéologie*, no. 2.

JACQUART, E. 1974. *Le théâtre de dérision*. Paris: Gallimard.

JACQUOT, J., ed. 1960. *Réalisme et poésie au théâtre*. Paris: CNRS.

– 1965a, ed. *Le théâtre tragique*. Paris: CNRS.

– 1965b. *Théâtre moderne: Hommes et tendances*. Paris: CNRS.

– 1968, ed. *Dramaturgie et société: Rapports entre l'œuvre théâtrale, son interprétation et son public aux XVIe et XVIIe siècles*. 2 vols. Paris: CNRS.

– 1972. 'Sur la forme du masque jacobéen.' Vol. 5 of *Actes des journées internationales d'étude du baroque*. Toulouse: Association des Publications de la Faculté des lettres et sciences humaines.

JACQUOT, J., and A. VEINSTEIN eds. 1957. *La mise en scène des œuvres du passé*. Paris: CNRS.

JACQUOT, J., and D. BABLET, eds. 1963. *Le lieu théâtral dans la société moderne*. Paris: CNRS.

JAFFRE, J. 1974. 'Théâtre et ideologie: note sur la dramaturgie de Molière.' *Littérature*, no. 13.

JAKOBSON, R. 1963. *Essais de linguistique générale*. Paris: Le Seuil.

– 1971. 'Visual and Auditory Signs.' In *Selected Writings*. Vol. 2. Paris and The Hague: Mouton.

– 1977. *Huit questions de poétique*. Paris: Le Seuil.

JAMATI, G. 1952. *Théâtre et vie intérieure*. Paris: Flammarion.

JAMESON, F. 1972. *The Prison-House of Language*. Princeton, NJ: Princeton University Press.

– 1981. *The Political Unconscious*. Ithaca, NY: Cornell University Press.

JANSEN, S. 1968. 'Esquisse d'une théorie de la forme dramatique.' *Langages*, no. 12.

– 1973. 'Qu'est-ce qu'une situation dramatique?' *Orbis Litterarum*, vols. 20–28, no. 4.

– 1984. 'Le rôle de l'espace scénique dans la lecture du texte dramatique.' In SCHMID AND VAN KESTEREN 1984.

JAQUES, F. 1979. *Dialogiques: Recherches logiques sur le dialogue*. Paris: PUF.

– 1985. *L'espace logique de l'interlocution: Dialogiques II*. Paris: PUF.

JAQUES-DALCROZE, E. (1919) 1965. *Le rythme, la musique et l'éducation*. Lausanne: Foetisch Frères.

JARRY, A. (1896) 1962. 'De l'inutilité du théâtre au théâtre.' In *Tout Ubu*. Paris: Le Livre de poche.

JAUSS, H.R. 1970. *Literaturgeschichte als Provokation*. Frankfurt: Suhrkamp.

– 1977. *Ästhetische Erfahrung und literarische Hermeneutick I*. München: Fink Verlag.

– 1982a. *Aesthetic Experience and Literary Hermeneutics*. Trans. of 1977 by Michael Shaw. Minneapolis: University of Minnesota Press.

– 1982b. *Towards an Aesthetic of Reception*. Minneapolis: University of Minnesota Press.

JAVIER, F. 1984. *Notas para la historia científica de la puesta en escena*. Buenos Aires: Editorial Leviatan.

Jeu: Cahiers de théâtre. 1985. No. 37 ('La photographie de théâtre').

JEAN, G. 1976. *Le théâtre*. Paris: Le Seuil.

JOHANSEN, D. 1986. See HELBO, ed. 1986.

JOHNSON, M. 1987. *The Body in the Mind*. Chicago: University of Chicago Press.

JOMARON, J. 1981. *La mise en scène contemporaine II: 1914–1940*. Bruxelles: La Renaissance du livre.

– 1989, ed. *Le théâtre en France*. Paris: Armand Colin.

JOURDHEUIL, J. 1976. *L'artiste, la politique, la production*. Paris: UGE.

Journal du théâtre national de Chaillot. 1982. no. 9 (décembre).

JOUSSE, M. 1974. *L'anthropologie du geste*. Paris: Gallimard.

JOUVET, L. 1954. *Le comédien désincarné*. Paris: Flammarion.

– 1968. *Tragédie classique, théâtre du XIXe siècle: extraits des cours de Louis Jouvet au Conservatoire (1939–1940)*. Paris: Gallimard.

JUNG, C. 1937. 'Über die Archetypen.' In *Gesammelte Werke*. Zurich: Rascher.

JUNG, U. 1994. *L'énonciation au théâtre: Une approche pragmatique de l'autotexte théâtral*. Tübingen: Narr Verlag.

KANDINSKY, W. 1975. 'De la composition scénique' and 'De la synthèse scénique abstraite.' In *Écrits complets*, vol. 3. Paris: Denoël-Gonthier.

KANT, E. (1790) 1959. *Kritik der Urteilskraft*. Hamburg: Vorlander.

KANTOR, T. 1977. *Le théâtre de la mort*. Ed. D. Bablet. Lausanne: L'Âge d'homme.

KANTOR, T. et al. 1990. *L'artiste à la fin du XXe siècle*. Paris: Acte Sud Papiers.

– 1991. *Ma création, mon voyage*. Paris: Plume.

KAYSER, W. 1960. *Das Groteske in Malerei und Dichtung*. Hamburg: Rowohlt.

KELLER, W. 1976. *Beiträge zur Poetik des Dramas*. Darmstadt: Wissenschaftliche Buchgesellschaft.

KENNEDY, A. 1983. *A Dramatic Dialogue*. Cambridge: Cambridge University Press.

KERBRAT-ORECCHIONI, C. 1980. *L'énonciation: De la subjectivité dans le langage*. Paris: Armand Colin.

– 1984. 'Pour une approche pragmatique du dialogue théâtral.' *Pratiques*, no. 41 (mars).

– 1990. *Les interactions verbales*. Paris: Armand Colin.

– 1996. *La conversation*. Paris: Armand Colin.

KESTING, M. 1959. *Das epische Theater*. Stuttgart: Kohlhammer.

– 1965. 'Gesamtkunstwerk und Totaltheater.' In *Vermessung des Labyrinths*. Frankfurt: Suhrkamp.

KIBÉDI-VARGA, A. 1970. *Rhétorique et littérature*. Paris: Didier.

– 1976. 'L'invention de la fable.' *Poétique*, no. 25.

– 1981, ed. *Théorie de la littérature*. Paris: Picard.

KIERKEGAARD, S. (1841) 1965. *The Concept of Irony, with Constant Reference to Socrates*. Trans. Lee M. Capel. New York: Harper.

KIPSIS, C. 1974. *The Mime Book*. New York: Harper and Row.

KIRBY, E.T. 1969. *Total Theatre: A Critical Anthology*. New York: Dutton.

KIRBY, M. 1965. *Happenings: An illustrated Anthology*. New York: Dutton.

– 1976. 'Structural Analysis/Structural Theory.' *Drama Review*, no. 20.

– 1982. 'Nonsemiotic Performance.' *Modern Drama* 25, no. 1 (March)

– 1987. *A Formalist Theatre*. Philadelphia: Pennsylvania Press.

KLEIN, M. 1984. 'De la théâtralisation comme travail du rythme.' *Le Rythme*, Colloque d'Albi, vol. 1.

KLEIST, H. von. (1810) 1978. 'Über das Marionettentheater.' In *Werke und Briefe*. Berlin: Aufbau Verlag.

KLIER, H. 1981. *Theaterwissenschaft im deutschsprachigen Raum*. Darmstadt: Wissenschafliche Buchgesellschaft.

KLÖPFER, R. 1979. 'Fluchtpunkt Rezeption.' In *Bildung und Ausbildung in der Romania*, ed. R. Klöpfer. München: Fink Verlag.

– 1982. 'Zu den Grundlagen des "dialogischen Prinzips" in der Literatur.' *Romanistiche Zeitschrift für Literaturgeschichte*, no. 3–4.

KLOTZ, V. 1969. *Geschlossene und offene Form im Drama*. München: Hanser.

– 1976. *Dramaturgie des Publikums*. München: Hanser.

KLÜNDER, J. 1971. *Theaterwissenschaft als Medienwissenschaft*. Hamburg: Lüdke Verlag.

KNAPP, A. 1993. *Une école de la création théâtrale*. Paris: Actes Sud Papiers; ANRAT.

KNOPF, J. 1980. *Brecht Handbuch*. Stuttgart: Metzler.

KNOX, N. 1961. *The Word Irony and Its Context, 1500–1755*. Durham, NC: Duke University Press.

KNUDSEN, H. 1971. *Methodik der Theaterwissenschaft*. Stuttgart: Kohlhammer.

Kodikas/code. 1984. Vol. 8, no. 1–2 ('Le spectacle au pluriel.' Eds. P. Delsemme and A. Helbo).

KOMMERELL, M. 1940. *Lessing und Aristoteles: Untersuchung über die Theorie der Tragödie*. Frankfurt: V. Klostermann.

KONIGSON, E. 1969. *La Représentation d'un mystère de la Passion à Valenciennes en 1547*. Paris: CNRS.

– 1975. *L'espace théâtral médiéval*. Paris: CNRS.

KOSTELANETZ, R. 1968. *The Theatre of Mixed Means*. London: Routledge and K. Paul.

KOTT, J. 1965. *Shakespeare, notre contemporain*. Verviers, Bruxelles: Marabout Université.

KOURILSKY, F. 1971. *The Bread and Puppet Theatre*. Lausanne: La Cité.

KOWZAN, T. 1968. 'Le signe au théâtre.' *Diogène* 61.

– 1970. 'L'art du spectacle dans un système général des arts.' *Études philosophiques*, janvier

– 1975. *Littérature et spectacle*. La Haye et Paris: Mouton.

– 1976. 'L'art en abyme.' *Diogène*, no. 96 (octobre-décembre).

– 1980. 'Les trois impromptus: Molière, Giraudoux et Ionesco face à leurs critiques.' *Revue d'histoire du théâtre*, no. 3.

– 1985. 'Iconographie-iconologie théâtrale: Le signe iconique et son réffrent.' *Diogène*, no. 130 (avril-juin).

– 1992. *Sémiologie du théâtre*. Paris: Nathan.

KREJCA, O. 1971. 'L'acteur est-il un singe savant dans un système de signes fermé?' *Travail théâtral*, no. 1 (octobre-décembre).

KRISTEVA J. 1969. *Semiotiki Recherches pour une sémanalyse*. Paris: Le Seuil.

KRYSINKSI, W. 1978. 'Entre l'éthique du langage et la grammaire générative: Le système sémiotique de Thomas Pavel.' *Semiotica*, no. 23, 3–4.

– 1981. 'Semiotic Modalities of the Body in Modern Theater.' *Poetics Today* 2, no. 3.

– 1982. 'Changed Textual Signs in Modern Theatricality.' *Modern Drama* 35, no. 1.

LABAN, R. 1960. *The Mastery of Movement*. London: Macdonald and Evans.

– 1994. *La maîtrise du mouvement*. Arles, France: Actes Sud.

LA BORDERIE. 1973. 'Sur la notion d'iconicité' Messages, no. 4.

LA BORDERIE and A. LE GALLOC'H, 'L'iconicité de la représentation et de l'évocation dans le théâtre classique.' *Messages*, no. 4.

LABORIT, H. 1981. 'Le geste et la parole: Le théâtre vu dans l'optique de la biologie des comportements.' *Degrés*, no. 29.

LA BRUYÈRE , J. DE. 1934. *Œuvres complètes*. Paris: Gallimard.

LAFON, D. 1991. *Le chiffre scénique dans la dramaturgie molièresque*. Paris: Klincksieck.

L'art du théâtre. 1986. No. 6.

LAGRAVE, H. 1973. 'Le costume de théâtre: Approche sémiologique.' *Messages*, no. 4.

– 1975. 'Du côté du spectateur: Temps et perception théâtrale.' *Discours social*, no. 5.

Langages. 1968. No. 10 ('Pratiques et langages gestuels').

– 1984. No. 73.

LANGER, S. 1953. *Feeling and Form*. New York: Scribner's.

Langue française. 1979. No. 42, May. ('La Pragmatique.' Eds. F. Recanati and A.-M. Diller).

– 1982. No. 56, Dec. ('Le rythme et le discours.' Ed. H. Meschonnic).

LARTHOMAS, P. 1972. *Le langage dramatique*. Paris: Armand Colin.

LASSALLE, J. 1991. *Pauses*. Arles: Arles Sud.

LAUSBERG, H. 1960. *Handbuch der literarischen Rhetorik*. München: Max Huber Verlag.

LAVER, J. 1964. *Costume in the Theatre*. London: George and Harrap.

Le théâtre européen face à l'invention: allégories, merveilleux, fantastique. 1989. Paris: PUF.

LEABHART, T. 1989. *Modern and Post-Modern Mime*. London: Macmillan.

LEBEL, J.-J. 1966. *Le happening*. Paris: Denoël.

LECOQ, J., ed. 1987. *Le théâtre du geste*. Paris: Bordas.

– 1996. *Jacques Lecoq au conservatoire*. Paris: Actes Sud Papiers; ANRAT.

LEFÈBVRE, H. 1972. *La vie quotidienne dans le monde moderne*. Paris: Gallimard.

LE GALLIOT, J. 1977. 'La scène et "l'autre scène."' In *Psychanalyse et langage littéraire. Théorie et pratique*. Paris: Nathan.

LEHMAN, H.T. 1989. 'Die Inszenierung: Probleme ihrer Analyse.' *Zeitschrift für Semiotik* 11, Heft 11.

– 1991. *Theater und Mythos*. Stuttgart: Metzler.

LEHMANN, H.T., and H. LETHEN. 1978. *Bertolt Brechts 'Hauspostille.' Text und kolleltives Lesen*. Stuttgart: Metzler

LEJEUNE, Ph. 1971. *L'autobiographie en France*. Paris: Armand Colin.

LEMAHIEU, D. 1995. 'Vaudeville.' In CORVIN 1995.

LEPSCHY, G. 1967. *La linguistique structurale*. Paris: Payot

LEROI-GOURHAN, A. 1974. *Le geste et la parole*. 2 vols. Paris: Albin Michel.

LEROY, D. 1990. *Histoire des arts du spectacle en France*. Paris: L'Harmattan.

LESSING, E. (1767) 1885. *Dramaturgie de Hambourg*. Paris: Perrin.

LEVIEUX, F. and J.-P. n.d. *Expression corporelle*. Marly: Éditions de l'INJEP.

LEVIN, S. 1962. *Linguistic Structures in Poetry*. Paris and The Hague. Mouton.

LÉVI-STRAUSS, C. 1958. *Anthropologie structurale*. Paris: Plon.

LEVITT, R.M. 1971. *A Structural Approach to the Analysis of Drama*. Paris and The Hague. Mouton.

LINDEKENS, R. 1976. *Essai de sémiotique visuelle*. Paris: Klincksieck.

LINDENBERGER, H. 1975. *Historical Drama: The Relation of Literature and Reality*. Chicago: University of Chicago Press.

LINDLEY, D., ed. 1984. *The Manchester Court Masque*. Manchester: n.p.

Linguistique et sémiologie. 1976. No. 2 ('L'ironie').

LIOURE, M. 1973. *Le drame de Diderot à Ionesco*. Paris: Armand Colin.

LISTA, G. 1973. *Futurisme: Manifestes, documents, proclamations*. Lausanne: L'Âge d'homme.

Littérature. 1985. No. 57 ('Logiques de la représentation').

LOCKEMANN, W. 1973. *Lyrik-Epik-Dramatik*. Meisenheim: Hain.

LORELLE, Y. 1962. 'Les transes et le théâtre.' *Cahiers Renaud-Barrault*, no. 38.

– 1974. *L'expression corporelle du mime sacré au mime de théâtre*. Bruxelles: La Renaissance du livre.

LOTMAN, J. 1977. *The Structure of the Artistic Text*. Trans. Ronald Vroon. Ann Arbor, MI: UMI Research Press.

LOUYS, M. 1967. *Le costume: pourquoi et comment?* Bruxelles: La Renaissance du livre.

LUKÁCS, G. 1914. *Die Soziolegie des modernen Dramas*. Archiv fur Sozialwissenschaft. Reprint in *Gesammelte Werke*. Luchterand Verlag.

– 1956 (1965). Le roman historique. Paris: Payot.

– 1961. *Schriften zur Literatursoziologie*. Neuwied, Germany: H. Luchterhand.

– 1963. *The Historical Novel*. Trans. Hannah and Stanley Mitchell. Boston: Beacon Press. Reprint 1983 Lincoln: University of Nebraska Press.

– 1964. *Realism in Our Time: Literature and the Class Struggle*. Trans. John and Necke Mander. New York: Harper.

– 1975. *Problèmes du réalisme*. Paris: L'Arche.

LYONS, J. 1977. *Semantics*. 2 vols. Cambridge: Cambridge University Press.

LYOTARD, J.-F. 1971. *Discours, figure*. Paris: Klincksieck.

– 1973. 'La dent, la paume.' In *Des dispositifs pulsionnels*. Paris: UGE.

MACHEREY, P. 1966. *Pour une théorie de la production littéraire*. Paris: Maspéro.

– 1978. *A Theory of Literary Production*. Trans. of 1966 by Geoffrey Wall. London: Routledge and K. Paul.

MADRAL, P. 1969. *Le théâtre hors les murs*. Paris: Le Seuil.

MAINGENEAU, D. 1976. *Initiation aux méthodes de l'analyse du discours*. Paris: Hachette.

– 1981. *Approche de l'énonciation en linguistique française*. Paris: Hachette.

MALPURGO, V. 1984. *L'avventura del sipario*. Milano: Ubulibri.

MAN, P. DE. 1971. *Blindness and Insight: Essays in the Rhetoric of Contemporary Criticism*. New York: Oxford University Press.

MANCEVA, D. 1983. 'Considérations sur l'analyse du texte dramatique contemporain.' *Philologia*, no. 12–13, Sofia.

MANN, Th. 1908. 'Versuch über das Theater.' Vol. X of *Gesammelte Werke*. Frankfurt: Fischer Verlag.

MANNONI, O. 1969. 'L'illusion comique ou le théâtre du point de vue de l'imaginaire.' In *Clés pour l'imaginaire*. Paris: Le Seuil.

MARCEAU, M. 1974. *M. Marceau ou l'aventure du silence: Interview de G. et T. Verriest-Lefert*. Paris: Desclée de Brouver.

MARCUS, S. 1974. *Mathematische Poetik*. Frankfurt: Athenäum.

– 1975. 'Stratégie des personnages dramatiques.' In HELBO 1975.

MARIE, M. 1977. 'Montage.' In COLLET et al. 1977.

MARIN, L. 1985. 'La sémiotique du corps.' *Enyclopædia Universalis*, Paris.

MARIVAUX. 1969. *Journaux*. Paris: Garnier.

MARMONTEL, J.-F. 1763–1787. *Éléments de littérature*. 6 vols. Paris: Née de la Rochelle.

MARRANCA, B., ed. 1977. *The Theatre of Images*. New York: Drama Book Specialists.

MARS, F. 1964. *Le gag*. Paris: Editions du cerf.

MARTIN, Bernard. 1993. *La théâtralisation de l'écrit non théâtral*. Thesis, Université de Paris 8.

MARTIN, JACKY. 1984. 'Ostension et communication théâtrale.' *Littérature*, no. 53 (février).

MARTIN, JACQUELINE. 1991. *Voice in Modern Theatre*. London: Routledge and K. Paul.

MARTIN, JOHN. 1966. *The Modern Dance*. New York: Barnes.

MARTIN, MARCEL. 1977. *Le languge cinématographique*. Paris: Éditeurs français réunis.

MARTY, R. 1982. 'Des trois icônes aux trois symboles.' *Degrés*, no. 29.

MARTY, R., W. BURZLAFF, C. BRUZY, K. RHETORÉ, and F. PERALDI. 1980. 'La sémiotique de C.S. Peirce.' *Langages* (juin: special issue on Peirce).

MARX, K., and F. ENGELS 1967. *Über Kunst und Literatur*. 2 vols. Berlin: Dietz Verlag. Particularly, 'Die Sickingen Debatte' (1859). French translation in letters from April 19th to May 18th, vol. 5 of *Correspondance Marx-Engels*. Paris: Éditions sociales.

MATEJKA, L., ed. 1976. *Sound, Sign and Meaning: Quinquagenary of the Prague Linguistic Circle*. Ann Arbor: UMI Research Press.

MATEJKA, L., and I. TITUNIK, eds. 1976. *Semiotics of Art: Prague School Contributions*. Cambridge, MA: MIT Press.

Matérialités discursives: Colloque des 24, 25, 26 avril 1980, Universite Paris X, Nanterre. 1981. Lille: Presses Universitaires de Lille.

MATHERS, P.W. 1985. 'Extending the Couragemodell: Computer-aided Design and Theatre Work.' Paper read at the Congrès Internacional de Theatre a Catalunya.

MATHIEU, M. 1974. 'Les acteurs du récit.' *Poétique*, no. 19.

MATHIEU-COLAS, M. 1986. 'Frontières de la narratologie.' *Poétique*, no. 65.

MAURON, C. 1963. *Des métaphores obsédantes au mythe personnel: Introduction à la pychocritique.* Paris: Corti.

MAUSS, M. 1936. 'Les techniques du corps.' *Journal de psychologie* 72, no. 3–4 (mars–avril).

MCAULEY, G. 1984. 'Freedom and Constraint: Reflections on Aspects of Film and Theatre.' In *Aulla XXII.* Australian National University: Camberra.

– 1985. 'Performance Studies: A Personal View.' *Australian Drama Studies*, no. 7.

MCGOWAN, M. 1978. *L'art du ballet de cour en France.* Paris: CNRS.

MEHLIN, U. 1969. *Die Fachsprache des Theaters: Eine Untersuchung der Terminologie von Bühnentechnik.* Dusseldorf: Schauspielkunst und Theaterorganisation, Pädagogischer Verlag Schwann.

MELDOLESI, C., and L. OLIVI. 1989. *Brecht Regista.* Bologna: Il Mulino.

MELEUC, S. 1969. 'Structure de la maxime.' *Langages*, no. 13.

MELROSE, S. 1983. *Une analyse fonctionnelle systémique de deux mises en scène de 'No Man's Land' (Planchon et Hall).* Thesis, 3^{d} cycle, Université de Paris 3.

MERLE, P. 1985. *Le café-théâtre.* Paris: PUF.

MESCHONNIC, H. 1982. *Critique du rythme: Anthropologie historique du langage.* Paris: Verdier.

MESGUICH, D. 1991. *L'éternel éphimère.* Paris: Seuil.

METZ, Ch. 1977. *Le signifant imaginaire.* Paris: UGE.

MEYER-PLANTUREUX, C. 1984. 'Les métamorphoses de la photo de théâtre.' *Art-Press*, no. 79

– 1992. *La photographie de théâtre ou la mémoire éphémère.* Paris: Paris-Audiovisuel.

– 1995. See PIC, R.

MEYERHOLD, V. 1963. *Le théâtre théâtral.* Paris: Gallimard.

– (1969) 1972. *Meyerhold on Theatre.* Trans. Edward Braun. New York: Hill and Wang.

– 1973, 1975, 1980, 1992. *Écrits sur le théâtre.* 4 vols. Lausanne: La Cité-L'Âge d'homme.

MIC, C. 1927. *La commedia dell'arte.* Paris: Éditions de la Pléiade.

MICHAUD, G. 1957. *L'œuvre et ses techniques.* Paris: Nizet.

MIGNON, P.-L. 1986. *Le théâtre au XXe siècle.* Paris: Gallimard.

MILLER, J. 1972. 'Non-verbal Communication.' In *Non-verbal Communication*, ed. R.A. Hinde. London: Cambridge University Press.

MILLER, J.G. 1977. *Theater and Revolution in France since 1968.* Lexington, KY: French Forum.

MILNER, J.-C., and F. REGNAULT. 1987. *Dire le vers.* Paris: Le Seuil.

Modern Drama. 1982. Vol. 35, no. 1 ('Theory of Drama and Performance').

MOHOLY-NAGY, L., and O. SCHLEMMER. 1925. *Die Bühne im Bauhaus.* München: A. Langen.

MOINDROT, I. 1993. *Dramaturgie de l'opéra.* Paris: PUF.

MOLES, A., ed. 1973. *La communication et les massmédia.* Verviers: Marabout.

MOLES, A., and E. ROHMER. 1972. *Psychologie de l'espace.* Paris: Castermann.

MOLINARI, C., and V. OTTOLENGHI. 1979. *Leggere il teatro.* Firenze: Vallechi.

MONOD, R. 1977a. *Les textes de théâtre.* Paris: CEDIC.

– 1977b. 'Les dramaturgies emboîtées.' *Travail théâtral*, no. 27 (avril–juin).

– 1983, ed. *Jeux dramatiques et pédagogie.* Paris: Edilig.

MONRO, D.H. 1957. *The Argument of Laughter.* Victoria: Melbourne University Press.

MORAUD, Y. 1981. *La conquête de la liberté de Scapin à Figaro.* Paris: PUF.

MOREL, J. 1964. *La Tragédie.* Paris: Armand Colin.

MORENO, J.-L. 1924. *Das Stegreiftheater.* Potsdam: Verlag des Vaters, G. Kiepenheuer.

– 1965. *Psychothérapie de groupe et Psychodrame.* Paris: PUF.

– 1973. *The Theatre of Spontaneity.* Boston: Beacon Press.

– 1984. *Théâtre de la spontanéité.* Paris: L'Épi.

MORVAN DE BELLEGARDE. 1702. *Lettres curieuses de littérature et de morale.* Paris: Guignard.

MOUNIN, G. 1970. *Introduction a la sémiologie.* Paris: Minuit.

MOUSSINAC, L. 1948. *Traité de la mise en scène.* Paris: Librairie centrale des beaux arts.

MRLIAN, R., ed. 1981. *Teória dramatických umeni.* Bratislava: Tratan.

MUECKE, D.C. 1982. *Irony and the Ironic.* London: Methuen.

MUKAROVSKY, J. 1933. 'L'intonation comme facteur du rythme poétique.' *Archives néerlandaises de phonétique expérimentale*, no. 8–9. English translation in Mukarousky 1977.

– 1934. 'L'art comme fait sémiotique.' *Actes du huitième congrès international de philosophie à Prague*. Reprint in *Poétique*, no. 3, 1970.

– 1941. 'Dialog a monolog.' Vol. 1 of *Kapitoly z Ceské poetiky*. Praha: n.p. English translation in 1977.

– 1977. *The Word and Verbal Art*. Trans. J. Burbank and P. Steiner. New Haven, CT: Yale University Press.

– 1978. *Structure, Sign and Function*. Trans. J. Burbank and P. Steiner. New Haven, CT: Yale University Press.

NADIN, M. 1978. 'De la condition sémiotique du théâtre.' *Revue roumaine d'histoire de l'art* 15.

NATTIEZ, J.-J. 1987. *Sémiologie générale et sémiologie*. Paris: Bourgois.

NELSON, R. 1958. *Play within a Play*. New Haven, CT: Yale University Press.

NICOLL, A. 1962. *The Theatre and Dramatic Theory*. New York: Barnes & Noble.

– 1963. *The World of Harlequin: A Critical Study of the Commedia dell'Arte*. Cambridge: Cambridge University Press.

NIETZSCHE, F. (1872) 1967. 'Die Geburt der Tragödie.' In *Werke in zwei Bänden*. München: C. Hanser.

– 1967. *The Birth of Tragedy and the Case of Wagner*. Trans. of 1872 by Walter Kaufmann. New York: Vintage Books.

Nouvelle revue de psychanalyse. 1971. No. 4 ('Effets et formes de l'illusion').

NORMAN, S.-J. 1993. 'Le Body Art.' In *Le Corps en jeu*. Paris: CNRS.

– 1996. [article] in *Cahiers de médiologie*.

NOVERRE, G. 1978. *Lettres sur la danse et les arts imitateurs*. Paris: Ramsay.

OBREGON, O. 1983. 'The University Clásico in Chile.' *Theater* 15, no. 1.

OGDEN, R., and I.A. RICHARDS. 1923. *The Meaning of Meaning*. London: Harcourt.

OLSON, E. 1968a. 'The Elements of Drama: Plot.' In CALDERWOOD and TOLIVER 1968.

– 1968b. *The Theory of Comedy*. Bloomington: Indiana University Press.

Organon 80. 1980. *Sémiologie et théâtre*. Ed. M. Corvin. Lyon: Presses de l'Université de Lyon.

ORLANDO, F. 1971. *Lettura freudiana della 'Phèdre.'* Torino: Einaudi.

ORGEL, S. (1965) 1981. *The Jonsonian Masque*. New York: Columbia University Press.

OSOLSOBE, I. 1967. *Muzikál je, kdyz...* Praha: Supraphon.

– 1974. *Divaldo, ktere mluví, spíva a tancí*. Praha: Supraphon.

– 1980. 'Cours de théâtristique générale.' In ed. SAVONA 1980.

OUAKNINE, S. 1970. 'Prince Constant: Étude et reconstitution du déroulement du spectacle.' Vol. 1 of *Les voies de la création théâtrale*. Paris: CNRS.

Oxford Companion to the Theatre. (1957) 1993. Ed. P. Hartnoll. 4th ed. Oxford: Oxford University Press.

PAGNINI, M. 1970. 'Per una semiologia del teatro classico.' *Strumenti critici*, no. 12.

– 1980. *Pragmatica della letteratura*. Palermo: Sellerio.

PANDOLFI, V. 1957–1961. *La commedia dell'arte*. 6 vols. Firenze: Sansoni

– 1961. *Regia e registi nel teatro moderno*. Universale Capelli. Bologna: Capelli.

– 1969. *Histoire du théâtre*. 5 vols. Marabout Université. Verviers: Gérard.

PAQUET, D. 1990. *Alchimie du visage*. Paris: Chiron.

– 1995. 'Pour un théâtre de fragrances.' *Comédie française*, no. 17.

PASSERON, R. 1996. *Naissance d'Icare: Éléments de poïétique générale*. Presses Universitaires de Valenciennes.

PASSOW, W. 1971. *Max Reinhardts Regiebuch zu Faust I*. München: Kitzinger.

PATSCH, S.M. 1980. *Vom Buch zur Bühne*. Innsbruck: Osterr Kommissionsbuchh.

PAUL, A. 1981. 'Theater als Kommunikationsprozess.' In KLIER 1981.

PAVEL, T. 1976. *La syntaxe narrative des tragédies de Corneille*. Paris: Klincksieck.

PAVIS, P. 1975. 'Problèmes d'une sémiologie du théâtre.' *Semiotica* 15, no. 3.

– 1976a. *Problèmes de sémiologie théâtrale*. Montréal: Presses de l'Université du Québec.

– 1976b. 'Théorie du théâtre et sémiologie: sphère de l'objet et sphère de l'homme.' *Semiotica* 16, no. 1.

– 1978a. 'Remarques sur le discours théâtral.' *Degrés*, no. 13, Spring.

– 1978b. 'Mise au point sur le gestus.' *Silex*, no. 7.

– 1978c. 'Des sémiologies théâtrales.' *Travail théâtral*, no. 31.

– 1978d. 'Débat sur la sémiologie du théâtre.' *Versus*, no. 21 (septembre)

– 1979a. 'Il discorso de la critica teatrale.' *Quaderni di Teatro*, no. 5.

– 1979b. 'Notes towards a semiotic analysis.' *Drama Review*, T84 (December).

– 1980a. 'Dire et faire au théâtre: Sur les stances du Cid.' In ed. J. SAVONA 1980.

– 1980b. 'Toward a Semiology of *Mise en scènes*.' Paper read at Conference on the Theory of Theatre, University of Michigan, 17–19 April. Reprint in PAVIS 1982b.

– 1980c 'Vers une esthétique de la réception théâtrale: Variations sur quelques relations.' In DURAND 1980a.

– 1980d. 'Le discours du mime.' In DE MARINIS 1980.

– 1981a. 'Problems of a Semiotics of Gesture.' *Poetics Today* 2, no. 3.

– 1981b. 'Réflexions sur la notation théâtrale.' *Revue d'histoire du théâtre*, no. 4.

– 1982a. *Voix et images de la scène: Essais de semiologie théâtrale.* Lille: Presses universitaires de Lille (2nd ed.: 1985e. Includes PAVIS 1978a, 1978b, 1978d, 1979a, 1979b, 1980a, 1980c, 1981a, 1981b.)

– 1982b. *Languages of the Stage: Essays in the Semiology of the Theatre.* New York: Performing Arts Journal Publications.

– 1983a. 'Production et réception au théâtre: La concrétisation du texte dramatique et spectaculaire.' *Revue des sciences humaines*, no. 189, 1.

– 1983b. 'Du texte à la scène: Un enfantement difficile.' Paper read at conference Scène, Signe, Spectacle, April 1983. In *Forum Modernes Theater*, 1986, no. 2.

– 1983c. *Marivaux à l'épreuve de la scène.* Thèse d'État, Université Paris 3. (Abridged in PAVIS 1986.)

– 1984a. 'Du texte à la mise en scène: L'histoire traversée.' *Kodikas/code* 7 no. 1–2.

– 1984b. 'De l'importance du rythme dans la mise en scène.' Paper read at Conférence sur le texte dramatique, la lecture et la scène. In PAVIS 1985e; in HEISTEIN 1986.

– 1985a. 'Le théâtre et les médias: Spécificité et interférences.' In eds. A. HELBO et al. 1987.

– 1985b. 'Questions sur un questionnaire.' In eds. A. HELBO et al. 1987.

– 1985c. 'Commentaires et édition de LA MOUETTE.' Paris: Livre de Poche.

– 1985d. 'La réception du texte dramatique et spectaculaire: Les processus de fictionnalisation et d'idéologisation.' *Versus*, no. 41. (Reprint in PAVIS 1985e).

– 1985e. *Voix et images de la scène: Pour une sémiologie de la réception.* Lille: Presses Universitaires de Lille. (Second edition of 1982a).

– 1986. *Marivaux à l'épreuve de la scène.* Paris: Publications de la Sorbonne.

– 1987. *Semiotik der Theaterrezeption.* Tübingen: Narr Verlag.

– 1990. *Le théâtre au croisement des cultures.* Paris: Corti.

– 1992. *Confluences: Le dialogue des cultures dans les spectacles contemporains.* Saint-Cyr: PPBBR.

– 1996a. *L'analyse des spectacles.* Paris: Nathan.

– 1996b. *The Intercultural Performance Reader.* London: Routledge and K. Paul.

PAVIS, P., and J.-M. THOMASSEAU, eds. 1995. *Copeau l'éveilleur.* In *Bouffoneries.*

PAVIS, P., and R. VILLENEUVE 1993. *Protée* 21, no. 3 ('Gestualité').

PEIRCE, C.S. 1931–1958. Vol. 2 of *Collected Papers.* Cambridge, MA: Harvard University Press.

– 1978. *Écrits sur le signe.* Ed. and trans. G. Deledalle. Paris: Le Seuil.

PERCHERON, D. 1977. 'Diégèse.' In COLLET et al., 1977.

PFISTER, M. 1973. 'Bibliographie: Theorie des Komischen, der Komödie und der Tragikomödie (1943–1972).' *Zeitschrift fur französische Sprache und Literatur*, no. 83.

– 1977. *Das Drama.* München: Fink Verlag.

– 1978. 'Kommentar, Metasprache und Metakommunikation im Hamlet.' *Jahrburch der Deutschen Shakespeare-Gesellschaft West.*

– 1985. 'Eloquence is action: Shakespeare und die Sprechakttheorie.' *Kodikas/code* 8, no. 3–4.

PIC, R. 1995. *Bertolt Brecht et le Berlinner Ensemble à Paris.* Paris: Arte Editions.

PICOT, E., ed. 1902–1912. *Recueil général des sotties.* Paris: Firmin Didot.

PIDOUX, J.-Y. 1986. *Acteurs et personnages.* Lausanne: l'Aire.

PIEMME, J.-M. 1984. 'Le souffleur inquiet.' *Alternatives théâtrales.* Bruxelles: Ateliers des Arts, no. 2021.

– 1989. *L'invention de la mise en scène.* Bruxelles: Labor.

PIERRON, A. 1980. 'La scénographie: décor, masques, lumières...' In COUTY and REY 1980.

– 1994. *Le théâtre: ses métiers, son langage.* Paris: Hachette.

PIGNARRE, R. 1975. *Histoire de la mise en scène.* Paris: PUF.

PISCATOR. E. 1980. *The Political Theatre.* Trans. Hugh Rorrison. London: Eyre Methuen.
PLADDOT, D. 1962. 'The Dynamics of the Sign System in the Theatre.' In HESS-LÜTTICH, 1981 vol. 2
PLASSARD, D. 1992. *L'acteur en effigie.* Lausanne: L'Âge d'homme et Institut international de la marionnette.
PLATO. 389–369 B.C. *The Republic,* Book III, 1.
POERSCHKE, K. 1952. 'Vom Applaus.' In *Mimus und Logos: Eine Festgabe für C. Niessen.* Lechte: Verlag.
PÖRTNER, P. 1972. *Spontanes Theater.* Köln: Kiepenheuer und Witsch.
Poetica. 1976. Band 8, Heft 3–4 ('Dramentheorie, Handlungstheorie').
Poetics. 1977. Vol. VI, no. 34 ('The Formal Study of the Drama').
Poetics Today. 1981. Vol. 11, no. 3 ('Semiotics and Theatre').
Poétique. 1973. No. 16 (' Le Discours réaliste').
– 1978. No. 36 ('L'ironie').
POLTI, G. (1895) 1981. *Les trente-six situations dramatiques.* Paris: Éditions Aujourd'hui.
POSTELWAIT, T., and B. MCCONACHIE, eds. 1989. *Interpreting the Past: New Directions in the Historiography of Performance.* Iowa City: University of Iowa Press.
POUGIN, A. 1885. *Dictionnaire du théâtre.* Paris: Firmin-Didot.
PRADIER J.-M. 1985. 'Bio-logique et sémiologique.' *Degrés,* no. 42–43 (été-automne).
– 1987. 'Anatomie de l'acteur.' *Théâtre/public,* no. 76–77.
– 1996. 'Ethnoscénologie: la profondeur des émergences.' *Internationale de l'imaginaire,* no. 5.
Pratiques. 1977. No. 15–16 (juillet: 'Théâtre').
– 1979. No. 24 (août: 'Théâtre').
PRATT, M.-L. 1978. *Towards a Speech Act Theory of Literary Discourse.* Bloomington: Indiana University Press.
PRIETO, L. 1966a. *Messages et signaux.* Paris: PUF.
– 1966b. 'La sémiologie.' In *Le langage.* Paris: Gallimard.
PRINCE, G. 1973. *A Grammar of Stories: An Introduction.* Paris and The Hague: Mounton.
Princeton Encyclopedia of Poetry and Poetics. 1974. Ed. A. Preminger. New Jersey: Princeton University Press.
PROCHÁZKA, M. 1984. 'On the Nature of the Dramatic Text.' In SCHMID and VAN KESTEREN 1984.
PRONKO, L.-C. 1963. *Théâtre d'avant-garde.* Paris: Denoël.
– 1967. *Theater East and West.* Berkeley: University of California Press.
PROPP, W. (1929) 1968. *Morphology of the Folktale.* Trans. Laurence Scott. Austin: University of Texas Press.
PRZYBOS, J. 1987. *L'entreprise mélodramatique.* Paris: Corti.
PUJADE-RENAUD, C. 1976. *Expression corporelle: Langage du silence.* Paris: ESF.
PÜTZ, P. 1970. *Die Zeit im Drama.* Göttingen: Vandenhoeck und Ruprecht.
QUERÉ, L. 1982. *Des miroirs équivoques: Aux origines de la communication moderne.* Paris: Aubier.
RADKE-STEGH, M. 1978. *Der Theatervorhang : Ursprung, Geschichte, Funktion.* Meisenheim am Glan: Hain.
Raison présente. 1982. No. 58 ('Théâtres, parcours, paroles').
RANK, O. 1971. *The Double: A Psychoanalytic Study.* Trans. Harry Tucker Jr. Chapel Hill: University of North Carolina Press.
RAPP, U. 1973. *Handeln und Zuschauen.* Darmstadt: Luchterhand.
RASTIER, F. 1971. 'Les niveaux d'ambiguïté des structures narratives.' *Semiotica,* 2, 4.
– 1972. 'Systématique des isotopies.' In *Essai de sémiotique poétique,* ed. A. Greimas. Paris: Larousse.
RASZEWSKI, Z. 1958. 'Partytura teatralna.' *Pamietnik Teatralny* VII, 3, 3–4: 380–412.
Reallexikon der deutschen Literaturgeschichte. 1955. Eds. Stammler and P. Merker. 4 vols. Berlin: De Gruyter.
REGNAULT, F. 1980. *Histoire d'un 'ring': Bayreuth, 1976–1980.* Paris: Laffont.
– 1996. *La doctrine inouïe: Dix leçons sur le théâtre classique français.* Paris: Hatier.
RÉGY, C. 1991. *Espaces perdus.* Paris: Plon.
REICHERT, G. 1966. *Die Entwicklung und Funktion der Nebenhandmung in der Tragödie vor Shakespeare.* Tübingen: n.p.
REINELT, J., and J. ROACH 1992. *Critical Theory and Performance.* Ann Arbor, MI: UMI Research Press.
REINHARDT, M. 1963. *Ausgewählte Briefe, Reden, Schriften und Szenen aus Regiebüchern.* Wien: Prachner Verlag.
REISS, T.J. 1971. *Toward Dramatic Illusion: Theatrical Technique and Meaning from Hardy to Horace.* New Haven, CT: Yale University Press.

Revue de psychologie des peuples. 1962. No. 1.

Revue d'esthétique. 1960. (Numéro spécial: 'Question d'esthétique théâtrale').

– 1977. No. 1–2 ('L'envers du théâtre').

– 1978. No. 3–4 ('Collages').

Revue des sciences humaines. 1972. No. 145 ('Théâtre dans le théâtre').

REY-DEBOVE, J. 1979. *Lexique sémiotique*. Paris: PUF.

REY-FLAUD, B. 1984. *La farce ou la machine à rire: Théorie d'un genre dramatique*, 1450–1550. Genève: Droz.

REY-FLAUD, H. 1973. *Le cercle magique: Essai sur le théâtre en rond à la fin du Moyen Âge*. Paris: Gallimard.

RICHARDS, I.A. 1929. *Pratical Criticism*. New York: Harcourt, Brace & World.

RICHARDS, T. 1995. *Travailler avec Grotowski sur les actions physiques*. Arles: Actes Sud.

RICŒUR, P. 1953. 'Sur le tragique.' *Esprit* (mars).

– 1965. *De l'interprétation*. Paris: Le Seuil.

– 1969. *Le conflit des interprétations*. Paris: Le Seuil.

– 1972. 'Signe et sens.' In *Encyclopædia Universalis*, Paris.

– 1983–1984–1985. Temps et Récit. 3 vols. Paris: Le Seuil.

RIGHTER, A. 1967. *Shakespeare and the Idea of the Play*. London: Penguin.

RISCHBIETER, H., ed. 1983. *Theaterlexikon*. Zürich: Orell Fussli Verlag.

RISCHBIETER, H., STORCH, W. 1968. *Art and the Stage in the 20th Century: Painters and Sculptors Work for the Theater*. Trans. Michael Bullock. Greenwich, CT: New York Graphic Society.

RIVIÈRE, J.-L. 1978. 'La déception théâtrale.' In BARTHES 1978b.

ROBICHEZ, J 1957. *Le symbolisme au théâtre*. Paris: L'Arche.

ROGIERS, P., ed. 1986. *L'écart constant*, Récit. Bruxelles: Didascalies.

ROKEM, F. 1986. *Theatrical Space in Ibsen, Chekov and Strindberg*. Ann Arbor, MI: UMI Research Press.

ROLLAND, R. 1903. *Le théâtre du peuple: Essai d'esthétique d'un théâtre nouveau*. Paris: Albin Michel.

ROMILLY, J. DE 1961. *L'évolution du pathétique d'Eschyle à Euripide*. Paris: PUF.

– 1970. *La tragédie grecque*. Paris: PUF.

ROOSE-EVANS, J. (1971) 1989. *Experimental Theatre from Stanislavsky to Today*. London: Routledge and K. Paul.

ROUBINE, J.-J. 1980. *Théâtre et mise en scène, 1880–1980*. Paris: PUF.

– 1985. *L'art du comédien*. Paris: PUF.

– 1990. *Introduction aux grandes théories du théâtre*. Paris: Dunod.

ROUCHÉ, J. 1910. *L'art théâtral moderne*. Paris: Cornély.

ROUGEMONT, M. DE, J. SCHERER, and M. BORIE. *Esthétique théâtrale: Textes de Platon à Brecht*. Paris: CDU-SEDES.

ROUSSEAU, J. 1984. 'À quoi sert le répertoire.' *Journal de Chaillot*, no. 16.

ROUSSEAU, J.-J. (1758) 1967. *Lettre à M. d'Alembert sur son article Genève*. Paris: Garnier-Flammarion.

– (1762) 1960. *Du contrat social*. Paris: Garnier.

ROUSSET, J. 1962. *Forme et Signifcation*. Paris: Corti.

ROZIK, E. 1986. 'Theatrical Irony.' *Theatre Research International* no. 2.

– 1992. *The Language of the Theatre*. Glasgow: Theatre Studies Publications.

RUDNITSKI, K. 1988. *Théâtre russe et soviétique*. Paris: Regard.

RUELICKE-WEILER, K. 1968. *Die Dramaturgie Brechts*. Berlin: Henschelverlag.

RUFFINI, F. 1974. 'Semiotica del teatro: La stabilizzazione del senso: Un approccio informazzionale.' *Biblioteca Teatrale*, 10–11

– 1978. *Semiotica del testo: L'esempio teatro*. Roma: Bulzoni.

– 1986. 'Remarques sur le montage au théâtre.' In HELBO 1986.

RUNCAN, A. 1974. 'Propositions pour une approche logique du dialogue.' *Versus*, no. 17.

RUPRECHT, H.G. 1976. *Theaterpublikum und Textauffassung*. Bern: Lang.

– 1983. 'Intertextualité.' *Texte*, no. 2.

RUSSELL, D. 1976. *Theatrical Style*. Palo Alto, CA: Mayfield.

RUTTKOWSKI, W. 1968. *Die loterarischen Gattungen*. Berne: Francke.

RYNGAERT, J.-P. 1977. *Le jeu dramatique en milieu scolaire*. Paris: CEDIC.

– 1984. 'Texte et espace: sur quelques aventures contemporaines.' *Pratiques*, no. 41.

– 1985. *Jouer, représenter*. Paris: CEDIC.

– 1991. *Introduction à l'analyse du théâtre*. Paris: Dunod.

– 1993. *Lire le théâtre contemporain*. Paris: Dunod.

SAÏD, S. 1978. *La faute tragique*. Paris: Maspéro.

SAISON, M. 1974. 'Les objets dans la création théâtrale.' *Revue de métaphysique et de morale* 79, no. 2 (avril–juin).

SALLENAVE, D. 1988. *Les épreuves de l'art*. Arles: Actes Sud.

SALZER, J. 1981. *L'expression corporelle: un enseignement de la communication*. Paris: PUF.

SAMI-ALI. 1974. *L'espace imaginaire*. Paris: Gallimard.

SANDER V. 1971. *Tragik und Tragödie*. Darmstadt: Wissenschaftliche Buchgesellschaft.

SANDERS, J. 1974. *Aux sources de la vérité du théâtre moderne*. Paris: Minard.

– 1978. *André Antoine, directeur de l'Odéon*. Paris: Minard.

SAREIL, J. 1984. *L'écriture comique*. Paris: PUF.

SARKANY, S. 1984. *Forme, socialité et processus d'information: sociopoétiquedu récit court*. Thesis, Université de Lille 3.

SARLES, H. 1977. *After Metaphysics: Toward a Grammar of Interaction and Discourse*. Lisse: Peter de Ridder.

SARRAZAC, J.-P. 1981. *L'avenir du drame: Écritures dramatiques contemporaines*. Lausanne: Éditions de l'aire.

– 1989. *Théâtres intimes*. Arles: Actes Sud.

– 1994. *Les pouvoirs du théâtre: Essais pour Bernard Dort*. Paris: Éditions théâtrales.

– 1995. *Théâtres du moi, théâtre du monde*. Rouen: Éditions Médianes.

SARRAZAC, J.-P., F. VANOYE, and J. MOUCHON. 1981. *Pratiques de l'oral*. Paris: Armand Colin.

SARTRE, J.-P. 1973. *Un théâtre de situations*. Paris: Gallimard.

SAUSSURE, F. DE. 1915. *Cours de linguistique générale*. Paris: Payot.

– 1986. *Course in General Linguistics*. Trans. of 1915. La Salle, IL: Open Court Publishing.

SAUTER, W., ed. 1988. *New Directions in Audience Research*. Utrecht: Institut voor Theaterwetenschap.

SAUTER, W., C. ISAKSSON, and L. JANSSON. 1986. *Theaterögon. Publiken möter föreställningenupplevelse, utbud, vanor*. Stockholm: Liber Förlag.

SAVONA, J., ed. 1980. 'Théâtre et théâtralité.' *Études littéraires* 8, no. 3 (décembre).

– 1980. 'Narration et actes de parole dans le texte dramatique.' *Études littéraires* 8, no. 3 (décembre).

– 1982. 'Didascalies as Speech Act.' *Modern Drama* 15, no. 1 (March).

– 1984. 'French Feminism and Theatre: An Introduction.' *Modern Drama* 17, no. 4.

SAWECKA, H. 1980. *Structures pirandelliennes dans le théâtre français, 1920–1950*. Sklodowskiej, Lublin: Uniwersytet Marii Curie.

SCHECHNER, R. 1972. 'Propos sur le théâtre de l'environnement.' *Travail théâtral*, no. 8 (octobre–décembre).

– 1973a. 'Kinesics and performance.' *Drama Review* 59, vol. 17.

– 1973b. *Environmental Theater*. New York: Hawthorn.

– 1977. *Essays on Performance Theory, 1970–1976*. New York: Drama Books Specialists.

– 1985. *Between Theater and Anthropology*. Philadelphia: University of Pennsylvania Press.

– 1988. *Performance Theory*. London: Routledge.

SCHERER, J. 1950. *La dramaturgie classique en France*. Paris: Nizet.

SCHERER, J.; Mélanges pour. 1986. *Dramaturgies, langages dramatiques*. Paris: Nizet.

SCHERER, K. 1970. *Non-verbale Kommunikation*. Hamburg: Buske Verlag.

SCHILLER, F. 1793. 'Über das Pathetische.' In *Sämtliche Werke*. 2 vols. München: Winckler Verlag.

SCHLEGEL, A.W. von (1814) 1971. *Cours de littérature dramatique*. Genève: Slatkine reprints.

SCHLEMMER, O. (1927) 1978. *Théâtre et abstraction*. Lausanne: L'Âge d'homme.

SCHMELING, M. 1982. *Métathéâtre et intertexte: Aspects du théâtre dans le théâtre*. Paris: Lettres modernes.

SCHMID, H. 1973. *Strukturalistische Dramentheorie*. Kronberg: Scriptor Verlag.

SCHMID, H., and A. VAN KESTEREN, eds. 1984. *Semiotics of Drama and Theatre*. Amsterdam: John Benjamins.

SCHNEILIN, G., and M. BRAUNECK. 1986. *Drama und Theater*. Bamberg: Buchners.

SCHOENMAKERS, H., ed. 1986. *Performance Theory*. Utrecht: Instituut voor Theaterwetenschap.

– 1990. 'The Spectator in the Leading Role.' In *New Advances in Theatre Research*, ed. W. Sauter. Copenhagen: Munksgaard.

SCOTTO DI CARLO, N. 1991. 'La Voix chantée.' *Recherche*, no. 235.

SEARLE, J.R. 1969. *Speech Acts: An Essay in the Philosophy of Language*. London: Cambridge University Press.

– 1975. 'The Logical Status of Fictional Discourse.' *New Literary History* 6, no. 2 (Winter).

– 1980. *Speech Act Theory and Pragmatics.* Dordrecht, Holland and Boston: D. Reidel.

SEBEOK, T., ed. 1986. *Encyclopedic Dictionary of Semiotics.* 3 vols. Berlin, New York, and Amsterdam: Mouton de Gruyter.

SEGRE, C. 1973. *Le strutture e il tempo.* Torino: Einaudi. (Particularly 'The Function of Language in Beckett's *Acte sans paroles*').

– 1980. 'A Contribution to the Semiotic of Theatre.' *Poetics Today* 1, no. 3.

– 1984. *Teatro e romanzo.* Torino: Einaudi.

SENTAURENS, J. 1984. *Séville et le Théâtre.* Bordeaux: Presses Universitaires de Bordeaux.

SERPIERI, A. (1977) 1981. 'Toward a Segmentation of the Dramatic Text.' *Poetics Today* 2, no. 3.

SERPIERI, A., et al. 1978. *Como communica il teatro: Dal testo alla scena.* Milano: Formichiere.

SERREAU, G. 1966. *Histoire du nouveau théâtre.* Paris: Gallimard.

SHARPE, R.B. 1959. *Irony in the Drama.* Chapel Hill: University of North Carolina Press.

SHAW, G.B. (1937) 1958. *Shaw on Theater.* New York: Hill and Wang.

SHETSOVA, M. 1993. *Theatre and Cultural Interaction.* Sydney: University of Sydney Studies.

SHLOVSKY, V. 1965a. 'L'art comme procédé.' In TODOROV 1965, 76–97.

– 1965b. 'Art as Technique.' In *Russian Formalist Criticism: Four Essays.* Trans. Lee T. Lemon and Marion J. Reis. Lincoln: University of Nebraska Press.

SHOMIT, M. 1992. *Systems of Rehearsal.* London: Routledge and K. Paul.

SIGAUX, G. 1970. *La comédie et le vaudeville de 1850 à 1900.* 5 vols. Évreux: Cercle du bibliophile.

SIGAUX, G., and P.-A. TOUCHARD. 1969. *Le mélodrame.* 2 vols. Évreux: Cercle du bibliophile.

SIMHANDL, P. 1993. *Bildertheater.* Berlin: Gadegast.

SIMON, A. 1970. *Dictionnaire du théâtre français contemporain.* Paris: Larousse.

– 1979. *Le théâtre a bout de soufle.* Paris: Le Seuil.

SIMON, R. 1979. 'Contribution à une nouvelle pédagogie de l'œuvre dramatique classique.' *Pratiques,* no. 24.

SINKO, G. 1982. *Opis przedstawienia teatralnego – Problem semiotyczny.* Wroclaw: Ossolineum. (See English synthesis, pp. 182–195).

SLAWINSKA, I. 1959. 'Les problèmes de la structure du drame.' In *Stil und Formprobleme in der Literatur,* ed. P. Bockmann. Heidelberg.

– 1978. 'La semiologia del teatro in statu nascendi, Praga 1931–1941.' *Biblioteca teatrale.*

– 1985. *Le théâtre dans la pensée contemporaine.* Louvain: Cahiers-théâtre Louvain.

SOBEL, B. 1993. *Un art légitime.* Arles: Actes Sud.

SOLGER, K. 1829. *Vorlesung über Ästhetik.* Leipzig: n.p.

SONREL, P. 1943. *Traité de scénographie.* Paris: O. Lieutier.

SOURIAU, E. 1948. 'Le cube et la sphère.' *Architecture et dramaturgie.* Paris: Flammarion.

– 1950. *Les deux cent mille situations dramatiques.* Paris: Flammarion.

– 1960. *Les grands problèmes de l'esthétique théâtrale.* Paris: CDU.

Spectacles à travers les âges, Les. 1931. 3 vols. Paris: Éditions du Cygne.

SPIRA, A. 1957. *Untersuchungen zum Deus ex Machina bei Sophokles und Euripides.* Frankfurt: Diss.

SPOLIN, V. 1963. *Improvisaion for Theater.* Evanston, IL: Northwestern University Press.

– 1985. *Theatre Games for Rehearsal.* Evanston, IL: Northwestern University Press.

– 1986. *Theatre Games for the Classroom.* Evanston, IL: Northwestern University Press.

STAIGER, E. 1946. *Grundbegriffe der Poetik.* Berlin: Atlantes Verlag.

STANISLAVSKY, C. 1952. *My Life in Art.* Trans. J.J. Robbins. New York: Theatre Arts Books.

– 1963a. *La formation de l'acteur.* Paris: Payot.

– 1963b. *An Actor's Handbook.* English of 1963a. Trans. Elizabeth Reynolds Hapgood. New York: Theatre Arts Books/Methuen.

– 1966. *La construction du personnage.* Paris: Perrin.

(1977) 1989. *Building a Character.* Trans. Elizabeth Reynolds Hapgood. New York: Routledge/ Theatre Arts Books.

– 1980. *Ma vie dans l'art.* Lausanne: L'Age d'homme.

– 1989. *An Actor Prepares.* Trans. Elizabeth Reynolds Hapgood. New York: Routledge/ Theatre Arts Books.

STAROBINSKI, J. 1970. *La relation critique.* Paris: Gallimard.

STATES, B.O. 1971. *Irony and Drama.* Ithaca: Cornell University Press.

– 1983. 'The Actor's Presence: Three Phenomenal Modes.' *Theatre Journal* 35, no. 3. Reprint in STATES (1985) 1987.

(1985) 1987. *Great Reckonings in Little Rooms.* Berkeley: University of California Press.

STEFANEK, P. 1976. 'Vom Ritual zum Theater: Zur Anthropologie und Emanzipation szenischen Handelns.' *Maske und Kothurn* 22, H. 3–4.

STEINBECK, D. 1970. *Einleitung in die Theorie und Systematik der Theaterwissensachft.* Berlin: De Gruyter.

STEINER, G. 1961. *The Death of Tragedy.* London: Faber and Faber.

STEINER, J. 1968. *Die Bühnenanweisung.* Göttingen: Vandenhoeck und Ruprecht.

STEINER, P., ed. 1982. *The Prague School: Selected Writings, 1929–1946.* Austin: University of Texas Press.

STEINER, R. 1981. *Cours d'eurythmie de la parole.* Paris: Éditions du Centre Triade.

STERN, D. 1973. 'On Kinesic Analysis.' *Drama Review* 59 (September).

STIERLE, K.H. 1975. *Text als Handlung.* München: Fink Verlag.

STRASBERG, L. 1969. *Le travail à l'Actors Studio.* Paris: Gallimard.

STRASSNER, M. 1980. *Analytisches Drama.* München: Fink Verlag.

STREHLER, G. 1980. *Un théâtre pour la vie.* Paris: Fayard.

STRIHAN, M. 1983. 'Semiotics and the Art of Directing.' *Kodikas/code* 6, no. 1–2.

STRINDBERG, A. 1964. *Théâtre cruel et théâtre mystique.* Paris: Gallimard.

STYAN, J.L. 1962. *The Dark Comedy.* Cambridge: Cambridge University Press.

– 1963. *The Elements of Drama.* Cambridge: Cambridge University Press.

– 1967. *Shakespeare's Stagecraft.* Cambridge: Cambridge University Press.

– 1975. *Drama, Stage, and Audience.* Cambridge: Cambridge University Press.

– 1981. *Modern Drama in Theory and Practice.* 3 vols. Cambridge: Cambridge University Press.

SUVIN, D. 1970. 'Reflexion on Happenings.' *Drama Review* 14, no. 3.

– 1981. 'Per una teoria dell'analisi agenziale.' *Versus: Quaderni di studi semiotici,* no. 30.

SWIONTEK, S. 1980. 'Genologiczne aspekty konstrukcji "teatru w treatrze."' *Acta Universalis Lodziensis,* no. 35.

– 1986. 'La situation théâtrale inscrite dans le texte dramatique.' *Zagadnienia Rodzajow Literackich* 29, 2.

– 1990. *Dialog – Drama – Metateatr.* Lodz: Uniwersytetv Lodzkiego.

– 1993. 'Le dialogue dramatique et le métathéâtre.' *Zagadniena rodzajów literackich,* vol. 36, no. 1–2.

SZEEMAN, H., ed. 1983. *Der Hang zum Gesamtkunstwerk.* Frankfurt: Berliner Kunstlerprogramm des DAAD.

SZONDI, P. 1956. *Theorie des modernen Dramas.* Franfurt: Suhrkamp.

– 1961. *Versuch über das Tragische.* Frankfurt: Insel.

– 1972a. 'Der Mythos im modernen Drama und das epische Theater.' In *Lektüren und Lektionen* Frankfurt: Suhrkamp.

– 1972b. 'Tableau et coup de théâtre: Pour une sociologie de la tragédie domestique et bourgeoise chez Diderot et Lessing.' *Poétique,* no. 9.

– 1973. *Die Theorie des bürgerlichen Trauerspiels im 18. Jahrhundert.* Frankfurt: Suhrkamp.

– 1975a. *Das Lyrische Drama des Fin de siècle.* Frankfurt: Suhrkamp.

– 1975b. *Poésie et poétique de l'idéalisme allemand.* Paris: Minuit.

– 1985. *L'acte critique.* Ed. M. Bollack. Études sur Szondi Lille: Presses Universitaires de Lille.

– 1987. *Theory of Modern Drama.* Trans. Michael Hays. Minneapolis: University of Minnesota Press.

TAIROV, A. 1974. *Le théâtre libéré.* Lausanne: l'Âge d'homme.

TALMA, F. (1825) 1856. *Réflexions sur Lekain et l'art théâtral.* Paris: A. Fontaine.

TARRAB, G. 1968. 'Qu'est-ce que le happening?' *Revue d'histoire du théâtre,* no. 1.

TAVIANI, F., and M. SCHINO. 1984. *Le secret de la commedia dell'arte.* Cazilhac: Contrastes Bouffonneries.

TAYLOR, J.R. 1966. *A Dictionary of the Theatre.* London: Penguin.

– 1967. *The Rise and Fall of the Well-Made Play.* London: Methuen.

TEMKINE, R. 1977–1979. *Mettre en scène au présent.* 2 vols. Lausanne: l'Âge d'homme.

– 1987. *Le théâtre au présent.* Paris: Bouffonneries.

TENSCHERT, J. 1960. 'Qu'est-ce qu'un dramaturge?' Interview with E. COPFERMAN, *Théâtre populaire,* no. 38.

TESNIÈRE, L. 1965. Éléments de syntaxe structurale. Paris: Klincksieck.

Texte. 1982. No. l ('L'autoreprésentation').

– 1983. No. 2 ('L'intertextualité').

– 1984. No. 3 ('L'herméneutique').

Theater und sein Publikum, Das. 1977. Wien: Verlag der Osterreichischen Akademie der Wissenschaften.

Theaterarbeit. 1961. Eds. Brecht et. al. Berlin: Henschelverlag.

Théâtre d'agit-prop de 1917 à 1932, Le. 1977–1978. 4 vols. Lausanne: La Cité.

Théâtre/Public. 1974. No. 5–6. ('Deux *Timon d'Athènes*').

– 1980. No. 32. ('Théâtre, image, photographie').

– 1985. No. 64–65 ('La direction d'acteur').

THOMASSEAU, J.-M. 1984a. 'Pour une analyse du para-texte théâtral.' *Littérature*, no. 53 (février).

– 1984b. *Le mélodrame*. Paris: PUF.

– 1984c. 'Les différents états du texte théâtral.' *Pratiques*, no. 41.

– 1994. 'Le vaudeville.' *Europe*, no. 786.

– 1995. *Drame et Tragédie*. Paris: Hachette.

– 1996. 'Les manuscrits de théâtre' In *Les Manuscrits de théâtre*, eds. J. Neefs and B. Didier. Vincennes: Presses de l'université de Vincennes.

THOMSEN, CH., ed. 1985. *Studien zur Ästhetik des Gegenwartstheaters*. Heidelberg: Carl Winter.

THORET, Y. 1993. *La Théâtralité: Étude freudienne*. Paris: Dunod.

TISSIER, A. 1976–1981. *La farce en France de 1450 à 1550*. Recueil de farces. Paris: CDU et SEDES.

TODOROV, T., ed. 1965. *Théorie de la littérature: Textes des formalistes russes*. Paris: Le Seuil.

– 1966. 'Les catégories du récit littéraire.' *Communications*, no. 8.

– 1967. 'Les registres de la parole.' *Journal de psychologie*, no. 3.

– 1968. 'Poétique.' In *Qu'est-ce que le structuralisme*? Paris: Le Seuil.

– 1970. *Introduction à la littérature fantastique*. Paris: Le Seuil.

– 1976. 'The Origins of Genres.' *New Literary History*, Fall.

– 1981. *Mikhail Bakhtine: Le principe dialogique*. Paris: Le Seuil.

TODOROV, T., and G. GENETTE, eds. 1977. *Poetique du recit*. Paris: Le Seuil.

TOMACHEVSKY, B. 1965a. 'Thématique.' In TODOROV 1965, 263–307.

– 1965b. 'Thematics.' In *Russian Formalist Criticism: Four Essays*. Trans. Lee T. Lemon and Marion J. Reis. Lincoln: University of Nebraska Press.

TORO, F. DE. 1984. *Brecht en el teatro hispanoamericano contemporáneo: Acercamento semiótico al teatro épico en hispanoamerica*. Ottawa: Girol Books.

– 1986. *Semiótica del teatro: Del texto a la puesta en escena*. Buenos Aires: Galerna.

– 1995. Theatre Semiotics: Text and Staging in Modern Theatre. Trans. John Lewis. Toronto: University of Toronto Press.

TOUCHARD, P.-A. 1968. *Dionysos: suivi de l'amateur de théâtre*. Paris: Le Seuil.

TRAGER, L. 1958. 'Paralanguage: A First Approximation.' *Studies in Linguistics*, no. 13.

Travail théâtral. 1978. No. 31.

Traverses. 1980. No. 20 (novembre: 'La voix, l'écoute').

TROTT, D. 1970. *The Interplay of Reality and Illusion in the Theatre of Marivaux*. Ph.D. thesis, University of Toronto.

TROUSSON, R. 1981. *Thèmes et mythes*. Bruxelles: Éditions de l'université de Bruxelles.

TRUCHET, J. 1975. *La tragédie classique en France*. Paris: PUF.

TURK, H. 1976. 'Die Wirkungstheorie poetischer Texte.' In *Literaturtheorie I*. Göttingen: Vandenhoeck und Ruprecht.

TURNER, V. 1982. *From Ritual to Theatre*. New York: Performing Arts Journal Publications.

TYNIANOV, J. 1969. 'La destruction.' *Change*, no. 1.

UBERSFELD, A. 1974. *Le roi et le bouffon*. Paris: Corti.

– 1975. 'Adamov ou le lieu du fantasme.' *Travail théâtral*, no. 20 (juillet).

– 1977a. Lire le théâtre. Paris: Éditions sociales. Nouv. ed. rev., Paris: Belin, 1996.

– 1977b. 'Le lieu du discours.' *Pratiques*, no. 15–16 (juillet).

– 1978a. *L'objet théâtral*. Paris: CNDP.

– 1978b. 'Le jeu des classiques.' In *Voies de la création théâtrale*, vol. VI. Paris: CNRS.

– 1981. *L'école du spectateur*. Paris: Éditions sociales.

– 1991. *Le théâtre et la cité: de Corneille à Kantor*. Bruxelles: AISSIASPA.

– 1993. *Le drame romantique*. Paris: Belin.

ULIVI, F. 1972. *La letteratura verista*. Torino: ERI.

URMSON, J. 1972. 'Dramatic Representation.' *Philosophical Quarterly* 22, no. 89.

URRUTIA, J. 1985. *Semio(p)tica: Sobre el sentido de lo visible*. Madrid: Hiperion.

USPENSKY, B. 1970. *Poetik der Komposition*. Frankfurt: Suhrkamp.

– 1972. 'Structural Isomorphism of Verbal and Visual Art.' *Poetics*, no. 5.

– 1973. *Poetics of Composition*. Berkeley: University of California Press.

VAÏS, M. 1978. *L'écrivain scénique*. Montréal: les Presses Universitaires du Québec.

VALDIN, B. 1973. 'Intrigue et tableau.' *Littérature*, no. 9.

VALENTIN, F.-E. 1988. *Lumière pour le spectacle*. Paris: Librairie théâtrale.

VANDENDORPE, C. 1989. *Apprendre à lire des fables: Une approche sémiocognitive*. Montréal: Éditions du Préambule.

VAN DIJK, T. ed. 1976. *Pragmatics of Language and Literature*. Amsterdam and Oxford: North-Holland Publishing Co.

VEINSTEIN, A. 1955. *La mise en scène théâtrale et sa condition esthétique*. Paris: Flammarion.

– 1968. *Le théâtre expérimental*. Bruxelles: Renaissance du livre.

– 1983. 'Théâtre, étude, enseignement: éléments de méthodologie.' *Cahiers Théâtre-Louvain*.

– 1984. *Bibliothèques et musées des arts du spectacle dans le monde*. Paris: CNRS.

VELTRUSKÝ, J. 1940. 'Clovek a predmet v divadle.' *Slovo a Slovesnost*, VI. English translation by P. Garvin in *A Prague School Reader on Esthetics: Literary Structure and Style*. Washington, DC: Georgetown University Press, 1964.

– 1941. 'Dramaticky text jako soucast divadla.' *Slovo a slovesnot* 7. English translation in MATEJKA and TITUNIK 1976.

– 1977. *Drama as Literature*. Lisse: Peter de Ridder.

VERNANT, J.P. 1965. *Mythe et pensée chez les Grecs*. Paris: Maspéro.

– 1974. *Mythe et société en Grèce ancienne*. Paris: Maspéro.

VERNANT, J.-P., and P. VIDAL-NAQUET. 1972. Vol. 1 of *Mythe et tragédie en Grèce ancienne*. Paris: Maspéro.

– 1986. Vol. 2 of *Mythe et tragédie en Grèce ancienne*. 2. Paris: La Découverte.

VERNOIS, P., ed. 1974. *L'onirisme et l'insolite dans le théâtre français contemporain*. Paris: Klincksieck.

VERNOIS, P., and G. HERRY. 1988. *La formation aux métiers du spectacle en Europe occidentale: Enquête et dossiers*. Paris: Klincksieck.

VERRIER, J., ed. 1993. *Le français aujourd'hui*, no. 103.

VERSUS. 1978. No. 21 ('Teatro e semiotica,' interventi di Bettetini, Gulli-Pugliati, Helbo, Jansen, Kirby, Kowzan, Pavis, Ruffini).

– 1985. No. 41 ('Semiotica della ricezione teatrale.' Ed. M. De Marinis)

VIALA, A. 1985. *Naissance de l'écrivain: Sociologie de la littérature*. Paris: Minuit.

VICKERS, B. 1973. *Towards Greek Tragedy*. London: Longman.

VICTOROFF, D. 1953. *Le rire et le risible*. Paris: PUF.

VILAR, J. (1955) 1963. *De la tradition théâtrale*. Paris: Gallimard.

– 1975. *Le théâtre, service public et autres textes*. Paris: Gallimard.

VILLENEUVE, R. 1989. 'Les îles incertaines.' *Protée* 17, no. 1.

VILLIERS, A. 1951. *La psychologie de l'art dramatique*. Paris: Armand Colin.

– 1958. *Le théâtre en rond*. Paris: Librairie théâtrale.

– 1968. *L'art du comédien*. Paris: PUF.

– 1987. *L'acteur comique*. Paris: PUF.

VINAVER, M. 1978. *Théâtre de chambre*. Paris: L'Arche

– 1982. *Écrits sur le théâtre*. Ed. Michelle Henry. Lausanne: Éditions de l'Aire.

– 1987. *Le compte rendu d'Avignon*. Arles: Actes Sud.

– 1988. 'La mise en trop.' *Théâtre/public*, no. 82–83.

– 1993. *Écritures dramatiques*. Arles: Actes Sud.

VITEZ, A. 1974. 'Ne pas montrer ce qui est dit.' *Travail théâtral* 14 (hiver).

– 1984. 'La traduction: désir, théorie, pratique.' *Actes des premières assises de la traduction littéraire*.

– 1991. *Le théâtre des idées*. Paris: Gallimard.

– 1994. *Écrits I – L'école*. Paris: POL.

VITEZ, A., and E. COPFERMAN. 1981. *De Chaillot à Chaillot*. Paris: Hachette.

VITEZ, A., and H. MESCHONNIC. 1982. 'À l'intérieur du parlé, du geste, du mouvement: Entretien avec Henri Meschonnic.' *Langue française*, no. 56 (décembre).

VODICKA, F. 1975. *Struktur der Entwicklung*. München: Fink Verlag.

Voies de la creation théâtrale, Les. 13 vols. 1970–1996. Paris: CNRS.

VOLTZ, P. 1964. *La comédie*. Paris: Armand Colin.

– 1974. 'L'insolite est-il une catégorie dramaturgique?' In VERNOIS 1974.

WAGNER, R. (1850) 1910. *L'œuvre d'art de l'avenir.* Paris: Delagrave.

– (1852) 1910. *Opéra et Drame.* Paris: Delagrave.

– (1852) 1995. Opera and Drama. Trans William Ashton Ellis. Lincoln. University of Nebraska Press.

WARNING, R., ed. 1975. *Rezeptionästhetik.* München: Fink Verlag.

WARNING, R., and W. PREISENDANZ, ed. 1977. *Probleme des Komischen.* München: Fink Verlag.

WATSON, I. 1993. *Towards a Third Theatre. Eugenio Barba and the Odin Teatret.* London: Routledge and K. Paul.

WEINRICH, H. 1974. *Le Temps.* Paris: Le Seuil.

WEISS, P. 1968. '14 Punkte zum dokumentarischen Theater.' Vol. 2 of *Dramen.* Frankfurt: Suhrkamp.

WEKWERTH, M. 1974. *Theater und Wissenschaft.* München: Hanser Verlag.

WILES, T.J. 1980. *The Theater Event: Modern Theories of Performance.* Chicago: Chicago University Press.

WILLIAMS, R. 1968. *Drama in Performance.* London: Penguin.

WILLS, J.R. 1976. *The Director in a Changing Time.* Palo Alto, CA: Mayfield.

WINKIN, Y., ed. 1981. *La nouvelle communication.* Paris: Le Seuil.

WINNICOTT, D.W. 1971. *Playing and Reality.* New York: Basic Books.

WINTER, M.H. 1962. *Le théâtre du merveilleux.* Paris: Olivier Perrin.

WIRTH, A. 1981. 'Du dialogue au discours.' *Théâtre/Public,* no. 40–41.

– 1985. 'The Real and the Intented Theater Audiences.' In THOMSEN 1985.

WITKIEWICZ, S. 1970. 'Introduction à la théorie de la forme pure au théâtre.' *Cahiers Renaud-Barrault,* no. 73.

WITTGENSTEIN, L. 1961. *Les investigations philosophiques.* Paris: Gallimard.

WODTKE, F.W. 1955. 'Katharsis.' In *Reallexikon der deutschen Literaturgeschichte,* eds. W. Stammler and P. Merker. Berlin: De Gruyter.

WOLFFLIN, H. 1950. *Principles of Art History: The Problem of the Development of Style in Later Art.* New York: Dover.

World Theatre. 1965–1966. 14, no. 6 and 15, no. 1 ('Théâtre total').

ZICH, O. 1931. *Estetika Dramatickeho.* Praha: Umeni Melantrich.

ZIMMER, C. 1977. *Procès du spectacle.* Paris: PUF.

ZOLA, E. (1881) 1968. 'Le naturalisme au théâtre.' Vol. 9 of *Œuvres complètes.* Paris: Cercle du livre précieux.

ZUMTHOR, P. 1983. *Présence de la voix: Introduction a la poésie orale.* Paris: Le Seuil.

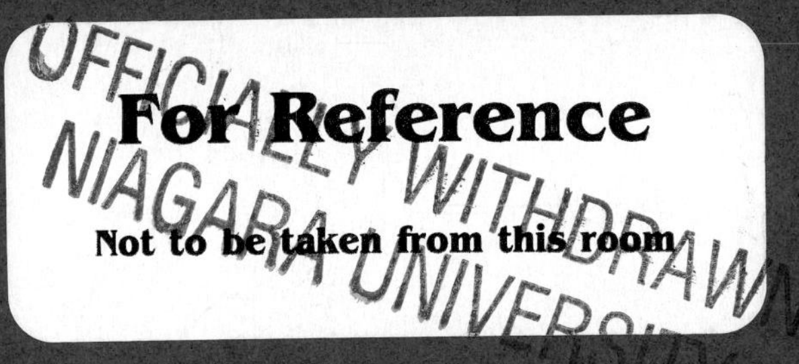